EUROCURRENCIES AND THE INTERNATIONAL MONETARY SYSTEM

A conference sponsored jointly by
the American Enterprise Institute for Public Policy Research
and the U.S. Department of the Treasury

EUROCURRENCIES AND THE INTERNATIONAL MONETARY SYSTEM

Edited by
Carl H. Stem, John H. Makin,
and Dennis E. Logue

American Enterprise Institute for Public Policy Research
Washington, D.C.

030759

0552391

ISBN 0-8447-2090-9 (Paper)
ISBN 0-8447-2091-7 (Cloth)

Library of Congress Catalog Card No. 76-29115

Printed in the United States of America

MAJOR CONTRIBUTORS

Robert Z. Aliber
Professor, Graduate School of Business, University of Chicago

Polly R. Allen
Professor, Department of Economics, Princeton University

Fischer Black
Professor, Graduate School of Business, University of Chicago

William H. Branson
Professor, Department of Economics, Princeton University

Deane Carson
Professor, Graduate School of Business, Columbia University

Richard N. Cooper
Professor, Department of Economics, Yale University

David I. Fand
Professor, Department of Economics, Wayne State University

Gottfried Haberler
Resident Scholar, American Enterprise Institute for Public Policy Research

Richard J. Herring
Professor, The Wharton School, University of Pennsylvania

Zoran S. Hodjera
Senior Economist, International Monetary Fund

Peter B. Kenen
Professor, Department of Economics, Princeton University

Dennis E. Logue
Professor, Amos Tuck School of Business Administration, Dartmouth College

John H. Makin
Professor, Faculty of Commerce and Business Administration,
University of British Columbia, and
Department of Economics, University of Wisconsin-Milwaukee

Richard C. Marston
Professor, The Wharton School, University of Pennsylvania

Helmut W. Mayer
Bank for International Settlements

Hamish McRae
Financial Editor, *The Guardian* (London)

Franco Modigliani
Professor, Department of Economics, Massachusetts Institute of Technology

Jurg Niehans
Professor, Department of Political Economy, Johns Hopkins University

Michael A. Salant
Economist, U.S. Department of the Treasury

Paolo Savona
Section Chief, Bank of Italy

Carl H. Stem
Dean and Professor, College of Business Administration, Texas Tech University

Richard J. Sweeney
Associate Director, Office of Policy Research, Office of the Assistant
Secretary for International Affairs, U.S. Department of the Treasury

Alexander K. Swoboda
Professor, Graduate Institute of International Studies, Geneva, Switzerland

Thomas D. Willett
Deputy Assistant Secretary for Research, Office of the Assistant
Secretary for International Affairs, U.S. Department of the Treasury

Paul Wonnacott
Professor, Department of Economics, University of Maryland

CONTENTS

PART THREE

PART FOUR

INTRODUCTION AND SUMMARY

John H. Makin

Overview

The Eurocurrency system has been intimately involved in the dramatic changes which have occurred over recent years in the shape of the international monetary system. The impact of its growth on national monetary independence and on global rates of inflation have been matters of considerable concern to architects of national and international monetary policy. In the view of some governments, it has proved both a curse (as a transmitter of national monetary disturbances) and a blessing (as a channel for large-scale financing of deficits, particularly those associated with the "oil crisis"). Frequent calls have been heard for regulation of the Eurocurrency system, generally expressing a wish to retain its benefits while reducing costs perceived to be associated with its activities.

In order to shed light on the role of the Eurocurrency system in affecting the workings of the international monetary system and thereby the problems faced by the national financial systems, a group of experts from universities, governments and international agencies was brought together under the joint sponsorship of the American Enterprise Institute for Public Policy Research and the U.S. Treasury. Four conference sessions were organized, each concerned with a specific aspect of the impact of Eurocurrencies on the international monetary system and on national financial policies. The papers and discussion in each of these four sessions compose the four parts of this volume.

In Part One, the major theme of the Makin paper is the role played by the growth of Eurocurrency operations in reducing the viability of independent national financial policies and the resultant acquiescence to an abandonment of rigidly pegged exchange rates. Both the paper and the discussion pay particular attention to the impact of increased flexibility of exchange rates upon world price levels and upon real world trade flows.

Part Two focuses upon the workings of international capital markets. The Logue-Salant-Sweeney paper employs factor analysis to investigate the degree of integration of international capital markets in a theoretical setting reflecting the theory of efficient financial markets. The Herring and Marston paper investigates the degree of integration between U.S. and Eurocurrency markets, within Eurocurrency markets, and between European and Eurocurrency markets, finding the former two sets of markets to be more highly integrated than the latter set.

The Willett paper in Part Three considers appropriate national monetary and fiscal policies under alternative exchange-rate systems. Both the paper and discussion point to the critical need for more empirical work on the determinants of capital flows and to the critical role of exchange-rate expectations in affecting international capital flows which in turn substantially determine the relative strength of monetary and fiscal policy measures under regimes of fixed and floating exchange rates.

In Part Four, the paper by Stem considers the advisability of imposing controls on the Eurocurrency system by employing instruments analogous to those employed to control national financial systems. While there was general agreement that such controls would at best be difficult to effect, there appeared to be some disagreement regarding the appropriateness of the "multiplier" view of the growth of Eurocurrency deposits. A brief separate paper by Makin attempts to reconcile the "multiplier" view and the "new view" of Eurocurrencies. Part Four also includes special notes by Gottfried Haberler on "Flexible Exchange Rates and the Recycling of Petrodollars" and by Dennis Logue on "Does It Make a Difference Whether Petrodollars Are Channelled to the Eurodollar Market or to U.S. Financial Markets?"

In the following part of this introduction, major themes of the conference are identified and briefly discussed. Conference participants were very much aware that a gathering of experts where discussion is focused on *Eurocurrencies and the International Monetary System* should produce a set of conclusions and an agenda for further work. Of course, complete consensus on any such items would only be an illusion, and no pretense to complete consensus is made here. Rather an attempt is made to identify a number of major themes particularly related to Eurocurrencies and the international monetary system and persisting throughout the conference in papers and discussions, and to suggest conclusions and some items for further analysis which may be derived from these themes. I shall not attempt to keep a complete running account of all names associated with an idea but will try to identify individuals whom I perceive to have been its major proponents.

The four themes to be considered, while closely interrelated, are distinguished by the nature of their implications for the Eurocurrency system and the international monetary system. First, considerable attention is devoted to the transformation of the international monetary system toward greater flexibility of exchange rates. The Eurocurrency system both affected and was affected by this transformation. Closely related is a second major theme, the question of integration of world money and capital markets. Here, the intimate connection between Eurocurrencies and national financial policies is perhaps most obvious. A third theme of considerable interest is the inflationary potential arising from the growth of the

Eurocurrency system. Finally, the question whether the Eurocurrency system should or can be regulated received considerable attention.

Eurocurrencies and the Transformation of the International Monetary System

This topic receives the most attention, at least in terms of the influence running from Eurocurrencies to the international monetary system, in the presentation and discussion of the Makin paper. Possible influence running in the opposite direction is covered in discussion of the Willett paper. Briefly, the point which the Makin paper tries to make is that the Eurocurrency system developed as a means to subvert national restraints on international capital flows. As such, it is possible that the system was effective enough by the early 1970s to preclude independent national monetary policies for the control of nominal money supplies by national monetary authorities. The implication of this possibility is seen to be the increased flexibility of exchange rates permitted to occur in order to regain some degree of national monetary control.

Of course, it can be pointed out, and is pointed out by Professor Swoboda, that the existence of the Eurodollar market (or more generally the Eurocurrency market) was neither a necessary nor a sufficient condition for the breakdown of fixed exchange rates, since such a breakdown could be envisioned in the absence of Eurocurrencies if only the misalignment of national monetary policies became sufficiently pronounced. The existence of Eurocurrencies might serve only to accelerate such a breakdown and then only if capital movements—in response to given disequilibrium situations in capital markets—were either more pronounced or more rapid in the presence of Eurocurrency markets than they would be otherwise. The answer to this question requires empirical evidence and is perhaps better discussed when considering the question of integration of national and international capital markets. But it is fair to say at this point that conclusive empirical evidence is not currently available on the question whether the existence of Eurocurrency markets has increased international capital mobility (although valuable studies such as those of Branson do exist for a single time span).

While it may be argued that Eurocurrency markets have played a catalytic role in transforming the international monetary system toward greater flexibility of exchange rates, the possibility of reverse causation exists. Richard Cooper raises such a possibility in his discussion of the Willett paper, noting that flexibility of exchange rates might reduce the sensitivity of international capital movements both to uncovered interest differentials and to differential movements in income. This possibility has also been suggested by John Williamson, as noted in discussion (in the Makin paper) of the relationship between accommodating capital flows and reserve demand under increased flexibility of exchange rates. If this were the case, we have the possibility that the Eurocurrency system has itself wrought changes in the very environment within which it operates that have erased the means by which the

3

changes were produced. That is, the circle of reverse causation is complete if the Eurocurrency system's possible positive impact on capital mobility has led to increased exchange-rate flexibility, which in turn has reduced capital mobility. Of course we do not have the full facts on the situation for capital mobility at any point in the circle, much less the net impact on capital mobility arising from a full traverse of the circle. As data accumulate for a period of global limited flexibility —which began in the spring of 1973—we may expect to obtain some answers on the state of capital mobility across exchange-rate regimes.

The impact of Eurocurrencies on the international monetary system and national financial policies is perhaps nowhere more clear than within the context of the Willett paper, which examines the changing effectiveness of monetary and fiscal policy measures under alternative exchange-rate regimes. Basically, floating improves the relative effectiveness of monetary policy in (say) effecting a change in aggregate demand if capital mobility is particularly high. However, as noted above, Cooper suggests the possibility that the increased flexibility of exchange rates, which may accompany floating, may in turn reduce capital mobility, thereby increasing the relative effectiveness of fiscal policy measures.

To compound uncertainty in this area, even while changes in interest sensitivity of capital flows remain a complicating factor, the effects of the income mobility of capital cannot be determined insofar as the sign of the effect of income changes on net capital flow is not even known with certainty, either a priori or empirically.[1]

The sign and magnitude of the effects of income changes on the relative effectiveness of monetary and fiscal policy measures can be considerable under either exchange-rate regime. For example, if higher income attracts a net capital inflow, then (even if interest mobility is high) monetary policy may become less effective in operating on aggregate demand under flexible rates, since the capital outflow induced by a lower interest rate resulting from monetary expansion may be reduced by an inflow effect associated with higher income. As a consequence, depreciation of the domestic currency would be reduced and less demand shifted onto domestic capacity.

Income mobility of capital, of course, also affects the relative value of policy measures in dealing with balance-of-payments disequilibria in a fixed exchange-rate setting. If higher income should attract a net capital inflow, there would be a reduction in the comparative advantage of monetary over fiscal policy in affecting

---

[1] An estimate does exist for the United States. Sung Kwack found that an increase of $1 billion in income would lead to about a $30 million increase in net capital outflow in the 1960s. (See "A Disaggregated Quarterly Model of U.S. Trade and Capital Flows," unpublished version, U.S. Department of the Treasury, 1973.) Some empirical work which I have done recently for Canada confirms Harry Johnson's suggestion (in *Essays in Honor of Marco Fanno*, Padua, 1966, pp. 345-59) that higher domestic income may attract capital from abroad for a country such as Canada, which may serve as an investment outlet for a proximate, large economy such as the United States. In any case, even the signs of the income mobility of capital are not constant from country to country.

4

the balance of payments. The reverse would hold true if higher income were to result in a net capital outflow.

Whatever the net effect of possible changes in interest and income mobility of capital as the exchange-rate regime changes, we need more hard information on the direction and degree of such changes, as well as a systematic framework within which to consider their implications for the relative effectiveness of monetary and fiscal policy.[2] With regard to this latter point, it is perhaps premature, simply on the basis of an assertion that fiscal policy measures may lead to monetary policy measures, to abandon a systematic approach to assessing the relative effectiveness of these instruments. Rather, it could be argued that better than giving up on Keynesian international policy models would be an attempt to improve them by incorporating flexible prices, the stock-adjustment model in international capital flows, and income mobility of capital—and then to reexamine conclusions regarding the relative effectiveness of monetary and fiscal policy measures in affecting aggregate demand under alternative exchange-rate regimes. In addition, improved empirical information will be required on the workings of such models.

Integration of World Capital Markets

Analysis of questions related to the integration of world money and capital markets centers on a pair of topics treated by the papers in the second session. First treated, in the Logue-Salant-Sweeney paper, is the question whether world money and capital markets are (or approach being) "efficient" or "perfect" in the formal sense that rational investors instantaneously diversify to eliminate all returns from bearing nonsystematic risk (that is, risk which can be avoided through portfolio diversification). Next, in the Herring-Marston paper, attention is given to integrating forward markets into a model treating determination of non-dollar Eurocurrency rates and non-dollar domestic interest rates.

While it is consoling to think that it does not matter where petrodollars go, given the ability of efficient capital markets to recycle funds, there does appear to be some skepticism among discussants of the Logue-Salant-Sweeney paper on what conclusions could be drawn from their results and what is meant by monetary independence in the first place. It is suggested that the conclusions drawn from an innovative application of a most promising technique may not have been directly inferable from the actual results obtained. Some questions are raised about making the leap from the Logue-Salant-Sweeney empirical result that 83 percent of the

---

[2] Annex A and Annex B of the Willett paper prepared by members of the Treasury Research Staff are representative of the type of empirical and analytical work that will be necessary to improve open economy models. Annex A by Willett and Kaylin, Piggott, and Sweeney examines how the effects of changes in uncovered short-term interest differentials are distributed among changes in spot and forward rates, changes in short-term capital flows and changes in home and foreign interest rates. Annex B by Victoria S. Farrell reports on studies of changes in the effectiveness of fiscal policy under alternative exchange-rate systems.

variance among interest rates in different countries was explained by a single factor to the conclusions drawn by the authors about the degree of integration of international capital markets.

Part of the problem with this transition can perhaps be explained by considering the disequilibrium dynamics of price and quantity adjustments. Professor Kenen's description of the limiting case of an efficient market is a description of a market in which no quantity adjustments occur because prices adjust instantaneously to their equilibrium levels in the face of any exogenous market shocks. In economic terms this means that information is in fact costless and that given such costless information about an exogenous shock, all market participants can and do instantaneously select the same new set of prices—which are, in addition, equilibrium prices. This limiting case is useful for what it suggests about conclusions on capital mobility to be drawn from arguments about the efficiency of capital markets. First, information regarding capital assets is disseminated rapidly but neither instantaneously nor at zero cost. Indeed, one can readily imagine that information flows would be faster and investors' perception of new equilibrium prices more uniform if large increases in funds flowed to the Eurodollar market instead of to the mythical Swaziland of the Logue-Salant-Sweeney paper. After all, investors are likely to have had a good deal more experience with the responses of the former to large inflows of funds than with the responses of the latter. It is the difference among perceived new sets of equilibrium prices, in turn determined by the speed and accuracy of information flows, which induces quantity adjustments (that is, capital flows) to exogenous shocks to markets. The quantity adjustments then feed back into subsequent price adjustments which, for stable markets, are on the second round more uniform and closer to equilibrium values than they were after the first response to an exogenous shock.

In a sense, then, there does exist a connection between the efficiency of international capital markets and the volume of capital flows. Perfectly efficient markets should see no flows in response (say) to a large increase in the U.S. money supply, since all market participants would merely readjust prices on capital instruments to their "new" equilibrium levels and the adjustments would all be correct. As markets become less efficient, larger capital flows should arise in response to such a disturbance, and they should last longer. This view suggests that the interesting question to consider is the possible changes in the degree of efficiency over time and across capital markets. Larger movements of capital—in response to given exogenous disturbances—may reflect a reduction in capital market efficiency.

Richard Cooper suggests, in his comments on Willett's paper, that capital mobility is reduced by flexible exchange rates. Such a result may be due to the increased efficiency of international capital markets, arising from a reduction in uncertainty about changes in capital controls below levels that exist in periods of fixed exchange rates. Increased efficiency, by the way, is not the reason for reduced capital mobility suggested by Cooper. His reason is tied to the increased risk attached to uncovered capital movements in the absence of credible parities.

Leaving aside for now the question whether parities are more "credible" under systems of fixed exchange rates or limited flexible exchange rates, the effect of a flexible regime—which allows exchange rates to adjust—may be to eliminate some of the uncertainty regarding large, discrete exchange-rate adjustments or controls in the minds of international portfolio managers. In short, flexible exchange rates may in fact increase the efficiency of international capital markets, and this—not increased uncertainty over exchange rates— may reduce observable movements of capital.[3] Indeed, uncertainty about exchange rates may be less in a regime of limited flexibility of exchange rates than where exchange rates are "fixed" but parities are incredible because of the low level of coordination of national monetary policies.

This discussion of capital market efficiency feeds back in a revealing way into the notion of capital market integration. One might say that an observation of increased movements of capital across national boundaries—such as has occurred in recent years—is suggestive of an increased degree of capital market integration. But this would be a claim fraught with potential error. First, the increased movement of capital might have arisen because of a higher degree of capital mobility, which would increase the capital flow occurring in response to a given change in rates of return. Or, holding constant capital mobility (so defined), larger capital movements may result from lowered efficiency of capital markets insofar as capital market efficiency determines the mix between price (rate of return) and quantity (capital flows) adjustments to exogenous shocks to capital markets. In any case, the relationship between capital market efficiency and integration as inferred from the volume of capital movements is not positive, but rather is inverse and holds only for a given level of capital mobility.

While the Logue-Salant-Sweeney paper considers the broad question whether it matters if petrodollars are initially deposited in any one of a large number of financial markets, Herring and Marston consider the narrower but important question whether it matters if funds go (say) to the U.S. dollar and the Eurodollar markets or to the German DM and Euro-DM (Euromark) markets. Herring and Marston find U.S. and Eurodollar rates closely related, conclude that a high degree of integration exists between U.S. and Eurodollar markets, and turn their attention

---

[3] Such a reduction in capital movements would arise from a smaller response of capital flows to a given exogenous shock to capital market equilibrium resulting from the fact that rate-of-return differentials which appear in response to the shock are smaller and persist over a shorter period of time. This notion of a change in observable capital movements is not the same as the notion of a change in capital mobility advanced by William Branson, who recalled Fritz Machlup's useful distinction between increases in capital mobility and capital movement. The former refers to the size of capital movement in response to a given change in interest rates, while the latter refers to increased movements in response to increased incentives to move. As markets become more "efficient," prices adjust more rapidly, in turn reducing incentives to move capital.

to German and Euromark markets. Their approach yields a conclusion—anticipated by interest parity theory—that all variation in the return on DM assets is determined by changes in the forward rate between dollars and DM, once the spot rate and return on dollar assets are given, although they do find evidence of a lower level of integration than that between U.S. and Eurodollar markets. Further, integrating Euromarks and German bonds into a model with a forward market simultaneously determines the German interest rate, the forward premium, and the Euromark rate, given the spot rate and the Eurodollar rate.

Exercises such as the Herring and Marston paper can be and are in the discussion section subjected to criticism related both to "unrealistic" assumptions (that is, what variables are taken to be exogenously determined) and to their easily anticipated conclusions. Such criticism is probably not terribly damaging. The basic advance contained in such efforts is methodological. Development of a formal approach, adapted to Eurocurrency markets—where endogenous variables include a domestic interest rate, a Eurocurrency rate, and a forward rate—is only one step removed from a full general equilibrium model of small country capital markets where the "foreign" Eurodollar rates can reasonably be taken as given. Addition of a spot market equation gives an appropriate general equilibrium specification in a world where exchange rates are free to move.

A problem remains, however, insofar as Eurocurrency markets do not develop for the currencies of countries whose capital markets are sufficiently small to take returns on other Eurocurrencies as given. This problem is recognized by Savona in comments on the Herring and Marston paper. The result is that a minimum of five equations is needed to determine for a non-dollar Eurocurrency the domestic interest rate, the Eurocurrency interest rate, forward rate, spot rate, and the interest rate on dollars. Even here, sterling rates—and, indeed, the U.S. dollar and Eurodollar rate differential— may be deemed endogenous, adding two more equations to the five already suggested. Obviously, the construction of a full general equilibrium model, such as is implied by criticism of "partial equilibrium" models like that of Herring and Marston, could produce a cumbersome device at best. Probably addition of a spot market to the Herring and Marston model, which they indicate is already under way, represents the best and perhaps last appropriate addition to their model of Eurocurrency and national money markets.

Perhaps as a final note, it is worth adding that the discussion of capital market integration produces a more precise notion of what may be meant by monetary independence. Monetary independence would imply, as Professor Carson notes, an ability of the central bank to control the nominal money supply and not necessarily to control interest rates. If a high degree of capital market integration resulted either in volatility of the nominal money supply under fixed exchange rates or volatility of the exchange rate and, thereby, of prices under flexible rates, in neither case would control of the real money supply be assured. Loss of monetary independence would be judged by loss of control of the real money supply, but this would undoubtedly be closely related to the degree of control of the short-run variability of interest rates, if not to the determination of their long-run equilibrium levels.

Eurocurrencies and Inflation

The possible inflationary impact of the growth of Eurocurrency markets is a topic which appears in all the sessions. While views are mixed, there does emerge an overall skepticism regarding the validity of arguments that the growth of Eurocurrency markets has resulted in sustained inflationary pressure on a global level.

Perhaps the most indirect link between Eurocurrency growth and inflation comes in the first session, where the catalytic role of Eurocurrencies is viewed as forcing a move to increased flexibility of exchange rates—which in turn cuts the private and official demand for reserves, leading to an inflationary potential in the form of redundant liquidity. This effect would only be temporary, however, and as Professor Carson pointed out, if increased flexibility provided central banks with better control over their nominal money supplies, inflation would become easier to control. It probably should be added that since exchange rate movements imply de facto price changes, control of inflation in countries where currencies are depreciating may remain a difficult problem. Further, if wages are rigid and the monetary authority is concerned about full employment, even a revaluation may be inflationary if the central bank increases the money supply when (as a result of revaluation) unemployment rises in domestic tradable goods industries.[4]

Other arguments about the inflationary impact of the Eurocurrency system essentially revert back to arguments among monetary theorists in the United States during the 1950s and 1960s about the inflationary potential arising from expansion of non-bank financial intermediaries. It is observed that most Eurocurrency holdings are not in the form of demand deposits and, indeed, since they bear interest, are closer to time deposits. Therefore, the argument is made that Eurocurrencies may become a vehicle of inflation by increasing the velocity of circulation of (say) M_1. Willett makes this argument more concrete by suggesting that increased capital mobility eases borrowing and thereby cuts demand for cash and increases velocity. This effect appears, however, not to have materialized; he produces evidence from nine industrial countries which suggests a general downward trend in velocity defined as GNP/M.[5] As Willett indicates, such a result is probably not surprising when one remembers Warren McClam's argument that the growth

---

[4] This point has been argued by Richard Sweeney and Thomas D. Willett in a paper to appear in the volume from a Treasury Conference held in April 1974 on *Effects of Exchange Rate Adjustments*.

[5] Here we would like to be assured that the M_1 definition in all countries uniformly excludes foreign-owned and foreign currency deposits. Further, demand deposits in some countries do bear interest, which tends to blur the implicit distinction drawn by some between "money" (non-interest-bearing claims on the issuer) and "credit" (interest-bearing claims on the issuer).

of the Eurocurrency system merely represents financial intermediation that would otherwise have been effected by some other—although probably less efficient—set of intermediaries.[6]

This approach has merit insofar as it produces some hard information about velocity trends across countries—although it is subject to the qualifications suggested in footnote 5. In focusing on the behavior of velocity, it is also suggestive of a frontal assault on the question of the inflationary impact of an increased volume of credit by Fischer Black. His point is simple, yet powerful, and deserving of careful consideration. It is that, because aggregate borrowing through intermediaries is equal to aggregate lending, there is zero net credit creation and therefore zero net impact on aggregate demand arising from the activities of intermediaries in the Eurocredit markets, as he has renamed the Eurocurrency markets.

This argument has considerable logical appeal of the sort held by the arguments about "efficient" capital markets precluding the need for capital movements. There is some abstraction from detail—desirable for the insights which it makes possible, but perhaps a bit risky in view of the details which it may involve regarding the real impact of possible market imperfections. More precisely, in a perfectly competitive market, the last loan extended by a financial intermediary before reaching a "loaned-up" equilibrium position would conform with Black's notion that credit creation has a zero net impact on aggregate demand. If, however, one backs up to look at the situation which brought Eurocurrency markets into existence in the first place—to the extent that it was cartelization of national financial intermediary systems—the growth of Eurocredits has meant that, at the margin, loans were made that would not otherwise have been made. And while at the margin, lending equals borrowing, there is some liquidity created in the process of moving to the margin by the willingness of the intermediary to borrow short and lend long. Otherwise, the net worth of new intermediaries would be zero. If a new group of intermediaries arises which is willing to extend this process on the basis of narrower spreads between borrowing and lending rates, an increase in liquidity results, which in turn bears on aggregate demand. The amount of liquidity creation is mirrored by the integral over time of the profits of a new set of financial intermediaries less the reduction in profits which those intermediaries have caused existing intermediaries.

This argument is not inconsistent with Black's argument. It simply relaxes his assumption that the total liabilities of intermediaries must equal their total assets, and it starts from a disequilibrium condition in which one set of national (non-Eurocurrency) intermediaries is earning monopoly profits. Further, it suggests that the liquidity-creating effects of Eurocurrency operations are in no way equal to their total liabilities (assets) and are small indeed in comparison with such figures. However, the rate of change of liquidity creation is related to the rate of

[6] See Warren D. McClam, "Credit Substitution and the Eurocurrency Market," *Banca Nazionale del Lavoro Quarterly Review,* no. 103 (December 1972).

growth of Eurocurrency operations. In short, growth of Eurocurrency operations creates some liquidity, but the volume of the liquidity in no way approaches the total liabilities of the system, and its inflationary impact may therefore be quite small indeed.

It is worth noting here that Black's argument is reminiscent of the outside/ inside money distinction which arose in assessing the potential for real balance effects. If an item is at once someone's asset and someone else's liability, it cannot, on net, affect aggregate demand. As Professor Harry Johnson has noted, to argue that creating demand deposits creates no net wealth because borrowing equals lending overlooks the fact that the process creates wealth for the economy taken as a whole in the form of a larger net worth for bank owners.[7] In this view, it is the owners of Eurocurrency institutions who affect aggregate demand as deposits rise, not their borrowers and lenders. However, as we have noted, while likely to be proportional to the total volume of Eurocurrency operations, such an effect is small relative to total Eurocurrency liabilities. Further, arguments to eradicate such net wealth would be indistinguishable from arguments to eradicate profits for firms in general.

Discussion of both the velocity and credit-creation arguments for the inflationary potential of Eurocurrency growth suggests that the markets' inflationary potential is small indeed. However, some further careful empirical work on both arguments would surely be worthwhile.

Regulation of the Eurocurrency System

Professor Stem argues strongly against regulation of the Eurocurrency system and in favor of deregulation of national banking systems, particularly in the United States. It comes through in the discussion of the regulation issue that the most notable feature of the pressure for regulation of Eurocurrency markets is the shift among the arguments for regulation away from the "problem" of international capital flows, to the inflationary potential of Eurocurrencies. As Helmut Mayer observes in his comments on Professor Stem's paper, increased flexibility of exchange rates and the role which the Eurocurrency system has played in recycling petrodollars have served to end official concern about the ability of the Eurocurrency system to enhance capital movements. However, if we agree with the discussion in the previous section regarding the limited inflationary potential of the Eurocurrency system, the new argument for regulation follows the old one into oblivion.

Pursuing the argument for regulation a bit further along lines suggested by Gottfried Haberler, it is probably correct to suggest that given fixed exchange rates, uncontrolled Eurocurrency markets undercut controls on capital flows, which in

---

[7] H. G. Johnson, "Inside Money, Outside Money, Income, Wealth and Welfare in Monetary Theory," *Journal of Money, Credit and Banking,* February 1969, pp. 30-45.

turn may have been imposed in efforts to maintain an overvalued or undervalued currency. But even such a questionable rationale for regulating Eurocurrencies disappears where exchange rates are permitted to change, as authorities abandon what may have been overly rigid and unrealistic exchange-rate targets. However, one might expect that for a country which desires to keep growth rates high by consistently undervaluing its currency and thereby gaining reserves from resultant capital inflows arising in anticipation of eventual appreciation, the Eurocurrency market—from which a massive volume of such inflows emanate—may seem to contain inflationary potential. The leader of such a country could be expected to call for regulation of Eurocurrencies because of their inflationary impact. Such a call would arise from precisely the same source as the call for controls on international capital flows: a desire to maintain control over the national nominal money supply and to maintain a disequilibrium exchange rate.

If one accepts the inflationary-potential argument regarding Eurocurrencies, the possibility of regulation raises the question how to control the aggregate liabilities of a system with no national boundaries. Professor Stem examines the possibility of reserve requirements and open market operations with the U.S. Federal Reserve playing a supra-national central bank role. The difficulties of agreeing on such a system, with its questionable effect on world inflation, lead Stem to suggest, instead, deregulation of U.S. commercial banks. An end to the prohibition on interest payments on less-than-thirty-day deposits and an end to effective reserve requirements on time deposits would better enable U.S. banks to compete with Eurodollar banks. If, as a result, a larger share of offshore dollar business were returned to the United States, the Federal Reserve would obtain direct control over a larger share of world credit creation.

While the argument for deregulation of U.S. banks is solidly based and would lead to an increase in world welfare, such a change would not be likely to have a major effect on the global inflationary potential of the activities of financial intermediaries, which is probably small in the first place. Offshore markets would continue to exist to frustrate efforts by national central banks simultaneously to maintain disequilibrium exchange rates and to maintain control over nominal money supplies. For this reason, actual inflationary effects aside, calls for control of Eurocurrencies would continue, even if the share of offshore dollar operations relative to total dollar operations fell.

A final set of arguments for regulation of the Eurocurrency system revolves about concern over a "credit collapse" of the system in the absence of a "lender of last resort." As the difficulties following the Herstatt failure and the failures of several other banks made clear, the need in this area is not so much for additional regulation as it is for a clear assignment of responsibilities under existing institutional arrangements—that is, the assignments of responsibilities of national central banks with respect to foreign branches and subsidiaries doing business within national boundaries. It appears that concern over the incidents occurring during the summer of 1974 has galvanized central banks to assign responsibilities to insure the liquidity and solvency of well-run financial intermediaries in the Eurocurrency system.

The regulation question perhaps is a fitting end to a discussion of the relationship between Eurocurrencies and the international monetary system. The Eurocurrency system grew up as an international system outside the control exercised by national financial policies and served to signal clearly to the architects of such policies the need to recognize the rapid growth of economic interdependence among nations since the 1950s. Under the Bretton Woods system of fixed parities, the system of Eurocurrencies came severely to constrain national financial policies that were conceived without adequate recognition of the growth of economic interdependence. The international monetary system has, however, been transformed with the acquiescence of national financial policy makers into a form which de facto —by virtue of increased permissible exchange-rate flexibility—has recognized the need, transmitted through the Eurocurrency system, for internationalization of national financial policies. It is heartening to note in closing that events which have transpired since the conference, where some serious doubts were expressed about the resiliency of Eurocurrency markets in the wake of the Herstatt difficulties, have tended to reconfirm the notion that the Eurocurrency system is a viable and valuable set of institutions which will be with us for some time.

PART ONE

EUROCURRENCIES AND THE EVOLUTION OF THE INTERNATIONAL MONETARY SYSTEM

John H. Makin

1. Introduction

This paper explores three major topics. First, consideration is given in Section 2 to the atrophy of the Bretton Woods system in the face of a degree of capital market integration that has become sufficient to preclude rigid exchange rates in the absence of systematic coordination of national monetary policy. Section 3 analyzes the impact of the new regime of increased permissible flexibility of exchange rates upon world prices and upon world trade flows. Finally, in Section 4, attention is given to devising a means for moving toward an optimal degree of limited flexibility of exchange rates over time.

In Section 2, the atrophy of the Bretton Woods system is seen to be intimately linked to the use of the dollar as international money, to the implied growth of the Eurocurrency markets, and to the Eurodollar market in particular with the attendant high degree of capital market integration. Considerable attention is given early in Section 2 to developments in contemporary monetary theory which attempt to rationalize the selection of a particular asset to be employed as money. This analysis is employed to help explain the evolution, since World War II, of the U.S. dollar, and subsequently of the Eurodollar, as international money. Such evolution is seen to parallel the development of a national money within the United States during the nineteenth century. Given the high level of integration of international capital markets, attendant upon the role of the dollar and hence the Eurodollar as international money or credit, the major shock to the requisite level of coordination of national monetary policies is seen to be the end of a passive U.S. balance-of-payments policy initiated in August 1971 in the face of pressures from producers of tradable goods.

In Section 3 it is argued that increased flexibility of exchange rates has probably had some inflationary impact but has had little measurable impact upon real trade flows. The inflationary impact of increased permissible flexibility of exchange rates is seen to have arisen from the attendant reduction in the demand for private as well as for official holdings of international money. There is, however, disagreement on the impact of exchange-rate flexibility upon the demand for private reserves. Even the generally assumed negative relationship between official reserves and the degree of exchange-rate flexibility has been questioned. Attention

17

is given to points raised on both sides of the question. No systematic relationship is discovered (see Appendix) between real trade flows and the increased flexibility of exchange rates for the four major open economies investigated.

In Section 4 the question of whether there may exist an optimal degree of limited flexibility of exchange rates is considered in view of the "in-between" system of some but not complete exchange-rate flexibility that has evolved since the Bretton Woods era. It is argued that both the unannounced target exchange rate around which limited intervention operations in the foreign exchange market are conducted and the degree of that intervention ought to be varied over time to remove what emerge as nonrandom portions of disturbances in the foreign exchange market. While such a procedure may not always be completely successful, it must represent an improvement over a system of rigid par values which assumes ex ante that all disturbances impinging on the foreign exchange market are reversible and ought not to be offset. The system of limited intervention, or equivalently, of limited flexibility, replaced "all" with "some" and thereby represents an improvement over the system of rigid rates.[1]

While the system of limited flexibility is not viewed as the ideal, it is viewed as the best possible system, in view of the constraints implied by the absence of an institutional framework for a world central bank which could conduct a world monetary policy over a world currency. In particular, the arguments advanced in this paper in favor of limited flexibility of exchange rates are employed to claim that the application of "optimum quantity of money arguments" by Clark and Grubel to suggest payment of interest on official international reserves is invalid.[2]

In short, the Eurocurrency markets will be seen here as a major catalyst in the transformation of the international payments system from a liquidity-oriented framework to an adjustment-oriented framework. The adjustment referred to here is not the sort involving domestic incomes, prices, and interest rates that is undertaken by nations in response to balance-of-payments disequilibria, but refers to permitted adjustment of exchange rates between national monies in anticipation of balance-of-payments disequilibria. In effect, trading nations have chosen to acquiesce to changes in relative prices of their monies in the face of their inability to prevent large changes in their relative quantities. This development is viewed as being due particularly to a combination of uncoordinated national monetary policies

---

[1] I do not mean to imply here that flexible exchange rates guarantee complete monetary autonomy. Flexible exchange rates give the central bank control over the nominal money supply, but not complete control over the real money supply since exchange-rate changes affect the price level.

It is, however, probably safe to say that the absence of intervention responsibilities in the foreign exchange markets does considerably ease the task of the monetary authority in controlling the nominal money supply.

[2] Peter B. Clark, "Interest Payments and the Return on International Fiat Currency," *Weltwirtschaftliches Archiv,* Heft 4 (1972), pp. 537-564; and H. G. Grubel, "The Case for Optimum Exchange Rate Stability," *Weltwirtschaftliches Archiv,* Heft 3 (1973), pp. 351-381.

and difficult-to-control Eurocurrency markets which readily transmit the effects of national monetary policies to frequently unreceptive trading partners.

2. Atrophy of the System of Fixed Exchange Rates

Evolution of the U.S. Dollar as an International Money. The Bretton Woods system survived for about a decade in the presence of a developing Eurocurrency system and a low level of coordination of national monetary policies partly because that was the amount of time required for the U.S. dollar to develop from an international unit of account into a full-fledged international medium of exchange and store of value. In order to see this, it is well to document the growth of the dollar as international money along the lines suggested by recent theoretical attempts to account for the use and holding of money on the basis of information costs and uncertainty.[3]

Briefly, such arguments for the existence of money envision households and firms faced with the problem of acquiring goods and services, initially in a barter situation. Assets which lower the cost of acquiring information about market opportunities and qualities of goods tend to be held for purposes of reducing resources devoted to acquiring information and effecting exchange. Eventually institutions develop which issue paper claims based on fractional reserves of such assets. These institutions come to serve as intermediaries between borrowers and lenders by lending a part of the proceeds obtained from those who exchange reserve money or assets for claims on the intermediary. The exchange is made conditional upon a guaranteed repurchase agreement offered by the intermediary for its liabilities in exchange for reserve money. A powerful nation-state may claim the right to issue reserve money based on either its holdings of the asset or, alternatively, on no more than its legal ability to designate legal tender. Evolution of such a system faces money-holders with the choices implied by transactions, precautionary, and speculative motives for holding money, *once the emergence of a dominant medium of exchange has been rationalized by the problem of minimizing the costs of acquiring information and effecting transactions.*[4]

This evolution is generally discussed within the context of a trading area defined by national boundaries. If the opportunity given to households and firms

---

[3] See J. Niehans, "Money and Barter in General Equilibrium with Transactions Costs," *American Economic Review*, December 1971, pp. 233-252; K. Brunner and A. H. Meltzer, "The Uses of Money: Money in the Theory of an Exchange Economy," *American Economic Review*, December 1971, pp. 784-805; and M. Perlman, "The Roles of Money in an Economy and the Optimum Quantity of Money," *Economica*, August 1971, pp. 233-252. In addition, the savings implicit in employing a single money for use as foreign exchange and competition for the implied "denomination rents" for dollars have been offered as an explanation for the growth of the Eurodollar system by A. K. Swoboda, "The Eurodollar Market: An Interpretation," *Essays in International Finance*, no. 64 (Princeton, N.J.: Princeton University Press, 1968). This argument is further developed below.

[4] This point is emphasized by Brunner and Meltzer, "Uses of Money."

for acquisition of goods and services is enlarged to include a number of national markets, each with its own national money, then the new optimization problem involves balancing the marginal benefits of access to a larger choice among goods and securities with the marginal costs of acquiring information about qualities and prices of goods and securities and of effecting transactions to obtain such items. A full understanding of this process will be seen here to be fundamental in understanding the evolution of the international monetary system, so a fuller examination of the implied theory of an optimum currency area based upon information and transactions costs is undertaken here.

A Theory of Optimum Currency Areas as Implied by Costs of Information and Transportation. The area over which a single asset or money may come to be held and used for purposes of effecting exchange will depend largely upon technological constraints upon the distance over which information can travel rapidly at low cost and upon the distance over which goods and services can travel at a non-prohibitive cost.[5] These conditions define the area over which a regional minimum-cost means of effecting transactions will be desired.

For example, in the first half of the nineteenth century in the United States, state banks or regional banks with a national charter existed as a reflection of the technological ability to deal with information and transportation costs at the time. Their notes circulated primarily within the locality of the issuing bank or at a discount beyond that area.[6] While some interstate commerce existed, the marginal costs of information and transportation for most households and firms exceeded the marginal benefits implicit in a larger choice set for goods and securities. Therefore a significant demand did not arise for a supra-regional currency and the relatively limited volume of such commerce could be carried on with specie which served as a national or supra-regional currency before establishment of the National Banking System.[7] With the development of lower costs of transportation over interstate distances and improved flows of information among states, the marginal benefits of interstate trade came to exceed the purely technological marginal costs. Conditions became ripe for evolution of a minimum-cost interstate money when a problem arose regarding maintenance of fixed rates of exchange among state or local monies over the new, enlarged, technically feasible trading area. If one set of state banks were

---

[5] Of course, "services" include the embodied services of labor for which ready mobility defines the optimum currency area for R. A. Mundell, "A Theory of Optimum Currency Areas," *The American Economic Review*, September 1961, pp. 657-665.

[6] See H. Rockoff, "The Free Banking Era: A Reexamination," *Journal of Money, Credit and Banking* (May 1974), p. 144. Discounts of state monies at Philadelphia generally fell over time as transportation and communication improved, except during crises such as suspension of specie payments.

[7] Rockoff, "Free Banking Era," found that the ratio of specie outside the U.S. Treasury to the total money supply fell from .41 in 1859 to .15 in 1884. The fall is attributed largely to the establishment of the National Banking System which was in operation by 1865, providing a single paper currency on a national scale. It became the minimum-cost medium of exchange in the increasingly integrated national U.S. market.

to expand its note issue at a rate which implied depreciation of notes in terms of goods, while another state did not, potential traders could face high costs of information in uncertainties regarding the terms upon which transactions may be effected—costs of uncertainties not unlike those faced in a barter economy or those between nations with rapidly fluctuating exchange rates. In such a case a process will operate whereby a choice among monies will be made upon the basis of the minimum costs of arranging interstate transactions, just as a choice among potential money assets was made upon the minimum cost of arranging intrastate or intra-area transactions. In effect, Gresham's Law will operate in reverse whereby "good (minimum variance) money drives out bad," *where no effort is made to maintain rates of exchange among state monies.*[8] Under such conditions it is likely that the money of that state which produces and sells the largest volume of goods and services will evolve as the dominant intrastate and interstate money simply because this minimizes the cost of arranging transactions for the largest bloc of commodities. If an attempt is made to maintain fixed exchange rates among state monies, it will prove most economical to employ a single intervention money which will likely be the money of the economically largest state. This process itself assures that the intervention state currency will be the least costly for private traders to use.[9]

Of course it is likely that this process, if left free from state, regional or national intervention, will evolve gradually over time with single monies for geographically proximate states, developing ahead of a non-specie, national money. The natural course of this evolution toward non-specie national money was replaced by government intervention and establishment of a de jure as opposed to de facto national money in 1865 in the United States.[10] The costs in terms of possible resource misallocation implicit in these steps were probably low in view of the likelihood that they merely accelerated a process that would have come to pass in a competitive setting. In fact it might be argued that the social benefits of such a move exceed the private benefits. The private sector would not find it profitable to incur the costs of supplying a single money over an area larger than that prescribed by information

[8] Of course the normal operation of Gresham's Law requires that some authority must intervene to maintain a fixed price between good and bad money which amounts in turn to a role for the authority as a residual supplier of good money for bad.

[9] The potential flexibility of the exchange rate between the intervention money and all others is one-half that between non-intervention monies. See Swoboda, "Eurodollar Market," and R. N. Cooper, "Eurodollars, Reserve Dollars and Asymmetries in the International Monetary System," *Journal of International Economics* (September 1972), pp. 325-344. Of course this assumes *some* flexibility around par for state monies.

[10] The first National Bank Act in the United States was passed in February 1863, spurred into being by the financial pressures upon the government arising from the Civil War. This act was poorly framed and was succeeded by a revised National Bank Act in 1864. The fact that this move was ahead of the rate of competitive evolution to a single money is demonstrated by the fact that complete dominance of the National Bank's notes over the notes of state banks was not established until the latter's notes were taxed out of existence by a 10 percent annual tax on their circulation passed in March 1865 and effective on 1 July 1866. The state banks themselves were generally absorbed into the national banking system and came to issue only national bank notes.

and transportation costs for a regional minimum cost means of effecting transactions. At the same time the existence of a state-decreed national money might serve to accelerate the development of inter-regional trade at a faster rate than would have occurred with market evolution of national money. The difference would probably be small, however, since with free entry into banking, such as existed in parts of the United States from about 1840 to 1860, the incentive would be strong for each bank in an existing currency area to expand as rapidly as possible into a growing, viable currency area as long as it was on the downward-sloping portion of its long-run average cost curve.

It is probably true that, given constant improvements in transportation and communication, the National Banking Act constituted little more than building ahead of demand. As noted by Mundell, the major problems for a large currency area would relate to regional discrepancies with regard to requirements for growth of the note issue.[11] A shift in demand away from the output of one region and onto that of another (say, occasioned by rapid regional industrial growth) would result in a chronic flow of funds from the relatively depressed area to the booming area unless or until resources moved between areas. With regional banks, the result would be a depreciation of the money of the depressed area against that of the boom area.

The Theory Applied to Evolution of International Money. The strong parallel between the state-national evolution of the optimum currency area and the national-international evolution is clear. The twentieth century has seen further advances in the process of reducing the costs of information and goods and security flows over distance. The period since World War II has seen an era of political stability sufficient to permit such technological developments to be used to expand trade. In fact it may be argued that while the transition from state or regional to national monies was speeded ahead by national governments at a rate in excess of that generated by the private sector, the same national governments have tried to slow the transition from national to international money below the rate generated by the private sector. The result has been the development of the Eurocurrency system as a device to produce private sector international money in the face of restrictions placed upon its evolution by national authorities. Dominant in the Eurocurrency system is, of course, the Eurodollar, which emerged because of the unique role of the U.S. dollar in the Bretton Woods system.

In a sense it can be argued that the Bretton Woods system, established as it was without the powers of a world central bank, contained the seeds of its own destruction. This is not to say that it deserved such a fate, but merely that the features of the system made its failure highly likely. The key to the difficulty lay with the intervention role that was necessarily assigned to a national currency, the U.S. dollar, in the absence of a separate note issue by a world central bank.

---

[11] Mundell, "A Theory of Optimum Currency Areas," pp. 657-665.

Swoboda has analyzed the evolution of "denomination rents" accruing to dollar intermediaries.[12] Establishment of the U.S. dollar as a preferable instrument for private or official international liquidity needs was given a powerful beginning by its convertibility into gold and the absence of general convertibility agreements for European currencies prior to 1958. After that date the role of the dollar as an intervention currency preserved its property as the denomination with the most stable value in terms of other currencies, not to mention the fact that dollars represented claims on the huge selection of goods and securities produced by the U.S. economy. Given these advantages and the economies of scale implicit in holding transactions balances in a single country (noted by Swoboda), there emerged widespread use of the U.S. dollar as a unit of account and medium of exchange. As international traders in goods, seeking to minimize the costs of holding transactions and precautionary balances, looked for a store of value, they found the large and resilient capital markets of the United States an attractive source of short-term assets.

These developments had the effect of providing "denomination rents" in the form of a larger spread between borrowing and lending rates to U.S. financial institutions dealing in dollar instruments. In the absence of barriers to entry, such monopoly profits attracted competitors in the form of financial intermediaries outside the United States which offered deposit and loan facilities denominated in dollars.[13] The growth of such competitors was probably enhanced by restrictions on short-term lending abroad placed upon U.S. financial institutions from 1963–64 and maintained in effect until early 1974.

The Eurodollar market would not have existed without the denomination rents implicit in the role of the U.S. dollar in the Bretton Woods system. In turn, such rents would not have accrued to a national money if the note issue of a world central bank had occupied the intervention role of the dollar. More fundamentally, however, no denomination rents for any money in a supra-national role would have existed unless the marginal benefits implicit in access to a larger, supra-national set of goods and securities exceeded the marginal costs of information and transportation for the bulk of households and firms in trading nations.

Throughout the 1950s the U.S. dollar had evolved from a role as an international unit of account to an international medium of exchange. This evolution, along with the sizeable U.S. capital markets, assured a significant role for dollar-denominated assets as an international store of value. By the early 1960s information costs to non-U.S. investors in dollar-denominated assets were lowered by the

---

[12] Swoboda, "Eurodollar Market."

[13] One may well ask why it is that such "denomination rents" are not eliminated by competition from domestic U.S. banks. The answer is that the U.S. banking industry is not perfectly competitive with entry limited to firms with a charter. Further, the few large U.S. banks operating in international dollar dealings are in effect an oligopoly as are the large banks with international dealings in most industrial countries. Indeed, the level of denomination rents available to Eurocurrency operators may serve as an index of the monopoly power of large banks in the country whose currency denominates a Eurocurrency instrument.

23

dollar activities of foreign banks. U.S. capital control programs enacted between 1963 and 1965 probably accelerated these activities while at the same time they lowered information costs for U.S. firms dealing in international securities by encouraging growth of U.S. branch banks abroad. All that was required to produce disruptive flows was a misalignment of monetary policies such as occurred on a manageable scale with U.S. tight money policies in 1966 and on an unmanageable scale with the rapid switch from U.S. tight money policies in 1969–70 to loose money in 1970–71.

The arrangements to effectively supply the dollar as a supra-national money for the private sector (as well as for central banks) were well in place by 1970, having arisen in response to the denomination rents implicit in dollar intermediation arising, in turn, from the desire for a currency area which exceeded national boundaries. The potential difficulty lay with the fact that the Bretton Woods system, although it had spawned the supra-national monetary role of the dollar, had not been intended to have the U.S. central bank operate as a world central bank. But the combination of fixed exchange rates and the rapid flow of information regarding security prices through the Eurodollar market, implicit in the dollar's role as an effective supra-national money, guaranteed in time to produce massive international capital flows. This resulted from the absence of policies to assure that national monetary authorities acted *as if* the western world were a single-currency area. The fact that the private sector had evolved a supra-national money coincident with an official system of national monies meant that the purveyors of national monies would either have to coordinate their activities or cease efforts to fix the prices of national monies in terms of each other. Understandably enough, the exigencies of national politics dictated the latter course. Information regarding unique, regional economic problems is not as readily transmitted among nations as information regarding the prices and qualities of goods and securities.

The final blow to the Bretton Woods system came in 1971 when unprecedented financial strains were accompanied by an end to an essentially passive balance-of-payments policy on the part of the United States.

Emergence of Inconsistent Balance-of-Payments Goals. The argument is advanced here that rapidly increasing international capital mobility, brought about by development of the Eurocurrency markets, constituted a necessary but not a sufficient condition for the breakdown of a system of fixed or ex post adjustment of exchange rates. Necessary and sufficient for the breakdown of the Bretton Woods system was the increased degree of private capital mobility in the presence of inconsistent balance-of-payments goals. A major shock to the consistency of balance-of-payments goals came when the United States ended its passive policy toward the balance of payments.[14] This was a major shock for two reasons. First, U.S. mone-

---

[14] Reasons for this change are discussed in J. H. Makin, "Capital Flows and Exchange-Rate Flexibility in the Post-Bretton Woods Era," *Essays in International Finance,* no. 103 (Princeton, N. J.; Princeton University Press, 1974).

tary policy had moved into a relatively expansionary phase with the annual rate of expansion of the money stock rising from 5.7 percent during the February 1970–January 1971 period to 11.6 percent in the January 1971–July 1971 period. This disturbance was rapidly transmitted to U.S. trading partners by the Eurocurrency markets, and dollar accumulation by foreign central banks rose from an annual rate of $7.5 billion in the third quarter of 1970 to $25.9 billion in the second quarter of 1971. It was not possible for major recipients of this inflow to approach full sterilization, and so from the point of view of many G-10 countries it was time to end the reserve currency role of the dollar by perhaps attempting conversion of large quantities of short-term dollar liabilities for gold. The response of the United States in ending the convertibility of the U.S. dollar into gold was undoubtedly intended to head off such action. But the action by the United States, as was discovered in the difficult negotiations in the fall of 1971, represented a more fundamental goal largely missed at first in the presence of more conspicuous financial symptoms for the U.S. actions. This goal, which constituted the second reason for the enormity of the shock to the Bretton Woods system, was to end the tax upon U.S. producers of tradable goods that was implicit in a chronically overvalued U.S. dollar. The second quarter of 1971 had showed a U.S. trade balance deficit at a $3.6 billion annual rate, the largest deficit in this account to have been reported up to that time.

In short, a massive financial shock to the Bretton Woods system, implicit in poorly coordinated national monetary policies and rapid intermediation through the Eurocurrency markets, and U.S. efforts to obtain some ability to adjust the dollar exchange rate combined to produce a breakdown of the system in 1971. Speculation is surely possible as to whether either cause would eventually have been sufficient by itself to cause a full breakdown, but in retrospect at least, the combination of both causes, intensely manifested in 1971, rationalizes the particular timing of the collapse.

3. Effects of Increased Flexibility of Exchange Rates on World Inflation and Real Trade Flows

Near-Term Effects of Increased Flexibility on Official Reserve Demand. Since an increase in the degree of exchange-rate flexibility has been accompanied by an increase in world inflation, it is worthwhile to consider whether any basis exists to suggest a causal link between these two events. It will be argued that increased flexibility of exchange rates has resulted in an excess of private and official liquidity which in turn may explain some of the inflation that has accompanied increased flexibility of exchange rates.

Beginning with the easiest case, there is general agreement, with one exception to be discussed below, that official demand for reserves will fall with increased exchange-rate flexibility. Such reserves are basically precautionary balances held to intervene in foreign exchange markets as a residual supplier or demander of foreign exchange in the process of fixing exchange rates. While general agreement exists regarding the negative impact upon official reserve demand of increased flexibility of exchange rates, there has been little systematic effort devoted to simultaneously viewing liquidity and adjustment properties of future international monetary arrangements in various proposed reforms that have been discussed. I have argued elsewhere that it makes no sense to talk about how to serve liquidity needs from various sources available without simultaneously determining just what those liquidity needs will be.[15] In turn, as will be shown below, the demand for official liquidity, as well as private liquidity, is intimately related to the exchange-rate regime which, in turn, must be determined by balancing the benefits of a single world money against the costs which individual nations perceive to be related to relinquishing control over their national money supplies.

Further, since we have moved to a system of limited rather than complete flexibility of exchange rates, there is a need for precise information regarding *how much* the official demand for reserves may fall in the face of an increased degree of exchange-rate flexibility. In my investigation of liquidity-adjustment alternatives (see footnote 15), I have employed a framework for analyzing the precautionary demand for international reserves by central banks which suggests an elasticity of demand for such reserves with respect to increased (permissible) flexibility of exchange rates of between minus one-half and minus one-third. For example, a doubling of the permissible width of the band about par would reduce the precautionary official demand for reserves by between 50 and 33⅓ percent. Calculations made on the basis of this approach suggested no shortage of official reserves among industrial countries in 1971, the inference being that subsequent increases in permissible flexibility of exchange rates may have led to a possible excess supply of official reserves in the 1972–74 period.

The analysis of official demand for precautionary reserves does not, however, explicitly take account of the possible role of capital flows in financing current account imbalances. The question of how much official reserve demand will fall in the presence of limited flexibility of exchange rates is perhaps not so easily answered, at least in the transitional period, once consideration is given to the role played by such accommodating flows of private financial capital. Theory suggests, and Kouri and Porter have adduced, considerable empirical evidence to support the notion that random disturbances in the current account over time are rationally financed by accommodating capital flows just as any discrepancy between receipts and payments gives rise to borrowing or lending.[16] To the extent that such accommodating capital flows are permitted to operate promptly and freely, official reserves held to offset

---

[15] See John H. Makin, "Exchange Rate Flexibility and the Demand for International Reserves," *Weltwirtschaftliches Archiv,* Band 110, Heft 2 (1974), pp. 229-243.

[16] P. J. Kouri and M. G. Porter, "International Capital Flows and Portfolio Equilibrium," *Journal of Political Economy* (May/June 1974), pp. 443-468.

foreign-exchange-market disequilibria may be reduced due to a resultant negative correlation between the net demand (supply) for foreign exchange for current account purposes and a net supply (demand) of foreign exchange through the capital account. Of course some official reserves will be required in the face of imperfect correlation and possibly some time lag in the responsiveness of accommodating capital flows. In addition, nonrandom or irreversible current-account disturbances will not consistently be financed by accommodating private capital flows and will require increased official intervention in the foreign exchange markets.[17] To the extent that official intervention has misjudged the permanence or transience of foreign-exchange-market disequilibria in the past, an end to or reduction of such intervention and replacement by exchange-rate flexibility will reduce official reserve needs.

A possible argument, related to private capital flows, for increased official reserve needs in the presence of limited floating has been advanced by John Williamson.[18] It is suggested that the sensitivity of accommodating private capital flows to a deviation from the actual equilibrium exchange rate may be reduced by the absence of a credible estimate of parity as represented by the par value in a system of official intervention. Evidence is presented that monthly reserve changes were actually larger for many countries during recent periods of floating than during periods of fixed rates.

Of course Williamson recognizes that his theoretical argument "is applicable only where the parity is a credible one." It seems, too, that the breakdown of Bretton Woods was due in no small part to the consistent incredibility of parities as manifest by the results produced by poor coordination of monetary policies in the presence of highly efficient Eurocurrency markets. It seems possible also to argue that the moderate increase in monthly reserve changes observed by Williamson is due largely to the uncertainty that prevailed regarding the very nature of the exchange-rate regime in particular and the shape of the international monetary system in general during most of his "floating" periods. General acquiescence to the system of limited flexibility really did not come until mid-1973, by which time the G-20 had begun to see the impossibility of the task it had set for itself. In such a world where the basic shape of the rules of the game is so unsure, it is not surprising that accommodating private capital flows may have been somewhat slow to occur, thus increasing the need for official intervention and resultant increases in official reserve variability even with more exchange-rate adjustment. It will be most important to repeat Williamson's tests as data for the period following 1974 become available. Of

---

[17] The question whether the private sector or the central bank is, ex ante, the best judge of whether or not disturbances are irreversible is crucial in determining the degree to which accommodating private capital flows can substitute for official reserves. The better the performance of the private sector the more official reserves can be reduced and oriented toward dealing only with the transitory disturbances in the foreign exchange market not financed by the private sector.

[18] J. Williamson, "Increased Flexibility and International Liquidity," presented to the Williamsburg Conference of the Bürgenstock Group, May 1974.

course care will have to be taken to allow for the effects of the oil crisis, which constitutes a major shock exogenous to the exchange-rate regime. For my part, I would argue that official reserve variability from October 1973 to June 1974—and therefore the need for official reserves—would have been considerably larger than it was in the absence of a ready ability to adjust exchange rates that existed during that period.

With the exception of Williamson's argument, there is general agreement that the demand for official reserves is *ceteris paribus* reduced by increased permissible flexibility of exchange rates, and there is even some theoretical basis for predicting how much of a reduction will take place when nonintervention bands are widened. The analysis is somewhat complicated by evidence that accommodating private capital flows can substitute for official reserves. First, as has been suggested, the development of Eurocurrency markets over time has probably enhanced this accommodating role of private capital flows. Also, the very period of increased flexibility under consideration has seen considerable changes regarding official restriction on private capital flows. On net, however, the reduction of U.S. controls on capital flows and the ability of Eurocurrency markets to generally avoid controls continuing in existence suggest a continuing increased ability for accommodating private capital flows to substitute for official reserves. This, along with increased permissible flexibility of exchange rates, suggests a reduction of official reserve needs in the evolving international monetary system.

Exchange-Rate Flexibility and the Demand for Private Reserves: Effect on the World Price Level. There is less agreement regarding the impact of increased exchange-rate flexibility upon the demand for private reserves. The difference of opinion appears to arise from a confusion between the degree of permissible flexibility of exchange rates and the actual flexibility of exchange rates. Machlup argues that free market determination of exchange rates would produce especially large private foreign balances because increased hedging in forward markets by risk-averse foreign traders will produce profitable opportunities for speculators who will hold large inventories of foreign exchange.[19] McKinnon suggests in an extension of Machlup's argument that "floating exchange rates are not a solution to the (private) international liquidity problem."[20] Based essentially on an argument (already made above) for the "denomination rents" on dollars, McKinnon argues that the U.S. dollar would be the private foreign balance demanded. Therefore flexibility of nondollar exchange rates would not reduce and may increase the U.S. deficit, a net result determined by an increased private demand and reduced official foreign demand for U.S. dollar balances. The net result may be an increased

---

[19] F. Machlup, *International Payments, Debts and Gold* (New York: Charles Scribner's Sons, 1964), Chapter XII.

[20] R. I. McKinnon, *Private and Official International Money: The Case for the Dollar,* Essays in International Finance, no. 74 (Princeton, N. J.: Princeton University, 1969).

demand for dollars in view of the likelihood that economies of scale in national holdings of the intervention currency would not be applicable to private holdings.[21]

In contrast to the Machlup-McKinnon position, A. A. Walters argues that a system of floating rates drastically reduces the demand for foreign exchange by both official and private holders.[22] The fall in demand by private holders is said to occur because "the profits from exchange rate operations are also considerably reduced." [23] In a convincing and cogent analysis, Walters argues that the system of pseudo-fixed parities in the 1960s (including restrictions placed on international capital flows) led to the development of the Eurodollar and Eurocurrency markets. The large supply of private liquidity in the form of Eurodollars was generated to attack "fixed" parities which presented inviting speculative opportunities. The resulting massive supply of private liquidity led to an increased demand for official liquidity and creation of currency swaps and Special Drawing Rights (SDRs). The increase in official liquidity was in some cases invested in the Eurodollar market which in turn reinforced the growth in the supply of private liquidity already chasing the speculative profits implicit in pseudo-fixed exchange rates. The result has been that so much private liquidity has been generated that floating has been required. This in turn has resulted in a large reduction of the private demand for liquidity due to reduced speculative opportunities. The largely dollar-denominated liquidity does not disappear as rapidly as the speculative demand for it and, seeking employment in domestic sectors of economies, it produces inflationary pressure. The most promising way to eliminate inflationary pressures of this sort, in Walters' view, is to improve efficiency of domestic banking systems by removing official barriers to free competition in the systems and by retaining flexibility of exchange rates to "diminish the bait offered by the Eurobanks." [24]

Walters' argument probably takes an overly singular view of the operation of the international monetary system by emphasizing only the speculative demand for private reserves. It is, however, instructive in pointing up the fact that predictions regarding the impact of exchange-rate flexibility upon the private demand for reserves depend largely on the analysts' belief as to whether an increased *permissible* margin for exchange-rate flexibility will be accompanied by more or less *actual,* predictable variation in exchange rates. Leaving aside McKinnon's assumption in 1969 that the dollar's par value could not be changed, the Machlup-McKinnon view is that private reserve holdings will increase under zero or reduced central bank intervention in the foreign exchange markets because profitable, speculative oppor-

---

[21] This argument seems to ignore the point made by F. Machlup, *International Payments,* Chapter XII, that the private sector can obtain economies of scale by pooling of exchange risks accomplished by a group of private banks engaging in the foreign exchange business for profit.

[22] A. A. Walters, "Floating Rates, World Liquidity and Inflation," *Euromoney* (July 1973), pp. 9-15.

[23] Ibid., p. 9.

[24] Ibid., p. 15.

tunities will be increased under such circumstances.[25] The Walters view is simply the reverse. If central banks are the best judge of the permanence or transience of disturbances in the foreign exchange markets, then the Machlup-McKinnon view is correct. Walters is correct if the private sector contains the best judges of the same issue. It has been the attempt by central banks to maintain a single currency area where none could exist in view of divergent monetary policies that has supplied the proof of their poor or unrealistic judgment. One is led to conclude, therefore, that the Walters view is substantially correct and goes some of the way toward explaining the high international level of inflation in 1973–74. One is also led to the conclusion, with Walters, that in the face of the surplus of private liquidity coincident with increased flexibility of exchange rates, and lacking a world central bank to absorb the surplus, it would be preferable to allow increased movement of exchange rates rather than attempt, with little success, to place prohibitive controls on international borrowing and lending by Eurobanks.[26] The (possible) costs associated with an increase in permissible flexibility of exchange rates would not exceed the costs associated with attempts to extinguish the Eurocurrency market through restrictive controls.

It has been argued that both the official and private demand for reserves is affected by the exchange-rate regime. Leaving aside the possible harmful impact on accommodating private capital flows suggested by Williamson, the official demand for reserves is reduced, virtually by definition, when more permissible flexibility of exchange rates reduces or removes the intervention requirements of the pegging authority in the foreign exchange market. For private reserves, if more flexibility of exchange rates means less official attempts to peg unrealistic parities, speculative opportunities relative to adjustments of exchange rates will be reduced, resulting in less private demand for liquidity. The total effect of a transition to a more flexible exchange-rate regime is, then, a likely reduction in both official and private demands for liquidity. A possible result, in the absence of some global means for absorbing liquidity, has been an increase in the rate of global inflation.[27] The conclusion which

---

[25] This view is suggested in R. I. McKinnon, "Private and Official International Money," by his statement: "If, in spite of its inability to alter the relative value of its currency, the United States adopts targets. . . ."

[26] A problem may exist here as well in terms of inflationary pressure. If, as has been suggested by Mundell and Laffer in J. Wanniski, "The Case for Fixed Exchange Rates," *The Wall Street Journal* (14 June 1974), prices are rigid downward and exchange-rate changes cannot affect real prices, then increased *movement* of exchange rates and not only devaluation is inflationary. It has also been argued by R. Sweeney and T. Willett, "The Inflationary Impact of Exchange Rate Adjustments: Some Theoretical Considerations," presented at the U.S. Treasury *Conference on Effects of Exchange Rate Adjustments* (April 1974) that revaluation as well as devaluation may be inflationary. The seemingly odd result for revaluation arises if it creates excess supply in export- and import-competing sectors. Unemployment may then arise due to a combination of factor immobility and wage rigidity, and if the monetary authority responds with an increase in the money supply, inflation may result. Of course here the proximate cause of inflation remains monetary expansion.

[27] If increased flexibility of exchange rates reduces the demand for reserves in the manner described by J. H. Makin, "Exchange Rate Flexibility," an excess supply of foreign exchange

30

emerges is that if further movement toward increased permissible flexibility of exchange rates is viewed as a possibility, then attention ought to be given to devising coordinated methods for contracting world liquidity in order to avoid further inflation. Of course the corollary proposition is that plans for increasing world liquidity only make sense within the context of a move toward less permissible flexibility of exchange rates.

As a final note, it should be added here that it is not by any means being claimed that the negative impact of increased exchange-rate flexibility upon the demand for official and private reserves accounts for all of the rapid increase in the rate of world inflation. Rapid rates of monetary expansion around the world, flexibility of exchange rates per se in a world of considerable downward rigidity of prices (see footnote 26), the once-for-all impact of oil price increases representing a sudden exercise of monopoly power, and the possible increase in the velocity of international money implicit in expanded Eurocurrency operations (as described by Walters) have all acted to increase the global rate of inflation. Of these causes, however, only the first can lead to sustained inflation. The middle two causes will not lead to sustained inflation unless effectively validated by accommodating increases in the money supply provided by the monetary authority to maintain real balances. However, it is very likely that such increases will be provided in view of real fears of the contractionary implications of not doing so. The last cause represents transitional development of financial intermediaries. Basically it is being suggested here that increased flexibility of exchange rates cuts the global demand for official and private international money so that, given all of these other demand and supply factors, with increased flexibility of exchange rates, the rate of world inflation is greater than it otherwise would have been.

The Impact of Increased Exchange-Rate Flexibility on World Trade. If it is acknowledged that increased permissible flexibility of exchange rates is currently a necessary feature of the international payments system, the view as to whether this state of affairs is to be considered a necessary evil to be endured for the minimum possible period or a desirable thing to be held to over a long term should depend upon whether such an arrangement permits the maximum unimpeded international flow of goods and securities, subject to the constraints imposed by desires for independence of national monetary policy. This qualification is necessary because given

---

reserves results *ceteris paribus* when more exchange-rate flexibility occurs. The effect on a national money supply of an exogenous shock reducing the demand for reserves in the presence of a given supply of reserves is the same as the expansionary effect of an increase in the supply of reserves where the demand for reserves is fixed. In both cases, allowing the nominal money stock to rise will lead to results which erase the excess supply of reserves, even though in both cases sterilization could offset the impact of effective changes in the supply of reserves on the money supply (given that accommodating capital flows do not completely preclude sterilization). This point is implicit in the argument by M. Friedman, *International Inflation: Four Commentaries* (Chicago: Federal Reserve Bank of Chicago, July 1974), linking increased flexibility of exchange rates with increased world inflation.

adequate mobility of factors of production, a strong case can be made for the gains implicit in the reduction in transactions costs implicit in either a single currency area or in a currency union with rigid rates among inclusive currency areas. No one would seriously argue that the United States would be better off with a reversion to floating exchange rates among states or to regional currencies such as effectively prevailed in parts of the 19th century. It could, however, be argued that the common market countries would, in view of a lack of ability or desire to coordinate monetary policies, be better off with some increased flexibility of exchange rates among them. The revealed preference for some floating displayed by the Italian, British and French governments, among others, suggests that this is so.

In addition to these points it can be said that, *ceteris paribus,* an increase in transactions costs will have a negative impact upon the volume of trade and that the degree of that impact will rise or fall with the similarity or differences of tastes and endowments among traders.[28] The transactions costs referred to here include search and information costs and storage costs for inventories of foreign exchange (or access thereto) and for goods involved in international trade.[29]

A move from truly fixed to flexible exchange rates will raise search and information costs due to increased difficulty in ascertaining real terms of trade for current, as well as future, dates for delivery or receipt of goods and/or securities. Storage costs will probably increase for both foreign exchange and goods and securities entering into international trade as a result of increased uncertainty regarding the value of such inventories in terms of a single unit of account. The result of increased storage and information costs will, for given differences in tastes and endowments, be a reduction in the volume of trade. However, the recent transition of the international monetary system has not been from a system of truly fixed rates to a system of truly flexible rates. Rather the transition has been from a system of discrete ex post adjustments occurring at uncertain intervals to one of more continuous ex ante adjustment of exchange rates. In this context, what needs investigation is the impact upon trade volume of changes in the actual and expected degree of exchange-rate flexibility over time.

Of course in an analysis of the impact of exchange-rate variability upon the volume of trade, it is necessary to control other important factors such as income, relative prices, capacity utilization, and perhaps the availability of credit to finance trade. Of these factors, most official discussions emphasize income.[30] As a broad and somewhat crude overall picture of recent trends, Table 1 presents recent, trade-

---

[28] See Niehans, "Money and Barter," p. 779.

[29] Niehans, "Money and Barter," takes transactions costs to include only search and information costs, and treats storage costs separately. This semantic difference has no impact upon our simplified analysis here. In a fuller analysis, the variability of search and information costs and storage costs would also enter into the determination of full transactions costs. Since these costs are not essential to the presentation here, they are omitted.

[30] See discussion of world trade growth rates in the *Annual Report* of the International Monetary Fund, 1973, and the *International Economic Report of the President,* 1974.

Table 1
GROWTH OF GNP AND TRADE, 1961–73

	Real GNP Growth Rate[a]	Real Trade Growth Rate[b]
1961–72	5.27	
1960–70		8.3
1971	3.66	6.1
1972	5.24	8.5
1973	6.52[c]	13.5[c]

[a] 1972 export weighted average for United States, United Kingdom, France, West Germany, Italy and Japan. Calculated from unweighted data in the *International Economic Report of the President* (Washington, D.C.: U.S. Government Printing Office, 1974). Weights calculated from IMF, *International Financial Statistics*, 1968-74, various issues.

[b] Measured as real exports (f.o.b.). Source: IMF *Annual Report,* 1973.

[c] Estimated from January through October data.

weighted average rates of growth of real GNP for major industrial countries accounting for 51.9 percent of world exports in 1972 along with real rates of growth of world trade. More detailed, country-by-country estimates of determinants of trade volume for some major countries are presented in the Appendix and discussed below.

Turning first to Table 1, two suggestions emerge. First, as is well known, rates of growth of world trade have exceeded overall economic growth rates during the 1960s and early 1970s. Second, and more important for our purposes here, the positive relationship between real GNP growth rates and real trade flows has surely not been disturbed by the early stages of the transition to limited flexibility of exchange rates. If anything, the sensitivity of real trade growth to real growth of GNP appears to have increased, although this result may be illusory as the more detailed empirical analysis in the Appendix will suggest. Still it is encouraging to note that from 1971 to 1972 the elasticity of real trade growth with respect to real income growth was 0.91 while from 1972 to 1973 it was 2.41.[31] Let me hasten to add that I do not regard such preliminary evidence as powerfully convincing, but rather as an encouraging indication that real trade flows are not highly sensitive to the exchange-rate regime.[32]

---

[31] The low responsiveness of trade flows from 1971 to 1972 may be partly accounted for by the sharp increase in restrictions on capital flows in response to the sharp increases in capital movements which accompanied uncertainties regarding some "pegged" exchange rates which occurred in 1971 and 1972. See Organization for Economic Cooperation and Development, "Controls on Capital Flows: The Recent Escalation," from *Economic Outlook* (December 1972).

[32] Further, there exists more systematic evidence regarding the failure of increased permissible flexibility of exchange rate to adversely affect trade flows. An empirical study by Peter B. Clark and Charles Haulk, "Flexible Exchange Rates and the Level of Trade," mimeographed

Turning to a more systematic investigation of the effect of increased flexibility of exchange rates on trade volume, the Appendix presents estimated, real-import-demand equations for Germany, Canada, Japan, and the United Kingdom. Included as an explanatory variable in each of these equations is the actual variability of spot and forward exchange rates of local currencies against the U.S. dollar. Leaving aside the qualifications to the analysis which are fully presented in the Appendix, the estimated equations do not support the hypothesis that exchange-rate variability, either actual (spot) or expected (forward), has any systematic impact upon trade volume. Based on the above discussion, it would be expected that increased exchange-rate variability would have a negative impact on real trade volume *if* increased exchange-rate flexibility raised actual search and information costs and/or storage costs involved in international trade. The evidence in the Appendix suggests that such costs have not risen significantly during the transition from the Bretton Woods system of adjustable parities to the current system of continuous limited flexibility of exchange rates.

Uncertainty with Limited Flexibility versus "Fixed" Rates. The key to understanding the transition from Bretton Woods to the current system lies with the nature and consequent level of uncertainty regarding availability of foreign exchange. The Bretton Woods system aimed at supplying unlimited quantities of foreign exchange at a fixed price. Where coordination of monetary policy prevented this, a confusion of means and ends set in and effectively only limited quantities were made available at a fixed price by controls, particularly on international capital flows. As we have seen, the effectiveness of such controls was sharply reduced by the growth of Euro-currency markets. The result was increased uncertainty regarding the price at which foreign exchange could be obtained or sold and continued uncertainty regarding quantity. These uncertainties and the attendant high level of transactions costs probably reached their peak in 1971 when real trade flows fell to a 6.5 percent annual rate of growth, significantly below the long-run trend of 8.3 percent from 1960–70. The advent of limited flexibility has served to reduce uncertainty regarding price over discrete intervals such as 90 or 180 days. The probability that the private sector can predict the timing and magnitude of exchange-rate changes is higher when the inputs for the prediction are market forces rather than guesses about political judgments.

All of this discussion is not meant to argue that, if the world moved to truly fixed exchange rates in the future, the volume of world trade would not rise. It

(Washington, D.C.: U.S. Treasury Dept., 1972), detected no reduction in the trade volume for Canada attributable to increased flexibility of exchange rates during its period of "floating" in the 1950s. This finding may, of course, be due to the fact that only a small increase in actual exchange-rate variability over time accompanied the reduced level of central bank intervention. The possibility that increased uncertainty regarding future exchange rates did not accompany the small increase in *actual* exchange-rate variability during the Canadian "float" may account for Clark's failure to detect any significant impact on the volume of trade.

surely would, due to the lower transactions costs implicit in unlimited availability of foreign exchange at a fixed price. But the world can be made better off by the relaxation of any constraint. To suggest a move to truly fixed exchange rates with a single world money necessarily implies relaxation of the constraint on the world payments system that is implied by desires for national monetary autonomy.

From the point of view of raising the productivity of money, the world would be better off with a single money and a single world central bank of any sort.[33] But a world central bank has to supply money which has evolved or will evolve to be the lowest-cost way of acquiring information about exchange opportunities and effecting transactions, and currently the U.S. dollar is the "only game in town." The world central bank role was fairly well served by the United States as long as it maintained a passive balance-of-payments policy and as long as inflation in the United States (and implicitly elsewhere) remained low. However, concern on the part of U.S. producers regarding their ability to sell abroad and the curse (to them and not to consumers) of "cheap" foreign goods ended the U.S. role as solver of the redundancy problem. A world ambivalent, yet acquiescent, to the international monetary role of the U.S. dollar was disturbed in 1971 by what may become an exchange of the reserve currency role of the dollar for an ability of the United States to alter its exchange rate. This move caused great confusion among international monetary managers because the G-10 countries, other than the United States, were not certain whether they wanted to continue to accumulate dollars and sell more to the United States or sell less to the United States and evolve a "new," as yet unspecified and very remote, international money. The United States, for its part, was and remains unsure whether it wants to relinquish entirely the reserve currency role of the dollar for complete freedom to adjust rates of exchange. In the period of great uncertainty that has resulted from this two-sided ambivalence, the expedient of limited flexibility of exchange rates has emerged as a fact of life that is consistent with the simple inability of all participants in the western trading world to make up their minds about what exchange-rate regime is most desirable. In addition, the U.S. dollar probably remains the best bet for serving private liquidity needs and will continue in that role unless or until some new "official reserve unit" such as new SDRs becomes the intervention currency. Since this step would require private holding of such instruments, the future for such an arrangement is uncertain. A highly successful new asset of this type would tend to dominate national monies since it would represent the minimum-cost means of obtaining information about worldwide market prices for goods and securities and would

---

[33] Allan H. Meltzer, "The Dollar as International Money," *Banca Nazionale del Lavoro Quarterly Review* (March 1973), pp. 21-28, has argued this case for the U.S. dollar. Such a case is also implicit in R. N. Cooper's "Eurodollars, Reserve Dollars" discussion of the fundamental changes that would be required in the international monetary system for a full restoration of the dollar to the role of a strictly national currency. See Harry Johnson, "Political Economy Aspects of International Monetary Reform," *Journal of International Economics* (September 1972), pp. 401-424, for an instructive parable of the cat-and-mouse role of the United States as a world central bank.

therefore emerge, like the dollar did in its intervention role, as a dominant unit of account and medium of exchange. The resultant demand for loans denominated in the official reserve unit would swell financial capital market activity and complete its establishment as the dominant world money with a superior store-of-value role. The evolution of such an official reserve unit to a status as the world money would be likely to parallel that of the U.S. dollar. In view of the level of understanding already extant regarding the evolution of the dollar and in the absence of any national identity, such an official reserve unit would also be likely to evolve faster and further than the U.S. dollar to a role as a dominant world money. This possibility suggests that national central banks may well be reluctant to collaborate in the production of some body which produces a money superior to the money which each national bank supplies to its residents.[34]

In short, we are abruptly returned to the constraint that the desire for national monetary sovereignty places on the configuration of the international monetary system. In the face of such a constraint and the likely continuation on all sides of ambivalence about the U.S. dollar's role as international money, we shall probably do best to stick with limited flexibility. This need not be a bad thing if the reduced restrictions on goods and capital flows made possible under such a system are permitted to occur. There are, however, different forms of limited flexibility and it is worth paying some attention to selecting the best one.

4. Toward an Optimal Degree of Flexibility of Exchange Rates

A System of Limited Exchange-Rate Flexibility. The primary dimensions of a system of limited exchange-rate flexibility are its degree and timing. Degree, of course, refers to the position of an exchange-rate system on the continuum from rigidly fixed exchange rates to freely flexible rates. Timing refers to whether or not exchange rates are adjusted, ex post in response to recorded disequilibria in the foreign exchange market as with adjustable peg systems, or whether exchange rates are permitted to change ex ante in anticipation of the likelihood that some part of any contemporaneous disturbance in the foreign exchange market will be nonrandom and therefore ought not to be offset.

To begin with the easiest issue, that of timing, the notion of ex post exchange-rate adjustment systems of the automatic, crawling, or adjustable peg type appears

---

[34] As F. Machlup, "The Official SDR Standard and Private SDR Money," *Euromoney* (November 1973), p. 29-33, suggests, governments may "take a dim view" of private, official-reserve-unit-denominated operations parallel to national-money-denominated operations if the former "begins to impinge on the use of national currency." He suggests, however, that toleration of Eurocurrency operations in the past may mean that official reserve unit operations would not be inhibited by governments. This suggestion, based on past actions, may well be incorrect. As integration of national economies is increased, the likelihood that an international money will permit least-cost transactions chains will increase, thereby establishing dominance over national monies.

to have been largely abandoned. The reason, anticipated by a number of analysts, is that the principle of substituting certainty of a small parity adjustment for uncertainty regarding a relatively large parity adjustment upon which ex post systems are based is intrinsically destabilizing. The expected returns to moving capital in response to a small but well-known parity change can be as large as those to moving capital in response to an unknown adjustment at an unknown time. If not fully as large as the latter, the former returns are large enough to induce capital movements in anticipation of "peg" adjustment of sufficient size to disrupt such a system. Even if the adjustable peg system does not produce destabilizing results, simulation analysis of adjustable pegs versus ex ante limited exchange-rate flexibility in a general equilibrium setting shows that the latter system produces faster convergence times for policy goals like real income (employment), interest rates, the price level, and balance-of-payments equilibrium.[35]

As has been suggested, the alternative to the adjustable peg or ex post adjustment system in a world of limited flexibility of exchange rates is the ex ante system of adjustment whereby some probability (which may be varied over time) is assigned to whether a typical disturbance impinging on the foreign exchange market is permanent and should be permitted to affect the exchange rate or is temporary and self-reversing and should be offset by intervention in the foreign exchange market. This way of viewing the nature of disturbances in the foreign exchange market really amounts to raising the question of just who ought to be making the decision as to whether exchange-market disturbances ought to be offset.

It may be argued, as by Porter and Kouri, that very little official intervention is required in the foreign exchange market under any exchange-rate system because accommodating private capital flows will arise to finance reversible current-account disturbances producing a zero net effect upon the excess demand (supply) for foreign exchange.[36] The implicit judgment is, of course, that where such accommodating flows do not arise, the disturbance does not have an expected long-run value of zero and therefore ought not to be offset in the first place. Such nonrandom disturbances should be permitted to affect the exchange rate in order to avoid chronic reserve gains or losses over time.

Even allowing for the notion that only nonrandom disturbances ought not to be offset, it is not apparent that advocates of the accommodating capital-flows approach mean to suggest that official reserves could be zero under a regime of fixity or limited flexibility of exchange rates. In the first place, simple time lags may exist between the time when random current-account disequilibria generate a requirement for accommodating capital flows and the time when those flows actually occur. Second, though it may be claimed that, in view of losses incurred

---

[35] See John H. Makin, "Alternative Exchange Rate Management Systems: A Simulation Study," a paper presented at the annual meetings of the Western Economic Association, Las Vegas, Nevada, June 1974.

[36] Porter and Kouri, "International Capital Flows," pp. 443-468.

by those who are wrong, judgments by the private sector as to the ultimate reversibility of current-account disturbances are superior to those which the official sector could make, insofar as information is imperfect, the inverse correlation between current-account disturbances and accommodating capital flows is not unity. In short, there exists some error term, ϵ, in the expression:

$$TC_t = b \ CAB_t + \epsilon_t \tag{1}$$

where
$$E[b] = -1 \qquad \sigma_b \neq 0$$
$$E[e] \neq 0$$
$$\sigma_\epsilon \neq 0$$

and TC_t = capital account at time t (net inflow),

CAB = current account surplus at time t.[37]

Some official reserves are required with fixity or limited flexibility of exchange rate so long as $R^2 \neq 1$ for equation (1). In short, it is highly unlikely that accommodating private capital flows obviate the need for official reserves where exchange rates are not completely flexible.

In terms of timing, then, the current widespread system of ex ante adjustment, which is referred to here as limited flexibility to avoid the inappropriately pejorative term, "dirty floating," represents an improvement over the Bretton Woods system where central banks chose to offset by intervention virtually all foreign exchange market disturbances in defense of rigidly fixed parities. The latter approach, which amounted to pretending that some irreversible disturbances in the foreign exchange market were only temporary, of course led to more uncertainty about exchange rates rather than less, as was intended. When the Eurocurrency markets had become fully developed by the late 1960s, the speculative capital flows which arose in response to central bank attempts to offset obviously irreversible disturbances led to the breakdown of the fixed parity system.

Having seen an improvement over the unlimited intervention system represented by Bretton Woods, the question which remains is whether we can do still better. This question amounts to raising the issue of the optimum *degree* of exchange-rate flexibility over time. Advocates of the accommodating private capital-flows approach might argue that the optimum degree of exchange-rate flexibility over time is really a red herring as a policy issue. In their view, one should really just offset, with official intervention, disturbances that are implied by $\sigma_\epsilon \neq 0$ in equation (1) and let accommodating private capital flows do the rest. How-

---

[37] In fact, based on Kouri and Porter, "International Capital Flows," pp. 443-468, equation (1) is mis-specified because of left-out exogenous variables including changes in domestic income, foreign interest rates, net domestic assets of central banks, and risk variables concerning expected exchange-rate changes. This need not trouble us here since equation (1) is only employed for exposition. The left-out variables will imply serial correlation in the equation so that $E[\epsilon] \neq 0$. The implication of this for limited flexibility of exchange rates is discussed below.

ever, a problem arises here if the private sector perceives that a series of disturbances in the current account is not random and ought not to be accommodated.[38] In such a case the net foreign-exchange-market disturbance facing the intervention authority has a random component from $\sigma_\epsilon \neq 0$ and a nonrandom component from the current account. As we shall see, it is possible to obtain information on the mix between these components, but at this stage it is at least possible to rule out the polar cases for disturbances confronting the intervention authority of complete randomness (logically implying full intervention) and complete nonrandomness (logically implying zero intervention). Therefore, even in the presence of accommodating private capital flows, some degree of limited intervention in the foreign exchange market is justified.

The conclusion that there exists some appropriate nonzero level of exchange-rate flexibility (or some appropriate degree of limited intervention) does not identify for us ex ante the optimal degree of exchange-rate flexibility over time. There are two ways to deal with this problem. The first approach is suggested by an allegorical plan for the optimal layout of campus walkways. The plan involves determining the routes which walkways should take by simply doing nothing until the grass is worn down over the routes determined by revealed preferences of intracampus travelers and then pave over the worn paths. The implied suggestion is, of course, simply to allow the degree of exchange-rate flexibility to evolve over time and adopt or "pave over" the one which emerges. While it may be forcing the analogy a bit, it does seem worthwhile to allow for the fact that desired paths may change over time on account of the relocation of mass lectures in another existing structure. It is the rigidifying of the arrangements which should cause uneasiness. Further, it seems a shame to put up with muddy and rutted paths for any period of time if some means exists to predict accurately the optimal locations for paths. In short, it seems worthwhile to try and explore the factors which might determine the optimal degree of exchange-rate flexibility over time, not with an eye to adopting a single, rigid system of intervention, but rather with an eye to speeding the transition from one system to another when factors affecting optimal flexibility change over time.[39]

---

[38] It is important also to bear in mind the terms upon which private accommodation, or, equivalently, private borrowing or lending can be conducted. If a current-account surplus suggests net private lending abroad, then interest rates at home and abroad must be such as to induce the implied acquisition of future goods in favor of expenditure on current goods. Conversely, given a deficit, net private borrowing from foreigners will depend upon relative interest rates. More generally, the terms of trade between current and future goods as represented by the real interest rate will affect the choice between net purchases of current and future goods by and from foreigners—represented by the decomposition of the balance of payments into current and capital accounts.

[39] Some of the following material is drawn from comments which I introduced at the September 1971 AEI Conference on International Monetary Problems. See J. H. Makin, "Comment on Exchange Rate Flexibility," in F. Machlup et al., *International Monetary Problems* (Washington, D. C.: American Enterprise Institute for Public Policy Research, 1972), pp. 102-104.

Real Resource Allocation and the Exchange-Rate Regime. When the issue of limited flexibility of exchange rates is raised, there is some recognition, implicit or explicit, that there exists some time interval of less than infinite duration over which exchange rates ought not to remain fixed. At one extreme, the neoclassical analysis generally assumes that resource adjustments, in terms of movements of resources in response to changes in market prices, occur very quickly and are therefore virtually costless. If one assumes that resources move costlessly, over any time period, there is no logical basis for the existence of inaccurate price messages like disequilibrium exchange rates regarding where resources ought to move. The Bretton Woods system, on the other hand, has been associated with fixity of exchange rates unless there exists some "fundamental disequilibrium." Such a view suggests that resources move more slowly than in the neoclassical case or, equivalently, at great cost, since there is a lower cost assigned to the movement of resources in response to a long-persisting disequilibrium exchange rate.

It has been suggested by Mundell and Laffer that devaluation leads only to changes in nominal prices which maintain equal real prices (see Wanniski).[40] Of course if this is the case, then real resource allocation is independent of exchange rates, and the resource movement in response to exchange-rate changes being discussed here would not be expected to occur.

Since interpretation here of the Mundell-Laffer view is only secondhand (by way of the Wanniski article on their views cited above) the response is only to a supposition that I have correctly perceived their position. There are two arguments to counter the asserted independence of real prices and therefore of real resource allocation from exchange rates. The first is dynamic. Granting the perceived Mundell-Laffer argument, how long does it take nominal prices to adjust in response to an exchange-rate change? If adjustment is not instantaneous, which seems likely, then transitional adjustment of real resources will occur, which in itself will result in a new equilibrium set of real prices. The second argument with the perceived Mundell-Laffer view is more fundamental. It is to argue directly that devaluation aims at creating an excess demand for home-produced tradables and tradable substitutes by raising the relative prices of imports at home expressed in the home currency and lowering the relative prices of exports abroad expressed in foreign currency. This does result in inflationary pressure in the devaluing country because prices of domestic import substitutes rise and prices of domestic exportables rise, both due to a shift of demand onto those products. But the inflation should not leave relative prices unaffected unless (1) there was full employment in the first place, in which case devaluation is completely unjustified, (2) no resource reallocation occurred in response to the transitional change in relative prices, if indeed that is all that occurs, and (3) hoarding is absent from the demand equations of all commodities and/or real balances passively adjust in the face of price-level changes. (Of course, if the monetary authority acts to

---

[40] J. Wanniski, "The Case for Fixed Exchange Rates," *The Wall Street Journal* (14 June 1974).

keep real balances unchanged, further inflation will result in the devaluing country.)

If one accepts the notions that exchange rates affect resource allocation, that the movement of resources through space requires time, and that the cost of such movement rises with the rate at which it is executed, the question arises as to whether there exists a positive net return from having resources ignore for some time the movements implied by disequilibrium prices which may not persist for very long. It may be that random events imply a smaller or zero net change in prices and that beginning the costly movement of resources in response to any change in exchange rates will become an ex post error if the short-run equilibrium rate is constantly fluctuating about some long-run equilibrium value.

Exchange-rate movements, of course, can be and currently are to some extent suppressed by substituting (presumably reversible) changes in the quantity of central bank holdings of foreign exchange for changes in the price of foreign exchange. This approach is implicit in the "liquidity" (relative quantity of money adjustment) response to balance-of-payments disequilibria.

What is important to note is that an answer to the question of what is the optimum time domain for exchange-rate fixity also implies an optimum mix between liquidity (quantity) and adjustment (price) responses to balance-of-payments disequilibria. Once the optimum period over which exchange rates ought to be held constant is selected, it is possible to select a liquidity stock which precludes, by some given margin, the possibility of running out of reserves. This decision would, of course, require information as to the maximum likelihood value of the amplitude of shocks expected to cause payments disequilibria at a given exchange rate. It is possible to narrow the bands between currencies as much as one likes so long as it is possible to arrange for accommodating private capital flows to finance current account disequilibria between countries and so long as one assumes over some finite time period a zero expected value of net payments disequilibria between countries. This amounts, as we have seen, to an unwarranted assumption of an expected value of zero for the error term in equation (1).

Determination of the Appropriate Degree of Exchange-Rate Flexibility. Determination of just how much exchange-rate flexibility to employ over time requires an operational procedure that will identify the mix between nonrandom disturbances and random disturbances not financed by accommodating private capital flows that impinge upon the foreign exchange market. Such a procedure could be put into effect by having the intervention authority, given some perceived equilibrium exchange rate, assign an ex ante probability to the permanence or self-reversing property of any given shift in the private demand or supply schedule for foreign exchange. This in turn would lead to an exchange-rate change given zero intervention or a reserve change at a given exchange rate. As we have suggested, this notion can only represent a qualitative improvement in intervention policy since ample evidence has been provided during the operation of fixed exchange-rate systems that ex ante all disturbances in the foreign exchange market at some par value for the exchange rate cannot be regarded as self-reversing. The quantitative question of what ex ante probability to assign to the permanence of an exchange-market disturbance away from some perceived equilibrium could be answered over time by observing whether chronic reserve changes accompany a given degree of intervention (based upon, say, a perceived probability that 50 percent of any quantity disturbance at a given perceived long-run equilibrium exchange rate is permanent). The intervention level should be reduced until evidence of chronic reserve changes is removed. If this proves impossible for a given perceived equilibrium exchange rate, of course, the suggestion is for an alteration in that rate with persistent reserve losses at a given level of intervention raising the perceived equilibrium exchange rate and persistent reserve gains lowering it.

In effect, such a system of limited intervention gives the central bank an additional instrument with which to resolve balance-of-payments disequilibria by means of a variable mix between reserve changes and exchange-rate changes. The central bank may operate with a perceived target exchange rate at which intervention falls to zero when the private market clears, but that rate should not be announced. With no announced target, the target itself may be gradually adjusted over time on the basis of evidence—derived from reserve changes—that the target exchange rate is inconsistent with a long-run path of the balance of payments about an equilibrium trend. Intervention should be employed only to smooth deviation from the trend. The additional instrument represented by a variable degree of limited intervention permits the use of monetary and fiscal policy instruments for domestic goals such as full employment, price stability or growth.[41]

In sum, the initial step for arriving at an answer to the question of the optimal degree of exchange-rate flexibility is essentially equivalent to waiting to see where paths are worn by intracampus travelers. The degree of intervention in the foreign exchange markets is set to reflect some perceived element of nonrandomness in exchange-market disturbances occurring at some perceived but unannounced equilibrium exchange rate. Both the degree of intervention in the short run and the perceived equilibrium exchange rate in the long run are then adjusted on the basis of feedback supplied by reserve changes until only random elements remain in reserve changes over and above those handled by the disturbances accommodated by private capital flows. In a stationary world the implication is that the perceived equilibrium exchange rate would be adjusted until it coincided with an actual equilibrium rate insofar as, at that rate, exchange-market disturbances could be viewed as random. From the theory of precautionary reserves, the appropriate level of official reserves could then be determined, based upon the variance of

---

[41] See J. H. Makin, "Alternative Exchange Rate Management Systems," for a fuller exposition comparing a system of limited intervention with adjustable pegs based upon parameter values for the United States.

random disturbances, the cost of holding reserves (future goods), or the interest rate and the cost of arranging coverage for a shortage of reserves.

But the world is, of course, not stationary and therefore neither is the equilibrium exchange rate. Indeed the unrealistic hope that the equilibrium exchange rate could be picked and remain undisturbed over time was at the heart of the failure of Bretton Woods. Neither the degree of intervention nor the perceived equilibrium exchange rate should be "paved over" or rigidified. The former should be free to change to adjust for alterations in the *rate* at which nonrandom disturbances impinge upon the foreign exchange market while the latter should be free to change to adjust for alterations in the cumulative effects of nonrandom disturbances upon the equilibrium exchange rate.

Other Approaches to Optimal Exchange-Rate Adjustment Over Time. There exists a class of arguments for an optimum quantity of international reserves and an implied "Case for Optimum Exchange Rate Stability" put forward by Grubel essentially extending the work by Clark to include in an international setting the optimum quantity of money arguments put forward by Friedman.[42] Clark argued (in his 1970 article) that if a social-welfare function is postulated in terms of the level and variability of the national income stream, the well-being of a risk-averse society is increased by a reduction in the variability of the income stream made possible by a stock of international reserves which permits financing of random payments imbalances. The marginal benefits of reduced income variability are equated with the marginal costs of earning reserves.

Leaving aside the fact that this argument takes no account of the fact that private capital flows are available to finance random payments imbalances and that therefore the costs of official reserve accumulation that lower income levels may be unjustified, it can be argued that larger official reserve holdings will actually increase rather than reduce the variability of the income stream. Arguments for a stabilizing large stock of official reserves presuppose two things: (1) that shocks are random and hence the expected value is zero, and (2) that maintenance of a disequilibrium exchange rate over a long period of time is both costless in terms of resource allocation and without impact on the likelihood that the economy can return to a condition of balance-of-payments equilibrium at the original par value that the central bank seeks to maintain.[43] These conditions are unlikely to be

---

[42] Grubel, "The Case for Optimum Exchange Rate Stability," pp. 351-381; Clark, "Interest Payments," pp. 537-564 and "Optimum International Reserves and the Speed of Adjustment," *Journal of Political Economy* (March/April 1970), pp. 356-370; Milton Friedman, "The Optimum Quantity of Money," in M. Friedman, *The Optimum Quantity of Money and Other Essays* (Chicago: Aldine Publishing Co., 1969).

[43] Note that the argument for accommodating private capital flows as a substitute for official reserves presupposes only that current-account shocks are random while the official reserves argument presupposes that overall balance-of-payments shocks are random. Indeed, if accommodating flows of private capital finance all random current-account balances, then the only

satisfied if it can be shown that random shocks will tend to be reinforced rather than reversed by a policy of maintaining a fixed exchange rate. I have argued elsewhere that both real and financial capital flows as well as real resource movements between tradable- and nontradable-goods sectors will reinforce the pressure of exogenous shocks on a given exchange rate over time.[44] The only way to avoid such reinforcing shocks is for the central bank to identify ex ante which disturbances will be temporary or, failing this, to assign some probability to the permanence or transitoriness of a typical exchange-market disturbance. In short, arguments suggesting the optimality of larger reserve holdings to lower the variability of the domestic income stream fail to recognize that resource movements which themselves affect the equilibrium exchange rate are not independent of its level. The equilibrium exchange rate is an endogenous variable whose equilibrium value is simultaneously determined along with the income and relative prices existing for an economy.

This view puts me in disagreement with Grubel, who bases his argument for the "social productivity of international reserves" on the notion that "one essential character of all the disturbances (unpredictable exogenous shocks to the national and international economies) described is that they tend to be self-reversing or offset by disturbances with opposite effects originating domestically or abroad." [45] It is claimed that it is not crucial to this argument for offsetting disturbances that they net to zero over time because once a country does run out of reserves, its beliefs regarding the permanent or transient nature of disturbances become immaterial and it must change its exchange rate anyway. Grubel's argument is valid ex post and is based on his explicit assertion that "the unsuccessful post-war attempts to define 'fundamental disequilibrium' basically faltered on the fact that it is impossible in principle to distinguish ex ante trends from cycles." [46] It has already been argued in the previous section that the Bretton Woods system faltered on the notion adopted by central banks that ex ante all disturbances were reversible, precisely Grubel's view. The system failed when this proposition was revealed to be false. This result strongly suggests that a system of limited flexibility which permits adjustment over time in the degree of foreign-exchange-market intervention and in the perceived equilibrium exchange rate will, among other things, reduce the demand for official reserves since nonrandom disturbances are no longer to be financed systematically.

In sum, it has been argued that the optimal degree of exchange-rate flexibility over time, or equivalently the optimal degree of official intervention in the foreign

---

disturbances left for official financing are disturbances perceived by the private sector to be nonrandom, leaving aside the imbalances which may arise from slack in equation (1).

The suggestion here is for a very low level of official intervention in the foreign exchange markets and therefore a negative marginal product for high levels of official reserves.

[44] See John H. Makin, "Capital Flows and Exchange-Rate Flexibility."

[45] Grubel, "The Case for Optimum Exchange Rate Stability," p. 353.

[46] Ibid., p. 359.

exchange market, is a function of two things: (1) the responsiveness to random current-account disequilibria of accommodating private capital flows, and (2) the degree of nonrandomness in the shocks impinging on the foreign exchange market which depends in turn on the degree of nonrandomness of shocks to the current account and on the imperfect correlation between random current-account shocks and accommodating flows of private capital. These criteria suggest that a variable degree of permissible exchange-rate flexibility is desirable. The corollary proposition is that the marginal productivity of existing high levels of official international reserves may be negative, since the levels are in excess of the quantity required to finance random disturbances to the foreign exchange market. If this is the case, Grubel's argument (based on the analogy with private domestic money balances) for paying interest on officially held SDRs in order to induce a larger equilibrium stock of official reserves is invalid. Such payment would further increase the net social cost implicit in holdings of official reserve stocks by increasing the ability to finance nonrandom foreign-exchange-market disturbances, thereby increasing the likelihood of a higher level of speculative capital flows and increasing the resource-misallocation costs implicit in disequilibrium exchange rates.

5. Summary and Conclusions

It has been argued here that the increased mobility of capital through the Euro-currency markets has been a major catalyst in transforming the international monetary system from a fixed-exchange-rate orientation to a flexible-exchange-rate orientation. The catalyst had its effect primarily from about 1969 to 1971 for two reasons. First, the evolution of the U.S. dollar to a status as an international unit of account, medium of exchange, and store of value had been completed since the early 1960s, and subsequent competition for the denomination rents implicit in that role had by the late 1960s greatly expanded the Eurodollar market which lay largely outside of the control of national monetary authorities. Second, the degree of coordination of national monetary policies fell to a low level while the United States, in the midst of an inflationary episode, abandoned its passive policy toward the balance of payments. The resultant increase in foreign official dollar holdings, paired with a desire on the part of the United States to achieve a balance-of-payments equilibrium, forced the exchange-rate changes which began in August 1971. An attempt to return to fixed rates in December 1971 proved impossible in view of the combination of a high degree of capital market integration in the presence of poorly coordinated national monetary policies.

It has been argued also that the resultant system of limited exchange-rate flexibility represents an appropriate and workable response to the set of circumstances which brought it about. Therefore a variable degree of limited exchange-rate flexibility should characterize the international payments system as an additional policy instrument to effectively validate any degree of revealed preference among nations for coordination of national monetary policies or, less likely, for establishment of a true world central bank.

Finally, the transition to limited flexibility of exchange rates has produced effects on world prices but no discernible effect on world trade flows. The effect on prices arises from the negative impact upon the effective demand for both private and official reserves caused by a transition to limited flexibility. Some of the worldwide inflation experienced after 1971 was due to the appearance of excess liquidity associated with the new exchange-rate regime. The implication is that in a world of changing degrees of exchange-rate flexibility, particularly where a major transition occurs such as that after August 1971, attention should be given to devising means of readily adjusting, downward as well as upward, the quantity of international liquidity.

Appendix: The Impact of Exchange-Rate Variability on Trade Flows in Four Industrial Countries

Import demand equations were fitted for four countries, Germany, Japan, United Kingdom, and Canada, for which data were readily available in order to assess systematically the impact of exchange-rate variability on trade. Included among the usual explanatory variables of income, relative prices, capacity utilization, and investment were indices of the variability of the spot and forward exchange rate of the country in question against the U.S. dollar. In no case did the estimated equations support the hypothesis that, in the presence of the usual explanatory variables, increased exchange-rate variability will reduce the volume of trade.

While the index of exchange-rate variability, expressed in terms of dollars, that was employed has some shortcomings in view of the fact that trade with the United States by no means exhausts the trade of countries in question, it is not unreasonable to assume that some non-U.S. trade has been conducted in dollars during the period under investigation (1960IV through 1973IV).[1] Variability against the dollar is the most comprehensive single index of exchange-rate variability available over the long term in view of the dollar's intervention role in the Bretton Woods system. New trade-weighted indices of currencies against a package of other currencies have only been available in recent years, particularly since 1971. Once longer series of such data are available, they will constitute a more comprehensive index of exchange-rate variability facing a nation of traders than does the dollar rate alone.

The index of exchange-rate variability employed here is a moving standard deviation calculated from six-month blocs of data. While such an index of varia-

Preparation of this appendix was expedited by the able programming of Paul Keuler of the Social Science Research Facility at the University of Wisconsin—Milwaukee. Discussion with Ragnhild Mowill of the Rand Corporation also proved valuable.

[1] The percentage of total imports from the United States in 1970 was 11.0 for Germany, 29.5 for Japan, 13.0 for United Kingdom, and 67.6 for Canada.

bility will likely be lower in the pre-1971 period, it can reflect any actual increases in crisis periods before 1971, in the period from August 1971 to December 1971, and subsequently, when wider bands were permitted. Also, the figures will reflect the impact upon exchange-rate variability of the Canadian float begun in May 1970, the U.K. float begun in June 1972, and the Japanese float begun in February 1973.

There is little doubt that actual variability of exchange rates has increased since 1971. My calculated indices of variability show this as well as a recent investigation by Hirsch and Higham.[2] The important question, however, is whether such an increase in variability constitutes an increase in actual uncertainty regarding future rates that will in turn increase the cost of conducting trade and thereby, *ceteris paribus,* reduced trade volume.

The import equations presented here are closely related to those employed by Clark.[3] Clark used this formulation to test the same hypothesis regarding the impact of exchange-rate variability on trade volume that is being tested here and found no negative impact in the case of Canada.[4] This study employs fifty-three quarterly observations for the period from 1960IV–1973IV. With the exception of the index of capacity utilization, all data are drawn from *International Financial Statistics* published by the International Monetary Fund. Symbols and descriptions of the variables are as follows:

$M/$ = real imports measured as nominal imports (cif) deflated by an index of import prices. Expressed in billions of units of local currency, except for the United Kingdom, where they are expressed in millions of pounds sterling.

$Y/$ = real GNP measured as nominal GNP deflated by the consumer price index. Expressed in billions of units of local currency, and seasonally adjusted at annual rates for Canada and Germany.

$P/$ = relative price of imports measured as the import price index divided by the consumer price index.

$CU/$ = index of capacity utilization from OECD biannual estimates. Quarterly data interpolated from biannual series.

$VS(VF)$ = moving standard deviation of spot (forward) exchange rate of local currency against dollars.

D_i = seasonal dummy variables $i = 1 \ldots 3$.

$\overline{R}^2$ = portion of explained variance adjusted for degrees of freedom.

---

[2] Fred Hirsch and David Higham, "Floating Rates—Expectations and Experience," *The Three Banks Review* (June 1974), pp. 3-34.

[3] Peter B. Clark and Charles J. Haulk, "Flexible Exchange Rates and the Level of Trade: A Preliminary Analysis of the Canadian Experience," mimeographed (Washington, D. C.: Department of the Treasury, 1972).

[4] Clark's and Haulk's figures were for quarterly standard deviations of the forward and spot rates. They investigated only the case of Canada in subperiods of "floating" and "fixed" rates from 1952-70.

DW = Durbin Watson statistic.

t-ratios are in parentheses below estimated coefficients.

The equation to be fitted for each of $i = 1 \ldots 4$ countries is:

$$M/_{i_t} = a_o + a_1 Y/_{i_t} + a_2 P/_{i_t} + a_3 I/_{i_t} + a_4 CU_{i_t}$$
$$+ a_5 VS_{i_t}(VF)_{i_t} + a_6 D_1 + a_7 D_2 + a_8 D_3 + e_t \qquad \text{(A.1)}$$

where hypothesized coefficient signs are $a_1, a_3, a_4 > 0$, $a_2 < 0$, $a_5 \gtrless 0$. Results are reported in Table A-1.

The import demand equations reported in Table A-1 suggest no statistically significant impact of exchange-rate variability upon imports of the four industrial countries investigated during the 1960IV–1973IV period. I hasten to add that these equations also display the difficulties associated with many empirical estimates of import demand equations. To the extent that import supply schedules facing these countries are not perfectly elastic, the one-stage least-squares estimates reported here will contain biased coefficients. Use of the gross relative price index may be inappropriate in view of the possibility that only a small portion of the commodities in the consumer price index may be import substitutes. The index of capacity utilization is employed as a proxy for waiting time for domestic goods which constitutes part of their cost. This index is quite crude in view of the fact, cited with respect to relative prices, that many non-import substitutes may be included in the index of capacity utilization. In addition, what really should be computed is an index of relative rates of capacity utilization since imports won't cut waiting times if both domestic and foreign suppliers have full order books. The fact that relative prices and capacity utilization variables are significant with the expected sign only for Germany probably reflects shortcomings in the data alluded to here.

In addition, two frequently cited explanatory variables for import demand analysis, foreign exchange reserves and credit, are absent from the equations presented here.[5] For developing countries, the foreign exchange reserve figure is generally taken to be relevant as an index of stringency of controls on access to foreign exchange. Therefore it is not appropriate for the highly industrialized countries under examination here. The credit variable is more easily employed in studies of aggregate exports where long-term capital outflows from the exporting country are taken as an index of credit ease. For import equations, data would be required on capital outflows from major import suppliers. In the cases at hand, a weighted average for capital outflows from groups of major import suppliers would be required. While such an effort would be desirable in a more complete study, it was not undertaken here where the main purpose has been to attempt to measure the impact, if any, of changes in exchange-rate variability upon trade flows. In

---

[5] See Edward Leamer and Robert Stern, *Quantitative International Economics* (Boston: Allyn and Bacon, 1970).

Table A-1
IMPORT DEMAND EQUATIONS 1960IV–1973IV

Country	Constant	Y/	P/	CU	VS	VF	D_1	D_2	D_3	$\bar{R}^2$	DW
						Explanatory Variables					
GERMANY	15.05 (2.34)	.0525 (13.04)	−21.01 (4.34)	.1993 (2.71)	−3.81 (1.52)		−.8172 (3.43)	−.3358 (1.31)	−1.34 (5.71)	.985	2.00[a]
	15.90 (2.35)	.0518 (12.04)	−21.57 (4.27)	.2032 (2.76)		−2.73 (1.00)	−.8110 (3.31)	−.3396 (1.29)	−1.34 (5.50)	.985	1.97[a]
CANADA	−4045 (1.86)	87.66 (10.10)	1863 (1.03)	1161 (0.45)	8636 (1.75)		−294.3 (5.96)	77.03 (1.39)	−266.3 (5.37)	.943	2.18[a]
	−3988 (1.83)	87.62 (10.06)	1805 (0.99)	10.29 (0.40)		7863 (1.60)	−291.6 (5.86)	78.74 (1.40)	−264.8 (5.28)	.943	2.19[a]
JAPAN	−996.5 (5.37)	.1694 (25.48)	319.5 (2.29)	−.00005 (0.68)	−3.703 (1.55)	[b]	330.0 (12.04)	373.9 (13.91)	309.1 (11.35)	.989	1.74
UNITED KINGDOM	−2037 (6.06)	350.7 (19.91)	463.8 (1.75)	−.00003 (0.68)	214.2 (0.68)		265.2 (10.29)	151.2 (5.77)	56.61 (2.36)	.923	1.91
	−2047 (6.33)	352.4 (20.62)	486.4 (1.87)	−.00003 (0.43)		158.9 (0.52)	268.9 (10.39)	151.5 (5.73)	57.08 (2.35)	.925	1.87

[a] Equation was reestimated using generalized least squares to adjust for autocorrelation.
[b] Data for forward rates on the yen were not available in *International Financial Statistics*.

49

view of the fairly high explanatory power of the equations reported, it seems unlikely that such an improved specification of the import demand equation would have a significant impact upon the major conclusions of this study.

It should also be noted that the export equations could have been employed along with import equations to test our hypothesis. This was done by Clark and Haulk. Aggregate export equations were not employed here because their specification entails more data problems than aggregate import equations in view of the fact that weighted averages of foreign values for some explanatory variables are required. Since there is no a priori reason why exchange-rate variability per se should affect exports differently from imports, and since Clark's results for exports were "essentially the same as those obtained for the import equation," little is lost by their omission.

As a final general comment, it is noted that no attempt has been made to experiment with various possible lag structures regarding the impact of explanatory variables upon imports. This omission is not meant to suggest that, a priori, a particular lag structure may be inappropriate. Studies like that by Junz and Rhomberg suggest that indeed the response of trade flows to price variables may be spread over a considerable period of time.[6] However, exploration of possible lag structures is not seen as essential to our purposes here.

Finally, a few specific remarks on the results reported in Table A-1 are in order. The income variable carries the hypothesized sign and, along with nearly all of the seasonal dummy variables, is a highly significant explanatory variable for imports in each of the countries tested. Real investment, which had been originally included as an explanatory variable, was in no case significant and was therefore omitted from the final set of equations estimated. The relative price variable performs well only for Germany. It carries a significant "wrong" sign for Japan which may be due to the shortcomings of such aggregate data alluded to earlier. The capacity utilization variable is significant and carries an expected sign only for Germany. The insignificant results for other countries probably reflects either shortcomings of the aggregate data or the absence of an index of *relative* rates of capacity utilization to which reference has already been made.

Exchange-rate variability (both forward and spot, as they are highly correlated) carries a statistically insignificant negative coefficient for Germany and Japan and a statistically insignificant positive coefficient for Canada and the United Kingdom.[7] As already noted, these results do not support the hypothesis of any systematic relationship between exchange-rate variability and trade volume. The

---

[6] Rudolph R. Rhomberg and Helen B. Junz, "Price Competitiveness in Export Trade among Industrial Countries," *International Finance Discussion Papers* No. 22 (Washington, D. C.: Board of Governors, January 1973).

[7] Even if the coefficients were significant, which of course they are not, the implied elasticities of trade volume with respect to increased variability of exchange rates are in all cases very small. For the variability of the spot rate, the actual elasticities calculated at the mean are as follows: Germany, -0.0065; Canada, $+0.016$; Japan, -0.0067; United Kingdom, $+0.00298$.

inconsistency of the results, moving from country to country, may reflect an unstable relationship across countries between exchange-rate variability and the direction of expected exchange-rate movements during the era of adjustable parities. The negative figures for Germany and Japan may reflect the tendency for increased variability in DM and yen (prior to mid-1973) rates to precede revaluations of these currencies. If such were the case, there would be some tendency to lower imports during such periods in anticipation of possibly lower local currency prices for imports after the anticipated revaluation.

In sum, the import demand equations presented here suggest that, in the presence of the usual explanatory variables, the real volume of imports bears no systematic relationship with the degree of actual variability of exchange rates. This result must be viewed only as preliminary evidence on the question of the impact of freely floating exchange rates on trade volume. The primary reason for such tentativeness lies with the fact that actual variability of exchange rates was confined, until the third quarter of 1971 or for about 80 percent of the time period studied, to a very low level by a high degree of central bank intervention at the edges of bands, as prescribed by the Bretton Woods system. The testing procedure here has assumed that any possible relationship between exchange-rate variability and trade volume is linear, which amounts to assuming that the nature of the relationship over a wide range of exchange-rate variability can be extrapolated from the response to changes in actual variability over a fairly narrow range. To the extent that such a relationship is nonlinear, the results obtained here could be misleading.[8] Further study is needed employing data from the third quarter of 1971 onward and, preferably, from mid-1973 onward in order to eliminate the possible extra effects on uncertainty regarding the exchange-rate regime.

---

[8] These remarks also apply to log linearity since fitting log linear equations gave substantially the same conclusions in terms of qualitative results for coefficients and significance of explanatory variables.

COMMENTARIES

Alexander K. Swoboda

Twenty minutes is an inadequate time in which to do justice to a sixty-page paper that contains, among other things, a synopsis of the causes of the rise, decline, and fall of the Bretton Woods system, a prognosis about the future, an analysis of the demand for international reserves, and an appraisal of exchange-rate flexibility. Instead of listing in detail the many points of agreement and disagreement I have with Professor Makin, I have organized my remarks into four main parts. First, I attempt to summarize what I see as the main points made by Makin; second, I offer some brief comments on these main points; third, I raise some broader methodological issues before concluding with a deliberately provocative alternative scenario to that offered by Professor Makin.

Six Major Themes

At the risk of being unfair to the author, let me distinguish six major themes, or theses, in Makin's paper. Three of these concern the past and three deal with contemporary developments and the future.

Looking at the past, Makin emphasizes three links between the growth of the Eurocurrency market and the evolution of the international monetary system. First, the Eurocurrency system is seen as a major catalyst in the transformation of the international monetary system from a liquidity- to an adjustment-oriented framework. Second, the growth of the Eurodollar market reflects the evolution of the dollar into an international money. At the same time, that market helps bid away some of the "denomination rents" which would be implicit in a "plain" dollar market. One major consequence of the growth of the Eurodollar market is an increase in capital mobility and the internationalization of capital markets. Third, Makin attributes the breakdown of the Bretton Woods system to two major causes. These are, to quote him, "uncoordinated national monetary policies" and the fact that it is "difficult to control Eurocurrency markets which readily transmit the effects of national monetary policies to frequently unreceptive trade partners."

Makin amplifies on this last theme by advancing more specific reasons for the breakdown of the system to occur in 1971 rather than earlier. These include the fact that the culmination of the Eurodollar market's evolution coincides with "the end of U.S. passive balance of payments policy." This shift in U.S. policy is ascribed, in turn, to an attempt by the United States to stave off major conversions of dollars into gold and, more importantly, to the desire to "end the tax upon U.S. producers of tradable goods that was implicit in a chronically overvalued U.S. dollar."

Turning to the future, Professor Makin advances three main theses that bear chiefly on the degree of exchange-rate flexibility and are only loosely related to the specifics of Eurocurrency markets. The first argues that the impact of the recent trend towards greater exchange-rate flexibility will be—and to some extent already has been—to diminish private and official demand for international liquidity. The side effect of this decrease is to provide additional fuel for world inflation. Second, Makin argues that additional exchange-rate flexibility has had no measurable negative effect on the volume of trade in goods and securities. Third, Makin concludes by arguing that what we need—and are likely to get—in the future is managed flexibility of exchange rates evolving towards an optimum mix of liquidity and price adjustments.

Some Specific Comments

Before turning to broader methodological issues, I should like to offer some specific comments related, on one hand, to Makin's analysis of the evolution of the Bretton Woods system and, on the other hand, to his discussion of the future and the demand for international money.

On the first of these topics, I can be brief since I shall touch on it again in the next two sections of my comments. A number of points are, however, worth emphasizing at the outset. First, the Bretton Woods system (by which, I take it, is meant roughly the international monetary system as it functioned in the late 1950s and early 1960s) started breaking down well before 1971, say, around 1966–68. Second, the breakdown of the Bretton Woods system would have occurred even if the Eurodollar market had not existed. In other words, the Eurodollar market was neither necessary nor sufficient for the breakdown to occur, although I would agree with Makin that the existence of a high degree of capital mobility did speed the process—in the sense that, although a high degree of capital mobility helps adjustment when governments follow equilibrium policies, it hinders adjustment when disequilibrium policies are pursued, as indeed they were, at least after 1968. Finally, and I will come back to this point later since it is quite important, I do not believe in the chronic overvaluation of the dollar in the 1950s and 1960s; the trouble was not a "dollar" problem in the traditional "individual-country-adjustment" approach, but a problem at the level of the functioning of the system as a whole, however badly or well that may have been understood at the time.

Turning to Makin's appraisal of the future demand for international money, a number of questions come readily to mind:

(1) It is easy to agree with Makin that official demand for reserves is likely to fall with increased exchange-rate flexibility, other things equal. However, there has been a significant fall in the supply of international liquidity to the extent that gold has become illiquid (on the other hand, its market value has increased). The general increase in uncertainty in the system over the past few years may well have increased the demand for international liquidity on that account. On balance, however, one might well conclude with Professor Makin that a temporary excess supply was created recently, resulting in increased inflation.

(2) Professor Makin argues that private demand for international liquidity would fall with increased flexibility of exchange rates because of lessened "speculative" incentives to hold international liquidity. Curiously, though, Makin fails to set off against this the possible increase in the "transactions" demand for money he rightly emphasizes in the first part of his paper.

(3) Actually, to give a well-defined meaning to the two questions above, one would first need to define what is meant by international liquidity or money, particularly under flexible exchange rates. This is a difficult enough task even under fixed rates where we can, however, agree to call "official" international liquidity those central bank assets with which the banks can purchase their own currency in the spot foreign-exchange market in order to stabilize their exchange rates. Under flexible rates, there is no clear-cut definition of international liquidity (or money), and the concept loses much of its usefulness. In particular, it might be much more helpful to speak of the private demand for foreign exchange— dollars, pounds, and so on (including specification of the type of asset), depending on the purpose of the analysis—rather than to speak of an unspecified "private demand for international liquidity." If we were to estimate outstanding private international liquidity or its growth rate, what series should we define or look at? Incidentally, if the answer is Eurocurrency holdings, the implication is a significant growth of private liquidity in spite of increased exchange-rate flexibility.

(4) Though Makin's arguments concerning the effect of increased flexibility of exchange rates on price levels and inflation rates via decreased demand for liquidity are interesting, the chains of causality involved may be much more complex than he suggests. Casual empirical evidence is just as consistent with the alternative hypothesis that increased flexibility of exchange rates is itself partly the result of an increased desire to inflate on the part of some countries. Furthermore, a fall in the demand for real money balances may well reflect stock adjustments due to an increase in the expected rate of inflation rather than to increased flexibility in exchange rates.

(5) Makin finds that increased flexibility has not led to a fall in the volume of trade—indeed, perhaps just the reverse. This is a reassuring and theoretically appealing finding. It should, however, be taken with at least three grains of salt.

First, rising inflation could be expected to cause an increase to the extent that it provides incentives for the accumulation of inventories of goods, some of which are acquired in international trade. Second, an increase in currency speculation may well increase the volume of trade since some of this speculation is effected through trade transactions and leads and lags. Third, normative conclusions should only be drawn very guardedly from an increase in the volume of trade since that increase may reflect trade diversion (or an increase in wasteful speculation) rather than trade creation.

(6) As a last point of detail, let me quarrel with Makin's equation (1) and the uses to which it is put. Beyond not being really needed, this equation tends to be misleading for heuristic purposes. It states that the capital account is equal to a coefficient, b, $(E[b] = -1)$, times the current account plus an error term. The nature of the error term should then, according to Makin, determine, in part at least, the choice of an exchange-rate regime and intervention system. This seems to me incorrect since the "error term" will itself depend on the exchange-rate regime. Thus, it is obvious that when there are no errors in variables, as Makin assumes, both the mean and variance of the "error term" must by definition be equal to zero under perfectly flexible exchange rates.

Adjustment, Overvaluation, and All That

Before concluding with an alternative scenario to that proposed by Professor Makin, I should like to raise some broader "methodological" points. These bear on the meaning of such concepts as "adjustment" and "overvaluation." An exact understanding of the context and way in which such concepts are used is essential if policy recommendations are to be based on analysis that draws on them.

(1) The term "adjustment" can be interpreted in a variety of ways. Makin begins his paper by arguing that the international payments system has evolved from "a liquidity-oriented framework to an adjustment-oriented framework." He is careful to emphasize in the next sentence that by this he means simply that more reliance is now put on variations in the price rather than in the quantity of foreign exchange. The very choice of words, however, suggests that there is more basic "adjustment" going on under flexible than under fixed exchange rates. Moreover, the term "adjustment" is given its usual broader meaning, at least implicitly, in later parts of the paper. Adjustment there refers to adjustment of absorption to income in order to bring about, for instance, a level of the current account compatible with long-term capital flows. The fact that the exchange rate fluctuates and the level of reserves is constant does not necessarily mean that adjustment—in that sense—is taking place. It will not occur if policy or some other factor keeps absorption from income (by more than some level compatible with "equilibrium" capital flows), however much exchange-rate flexibility prevails. Conversely, the fact that the exchange rate is fixed and the level of reserves varies

does not imply the absence of adjustment in the broader sense—provided, of course, that variations in reserves set in motion the changes in income or absorption required.

(2) In his discussion of the breakdown of the Bretton Woods system, Makin emphasizes the chronic overvaluation of the dollar and the tax on U.S. producers of internationally tradable goods that it implied. The concept of overvaluation or undervaluation of a currency is a slippery one—"weasel words and jargon" as Fritz Machlup would put it. In any event we have not seen any great dismantling of the barriers to trade presumably needed to keep a currency overvalued.

In the absence of increasing barriers to trade and payments, arguing that the U.S. dollar was chronically "overvalued" requires an operational definition of the expression. If by overvaluation it is meant that prices of export goods are kept "too high" relative to the prices of similar goods produced abroad *or* prices of traded goods kept "too low" relative to the price of nontraded goods at home, I would argue that such overvaluation is unlikely except over a time span of a few months at most. Goods arbitrage in integrated world markets would take care of the first type of overvaluation under fixed exchange rates, and the process by which the second is maintained has not been specified. I shall return to the implications of the absence of chronic overvaluation through goods arbitrage for "coordination" and "independence" in my fourth point below.

(3) Though this is only peripheral to the main part of Professor Makin's paper, let me emphasize the importance of distinguishing sharply between the devaluation of a fixed exchange rate and the depreciation of a currency under flexible rates. The essential difference is, of course, that with devaluation, causation runs from an autonomous (for analytical purposes) change in the exchange rate to the endogenous response of the price level and exchange reserves. With flexible exchange rates, on the contrary, it is the course of price levels in national currency which determines (partly) the exchange rate which thus becomes an endogenous variable in the analysis. Much confusion can be avoided by keeping these two cases clearly distinct.

In particular, keeping this distinction in mind helps understand why under *flexible* exchange rates a change in the general price level or in relative prices will tend to change the exchange rate, whereas an autonomous change in the exchange rate under *fixed* rates may in the long run have no effect on "real" variables but only on the general price level. This typically "monetarist" proposition about the effects of devaluation holds, of course, only if the initial position is one of equilibrium and under the assumption that there is no money illusion, in the sense that all real excess demand functions are homogeneous of degree zero in money prices and the money stock. The conclusion, then, is that once every market has cleared, relative prices return to their pre-devaluation value. But, of course, changes in relative prices will occur in the transition period—as many so-called "monetarists" have not only recognized but also emphasized—and these changes will have sizeable resource allocation effects. I would very much agree with Makin that these are indeed very important.

(4) Finally, let me comment on the role of goods market integration as it impinges on the "independence" issue.

The breakdown of the Bretton Woods system has often been attributed to a greater desire for independence of monetary policy than was available under fixed exchange rates. Though I would agree, at least partly, with this view, I would put less emphasis than most of its proponents do on the role of capital-market integration in frustrating national monetary independence under fixed exchange rates. For, even if there were no capital movements, goods market integration would rapidly frustrate the attempt to use monetary policy to keep national rates of inflation very significantly different from each other. In an important sense, the problem is not that uncoordinated monetary policies lead to the breakdown of fixed rates by creating divergent price trends, but that fixed exchange rates automatically entail a coordination of policies (or targets) that may not be desired. Of course, capital-market integration as embodied in the Eurodollar market does, in fact, play an important role in shortening even further the time or extent over which independent monetary policies may be exerted under fixed exchange rates.

Flexible rates are a means of gaining some independence, but it is important to be clear about what that independence is. During the period in which money illusion prevails, monetary policy gains some leverage on output, employment, and other real variables. During the period in which money illusion disappears—and that period may be fairly short chronologically in a generally inflationary period—the independence gained is over the price level and rate of inflation. Whether that independence is worth having—and I think it often is not—is not irrelevant to the alternative scenario that follows.

An Alternative Scenario

Like Makin's, my scenario concerns both past and future. It is given in bare outline, deliberately seeking contrast. Four features are worth noting concerning the past.

First, to reiterate a statement often made by many others in the past, the postwar international monetary system functioned quite well—even extremely well—until about 1966 or 1968. There were particular "problem" countries which tended to perform systematically better or less well than others, like Germany or the United Kingdom. On average, however, the majority of countries was satisfied with the general evolution of rates of inflation, unemployment, and growth in the world economy and with the corresponding rates implied for their economies. Only the "problem" countries were genuinely dissatisfied with having to maintain, or being unable to maintain, their rate of inflation within a band of a few percentage

58

points around the average dictated in large measure by the United States. The consequence was a number of episodic devaluations and revaluations.

The problem, however, was that of a number of countries, not that of the system as a whole. What happened to break this relatively happy state of affairs was not the abandonment of a passive United States balance-of-payments policy but, if anything, the adoption of one. This is the second feature of the past which I think is worth emphasizing. Up until 1966 the United States may not have consciously acted "positively" towards its balance of payments; its monetary policy, however, was on balance compatible with the maintenance of the system, and some attention was paid to limiting deficits.

In 1966–67 the United States initiated monetary and fiscal policies inconsistent with the maintenance of the Bretton Woods system, or acted as if it did not have a balance-of-payments constraint—and in the short run, it did not. For various reasons—financing the Vietnam War not the least among them—these policies implied a higher rate of monetary expansion and larger budget deficits and entailed a rising rate of inflation. It is striking to note that the worldwide tendency for the price of traded goods to start rising dates back to approximately 1968 and does not begin in 1971. The policy of benign (or not so benign) neglect was put in effect before its name was invented.

The consequence of quickening monetary expansion and inflation in the second half of the 1960s—and this is my third observation about the past—was increased dissatisfaction with the international monetary system on the part of the United States' partners. Inflationary policy adopted by the center country—whether appropriate or not on other grounds—is not a "country problem" but a system-wide one when, for a number of well-known reasons, the other countries are more or less pegged to the center country's rate of inflation. Some analysts have stressed seigniorage as one of the main reasons for dissatisfaction with the system. Except for the last years of massive U.S. deficits, I think seigniorage was only a minor issue—a by-product of the disagreement as to the proper rate of expansion of the system as a whole.

In any event, the final 1971 breakdown was rooted in a number of factors such as the rising economic power of the rest of the world, enabling it to express its dissatisfaction with the way the system was being run in the midst of a political vacuum. That meant that when the break finally came in 1971, it was a break not towards revising the existing or devising a new system of fixed rates, or adopting a clear and clean system of floating rates, but towards failure to agree on a properly devised system of fixed exchange rates.

Be that as it may—and this is my last point about the past—the breakdown of the Bretton Woods system was not due to the overvaluation of the dollar. Of course, the huge increase in the U.S. trade deficit in 1971 did play its role. But that increase is not surprising in view of the figures which Makin quotes about the increase in the U.S. rate of monetary expansion in the first half of 1971.

This view of the past has some implications for the future. Much hinges on the direction of U.S. policy. Given stability in the United States in terms of inflation, the rate of monetary expansion, and the rate of growth, I would guess that a number of developments will take place.

First, the more stable countries, which can best afford to do so, will again peg to the dollar. Second, the private uses of the dollar will again start expanding very rapidly. Third, perhaps after a fairly long time lag, the discovery that the freedom which flexible exchange rates affords is a difficult one to live with will lead some of the more profligate countries (the United Kingdom and Italy?) to want to come back to fixed exchange rates.

This scenario is predicated on economic stability in the United States. But even then the story may not end there, as the temptation to start the whole cycle again would be fairly high unless some agreement on a workable system is reached. Only with adoption of a clear system can the present uncertainty be alleviated and the messy dollar standard to messy flexible exchange rates and back scenario—perhaps the most likely one at present—be avoided.

From where we are, namely, messy flexible exchange rates, there are four "clean" alternatives to which we could go: a "clean" dollar standard, a world of major currency blocs linked by relatively flexible exchange rates, a system of "pure" flexible rates, and fixed rates with a world central bank. Unfortunately, I see little immediate likelihood of any of these systems being adopted. Rather, tendencies towards a messy dollar standard may well emerge. To my mind, that constitutes one compelling reason to work for a more satisfactory solution such as a world central bank.

Franco Modigliani

Professor Makin has provided us with a valuable and instructive survey of the formation of the Eurodollar market, of the circumstances leading to breakdown in the Bretton Woods system and eventually to the abandonment, *sine die,* of "permanently" fixed parities, of the experience under floating rates, and of the direction in which the international monetary system should, and could, evolve. While I find myself in agreement with much of his paper, because of limitation of space, I will concentrate on a few points of lesser agreement or points which strike me as in need of further clarification.

The International Role of the Dollar and Eurodollars

Professor Makin has endeavored (in Section 2) to apply some recent developments in monetary theory to explain the rise of the dollar to the role of international money, as well as the emergence of the Eurodollar market. I largely agree with his treatment of the first topic, but I have serious reservations about his contention that the role of the dollar provided "'denomination rents' . . . to U.S. financial institutions . . . [which] attracted competitors in the form of financial intermediaries outside the United States. . . ." (p. 23). While the developing international role of the dollar could account for an increased demand for the services of financial intermediaries offering assets and liabilities denominated in U.S. dollars, there is no good reason why it should give rise to profits which could not have been competed away by the expansion of intermediaries within the United States.

There is instead ample ground for holding that the formation of offshore institutions dealing in dollar-denominated claims was fostered initially by U.S. bank regulations. These include, in particular, Regulation Q, prohibiting the payment of interest on short-term deposits and limiting those on longer maturities, and later on, restrictions designed to improve the U.S. balance of payments. Of course, once started, the vigorous development of the Eurocurrencies market was also fostered by the absence, or looseness, of government regulations governing Eurocurrency bank transactions, and in the case of Eurodollars, by the advantage of proximity to a large portion of the customers. As a result, it is now widely held that even if Regulation Q were to be abolished or greatly relaxed (as it has already been, to some extent), the London Eurodollar market would not wither away and be reabsorbed by New York. Only regulations of the Eurodollar market appreciably more onerous than those in the United States could conceivably achieve this result.

A second point on which I am inclined to differ with Makin's interpretation of history concerns the circumstances which led to the demise of the Bretton Woods system in August 1971. In my view he greatly overstresses the importance of U.S. mercantilistic pressures to reduce the parity of the dollar in order to improve the U.S. competitive position. Surely such pressures had been developing gradually and had gathered momentum during the economic slowdown of 1970–71. But stresses in the system had started much earlier, largely under the leadership of France. One can point in particular to the recurrent concern with excessive U.S. deficits and the consequent growth of dollar reserves and to the jealousy for the asymmetric position of the United States enabling it, supposedly, to pursue its economic policies totally unconstrained by balance-of-payments considerations. Some of these stresses can, in fact, be traced as far back as the end of the 1950s. It was then that we suddenly moved from the era of worldwide dollar shortage to the era of dollar surplus and that U.S. monetary policy began to be seriously conditioned by balance-of-payments considerations.

The U.S. position grew worse in the second half of the 1960s with the Vietnam War, though it was papered over in 1969 by skyrocketing interest rates and heavy U.S. borrowing from the Eurodollar market. With the easing of monetary policy, these flows were reversed, giving rise to huge U.S. payments deficits in 1970 and the first half of 1971. In the meantime, massive speculative attacks on currencies, usually followed by changes in parities, were becoming more frequent, producing growing disenchantment with the notion of parities rigidly fixed except under conditions of "fundamental disequilibrium." "Benign neglect," reflected partly in the expansionary monetary policy episode recounted by Makin, was but the straw that broke the camel's back. Had U.S. dissatisfaction with its parity for competitive reasons been the only problem, a solution could undoubtedly have been found other than unilateral suspension of convertibility—a move which could not but destroy the Bretton Woods system as well as any possible remaining willingness on the part of the other industrial countries to give the United States any asymmetrical position (except possibly an asymmetrical disadvantage).

Alternate Exchange Systems

The issue to which I would like to devote my major comments involves Makin's analysis of alternative exchange systems. Let me first note that Makin—in common with many others favoring floating rates—tends to approach the problem in terms of inexorable natural economic laws, thus failing to recognize its great dependence on economic policies which in turn may be significantly shaped by the nature of the exchange mechanism. This failure tends to bias his judgment against any system requiring the monetary authority to intervene in the market in order to maintain the exchange rate within some limits. To illustrate, even though I am not in favor of fixed exchange rates, I feel that criticizing the Bretton Woods fixed parity system as being based on the untenable assumption that the equilibrium rate never changes misses the essence of that system.

Rather, what Bretton Woods assumed was that as a rule, countries could—by pursuing appropriate policies—adjust their economies so as to make them consistent with a stable equilibrium rate; the exception to the rule was, of course, the case of fundamental disequilibrium. A good illustration of this approach and its problems is provided by the case of Italy in 1963–64. When a combination of excess demand and aggressive unions, spurred by political developments, boosted domestic production costs to a level inconsistent with full employment and balance-of-payments equilibrium, the authorities, instead of depreciating the exchange rate, resorted to deflationary monetary and fiscal policies, which eventually made good the preexisting exchange rate—though at the cost (in my view excessive) of a slowdown in output and substantial unemployment.

I suggest, therefore, that the real objection to a system of permanently fixed parities is not its assumption that the equilibrium exchange rate is constant, but rather the fact that, under present conditions of widespread price-wage rigidities, the policies required to make that assumpton valid tend to be too costly in terms of domestic output and employment. The system is also likely to involve costs in the form of misallocation of resources, both by inviting recourse to restrictions on trade and capital movements to defend the parity and by encouraging stabilization policies having distorting effects on long-term real capital flows. (See Modigliani and Askari in the *Quarterly Review of Economics,* December 1973.)

Failure to recognize adequately the interaction between types of exchange regimes, policies pursued, and the equilibrium exchange rate also affects Makin's analysis of other exchange systems. It also weakens his case for rejecting crawling pegs in favor of what he calls "limited flexibility," though perhaps it could be better characterized as limited floating.

I must acknowledge some difficulty in understanding the detailed workings of his preferred exchange system. It seems to involve central bank intervention to offset some fraction "of any quantity disturbance at a given perceived long-run equilibrium exchange rate." I cannot see how the authority operationally could measure the size of the disturbance in order to offset a stated portion. However, in broad terms, what Makin seems to have in mind is that central bank intervention would grow in size as the difference between the market rate and the perceived equilibrium rate became larger. At the same time, persistent reserve gains or losses should lead the central bank to modify its view of the equilibrium rate, which in turn implies reducing intervention for a given market rate. If I am correct in this interpretation, Makin's system is clearly not so different from a crawling peg system in which the central bank would normally not intervene significantly until the market rate reached either limit of the band—leaving scope for private capital movements to offset short-term variations in the trade balance—but would fully support the rate at either limit while at the same time changing the parity itself in the appropriate direction, though at a limited rate.

The objections to the crawling peg reviewed by Makin—centering on the contention that knowledge that the parity will change at some given rate would unleash massive destabilizing capital movements—do not seem convincing. In the first place, even if the parity were expected—with great confidence—to depreciate for a sizable period at a rate of, say, 3 to 4 percent per year, the size of short-term capital movements generated by returns of this magnitude (or even smaller, if offset by interest-rate differentials) would likely be of a manageable order of magnitude, especially if central bank cooperation would persuade speculators that they cannot "break the bank." In the second place, the fact that the parity *can* slide at some maximum rate does not mean that the market exchange rate *will* continuously slide at that rate. Hence the return is not only modest but also uncertain, especially since the central bank would not be required to purchase the return flow, except at the opposite limit of the band whose width would be commensurate with the maximum rate of crawl. Serious problems could arise only if some unexpected event occurred which was widely recognized as implying an equilibrium parity substantially different from the current parity. But, in this case, a well-designed system would call for temporary suspension of intervention, letting the currency float until it found a new equilibrium.

The advantage of some form of limitation on the rate of change of parities—of limited stability, to contrast it with Makin's limited flexibility—is that it would provide a climate of greater stability for trade and financial transactions and even encourage stabilizing speculation. It would do so by requiring the commitment to policies that would keep the equilibrium exchange rate within, or close to, the bounds required by the rules of the game. As a consequence, countries would also be limited in their ability to pursue countercyclical policies which tend to shift domestic disturbances to the rest of the world. (See Modigliani and Askari, *Quarterly Review of Economics,* December 1973.) To the extent that countries succeeded in abiding by their obligations, the central bank's intervention would also be validated.

It may be argued that if countries are prepared to follow policies preventing significant and rapid changes in the equilibrium exchange rate, then a system of limited—or even of unlimited—floating would most likely produce the same advantages. If one takes this view, then, in the last analysis, the choice between alternative exchange systems must revolve around one's judgment as to whether *formal* commitment to a system requiring limited stability in equilibrium rates is likely (1) to generate greater actual stability that might result from a *moral* obligation and goodwill, and (2) to achieve this result without unduly large costs.

In concluding, let me note that the difference between limited flexibility and limited stability is further reduced when one recognizes that, just as under certain conditions crawling pegs should temporarily be suspended in favor of floating, so in some circumstances, floating—whether total or limited—would be best suspended in favor of unqualified intervention. A case in point is the massive balance-of-payments surpluses and deficits generated suddenly by the recent many-fold increase in oil prices. As a result, the non-oil countries face unavoidable balance-of-trade deficits of many tens of billions of dollars.

I would argue that, to a first approximation, major countries should aim at target deficits commensurate with their incremental imported oil bill. To be sure, if prices hold, the higher oil bill will eventually have to be paid in commodities—to the extent that the oil countries' surpluses disappear—or by long-term capital flows, for example, from some oil countries to underdeveloped countries. But it is yet too early to know just how the problem will eventually be settled, and it would therefore be premature to undertake large-scale reshuffling of resources in order to redistribute the deficit within the non-oil countries. I can see no grounds for holding that private capital movements could undertake to finance these "target" deficits at rates of exchange consistent with the deficits. Hence, there is the need for large-scale intervention in the exchange markets by central banks—using initial reserves plus borrowings, which, so far, have been haphazard but hopefully can soon be replaced by recourse to appropriate types of internationally arranged "oil facilities."

Professor Makin has presented a wide-ranging and stimulating paper covering an area where suggestive ideas have not yet crystallized into hard analysis. However, my tentative interpretation of recent developments is in several respects different from his. The following comments will make specific what I have in mind.

Choice of a Medium of Exchange

It is now fairly well understood that the choice of a medium of exchange depends on transactions costs and yields. The following propositions are also widely accepted, though they have not been fully incorporated into the theory:

(1) Transactions costs are, in part, information costs.

(2) An important component of the yield is expected future capital gains or losses, which introduce speculative elements into the demand for money.

(3) Uncertainty about yields and about any other aspects of the situation is also a potentially important factor, which introduces precautionary motives into the demand for money.

If some medium of exchange dominates the others in all respects, we do not need an elaborate calculus to conclude that it will indeed be used. But this is an exceptional case. Usually, some medium is better in one respect, while another is better in others. To determine to what extent a given medium will be used would then require a solution to an extremely complex general equilibrium problem. In such a case, references to cost minimization, marginal benefits, marginal costs, opportunity sets, and the like are just figurative speech without well-defined meaning.

Makin gives special prominence in his analysis to transportation costs for goods and information. This would be a very fruitful area for theoretical analysis. The monetary history of antiquity and of the Middle Ages seems to show that monies may have wide international use even with high transportation cost, the main requirement being confidence in their metallic content (that is, low risk of capital loss in terms of commodities). However, the costs of information transmission seem to be important for credit instruments where proximity of the borrower and lender can be a major consideration. The United States, in fact, had a common currency, consisting of gold and/or silver money, at the time when Makin says it had only regional money. What Makin actually describes is the competition between different bank notes, all promising convertibility into commodity money, but with different risk.

International Money

It is clear that there is no international money today. In particular, the dollar is not an international currency to any significant extent, as any traveler, trader, and foreign exchange dealer knows. Eurodollars are claims to U.S. money, like any American deposit or loan. The fact that somebody borrows dollars from a British bank does not make these dollars any more "international" than Manitoba No. 1 wheat traded in Zurich and stored in Antwerp. For hundreds of years there were international markets in which different monies were traded against each other. The Eurocurrency market developed a new dimension inasmuch as banks in country A would now borrow and lend currency B. However, this does not make the dollars, pounds, and francs traded in these markets international money.

There was indeed a time when there was something like international money. This was when a number of countries were on a gold standard or gold-exchange standard with high confidence in the convertibility of their currencies. In that case, national currencies were almost perfect substitutes. (In some cases, as in the Latin Currency Union, they were perfect substitutes, circulating across national boundaries.) At certain times in the postwar period, the dollar seemed to be in the process of becoming an international money. This was when the dollar holdings of other countries were still depleted by the war and the high gold reserves of the United States seemed to guarantee continued convertibility. It should be noted, however, that the international character of the dollar, to the extent it existed, was borrowed from gold, just as in the 19th century the national character of American bank notes was borrowed from gold. With the breakdown of the gold-exchange standard, the dollar has again lost its international qualities, and the Western world is further away from international money than at any time in modern history. There is perhaps a chance that the dollar may again become an international money if its purchasing power can be held roughly constant in the long run.

The Eurodollar Market

I do not think that the Eurodollar market owes its existence to a "denomination rent" of the dollar as an international money. At first, an increase in the foreign demand for dollars would indeed produce an enlarged spread between borrowing and lending rates in the United States. The crucial question is, however, why this spread does not close rapidly under the pressure of competition among American banks but rather leads to the entry of European banks. Once we know the answer, we do not have to appeal to "denomination rents" at all, because the difference in interest margins to which the Eurodollar market owes its existence does not depend on such rents. I believe the main reasons why Eurobanks can work with smaller interest margins than U.S. banks *for some types of funds* should be sought among the following: (1) differences in legislation, including interest ceilings and reserve requirements; (2) higher efficiency of banking operations; and (3) greater proximity to certain borrowers and/or lenders, lowering information costs.

Factor (1) was probably most important in the initial stage of Eurocurrency development, but it may turn out to be temporary. I am not sure that (2) plays an important role. The long-term future of the market will largely depend on factor (3). This factor means that for the transmission of dollar funds from, say, a firm in Sweden to a firm in Italy, it is often cheaper to go through the Eurobank network than through New York. The same reasoning explains, conversely, why the Eurobanks have attracted only a limited part of the U.S. credit business. In this sense, the Eurocurrency system, by making the nationality of the banks independent of the nationality of the funds, promises a permanent improvement in the efficiency of credit distribution.

This distribution network does not produce a large amount of credit creation, since in the Eurocurrency market proper there seems to be relatively little "borrowing short" in order to "lend long." [1] (The frequent assertion to the contrary seems to be based on a misleading analogy with textbook models of national money creation.) As a consequence, the Eurocurrency market also promises to be a relatively stable part of the credit system. It is significant that recent cases of conspicuous bank losses have not arisen out of the Eurobusiness, but from traditional forward-exchange dealings.[2]

Speculative Capital Flows

It is not clear whether the expansion of the Eurocurrency market has had a significant effect on the volume of speculative capital flows. What is important for speculative flows is the foreign exchange market, where one currency is traded against another, spot or forward. In the Euromarket, however, spot funds are traded against forward funds, both denominated in the *same* currency. The main effect of the Euromarket has been the lowering of the margins between borrowing and lending rates for certain transactions. To the extent that speculative capital flows move through the forward exchange market, they depend on a comparison between the forward rate and the expected future spot rate. What matters here is the spread between bid and ask prices in the exchange markets, on which the Euromarket seems to have no significant influence. If speculators operate through the spot market, the interest margin may also play a role. I find it hard to believe, though, that the narrowing of this margin, modest as it is relative to the expected gains, has had a major effect on the size of speculative flows.[3] In the absence of the Euromarket, these flows would just have been channeled through the respective

---

[1] This statement is based on (1) comparisons of the maturity structure of assets and liabilities in the Eurodollar market and in national credit markets, and (2) the prevalence of "roll-over" arrangements which reduce what appears as a long-term loan to a sequence of short-term loans.

[2] It should be noted that these statements relate to *liquidity* risks; of course, Eurodollar banks are exposed to *default* risks like any other banks.

[3] However, the Eurodollar market, by lowering interest margins, may have induced speculators to operate through the spot market rather than the forward market, thus helping to explain the shrinking of forward markets observed by some bankers.

domestic markets, as they were in the case of the large hot-money flows in the 1930s. Of course, in addition to its Eurocurrency operations, a bank may decide also to engage in speculative exchange operations, but these are not a part of the Euromarket itself and could well have taken place in the absence of a Euromarket.

The Collapse of the Gold-Exchange Standard

Makin argues that the breakdown of the gold-dollar standard was, in part, due to the increasing volume of speculative capital flows. I would rather be inclined to take the opposite view—that the large volume of speculative capital flows was the consequence of the increasing risk of a breakdown of the system. Makin also assigns a major role to the abandonment by the United States of the policy of "benign neglect" with respect to its balance of payments. Again, I would rather take the opposite view—that U.S. adherence to a policy of "benign neglect" was one of the principal reasons for the breakdown.

In fact, the breakdown of the Bretton Woods system is a rather simple story. While in the early postwar period, the rate of expansion of domestic credit by the Federal Reserve System had been quite moderate, it increased about seven-fold in the early 1960s, reaching a level of 35 to 40 percent (for four years) under every administration since Kennedy's. There is probably no system that could have preserved the convertibility of the dollar into gold at a fixed price under these conditions. In particular, international "harmonization" of monetary policy would not have helped. The degree of international harmonization is indeed a crucial (and often fatal) problem for a fixed-rate system without gold (as, for example, for the European currency bloc). It is not essential—though perhaps desirable— under a gold standard (because harmonization is brought about automatically) or with flexible exchange rates. One of the major deficiencies of U.S. policy in the late 1960s was that the United States tried to avoid a breakdown of the international monetary system by appeals for "harmonization" in a situation where this could not possibly help.

The Inflationary Effect of Floating Exchange Rates

I am not convinced by the Makin-Walters argument that the transition to fluctuating exchange rates—by reducing the demand for speculative cash balances—has been inflationary. First, a large volume of currency speculation is not inherent in a fixed-rate system, but rather a concomitant of its breakdown. While the volume of speculative positions under freely fluctuating rates may well be smaller than under a moribund adjustable peg with increasingly frequent adjustments, it is probably still much larger than under a workable fixed-rate system. More important is another point. Since currency speculation relates to one currency relative to another (and not, as in the Keynesian speculative motive, cash relative to securities), its main effect will be on the *composition* of cash balances with respect to different currencies and not on the aggregate demand for cash balances. One of the more important problems of flexible exchange rates will indeed be the effect they have on the international diversification of liquid assets. There are rather strong reasons to believe that this effect will be in the direction of increased diversification, since firms, banks, and households will want to reduce their exchange risks.

This may have potentially far-reaching consequences for national monetary policies. One of the main effects of flexible exchange rates is to give each central bank national autonomy over its monetary base (and not only over the domestic credit component). In the absence of portfolio diversification—that is, if liquidity consists only of domestic money—control over the monetary base would also give the central bank control over the liquidity of the domestic economy. This is not so, however, if liquidity consists to a significant extent of foreign money because the liquidity of any one economy depends jointly on all money supplies. As a consequence, international diversification of liquid portfolios would tend to rob the system of one of the main advantages of flexible exchange rates. (For illiquid assets, diversification often takes the form of multinational corporations; the breakdown of the fixed-rate system was thus associated with a rapid proliferation of MNCs.)

Intervention Rules for a Managed Float

To derive rules of optimal intervention for a flexible exchange-rate system would, by itself, be a major analytical undertaking. The problem could perhaps be posed in the following way. The government has two objectives, namely, domestic stabilization and the control of the exchange rate. It can expand or contract its money supply in at least three ways (not counting gold transactions), namely, by trading in domestic securities, by trading in foreign securities (for example, Eurodeposits or Treasury bills), and by trading in foreign currencies. What are the rules for the optimal "policy mix" in such a case? If central bank A buys and sells currency B, it has an immediate influence on the money supply in B, very much as if central bank B had used open market operations. As a consequence, if all central banks operate in the foreign currency market, the national autonomy of monetary policy is again lost.[4] There may thus be a good reason to postulate that central banks should not operate in the foreign currency market. This would still leave the choice between open market operations in the domestic market and operations with foreign

---

[4] It is now well understood how central banks increased the supply of dollars when they switched some of their dollar holdings from currency to Eurodeposits. It is not always realized, however, that the inflationary effect had nothing to do with any particular characteristics of the Eurodollar market and would have been essentially the same if the banks had bought U.S. Treasury bills instead.

securities. The principles which should guide this choice seem to be an urgent topic for research. It may be that Mundell's assignment principle takes us part of the way, but a preliminary study has not turned up clear-cut comparative advantages. It may well be, therefore, that a different type of analysis will have to be developed.

Robert Z. Aliber

When I heard Professor Makin describe his paper, it came as a relief, for I had read the paper several times and had been confused. The source of my confusion was that the substance of the paper has little to do with the title. The basic topic of the paper is fixed and floating exchange rates. The title of the paper is "Euro-currencies and the Evolution of the International Monetary System."

I want to make three points. The first deals with the question of whether the Eurocurrency system has anything to do with international finance or whether it primarily involves industrial organization.

Let me make a very simple proposition. Imagine a world that consisted of one country, the United States, one group of islands, the Virgin Islands, and two monetary authorities, the U.S. monetary authority and the Virgin Islands monetary authority. It is inevitable in this world that a Eurodollar market or a Virgin-dollar market would develop. The reason for the development of the Virgin-dollar market is that in every country the organization of the banking system is cartelized and the smaller banks put pressure on the political authority to limit the competitive position of the larger banks.

Well, now, let's open the world up. It is intriguing, I think, to look at Professor Makin's paper because while the title mentions the Eurocurrency system, the paper is basically about Eurodollars. He may believe that that distinction is unimportant, but I think it is important. There is substantial evidence which suggests that the growth of external currency banking denominated in three or four other major currencies has been about as rapid—from about the beginning—as has been the growth of external currency banking denominated in U.S. dollars.

External markets are likely to arise in the currencies of major trading countries, as larger international banks begin to compete against smaller national banks for deposit-loan business. The total share of U.S. dollar deposits issued by the First National City Bank has undoubtedly increased because of the growth of the external U.S. dollar market. We then have to ask whether the existence of an external dollar market has altered investor currency preferences or has only meant that investors in various countries more quickly shift from holding domestic deposits to external deposits denominated in the same currency. Investors might alter their currency preferences because the market is a source of information that was not otherwise available or because the market makes information available more

70

cheaply than it was before, therefore making investors more likely to change their asset preferences.

It is hard to test this proposition. The proposition that we might want to test and that can be tested by the use of interest-rate data involves the following question: in a world without external currencies and with a given set of monetary policies, there is a given set of interest rates on assets denominated in different currencies. When we move to a world with external currencies, we then have to ask: has the interest-rate relationship among assets denominated in different currencies changed and has investor perception of risks attached to changing the currency mix of their portfolios changed?

I believe there is relatively little evidence to suggest that investors have altered the currency mix of their portfolios because of this institutional innovation —the development of external deposit-loan markets—for the major currencies taken as a group. What has happened is that there has been a switch—an increase perhaps—in investor demand for currencies of six or eight of the major countries relative to the currencies of other countries.

Two more issues are relevant to the discussion at hand. One concerns whether the move to floating rates has affected world trade. We know the direction of the answer to the question on an a priori basis. The reason for moving to floating rates is to increase uncertainty in international markets in a way to insulate national currency areas from each other. Makin's test of this proposition in a period of world inflation is really naive.

The other issue involves the impact of the Eurocurrency system on the composition of reserve assets. Makin mentioned the Eurco and the SDR. It is now possible for any investor to obtain any sort of portfolio—any market basket of currencies—that he wishes. Eurco is basically a mutual fund arrangement for reducing the cost to any one investor of obtaining a multi-currency market basket. The question we might want to ask is whether there is anything to suggest that there are economies of scale in having a mutual fund perform this function?

The same sort of question can be asked about the SDR, and it is an interesting question: would investor demand for an SDR-type market basket of currencies be greater than investor demand for assets denominated in the various currencies which currently comprise the SDR market basket?

Incidentally, one institutional point: if one desires that central banks intervene in the SDR market, it seems to me that it is almost inevitable that everyone, or at least the commercial banks, will wind up holding SDRs. It would be difficult to have effective exchange-market intervention in SDRs without having the interplay of private parties and central banks which necessitates the holding of SDRs by both.

Along these lines I would also like to point out that Makin has in essence said that if the SDR is superior to the dollar, it will be superior to the dollar. Makin's position is basically definitional. I suggest that one who takes that view should look at two things. First, look at the yield on World Bank bonds issued in various currencies and ask the question: why don't investors prefer these bonds to national bonds denominated in the same currencies? The World Bank bond is a development in the direction of the SDR. Secondly, ask the following question: if one wanted to move toward an SDR-type international financial system, what kind of underlying agreement must there be among central banks, and what kind of underlying political structure would be required?

An SDR asset—commonly held—will, in its initial stages, only have credibility if it has the backings of national governments, unless there is a world government. One might ponder the political implications upon national sovereignty of an SDR as world money, both private and public. I do not believe it is very useful to move in this direction. It seems to me that in a conference of this sort, economists should take the political structure as more or less given and ask, "Within that structure, what is the feasible set of international monetary arrangements?"

REJOINDER

John H. Makin

Let me start with Professor Swoboda's comments. I would not disagree with the notion that the breakdown of the Bretton Woods system was neither entirely accomplished nor begun in 1971. Professor Swoboda argued, and I think with merit, that the breakdown probably began as early as 1968. He pointed out that the Euro-dollar market, or the Eurocurrency system, is neither necessary nor sufficient for the breakdown of the Bretton Woods system, and I would not seriously quarrel with that position.

I think the necessary condition for a breakdown would be the lack of something more fundamental—the lack of coordination of national monetary policies. The Eurocurrency system is merely a showplace that puts the spotlight on the consequences of such lack of coordination.

A number of the discussants have questioned whether there can be chronic overvaluation of a currency—such as I claimed for the U.S. dollar—with the ability for arbitrage to occur through the goods markets. What this really amounts to is an argument about markets in which disequilibrium can be resolved either by a change in prices or by a change in quantities. If there is not the change in prices, the change in quantities occurs. Indeed, the adjustments vis-à-vis the United States had been taking place through the goods markets to the extent that U.S. producers of international tradables were, as I noted, clamoring for some change to restore their price competitiveness in world markets. This pressure constituted a necessary but not a sufficient condition for the sharp changes that occurred in 1971.

Questions have also been raised regarding the impact of exchange-rate flexibility on the volume of trade. I mean by "volume" the real value of world trade. In the Appendix, which is devoted, as I mentioned earlier, to a rough assessment of the impact of increased flexibility of exchange rates on trade, prices are washed out of all of the nominal variables so the analysis is in real terms. In the presence of a high degree of flexibility, and given an accompanying high level of inflation, problems would arise if nominal values were employed. Therefore, since variables are all expressed in real terms, I do not think the concern about inflation affecting the outcome of my analysis is valid.

As Professor Swoboda noted, equation (1)—that is, the one that relates the current account to capital flows—is indeed mis-specified, as I indicate in the footnote right next to it. I had intended to use the equation as a heuristic device to discuss the inability of accommodating capital flows fully to offset current-account disturbances and, further, to argue that with fixed and partly flexible exchange rates, even the presence of accommodating private capital flows would not obviate the need for official reserves.

Professor Swoboda also commented on my discussion of the possible costs of disequilibrium exchange rates in an illuminating way. One is perhaps tempted, recalling a sort of classical dichotomy, to think that a change in the quantity of money will not have any long-run real effects. But I think it also is necessary to keep in mind that markets do not adjust instantaneously and that the transitional real effects of price changes which are induced by exchange-rate changes stay with us always. It is the same type of thing that occurs in discussions of labor markets: If one waits long enough, the labor market will clear. This may be so, but the intervening unemployment may be an expensive proposition indeed and governments may fall as a result.

Even within the context of the monetarist approach to devaluation—which, of course, avoids the question of elasticities with regard to demand for exports and imports—there are cases in which there can be, at least in my view, long-run relative price effects arising from a devaluation. These occur if the income elasticity of demand for traded goods—that is, exportables, importables and nontraded goods —are not all the same. The relative price effects are distinct. The primary effect of the devaluation is to raise all prices but not necessarily by the same percent. Murray Kemp's article in the *Review of Economic Studies* (1970) has a rather neat look at that question, and he comes out with that type of conclusion. All of this is not meant to deemphasize, however, the fundamental negative effect on the excess demand for foreign goods caused by an eventual increase in all prices.

Finally, on Professor Swoboda's remarks, let me comment on the possible future scenarios involving dollar system blocs, pure flexibility, quasi-flexibility, or a world central bank. I agree that the current system is messy. I think economists who attempt analytical work in the area would prefer either fixed or flexible rates, simply because analytical work is easier with a well-defined system. We do not have a well-defined exchange-rate system now, and I think some of the difficulty with my attempt to sketch out an optimum intervention system reflects the difficulty of capturing the system within a coherent model. I do, however, believe that attempts to describe systematically the hybrid system of limited flexibility, which has evolved to the surprise of many of us, ought to be pressed forward.

Professor Modigliani's point that my model of optimum intervention lacks a trigger mechanism is well taken. As he was talking, it occurred to me that one could argue that the optimum system in an open economy—and one that would be consistent with Bretton Woods—would be a system in which the central bank had absolutely nothing to do. By that I mean the central bank could simply sit back and trust in the ability of the private sector to perceive those disturbances in the foreign exchange markets which were ultimately reversible. This would be workable since an ultimately reversible difference between current expenditures and receipts is the basis for borrowing and lending in any type of situation, be it between individuals or between nations.

The real bugaboos to a fixed exchange-rate system are disturbances which turn out to be irreversible. Therefore, if trust is placed in the ability of profit-maximizing borrowers and lenders to identify those things which they should finance—where they could lend money, get interest and indeed get the principal repaid—there is not anything for the central bank to do. The reason for this is that intervention over and above intervention to finance reversible disturbances would be intervention to finance irreversible disturbances and, of course, that kind of financing represents the crux of the problem of a fixed exchange-rate system. The criterion for fundamental disequilibria suggests that irreversible disturbances should not be financed in the first place.

The question of a trigger mechanism requires consideration of the optimum intervention system outlined in my paper. The determination of just how much exchange-rate flexibility to employ over time requires an operational procedure that will identify the mix between nonrandom disturbances and random disturbances not financed by accommodating private capital flows impinging on the foreign exchange market.

Such a procedure could be put into effect by having the intervention authority —given some perceived and unannounced equilibrium exchange rate—assign an ex ante probability to the permanence or self-reversing property of any given shift in the private demand or supply schedule for foreign exchange. The problem with this is, as Professor Modigliani points out, determining what will signal just how large that shift is. However, the intervention authority need not actually measure the size of a potential foreign-exchange-market disequilibrium at a given exchange rate to know when the rate ought to change. Its response would be to allow the exchange rate to move in a manner which effects an adjustment to the disequilibrium by means of both reserve and exchange-rate changes, but where the mix between such changes is conditioned by the perception of the intervention authority as to the permanence or self-reversing nature of disturbances impinging on the foreign exchange market.

In other words, it goes back to the fundamental method of erasing disequilibria in any market. Offset part of the net excess demand for foreign exchange on a given day with intervention and simply let the rate change resolve the rest. If a given price-quantity mix in the adjustment process seems to leave evidence of continued chronic reserve changes, allow more price adjustment with less intervention. Quantitative information is not required about the actual size of any given disturbance, rather only qualitative information about the irreversibility of some disturbance over time which can, in turn, be read from the behavior of reserves. This sort of smoothed adjustable peg mechanism has been widely used since the spring of 1973.

I am simply suggesting a continuous mix between quantity and price changes in response to foreign-exchange-market disequilibria. As I noted, in effect, the adjustable peg system is a discontinuous version of what I have in mind; that is, it is more of a step function arrangement. I have always been uneasy about that because the danger, I think, of destabilizing capital flows is greater where there is a type of framework in which it is known that there will be some discrete adjustment of the exchange rate, however small.

The point that Professor Aliber raised that is of most interest to me is the statement to the effect that if intervention is conducted in SDRs everyone is going to end up holding SDRs. I wholly agree. In fact, I think such a possibility is the major reason why intervention in SDRs is never going to materialize. Central banks will get rather uneasy about the notion of a private sector international money that could dominate any national money. Particularly, the role of the dollar in the international monetary system would be severely affected by an SDR which was truly a superior asset.

I think that moving in the direction of intervention with SDRs would be moving in the direction of the kind of authority for a world central bank that would lead to a world money of the type Keynes had·in mind in his proposals at Bretton Woods. From the point of view of having a workable international money, intervention in SDRs seems the easiest way to go. However, the implications of such practice for national monies are what may indeed prevent it from materializing.

Speaking more generally, I should add that although the remarks in my paper obviously favor increased flexibility of exchange rates and this in turn reduces—or in the limiting case of complete flexibility removes—the need to consider questions of reserve adequacy or form, all such remarks are predicated on an observed inability of national authorities to coordinate monetary policies. A number of arrangements, either in the form of a world central bank or presumptive criteria for automatically adjusting national money supplies in response to balance-of-payments disequilibria, could make a fixed exchange-rate system fully workable. It seems, however, and perhaps the view is not without merit, that nations prefer not to let domestic prices, incomes, and interest rates adjust to accommodate exogenous shocks to the equilibrium of the foreign exchange market. Rather, to avoid letting the foreign "tail" wag the domestic "dog," the aim is to absorb such shocks with exchange-rate changes, even though these changes are indeed transmitted to domestic prices and thereby, through real balance effects, to domestic interest rates and incomes.

Finally, among Professor Niehans' comments, there was one that I wanted particularly to address. His final remarks with regard to deriving rules for optimum intervention were very suggestive to me of approaches that I believe may be fruitful. These approaches involve using the target-instrument analytical framework within which to employ intervention in the foreign exchange market as an instrument directed at an exchange-rate goal among a number of goals in a general equilibrium setting.

Niehans suggests the work of Mundell and the principle of effective market classification. I would extend that by suggesting that one might want to set up a model in which intervention in foreign exchange markets and the level of government expenditure are perhaps two instruments which might be aimed at an equilibrium exchange rate and a full employment level of income. In such a variable-targets model—one in which targets may be traded off in the policy makers' welfare function—there is a little more flexibility in the formulation of the problem because the number of goals and instruments need not be equal as in the case of the fixed-targets approach. In fact the number of targets may be greater than or equal to the number of instruments in a variable-targets model and there still be a unique solution to the model.

DISCUSSION

Reasons for Emergence of Eurodollars

PROFESSOR MAKIN: Professor Niehans' comments on why denomination rents are not bid away from Eurobanks by the U.S. banking industry are very relevant. Professor Niehans suggested that in a competitive system, the denomination rents of the Eurobanks would be bid away. But if the degree of competition in the U.S. banking system is less than the degree of competition in the banking system of the world as a whole, then, opening up the area over which competition for denomination rents is conducted would, of course, explain part of the discontinuity in the way in which denomination rents are to be bid away.

PROFESSOR STANLEY BLACK: I would like to argue that the denomination rent question—relative to the development of the Eurodollar system—has been somewhat misdirected in this discussion. The question is not solely one of denomination rents arising from the international use of the dollar but, rather, denomination rents arising in all national banking systems. Actually, the difference between borrowing and lending rates in many countries is wider than the difference in the United States, and a major impetus behind the development of the Eurodollar market was to exploit this differential in deposit-lending margins to make available a more competitive banking system to the residents of most countries.

PROFESSOR SWOBODA: My comments deal with the denomination rent question and the unimportance, as Professor Modigliani puts it, of the money-theoretic approach in explaining the existence of the Eurodollar market. One can get—it is quite true—some satisfactory answers to why the Eurodollar market has grown at particular historic periods and neglect the theoretical considerations. But I think we still have to address three questions, to which a money-theoretic approach might provide the beginnings of an answer.

The first question is why there is a growing demand for U.S. dollar holdings, or more generally, for foreign-exchange assets, as transactions balances. The explanation may be sought either in a Brunner-Meltzer type of information-cost theory or in Niehans' general-equilibrium-of-money approach.

The second question is why people are willing, or prefer, to hold those dollars in Europe. Here, one probably wants to concentrate on factors such as proximity, business hours, and like factors, as Professor Niehans has emphasized.

The third question is why Europeans are willing and able to supply part of the demand for dollars. This is where I introduce the idea of denomination rents. Professor Niehans' comment is quite to the point, that is, some of the rents at the margin will be competed away by U.S. banks. European banks, however, can get at some of the intramarginal rents which would exist in their absence. This can be done either because of regulations or because in some respects they are more efficient, because of such factors as proximity, et cetera.

PROFESSOR ADOLF NUSSBAUMER: If we look at the history of the Euro-dollar system, it may tell us something about the system's future growth potential. I believe the development of the Eurodollar market in the latter part of the 1960s was largely due to the fact that yields in Europe were higher and that banks were able to operate more efficiently because of a strong belief in economic stability which was emanating from the policies being followed by the major European central banks at the time. Whenever confidence in stability begins to disappear, as was the case this year, the Eurodollar market begins to shrink and money is repatriated to the United States.

If my observation is correct, it would support an argument in favor of some sort of adjustable peg system. Whether it is called an adjustable peg and is institutionalized as Professor Modigliani has proposed, or whether the central banks follow such a policy but keep the pegs secret—as Professor Makin has suggested —would not matter. The advantage of the system would not be only as Professor Modigliani has suggested, that no one country could destabilize the world, but that the cost of instability and the losses experienced would be less for banks operating within relatively stable pegs. Combine this with the higher profit which there is in Europe because of the somewhat wider margin between lending and borrowing rates, and you may have some factors which explain the strength of Eurodollar growth and which are relevant to its future growth.

Alternative Exchange-Market Intervention Systems

PROFESSOR ALIBER: It is assumption-begging to make a statement, as Professor Makin has made, to the effect that if the SDR is superior to the dollar, it will be superior to the dollar. Such a statement is basically a definition. I suggest that if one takes the view that we perhaps should look towards an SDR world, one should do two things.

First, one should look at the yield on World Bank bonds issued in various currencies and ask the question, "Why don't investors prefer these bonds relative to national bonds denominated in the same currencies?" The World Bank bond

80

is a movement in the direction of a privately held SDR. Secondly, one should ask the question, "If we want to move toward an SDR international monetary system, then what kind of underlying agreement among central banks and underlying political structure is required?" An SDR asset, commonly held, will in its initial stages only have credibility if it has the backing of a national government, unless some type of world government is assumed. Also, we must be concerned with the political implications of SDRs as world money—private and public—and the problem of national sovereignty. I do not believe it would be very useful to move in the direction of a privately held SDR. It seems to me that economists ought to take —in a conference of this sort—the political structure as more or less given and ask, within that structure, what is the feasible set of monetary arrangements?

PROFESSOR MAKIN: Basically the framers of the SDR suggestion are saying, "Look, the dollar is not as stable in terms of a basket of international currencies as it once was, so we are suggesting a new asset which may have a lower rate of return. But it is an asset which also has a lower variance in terms of the things that one wants to buy with it simply because it has implicit in it a package of currencies." In my opinion, the properties of that type of currency basket—given the rate of return and perhaps reduced variance of purchasing power—are not going to dominate something like a dollar asset with a rate of return of 10, 11, or 12 percent.

PROFESSOR ALIBER: That is an unfair comparison; it is unfair to compare current market rates in an inflationary environment with rates of two assets in a stable interest-rate environment.

PROFESSOR MAKIN: One can compare two nominal interest rates in an inflationary environment. In that case, both need to be adjusted.

About the political setting, I agree that the political setting does not bode well for world money. But I feel that in this kind of conference, we should try to abstract from the political setting. It was concern with the political setting in the late 1960s which limited our consideration of flexible exchange rates. Everyone then was saying, "We know how interesting flexible rates are, but let us be realistic and talk about the real world. They are not feasible in the real world." It is not my job to talk about the real world now; it is my job to talk about possible states of the world, and a possible state of the world at some point in the future is to have an international central bank. And, if we do not want that—if we live in a nationalistic world—then the logical system is flexible rates.

PROFESSOR SWOBODA: Professor Makin has said that economists working in the international money area would prefer to deal with pure systems because they are analytically more manageable. This is, of course, one reason for the preference, but it is not the main one. The main reason some economists do not like the messiness of impure systems is because of the belief that uncertain situations

—shot through with numerous and, especially, changing regulations—are likely to cause disturbances to economic relationships which entail very real costs.

PROFESSOR MODIGLIANI: With regard to the breakdown of the Bretton Woods system, there is the sort of crude moralist notion—as voiced by Professor Niehans and others—that the breakdown of Bretton Woods was related to the overexpansion of either the money supply or the supply of credit. Professor Niehans quoted some data on money supply growth in his comments.

Let me remind you, however, that the first strains in the Bretton Woods system began in 1958. It was then for the first time that preoccupation about the viability of Bretton Woods cropped up. Throughout the 1958-60 period, the Federal Reserve tried to pursue a relatively high interest-rate policy—relatively high for a recession—because of concern with short-term capital movements out of the United States. That was the beginning of our concern—which eventually led to controls —about capital movements. Between 1960 and 1964 the U.S. payments position actually improved, and then the real trouble began with the Vietnam War in 1966. That was when things really began to get out of line.

And now a word about the problem of speculation and moving pegs, which Professor Makin discussed and does not favor because the direction of movement of the parity can be guessed. This is really not quite true in the case of moving pegs because the outcome depends on whether the parity is changed when the market rate is at the limit. If the rate stays at the limit, the peg will tend to slide —upward if the rate is at the upper limit—but only if the rate stays at the limit. If the rate comes down, the peg will not move any more.

In any event, the slide is supposed to be minimal, perhaps something like 3 percent a year. That is really not enough to justify significant capital movements in a world in which the market rates themselves are uncertain because there is a band within which they move. Of course, it should be said—and this will make our two approaches even closer—that anyone who believes in moving pegs will also believe that, under certain circumstances, the peg has to be abandoned for a while. Some major new event may occur, for example, which clearly makes the 3 percent inadequate for the achievement of the necessary adjustment within a short time. Then the sliding peg system must be dropped.

PROFESSOR MAKIN: The view that the breakdown of the Bretton Woods system was due largely to overexpansion of the U.S. money supply has been taken by previous discussants to be contradictory to my view that the breakdown is explained by an end to a passive U.S. balance-of-payments policy. On the contrary, I think my view is consistent with that view. The increase in the rate of expansion of the U.S. money supply in a sense directed foreign central banks to the choice of either letting their currencies appreciate or absorbing a very large quantity of dollars. This development, I believe, was a manifestation of a desire by the United

States, either consciously or unconsciously, to bring about devaluation of what they saw as an overvalued dollar.

With regard to Professor Modigliani's comments about intervention systems —adjustable pegs, et cetera—the goal of an intervention system is to adjust by enough to keep exchange rates fairly steady but not to give the speculators a target. We are really into a discussion of ways to avoid targeting speculators on what seems to be a disequilibrium exchange rate. Going back to my earlier comments, the more I think about it, the more I think that the best way to deal with the problem of how much exchange-rate adjustment to allow is to let private borrowers and lenders decide what imbalances they are going to finance and then let the exchange rate adjust to deal with the rest, which sort of squeezes the central bank out of the picture.

PROFESSOR FISCHER BLACK: Professor Makin keeps flirting with the idea that central banks perhaps should get out of the business of exchange-market intervention, which I take to mean to go all the way to floating rates. But there are no arguments in his paper or his comments telling why a pure floating system will not work. He has talked about a very elaborate scheme for an optimum mix of price and quantity adjustment. But would it not be optimum to have the mix entirely price-adjusted?

PROFESSOR MAKIN: Let me acknowledge inconsistency in the limited intervention scheme that I suggested in my paper and the tentative conclusion I have come to that perhaps it would be better if central banks got out of the business of exchange-market intervention entirely. It seems to me the conclusion one comes to depends on how good one thinks the private sector is in judging whether a disturbance is reversible or irreversible and whether it should finance it or not.

PROFESSOR FISCHER BLACK: The correct answer to this question will come directly out of an optimization problem, which you have posed but perhaps not solved. If one tries to devise an optimal exchange-market intervention strategy and the optimum turns out to be close to zero, then we know that no intervention is required. But if the optimum turns out to be far away from zero, then we know that intervention is required. That is exactly why we should try to solve such an optimizing problem.

PROFESSOR KENEN: "Optimum," or "optimal," or "optimization" implies the existence of an objective function. If the mix of price and quantity adjustments in international transactions is to be optimized, it has to be optimized with respect to some objective function, which is surely not our own as economists. If we are to come up with a relevant rule, we must optimize with respect to some social welfare function that we recognize to be politically acceptable or which is articulated by our political masters. Otherwise, we are playing a game that bears no relationship to reality.

With regard to Professor Makin's suggestion that well-informed private lending and borrowing might be allowed to smooth movements in exchange rates—in other words, the ultimate free-floating system—I would be much more sympathetic to that proposal if I were persuaded that the consequence of ill-informed private speculation is trivial. Perhaps we should recall what Jurg Niehans has already pointed out, namely, that the foreign exchange losses suffered recently by some of the large banks and the uncertainties generated in many countries about the future of the banking systems derive precisely from the mistakes made by banks in foreign-exchange speculation—mistakes defined in the sense that their bets proved to be unprofitable given the constraints and rules under which they were operating.

If I were persuaded that the failure of private institutions engaged in speculation was of no consequence, I would be fully willing to agree to let the private sector do the job. I am not sure, however, that we have learned yet how to bail ourselves out of disasters that can be created when private institutions make mistakes. When the private institutions are large, the social costs of their mistakes may be just as great—though the incidence may be somewhat different—than the social costs of mistakes by central banks.

PROFESSOR MAKIN: I agree, to discuss optimization one has to have an objective function, which—I confess—is not present in my paper. However, my comments to Professor Niehans' remarks contained an objective function where, in a sense, the policy maker is willing to trade off among the objectives that he is perceived to have. Interestingly enough, this approach can also lead one—consistent with a body of literature that was done in the mid-1960s—to an *ex post* measurement of exactly what weights the policy makers assigned to each of the goals in their proposed objective function. It provides a fascinating way to compare what policy makers really wanted to do with what they said they wanted to do.

Finally, the consequences of ill-informed market behavior, either by private or public factors—in this case in the exchange market—can, of course, be serious. I believe it comes back to whether or not one is willing to trust the judgment of the private sector or the public sector. I go with the private sector because at least the people who make mistakes in the private sector—serious mistakes—tend to disappear from the scene, whereas governments that make serious mistakes—at least, serious economic mistakes—may or may not go.

DR. ROBERT SOLOMON: I want to point out that the question of exchange-market intervention in SDRs was examined by a working group of the Committee of Twenty, and these documents are now available. Their study showed that it is not necessary to let holdings of SDRs go all the way to savings and loan associations in order to have an effective exchange-market intervention system in SDRs.

Also, it seems useful to recognize at least that the IMF has agreed in fact to a set of guidelines for floating which are supposed to influence the behavior of central banks. That fact is not completely irrelevant to our discussion this morning.

PROFESSOR WILSON SCHMIDT: Ever since the failure of the Smithsonian Agreement, I have been concerned with the very practical question of how one forms a judgment as to what an equilibrium range of exchange rates is. With respect to the IMF guidelines to which Mr. Solomon referred, it should be noted that these guidelines call for the Fund and for the governments involved to look as much as three or four years ahead and estimate cyclically employment equilibrium rates.

We should be aware of the problems with the data on which we must depend in making such long-range estimates. For example, Edward Dennison's remarkable book, *Accounting For Economic Growth,* gives a new series of full-employment GNPs for the United States which, on casual inspection, imply very different equilibrium rates of exchange than those which would be implied by the Council of Economic Advisers' full-employment GNP levels. There are very serious data problems with regard to the terms of trade, the import unit value indices, et cetera. Those who believe in central bank intervention—particularly this long-term kind —should call for substantially increased budgetary support for agencies around this town (Washington) so that the quality of economic data can be very greatly increased; otherwise, we are going to have another Smithsonian.

At the other extreme, I call your attention to July 24, 1974, when the Supreme Court decided against our recent President with respect to the tapes. That afternoon, if my foreign exchange sources tell me correctly, late in the afternoon—why late, I do not understand—the Fed intervened in the foreign exchange markets. I ask, how in the world could a central banker know what happened to the equilibrium exchange rate that afternoon, given the extraordinary political turmoil in this country at that time? I do not think anybody could. The market might give us some consensus, but I doubt that a small number of men could.

The Oil Financing Problem

DR. HELMUT MAYER: I feel the panelists' discussion of the optimal exchange-rate system is a little bit esoteric because it does not make reference to factors which, in my view, are going to influence fundamentally the kind of exchange-rate system the world will have in the near future. One is the oil situation. It is generally agreed that floating by the oil-importing countries, vis-à-vis oil-exporting countries, is not an effective way to eliminate these huge payments problems. I admit that floating is a way to bring the payments deficit of the oil-importing countries—of individual oil-importing countries—somewhat better into line. But I do not think that day-to-day floating is the way to meet the international payments problem associated with the increased price of oil.

With day-to-day floating, we could not separate the floating among the oil-importing countries and the floating vis-à-vis the oil-exporting countries. The floating among the oil-importing countries would probably lead to competitive downward floating of exchange rates—resulting in a downward movement of rates vis-à-vis the oil-exporting countries—which would be useless and would just unsettle international monetary conditions even more.

Another factor is the inflation rate. If the world economy is stable with low rates of inflation, it does not make much difference whether fixed or floating rates exist. But if there is rampant inflation like we have had in the recent past, then the only thing which works, I believe, is floating rates. They will not give good results, but they are the only possibility under those conditions.

Thus governments do not really have too much freedom in choosing the exchange-rate system. They are pushed by events. So, I think that the issue of floating versus fixed or pegged rates is to a large extent an esoteric one. Rather it is a matter of what kind of economic environment we have with which to work.

PROFESSOR MODIGLIANI: I am glad Dr. Mayer brought up the question of oil, because I was trying to work out in my mind an answer to Professor Fischer Black's question: "Why not have complete floating?"

Fundamentally, I do not have—and I think many people would agree—complete confidence in the rationality and the efficiency of speculation. Wrong speculation is costly. What I saw during 1973 under the system of floating rates does not persuade me at all that speculation did a good job. I believe speculators very much overreacted. It was pretty clear. And what I see happening to the stock market now does not convince me of the rationale of speculation.

It is quite clear to me that there is no way to handle a situation like the oil situation under a system of floating exchange rates. Governments must intervene in exchange markets. The problem cannot be handled by private movement of capital—at least not on this order of magnitude. There would be complete collapse.

Let me, however, make a suggestion. It could be that the optimal solution—I said before, the optimal solution is a system with movable pegs and intermittent floating when necessary—is one in which currencies are floated, but every now and then there is reversion to movable pegs. In other words, when a crisis comes along, like the oil problem, then the system moves to something like movable pegs.

Of course, these systems shade into each other. If the bed is made large enough, then everything comes together. Perhaps I would be willing to go along with an exchange-rate system which is normally floating, but which, when a crisis occurs, reverts to some kind of floating peg.

PROFESSOR SWOBODA: I am sorry to intervene here, but is not the real problem a matter of a change in the terms of trade which implies a transfer of real income, which has to be effected in some way? It cannot be effected in the short run because the absorbtive capacity of the oil-exporting countries is too low.

Now, why should there be concern about whether fixed or flexible exchange rates exist? That concern really detracts from the real problem. Neither exchange-rate system by itself can deal with the problem.

PROFESSOR MODIGLIANI: Given the fact that the oil-exporting countries are not going to buy enough goods, they will simply acquire assets. Someone then has to be induced to acquire assets in Italy, for example.

Think of two groups of countries. There are the Arab countries that want to sell oil but do not want to buy equivalent amounts of commodities, and there are the other countries. There must be capital movements from the exporting countries to the importing countries—individually—until the Arab countries are ready to buy commodities. Unless you want the whole oil deficit to be shifted to the United States, is that what you would like? That is a possibility. But can you imagine the consequences of that—what it would mean in terms of employment in the United States, et cetera?

So, essentially, there have to be large capital movements. Now, whether they are as large as the oil deficit—a little larger, a little smaller—that is a detail. But there must be huge capital imports in the oil-importing countries, which is what the government has been doing in Italy—some directly and some through various government-controlled corporations. It could not occur through the private market—through Italian firms. And I do not think any exchange depreciation would do that. There would be a tremendous exchange depreciation, which would quite likely create a tremendous inflation in the country.

PROFESSOR SWOBODA: I do not understand why exchange depreciation would necessarily produce inflation. There is always some rate of currency depreciation at which it becomes profitable to import capital because people expect a huge revaluation to occur.

PROFESSOR MODIGLIANI: I quite agree. But given that the oil countries are not going to buy enough goods—no matter what—what is that rate?

Inflationary Impact of Eurocurrencies

DR. ROBERT HELLER: It has been asserted that overexpansion of the U.S. money supply contributed to the downfall of the international monetary system. To what extent has the existence of multiple money and credit expansion through the Eurocurrency system contributed to monetary expansion? In particular, what is the effect of the existence of the Eurocurrency market on the ability of central banks to conduct independent monetary policy and to counter inflationary tendencies otherwise present?

PROFESSOR MAKIN: In the late 1960s, of course, rapid U.S. monetary expansion—when it reached the point where nominal interest rates got up against the

Regulation Q ceiling—led to some short-circuiting through the Eurocurrency markets. That is, money went to London and then came back to the United States with no reserve requirements behind it. I would suggest that as far as the United States is concerned, probably the ability to short-circuit—to pump money back into the system and give it a little extra kick—would have had some effect.

PROFESSOR SWOBODA: I believe that most of the likely feelers we can put on it indicate that the inflationary impact of Eurocurrencies is very small. I recently constructed a model, which is fairly complete—a kind of world money supply model—and plugged in some likely figures. What turned out was that the effect of the Eurodollar market is to change the world money supply multiplier from something like four to four and a half, going from no Eurodollar market at all to a system that has a fairly high Eurodollar content. But what also turns up in that paper is that the effect of the dollar standard is very significant; it doubles the multiplier figure.

PART
TWO

INTERNATIONAL INTEGRATION OF FINANCIAL MARKETS: SURVEY, SYNTHESIS, AND RESULTS

Dennis E. Logue, Michael A. Salant, and Richard James Sweeney

Summary

This paper identifies three alternative views of international capital-market integration. Briefly, these are the sensitivity of international capital flows to interest-rate differentials, the degree to which domestic monetary authorities can pursue independent monetary policies in the face of foreign disturbances, and the similarity in interest-rate levels and interest-rate movements among countries. Following brief remarks about these views, this paper reviews and critiques prior studies focusing on interest-rate integration. These studies may be classed into two broad categories: those concerned with the testing of interest parity theory and those which examine levels of interest rates in groups of countries.

An alternative concept of interest-rate integration is introduced. In particular, this approach is derived from capital-market theory and concentrates on the covariability of interest rates and interest-rate changes. Support for this theory is obtained by applying factor analysis to interest-rate data for seven developed countries. A single "factor" is found which explains a statistically significant portion of the variation in interest rates among countries through time. From this it is inferred that international capital markets are highly integrated.

1. Introduction

There is wide agreement among economists that the principal benefit of international financial-market integration is increased efficiency in the allocation of scarce capital resources throughout the world.[1] Additionally, integrated capital

The views expressed here are the authors' own, and do not represent official Treasury Department or U.S. government policy. Logue gratefully acknowledges the support during a portion of this research of the Tuck Associates program of the Amos Tuck School of Business Administration at Dartmouth College. Sincere thanks are extended to Thomas Willett for many helpful suggestions and to Amnon Igra for his generous and knowledgeable advice on the theory and application of multivariate statistical technique; we, however, remain responsible for remaining errors.

[1] For an elaboration of both benefits and costs, see Richard N. Cooper, "Towards an International Capital Market?" in C. P. Kindleberger and A. Schonfield, eds. *North American and Western European Economic Policies*, proceedings of a conference held by the International Economics Association (New York: St. Martin's Press, 1971), pp. 192-208, and Robert G. Hawkins, "Intra-EEC Capital Movements and Domestic Financial Markets," in F. Machlup, W. S. Salant, and L. Tarshis, eds. *International Mobility and Movement of Capital* (New York: Columbia University Press, 1972), pp. 51-77.

markets tend to facilitate larger underwritings of securities, narrower specialization by financial institutions, or lower unit costs in obtaining financial information; hence the economic resources actually employed in transforming a given amount of foregone consumption into net investment are reduced.

There is similarly broad agreement that internationally integrated capital markets reduce the scope for independent monetary policy.[2] A central bank which wants, for example, to raise interest rates or reduce the rate of growth in the domestic money supply may find its efforts frustrated because of the relationship of its market to all others. Hence, in planning monetary policy, full account of possible international financial repercussions must be made. Similarly, countries which want no change in their monetary aggregates and policy targets may have to take positive steps to offset phenomena occurring abroad, often with unsatisfactory results. A second cost of international integration is a reduction in the ability of a country to pursue policies designed to channel the flow of savings into preferred types of investment; though potentially important, this type of cost will not be considered further.

Concerning the notion that the more integrated the international capital markets the greater is the prospective difficulty in pursuing independent domestic monetary policies, there is little dispute. The question of degree seizes attention, but before turning to this, it is important to identify different concepts of international capital-market integration, for each tells a different story regarding independence and its nature.

Concepts of Integration. It is useful to distinguish among three broad concepts of international financial-market integration. The first focuses upon the sensitivity of international capital flows to covered interest-rate differentials[3] or in some instances uncovered interest-rate differentials. The logic supporting this view is that as interest rates change in different countries in response to monetary policies, capital will flow

---

[2] For a complete description of why this is so and what the broad policy implications are, consult Robert Mundell, "The Appropriate Use of Monetary and Fiscal Policy for Internal and External Stability" *IMF Staff Papers*, March 1962, pp. 70-79, and Thomas D. Willett and Francesco Forte, "Interest Rate Policy With External Balance," *Quarterly Journal of Economics*, May 1969, pp. 242-262.

[3] For a thorough analysis of the work done under this concept see Zoran Hodjera, "International Short Term Capital Movements: A Survey of Theory and Empirical Analysis," *IMF Staff Papers*, November 1973, pp. 683-740. The original impetus of this work in this area came from Robert Mundell, "The Appropriate Use of Monetary and Fiscal Policy." Among the large number of excellent empirical studies using this concept as the basis of integration are: Peter B. Kenen, "Short Term Capital Movements and the U.S. Balance of Payments," *The United States Balance of Payments*, Hearings before the Joint Economic Committee, 88th Congress, 1st session, 8-9 July, 1963, Part I, pp. 153-191; Norman C. Miller and Marina v. N. Whitman, "A Mean-Variance Analysis of United States Long Term Portfolio Investment," *Quarterly Journal of Economics*, May 1970, pp. 175-196; "The Outflow of Short-Term Funds from the United States: Adjustment of Stocks and Flows," in Machlup, Salant and Tarshis, eds., *International Mobility and Movement of Capital*, pp. 253-286; and "Alternative Theories and Tests of U.S. Short Term Foreign Investment," *Journal of Finance*, December 1973, pp. 1131-1150; William H. Branson, *Financial Capital Flows in the U.S. Balance of Payments* (Amster-

among the countries. The greater the sensitivity of capital flows to covered differentials and the greater the magnitude of those flows, the less scope for independence a country has. But here the analysis stops. In general the capital flow approach per se does not directly confront the issue of what ultimately happens in the countries between which flows are occurring.

The second view of integration engages in such a confrontation. This view might be termed the "capital reflow" approach. It primarily concentrates on domestic effects of international responses to domestic policy decisions, but also on the extent to which there is an independent foreign influence on domestic conditions that is not initially prompted by domestic policy.[4]

A third view of international capital-market integration measures integration by examining the relationship among interest rates in various countries. Under this general concept, there are several distinct approaches. First, there is the interest parity approach. Here, interest-rate differentials on assets of comparable risk are related to the forward premium or discount on one of the two currencies of asset denomination vis-à-vis the other.[5] Given the two interest rates, the forward rate of currency exchange may be analytically derived; the smaller the difference between the theoretical and actual level, the more integrated are the two markets. Second, some researchers have examined the level of interest rates among several countries.[6] The less the divergence among interest rates, the greater will be the degree of

dam: North Holland Publishing Co., 1968); "Monetary Policy and the New View of International Capital Movements," *Brookings Papers on Economic Activity* 2, 1970, pp. 235-262; and William Branson and Thomas D. Willett, "Policy Toward Short-Term Capital Movements: Some Implications of the Portfolio Approach," in Machlup, Salant, and Tarshis, eds., *International Mobility and Movement of Capital*, pp. 287-309.

[4] Quite interesting research has been conducted within this general framework. Representative work includes the following: Pentti Kouri and Michael G. Porter, "International Capital Flows and Portfolio Equilibrium," *Journal of Political Economy*, May/June 1974, pp. 443-467; Michele Fratianni, "Domestic Bank Credit, Money and the Open Economy," paper presented at the Conference on Bank Credit, Money and Inflation in Open Economics, Katholieke Universiteitte Leuvens, September 1974; Richard J. Herring and Richard C. Marston, "Monetary Interdependence Among Industrial Countries: A Study of Interest Rate Linkages," unpublished paper, 1974, and "The Integration of National and International Money Markets: A Study of Interest Rate Linkages," paper presented at the Econometric Society Meetings, December 1973; and Dennis E. Logue and Richard James Sweeney, "Aspects of International Monetary Influences," unpublished paper, 1975.

[5] For example, Herbert G. Grubel, *Forward Exchange, Speculation, and the International Flow of Capital* (Stanford, Calif.: Stanford University Press, 1966); Hans R. Stoll, "An Empirical Study of the Forward Exchange Market under Fixed and Flexible Exchange Rate Systems," *Canadian Journal of Economics*, April 1965, pp. 55-78; Jerome L. Stein, "The Forward Rate and the Interest Parity," *Review of Economic Studies*, April 1965, pp. 113-126; Frederick R. Glahe, *An Empirical Study of the Foreign Exchange Market: Test of a Theory*, Princeton Studies in International Finance, No. 20 (Princeton, N. J.: Princeton University Press, 1967); Robert Z. Aliber, "The Interest Rate Parity Theorem: A Reinterpretation," *Journal of Political Economy*, November/December 1973, pp. 1451-1459; and J. A. Frenkel and R. M. Levich, "Covered Interest Arbitrage: Unexploited Profits," *Journal of Political Economy*, April 1975, pp. 325-338.

[6] For example, Cooper, "Towards an International Capital Market?" Hawkins, "Intra-EEC Capital Movements" and Winthrop G. Minot, "Tests for Integration Between Major Western European Capital Markets," *Oxford Economic Papers*, November 1974, pp. 424-439.

integration. A third approach examines the covariability of interest rates; its logic derives from capital-market theory [7] as well as new views of international integration in general.[8] The covariability view implies that prices of financial assets in particular countries move sympathetically, but does not require similarity of actual interest-rate levels. It contrasts with the former approaches in that it accepts the notion that different interest-rate levels may prevail because of different levels of risk—that is, that financial assets may not be perfect substitutes because of risk. Accordingly, international financial-market integration may exist if the covariability among interest rates and changes in interest rates is high, even though levels may not be similar.

There are several problems associated with both the capital flow and capital reflow approach. These problems are, however, largely of a technical nature. In general, analysts studying either capital flows or the capital reflow problem obtain remarkably good empirical results. But their results are of limited usefulness because the studies typically cannot distinguish causality. For example, in the capital flow approach it is impossible to isolate the explicit effects of interest-rate differentials, investor wealth, exchange-rate expectations (particularly under fixed exchange rates), and risk, because of the difficulty of obtaining reliable data on most of these variables. A second problem with using these findings as a basis for policy is that available methodology allows only for investigating flows between two countries, or more typically between one country and the rest of the world.

The capital reflow approach suffers from these same problems. Empirical counterparts for theoretical variables are often impossible to obtain, and when apparently available, may conceivably be quite misleading. Investigated relationships focus on two countries or one country and the rest of the world. Finally, in the reflow approach, because of the structure of the test equations, it is really impossible to distinguish whether policy was offset by international capital flows or disturbances were in fact being offset by monetary policy.

These two approaches yield quite elegant theoretical models and use very sophisticated empirical methods. Ultimately these may be extremely useful in the formulation and implementation of monetary policies, since they presumably will offer guidance as to what a monetary authority must do in order to offset international disturbances. At the current stage of development, these approaches may not be particularly useful to policy makers, primarily because of the divergent policy implications that result from different interpretations of the empirical findings. Accordingly, in much of what follows, we concentrate on the interest-rate

---

[7] For a full treatment of the theory with references to important early theoretical and empirical work, see William F. Sharpe, *Portfolio Theory and Capital Markets* (New York: McGraw Hill Book Co., 1970), or Jan Mossin, *Theory of Financial Markets* (Englewood Cliffs, N. J.: Prentice Hall Inc., 1973).

[8] For such insights as well as an excellent survey and critical review of much of this literature see Robert D. Tollison and Thomas D. Willett, "International Integration and the Interdependence of Economic Variables," *International Organization*, Fall 1973, pp. 255-271.

approach to measuring integration of international financial markets. In particular, we subsequently develop a theory and test of the covariability approach to international integration.

A Question of Degree. The interest-rate approach to integration is considerably more straightforward than the alternative approaches. Whereas alternative approaches focus on the flow of capital, this concept of integration ignores flows and concentrates on prices, specifically on interest rates. This concept involves, in essence, a notion of market efficiency which suggests that the prices of financial assets adjust instantaneously to new information, perhaps even in the absence of international capital flows. However, it should be noted that this approach tells us little about other objects of policy and how they might be affected simply because interest rates behave in a particular way.

It is desirable to know the degree of monetary autonomy—that is, whether policy actions are being fully offset, partially offset, barely offset, or offset not at all. The degree of offset ultimately determines the force with which a particular policy must be pursued. Indeed, if because of international influences a given policy will have only 50 percent of the effectiveness it would have if the country were insulated from such influences, then the authorities should know in advance that their implementation of the policy must have double strength. This issue poses some quite interesting policy trade-offs involving, among other things, the choice between (say) a weak policy instrument which is not offset by international forces and a potentially strong one which is.

Additional distinctions concerning the efficacy of policy may also be drawn with respect to the country's own situation. Under rigidly fixed exchange rates and no extant or threatened barriers to capital mobility, investors may tend to view all financial assets as substitutes. In this case, interest rates are likely to be similar among countries and the scope for independent monetary policy will hinge almost totally upon different countries having different domestic responses to similar interest rates. This is nearly equivalent to saying that the demand for money functions in different countries must be dissimilar for domestic monetary authorities to have any independence.

A second case may be that of fixed exchange rates with barriers to capital mobility or the threat of such barriers. Interest-rate differences may exist under such a situation and this may lead to greater monetary independence. However, the conclusion should not be drawn that the country certainly has independence because of interest-rate differences. The interest-rate difference may reflect the fact that investors no longer view the country's assets as perfect substitutes for those of other countries—that is, the perceived degree of risk may be altered considerably by controls or the threat of controls. In this instance, the domestic rate could still vary with the set of foreign rates, thus reducing independence, at least so far as interest rates are policy targets or determine things which are.

A floating-exchange-rate regime offers a third case. Once again, interest-rate levels may differ from country to country under flexible rates, thus providing some independence. But real independence would depend upon the portfolio behavior of investors, and there are plausible circumstances in which investors will behave such that the covariability of rates among countries remains high. In this instance, complete monetary independence may not be fully achieved. Similarly, as Niehans argues,[9] if price elasticities of the demand for exports and imports are affected by a transition to floating rates, and capital flows are dependent on the exchange rate, monetary policy may not be efficacious in controlling employment and output in the short run, but may be useful in controlling long-run price trends.

Policy concern must necessarily be focused upon degrees of monetary independence under alternative situations. Examination of interest rates offers some insight, but not substantive answers to this broad and important question. Nonetheless, interest-rate integration forms an important component of this fundamental question and, just as significant, is an important issue in and of itself because of its bearing on the benefit side of capital-market integration.

Barriers to Integration. It was implicitly assumed above that barriers to international capital-market integration essentially took the form of government-imposed controls. There are, however, other types of barriers and for completeness' sake, these should at least be mentioned.

Such barriers to international financial-market integration include transactions costs: the cost of doing investment business abroad. Indeed transactions costs are sufficient to obscure the validity of many of the tests directed at interest rates. Additionally, available measures of risk may be inadequate, thus making yield comparisons even on a risk-adjusted basis inappropriate.

Many have claimed, however, that the chief non-government control impediment to integration has to do with lack of knowledge about foreign investment opportunities or foreign borrowing opportunities on the part of domestic actors and the costs of obtaining that knowledge. Because of the costs of acquiring appropriate information, there are limits on the willingness of investors to hold financial instruments issued by nonresidents and limits also on their ability to do so.

Legal differences among countries also act as barriers to integration. At least two juridical dimensions to the differences between foreign and domestic investment can be identified, and these bear on the costs of investing or borrowing abroad. First, laws determine the treatment of issuers and borrowers and may even discriminate on the basis of nationality. Second, debt instruments are defined and issued under specific laws which govern borrowers' and lenders' rights and obligations; laws also regulate accounting practice, the publication of financial information, and the priority of claims in instances of default.

---

[9] Jürg Niehans, "Some Doubts About the Efficacy of Monetary Policy Under Flexible Exchange Rates," *Journal of International Economics* 5 (1975), pp. 275-281.

Despite the persuasiveness of these arguments, it is uncertain how great an effect these phenomena have actually had on segmenting international capital markets. Prices are determined by the marginal investor and by securities and exchange-market dealers. Even if the marginal investor were willing to pass up an opportunity for a sure profit, dealers would not; hence the bid-asked prices they set for the securities or forward exchange contracts they deal in should generally not show any opportunities for systematic profit by outside investors. That is, assets of identical risk would have identical expected returns.

The one reason for seemingly imperfect market integration which is most likely the most important in explaining the greatest portion of observable yield differences is the portfolio rebalancing phenomenon.[10] As investors rebalance to accommodate changes in outstanding stocks of securities, the riskiness of their portfolio changes. Moreover, since securities are valued on the basis of their risk within a portfolio, rather than their risk in isolation of other securities, one would anticipate yield differentials to change as a result of monetary policies aimed at increasing or reducing the volume of the securities outstanding: the overall risk of the portfolio as well as the risk of that security within the portfolio has changed.

The Remainder of the Paper. The theory pursued later in this paper is the theory of efficient financial markets or capital-market equilibrium under conditions of risk. (This theory is elaborated verbally in Section 3 and mathematically in Appendix A.) Our empirical tests involve the estimation of the latent structure of international interest rates.

Specifically, we explore the interrelationships of interest rates in seven developed countries. The data are quarterly data on the level of uncovered interest rates and changes in those interest rates for the years from 1958 through 1973. Factor analysis is the statistical technique used. With this technique it is possible not only to determine the latent structure of interest rates and changes in interest rates but also to impute the variation among interest rates to otherwise unobservable common factors. It is possible to observe the correlations between these unobservable factors and the observed interest rates, so that one can determine which factors are common to all interest-rate series and which are specific to fewer series or to an individual series.

Our results show that most of the explainable variation in the observed interest-rate series can be related to a single factor, from which we draw the inference that there is a considerable degree of integration among the seven major international financial markets examined. Moreover, our quantitative results compare quite favorably to those obtained by researchers looking at yields in different financial markets in a single economy. When this single factor shifts for the world

---

[10] See Robert Officer and Thomas D. Willett, "The Covered Arbitrage Schedule: A Critical Survey," *Journal of Money, Credit and Banking,* May 1970, pp. 244-257 for an elaboration of this argument.

as a whole, interest rates in the seven countries shift also, whether or not capital flows occur. The shifts in interest rates obviate the need for such flows, and responsiveness of interest rates in separate national markets to changing international conditions is essentially what we mean here by international integration of financial markets.

Our empirical work does not represent the uniformly most powerful test of our view of integration, though the strong formal relationship between our theory and statistical tests is demonstrated in Appendix B. In a sense, however, our findings are necessary but not sufficient. Our work is a logical precursor to more robust tests of the efficient markets view of international financial-market integration.

While we found that a single international factor explained a substantial proportion of the variability of international interest rates, we also found traces of a "Germanic" factor which further linked interest rates in the Netherlands, Switzerland, and Germany and an "Atlantic" factor tying interest rates in France, the United Kingdom and the United States together. These second factors—that is, those in addition to the world factor—are distinctly less important quantitatively, but the fact of their existence might be important from a policy maker's perspective.

The remainder of this paper is organized as follows. Section 2 ("Interest Rate Studies") examines empirical work on interest parity and interest-rate similarity. Section 3 ("The Theory of Efficient Markets and International Integration") sets forth the theoretical underpinnings of this study. Section 4 ("Empirical Results") reports and analyzes our empirical findings. Section 5 ("Concluding Remarks") summarizes the paper. Two technical appendices are also included. Appendix A offers a brief formal review of the theory of equilibrium capital asset prices under uncertainty. Appendix B concisely discusses the technique of factor analysis and relates it to the formal model of Appendix A, showing that factor analysis is in fact a valid test of the extent to which the markets are integrated under the concept of the model in Appendix A.

2. Interest-Rate Integration

Acceptance of the view that capital-market integration is least ambiguously measured by the similarity in interest rates among countries does not mean that there is one uniformly best empirical test of the fact and measure of the degree of capital-market integration. As noted, three quite separate approaches have been used to assess the degree and the trend of capital-market integration.

The first is a direct test of the interest parity theory. The theory holds that the difference in yields between identically risky securities in two different countries should offset the difference in the forward exchange rate between the two currencies of security denomination. In equilibrium an arbitrageur in one country should be indifferent between buying a domestic security and purchasing both a foreign security and a forward exchange contract to convert the foreign currency into domestic currency.

A second test examines levels of interest rates and the degree of similarity in interest rates among countries. In particular, it examines the variation in interest rates among countries at a particular point in time. This provides some measure of the degree of integration, and by examining several successive time periods, inferences about the changing degree of integration can be made.

A third approach does not focus on differences in interest rates between two countries, as the interest parity approach does, nor does it concern itself with interest-rate levels as the second approach does, but rather concentrates on simultaneous changes in interest rates among countries. This view is not so concerned with the absolute level of interest rates as with changes and the extent to which changes occur in several countries at one time. This is elaborated upon in Sections 3 and 4.

Despite the differences in approaches and the fact that several different analysts have employed these approaches, the pertinent studies tend to show: (1) that capital markets tend to be highly integrated; (2) that there has not been a significant trend toward greater capital-market integration in recent years; (3) that there is some scope for independence of monetary policy; and (4) in the one recent study which addressed this issue, that recent convergences in nominal interest rates—which prompted casual empiricists to suggest that capital-market integration has increased in recent years—have been a consequence of greater congruence among inflation rates in industrial countries. Unfortunately, extant studies do not shed substantive light on the reasons for this phenomenon.

Interest Parity. We may conveniently define the condition of interest parity by a four-variable equation. In equilibrium, the following relationship should hold:

$$(1 + i_d) = (1 + i_f) \cdot r_{fd}/r_s \qquad [1]$$

where　　i_d = domestic interest rate
　　　　　i_f = foreign interest rate
　　　　　r_{fd} = forward exchange rate
　　　　　r_s = spot exchange rate.

The empirical form of this relationship is:

$$(r_{fd} - r_s)/r_s = a + b[(i_d - i_f)/(1 + i_f)] + E \qquad [2]$$

This says that the forward premium or discount rate is a function of the difference between the domestic interest rate and the foreign interest rate divided by the foreign interest rate plus unity. E is a normally distributed error term, with mean zero.

The theory asserts that if capital markets are integrated, the estimate of the parameter, a, should be zero and the estimate of the parameter, b, should be unity.

In other words, once all adjustments to new information have taken place, there should be no systematic advantage to an arbitrageur to investing funds in one country or another; whatever difference there is in interest rates should be offset by the premium or discount on forward exchange rates.

Early tests [11] of the theory were uniformly unsuccessful in the sense that they showed significant unexploited opportunities for systematic excess profit. That is, their coefficient estimates did not conform to those predicted by the theory. Indeed, they seemed to show that traders and forward-exchange-market makers were not reacting appropriately to new information and that as a result the markets were not integrated. In particular, these tests showed that the period of adjustment of the forward premium or discount was quite short: by itself this implies a high degree of integration. However, they also found that the magnitude of the coefficient, b, was less than unity, implying incomplete adjustment. This prompted many of those doing research to conclude that international capital markets were inefficient and that arbitrage schedules were less than perfectly elastic.[12] However, this same finding lent some support to the modern view of forward-exchange-rate determination under which the forward rate was determined not only by covered arbitrage but also by speculative expectations.[13]

More recent tests of the theory have found these earlier empirical results to be misleading. Indeed, the tests of Aliber,[14] Frankel and Levich,[15] and Minot [16] have been quite successful in showing the validity of the interest parity theory. Each of these pointed out the principal deficiency of the earlier empirical work. In particular, early tests used interest rates on U.S. and foreign government securities to measure interest differentials. But money invested in a particular country in government securities of that country is subject to different degrees of political risk—that is, because the probabilities that different countries may impose capital controls preventing funds from leaving the country differ, the early research did not compare assets of equal risk, as required by the interest parity theory. The later studies used rates prevailing in private markets largely beyond the direct influence of domestic monetary authorities. For example, Aliber compared rates on dollar-denominated securities issued in London and rates on pound-denominated securities issued in Paris as well as several other pairs; along these lines, Minot examined bank-quoted Eurocurrency rates on dollar- and pound-denominated securities.

---

[11] Grubel, *Forward Exchange*; Stoll, "An Empirical Study"; Stein, "The Forward Rate"; and Glahe, *An Empirical Study of the Foreign Exchange Market*.

[12] See Officer and Willett, "The Covered Arbitrage Schedule" for a critique of much of this literature.

[13] Thomas D. Willett, "The Eurodollar Market, Speculation, and Forward Exchange," *Journal of Money, Credit and Banking*, August 1972, pp. 636-642.

[14] Aliber, "The Interest Rate Parity Theorem."

[15] Frankel and Levich, "Covered Interest Arbitrage."

[16] Minot, "Tests for Integration."

While the early tests suggested some scope for independence the latter tests revealed that among private credit markets interest parity appeared to hold.[17]

Because of this conflict in the results, depending on the type of securities considered, it is difficult to infer with a high degree of confidence much about the independence of domestic monetary policy from international influences. Specifically, judgment must be withheld whether it is the government rate or private rate that exerts the greatest influence on domestic economic activity and whether the yield premia of private securities over government (default-free) securities is relatively stable.

Beyond this, there are several technical disadvantages to the interest parity approach to testing for capital-market integration. First, it considers only two countries at a time, so it does not provide direct insight into the overall degree of integration among major capital markets. Second, and more important, it is difficult to distinguish whether adjustments to new information are reflected in interest rates or in the forward rate. For example, suppose in an initial equilibrium the interest rate in country A is 5 percent, the rate in country B is 3 percent, and the forward-exchange-rate premium (from the point of view of country B) is 1.94 percent (from equation [1] or [2]); that is, interest parity prevails. This relationship is then shocked by the central bank in country A in an attempt to raise the domestic interest rate to 6 percent. Using the econometric approach of equation 2, even if the coefficients are correct, no insight can be obtained into whether country B's interest rate changed in response to country A's initial shock, or whether the forward premium adjusted. A case-by-case examination would reveal what actually happened, but the statistical test of the interest parity theory will not. Indeed, if the forward premium alone adjusted, then both country A and country B would have some degree of independent control over domestic interest rates and a "successful" test of the interest parity theory would yield no understanding of the degree to which capital markets are integrated.

Interest-Rate Levels. One of the more interesting early tests of capital market integration is performed by Cooper.[18] He examined the standard deviations of two sets of interest rates—short-term government or call money rates and long-term governments—across countries for several different years in the period between 1958 and 1968. The greater the standard deviation, the greater is the divergence among national rates, and the less the degree of capital-market integration. Analogously, the smaller the standard deviation, the greater is the degree of integration. Observations are based on average rates in June of the particular year. Cooper's results are reproduced in Table 1, which also includes our own extension

---

[17] Herring and Marston, "The Integration of National and International Money Markets," though not using an interest parity approach, appear also to have found a closer relationship between yields of financial assets traded in international markets than those traded in national markets.

[18] Cooper, "Towards an International Capital Market?"

Table 1

INTERNATIONAL CONVERGENCE OF INTEREST RATES,[a] 1958–74

Year	Short-term[b]			Government Bonds[c]		
	Mean	Standard deviation	Coefficient of variation[d]	Mean	Standard deviation	Coefficient of variation[d]
1958	2.86	1.22	0.43	4.48	0.94	0.21
1960	3.37	1.21	0.36	4.66	0.93	0.20
1962	2.96	0.95	0.32	4.80	0.89	0.19
1964	3.66	0.74	0.20	5.36	0.93	0.17
1966	4.80	0.83	0.17	5.89	1.13	0.19
1968	4.74	1.75	0.37	5.97	0.81	0.14
1970[e]	7.4813	1.32281	0.177	8.059	1.08022	0.134
1972[e]	8.18	1.34296	0.164	7.36	0.907855	0.123
1974[e]	9.9157	1.92428	0.197	9.429	2.13155	0.226

[a] Average rate for June of indicated year.

[b] Unweighted mean and standard deviation of three-month Treasury bill or call money rates for Belgium, Canada, France, West Germany, Netherlands, Switzerland, United Kingdom and United States.

[c] With maturity in excess of twelve years; for countries listed in preceding footnote plus Italy and Sweden.

[d] Standard deviation divided by mean.

[e] Our extension of Cooper's results for these three years uses virtually the same assets.

Source: Underlying data from *International Financial Statistics*. Adapted from R. N. Cooper, "Towards an International Capital Market."

of the data through 1974. Hawkins [19] uses a similar approach in studying integration in the European Economic Community. Both Cooper's and Hawkins' findings show no secular downward trend in the standard deviations of interest rates. Cooper, however, suggests that coefficients of variation are low enough to support the view that the relevant markets are reasonably integrated.

Cooper's original intent was to use the standard deviation and coefficients of variation on average rates during a particular month as measures of integration. Unfortunately, this approach does not provide a powerful test. Consider this case. Suppose in one country rates on the first day of June were 1 percent and rose by 10 basis points every day during June, finishing the month at 4.0 percent; further suppose in another country interest rates were 4.0 percent on June 1 and dropped by 10 basis points each day, finishing the month at 1.0 percent; finally suppose that in a third country they were a constant 2.5 percent during the month. Computing the standard deviation of the averages for the month gives a value of zero, implying perfect integration, when, indeed, the rates were quite divergent.

Aside from this problem, which may or may not be empirically serious, Cooper uses interest rates on government securities which Minot and others suggest are

[19] Hawkins, "Intra-EEC Capital Movements."

inappropriate because of the political risk and the direct and immediate influence of monetary policy on them. In Cooper's favor, however, is the fact that he uses uncovered rates, thus allowing for insight into the interdependence of domestic monetary conditions. That is, his test distinguishes whether it is the forward exchange rate which accommodates integration (as found by the interest parity tests) or the domestic interest rate.

Momentarily leaving aside the problems with Cooper's approach, note that the trend in standard deviations [20] does not indicate a strong increase in capital-market integration in recent years. In fact, it shows just the reverse: that capital-market integration has declined in recent years. It is also important to notice that the standard deviations were largest during the period of generalized floating of exchange rates, 1973 and 1974. This is as theory would predict: floating exchange rates increase the monetary authority's ability to exert independent influence on domestic monetary conditions.

In a conceptually similar (but much more powerful) statistical examination, Minot obtains quite similar results for the period 1957 through 1971 using call money rates. That is, he does not find a strong trend to greater integration. Minot uses a technique known as Model II testing to measure dispersion among rates. In his own words:

> The procedure assumes that one observes a single variable over time but has several observations on that variable at any given moment. Its objective is to estimate the variance due to the error in measurement. These assumptions clearly dovetail with the hypothesis we are testing: the interest rate of each country could be considered an observation on the "European" rate, differing from it only by an error of measurement based on a lack of financial integration.

> Model II testing is essentially an application of analysis of variance. Let each month's observations be given by a row of the matrix $[(x_{ij})]$. The first step is to calculate the row means which estimate the "European" rate of interest:

$$\overline{X}_{i.} = (1/m) \sum_{j=1}^{m} x_{ij} \qquad\qquad i = 1, n$$

> where there are n rows (in a two-year period $n = 24$) and m columns. We then calculate the variance due to the different observations on this mean rate by calculating:

$$s_{\delta}^{2} = [1/\{n(m-1)\}] \sum_{i=1}^{n} \sum_{j=1}^{m} (x_{ij} - \overline{X}_{i.})^2$$

> since s_{δ} allows for movements common to all countries in its calculation, it can be seen that s_{δ} is an unbiased estimator of σ_{δ} or the standard deviation between countries. This procedure should yield results different

---

[20] The coefficients of variation tell us very little for they can decline either as a result of a decrease in the standard deviation or as a result of an increase in the mean level of interest rates. In Table 1, it appears that the latter was responsible for the general downward trend in the coefficients of variation in government bonds over the period.

Table 2

STANDARD DEVIATION OF COUNTRY-TO-COUNTRY DIFFERENCES IN CALL MONEY RATES FROM MODEL II TESTING

Belgium, France, West Germany, Netherlands

	Call Money Rates[a]					
	Not Including Great Britain			Including Great Britain		
Period	s_δ	$X..$	$s_\delta/X..$	s_δ	$X..$	$s_\delta/X..$
1957–58	2.01	3.54	.568	1.81	3.65	.496
1958–59	1.90	2.86	.664	1.69	2.97	.569
1959–60	1.41	2.78	.507	1.26	2.91	.433
1960–61	1.32	2.88	.458	1.35	3.16	.427
1961–62	1.09	2.49	.438	1.23	2.80	.439
1962–63	1.07	2.55	.420	1.04	2.70	.385
1963–64	1.09	3.05	.357	1.00	3.12	.319
1964–65	0.864	3.55	.243	0.988	3.77	.262
1965–66	0.693	4.14	.167	0.879	4.39	.200
1966–67	0.797	4.25	.188	0.885	4.46	.198
1967–68	1.42	3.90	.364	1.55	4.28	.362
1968–69	2.04	5.14	.367	1.97	5.43	.363
1969–70	1.89	6.94	.272	1.73	6.85	.253
1970–71	1.56	6.17	.253	1.45	6.07	.239

[a] S_δ gives the square root of the variance calculated under the Model II testing. $X..$ is the mean rate prevailing during a particular period. Call money rates are in percent per year; call money data are monthly averages from *Federal Reserve Bulletin* or *U.N. Monthly Bulletin of Statistics.*

Source: Adapted from Minot, "Tests for Integration," p. 434.

from the simple standard deviation figure commonly used since what is usually done is to take the deviation of the column means. This assumes a model for the analysis of variance that is not as applicable in this case as the one used by Model II testing since it does not recognize that the rates themselves move over time.[21]

This method was applied to rates from Belgium, France, West Germany, and the Netherlands and when indicated, included Great Britain's rate because it was hoped that a comparison of these two sets would indicate different factors affecting integration. His findings are reproduced in Table 2. In general, they do not show a strong and persistent trend to greater integration, suggesting that domestic authorities do have some control over monetary conditions at home. Note, however, that such a trend was evident before 1967. Why it reversed itself is not addressed by Minot, nor is it further considered here.

[21] Minot, "Tests for Integration," pp. 432-433.

Table 3

STANDARD DEVIATION OF COUNTRY-TO-COUNTRY DIFFERENCES IN INFLATION RATES FROM MODEL II TESTING
Belgium, France, West Germany, Italy, Netherlands

	Inflation Rates[a]					
	Not Including Great Britain			Including Great Britain		
Period	s_δ	$X..$	$s_\delta/X..$	s_δ	$X..$	$s_\delta/X..$
1957–58	.543	.282	1.926	.508	.279	1.823
1958–59	.439	.222	1.981	.419	.198	2.112
1959–60	.302	.170	1.776	.303	.155	1.954
1960–61	.263	.139	1.889	.260	.161	1.615
1961–62	.292	.266	1.097	.281	.270	1.040
1962–63	.314	.344	0.914	.264	.318	0.831
1963–64	.361	.338	1.067	.340	.327	1.040
1964–65	.371	.325	0.963	.351	.366	0.960
1965–66	.348	.293	1.186	.341	.301	1.131
1966–67	.336	.247	1.338	.326	.299	1.092
1967–68	.295	.263	1.121	.292	.274	1.066
1968–69	.291	.330	0.881	.281	.348	0.807
1969–70	.254	.382	0.664	.248	.407	0.609
1970–71	.178	.434	0.410	.213	.474	0.449

a Inflation data are moving averages of consumer price indexes from *U.N. Monthly Bulletin of Statistics.*
Source: Adapted from Minot, "Tests for Integration," p. 434.

Note also that there is a strong and persistent trend in the coefficients of variation (standard deviations divided by mean levels of interest rates—$(S_\delta/X..)$ in Table 2). This suggests a very strong upward trend in integration. However, the coefficient of variation is, in this case, a very misleading statistic in that it can decline either as a result of increased capital-market integration (lower standard deviation) or higher average levels of rates. In the case at hand, it appears that the secular decline in coefficients of variation is attributable to higher mean rates of interest.

A second of Minot's results worth reporting on has to do with an analogous analysis of inflation rates. (In addition to the countries noted above, Italy was included here.) The results are reproduced in Table 3. Quite clearly, they show a very strong secular downward trend in the cross-sectional standard deviation of inflation rates. Indeed, a quite forceful agreement could be made that the perceived convergence of nominal interest rates is a result of the convergence of inflation rates among many developed countries.[22]

This raises several fundamental issues. First, if nominal interest rates are perceived as converging, but in fact they are not, why are many casual observers wrong? One explanation is that such observers have what might be termed a "relative" bias. That is, they perceive the difference between a 10 percent and a 9 percent interest rate as being somehow smaller than the difference between a 5 percent and a 4 percent interest rate. If such a bias exists, then inflation has played a substantial role in forming it. This leads to a second point.

If nominal interest rates (which most analysts agree are approximated by the sum of the real rate of interest—the marginal productivity of capital—and the inflation rate) are not converging, but inflation rates are, then there must be a widening divergence among real rates of interest. If this, in fact, is the case (and no direct evidence exists on this point), and if the presumption is made that the proper role for monetary authorities within the context of interest-rate determination is the control of the real rate of interest, then the scope for independent monetary policy has increased dramatically within recent years.

This should not, however, be taken to imply that capital markets have become that much less efficient in recent years. Real rates of return can be different among countries either because of capital-market inefficiencies or governmental impediments hindering the free flow of capital or because policy actions taken by governments have affected the level of risk in the economy relative to the risk or uncertainties associated with other economies. In fact, a plausible case might be made that divergences have not been so much a "benefit" of monetary independence as a result of erratic behavior by most countries' monetary authorities.

We now turn to the development of a theory of international financial-market integration and a test of that theory.

3. The Theory of Efficient Markets and International Financial-Market Integration

Our measure of financial-market integration is the covariability of interest rates among countries. We define integration as the degree to which uncovered interest rates vary together in response to common underlying forces. Uncovered interest rates receive our attention because they more accurately reflect monetary conditions within a country than do covered rates, and one of the key reasons for examining

---

[22] Note, however, that Ronald L. Teigen, "Interpreting World Inflation," *American Economic Review*, May 1975, pp. 129-132, points out that during the period 1971-1973, there has been a modest divergence among inflation rates. He found that over the period 1945-1965 the cross-sectional standard deviation of inflation rates was .9 percent, during the period 1965-1971 .9 percent, but during the 1971-1973 period 1.1 percent. However, this moderately greater dispersion occurred at a considerably higher annual average rate—7.0 percent versus 2.7 percent in 1945-1965 and 4.3 percent in 1965-1971.

financial-market integration is the determination of how independent a single nation can be of other nations in the conduct of its domestic financial policies.

The motivation for focusing upon interest-rate covariability stems primarily from modern finance and capital-market theory. However, on much more intuitive grounds, there is sound rationale, as demonstrated by Tollison and Willett, for using covariability of interest rates among countries rather than any of the other measures of integration.[23] For defining integration they argue that "if the average level of prices of a set of products or factors of production converges between two countries, or if *fluctuations in these prices move closely in line* (emphasis added), then the level of integration . . . has increased." (p. 268). Let us now turn to an elaboration of the essential elements of the finance theory that establishes a foundation for the view that it is covariability, rather than the magnitude of differentials or measured capital-flow elasticities, which measures integration.

Theory. As formally pointed out by Harry Markowitz in his seminal work on portfolio theory, risk-averse, utility-maximizing investors will tend to hold efficiently diversified portfolios of financial assets.[24] In essence, if the correlation of returns between two assets is less than perfectly positive, then there are risk-reducing advantages to holding some of each rather than investing entirely in one or the other. Indeed, Markowitz showed how one might go about identifying what securities held in what proportions would comprise an efficient portfolio: a portfolio which has the highest expected return for a given amount of risk or minimum risk for a given level of return.

Markowitz' normative work required the specification of an individual's utility function. Extensions, however, were more in the spirit of positive economics. Tobin [25] reasoned that if investors have access to a riskless security, then the choice of an optimal portfolio of risky assets is independent of an investor's utility function. The optimal portfolio of risky assets is the efficient portfolio which comprises all securities available. With a constraint on wealth, the investor would simply hold a portfolio of risky assets which was proportional to the value of assets outstanding. Risk preferences would be accommodated by putting a greater or lesser portion of wealth into the risky portfolio and the riskless asset.

Sharpe and Lintner,[26] acting independently, developed a robust theory of capital-market equilibrium based on the initial Markowitz model and Tobin's extension. In sum, they argued that the risk of any given asset is decomposable into

---

[23] Tollison and Willett, "International Integration."

[24] Harry Markowitz, *Portfolio Selection: Efficient Diversification of Investments* (New York: John Wiley and Sons, 1959).

[25] James Tobin, "Liquidity Preference as Behavior Toward Risk," *Review of Economic Studies,* February 1958, pp. 65-86.

[26] William Sharpe, "Capital Asset Prices: A Theory of Market Equilibrium Under Conditions of Risk," *Journal of Finance*, September 1964, pp. 425-442; and John Lintner, "Security Prices, Risk, and Maximal Gains from Diversification," *Journal of Finance*, December 1965, pp. 587-615.

two components. The first component is called the systematic risk, the second the unsystematic or specific risk.

The systematic risk is the risk of the asset which cannot be avoided by portfolio diversification. If an investor holds a perfectly diversified portfolio, systematic risk must be borne. This type of risk is a general risk and one might conveniently think of it as macroeconomic risk. For example, if one holds a diversified portfolio of all U.S. financial assets, then all actions taken by the U.S. fiscal and monetary authorities will have an impact on the value of the portfolio. Individual securities may be more or less sensitive to macroeconomic fluctuations, but all have some sensitivity. Unsystematic or specific risk is the risk attaching to a particular asset. In considering common stocks, it is the risk associated with the firm's winning an antitrust battle, the firm's president jumping out of a window, or the firm's receiving a major new contract. The effect of bearing unsystematic risk can be good or bad in the rewards earned for risk-bearing, but whichever it will be can normally not be known beforehand. That is, the expected reward for bearing unsystematic risk, because such risk is largely a consequence of serendipitous events, is zero.

In this context total risk is defined as the variability or variance of returns when holding a financial asset. Systematic risk is a function of the covariability of returns between a particular security or portfolio and the return on the market portfolio. Unsystematic risk is simply the difference between the total and the systematic risk. (See Appendix A for a formal treatment of these notions.)

Because rational, risk-averse investors will tend to hold perfectly diversified portfolios whose returns are perfectly or nearly perfectly correlated with those of the market portfolio, there should be no predictable advantage to holding any portfolio other than a perfectly diversified one. Accordingly, the expected return on any security (because at the margin it is held in a perfectly diversified portfolio) or on any portfolio (being composed of such securities) will be a linear function of the degree of systematic risk inherent in that security or portfolio. Formally, this is an equilibrium condition and may be expressed thus:

$$E(R_j) = R_F + \beta[E(R_m) - R_F] + E(\epsilon_j) \qquad [3]$$

where:

$R_j =$ the return on the jth security or portfolio.
$R_F =$ the riskless rate of interest.
$R_m =$ the return on the optimally diversified portfolio.
$\epsilon_j =$ stochastic error term, reflecting unsystematic risk, $E(\epsilon) = 0$.
$\beta =$ Cov $(R_j R_m) / \text{Var}(R_m)$, measuring relative volatility,
$E(\cdot) =$ the expectations operator.

In essence, the model implies that there are no opportunities for making systematic excess profits—that is, profits or returns greater than those attaching to the degree of systematic risk borne—inasmuch as the expectation of the contribution to returns provided by bearing unsystematic risk is zero.

108

Since the development of this model, there has been an abundance of theoretical research raising questions concerning the model's viability,[27] but empirical evidence still generally supports the model and its implications.[28] Thus while expecting exciting refinements and improvements, we expect this model and the international extensions begun here to be fruitful avenues of research, particularly of empirical research. Let us now turn to an examination of this model in the context of international financial-market integration.

International Markets. Financial-market integration exists when financial assets are perfect substitutes for each other, in proportion to the degree of systematic risk. Referring to [3] above, markets are integrated when

$$\partial(R_j)/\partial(R_i) = \beta_j/\beta_i \qquad [4]$$

But this condition would be expected to hold only on the basis of anticipated returns. After the fact, two assets of similar risk might have yielded substantially different returns during any given time period, owing to their unsystematic risk, but, as noted, since this is unpredictable, the differential returns are similarly unpredictable. If there is no foreknowledge of differential net returns, the assets were appropriately priced relative to each other at the time of the original investment.

The specific requirement that there are no opportunities for investors to earn systematic excess profits is essential for the existence of an internationally integrated financial market. The existence of a covered interest differential between financial assets of identical riskiness in two countries implies that investors in one country are forsaking profit opportunities, and this is simply not understandable except under circumstances such as sovereign or political risk. On an ex post basis, we may often observe situations where sure excess profits could have been made, but the fact that such investments were not made suggests that something was amiss on an ex ante basis: our perceptions of risk were perhaps substantially different from the actual risk of the security, or else realized returns in any one case simply represent one realization of nonsystematic risk that tends to be zero over many realizations.

Observed covered-interest-rate differentials have prompted some observers to conclude that capital markets are imperfectly integrated. However, in view of the theory sketched above, persistent differentials might simply reflect differences between the systematic risk of one country's financial asset and the systematic risk

[27] See, for example, Fischer Black, "Capital Market Equilibrium with Restricted Borrowing," *Journal of Business*, July 1972, pp. 444-455; John Lintner, "The Aggregation of Investor's Diverse Judgments and Preferences in Purely Competitive Security Markets," *Journal of Financial and Quantitative Analysis*, December 1971, pp. 1173-1195; Dennis E. Logue and Larry J. Merville, "General Model of Imperfect Capital Markets," *Southern Economic Journal*, October 1973; Robert C. Merton, "An Intertemporal Capital Asset Pricing Model," *Econometrica*, September 1973, pp. 867-887.

[28] Eugene Fama and James D. MacBeth, "Risk, Return and Equilibrium: Empirical Tests," *Journal of Political Economy*, May/June 1973, pp. 607-636.

of the second country's financial asset and the requisite forward contract. Many authors have presumed that forward contracts and the two financial assets are identically risky, but this need not be the case, especially in the probability of default and the probability of the imposition of some type of capital controls. Indeed, persistent covered-interest-rate differentials imply either irrational investors foregoing certain profits or differing degrees of risk. (Our approach does not, in contrast to many other approaches, preclude the possibility of the latter.)

The foregoing observation also suggests a second reason for examining uncovered rather than covered interest rates. It is that covered rates involve complex assets—that is, financial assets plus forward contracts. Interest parity presumes, however, that the combination of foreign asset and a forward contract is identically risky to a domestic asset. This may not generally be the case. However, to account for the differences in the systematic risk of financial assets, it is not satisfactory to look at single observations of interest rates or differentials at a particular point in time. Instead, attention must be turned to the relative behavior of interest rates over time. This leads to covariability as a measure of integration.

The systematic risk of an asset may be taken as represented by the degree of relationship of the financial asset's yield to the world economy, or more precisely, by the strength of common international factors affecting each country's domestic interest rates. Differing degrees of relationship may be attributable to the relative size of the domestic financial markets, the existence of various capital control programs, and the like. The unsystematic risk may be viewed as the specific risk of the country of issue, and indeed may even reflect the risks inherent in the firm which issued the financial asset in question. Changes in expected net return should not be related to changes in specific risk; the overall risk of financial assets issued by what may be termed "open economies" would tend to have a relatively greater proportion of systematic risk than of unsystematic risk. Conversely, the overall riskiness of financial assets issued by closed economies would have a relatively greater proportion of nondiversifiable or unsystematic risk. An open economy, other things equal, would likely be more responsive to the behavior of all other economies, whereas a closed economy may have purposely attempted to isolate itself from events in the world economy.

A given type of financial asset issued by agents in (say) two different open economies need not have identical systematic risk. The value of some assets will be much more volatile relative to the world economy than the value of others, and often this will be so because of the nature of the issuing agent, the product the agent produces, or how or where it is sold. Similarly, the unsystematic component of the risk of financial assets issued in relatively closed economies need not be identical.

If all economies were perfectly open, their business cycles fully synchronized, and all at the same stage of development, then we would readily expect (given the assumption of risk-averse investors holding fully diversified portfolios) that all financial assets would yield equal returns in capital markets that are integrated internationally. Barriers to capital flows and trade and differences in the synchronization of business cycles and stages of development should change the degree of the relationship between an asset's yield and the yield on an internationally optimally diversified portfolio, but they should not alter the fact that the expected return on an asset is still a function of its systematic risk. In other words, the β of equation [3] may be high or low, but the overall relationship should still hold. Indeed, if a country were able to cut off its affiliation with the rest of the world completely, its financial assets would have zero systematic risk. (Logically this would also lead to zero returns to foreign investors because they would not be able to buy the assets.) Within the country, there would still be production, hence there would still be positive nominal yields on domestic financial assets, but these would not form a part of an international portfolio. This kind of situation is more a curiosity than an actual phenomenon.

Perfect Markets. A natural corollary to the view that the expected return on an asset is a function of its systematic risk is the notion that in an efficient market, the price of an asset immediately reflects all new information pertaining to that asset.[29] If it did not, then there would be opportunities to earn returns for bearing unsystematic risk, and this is precluded by our model. In the model exposited above, new information about a particular asset manifests itself through an effect on the instantaneous stochastic term, ϵ of equation [3]. For example, if a firm reported profits substantially greater than those the market anticipated, ϵ at that instant would be large and positive, since the price of the asset would increase in response to the new announcement. If there were lags in the adjustment of prices to new information, an investor could predict future ϵ's by observing past ϵ's. Hence, the notion of instantaneous adjustment of prices is quite closely related to the equilibrium theory sketched above. This notion suggests that the role of international capital flows is not to maintain integration of the international capital market; with instantaneous price adjustments, the rationale for capital flows is considerably reduced.

Under the interest-elasticity-of-capital-flows approach to integration, two assets of identical systematic risk could for some exogenous reason suddenly carry different yields. Investors would sell assets in the country of disadvantage and buy assets in the country with the higher interest rate. Yields in the country initially having the lower interest rate would gradually increase as investors sold their holdings of these securities, and interest rates in the inflow-receiving country would gradually decline until the net expected returns on both identically risky assets were equilibrated.

---

[29] Eugene Fama, "Efficient Capital Markets: A Review of Theory and Empirical Work," *Journal of Finance*, May 1970, pp. 383-417.

The notion that capital must flow to integrate and equilibrate financial markets raises some interesting questions, one of the more important of which is why investors would buy the financial assets being sold in the lower interest-rate country when these have an inferior yield to those in the higher interest-rate country—at least during the adjustment period. Similarly, why would investors sell assets at a low price initially in the high yield country, when simply by waiting they could obtain a higher price (when net yields between the two countries were equalized). Certainly, there is scope for some of this type of activity based on liquidity needs of investors, incomplete information, transactions costs, fear of waiting, and so on [30] but it is unlikely to result in very substantial international capital flows. In general, graduality of adjustment in the prices of financial assets implies that some investors are making consciously bad decisions and that they have significantly greater weight in the market than speculators who will exploit such behavior for their own profit. In those cases where price adjustments appear to be gradual, this could, of course, be due to central bank intervention in financial markets. In this case, it could be that to accomplish "the greater social good," central banks are willing to sustain losses. But the changing size of the market for financial assets may also change the systematic risk and hence the expected equilibrium return of the financial asset in question. Accordingly, what seem to be lags in adjustment of prices to all new information could indeed simply be the reflection of gradually changing asset risk due to central bank alterations in the stock of outstanding financial assets.

The implications of this view for substantial independence of monetary policy are somewhat harsh. This perspective suggests that interest rates are independent of capital flows, hence the raising or lowering of interest rates by controls or reserve policy, for example, may have very slight effects on the international flow of investor capital because it will also change risk. Where domestic policy may have an effect, however, is on the choice of place in which to borrow. To the extent that for borrowers actual and realized net nominal costs of borrowing tend to coincide, and because borrowers may not be concerned with the relationship of the financial markets in the country where they borrow to world financial markets, their actions may result in international capital flows in directions desired by the monetary authorities, but perhaps with a very long lag—since, for example, the decision to float a bond issue may be made only after much consideration. However, such international shopping for credit may still not have any particular effect on the level of interest rates anywhere.

To the extent that monetary policy is directed towards interest rates, it is unlikely that policy measures which do not substantially alter the stock of outstanding assets will change interest rates by very much. And changing the stock of financial assets will merely prompt a reassessment of the expected yield of a country's financial assets, causing a once-and-for-all global price change and

---

[30] See Dennis E. Logue, "Market Making and the Assessment of Market Efficiency," *Journal of Finance*, March 1975, pp. 115-123, for an exposition of these reasons.

some modest changes in covariability. It may not—at least within the range over which outstanding stocks of financial assets can be reasonably adjusted—lead to any major changes in covariability among international interest rates; thus there would most likely be very little reduction in financial-market integration. What this means for a small country is that without imposing a wide variety of controls and other nefarious devices, it simply cannot pursue an independent monetary policy on interest rates. And for a very large and relatively open economy, it means that it can dominate world financial-market conditions.[31]

Integrated Markets Asset Substitutability and the Capital Reflow Question: A Minor Digression. The "capital reflow problem" is of major theoretical and policy interest. Briefly, under fixed exchange rates, do capital flows react to offset virtually completely any change in monetary policy a country undertakes? From the viewpoint of capital-market theory, the question turns (1) on whether the initiating country's government bonds are virtually perfect substitutes for other governments' bonds and (2) on other countries' sterilization policies.

From another viewpoint, changes in a country's monetary policy will have no effect if such changes result in no economic change in the outstanding portfolio the world must hold. A simple example illustrates the essential considerations. Suppose there are two countries, the United States and Germany. Germany decides to expand its money supply, doing so by replacing $X worth of its bonds with an equivalent value of DMs. Now, suppose Germany does not sterilize reserve flows while the United States does so completely. Then a reserve outflow from Germany of $X results in a return of German base money to the same level as before; U.S. base money remains unchanged and the quantity of the U.S. government bonds outstanding rises by $X. The net effect of the German monetary experiment and the ensuing reserve flows and their financing is to leave the outstanding world portfolio unchanged save for the replacing of $X worth of German government bonds by the same value of U.S. government bonds. If this change is to have no effect on financial asset prices and thus on real activity, the U.S. and German government securities must be perfect substitutes (economically identical). The question of the degree of substitutability resolves itself into two aspects, exchange risk and the expected return/systematic risk equivalence of the assets (see equation [4]).

Taking the latter condition first, suppose both assets have the same expected return, the risk of both returns is equal, and the correlation of the returns is perfect (the correlation coefficient of the two returns is unity). Then the assets are identical in terms of the only two characteristics considered, hence (1) are economic equiva-

---

[31] See Logue and Sweeney, "Aspects of International Monetary Influences." Here evidence is provided that growth in United States monetary aggregates, namely the money supply, explains a greater portion of the variance of nominal income than does domestic money supply growth in twelve of fifteen OECD countries and is a statistically significant determinant in all fifteen countries.

lents, (2) bear the same per-unit price, and (3) can be freely substituted for each other.

As for exchange risk, holders of U.S. government bonds have smaller exchange risk and holders of German government bonds have greater, under the substitution. But both sides can use forward contracts to return to the previous position if the two assets are otherwise perfect substitutes. If the assets are perfect substitutes otherwise, and if forward markets are costless, then rationality implies that the denomination of the assets in one currency rather than the other will have no effect. Any such effect would arise then only through some sort of exchange-market illusion.

Using the forward market adds extra risk, because there is no assurance that the contract will be honored. (Note that there remains the possibility that the joint asset—the German bond and the forward contract—may be a perfect substitute for the U.S. bond.) Nevertheless, this qualification should have no more weight than if the two sorts of bonds were "almost perfect" substitutes. In either case, the substitution should cause only very minor asset price adjustments, and reserve flows should almost perfectly offset German monetary policy. (Since the current account can be taken as almost completely invariant to this short-run policy, the reserve flows imply complementary capital flows. Thus, the reduction in German bonds of $X diverts foreign investors and German investors who would have taken these bonds to U.S. bonds of equal value. The magnitude of these foreign investors' flows is entirely dependent on their share in the world's portfolio.) Given a non-zero price response to German policy, any given magnitude of response can be obtained by making the policy more massive to offset any increasing substitutability between German and U.S. government bonds. However, the more massive the policy must be, the larger the reserve flows and the greater must be a country's reserve position in order to withstand the flows which policy will generate.

In this example, if Germany partially sterilizes its reserve flows, then in the case of perfect substitutability it takes proportionately greater reserve flows to return the German money supply and the world portfolio to their previous equilibrium condition. Consequently, the more sterilization is attempted, the greater the measured "sensitivity" of capital flows, and the more ruinous is monetary action to the country's reserve position. More generally, assume that the ultimate configuration of assets after a monetary action is invariant no matter what reserve flows are, though the ultimate and initial positions may differ depending on the degree of substitutability. (Such an assumption of invariance is not out of keeping with either the financial or international literature, but need not be at all valid or useful. However, to go into the matter involves (1) questions of the degree to which future tax liabilities are known and discounted, (2) distribution effects across countries, and (3) the nature of governments' intertemporal real demand for reserves, which cannot be handled here.) Then, the more Germany tries to sterilize, the greater are reserve losses and the "sensitivity" of capital flows.

On the other hand, suppose the United States does not sterilize completely. Then the world cannot return to the initial portfolio even if the U.S. and German government bonds are perfect substitutes, since the reserve flows that act to reduce the German monetary base to its old level also act to increase the U.S. base. Rejecting the notion that U.S. and German base monies are perfect substitutes, the system must be affected; but even if the monies were perfect substitutes, reserve flows would now lead to increases in the total stock of base money relative to bonds and hence impinge on the array of asset prices.

If German and U.S. government monies are not perfect substitutes but their bonds are perfect substitutes, their prices must remain equal. With less than total sterilization by the United States, German monetary policy will have an impact even under perfect substitutability, and only under the most unusual of circumstances will the German (and U.S.) interest rate not change. But even supposing that by chance this interest rate does not change, this will be the result of offsetting changes in other asset prices, and monetary policy thus will have had its effect through prices of assets that are not its initial instruments.

It might be argued, however, that government interest rates remain constant under perfect substitutability because the U.S. rate is constant. This has two interpretations. In the first, as we have noted, the United States may simply sterilize completely. In the second, the United States may act only to offset the open-market aspects of Germany's monetary policy by increasing its bond supply (and reducing its money) when Germany reduces its bond stock. When reserves then flow from Germany to reduce its monetary base, the United States maintains its bond stock constant and reexpands its monetary base. This interpretation of the capital reflow problem emphasizes the non-initiating country's determination to frustrate the other's monetary policy and the way the perfection of bond substitutability facilitates this goal.

Another way to argue that the U.S. rate will remain constant, supposing the United States does not sterilize, is to argue that Germany is a "small" country relative to the United States and hence that whatever the United States does about sterilization, Germany and its reserve flows have so small an effect on the United States that the U.S. and (given perfect substitutability) German interest rates are only negligibly affected. In this scenario, Germany reduces its money supply by X percent, and reserve flows of $X \cdot M_g^s$ (where M_g^s is Germany's stock of base money) occur to increase the U.S. stock of money (M_{us}^s) by $X \cdot M_g^s$ (assuming an exchange rate of unity for convenience) or in percentage terms to increase the U.S. stock by $X \cdot M_g^s / M_{us}^s$. Thus, given the elasticity of the interest rate to the U.S. stock of base money, the smaller is M_g^s / M_{us}^s (the smaller is Germany relative to the United States), the more minor is the impact on the interest rate of a given percentage change in German monetary policy. At the limit, then, Germany would require massive changes in its base money to gain modest changes in the interest rate, even if it were to sterilize completely.

We can fairly well reject the notion that the actual Germany is small relative to the actual United States. It is fairly well recognized, though, that there is a tendency for European governments to deposit their dollar reserves in the United States and a tendency for the United States to leave with banks the deposits other countries transfer as reserve inflows. This pattern amounts virtually to complete sterilization of reserve flows by the United States—though, clearly, it depends in substantial part on European behavior. Thus, the empirical question in this case is the degree of the perfection of substitutability of financial assets.

It is useful to extend the example briefly in two directions. If there are several countries, but U.S. and German bonds are perfect substitutes and the United States sterilizes completely and Germany not at all, then the analysis of the total ineffectuality of German monetary policy applies. However, there is the possibility that some basket of $X worth of non-German government bonds is the economic equivalent of $X worth of German government bonds. Then, if no other government sterilizes, appropriate reserve flows will leave the world's portfolio unchanged and hence asset prices will be unchanged in the face of any German monetary policy that is not backed by complete German sterilization. Clearly, if some of the relevant countries sterilize completely, German monetary actions have an effect.

Another interesting qualification is to note that each government may have a range of maturities (and even types of assets) in which it may operate. Unless the term structure of assets outstanding does not affect asset prices (that is, the term structure of prices is invariant to relative supplies), a government's decisions on how to finance reserve flows can affect asset prices. Similarly, all assets in which a government may finance its reserve flows must be perfect substitutes if the choice of the financing asset is not to affect prices even if some assets are perfect substitutes across countries.

We have argued that the relevant criterion for the integration of financial markets is their covariability and equivalence of ex ante expected return. We have further argued that ex post tests of financial assets' yields or yield differentials are improper tests of the markets' efficiency. However, such tests are at least a crude measure of the degree of substitutability. In this connection, Cooper's results on the variability of nominal interest rates across countries argue for somewhat imperfect substitutability or for inefficiencies in the market (though we reject this possible interpretation because of our empirical results). The random pattern of variation in the coefficient of variation in Table 1 seems to be a sign of substitutabilities rather than fluctuations in the integration of markets.

The Empirical Beginning. While we do not attempt to perform a complete set of tests of the efficient markets view of capital-market integration, we do test the degree to which interest rates move together among many countries. In terms of our theoretical concepts, our tests are tantamount to separating the systematic from specific components of risk and determining the extent of international influence on

116

domestic interest rates—that is, the power of international systematic risk (βR_m, in terms similar to those of equation [3]) to explain variations in domestic interest rates. This approach also allows some inference as to the efficiency of the international market, in the sense that there are no opportunities for systematic excess profits. Before we would be able to conclude that international financial markets are in reality components of a single integrated worldwide financial market, many other tests would be necessary, but the one reported upon represents a logical first step.

4. Empirical Results

Summary. Quarterly interest rates on medium-long-term government bonds in seven OECD countries—the United States, France, West Germany, the Netherlands, Sweden, Switzerland, and the United Kingdom—over the period from first quarter 1958 through second quarter 1973 were obtained from the International Monetary Fund.[32] A factor analysis of these rates revealed that a single factor explained 82 percent of the variance in the level of interest rates in the fixed-rate period of first quarter 1958 through first quarter 1971 and 85 percent of the variance in the combination fixed/floating period of first quarter 1958 through second quarter 1973. Analysis of the first differences and percentage changes in interest rates gives very similar results, and yields two factors; the first factor explains 38 to 41 percent of variance, while the second factor is bipolar and shows the influences of variations in four "Germanic" countries versus variations in the United States, United Kingdom and France. This is interpretable as an index of the unsystematic or diversifiable risk discussed above. The second factor's relationship between the last three countries' rates is interpreted as an expected relationship between the United States and United Kingdom (given similar language, culture, and particularly financial development) plus a financial relationship between the United Kingdom and France, so that the United Kingdom seems to act as a transmission point (as well as an originating point) of influences between the United States and France. The relationship among the "Germanic" countries—Germany, the Netherlands, Sweden and Switzerland—seems explicable on the basis of claims of relationships based on culture, language, and financial integration.

Note that uncovered interest rates were studied, rather than covered rates. The rationale behind this was that we were concerned with the rates facing borrowers and lenders in particular countries and the potential degree of central bank control over those rates, not with external interest rates (that is, covered interest rates) because the cost of cover would obscure the actual degree to which countries have interest-rate autonomy.

Data. This study is one of the first in a series of ongoing studies of capital and reserve flows among OECD countries. Some immediate restrictions on data were

---

[32] We are grateful to the IMF for furnishing the data in machine readable form.

that (1) they must all start after the general return of Europe to convertibility, and (2) they must be uniformly accessible, must be from the same source, and must involve only minimal interpolations. This ensures replicability of results, a moderately coherent system of descriptive statistics, and a minimum of bias introduced by methods of interpolation.

Given these criteria, it was decided to use the *International Financial Statistics* for 1958 through mid-1971 in order to survey the fixed-rate period, and for mid-1971 through mid-1973 to include part of the floating-rate period, though it was recognized that the period between mid-1971 and mid-1973 was not long enough to be examined by itself and that the differences in results from including or excluding mid-1971 to mid-1973 would almost inevitably be statistically insignificant.

The criteria listed above generally allowed data for Austria, Belgium, France, West Germany, Italy, Japan, the Netherlands, Sweden, Switzerland, the United Kingdom and the United States. However, for interest rates, some of the corresponding interest-rate series have significant gaps and the country list is reduced to France, Germany, the Netherlands, Sweden, Switzerland, the United Kingdom and the United States.

This list, however, seems satisfactory in light of the factors hypothesized before statistical analysis: (1) an international factor, dependent on the general interconnectedness of the international economy, but represented in this period of analysis and for the particular variable analyzed in this period of analysis by whatever variable seemed a priori relevant—in the case of interest rates it would seem best to refer to this factor as the international marginal monetary productivity of capital; (2) a European Economic Community factor reflecting the general interconnectedness of the Six and relating their variations to those of the dominant members, France and West Germany—the factor analysis, however, cast strong doubts on this factor, suggesting a separate role for Germany as a nucleus of EEC and non-EEC Germanic countries, and a role for France in a separate relationship with the United States and United Kingdom; (3) a "trans-Atlantic" factor in which variations in U.S., Canadian, and U.K. variables were significant—while Canada has to be omitted from analysis because of data limitations, the U.S.-U.K. relationship was found to be as hypothesized, with the addition of an unexpected relationship to France, the United Kingdom seemingly acting as the link between the United States and France.

Meaning and Use of Factor Analysis. This section briefly describes the statistical meaning of factor analysis, and then describes the problem of its interpretation in the context of the problem under discussion. (See Appendix B for a more detailed description of this technique.) [33]

---

[33] See Donald F. Morrison, *Multivariate Methods* (New York: McGraw-Hill Book Co., 1967) for a more detailed description of factor analysis.

In short, using a factor analytic model, each observation (interest rate) can be represented as a linear function of unobservable common-factor variates (which it shares with other interest rates) and a single latent specific variate. The common factors generate covariances among observations (interest rates for a group of countries observed at a particular time), while the specific terms contribute only to the variances of particular observations.

Output from such an analysis includes a percentage of variance explained in an (MXT) matrix of T observations of M different interest rates by any given "unobserved" factor. These percentages are ordered, with the first factor explaining more of the variance than successive factors and so on. Also of interest is the "factor load." This is simply the correlation between the time series of observations of interest rates from a single country and the factor. For example, if two countries' interest rates have factor loads of .65 and .95, respectively, with a given factor, then the correlation coefficient between the first country's interest rate and this factor is .65 and the second country's interest rate has a .95 correlation.

Factor analysis has been used quite frequently in investigations of this type. Duncan Ripley examined rates of return on stock market indexes from various countries, with quite powerful results, showing a strong international factor.[34] Fase explored twenty market interest rates in the Netherlands using principal components analysis—a type of factor analysis.[35] He found that the rates examined were so closely related that "it is not very meaningful in econometric model building to distinguish a large number of different interest rates as explanatory variables. Hester analyzed eleven U.S. interest-rate series—five short-term and six medium- to long-term.[36] The first principal component accounted for at least 83 percent of the total variation in interest rates. He terms this "the rate of interest."

King performed one of the more elaborate studies using factor analysis in attempting to explain the latent structure of monthly stock market returns over the period May 1927 through December 1960.[37] His first factor, labeled the "market factor" (consistent with our notion of the first factor as reflecting the systematic element which affects all financial markets) accounted for nearly 40 percent of the variance in security returns. A second factor, the "industry factor," accounted for nearly 11 percent of the variance of security returns. This prompted him to argue for two components to so-called systematic risk: a general component and a more specialized component.

[34] Duncan Ripley, "Systematic Elements in the Linkage of National Stock Market Indices," *Review of Economics and Statistics*, August 1973, pp. 356-361.

[35] M. M. G. Fase, "A Principal Components Analysis of Market Interest Rates in the Netherlands," *European Economic Review*, June 1973, pp. 107-134.

[36] Donald D. Hester, "On the Dimensionality of Market Interest Rates and Price Movements," Paper 6956, Social Systems Research Institute, University of Wisconsin, November 1969.

[37] Benjamin King, "Market and Industry Factors in Stock Price Behavior," *Journal of Business*, January 1966, pp. 139-190.

In our analysis we have found a more specialized component as well—a regional type of component. It implies that net expected returns on financial assets vary predictably with nondiversifiable or general systematic elements which are here represented by two factors. It should be noted that this empirical finding does not invalidate our general theoretical arguments. These arguments were advanced to emphasize a dichotomy of risks, but separation of risks is still possible even if there are three or four factors of statistical significance, provided each is identifiable and useful in predicting future returns.

The factors in a factor analytic model are orthogonal—that is, each factor is independent of each other. Hence the model allows for separation or disentanglement of effects. In terms of international financial-market integration, we are most concerned with the first factor—the international factor. High factor loadings on the first factor—that is, high correlations, between national interest rates and the first factor—suggest this, no matter what else is occurring or what other systematic influences there are.

The mechanics of factor analysis do not specify the factors found. Indeed, the intellectual problem of a factor analysis that is statistically significant is to "give a name" to the factors. This problem has two levels of difficulty. This project to use factor analysis assumed that an "international factor" would be the first factor, and that this first factor would represent the international marginal monetary productivity of capital; this conjecture seems very well sustained (see below).

In our analysis of first differences and percentage changes, it is easy to label the second factor as the "Germanic" factor—meaning that Germany, the Netherlands, Sweden, and Switzerland seem to be separately interrelated. On a deeper level, it is necessary to examine the interrelationships of the Germanic countries, in the correlation matrix, with loadings and in the light of international importance, to determine the "true" meaning of the factors. The same is true of the U.S.-U.K.-France relationship, which is found to have a more significant meaning than the tripartite "U.S.-U.K.-France" factor.

It is important to notice that the Vari-Max rotation does not improve statistical fit, but is intended only as a device in interpreting the statistical results already achieved. Thus, the original unrotated matrix "contours" all the statistical results, and if this matrix is easier to interpret than the rotated matrix, it is clear that there is no difficulty in relying strictly on the unrotated matrix, while the rotated matrix can, with clear conscience, be rejected on the pragmatic grounds that it does not enhance interpretation. This is, in fact, the result for first differences and percentage changes.

The correlation matrix—which in this case shows simple correlations between interest rates (or changes in them) for all the various countries—can be unenlightening by itself: it has no statistical significance beyond that of each element. Nevertheless, when combined with patterns of factor loadings, it can suggest powerful conclusions, as seen below.

Table 4
INTEREST-RATE LEVELS: FIXED-RATE PERIOD

A. *Correlation Matrix*

	France	West Germany	Nether- lands	Sweden	Switzer- land	United Kingdom	United States
France	1.000						
West Germany	.582	1.000					
Netherlands	.826	.691	1.000				
Sweden	.656	.557	.902	1.000			
Switzerland	.832	.689	.965	.866	1.000		
United Kingdom	.860	.526	.918	.914	.883	1.000	
United States	.834	.434	.920	.876	.883	.938	1.000

B. *Cumulative Percentage of Variance Explained by Each Factor*

Factor 1—82.7 percent

Factor 2—no second factor

C. *Unrotated-Matrix Factor Loadings: Correlation of Interest Rates with Factors*

	Factor 1
France	.882[a]
West Germany	.685[a]
Netherlands	.983[a]
Sweden	.915[a]
Switzerland	.965[a]
United Kingdom	.959[a]
United States	.938[a]

D. *Rotated-Matrix Factor Loadings: Correlation of Interest Rates with Factors*

No rotation—only 1 factor

[a] Statistically significant at .01 level.

Results and Interpretations. Tables 4 through 9 list the correlation coefficients matrix in Panel A, the cumulative percentage of variance explained by each factor (derived from eigenvalues) in Panel B, the factor matrix factor loadings in Panel C, and the rotated factor matrix (new factor loadings) in Panel D, for the levels, first differences, and percentage rates of change of the interest rates over the two periods 1958 through 1971 (Tables 4, 6, and 8) and 1958 through 1973 (Tables 5, 7, and 9).

For the levels in Tables 4 and 5, the high loadings or correlations of interest rates with factors for each period suggest a single "international" factor, most appropriately interpreted as the international marginal monetary productivity of capital. This is strong evidence of a high degree of financial-market integration. The somewhat lower loading for West Germany suggests that there may be a second and bipolar "Germanic v. trans-Atlantic" factor which is not statistically

Table 5
INTEREST-RATE LEVELS: FIXED/FLOATING-RATE PERIOD

A. Correlation Matrix

	France	West Germany	Netherlands	Sweden	Switzerland	United Kingdom	United States
France	1.000						
West Germany	.679	1.000					
Netherlands	.854	.742	1.000				
Sweden	.746	.655	.915	1.000			
Switzerland	.863	.754	.967	.891	1.000		
United Kingdom	.887	.644	.913	.929	.903	1.000	
United States	.859	.540	.931	.896	.902	.935	1.000

B. Cumulative Percentage of Variance Explained by Each Factor

Factor 1—85.8 percent

Factor 2—no second factor

C. Unrotated-Matrix Factor Loadings: Correlation of Interest Rates with Factors

	Factor 1
France	.910[a]
West Germany	.763[a]
Netherlands	.978[a]
Sweden	.935[a]
Switzerland	.971[a]
United Kingdom	.963[a]
United States	.943[a]

D. Rotated-Matrix Factor Loadings: Correlation of Interest Rates with Factors

No rotation—only 1 factor

[a] Statistically significant at .01 level.

significant, so not listed, but which would be particularly important for West Germany (and West Germany bulks large in the group of West Germany, the Netherlands, Sweden and Switzerland).

Note that the single factor is found to explain a larger percentage of variance in the longer period that includes both the floating- and fixed-rate periods than in the shorter period. While the increase in the percentage of variance explained is not significant, the fact that the entries in the correlation matrix all rose or did not decline is qualitatively significant, and lends at least tenuous strength to the conjecture that the international marginal monetary productivity of capital has a more powerful effect on interest rates, and the international allocation of capital is hence more efficient, under flexible than under fixed exchange rates. Similarly, six of seven factor loadings increased in the longer period, adding further support for this view.

Table 6

INTEREST-RATE FIRST DIFFERENCES: FIXED-RATE PERIOD

A. *Correlation Matrix*

	France	West Germany	Nether-lands	Sweden	Switzer-land	United Kingdom	United States
France	1.000						
West Germany	.138	1.000					
Netherlands	.220	.505	1.000				
Sweden	.225	.410	.385	1.000			
Switzerland	.248	.300	.467	.221	1.000		
United Kingdom	.395	.237	.358	.496	.228	1.000	
United States	.319	.132	.501	.235	.345	.313	1.000

B. *Cumulative Percentage of Variance Explained by Each Factor*

Factor 1—41.9 percent

Factor 2—56.8 percent

Factor 3—no third factor

C. *Unrotated-Matrix Factor Loadings: Correlation of Interest Rates with Factors*

	Factor 1	Factor 2
France	.529[a]	.612[a]
West Germany	.604[a]	−.611[a]
Netherlands	.786[a]	−.246
Sweden	.665[a]	−.166
Switzerland	.618[a]	−.087
United Kingdom	.672[a]	.288
United States	.631[a]	.332

D. *Rotated-Matrix Factor Loadings: Correlation of Interest Rates with Factors*

	Factor 1	Factor 2
France	.006	.809[a]
West Germany	.856[a]	−.073
Netherlands	.758[a]	.322
Sweden	.614[a]	.305
Switzerland	.527[a]	.334
United Kingdom	.325	.655[a]
United States	.264	.662[a]

[a] Statistically significant to .01 level.

Table 7

INTEREST-RATE FIRST DIFFERENCES: FIXED/FLEXIBLE-RATE PERIOD

A. *Correlation Matrix*

	France	West Germany	Nether- lands	Sweden	Switzer- land	United Kingdom	United States
France	1.000						
West Germany	.147	1.000					
Netherlands	.208	.471	1.000				
Sweden	.207	.357	.333	1.000			
Switzerland	.217	.361	.461	.220	1.000		
United Kingdom	.278	.305	.248	.449	.333	1.000	
United States	.347	.139	.437	.239	.345	.319	1.000

B. *Cumulative Percentage of Variance Explained by Each Factor*

Factor 1—40.8 percent

Factor 2—55.3 percent

Factor 3—no third factor

C. *Unrotated-Matrix Factor Loadings: Correlation of Interest Rates with Factors*

	Factor 1	Factor 2
France	.496[a]	.630[a]
West Germany	.631[a]	−.549[a]
Netherlands	.732[a]	−.192
Sweden	.628[a]	−.184
Switzerland	.672[a]	−.089
United Kingdom	.656[a]	.072
United States	.631[a]	.480[a]

D. *Rotated-Matrix Factor Loadings: Correlation of Interest Rates with Factors*

	Factor 1	Factor 2
France	.054	.800[a]
West Germany	.831[a]	−.097
Netherlands	.712[a]	.254
Sweden	.622[a]	.203
Switzerland	.605[a]	.306
United Kingdom	.501[a]	.430[a]
United States	.250	.752[a]

[a] Statistically significant at .01 level.

124

Table 8
INTEREST-RATE PERCENTAGE CHANGES: FIXED-RATE PERIOD

A. *Correlation Matrix*

	France	West Germany	Nether- lands	Sweden	Switzer- land	United Kingdom	United States
France	1.000						
West Germany	.121	1.000					
Netherlands	.192	.451	1.000				
Sweden	.208	.367	.338	1.000			
Switzerland	.239	.283	.474	.218	1.000		
United Kingdom	.393	.192	.359	.472	.279	1.000	
United States	.235	.009	.424	.196	.291	.279	1.000

B. *Cumulative Percentage of Variance Explained by Each Factor*

Factor 1—39.4 percent

Factor 2—54.9 percent

Factor 3—no third factor

C. *Unrotated-Matrix Factor Loadings: Correlation of Interest Rates with Factors*

	Factor 1	Factor 2
France	.513[a]	.464[a]
West Germany	.548[a]	−.698[a]
Netherlands	.766[a]	−.173
Sweden	.648[a]	−.209
Switzerland	.644[a]	−.033
United Kingdom	.692[a]	.230
United States	.544[a]	.505[a]

D. *Rotated-Matrix Factor Loadings: Correlation of Interest Rates with Factors*

	Factor 1	Factor 2
France	.082	.687[a]
West Germany	.871[a]	−.167
Netherlands	.693[a]	.372[a]
Sweden	.626[a]	.268
Switzerland	.508[a]	.397[a]
United Kingdom	.372[a]	.628[a]
United States	.079	.738[a]

[a] Statistically significant at .01 level.

125

Table 9

INTEREST-RATE PERCENTAGE CHANGES:
FIXED/FLEXIBLE-RATE PERIOD

A. Correlation Matrix

	France	West Germany	Nether-lands	Sweden	Switzer-land	United Kingdom	United States
France	1.000						
West Germany	.125	1.000					
Netherlands	.188	.432	1.000				
Sweden	.199	.328	.311	1.000			
Switzerland	.218	.329	.473	.218	1.000		
United Kingdom	.311	.248	.290	.443	.341	1.000	
United States	.261	.022	.391	.201	.295	.280	1.000

B. Cumulative Percentage of Variance Explained by Each Factor

Factor 1—38.9 percent

Factor 2—54.1 percent

Factor 3—no third factor

C. Unrotated-Matrix Factor Loadings: Correlation of Interest Rates with Factors

	Factor 1	Factor 2
France	.486[a]	.495[a]
West Germany	.574[a]	−.649[a]
Netherlands	.736[a]	−.172
Sweden	.623[a]	−.151
Switzerland	.680[a]	−.080
United Kingdom	.680[a]	.143
United States	.549[a]	.562[a]

D. Rotated-Matrix Factor Loadings: Correlation of Interest Rates with Factors

	Factor 1	Factor 2
France	.103	.686[a]
West Germany	.846[a]	−.189
Netherlands	.696[a]	.293
Sweden	.593[a]	.244
Switzerland	.598[a]	.335
United Kingdom	.466[a]	.515[a]
United States	.115	.777[a]

[a] Statistically significant at .01 level.

126

To consider changes in levels of interest rates, begin with Table 6, which covers first differences in the fixed-rate period. Again, the first factor seems to be an international factor, given the relatively uniform and moderately high pattern of loadings in the unrotated factor matrix, and is interpreted again as the marginal monetary productivity of capital. The high loadings suggest very strong international influences on domestic interest-rate changes.

The second factor has an eigenvalue (not given in the table) close to unity and thus seems on the verge of becoming insignificant—it alone explains only 15 percent of the variance. However, the consistent pattern of eigenvalues for both the first and second factors in Tables 6 through 9 makes it seem likely that the second factor is generally significant. (It also seems plausible that a second factor, similar to the bipolar one to be discussed, may sometimes be significant for levels, helping to explain West Germany's relatively low loading in Tables 4 and 5.) The second factor is clearly bipolar, with West Germany at one extreme and France at the other. It seems plausible to group the Netherlands, Sweden, and Switzerland in a "Germanic" group with West Germany, and the United States and United Kingdom with France in what will later be seen to be a "trans-Atlantic" group. (The same result shows up for the second factor, perhaps more clearly, in the rotated factor matrix—though the rotation obscures the first factor.)

Merely discovering the bipolar factor, grouping countries at either pole, and then labeling the groups does not explain the factor. Examination of the communalities (not shown) shows West Germany's to be largest, and the Netherlands' to be second largest; the Netherlands' disproportionate influence is interpreted as a reflection of her relatively close correlation with West Germany and the United States, two large, important countries, with West Germany itself having a high communality. France also has a high communality, but has a correlation with West Germany that is not significantly different from zero (see the correlation coefficients matrix), and the United States and the United Kingdom also have low correlations with West Germany: the United States has its lowest correlation with West Germany, and the United Kingdom has virtually its lowest with West Germany. On the other hand, though France has relatively low correlation in general, its highest correlations are with the United Kingdom and the United States. The correlation coefficients matrix also seems to reveal a general pattern of connectedness among the countries in the Germanic group.

It thus seems plausible to identify the second factor as the Germanic factor— it represents the role of economic forces in the capital markets of West Germany. In this light, it seems natural that West Germany should be at one pole and France, the country that shows the least relationship with West Germany, should be at the other pole. Clustered with West Germany are the countries that by language and culture, as well as economic size, might be expected to yield some dominance to German influences. Clustered with France are two countries that are economically large enough to resist German influence, which have much weaker cultural and linguistic ties with West Germany and which additionally have a modest positive relationship with France.

Examination of either set of second-factor loadings shows the United Kingdom and United States a good deal closer to each other than to France. The generally stronger correlation between France and the United Kingdom than between France and the United States suggests that the United Kingdom is a transmission point between the United States and France, rather than that the United States directly affects France (or vice versa). Notice that the loadings of the other "Germanic" group countries decline directly with their lack of correlation with West Germany, rather than in some discernible pattern of strength of correlation with some other country such as the United Kingdom or the United States.

Table 8 lists statistical results for percentage changes in interest rates over the same period as Table 6: the basic patterns remain, but some variations should be pointed out and used in the interpretation. A major change is the increase in the second-factor loading for the United States. From the correlation coefficients' matrix, it seems likely that this is due to the quite low correlation between the United States and West Germany, thus reinforcing the interpretation that the second factor shows West Germany's influence and the high loadings in this factor for the United States and France result from their being out of step with West Germany, rather than in step with each other and the rest of the countries out of phase with a U.S.-France factor. Note that the new, lower U.S.-France correlation emphasizes the German factor and the role of the United Kingdom in a transmission mechanism between the United States and France.

Another change is that although West Germany remains somewhat more highly correlated with the Netherlands than with Sweden, the second-factor loading for Sweden is marginally higher (in absolute value in the unrotated-factor matrix) than for the Netherlands. But recall that the previously noted relationship between correlation with West Germany and strength of factor loadings was adduced as mere corroboration for a much more plausible case that the second factor represented German influence. In Table 8, the same case can be made, but for a "rough" relationship between correlation with West Germany and size of factor loadings. Indeed, it seems more to the point to observe that this illustrates two notions: (1) in the interpretation of factors, the correlation coefficients matrix is of much use, but hardly gives unqualified indications, and (2) for this reason among others, it is useful to cast a factor analysis in several similar but not identical forms, as done here, so that one form may illuminate the obscurity of others.

Tables 7 and 9 show the same patterns as Tables 6 and 8, but for the longer period that contains a period of flexible rates. The period of flexible rates is too short for significant conclusions to be drawn independently, but comparing Tables 6 through 9, it is clear that flexible rates caused no significant change—the percentages of variance explained are remarkably similar, for instance. In Table 8 the pattern between correlation with West Germany and second-factor loadings

128

reasserts itself for the Netherlands and Sweden, and while this is also in Table 9, it reverses itself in a wholly insignificant way for Sweden and Switzerland.

The one conjecture about the period of flexible rates that seems interesting is the decline in both Tables 7 and 9 of the number of correlation coefficients greater than .35 in absolute value. This suggests that the generally supposed greater freedom of interest-rate policy under flexible rates may manifest itself in the future, if flexible rates continue, though it certainly did not in the period considered. (Floating rates have, of course, unquestionably given individual countries greater scope for control of their national money stocks.)

One of the conclusions of this study is negative, but of some importance: there is no "EEC factor" that represents the influence on interest rates of the combined weight of the Six.[38] Before data limitations reduced analysis to the seven countries considered here, it was conjectured that the first factor would be an "international" factor (the international marginal monetary productivity of capital), the second would be an "EEC" factor (the integration of the Six into a bloc that rivaled the United States in importance and international economic influence) and the third, an "English-speaking" factor (the close relationship among the United States, the United Kingdom, and Canada, fostered by history, geography, culture and language). Data limitations ruled out the third factor in its original form, and no third factor was found to be significant. (Indeed, the interpretation above of the second factor made any U.K.-U.S. factor seem quite weak.) But it still seemed plausible that an EEC factor could be found, since only Italy and Belgium-Luxembourg were excluded. However, the failure to find an EEC factor is utterly convincing, and in its place is found a very plausible Germanic factor to which France shows strong antipathy. Rather than the Six melding into a single super-economy, there seems to persist this marked dichotomy between West Germany and France; moreover, lengthening the period does not diminish the divergence. On this basis the outlook for integration and harmonization is grim. Note that the addition of the United Kingdom to the EEC seems likely only to intensify this split (though the notion that the United Kingdom will act as a counterweight to West Germany, and thus on France's side, has some marginal plausibility).

Some Conclusions and Caveats. As noted previously, our empirical work does not explicitly test our theoretical notions of financial-market integration. Among other things, the factors are unweighted, whereas we previously indicated that an optimally diversified international portfolio—which the first factor represents—would contain assets in proportion to the relative outstanding stock of those assets. Nor do we explicitly test the speed of adjustment of interest rates in one country to interest-rate changes in another country. But we do provide strong evidence of

---

[38] This finding is consistent with those of Hawkins, "Intra-EEC Capital Movements," who was unable to find any real increase in financial-market integration after the first few years of the EEC's existence.

Table 10

CORRELATION MATRIX OF INTEREST-RATE LEVELS: FIXED/FLOATING PERIOD

	Nether-lands	Sweden	Switzer-land	United Kingdom	United States	West Germany	France
Netherlands	1.000						
Sweden	.915	1.000					
Switzerland	.967	.891	1.000				
United Kingdom	.913	.929	.903	1.000			
United States	.931	.896	.902	.935	1.000		
West Germany	.742	.655	.754	.644	.540	1.000	
France	.854	.746	.863	.887	.859	.679	1.000

financial-market integration by applying a technique allowing for simultaneous investigation of a number of domestic interest rates.

In every instance the factor loadings of domestic interest rates with the first factor of the unrotated matrix (the correlation) is highly positive and statistically significant. (Given our degrees of freedom, Piersonian correlation coefficients must be greater than .35 for statistical significance at the .01 level [from tables].) So even with an imperfect index (the unweighted by size first factor), we obtain quite powerful results which suggest extremely high covariability of interest rates, hence an extremely high degree of international financial-market integration.

We also note that in all instances the correlation of German interest rates with the first factor was lower than for any other country, suggesting that within the framework of international integration, West Germany was relatively able to influence international financial markets. This finding is at variance with conclusions reached by, say, Kouri and Porter who found a total inability of the German central bank to extricate German financial conditions from international influences.[39] To reinforce this finding, we reproduce Table 4, Panel A, the correlation matrix, as Table 10, but now arranged in a more revealing format. Notice that just on the basis of this fragment of our evidence France and particularly Germany seem to be less correlated to other countries' international influences than are other countries.

Our results on levels of interest rates compare quite favorably with those of Fase (90 percent of the variance explained by the first factor), who studied only rates in the Netherlands, and Hester (83 percent), who studied only the United States—and both these authors concluded that their results suggested a single interest rate. We obtain similar magnitudes in our analysis, implying a single international interest rate.

---

[39] Kouri and Porter, "International Capital Flows."

In terms of our first difference and percentage-change results, our findings of roughly 40 percent of the variation explained by the first factor compare favorably to the findings of King, who studied rates of return (percentage changes plus unity) in the U.S. stock market. To the extent that most researchers accept the notion that the U.S. stock market is highly integrated and indeed efficient, our results seem to merit a similar conclusion.

A major caveat: the parallel studies used monthly data; we used quarterly. If we had used monthly data, our findings might have been weakened if indeed the speed of price adjustment is not instantaneous—in fact if it takes more than one month, but occurs within a quarter. Nevertheless, price adjustment within a quarter is somewhat quicker than many in the capital flow school of price adjustments seem to imply.

In spite of this caveat, our analysis based on systematic risk reasoning seems to reveal strong financial-market integration, at least among those seven industrial countries. Moreover, to the extent that they are not weakened appreciably—in fact the interest-rate-levels analysis is strengthened—when the period of floating exchange rates is incorporated, our findings have implications concerning the actual degree of international monetary interdependence. Unfortunately, we were not able to test explicitly for this (floating exchange rates are too recent a phenomenon), but we view these findings as suggestive.

5. Conclusion

To summarize, we argued in favor of a concept of international financial-market integration which is based on the capital asset pricing model—an equilibrium model of asset prices under uncertainty. Applying this construct allows for a distinction between two types of risk—nondiversifiable and diversifiable risk—and suggests that expected returns are a function only of the former, but that ex post returns may reflect both types. We also reviewed and examined existing theory and direct empirical work on international financial-market (interest-rate) integration and pointed out some differences between extant work and our concept of financial-market integration. Finally, we reported our own empirical findings which, while not a direct test of our theoretical notions, did demonstrate that financial markets are indeed quite highly integrated internationally. The statistical technique employed was factor analysis, which allows for the simultaneity of price changes and indeed uses this simultaneity to allow inferences concerning interrelationships among financial markets.

More questions than answers have most likely been offered in this paper, and this may be to the good. At the very least, we hope we have demonstrated that we all have a lot further to go in understanding the nature, mechanics, and implications of international financial-market integration.

Appendix A: The Capital Asset Pricing Model

The capital asset pricing model asserts that the rate of return on the nth security, R_n, is a linear function of a risk-free rate, R_F, and the return on a broad-based index of economic activity of a fully diversified market portfolio, $\tilde{I}$, under the following sufficient, but not necessary assumptions:

(a) All investors are risk-averse, single-period, expected-utility maximizers where utility is a quadratic function of returns or the distribution of returns is normal.

(b) All investors have access to identical information and hold identical probability beliefs concerning future states of nature.

(c) There are no transactions costs and all investors may lend or borrow as much as they want at a single risk-free rate. It may be written as follows:

$$R_n = R_F + \beta_n (\tilde{I} - R_F)$$

where
$$\beta_n = \frac{\text{Cov} (R_n, \tilde{I})}{\text{Var} (\tilde{I})} . \qquad [A.1]$$

The statistical or empirical form of the capital asset pricing model, the market model, represents the stochastic behavior of security returns over time. It may be written:

$$R_{nt} - R_F = a_n + \beta_n (\tilde{I} - R_F) + \epsilon_{nt} \qquad [A.2]$$

where a_n, β_n are parameters and

$$E (a_{nt}) = 0 \text{ for } n = 1 \ldots N \qquad [A.3a]$$
$$E (\epsilon_{nt}) = 0 \qquad [A.3b]$$
$$E (\epsilon_{nt}, \epsilon_{nt-1}) = 0 \text{ for } n = 1 \ldots N, \text{ for all } t \qquad [A.3c]$$
$$E (I_t, \epsilon_{nt}) = 0 \qquad [A.3d]$$
$$E (\epsilon_{nt}, \epsilon_{n't}) = 0 \text{ for } n \neq n' \qquad [A.3e]$$

[A.3a] and [A.3b] are necessary to the idea of a competitive market where securities are, aside from systematic risk, β, perfect substitutes for one another. These assumptions suggest that "excess" returns should, on average, equal zero. [A.3c] is also necessary for the existence of a competitive market, for if returns were serially correlated over and above the serial correlation of $\tilde{I}_t$, but see [A.3d]), the random walk hypothesis would be untenable. These three assumptions are generic, therefore, to virtually all models developed using the foundation of a competitive market.

Statistical assumptions [A.3d] and [A.3e] summarize two of the more important aspects of the contributions to capital-asset theory of the positive model of [A.1]. [A.3d] states that the independent variable $\tilde{I}_t$ is uncorrelated with the error term ϵ_{nt}. [A.3e] asserts that the unexplained variation of the nth firm's return—Var (ϵ_n)— is uncorrelated with the unexplained variation of the nth firm's return. Together [A.3d] and [A.3e] allow all covariation between the nth and n'th firm's returns to be defined by Var $(\tilde{I}) \beta_n$ and $\beta_{n'}$, and this is the single most important aspect of

132

the model. If [A.3d] and [A.3e] do not hold, but [A.3a], [A.3b], and [A.3c] hold, then it can be shown that the covariation between R_n and $R_{n'}$ can be written as:

$$\text{Cov}\ (R_n\, R_{n'}) = \beta_n\beta_{n'}\,\text{Var}\ (\tilde{I}) + \text{Cov}\ (\epsilon_n\, \epsilon_{n'}) \qquad [A.4]$$
$$+\ \beta_{n'}\,\text{Cov}\ (\tilde{I}\,\epsilon_n) + \beta_n\,\text{Cov}\ (\tilde{I}\,\epsilon_{n'}).$$

[A.3e] requires the second term on the right-hand side of [A.4] to be zero for $n = n'$, and [A.3d] requires the final two terms to be zero as well.

In general, both the capital asset pricing model and its empirical counterpart dichotomize the variation of and covariation between securities into two components: one a parameter of the variation of the index $\tilde{I}$, the so-called systematic or nondiversifiable risk, and the other a parameter of the variation of the residuals, the unsystematic or diversifiable risk. Cooper's model, for example, does not recognize this distinction.

Thus the variance of R_n is:

$$\text{Var}\ (R_n) = \beta^2_{n}\,\text{Var}\ (\tilde{I}) + \text{Var}\ (\epsilon_n) \qquad [A.5a]$$

and the covariance between R_n and $R_{n'}$ is, in the model,

$$\text{Cov}\ (R_n\, R_{n'}) = \beta_n\, \beta_{n'}\,\text{Var}\ (\tilde{I}). \qquad [A.5b]$$

Of critical importance to the analysis at this stage is the nature and composition of the index, $\tilde{I}$. The literature pertaining to the subject has variously described $\tilde{I}$ as (a) an index of general economic activity, (b) an index of security prices or returns, or, similarly, (c) the return on a "market portfolio," and (d) an index which best "explains" the variance of security returns. The most generally accepted definitions and those most often used in empirical tests, are (b), (c), and (d), each of which implies an index $\tilde{I}$ which is *derived* from the returns on the securities it is supposed to represent in the aggregate.

Extending these results, the capital asset pricing model for M securities with T time periods may be written with R_F incorporated in R and $\tilde{I}$, as:

$$R = \alpha + \beta\,\tilde{I} + \Theta \qquad [A.6]$$

where $R = M \times T$ matrix of rates of return in excess of the risk-free rate.

$\alpha = M \times 1$ matrix of intercept terms (assumed to be zero), that is $E(\alpha) = 0$.

$\beta = M \times 1$ matrix of coefficients; measures of systematic risk.

$\tilde{I} = 1 \times T$ matrix of rates of change of the index.

$\Theta = M \times T$ matrix of measures of unsystematic risk.

As noted before, $\tilde{I}$ may be (and most often is) a linear combination of security returns, thus,

$$\tilde{I} = \alpha' R \qquad [A.7]$$

where $\alpha = M \times 1$ matrix of weights.

The variance-covariance may thus be written as:

$$E(R\,R') = \beta\,\tilde{I}\,\tilde{I}'\,\beta' + 2\beta\,\tilde{I}\,\Theta' + \Theta\,\Theta' \qquad\text{[A.8a]}$$

or substituting [A.7]:

$$E(R\,R') = \beta\,\alpha'\,R\,R'\,\alpha\,\beta' + \Theta\,\Theta' + 2\beta\,\alpha'\,R\,\Theta'. \qquad\text{[A.8b]}$$

Since it is assumed by [A.3d] in the stochastic market model that $E(\tilde{I}\,\Theta') = 0$, and generally in the positive model that systematic and unsystematic risk are unrelated, substituting the transposed [A.6] and using [A.7] we can conveniently write [A.3d] as

$$\alpha'\,R\,(R' - R'\,\alpha\,\beta') = 0 \qquad\text{[A.9a]}$$

and therefore

$$\alpha'\,R\,R'\,(I - \alpha\,\beta') = 0 \qquad\text{[A.9b]}$$

where I is an identity matrix. Since it is easily assumed that the T observations of $\tilde{I}$ are not identical, by necessity $I = \alpha\,\beta'$. For there to be two vectors, α and β, such that $\alpha\,\beta' = I$, would imply that once the index weights are chosen, the measures of systematic risk, the β matrix, would be determined *without regard to observations on returns*. Hence, with either the positive assumption or market model assumption [A.3d] and *when the index is a linear combination of security* returns, the model does not fully hold. This finding reflects an *over-specification* of the theoretical model. Empirically, this suggests that the β estimated for a given security is a function of the weights accorded the securities in the time series index against which the security's time series returns are regressed. In sum then, perhaps a more appropriate index would be one of general economic activity, unless one, as we propose, is simply interested in the degree of purely *financial* interrelation.

The key feature of the capital asset pricing model is that it facilitates the decomposition of risk into systematic and unsystematic components and forces focus on the systematic, or unavoidable component as the only relevant source of risk. Equation [A.8a] separates the variance-covariance matrix of security returns, $R\,R'$, into three kinds—specifically, its three right-hand terms. The first is the systematic risk which is based upon the variation of an index; the second is the unsystematic risk, namely the variation of the residuals; and the third form of risk is the covariation between the index and the residuals which has been assumed away by the model.

More explicitly, letting Γ be a $(l \times m)$ vector of proportional weights (i.e., the percentage of wealth invested in each security) such that $\sum_{i=1}^{m} \gamma_i = 0$, the risk associated with a portfolio may be written as:

$$\text{Risk}\,(\Gamma) = \Gamma\,\beta\,\tilde{I}\,\tilde{I}'\,\beta'\,\Gamma' + \Gamma\,\Theta\,\Theta'\,\Gamma + 2\Gamma\,\beta\,\tilde{I}\,\Theta\,\Gamma'. \qquad\text{[A.10]}$$

The last term disappears by assumption, and the second right-hand term may, since $\Theta\,\Theta' = \tilde{I}\,U\,\tilde{I}'$, be written as:

$$\Gamma\,\Theta\,\Theta'\,\Gamma' = \Gamma\,\tilde{I}\,U\,\tilde{I}'\,\Gamma' = \sum_{i=1}^{m} \gamma_i^2\,u_{ii} = 0. \qquad\text{[A.11]}$$

As the value of each γ_i approaches zero, this term approaches zero. Accordingly, in a portfolio where a sufficient number of securities are held, $\gamma_i \to 0$, the unsystematic risk of the portfolio, the second right-hand term of [A.10], approaches zero. Hence, for a well-diversified portfolio, the risk is simply:

$$\text{Risk} \cong \Gamma \beta \tilde{I} \tilde{I}' \beta' \Gamma. \qquad [A.12]$$

The rationale for going through the more complex matrix algebra, rather than stopping with the simpler exposition, is that the matrix algebra helps in the understanding of why a factor-analysis approach is an appropriate one.

Appendix B: An Overview of the Technique of Factor Analysis [1]

Assume p simultaneous observations at time t on p interest rates: $I, \ldots I_p$. Further assume the I_i are drawn from a multivariate normal population which for empirical purposes is assumed to be the same over time. Then we can write:

$$\begin{aligned} I_1 &= \lambda_{11} Y_1 + \ldots + \lambda_{1m} Y_m + e, \\ I_p &= \lambda_{p1} Y_1 + \ldots + \lambda_{pm} Y_m + e_p \end{aligned} \qquad [B.1]$$

where $Y_j = j$th common factor variate

$\lambda_{ij} = $ parameter reflecting importance of jth factor in composition of ith response

$e_i = i$th specific factor variate.

λ_{ij} is the loading of the ith response on the jth common factor. In matrix notation of this linear model let:

$$\begin{aligned} i &= [I, \ldots, I_p] \\ y' &= [Y_1, \ldots, Y_m] \\ \epsilon' &= [e_1, \ldots, e_p] \end{aligned}$$

and

$$\Lambda = \begin{bmatrix} \lambda_{11} \ldots \lambda_{1m} \\ \lambda_{p1} \ldots \lambda_{pm} \end{bmatrix} \qquad [B.2]$$

Then the model may be written as:

$$i = \Lambda y + \epsilon \qquad [B.3]$$

Let the m common factor variates in y be independently and normally distributed with zero means and unit variances. Assume elements of Λ are normally and independently distributed with zero means and variances, so that

$$\text{var} (e_i) = \Psi_i \qquad [B.4]$$

where Ψ_i is the specific variance as in the terminology of Appendix A, the diversifiable risk.

---

[1] This review draws heavily on Donald F. Morrison, *Multivariate Methods* (New York: McGraw-Hill Book Co., 1967), pp. 261-264.

It is convenient to write these parameters as the diagonal matrix

$$\Psi = \begin{bmatrix} \Psi_1 & & \\ & \cdot & \\ & & \cdot \\ & & \Psi_p \end{bmatrix} \qquad\qquad [B.5]$$

Finally, y and ϵ are independently distributed. (Thus, the separation of systematic from unsystematic risk may be accomplished as in Appendix A.)

The variance of the ith observation can be written:

$$\sigma_i^2 = \lambda_{i1}^2 + \ldots + \lambda_{im}^2 + \Psi_i \qquad\qquad [B.6]$$

and the covariance of the ith and jth observations as:

$$\sigma_{ij} = \Psi_{i1}\Psi_{j1} + \ldots + \Psi_{im}\Psi_{jm}. \qquad\qquad [B.7]$$

In matrix form:

$$\Sigma = \Lambda\Lambda' + \Psi. \qquad\qquad [B.8]$$

The covariance depends on specific risk. Compare [A.8a] and [B.8], recalling that the capital asset pricing model requires the second term in [A.8a] to approach zero. It is clear that the capital asset pricing model is satisfied in factor analytic terms. When Ψ is zero, or empirically, the significant factors explain a relatively large percentage of the variance of the interest rates. Under the factor model, the diagonal elements of $\Lambda\Lambda'$ are:

$$\sigma_i^2 - \Psi_i = \sum_{j-1}^{m} \lambda_{ij}^2 \qquad\qquad [B.9]$$

and are referred to as communalities of observations.

The parameter λ_{ij} is the covariance of the ith observation with the jth common factor. Note, however, that if Σ of [B.8] is the population correlation matrix (as we use in our analysis), the λ_{ij} are the correlations of the time series observations of a given domestic interest rate with the time series observation of a given factor.

The idea behind factor analysis is the determination of the elements of the loading matrix Λ, with the elements of Ψ following from constraint [B.6] imposed upon the communalities. This is accomplished by orthogonalizing the correlation matrix Σ and rotations of this matrix. In essence then, the notion strives to break down the elements of the variance-covariance or correlation matrix Σ, in two terms, a common part and a unique part, with part of the variance of the time series of each I_i "explained" by the term $\lambda_i f_t$, when f_t is the value of factor i at time t.

Recall from Appendix A, the measure of systematic risk of the capital asset pricing model, β, was defined as:

$$\beta = \frac{\text{Cov } (R_n \tilde{I})}{\text{Var } (\tilde{I})}. \qquad\qquad [B.10a]$$

Redefining terms: let $R_n = I_t$ for a time series of interest rates. Let $\tilde{I} = \Lambda\, y_t$ for a weighted index of common factors—the market portfolio in Appendix A. Then β may be written as:

$$\beta = \frac{\text{Cov } (I_t\, f_t)}{\text{Var } (f_t)} \qquad\qquad \text{[B.10b]}$$

and λ_{ij}, the factor load, may be written as:

$$\lambda_{ij} = \frac{\text{Cov } (I_t\, f_t)}{\sqrt{\text{Var } I_t}\ \cdot\ \sqrt{\text{Var } f_t}} = \frac{\beta\sqrt{\text{Var } f_t}}{\sqrt{\text{Var } I_t}}\,. \qquad\qquad \text{[B.11]}$$

Therefore

$$\lambda_j = \frac{\text{Var } (f_t)}{\sqrt{\text{Var } (I_t)}\ \cdot\ \sqrt{\text{Var } (f_t)}}\,. \qquad\qquad \text{[B.12]}$$

So there is essentially only a scale factor separating the two measures. Hence our interpretation of λ_{ij} as being a measure of the systematic relationship is meaningful.

THE FORWARD MARKET AND INTEREST RATES IN THE EUROCURRENCY AND NATIONAL MONEY MARKETS

Richard J. Herring and Richard C. Marston

Despite enormous shocks to the international monetary system during the past decade, forward exchange rates have remained at interest-rate parity with respect to Eurocurrency interest rates.[1] In contrast, forward exchange rates have occasionally diverged quite markedly from interest-rate parity with respect to national interest rates. Arbitrage is effective in holding forward rates at interest parity with respect to Eurocurrency rates primarily because (a) the Eurocurrency markets are largely free of the restrictions which inhibit arbitrage between national markets, and because (b) the Eurocurrency markets share an equal vulnerability to future capital controls; thus expectations of future controls do not inhibit arbitrage *between* Eurocurrencies.[2]

Knowing that interest parity holds for Eurocurrency interest rates, however, does not explain how transactions in the Eurocurrency markets and the forward exchange markets interact to determine Eurocurrency interest rates and forward exchange rates. While it is likely that increases in the demand for a particular

For discussions concerning current practices in the Eurocurrency and foreign exchange markets, we would like to thank without implicating Martin Griffin, Norman Klath, Nancy Shaw, and Dennis Weatherstone of Morgan Guaranty Trust Company of New York, and Robert Crowley, Roger Kubarych, and Scott Pardee of the Federal Reserve Bank of New York. We would also like to thank Charles Freedman, Hans Stoll, and the discussants of this paper at the Conference on Eurocurrencies and National Financial Policies for their valuable comments. We gratefully acknowledge the financial assistance of the American Enterprise Institute for Public Policy Research, the Rodney L. White Center for Financial Research, and the National Science Foundation (SOC 74-19271).

[1] In Appendix B, we discuss the recent behavior of forward exchange rates and Eurocurrency and national interest rates in the D-mark and dollar markets. Statistical evidence establishing that the forward rate and Eurocurrency interest rates are maintained at interest parity is given in Robert Z. Aliber, "The Interest Rate Parity Theorem: A Reinterpretation," *Journal of Political Economy* (November/December 1973), pp. 1451-1459; Richard C. Marston, "The Structure of the Eurocurrency System" (Ph.D. diss., Department of Economics, Massachusetts Institute of Technology, 1972), Chapter VI; Richard C. Marston, "Interest Arbitrage in the Eurocurrency Markets," *European Economic Review*, January 1976, pp. 1-13.

[2] The risk that capital controls might be imposed on financial centers is an important factor limiting arbitrage involving *national* investments. But the risk of capital controls is of minimal importance in transactions *between* Eurocurrencies simply because it is unlikely that future capital controls would be applied to one Eurocurrency and not another. Although governments have compelling reasons to formulate special regulations for transactions in securities denominated in the home currency, there is no incentive for them to formulate regulations which discriminate among securities denominated in different foreign currencies. See Aliber, "Interest Rate Parity Theorem"; Marston, "Structure of Eurocurrency System"; and Marston, "Interest Arbitrage."

Eurocurrency will affect the forward exchange rate, it seems equally likely that an increase in the speculative demand for a particular forward currency will affect Eurocurrency interest rates.[3] Unfortunately there is no standard framework for examining these interactions because most formal analyses of the forward exchange market have focused on the impact of interest rates on the forward rate while ignoring the impact which the forward rate itself may have on interest rates.[4]

In this study we reformulate the traditional analysis of the forward market to take into account the interaction among interest rates and the forward rate.[5] Our model integrates an analysis of the Eurocurrency operations of banks with the traditional model of forward exchange transactions in order to explain why the forward rate and Eurocurrency interest rates are maintained at interest parity. The model is then extended to explain the joint determination of forward rates and national interest rates. The model is used to show how national and Eurocurrency interest rates each respond to speculation in the forward market, and how the forward rate responds to disturbances in the national and Eurocurrency money markets.

The analysis is developed in two stages. In Section 1, we consider a case in which the national financial market in the foreign country is closed to all but trade transactions, and show how the forward rate and the non-dollar Eurocurrency rate are jointly determined. In Section 2, the national market is then opened to international capital movements, and the interaction among the forward rate, the Euro-

---

[3] The inherent simultaneity in the relationship between the forward rate and Eurocurrency rates is evident from the way in which transactions are conducted. In a series of interviews we conducted at a major New York bank, we found that Eurocurrency and forward-exchange traders each based quotations in their own market on rates established in the other market. Foreign-exchange traders said that Eurocurrency rate differentials determined the forward rates that they quoted, while Eurocurrency traders said that forward exchange rates determined differentials between non-dollar Eurocurrency rates and the Eurodollar rate. It is clear from the way in which rates are quoted that neither the impact of forward rates on Eurocurrency interest rates nor the impact of Eurocurrency rates on forward rates can be ignored.

[4] For the development of the modern theory of forward exchange see: A. E. Jasay, "Bank Rate or Forward Exchange Policy," *Banca Nazionale del Lavoro Quarterly Review*, March 1958, pp. 56-73; J. Spraos, "Speculation, Arbitrage, and Sterling," *Economic Journal*, March 1959, pp. 1-21; S. C. Tsiang, "The Theory of Forward Exchange and Effects of Government Intervention on the Forward Exchange Market," *International Monetary Fund Staff Papers*, April 1959, pp. 75-106; H. G. Grubel, *Forward Exchange, Speculation, and the International Flow of Capital* (Stanford, Calif.: Stanford University Press, 1966); P. B. Kenen, "Trade, Speculation, and the Forward Exchange Rate," in R. E. Baldwin et al., *Trade, Growth, and the Balance of Payments* (Chicago: Rand McNally, 1965), pp. 143-169; H. R. Stoll, "An Empirical Study of the Forward Exchange Market Under Fixed and Flexible Exchange Rate Systems," *Canadian Journal of Economics*, February 1968, pp. 55-78; and J. Kesselman, "The Role of Speculation in Forward Rate Determination: The Canadian Flexible Dollar 1953-1960," *Canadian Journal of Economics*, August 1971, pp. 279-298. An exception to this tradition is a study by Stanley W. Black, *International Money Markets and Flexible Exchange Rates*, Princeton Studies in International Finance, no. 32 (March 1973), which presents a fully simultaneous model in which the spot and forward exchange rates and national interest rates are jointly determined.

[5] Because we wish to focus on simultaneous interactions between the forward rate and interest rates, we shall follow the tradition in the forward-exchange-market literature of treating the spot exchange rate as fixed by official intervention.

currency rate, and the national interest rate is analyzed. We conclude with a brief summary of the analytic results. A statistical appendix reviews recent trends among interest rates and exchange rates in the D-mark and dollar markets.

1. Equilibrium in the Forward and Eurocurrency Markets

For simplicity we shall analyze a model in which there are only two countries, America and Germany, and only two currencies, the dollar and the D-mark. In this section we assume that the foreign market (Germany) is closed to all but trade transactions.[6] This assumption enables us to study the interaction between the Eurocurrency and forward markets alone. The aim of the analysis is to explain the determination of the interest rate on Eurocurrencies denominated in D-marks (Euromarks) and the forward D-mark rate as functions of the Eurodollar rate (or the U.S. interest rate) and non-interest-rate factors. In order to focus upon the Euromark interest rate and the D-mark forward rate, we shall assume that the U.S. interest rate is controlled by Federal Reserve policy. Interest rates in the Eurodollar and U.S. markets, moreover, are assumed to be tightly linked by flows of funds between the two markets so that, in effect, the Eurodollar rate can be considered exogenous to the rest of the world.[7]

The Market for Euromarks. Eurocurrency banks are assumed to offer both Eurodollar and Euromark deposits and loans at interest rates $i_\$$ and i_m, respectively. The demand for Euromark deposits by nonbank investors is denoted by M^d, and the supply of Euromark loans by nonbank borrowers is denoted by M^L.[8] All assets and liabilities are assumed to be gross substitutes; for example, the nonbank demand

---

[6] German residents are assumed to hold no foreign (including no Eurocurrency) assets and liabilities, and American residents are assumed to hold no German assets or liabilities.

[7] It might be argued that the U.S. interest rate is insulated from foreign economic conditions because of the dollar's role as a reserve currency. To the extent that foreign exchange reserves are held in the form of U.S. securities or bank deposits, U.S. balance-of-payments surpluses or deficits are effectively sterilized without any discretionary action on the part of the U.S. authorities. Alternatively, one might argue that the U.S. market is sufficiently large in comparison to any other financial market that the impact of shocks in any one of the non-dollar markets on the U.S. interest rate may be neglected. The additional assumption that Eurodollar and U.S. interest rates are tied closely together is an approximation to reality which considerably simplifies the analysis. Note that in recent months, since the dismantling of controls on investment by U.S. residents, U.S. and Eurodollar rates on comparable assets have diverged by much less than the interest rates on U.S. bank instruments and U.S. Treasury securities. See Appendix B for a description of recent interest-rate movements in the two dollar markets.

[8] We assume that the margin between the deposit and loan rates for either Eurocurrency is fixed by competitive bidding among Eurocurrency banks. (C. Freedman, "A Model of the Eurodollar Market" [Discussion Paper No. 25, Center for Economic Research, University of Minnesota, February 1973], adopts a similar assumption about deposit and loan rates in his model of the Eurodollar market.) For simplicity we assume that the margin is zero. Note that we have adopted the Freedman terminology in referring to nonbank investors *demanding* Eurocurrency deposits and nonbank borrowers *supplying* Eurocurrency loans. This terminology reverses that found in Marston, "Structure of Eurocurrency System"; and Marston, "Interest Arbitrage."

Figure 1

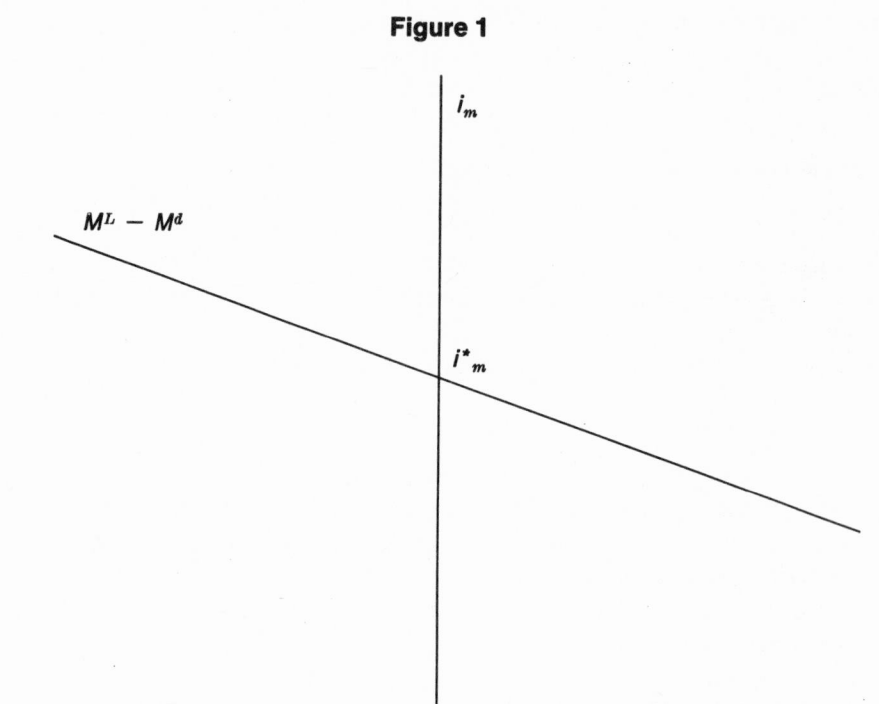

Excess supply of Euromark
loans by nonbanks

for Euromark deposits is positively related to the covered $(i_m + fp)$ and uncovered $(i_m + sp)$ returns on Euromarks and negatively related to the Eurodollar rate, $i_\$$.[9]

If Eurobanks insisted on matching deposits and loans in each Eurocurrency market, then the Euromark interest rate, i_m, would be determined by the interaction of nonbank investors and borrowers in that market alone. Under this simplifying assumption, the Euromark interest rate would be determined as in Figure 1 where the nonbank excess supply of Euromark loans, $M^L - M^d$, is zero.[10]

Since Eurobanks generally operate in several Eurocurrency markets at the same time, the market for Euromarks is not independent of the other Eurocurrency

---

[9] The forward premium, "fp", is defined as $(F - S)/S$ where F is the forward exchange rate and S is the spot rate. Both exchange rates are expressed in $\$/DM$. The speculative premium, "sp", denotes the expected return from holding a spot position in D-marks. Thus, $sp = ((S^e - S)/S)$ where S^e is the expected future spot rate. For easy reference, all symbols and their definitions are listed in Appendix A.

[10] Eurobanks also maintain transactions balances with U.S. and German banks. Most investigators have found that these balances are very small relative to the volume of Eurocurrency deposits outstanding. (See J. Hewson and E. Sakakibara, "The Eurodollar Deposit Multiplier: A Portfolio Approach," International Monetary Fund *Staff Papers*, July 1974, p. 315, and the references listed there.) Hence, to simplify the notation, we shall omit them from the analysis.

markets. Eurobanks, in fact, often maintain a net loan position in one currency by converting funds obtained in another Eurocurrency market. For example, Eurobanks may convert an excess of Eurodollar deposits over loans into marks to increase their Euromark loans. The banks then end up with a net mark loan position, *NMP*.

With Eurobanks willing to convert dollar deposits into marks, mark loans can come from two sources: (1) Euromark deposits and (2) marks converted from dollars by Eurobanks. Hence in equilibrium, Euromark loans must now equal the sum of Euromark deposits *and* the net mark position of the Eurobanks:

$$M^L = M^d + NMP, \text{ where } M^L_{mf}, M^L_{ms}, M^d_\$ < 0; \text{ and} \qquad [1]$$
$$M^L_\$, M^d_{mf}, M^d_{ms} > 0.^{11}$$

As a result of the currency conversions by Eurobanks, the interest rate on Euromarks is closely tied to the interest rate on Eurodollars. To understand how these rates are related, consider the case where Eurobanks are induced to convert dollar funds into marks. In order for the banks to avoid the exchange risk associated with a net mark loan position, they will normally cover that position with an equivalent purchase of forward dollars. The whole transaction will be profitable as long as the interest rate on Euromark loans adjusted for the forward premium exceeds the interest rate paid on Eurodollar deposits. Ignoring transactions costs, the transaction thus will be profitable as long as

$$i_m + fp \geqq i_\$,$$

where *fp* is the forward premium on marks.[12] Competition between Eurobanks, in fact, keeps the interest rate charged for Euromark loans at the interest parity level.[13]

$$i_m = i_\$ - fp.^{14}$$

If the Eurodollar rate and the forward premium are taken as given, then the Euromark rate offered by the Eurobanks is determined as well. Eurobanks stand

---

[11] M^L_{mf} and M^L_{ms} denote the partial derivatives of M^L with respect to the covered $(i_{mf} = i_m + fp)$ and uncovered $(i_{ms} = i_m + sp)$ returns on Euromark loans. $M^L_\$$ is the partial derivative with respect to the Eurodollar interest rate. The partial derivatives of M^d are defined analogously. The behavior of *NMP* is discussed below.

[12] The Eurobanks may require some margin between the rate paid on Eurodollar deposits (adjusted for forward cover) and the rate of interest on Euromark loans, but that margin is assumed to be constant over the relevant range of net currency positions undertaken by Eurobanks. For convenience, we have assumed the margin to be zero.

[13] In Marston, "Structure of Eurocurrency System" and Marston, "Interest Arbitrage," the relationship among Eurocurrency rates and forward premiums is investigated in detail. Over the seven-year period, 1965-71, the Eurocurrency rates and forward premiums for the three principal Eurocurrencies, the D-mark, Swiss franc, and sterling, are shown to adhere closely to interest parity with respect to the Eurodollar rate.

[14] The Eurocurrency rates are said to be at interest parity if the covered return on Euromarks $(1 + i_m)\dfrac{F}{S}$ is equal to the return on Eurodollars $(1 + i_\$)$. If second order terms are neglected, then the interest parity condition reduces to $i_m = i_\$ - fp$, where $fp = (F - S)/S$.

Figure 2

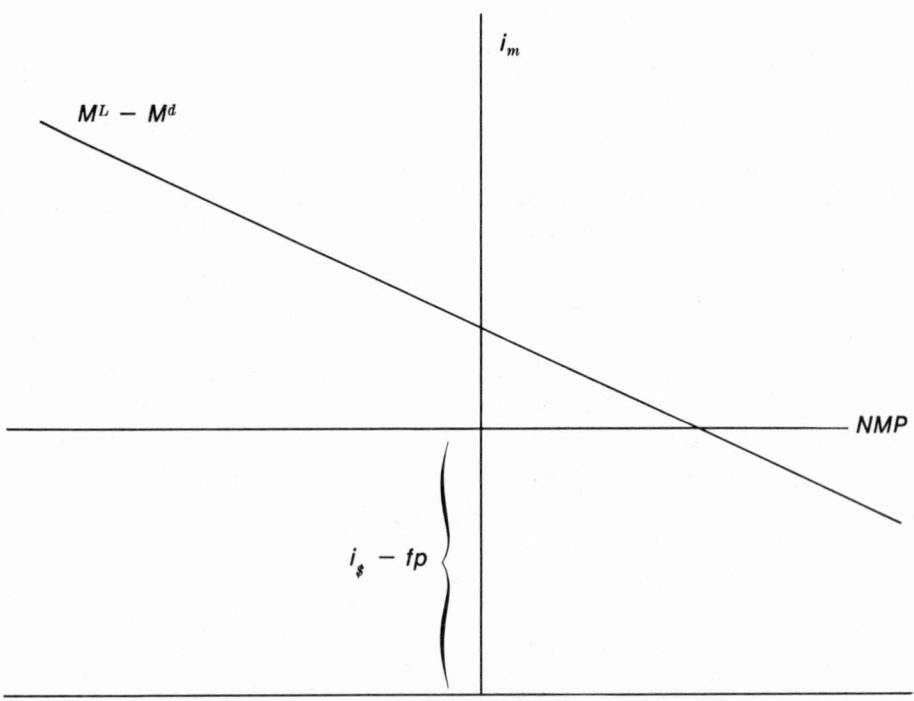

Excess supply of Euromark loans
by nonbanks *and*
net mark loan position of Eurobanks

ready to offer Euromark loans and deposits at an interest rate of $i_m = i_\$ - fp$, so the *NMP* schedule of the Eurobanks is horizontal at this rate. Equilibrium in the market for Euromarks, therefore, is achieved when the nonbank excess supply schedule intersects the *NMP* schedule at the interest parity rate.

Since the Euromark rate offered by the Eurobanks depends on the forward premium (as well as the exogenous Eurodollar rate), we must look at the forward market to understand how the Euromark rate is determined, and treat the markets for Euromarks and forward marks as two interdependent markets.

The Forward Exchange Market. The model of the forward market which we will introduce is a simple one which distinguishes between the excess demand for forward marks on the part of speculators and traders, and the excess supply provided by Eurobanks. The excess demand of speculators and traders (ST) is a function of orders for German exports (X^g) and German orders for imports from the rest of the world (I^g), as well as the forward and speculative premiums (fp and sp):

$$ST = ST(X^g, I^g, fp, sp), \text{ where } ST_X, ST_s > 0; ST_I, ST_f < 0. \qquad [2]$$

Eurobanks supply forward marks in connection with their Eurocurrency operations.[15] Under the simplifying assumption that Eurobanks fully cover their net Eurocurrency positions, the excess supply of forward marks provided by Eurobanks is given by NMP, their net Euromark loan position. NMP, in turn, must equal the excess supply of Euromark loans by nonbanks, $M^L - M^d$. That is, since the Eurobanks are willing to accept whatever Euromark deposits or loans are offered at the prevailing interest parity rate, the excess supply of forward marks provided by the Eurobanks must reflect the underlying excess supply of Euromark loans ($M^L - M^d$) by nonbank borrowers and investors.[16]

In equilibrium, the excess demand by traders and speculators for forward marks must equal the excess supply by nonbanks for Euromarks (which generates an equivalent excess supply of forward marks by Eurobanks):[17]

$$ST = M^L - M^d. \qquad [2.a]$$

The equilibrium in the forward market is illustrated in Figure 3. Given the level of the Eurodollar rate (and other exogenous variables), the forward market is in equilibrium at a forward premium of fp^*. Once the forward premium is determined, the Euromark rate is determined as well by the interest parity relationship.

Shifts in either curve, ST or $M^L - M^d$, lead to adjustments in the forward premium and corresponding adjustments in the Euromark rate. Thus an increase in orders for German exports leads to an upward shift in ST in Figure 4, raising the forward premium to fp^{**}. The Euromark rate then has to adjust downward to i_m^{**}, since Eurobanks maintain the Euromark rate at parity.

The effect of a change in the Eurodollar rate on the Euromark rate and forward premium is more complicated to analyze. First consider the adjustment of the Euromark rate alone under the assumption that the monetary authorities fix the forward premium $(\overline{fp})$. An increase in the Eurodollar rate leads to an equivalent upward shift in the NMP schedule as the Eurobanks adjust the rate charged on Euromarks, and to a reduction in the nonbank excess supply of Euromark loans. In addition, nonbanks respond directly to the increase in the Eurodollar rate by increasing their net borrowing of Euromarks (a rightward shift of $M^L - M^d$ in Figure 5).

---

[15] Since the Eurobanks set i_m equal to $i_s - fp$, *covered* investment (or borrowing) of Euromarks by nonbanks is generally unprofitable, and therefore can be neglected. Denoting covered investment (borrowing) by $\hat{M}^d$ ($\hat{M}^L$), we assume that $\hat{M}^d = \hat{M}^L = 0$.

[16] Since Eurobanks are willing to provide an indefinite quantity of Euromark loans (or deposits) at the interest parity rate, the actual quantity of loans (and hence the quantity of D-marks offered by Eurobanks in the forward market) is determined by the net supply of loans by nonbank investors and borrowers.

[17] The excess supply of Euromark loans by nonbanks is a function of the Euromark rate, not the forward premium. But the arbitrage operations of Eurocurrency banks ensure that the Euromark rate and forward premium are tied together in the interest parity relationship. So $M^L - M^d$ can be expressed in terms of either fp or i_m.

Figure 3

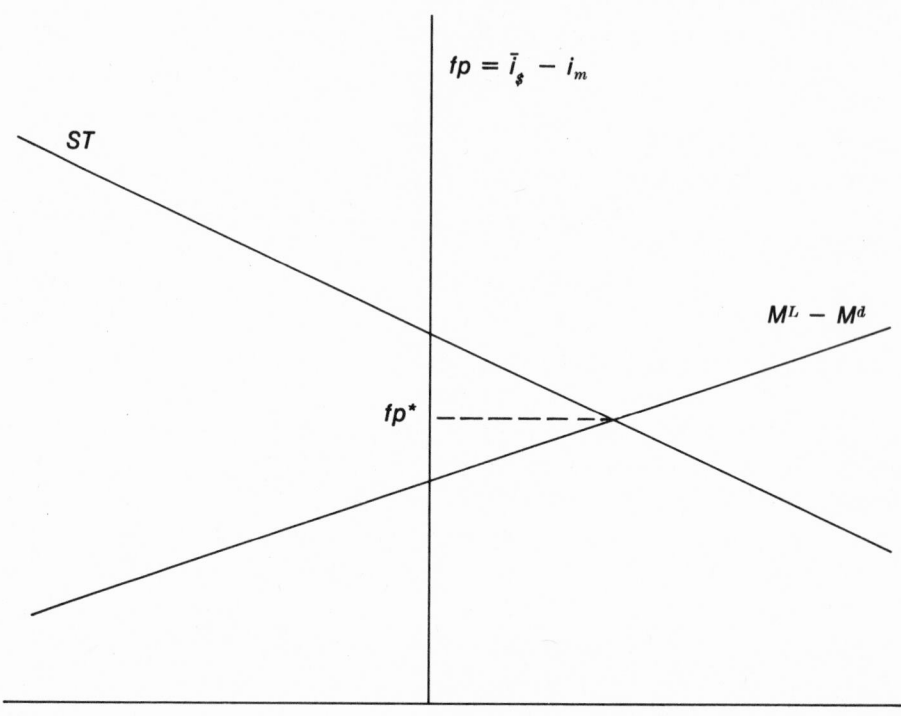

Excess demand by speculators and traders *and* excess supply by Eurobanks

Figure 4

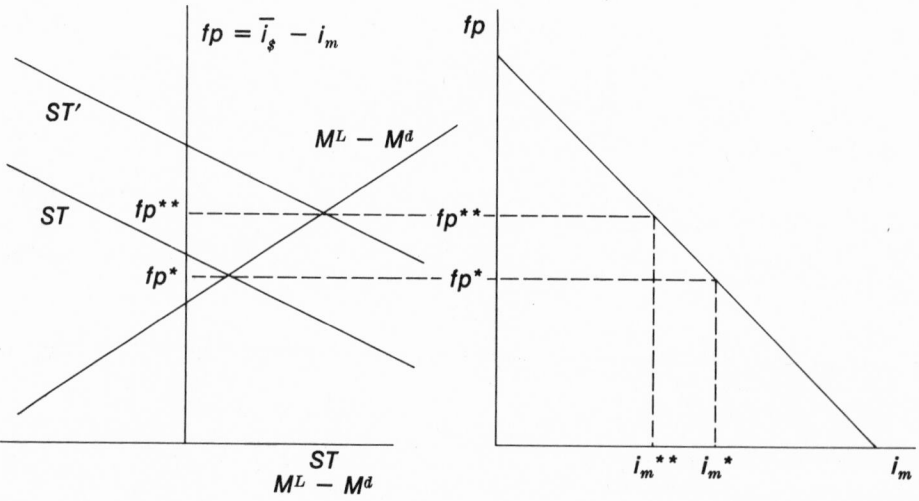

146

Figure 5

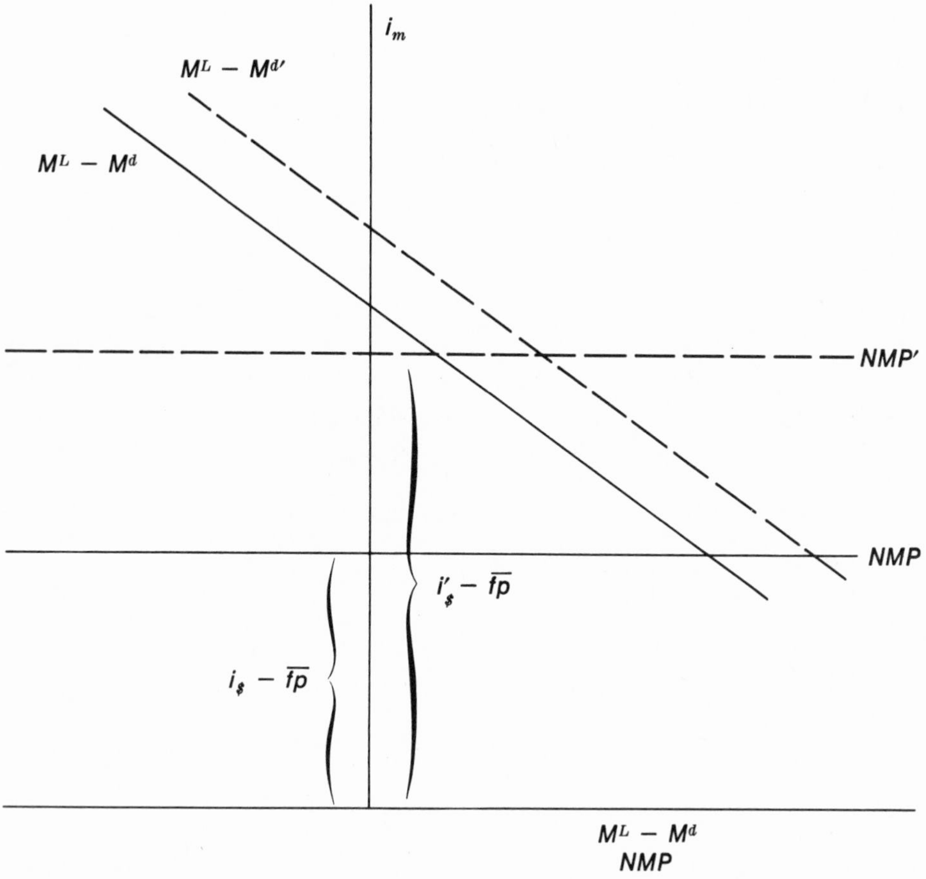

The result is an increase in the Euromark rate equal to the exogenous increase in the Eurodollar rate, and a *net decrease* in the nonbank excess supply of Euromark loans.[18] If the forward premium is also allowed to vary, then the Euromark rate will adjust by *less than* the Eurodollar rate. The net decrease in Euromark loans will cause Eurobanks to reduce their supply of forward marks. As a result, the forward premium will rise, reducing the necessary adjustment of the Euromark rate.[19]

---

[18] There is a net decrease in $M^L - M^d$ as long as the excess supply of Euromarks responds more to a change in the Euromark rate than to an equal change in the Eurodollar rate (i.e., as long as $-M_{ms}^{L-d} > M_{\$}^{L-d}$).

[19] The rise in the Eurodollar rate, by reducing the nonbank excess supply of Euromark loans, leads to a leftward shift of the Euromark schedule in the forward-market diagram (Figure 5′ below), and a rise in the forward premium. If the forward premium were not allowed to

As the analysis indicates, the traditional view of the forward market, where changes in interest rates caused changes in the forward premium, has to be amended once the Eurocurrency markets are introduced. In place of the traditional view, we have presented an integrated analysis of the forward and Eurocurrency markets which recognizes that the forward premium and the Euromark rate are jointly determined.[20] In the next section, we introduce a further modification of the traditional model of the forward market which allows national interest rates to be simultaneously determined with the Eurocurrency and forward exchange rates.

2. The German Bond Market, the Euromark Market, and the Forward Market

In order to focus on the interaction between the Eurocurrency markets and the forward market, we assumed in Section 1 that capital controls separate the German market from external financial markets. By assumption, the forward premium and the Euromark rate have been determined independently from the interest rate in

---

adjust, the Euromark rate would have to increase by the same amount as the Eurodollar rate (to i_m'' in Figure 5'). But with the forward premium adjusting upward to fp', the Euromark rate adjusts only to i_m'.

Figure 5'

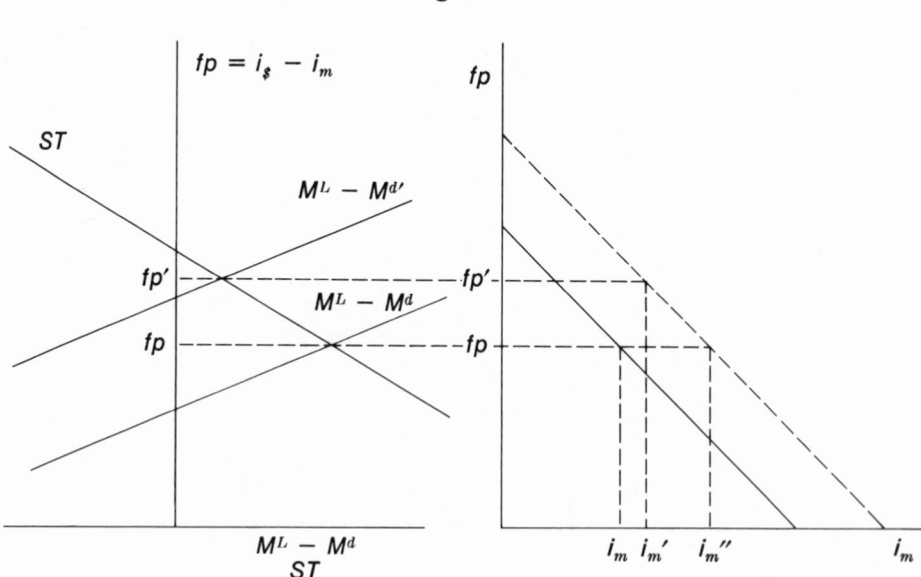

148

Germany. If we now relax this assumption by permitting foreign holdings of German securities, we can investigate how the forward premium will be affected.[21]

The German Bond Market. To consider these questions, we shall incorporate a simple model of the German monetary sector in our analysis. In this model, private German nonbanks hold assets consisting of demand deposits at German banks, DD^g, and bonds issued in the German market, G^{pd}. They may borrow by issuing bonds in the German market, G^{ps}. Their total wealth, $\overline{W}^g$, is assumed to be determined by factors exogenous to the model (although it may, of course, be augmented by a favorable trade balance).

German banks have liabilities consisting of demand deposits, DD^g, and assets consisting of bonds issued in the German market, G^{bd}, and reserves at the central bank, R^g, which are determined by the volume of demand deposits and the official required reserve ratio, q, $R^g = q\, DD^g$.[22]

The German monetary authority has liabilities consisting of the reserves of the banking system, R^g, assets consisting of foreign exchange reserves, SDR^g, and bonds issued in the domestic market, G^{md}. The assets and liabilities of those three entities are schematically presented in the balance sheets below:

Private German Nonbanks		*German Banks*		*German Monetary Authority*	
Assets	Liabilities	Assets	Liabilities	Assets	Liabilities
DD^g	G^{ps}	R^g	DD^g	SDR^g	R^g
G^{pd}	$\overline{W}^g$	G^{bd}		G^{md}	

As in the preceding section, all assets are assumed to be gross substitutes; private holdings of German securities, G^{pd}, for example, are assumed to be positively related to the return on German securities, i_g, and negatively related to the volume of transactions, y^g (the principal determinant of the imputed return on holdings of demand deposits). Because foreigners can hold both German securities and foreign securities, the foreign demand for German bonds (G^{ad}) depends positively on the covered and uncovered German rates, $i_g + fp$ and $i_g + sp$, negatively on the Eurodollar rate, $i_\$$, and negatively on the uncovered Euromark rate, $i_m + sp$.[23]

Equilibrium in the German securities market is established when the policy-determined net government supply of securities (the supply offered by the treasury,

---

[21] In particular, we can determine whether the fact that the forward premium is maintained at interest parity with respect to the Eurocurrency rates necessarily implies that it is not influenced by the rate of interest in Germany.

[22] These assumptions imply that banks neither borrow reserves nor hold excess reserves. Although free reserve behavior could easily be accommodated, it would complicate the exposition without altering the basic conclusions of the analysis.

[23] With i_m maintained equal to $i_\$ - fp$, there is no incentive for nonbanks to hold Euromarks on a covered basis. Thus, we have omitted $i_m + fp$ as a factor in the nonbank functions. Its inclusion would not reverse any of the conclusions below.

149

Figure 6

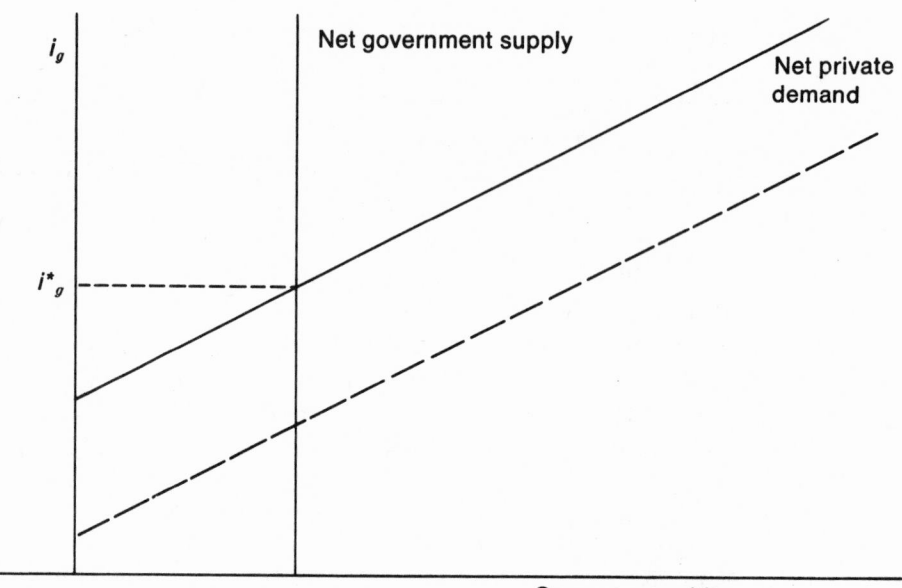

$\overline{G}$, net of the demand by the monetary authority, $\overline{G}^{md}$) is equal to the net private demand:

$$\overline{G} - \overline{G}^{md} = G^{pd} - G^{ps} + G^{bd} + G^{ad}.^{24}$$

By making use of the balance sheet identities for the German private sector and the required reserve identity, we may rewrite the equilibrium condition in terms of demand deposits, the stock of wealth, and the foreign demand for bonds:

$$\overline{G} - \overline{G}^{md} = \overline{W}^g - q\,DD^g + G^{ad}, \text{ where} \qquad [3]$$
$$DD_g^g < 0;\, G_{gf}^{ad},\, G_{gs}^{ad} > 0;\, G_{mf}^{ad},\, G_{ms}^{ad},\, G_{\$}^{ad} < 0.$$

The equilibrium is illustrated in Figure 6. With external interest rates and the forward premium given, the net government supply and the net private demand for German securities together determine the level of the German rate (i_g^*). An increase in the forward premium (accompanied by a reduction in the external mark rate because Eurobanks maintain i_m equal to $i_\$ - fp$) will, in the first instance, lead to a decline in the German rate as foreigners increase their demand for covered

---

24 For simplicity, we have assumed that the German monetary authority does not attempt to sterilize capital flows. This assumption could be relaxed to reflect more complex central bank behavior. See Richard J. Herring and Richard C. Marston, *National Monetary Policies and International Financial Markets* (Amsterdam: North-Holland Publishing Company, forthcoming), chapter 2.

holdings of German securities.[25] Thus a *higher* premium is associated with a *lower* German interest rate. In the footnote below, we show that the decrease in the German interest rate is always less than (or equal to) the increase in the forward premium.[26]

The Forward Market. Covered purchases of German bonds give rise to an additional supply of forward D-marks which must be represented in the equilibrium condition for the forward market. At equilibrium the excess demand for forward D-marks by speculators and traders, ST, must now be equal to the excess supply of forward D-marks by arbitrageurs—that is, by Eurobanks, $M^L - M^d$, and by investors who have made covered purchases of German securities, $\hat{G}^{ad}$:

$$ST = M^L - M^d + \hat{G}^{ad}. \qquad [2.b]$$

The equilibrium in the forward market is illustrated in Figure 7. Given the level of the Eurodollar and German rates, the forward market is in equilibrium at the forward premium fp^*. An *increase* in the German interest rate will lead to an increase in covered holdings of German bonds (a rightward shift in the arbitrage supply curve) and a *decrease* in the forward premium.[27] In the footnote below, we show that the decrease in the forward premium is always greater than (or equal to) the increase in the German rate.[28]

---

[25] This shift in net private demand will not be the final equilibrium position, however, since the increased demand for covered holdings of German securities will lead to an increased supply of forward D-marks and further changes in fp and i_m. The forward market and the German bond market must be solved simultaneously to determine the equilibrium set of rates.

[26] If equation [3], the equilibrium condition in the bond market, is differentiated with respect to i_g, fp and i_m (with dfp equal to $-di_m$), and the expression is solved for dfp/di_g, we obtain:

$$\frac{dfp}{di_g} = \frac{(-qDD_g^g + G_{gf}^{ad} + G_{gs}^{ad})}{-(G_{gf}^{ad} - G_{ms}^{ad})}.$$

It is evident that

$$\frac{dfp}{di_g} \leq -1$$

as long as $-qDD_g^g + G_{gs}^{ad} \geq -G_{ms}^{ad}$. A sufficient condition for this inequality to hold is that an equal rise in the uncovered returns on German bonds and Euromark deposits lead to an increase (or no change) in holdings of German bonds (i.e., $G_{gs}^{ad} + G_{ms}^{ad} \geq 0$). Note that if German bonds and Euromark deposits are close substitutes (i.e., G_{gs}^{ad} and G_{ms}^{ad} are very large in absolute value), $\frac{dfp}{di_g}$ will approach -1; i_g will be (approximately) equal to i_m, and both rates will be maintained at interest parity with respect to i_s.

[27] Of course, the initial shift in the arbitrage supply curve will not be the final equilibrium position, since adjustments will occur in both the bond market and the forward market.

[28] Equation [2.b], the equilibrium condition in the forward market, is differentiated with respect to i_g, fp, and i_m, and di_m is set equal to $-dfp$. If this expression is solved for $\frac{dfp}{di_g}$, we obtain:

$$\frac{dfp}{di_g} = \frac{-(\hat{G}_{gf}^{ad} + \hat{G}_{gs}^{ad} - M_{gf}^{d-L} - M_{gs}^{d-L})}{(-ST_f + \hat{G}_{gf}^{ad} - M_{gf}^{d-L} - \hat{G}_{ms}^{ad} + M_{ms}^{d-L})}$$

Footnote [28] *continued on page 152*

151

Figure 7

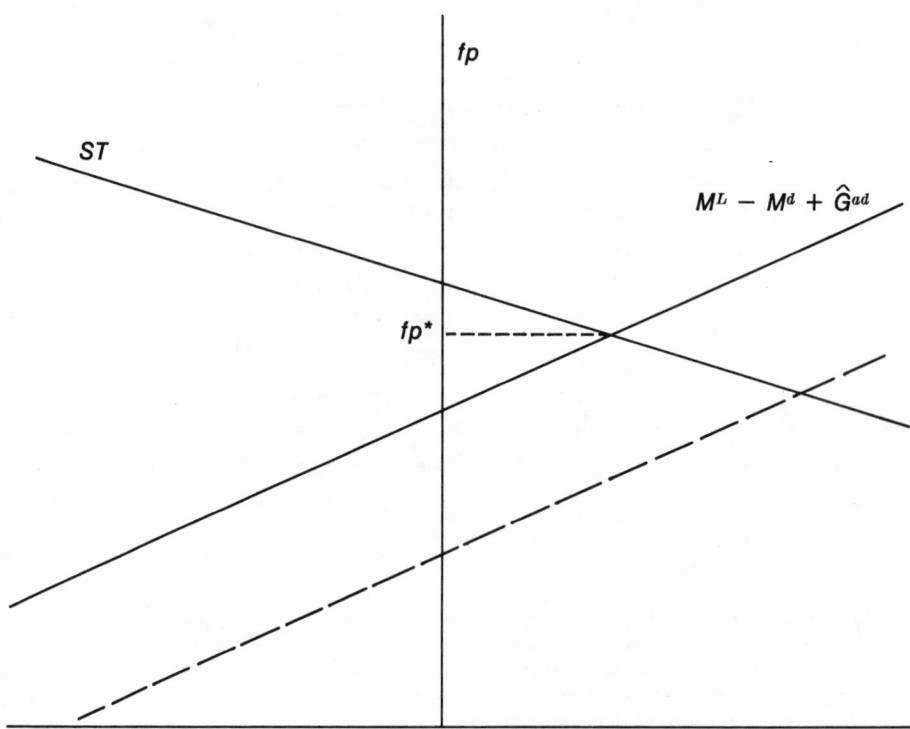

Net demand by speculators and traders *and* net supply by arbitrageurs

In Figure 8, we show the relationship between the German interest rate and the forward premium implicit in the equilibrium conditions for the German bond market [3] and forward market [2.b]. As we have demonstrated above, the forward market curve, *FF*, has a negative slope of absolute value less than unity, while the German bond market curve, *GG*, has a negative slope of absolute value greater than unity.[29] *GG* is the locus of all combinations of i_g and *fp* that will clear the

---

Footnote [28] *continued.*

It is evident that $-1 \leq \dfrac{dfp}{di_g} < 0$ as long as:

$$-ST_f + \hat{G}_{gf}^{ad} - \hat{G}_{ms}^{ad} + M_{ms}^{d-L} \geq \hat{G}_{gf}^{ad} + \hat{G}_{gs}^{ad} - M_{gs}^{d-L} \geq 0.$$

Sufficient conditions for this inequality to hold are that:

$$\hat{G}_{gs}^{ad} + \hat{G}_{gf}^{ad} \geq 0 \text{ and } M_{ms}^{d-L} + M_{gs}^{d-L} \geq 0.$$

These conditions are analogous to those discussed earlier. Note that if Euromark deposits and German bonds are close substitutes (i.e., M_{ms}^{d-L} and M_{gs}^{d-L} are large in absolute value), the ratio will approach negative one.

[29] Thus, we have established that the German bond market curve (*GG*) must be of steeper (negative) slope than the forward market curve (*FF*). Note that the *GG* schedule must be of steeper slope than *FF* if equilibrium in the two markets is to be stable.

Figure 8

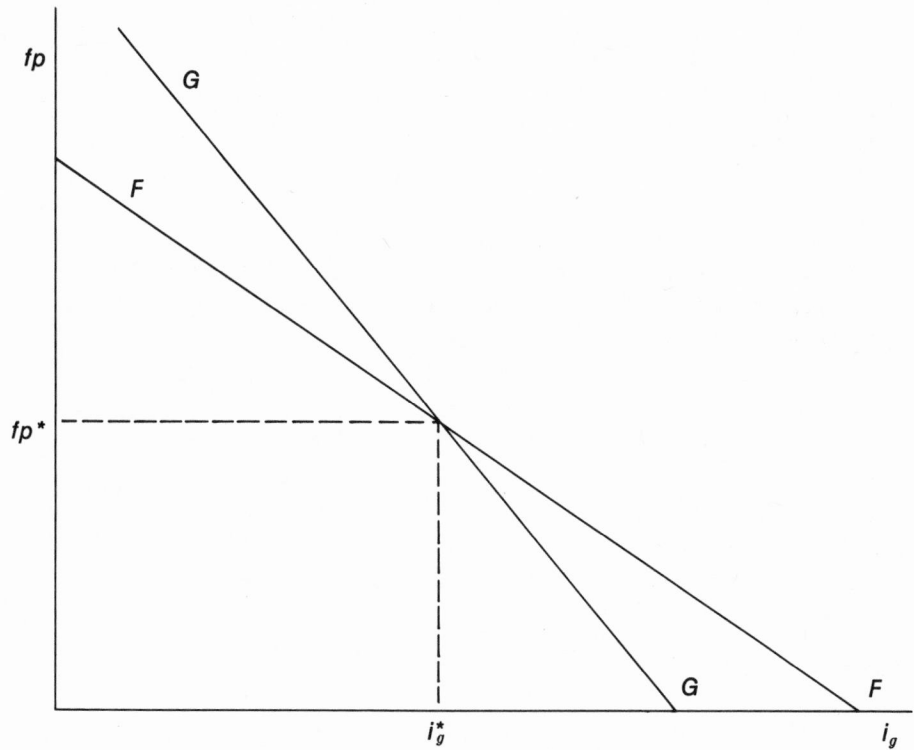

German bond market. *FF* is the locus of all combinations of i_g and *fp* which will clear the forward market. Together the two curves determine the German interest rate and the forward premium (given the Eurodollar rate and values of other exogenous variables). The level of the Euromark rate is also implicitly determined since Eurobanks will maintain this rate at interest parity with respect to the Eurodollar rate.

If equilibrium is disturbed in either of the two markets, in D-mark denominated assets or in the forward exchange market, both interest rates and the forward premium, in general, will change. If the German monetary authority, for example, institutes a tighter monetary policy by selling bonds to the public, there will be adjustments in all three markets. This change in policy may be represented by a rightward shift in *GG*; given the level of *fp*, i_g must be higher to induce German and foreign residents to hold the increased supply of bonds. The tightening of monetary policy will lead to a higher equilibrium level of i_g, and a lower level of *fp*.[30]

---

[30] The fact that *fp* falls in response to the tightening of German monetary policy is in accord with the traditional theory of the forward market. In the present model, however, the fall in *fp* is accompanied by simultaneous adjustments in the Euromark and German markets.

From this example, it is evident that events in the German financial market can influence the forward premium even though it is maintained at parity with respect to the Eurocurrency rates. Moreover, the shift in German monetary policy which led to a fall in the forward premium will automatically lead to a rise in the Euromark rate as Eurobanks arbitrage between the Eurodollar and the Euromark markets. Through this channel, movements in the German rate can influence the Euromark rate even if there are no direct flows between the two markets in D-mark denominated assets.

An increase in orders for German exports (or an increase in the expected return on speculative purchases of forward marks) will lead to an upward shift in FF. Once equilibrium is reestablished, the forward premium will be higher and the German and Euromark interest rates will be lower than previously. In the case where capital controls limit the flow of funds to and from the German market, the FF schedule will be relatively horizontal and the GG schedule relatively vertical. Shifts in FF then will induce relatively large adjustments in fp while leaving i_g virtually unchanged. Under such conditions, a German export boom (or speculation in favor of the mark) could lead to a large increase in the forward premium combined with a large decline in the Euromark interest rate *even though* the German interest rate remains relatively constant. This may, in fact, illustrate what happened in February and March 1973, when the D-mark forward premium rose sharply, the Euromark rate fell to a very low, occasionally negative, level, and the German interest rate remained at a high level.[31]

On the other hand, a complete relaxation of capital controls is likely to enhance the importance of arbitrage flows in determining the German interest rate. If external flows are quite sensitive to the covered differential between dollar securities and German securities, then fp and i_g are likely to adjust to parity with respect to the Eurodollar rate. GG and FF will nearly converge at a slope of negative one. This convergence is even more likely if there is also a high degree of substitutability between Euromarks and German securities.[32] If FF and GG do converge at a slope of negative one, the Euromark and German rates will be identical. Both will be jointly determined with the forward premium; each interest rate and the forward premium will be maintained at interest parity with respect to the Eurodollar rate. This seems to characterize the period following the relaxation of German capital controls early in 1974, when the covered Eurodollar rate, the German rate, and the Euromark rate converged.[33]

Finally, it should be noted that the fact that D-mark interest rates are maintained at interest parity with respect to the Eurodollar rate does not imply that the

[31] Note that the German spot rate was not fixed during this period, so adjustments in that exchange rate may also have occurred.

[32] In fact, strictly speaking, either condition is sufficient alone. For an algebraic description of this convergence, see footnotes 26 and 28.

[33] See Figure A-4.

Figure 9

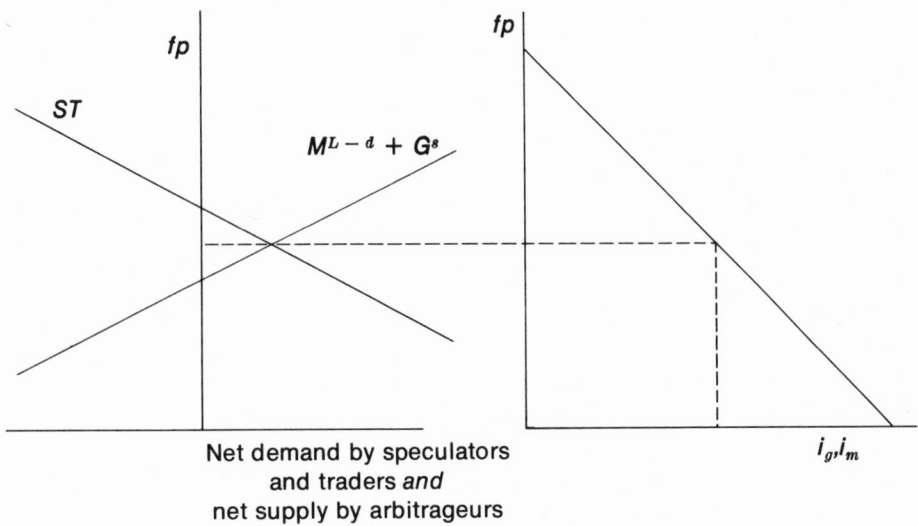

Net demand by speculators
and traders *and*
net supply by arbitrageurs

interest arbitrage schedule is perfectly elastic at the interest parity forward rate.[34] Given $i_\$$, the forward premium may vary so long as the D-mark interest rates vary inversely to fp. For example note that in Figure 9 a change in the speculative demand for forward D-marks, or an exogenous change in the supply of Euromark loans or in the supply of German bonds to arbitrageurs, can influence fp and hence i_g and i_m as well.[35] The arbitrage schedule becomes infinitely elastic *only when* the German government fixes i_g by offering an infinite supply of bonds. In this case, we return to the traditional analysis of the forward market in which, given the exogenously determined interest rate, an infinitely elastic arbitrage schedule determines the forward exchange rate.[36]

3. Conclusion

In this study we have reformulated the traditional analysis of the forward market to take into account the interaction among interest rates and the forward premium.

[34] Nor does it imply that the German interest rate is determined solely by the Eurodollar rate. The German interest rate may vary so long as the forward premium varies inversely to it.

[35] When the arbitrage demand for German bonds is infinitely elastic at the covered Eurodollar rate, the actual quantity of bonds purchased, and hence the quantity of forward exchange supplied by arbitrageurs, is determined by the quantity of bonds supplied in the market by non-arbitrageurs (G') at $i_g = i_\$ + fp$. This quantity will equal the net government supply ($\overline{G} - \overline{G}^{md}$) less the demand by private German residents ($\overline{W} - qDD^g$) less the demand by foreign speculators ($\tilde{G}^{ad}$).

[36] For an analysis of the interest arbitrage schedule, see Lawrence H. Officer and Thomas D. Willett, "The Covered Arbitrage Schedule: A Critical Survey," *Journal of Money, Credit and Banking*, April 1970, pp. 247-257.

The model which we have developed integrates an analysis of the Eurocurrency operations of banks with the traditional model of forward exchange transactions. A key element in the analysis is the competitive behavior of Eurobanks which ensures that each non-dollar Eurocurrency rate and the corresponding forward premium are maintained at interest parity with respect to the Eurodollar rate. With the Eurodollar rate given, Eurobank behavior fixes each non-dollar Eurocurrency rate relative to the forward premium, and Eurocurrency and forward market transactions by nonbanks together determine the forward premium.

Once arbitrage involving a national market is introduced, the analysis is broadened to include the simultaneous determination of the national interest rate as well as the Eurocurrency rate and forward premium. Shifts in either the excess demand for forward exchange or the excess demand for national securities induce adjustments in all three markets. One implication of the analysis is that forward premiums and national interest rates can adjust to interest parity as a result of two different forms of arbitrage. Traditional covered arbitrage involving movements of funds between national markets exclusively may bring about the necessary adjustment of forward premiums and national rates. Alternatively, arbitrage between Eurocurrency and national markets offering securities in the *same currency* may also bring about interest parity between national rates *even if* there are no direct flows between national markets. In the latter case, adjustments occur in all three markets, with adjustments in the forward premium relative to Eurocurrency rates ensuring that the interest parity relation now holds for both the Eurocurrency and national markets.

Appendix A

Symbols used in more than one section of the text are defined below for quick reference.

$\hat{\ }$: a covered holding; for example, $\hat{M}^d$ denotes covered Euromark deposits.

DD^g: demand deposits at German banks held by German residents.

fp: the forward premium defined as $(F-S)/S$ where F is the forward rate and S is the spot rate. Both exchange rates are expressed in $\$/DM$.

$\overline{G}$: the supply of bonds by the German treasury.

G^{ad}: the foreign demand for bonds issued in the German market.

G^{bd}: German bank holdings of bonds issued in the German market.

G^{md}: the German monetary authority's holdings of bonds issued in the German market.

G^{pd}: holdings of bonds issued in the German market by German nonbanks.

G^{ps}: issues of bonds in the German market by German nonbanks.

I^g: German orders for imports from the rest of the world.

i_g: the interest rate on bonds issued in the German market.

i_m: the Euromark rate.

$i_\$$: the Eurodollar rate.

M^d: the nonbank demand for Euromark deposits.

M^L: the nonbank supply of Euromark loans, that is, desired borrowing in Euromarks from Eurobanks.

NMP: the net mark loan position of Eurobanks.

q: the official required reserve ratio.

R^g: required reserves.

SDR^g: Official German foreign exchange reserves.

sp: the speculative premium, the expected return from holding a spot position in D-marks.

$sp = ((S^e - S)/S)$ where S^e is the expected future spot rate.

ST: the excess demand for forward marks by speculators and traders.

$\overline{W}^g$: wealth of German nonbanks.

X^g: orders for German exports.

Y^g: the volume of transactions in Germany.

Appendix B

In this appendix we present a brief graphical analysis of recent interest-rate trends in the U.S. and Eurodollar markets and in the German and Euromark markets.

Interest-Rate Relationships between Eurodollar and U.S. Markets. From the accompanying graphs (A-1, A-2 and A-3), it is apparent that Eurodollar rates and comparable New York interest rates have moved almost in tandem over the last three years. The close correspondence between external and domestic dollar interest rates is particularly striking in the very short-term end of the market. Figure A-1 displays movements in the overnight Eurodollar and federal funds rates over the period from January 1971 through July 1974. Discrepancies between the two rates are slight, as one would expect from the fact that large U.S. banks are continually dealing in both markets.

A comparison of three month rates reveals a looser correlation, although the covariation is still quite impressive. Figure A-2 charts movements in the U.S. Treasury bill rate, and the Eurodollar and U.S. certificate of deposit rates. Both of the latter two interest rates are adjusted for marginal reserve requirements to reflect the effective cost of each source of funds to large U.S. banks. The Treasury bill rate is included to illustrate that changes in lender preferences can lead to widening spreads between interest rates even within the U.S. market where barriers to arbitrage are minimal. In contrast to the pattern during 1971, toward the end of the period, the two bank deposit rates are more tightly linked than the certificate of deposit (CD) and Treasury bill rates.

Because nonbank lender arbitrage may also have an important influence on the relationship between the internal and external deposit rates, Figure A-3 displays

157

movements in the unadjusted Eurodollar and certificate of deposit rates (and the Treasury bill rate). In the period preceding June 1973, the pattern of covariation is even stronger than for the adjusted deposit rates, suggesting that lender arbitrage played a predominant role.[37]

Comparisons of rates charged nonbank borrowers are more difficult because of the difference in pricing practices in the internal and external dollar markets. However, most analysts have concluded that, when average compensating balances in the United States and the typical mark-up over the London interbank rate are taken into account, borrowing costs in New York and in the Eurodollar market have been quite similar.[38]

The Covered Eurodollar, Euromark, and German Interest Rates. In Figure A-4 the relationship among Eurodollar, Euromark, and German interest rates is shown for the recent period. The Eurodollar interest rate is adjusted for forward cover by subtracting the forward premium (*fp* in the text). As is evident from the figure, the covered Eurodollar rate and the Euromark rate follow closely together through time with only minor discrepancies between the rates. German interest rates, in contrast, are at markedly higher levels than the Euromark rate or covered Euro- dollar rate through most of 1973. But with the relaxation of German controls on capital inflows in early 1974, German interest rates move into line with Euromark rates.[39] German and Euromark rates both remain close to interest parity with respect to the Eurodollar rate through the rest of the period. Figure A-5 suggests that the Euromark rate and forward premium often respond to exogenous forces other than the Eurodollar rate, even though the three rates adhere closely to the parity relationships.

---

[37] To the extent that marginal reserve requirements differ between the Eurodollar and certificate of deposit markets, incentives for arbitrage by bank borrowers will differ from incentives for arbitrage by nonbank lenders. In the period prior to June 1973, the marginal reserve require- ment on U.S. bank borrowing from foreign branches (20 percent) was substantially higher than the reserve requirement against large certificates of deposit (5 percent). However, during June 1973, the marginal reserve requirement on foreign borrowing was reduced to 8 percent and a marginal reserve requirement of 8 percent was introduced on large certificates of deposit. With certain temporary exceptions, the marginal reserve requirements remained equal through- out the remainder of the period.

[38] See, for example, Morgan Guaranty Trust Company, *World Financial Markets*, July 1974, p. 13.

[39] In early January 1974, the German authorities abolished the 60 percent marginal reserve requirement on bank liabilities to foreigners and lowered the average reserve requirement on foreign liabilities. Effective on 30 January 1974, administrative restrictions on capital move- ments were largely abolished. In addition, the cash deposit ratio required on foreign borrowing was lowered from 50 percent to 20 percent, and other provisions of the cash deposit scheme were liberalized. See the *Monthly Report of the Deutsche Bundesbank*, various issues, and the *Report of the Deutsche Bundesbank* for 1973.

158

Figure A-1

OVERNIGHT EURODOLLAR AND FEDERAL FUNDS RATES,
JANUARY 1971–JULY 1974

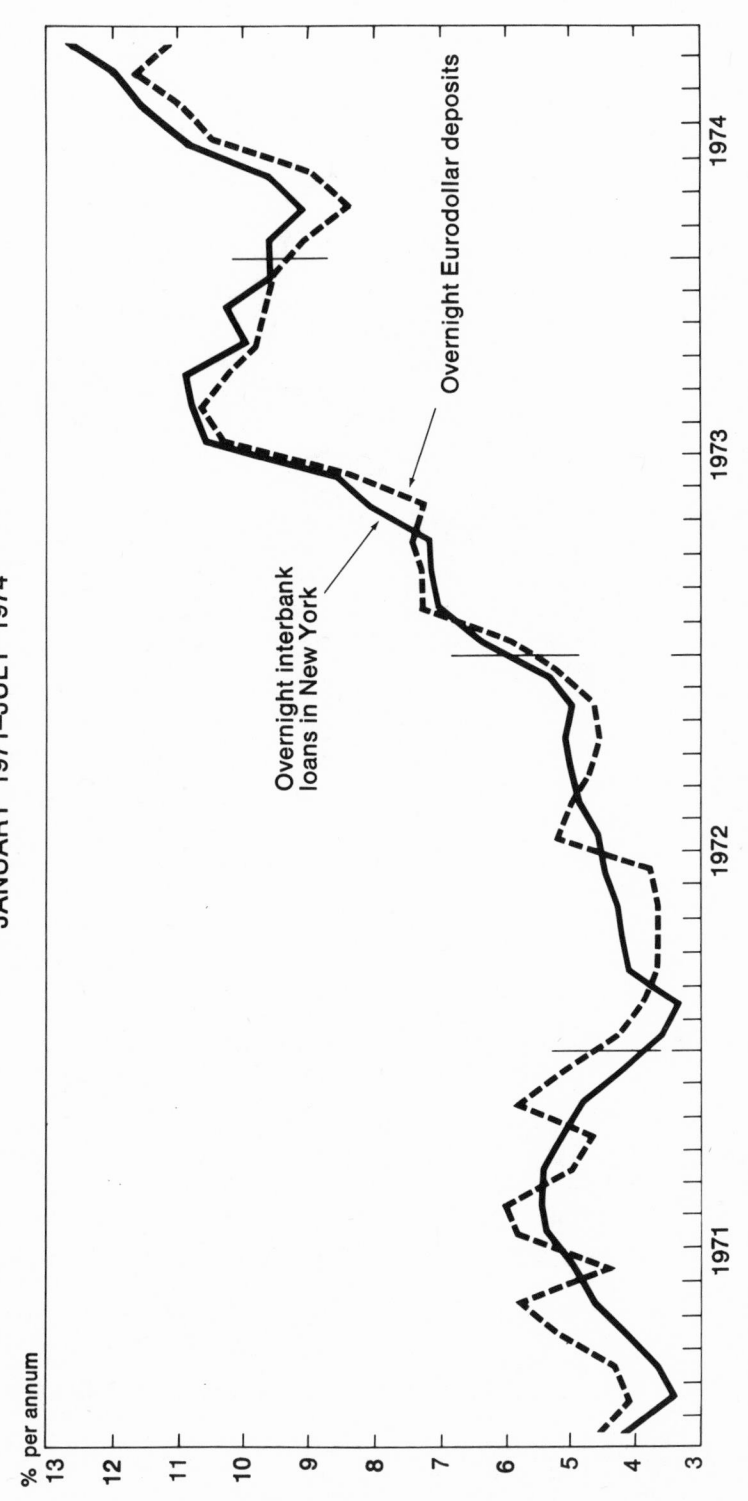

Note: call Eurodollar deposits—weekly averages (Thursday-Wednesday) of broker's bid rates in London through April 1971; overnight Eurodollar deposits—beginning May 1971, weekly averages (Thursday-Wednesday) of broker's bid rates in London; federal funds—weekly averages (Thursday-Wednesday) of overnight interbank loans in New York City.

Source: Federal Reserve Board.

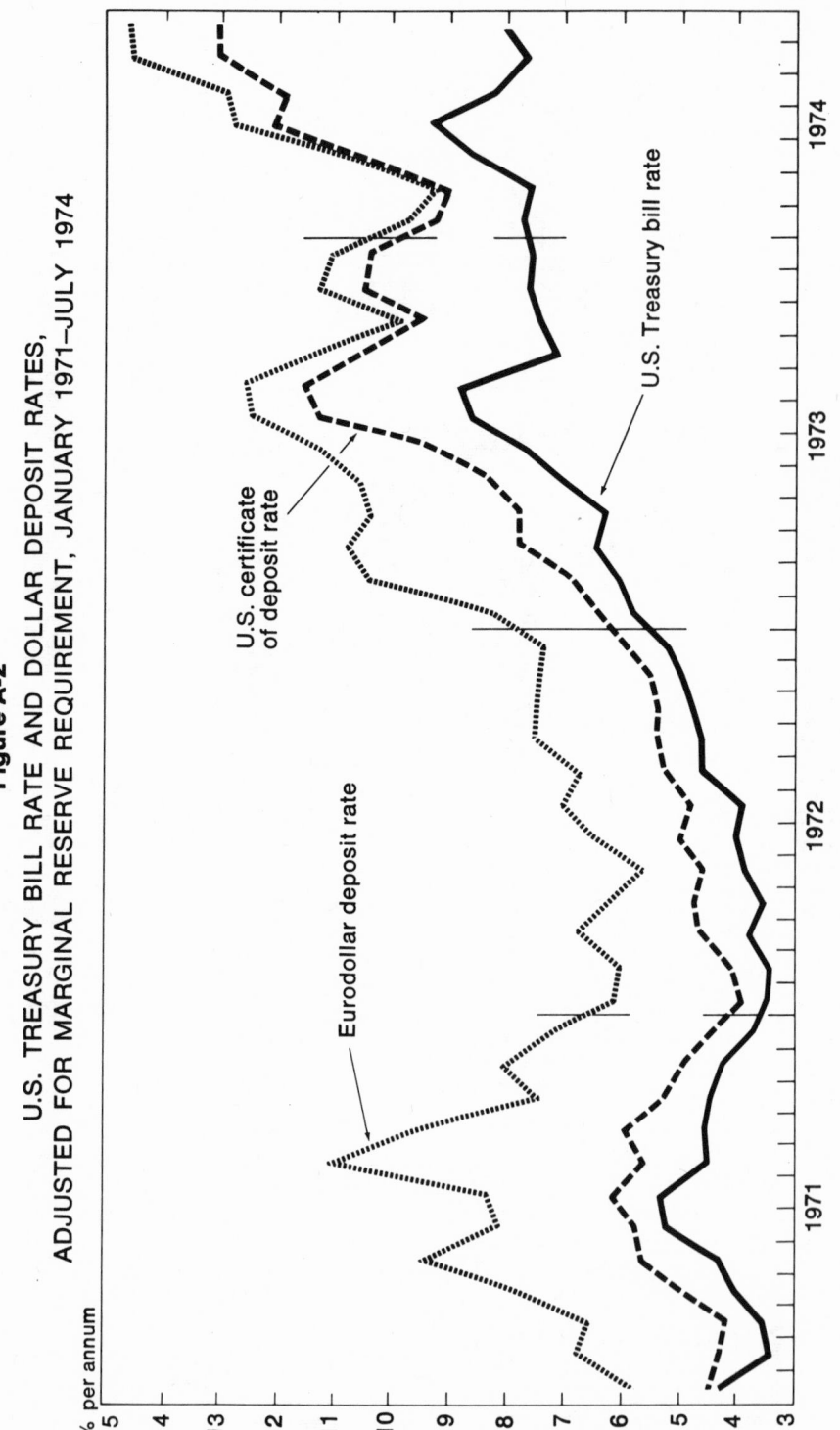

Figure A-2

U.S. TREASURY BILL RATE AND DOLLAR DEPOSIT RATES,
ADJUSTED FOR MARGINAL RESERVE REQUIREMENT, JANUARY 1971–JULY 1974

Source: *World Financial Markets* for interest rates; *Federal Reserve Bulletin* for reserve requirements.

160

Figure A-3

U.S. TREASURY BILL RATE, CERTIFICATE OF DEPOSIT RATE, AND EURODOLLAR RATE, JANUARY 1971–JULY 1974

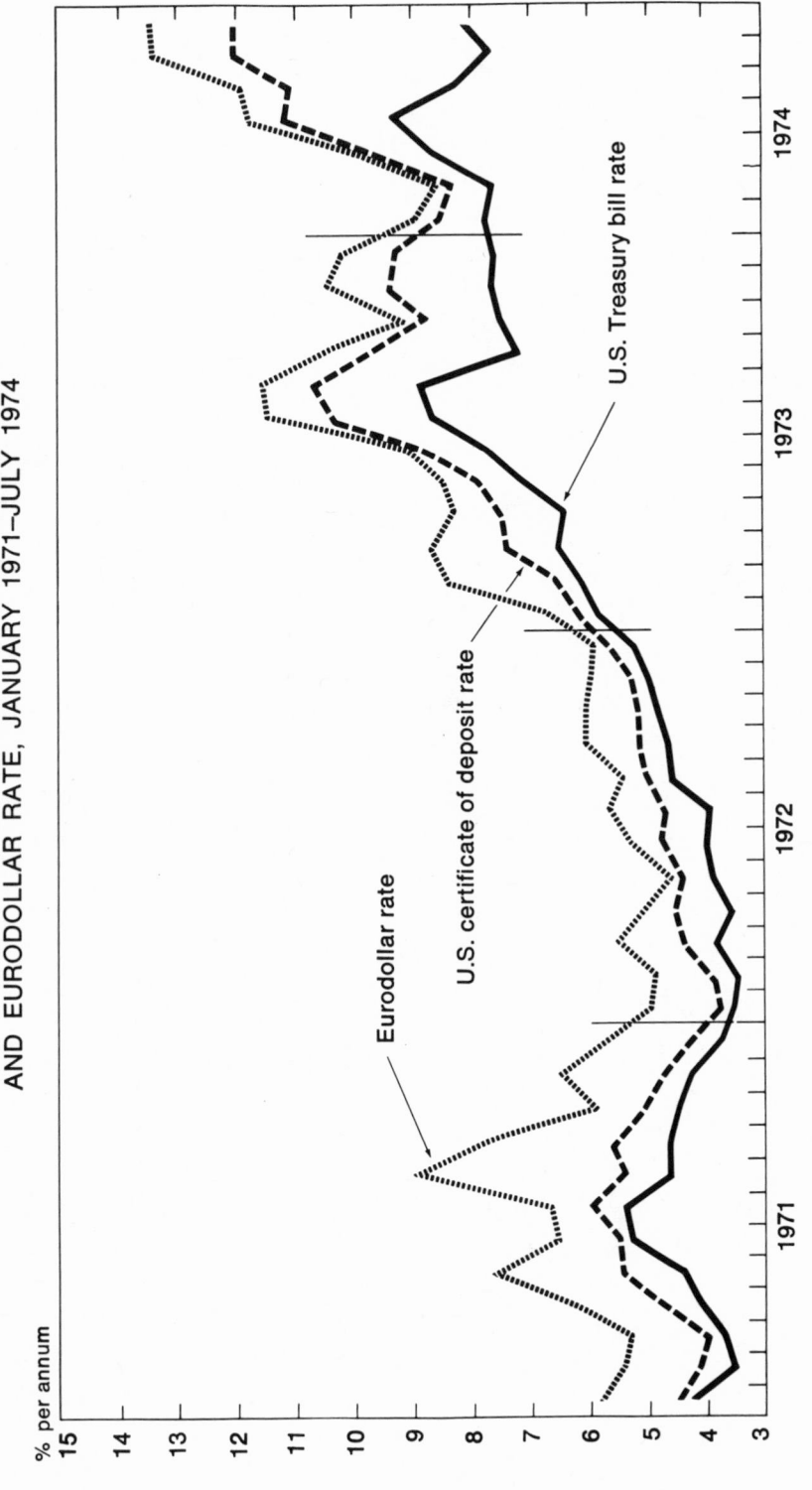

Source: *World Financial Markets.*

161

Figure A-4

THE EUROMARK, COVERED EURODOLLAR, AND
GERMAN INTERBANK RATES, JANUARY 1973–AUGUST 1974

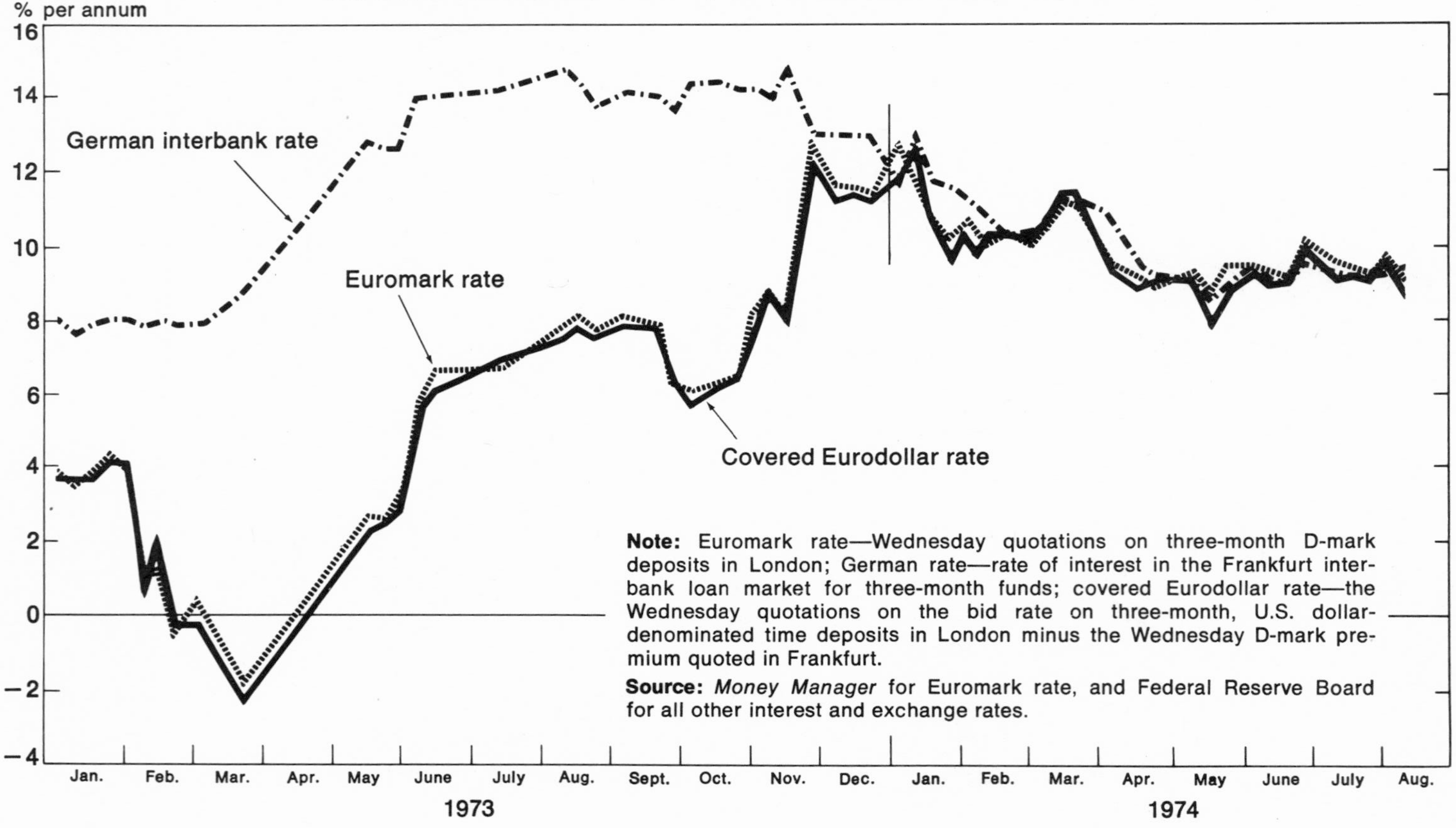

% per annum

German interbank rate

Euromark rate

Covered Eurodollar rate

Note: Euromark rate—Wednesday quotations on three-month D-mark deposits in London; German rate—rate of interest in the Frankfurt interbank loan market for three-month funds; covered Eurodollar rate—the Wednesday quotations on the bid rate on three-month, U.S. dollar-denominated time deposits in London minus the Wednesday D-mark premium quoted in Frankfurt.

Source: *Money Manager* for Euromark rate, and Federal Reserve Board for all other interest and exchange rates.

1973   1974

162

Figure A-5

THE EUROMARK, EURODOLLAR, AND GERMAN INTERBANK RATES, AND THE D-MARK FORWARD PREMIUM, JANUARY 1973–AUGUST 1974

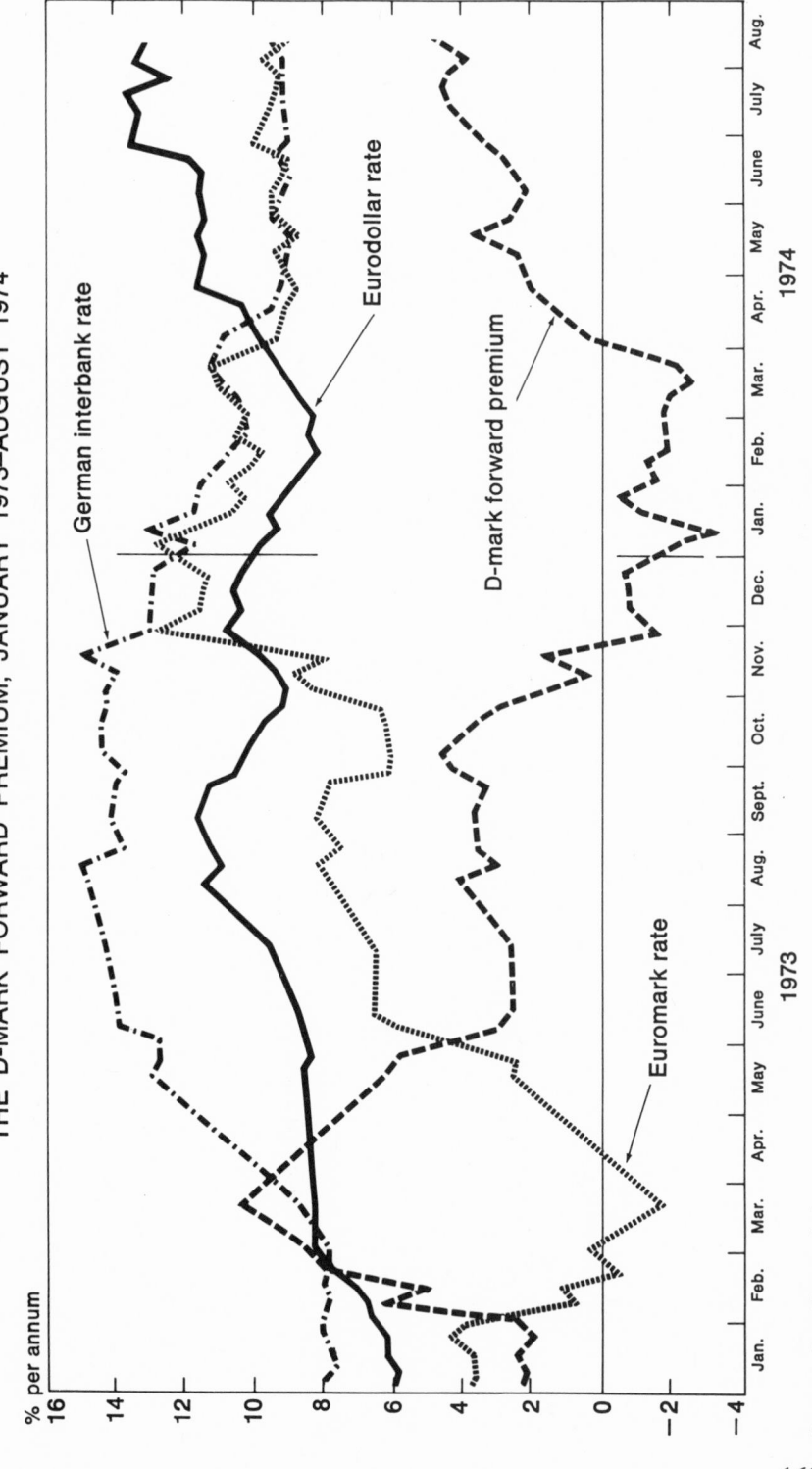

Source: See Figure A-4.

163

COMMENTARIES

Peter B. Kenen

Each of the two papers presented at this session makes an important contribution. Herring and Marston show how to link national credit markets, forward foreign-exchange markets, and Eurocurrency markets. Logue, Salant, and Sweeney apply the theory of efficient markets to the definition and measurement of international financial integration. But I am not happy with either paper. The first draws too few implications from the exercise. The second draws too many.

Herring and Marston seek to integrate two views of the relationship between Eurocurrency interest rates and forward exchange rates. Dealers in Eurocurrencies and dealers in forward exchange perform interest-parity calculations. The former, however, say that they use forward exchange rates and the Eurodollar rate to set each of the other Eurocurrency interest rates. The latter say that they use the Eurodollar and other Eurocurrency interest rates to determine forward exchange rates. Herring and Marston develop a model in which both groups of dealers can do what they claim to do. The markets in which they operate act to reconcile their independent and seemingly inconsistent calculations.

Members of our audience familiar with these markets may argue that Herring and Marston have not been sufficiently sophisticated—that their model is too simple to describe relationships among the many participants in the markets under study. I am unsympathetic to this complaint. One can never construct a manageable model without abstracting from a number of intriguing realities. Those asking for more elaborate models must be able to prove that these models are needed to explain the phenomena under consideration. Models are not meant to replicate reality in all of its detail; they are meant to fix attention on the particular subset of actors and transactions that is most directly relevant to the problem at hand.

My complaint is different. Herring and Marston have led us on a tour of three markets but have not told us why we had to visit them. What do we know after the tour that we did not know before? On the way here this morning, I might have climbed to the top of the Washington Monument. Had I done so and told you about it, you might have praised me for my energy, but wondered about my sanity. But had I been able to tell you that the Potomac has overflowed its banks

165

and threatens to drown us this afternoon, you would have thanked me for making the trip. In the same spirit, I ask our two authors whether we have learned anything new about the behavior of national and Eurocurrency interest rates and of forward exchange rates that we could not have learned without traipsing through all three markets.

Herring and Marston append tables to their paper which show the relationships among the relevant rates. There is, as they say, a startling stability. The Euromark rate never strays very far from the covered Eurodollar rate (Figure A-4). But each of the two naïve theories they mention would have predicted this result. If Eurocurrency dealers act as they say they do, the Euromark rate could not deviate from interest parity; if forward-exchange dealers act as they say they do, it could not do so either. Herring and Marston should show us that their more general model does something more than explain this stability. They should show us that the ways in which the several rates adjust to maintain interest parity is different from the way they would adjust under either naïve theory.

Allow me to illustrate my point precisely. If Eurocurrency dealers act as they say they do, any change in the Eurodollar rate would lead to an equal change in the Euromark rate; the forward dollar-mark rate would not change. If forward-exchange dealers act as they say they do, any change in the Eurodollar rate would cause an equal change in the dollar-mark rate; the Euromark rate would not change. To show that their model furnishes new knowledge, Herring and Marston should demonstrate that any exogenous change in one of the three rates will alter *both* of the others. They could do so easily by deriving the changes in the Euromark and forward dollar-mark rates caused by an exogenous change in the Eurodollar rate ($i_\$$ in their model). They should also show us why the sum of the changes in Euromark and dollar-mark rates will serve always to restore interest parity. Which parameters are vital to this outcome? There is nothing wrong with their model. It does, I believe, generate the right results when the Eurobanks' net mark asset position is infinitely elastic with respect to a change in the covered interest differential. But they have not used their model effectively. They have not shown *why* the trip was worthwhile.

If Herring and Marston do too little with their model, Logue, Salant, and Sweeney try to do too much. Their paper is important because it introduces a new notion of international financial integration and shows that this notion is at least consistent with the behavior of various interest rates. For this very reason, however, they may make mistakes when they connect their own conclusions with those that others have reached using different definitions of financial integration. They would have been well advised to repeat Humpty Dumpty's famous statement: "When I use a word, it means just what I choose it to mean—neither more nor less." We cannot reply, as Alice did, that no one has a right to make words mean so many things. We can complain, however, that authors and readers can both be misled when the authors themselves are unsure of their meaning.

166

There are several semantic snarls in this paper. One of them, encountered often, involves the meaning we attach to the assertion that flexible exchange rates can confer autonomy. Logue, Salant, and Sweeney deny this assertion, because the covariation among national interest rates described by their factor analysis survives with undiminished strength the introduction of flexible exchange rates. (It is, indeed, somewhat stronger in their long-period computations.) Here, however, they are using "monetary autonomy" to denote control over national interest rates, and this is not what was meant by writers who said that flexible rates would grant autonomy. Those writers seem to have had in mind domestic control over the stock of high-powered money, and this control can be asserted with flexible rates, since central banks do not have to alter their own assets (and the supply of high-powered money) whenever there is excess demand or excess supply in the foreign-exchange market.

More generally, Logue, Salant, and Sweeney make statements concerning the conventional wisdom about capital mobility and international financial integration which involve comparisons between conclusions drawn from models based on noncomparable concepts or definitions.

The origin of this confusion is also the enduring contribution of their important paper—its adaptation of the theory of efficient markets to the analysis of international financial integration. An efficient market is one in which all participants can acquire information without giving any one group of participants substantial and continuing profit opportunities. In the limiting case, prices in efficient markets would adjust instantaneously, without any arbitrage transactions, because each participant would anticipate the arbitrage demands or supplies of all other participants and would adjust his bid and asked prices accordingly.

If I understand them correctly, Logue, Salant, and Sweeney equate efficiency with integration. International capital markets are integrated if they behave in a fashion akin to a single efficient market. For this to happen, of course, participants in each of the national markets would have to have prompt, accurate knowledge of every event that could influence all markets in common and would also have to know about all localized events—those affecting other markets—that might impinge through arbitrage on their own markets.

The emphasis, then, is on the international mobility of knowledge, not on the international mobility of capital. On first reading, indeed, I thought that Logue, Salant, and Sweeney were saying that international financial markets could be integrated (that is, efficient) even if there were no possibility of international capital movements. This, however, is not so. If financial assets were not tradable, there could be no arbitrage, and information specific to a single market would have no significance for other markets. The mobility of capital, however, is not the measure of financial integration, as Logue, Salant, and Sweeney redefine it. The interest-elasticity of capital flows, the parameter upon which we have lavished

167

so much human and computer time, has only secondary importance. And this new view of integration is, therefore, different in many of its implications.

Consider the quite different implications of this view for one important proposition in macroeconomics. If capital flows are sensitive to interest rates—the old view of integration—an increase of one country's interest rate will cause its exchange rate to appreciate and its trade balance to deteriorate. Monetary policy has a strong effect on output and employment because it can influence the trade balance. The effect in question might, of course, be short-lived; the capital inflow might come to an end once portfolio balance had been restored in all countries. But it is deemed to be important in the short run. In the new view taken by Logue, Salant, and Sweeney, however, the flow of information across national boundaries—the knowledge of an increase in one country's interest rate—could suffice to align national interest rates. There would be no capital flow, no effect on the exchange rate, and no change in the trade balance, even in the short run. The anticipation of arbitrage would be enough to alter the prices of capital assets, achieving long-run portfolio balance without any flows of securities.[1]

One can draw an analogy, not too far-fetched, between this new notion of integration and the famous factor-price-equalization theorem that falls out of the Heckscher-Ohlin model. It is, I believe, a proper deduction from the new notion that the free flow of information across national boundaries would equalize interest rates on comparable assets, rendering movements of securities redundant. One would have to make subsidiary suppositions about the degree to which investors in various countries hold claims on other countries in their portfolios. These suppositions would play the same role in the proof that suppositions about specialization play in the proof of factor-price equalization. The same analogy, however, leads me to a second—one that is not complimentary to the empirical work reported by Logue, Salant, and Sweeney. They believe that their factor analysis is *prima facie* evidence that international capital markets are efficient. The existence of a strong first common factor explaining much of the movement in interest rates is deemed to say that there is a rapid dispersion of information from market to market, causing the prompt realignment of interest rates in all markets.

Consider, however, another interpretation. Assume that international capital markets were segregated—that there could be no arbitrage between them. It would still be possible for interest rates to move together, and one might be able to extract

---

[1] There is one important qualification which Logue, Salant, and Sweeney take into account obliquely in their discussion of monetary policy and international capital movements. If the disturbance affecting interest rates in one country is a change in the total supply of debt issued in that country (caused, for example, by government borrowing or open-market sales by the central bank), some part of the additional supply will have to be exported to equalize interest rates in all countries. The equalization of interest rates by flows of information alone can occur only when the change in one country's rate is due to some other disturbance (including, of course, a change in *expectations* concerning future borrowing by the government or open-market operations by the central bank).

a strong first common factor like the one they have found. Suppose that commodity markets were thoroughly integrated in the conventional sense—that there were no significant barriers to trade, and tradable goods comprised a large part of each country's output. Suppose, further, that nominal interest rates responded rapidly to changes in rates of inflation. Under these two suppositions, an acceleration of inflation in one country would lead rapidly to a similar acceleration in all other countries, and there would be an increase of nominal interest rates in all markets. The alignment of interest rates would be accomplished by the transmission of inflation through commodity trade, without any capital movements, yet the covariation of interest rates would give the appearance of capital-market integration.

It could, of course, be answered that an argument like this applies only to a system of fixed exchange rates. Flexible exchange rates like those we have had in recent years should prevent or weaken the transmission of inflation through international commodity markets. We have learned to our dismay, however, that flexibility is not sufficient for this purpose. The reasons lie beyond the scope of these comments. We know, moreover, that inflation rates have accelerated everywhere during the last few years. We should not be surprised, then, to find that the first common factor discovered by Logue, Salant, and Sweeney is no less powerful over the long period, including the years of flexibility, than it was in the short period. The apparent integration of capital markets may be in the main a common response to the influence of more rapid inflation on nominal interest rates everywhere.

I do not mean to disparage the important contributions made by Herring and Marston, and by Logue, Salant, and Sweeney. I seek only to urge that they identify carefully the limits to which they can carry their arguments. Herring and Marston have not gone far enough; I hope that they will show us that their model can do more. Logue, Salant, and Sweeney should perhaps draw back a bit.

Zoran Hodjera

Both papers presented at this session examine issues of importance, not only for the treatment of the Eurocurrency market but also for the general analysis of international capital movements. The formal analysis in this area has only quite recently outgrown a partial equilibrium framework within which capital movements were treated in isolation, and variables determined by domestic economic developments, such as national interest rates, were taken as exogenous to the underlying model. The new approach examines the issues within an open-economy framework so that monetary variables—both at home and abroad—are incorporated in the

The views expressed in these comments are personal and not necessarily those of the International Monetary Fund.

process of determination of international capital flows. In particular, the inter-dependence between domestic and foreign interest rates is explicitly taken into account.

Herring and Marston have taken this work one step further and have inte-grated international Eurocurrency transactions into such a framework. What is particularly interesting from a methodological point of view is that they have included forward-exchange transactions as well. Their treatment represents an advance in this area of analysis, since (with the possible exception of Jay Levin and Stanley Black) most formal open-economy models have been able to incor-porate international capital movements into a general equilibrium framework only at the expense of dropping a much more complex treatment of forward-exchange operations.

The carefully specified model by Herring and Marston involves the following three closely related markets:

(1) A traditional domestic financial market of an open economy in which domestic private demand for assets (that is, government bonds) is a function, among others, of the national interest rate. Supply is determined by the monetary authorities, while net foreign demand is a function of the domestic and foreign interest rates, covered forward, and of the incentive to speculate on the foreign exchange market.

(2) A close to perfect Eurocurrency market in which a net demand for borrowing in any one currency is a decreasing function of that Eurocurrency interest rate, covered forward, and an increasing function of the foreign Euro-currency rate—that is, the Eurodollar rate. The distinctive feature of this market is that the net supply function of deposits by Eurobanks in any one currency is perfectly elastic, indicating these banks' willingness to deal in different Euro-currencies at interest-rate differentials reflecting the cost of forward cover alone.

(3) A somewhat more complex market for forward exchange in which a perfectly competitive situation among Eurocurrency markets leads to Eurobanks providing all the required forward cover at a rate exactly equal to the differential between the interest rates in the two Eurocurrencies. Instead of affecting directly the forward rate, as in the usual partial equilibrium models, speculation affects interest rates in the Eurocurrencies transactions and may in this way change the forward premiums, while maintaining the perfectly competitive constraint that the forward premium is at all times exactly equal to the interest-rate differential.

Herring and Marston, however, drop the assumption of perfect competition in their treatment of forward transactions between national capital markets, other than Eurocurrency transactions. National markets are assumed to be subject to various institutional imperfections and to interferences by the government.

This three-market model basically treats the case of a small open economy, since the Eurodollar rate, which serves as an exogenous "foreign Eurorate," is uniquely determined by the U.S. monetary authorities. The other interest rates (that is, the national rate and the Eurorate denominated in that country's currency) and the forward premium are determined simultaneously in the three markets. Since the Eurocurrency market is perfect, while the national market is not, the transactions among Eurobanks dominate the determination of the forward premium. Thus if the degree of imperfection in the national financial market is large, the forward premium will still equal the differential between the two Eurocurrency interest rates, but may differ widely from the differential between the two *national* interest rates. On the other hand, speculation and intervention by national governments will influence domestic interest rates and in this way will affect indirectly the forward premium.

In addition to introducing explicitly the Eurocurrency market in the formal analysis of international capital movements, the main contribution of the two authors consists of focusing on the simultaneous determination of the forward rate and the interest rate in the same currency. Thus in case of a shift in one of the two functions determining the forward premium, the competitive behavior of the Eurobanks will insure that the covered interest-rate parity is preserved. The change in the forward exchange rate will be followed by a compensating adjustment in the Euro-interest rate denominated in the same currency and also, to a lesser degree, by the adjustment in the national interest rate. This simultaneous adjustment between the forward and the interest rates suggests a limitation of government intervention in the forward exchange market under conditions of relatively high capital mobility.

It should be pointed out that this interesting model is based on the assumption of fixed exchange rates. Flexible exchange rates could be introduced in the model, as shown by Tsiang, by providing an additional market for spot exchange. The authors should consider such an extension since it would make their model more relevant for the present conditions in international monetary relations.

The key element in this analysis of the Eurocurrency market is the high degree of competition among the Eurocurrency banks. The underlying conditions reflect low risk, other than the foreign-exchange risk. They also reflect substantial funds available to banks for Eurolending and for interest arbitrage among various Eurocurrencies. In other words, portfolio selection constraints entail almost constant opportunity costs of shifting funds on a covered basis among various Eurocurrencies and among Eurobanks. The question should be raised to what extent recent developments in the Euromarkets have modified these underlying conditions. The risk of increasing positions, even on a covered basis, in some Eurocurrencies and with some banks may have increased in recent months. This has resulted in a decreased flow of deposits to a number of medium and smaller banks so that they have had to offer higher deposit rates as compared to the rates offered by large banks. These imperfections among the Eurobanks suggest that a model which departs from a perfectly elastic bank arbitrage function and which allows for some discrepancy between interest-rate parities may be more realistic. Thus in such conditions, the difference between the Herring-Marston model and a tradi-tional approach is one of degree only. However, a general equilibrium treatment of the forward-rate and interest-rate determination in their model is an interesting contribution.

The paper by Logue, Salant, and Sweeney develops an interesting statistical technique in order to test the degree of financial integration among seven major industrial countries. The multivariate approach provided by factor analysis permits an exploration of the interrelationships between a large number of variables that is superior to the approach used in the past. I, however, have some misgivings regard-ing the rationale used in selecting uncovered interest rates as the relevant variables to be used for testing the degree of integration. Although the authors do not state this explicitly, it appears that they treat forward cover as a specific diversified risk which can therefore be disregarded in testing for the degree of integra-tion. I disagree with such a position because, in view of the important simultaneous relationship between the forward rate and the national interest rate, the former cannot be taken as independent of the latter. It would appear to me that a more complex approach is needed that would take into account the relationship between currencies and yields in the foreign exchange markets.

When levels of interest rates of the seven countries are tested, the results in the paper appear quite good, with over 80 percent of the percentage of variance explained by the international marginal monetary productivity of capital. Also, the correlation of individual interest rates with this factor is quite high. However, as Ripley has pointed out, the use of interest-rate levels is open to a high degree of first-order serial correlation which may give rise to spurious inferences about the cause of common movement.[1] The use of percentage changes in interest rates is free from the first-order serial correlation. The percentage of variance explained by this factor is about 40 percent, and the correlation coefficients of interest rates are also lower. These results are more consistent with those of other studies; they suggest a degree of financial integration between major industrial countries, but this integration appears to be far from perfect.

Deane Carson

There is an unconscious division of labor on the panel of discussants. My col-leagues who have already spoken have emphasized and approached their task from the standpoint of methodological issues. I will spend most of my time examining some of the policy implications for money and capital markets which are touched on in these two papers.

[1] D. M. Ripley, "Systematic Elements in the Linkage of National Stock Market Indices," *Review of Economics and Statistics*, August 1973, pp. 356 ff.

The first point I want to discuss is the cost of integration, which is brought up in the Logue, Salant, and Sweeney paper. The authors point out correctly that "any efforts by an individual nation to lower its domestic interest rates by open market operations will be unavailing—except in the immediate run—and will ultimately lead to excessive monetary issue and perpetuate inflation."

The point I would like to raise is whether this implied loss of interest-rate control is properly attributable to the integration case. To do so implies that such cost could not or would not accrue in a closed economy, an implication that I would reject. In a closed economy, as in an open one, the central bank has little permanent control over market yields. An attempt to lower interest rates will succeed in the short run, but only so long as the liquidity effect of an increase in the money supply is not washed out by the price expectations effect and actual increases in the general price level. When these latter effects take hold, interest rates stop declining and begin to rise in spite of, and often because of, attempts by the central bank to prevent the rise from occurring.

Thus, if central banks have little permanent effect on market yields in a closed economy, it seems somewhat erroneous or questionable to me to assign this loss as a cost of integrated markets. In fact, the existence of integrated world markets has the effect of accelerating the process described above. In the absence of integration, the central bank can maintain somewhat longer the illusion of controlling interest rates, since the international effects do not operate. But in the end, the results will be quite similar.

The Logue, Salant, and Sweeney paper further suggests that international integration of capital markets imposes a constraint on the ability of national governments to allocate resources towards socially desired projects which would not, presumably, be undertaken in a free market. The authors consider this to be one of the costs of integration. It is only a cost, however, if one happens to believe that central governments can and do make investment judgments that are superior to the free-market alternatives. There is very little evidence that this is the case in the long run and a great deal of evidence to the contrary. Thus, I for one would place this effect of integrated capital markets in the benefits column of the balance sheet with one potential reservation.

There is some danger that national governments may respond to the frustrations of their attempts to direct resources by imposing even greater controls on the flow of capital than now exist. This would certainly impose a cost on the world economy which we would like to avoid. But, in effect, my point is that you really cannot tell whether this is a cost or a benefit unless you make some projection of the behavioral reaction of the government in advance. I do not believe anyone can do that. There is some reason, I suppose, to believe that the tendency would be—where resource allocation is frustrated—to impose controls.

A far more important consideration, it seems to me, is the effect of integration on the ability of individual central banks to control domestic money supplies and their own rates of inflation. This is properly the topic for tomorrow, so I will not discuss it in detail now. Nevertheless, one of the interesting implications of the Herring and Marston paper—which they do not explicitly mention—is based on their Figure A-1, where one finds displayed an impressive correlation between the Eurodollar rate and the U.S. federal funds rate, a relationship which their model is designed to explain. Similarly, in their Figure A-4, a high degree of covariation exists between the Eurodollar, Euromark, and German interbank rates for recent periods.

As we all know, in recent years the Federal Reserve has exercised a great deal of control—perhaps management is the better word—over the federal funds rate. This rate is the key to the Federal Reserve's money market strategy for control of the U.S. monetary aggregates. One might infer from this, or at least hypothesize, that German money market rates are also determined by the Fed's position with regard to the appropriate level of the federal funds rate. If this is a correct inference, it implies that U.S. monetary policy has a substantial influence on the German money supply—not interest rates, but money supply—to the extent that interest rates determine the desired composition of portfolios between monetary and non-monetary assets.

An opposing hypothesis would be that the Federal Reserve's money market stance has been influenced by European money market rates. While this seems less likely, the hypothesis should not be rejected out of hand. In other words, there may be some feedback effects on Fed policy which account for this. When one is seeking the cause of the incredibly poor performance of the Fed in controlling the U.S. money supply in the period 1970 to 1973, one should throw out no possibility.

There is an important difference in the findings of the Logue, Salant, and Sweeney paper and the Herring and Marston paper. The Herring and Marston paper finds very considerable interdependence between U.S. and German short-term interest rates. This does not appear to be the case, however, for long-term rates if we are to take the evidence of the Logue, Salant, and Sweeney paper. Indeed, for the latter, which has to do with long-term rates, the German-U.S. relationship is the weakest of all. I am not sure that—from listening to my colleagues—we can attach any significance to this weak relationship, but it does raise some interesting questions of interpretation about the interdependence of financial markets and of monetary policy.

Paolo Savona

Let me start by recalling that—as stated in the paper—Herring and Marston's model explains why the forward rate and Eurocurrency interest rates are maintained at interest parity, and shows how national and Eurocurrency interest rates each respond to speculation in the forward market, and how the forward rate responds to disturbances in the national and Eurocurrency markets. (See p. 140.) I am satisfied as to the "whys" but not entirely as to the "hows" of this paper. This does not imply that the Herring and Marston exposé is not correct but casts some doubts on the usefulness of the economic policy implications of the study.

Before entering into details, let me also recall that Herring and Marston intend "to analyze a model in which there are only two countries, America and Germany, and only two currencies, the dollar and the D-mark." Nevertheless, throughout the paper the comparisons are drawn among dollar and D-mark interest rates and the Eurodollar and Euromark interest rates. This implies a third country, the United Kingdom, for example. In fact neither D-marks in New York nor D-marks in Frankfurt—which are the only two possibilities that we have in the model—are Eurocurrencies.

This is a minor point for the Herring and Marston analysis by itself, but it is not so minor if we introduce Aliber's political risk and other "modern" animals— such as lender-of-last-resort problems, Arabs' behavior, and so on—which reduce the crucial assumption of perfect substitution among the various national currency and Eurocurrency denominated assets. But, apart from this, Herring and Marston's paper is so formally elegant that it should not be spoiled by such lack of grace.

To remain for a while in the field of formal elegance, I found the assumption that U.S. interest rates are insensitive to every amount of demand for D-mark-denominated assets (infinite elasticity)—which plays such an important role in the Herring and Marston model—too restrictive for the model and too "heroic" for the reader. I would prefer to replace it with a less restrictive "operational" assumption of the following type: the present model can explain only market conditions characterized by a volume of D-mark-denominated assets which leaves unchanged U.S. interest rates (and obviously the U.S. exchange rate).

Now to come back to my dissatisfaction with the "hows." A study of the empirical relevance of the interest parity theory should above all be checked by (what we can call) the t-Tsiang (from the first scholar, if I am not wrong, who exhaustively developed the problem). If the interest parity theory is to be applied, the observed differentials among interest rates must belong to a period of covered foreign-exchange positions. If the speculation is on an "open" basis, not interest rates, but only expectations of exchange-parity variations are involved.

If we limit ourselves to the "surface" knowledge of the events during the sample period taken by Herring and Marston, we ought to reject as "casual" the empirical evidence produced to support the interest parity theory. Conversely, if we carefully document how speculation works in the Eurocurrency market, we are able to demonstrate a favorable t-Tsiang for the Herring and Marston empirical analysis. But this has not been done in the paper. These are the reasons for my dissatisfaction.

In the Eurocurrency market, speculation begins with Eurodeposits and is uncovered, and ends up covered, because of the banks' behavior. Among the banks, only a few—a small share of the total—work on "open" positions in the foreign exchange market. And recent developments have shown us that many of these "few" regularly go bankrupt.

I have published, in Italian, a comment on a recent paper written by Modigliani and Askari, in which I explain my view on this matter. I will now try to summarize this for you.

The basic assumption of my argument is that Eurobanks react to every loss of Eurodeposits by accepting new conditions. If depositors prefer to convert dollar-denominated Eurodeposits into D-mark-denominated ones, the banks offer no opposition but normally end up uncovered in terms of exchange risks if their assets are also, as usual, dollar-denominated. When this happens, the Eurobanks have three choices to cover their foreign-exchange position. They may: (1) convert their own liquidity, if any, into international monetary base (IMB)—using Fratianni-Savona language—for an amount equivalent to the above-mentioned conversions; or (2) buy forward an amount equivalent to the same above-mentioned deposit conversions; or (3) borrow dollars in New York (or elsewhere in the United States) in order to deposit these dollars in Frankfurt (or elsewhere), asking for D-mark conversions at the current exchange rate.

The first two solutions can only cope with very mild speculation. They perform an *ordinary* service for an *ordinary* business in the Eurocurrency market. But they cannot cope with extraordinary speculative attacks against the D-mark, such as those we experienced during the last three years. This is why the third possibility, that is, to borrow dollars in New York, is the "common" reply of the banks to the conversion required by clients and one which justifies the use of the interest parity theory to explain dollar-D-mark interest-rate differentials.

Using T-accounts, the operation runs as follows (stocks):

Starting point:

Eurobanks			
$ Assets	100	$ Deposits	100

Conversion point:

Eurobanks			
$ Assets	100	$ Deposits	90
		DM Deposits	10

(Note: Either the clients' or the banks' foreign exchange positions are "open.")

Covered point:

Eurobanks			
$ Assets	100	$ Deposits	90
		DM Deposits	10
DM Assets	10	$ Borrowing	10

Note that: (1) U.S. banks do not have an exchange risk because they have a dollar deposit position vis-à-vis their dollar lending to Eurobanks, and (2) German banks do not have an exchange risk because they are able to convert dollar deposits at the Bundesbank at fixed rates.

We can now conclude that the described operation satisfies the t-Tsiang, that is, it is a covered transaction in foreign exchange which involves interest rates (for the banks) together with expectations of exchange-rate variations (for the Eurodepositors). And this is the framework, according to my knowledge of the Eurosystem, which should be used to demonstrate how some operators respond to speculative attacks on the D-mark and to support the validity of the interest parity theory in explaining the behavior of forward exchange rates for some currencies.

DISCUSSION

International Financial Integration

PROFESSOR LOGUE: Let me address a number of the points raised in the discussion of our paper. I agree with Professor Carson about the costs of capital-market integration. I really don't think the items we mentioned are costs, and I really don't believe that the government makes better decisions than the private market. But these are the sort of costs which have been discussed in the literature, and to the extent that our paper was supposed to be a survey and a synthesis, we felt these "costs" of integration should be mentioned.

Now, as to whether we should have examined uncovered or covered interest rates: our objective was to examine interest rates within national financial markets, domestic rates—the rates facing domestic investors, borrowers and lenders—to get some idea of the scope for independent domestic financial policy. Uncovered rates were much more relevant than covered rates in our analysis.

If one, for example, were concerned with the elasticity of the covered interest arbitrage schedule—if he were to work within the context of capital flows which generate interest-rate changes—then indeed, covered rates would be much more appropriate. However, examining the elasticity, as it were, of the supply of funds within a country—which we did—we find that uncovered rate comparisons are likely to yield better results.

Just a comment on the question of oil money and the Eurocurrency market. The major effort we made in our model was to introduce portfolio and efficient capital-market concepts into the realm of international finance. We applied them to see what kind of implications they would have in international finance.

With respect to the oil funds, we would argue that rates of return would be related to the systematic risk of the asset. And to the extent that our empirical results tend to support this notion, there tends to be a predominant, very strong factor which determines rates of return. There are some implications in our work and some implications in the portfolio literature relating to how funds will get divided up among investment alternatives. Indeed, if we find that rates of return and only systematic risks are related, then we could presume that, as funds—oil funds, for example—are introduced into the system, they too will be channeled into various investments on a risk-return basis rather than on a more arbitrary basis.

179

DR. SWEENEY: The matter of the independence of monetary policy was raised in the discussion of our paper. We examined in our paper the problem of monetary policy independence under fixed exchange rates using financial portfolio theory. The problem turned out to be a matter of how good different financial assets are as substitutes for each other in a two-country world, that is, the assets in which the two governments make open-market operations.

We then distinguished financial-market integration from substitutability among financial assets. Markets can be perfectly integrated, and the assets not perfect substitutes. For example, a great many people think that the stock markets are efficient and integrated, but one stock is not a perfect substitute for another stock from a different firm and different industry. Individual stocks have different degrees of risk.

The problem of monetary policy independence turns out, then, to be a complex one turning on the degree of substitutability among financial assets, expected returns, and covariances, and also—this, I think is important—on the sterilization policies of the two governments considered.

Finally, I would like to mention that Professor Kenen's suggestion of the monetary equivalence of the factor-price equalization theorem is interesting though not, I think, very promising within our factor-analysis framework. As I understand it, within the context of that theorem, the scenario would go something like this: assume that there is one country in this world where there is no capital mobility whatsoever; this country experiences some monetary expansion, which in turn causes inflation, and thus causes interest rates to rise. (We used quarterly data in our analysis. Presumably, all this would occur within the same quarter.) The higher prices in this country are transmitted abroad—within the same quarter— causing prices abroad to rise and interest rates to follow along. If this series of developments takes somewhat longer than a quarter to occur, it will not get caught in the quarterly factor analysis, for in this type of analysis you are not running a time-series regression.

We have run another factor analysis, using short-term interest rates and weekly observations. This analysis produced somewhat better explanation. The first factor explains 88 percent of the total variance of the observations, which would mean that inflation is being transmitted through the goods markets in something less than a week. We have hopes of getting some daily data for analysis and finding that inflation is being transmitted in not more than a day!

DR. BRYANT: Professor Kenen asserted rather strongly that Logue, Salant, and Sweeney might be using the concept of monetary independence somewhat differently than we have traditionally used it. Do they question the traditional result that under flexible exchange rates, for example, a given size open-market operation will have more impact on domestic incomes and prices and less on foreign incomes and prices than would be the case under a fixed-exchange-rate regime?

DR. SWEENEY: Let me break that question into two parts. First, what effect will financial operations have on financial asset prices? Second, how does that work through to the real sector? And the answer to this second part is dreadfully unclear in my own mind.

I believe we would agree with the proposition that, although some people advocate one look at interest rates as an indicator of monetary policy, it is perhaps more plausible to look at monetary aggregates as the indicator (or target) for monetary policy, and that with flexible exchange rates a country is relatively independent to determine its own monetary and credit conditions. We would agree with the standard propositions that the real rate of interest is fixed by inflation, that the monetary authorities can control only the nominal rate, and that the exchange rate suffers as a consequence of overexpansion in the money supply. As for the effects of monetary policy, they become dreadfully complicated if you are considering a portfolio inclusive of international assets, because if the open-market operations of the two governments take place in assets that are not perfect substitutes, then the general prediction you would get would be a change in the whole array of asset prices—not a change in one country's national interest rate. All the asset prices in the international system would change in response to one country's open-market operations. The final state of affairs is very complicated to work out.

PROFESSOR SWOBODA: Recent and mainly theoretical work by various people—William Branson, Peter Kenen, Lance Girton and Dale Henderson, and Rudiger Dornbusch—on traded and non-traded assets could be quite relevant to the observed short-run independence of interest rates.

Second, I would like to add two remarks to Professor Kenen's assertion about what would happen to interest rates even if capital were not mobile. The first is the theoretical observation that under fixed exchange rates, even in a static world with zero inflation rates and no international capital movements, interest rates in various countries will tend to move together, because the essential characteristic of the fixed exchange-rate system is that monetary policy in any one center becomes generalized through the world as a whole and will tend to affect aggregate demand and interest rates in the world as a whole.

My second remark is an empirical one. A colleague of mine in Geneva, Hans Genberg, has just completed a preliminary study (as part of a larger empirical project) which analyzes inflation rates in a manner very similar to that in which Logue, Salant, and Sweeney have analyzed interest rates. He has computed principal components for levels of consumer price indexes for, I think, twenty-one major OECD countries using quarterly data and has found that the first principal component explains an even higher proportion of the variance in the original variables than do the principal components of Logue, Salant, and Sweeney for interest rates. The proportion explained is above 90 percent. He has done the same thing on yearly rates of change and has found that the first principal component explains only slightly less than the Logue, Salant, and Sweeney study, but that the two first components account for over 60 percent of the variance in a no-parity-change period, which is somewhat higher than what is accounted for by Logue, Salant, and Sweeney.

From the recognition of the importance of a second principal component, we have come to the conclusion that there might be some point in trying to separate a European area—where the German rate tends to dominate—from a U.S. area in short-run analysis. Quantifying and documenting this is part of a larger work we currently have under way on inflation rates.

And, finally, Genberg also has another type of study under way where he examines the variation in inflation rates within a country—as measured in fifteen major U.S. cities, for example—and compares it to the variation in inflation rates among countries. He has found that there is no significant difference between the variability of price levels within a country (as measured by the city consumer price indexes) and the variability among countries under fixed exchange rates.

That is not proof, of course, that the price inflation effect dominates and determines the Logue, Salant, and Sweeney results on interest rates. It may be that both things go on. I would add, in any event, that to my mind the Logue, Salant, and Sweeney test is an important one because a theory that says that capital markets are integrated, whatever the reason, should be able to pass the principal-components test first. I would also agree with Peter Kenen that there are some other issues that one would want to look at, however.

DR. SWEENEY: We did essentially the same things as Professor Swoboda's colleague. However, we used percentage changes in prices instead of price levels because of the bias which tends to show up when levels are used. We used percentage changes with money supplies, too, and found that we got a very good first factor, somewhat better than we got in the case of prices. (There are difficulties with prices—like wholesale price index versus consumer price index, and because some countries are quite biased in the construction of their indexes.)

We found that for money supplies and prices, for example, we got a first and second factor and even a third factor—which was France. We started the factor analysis so as not simply to be fishing around. We hypothesized that we would likely find a strong first factor which was an international factor. Then we hypothesized that we would likely find a European factor, representing the combined interaction of the EEC, and perhaps a factor for the Anglo-Saxon world— the United Kingdom, the United States, and Canada. But we found that there simply was not any EEC factor. They just are not dreadfully well integrated. And there was not much of an Anglo-Saxon factor either.

Let me discuss for a minute what constitutes good results. When we used percentage changes, we got results that were somewhat better than when we used absolute changes. I do not know whether our results were better than what one would get if he used percentage changes for the stock market. However, it seems to me we got results that are comparable to what would be gotten with markets which we have a high disposition to believe are very integrated and efficient.

DR. BRYANT: I thought Professor Niehans said something in his earlier comments about diversification into foreign currency assets by residents of a "home country" which indicated that he thought such diversification might rob the flexible rate system of some of its advantages. I wonder if he could comment more fully on his point.

PROFESSOR NIEHANS: Let me try with an extreme example. Suppose American households and firms hold all their liquid assets in the form of, say, 30 percent dollars, 20 percent marks, 10 percent lire, and so on, up to 100 percent, widely diversified, and that the same is true for Germans, Italians, and so on. Under flexible exchange rates, the Federal Reserve would have complete authority over the nominal money supply in the United States, and the same would be true for central banks in Germany, Italy, and so on. But since the liquidity supply of U.S. households does not depend only on the dollar supply, et cetera, the U.S. Federal Reserve no longer has complete authority over the nominal liquidity supply of U.S. firms and households. Even in the case of fixed exchange rates—where the liquidity supply of countries, in a nominal sense, is determined by all the central banks tied together—we have much the same situation.

Now I am using an extreme example to make my point clearer. The more firms and households diversify into multiple currency holdings of liquid assets—deposits with multiple denominations and combined currency baskets, and so forth—the more this state of affairs will develop. For the next few years, this will probably not be a very important consideration. (In countries like Switzerland, with a very large financial market and a small economy, I suppose this state of affairs already exists to some degree.) However, in ten to fifteen years it may be a significant factor and, again, we may move back to some of the same independence problems we had with us in the 1960s.

PROFESSOR CARSON: About liquid-asset diversification into multiple currencies, research results have shown that there is no predictable return attributable to holding assets outside of a diversified portfolio. In other words, there is no benefit to nondiversification. Professor Niehans suggested that in a flexible-exchange-rate world, we would find people holding portfolios of financial assets diversified into several currencies. Research results would support this contention. There is no reason why investors should not be expected to diversify into many currencies.

Now, getting back to the point about fixed versus flexible exchange rates and monetary policy independence: we have to presume that the optimal composition of an international portfolio would be weighted by the relative proportion of outstanding assets of each country to the total volume of outstanding financial assets of all countries together. In other words, if U.S. dollar-denominated assets accounted for 50 percent of the aggregate dollar-translated world portfolio of financial assets, then the dollar-denominated assets would make up 50 percent of this optimally diversified international portfolio.

When central banks engage in open-market operations—either buying or selling dollar-denominated assets—there is an impact on the composition of this optimal portfolio. Via the change in composition—and this is where Professor Niehans' notion comes in, I guess—we find some relationship among financial returns in individual countries even under a flexible exchange-rate system. This is because even under a flexible exchange-rate system, there is the optimal portfolio, although the weights change much more rapidly in response to changes in currency exchange rates. In applying this portfolio notion, even in a world of flexible exchange rates, we would expect to find very, very closely related interest-rate movements.

International Interest Arbitrage

PROFESSOR MARSTON: I have a couple of points to make, and then Professor Herring will take up one further point. The first point, which Dr. Savona brought up, concerns what happens to our model when U.S. assets and Eurodollar assets are not perfectly substitutable. In such a case, we would have to add an equation to the model to explain the Eurodollar rate, and it would complicate the exposition of the model. But as long as the degree of substitutability between U.S. and Eurodollar assets is greater than the degree of substitutability between U.S. assets and Euromarks, for instance, then all of our results still hold. So what is at issue is not whether there is perfect substitution between the U.S. and Eurodollar markets, but the degree of substitutability between those two markets.

The second point has to do with a question which Dr. Hodjera raised. That is how our empirical results—or, more specifically, the results that I obtained in an earlier study of the Eurocurrency markets—would hold up under a regime of flexible exchange rates. In fact, on the basis of some regressions which Professor Herring and I ran a few months ago, the interest arbitrage relationship in the Eurocurrency market tends to hold in the recent flexible period as well as in the past fixed-exchange-rate period. So there is really no change.

At this point, the question arises, and Dr. Hodjera has also brought it up, as to why Eurobanks are willing to perform this arbitrage function in flexible periods or in fixed periods. The basic reasons, which I discussed in my earlier paper, involve the fact that generally there have not been any restrictions on the

Eurocurrency markets, at least compared with the restrictions which have existed on arbitrage involving national markets. So, first, there is the absence of restrictions.

Secondly, there is the fact that in switching between currencies, Eurobanks do not increase or decrease the amount of political risk attached to having assets or liabilities in the different currencies. As long as they maintain the deposits or loans in a particular center, it doesn't matter whether the deposits or loans are denominated in dollars or marks and so on, unless investors believe that it is more likely that the labor government in England will clamp controls on Euromark deposits, for example, than on other Eurocurrency deposits. As long as you are talking about arbitrage within the Eurocurrency market, political risk is not going to be a significant factor.

Finally, a point which was raised by Professor Carson. In our model we assumed that the U.S. interest rate is controlled by the Federal Reserve; secondly, that the Eurodollar and U.S. interest rates are very closely arbitraged so they can effectively be considered the same interest rate. Of course, that's not true in reality. The assumption comes down to assuming that the Federal Reserve is able to control the Eurodollar rate. However, as I mentioned earlier, that is not a crucial assumption to the model, though it greatly simplifies the exposition. But there is no additional implication that the Federal Reserve controls the German interest rate. Although the Eurodollar rate is controlled, the German rate is free to vary, even in the case where interest parity holds, as long as the forward rate is allowed to vary as well.

PROFESSOR HERRING: I have only a small point to add. Professor Kenen pointed out that we had neglected to talk about one of the most interesting kinds of shocks that might be analyzed in this kind of model, namely, what happens when the Eurodollar rate changes. This kind of shock can, in fact, be shown graphically pretty simply. As might be expected from the general analysis, both the forward premium and the Euromark rate change, and they change in a predictable sort of way.

Looking first at the forward market, we have the speculator-trader demand curve and the arbitrage supply curve noted by the net offerings of loans by private citizens in the Euromark market. And we get this schedule, remember, because we've assumed that Eurobanks have an infinitely elastic net mark asset demand.

The other part of the story, then, is how Eurobanks link the Euromark rate and the forward premium with the Eurodollar rate. This line is simply the interest parity line. It is given by the equation: $i_m = i_s - fp$ or the Euromark interest rate equals the Eurodollar rate less the forward premium.

What happens in this type of system when the Eurodollar rate is changed? A change—decrease—in the Eurodollar rate will make it more attractive to borrow Euromarks than Eurodollars. There will be an increase in the net supply of Euromark loans by nonbanks to Eurobanks, and this will tend to drive the forward premium down from its initial level. The whole relationship will have shifted because the Eurodollar term has been changed. If the Eurodollar rate has been decreased, the whole line will simply shift out. The equilibrium Euromark rate is determined at a lower level. So, it is a fully general system. A Eurodollar rate shock brings about changes in both sets of rates: Euromark rates and forward exchange rates. It is all simultaneous.

PROFESSOR KENEN: My point was that it seems to me that the exposition of the paper does not sufficiently emphasize the fact that the results gotten by Herring and Marston were quite different from what would have been gotten with the naïve theory, which is parodied in footnote 3 of the paper. There is a movement when the Eurodollar rate changes, not just in the Euromark rate but in both the Euromark rate and the forward rate, the two together restoring interest parity—thanks to the assumption of infinite elasticity of net mark asset demand. There is nontrivial adjustment involving the forward rate, which has implications for other markets which are, in turn, connected to the forward market. That is the nature of the Herring and Marston contribution. It's not that they have done a more comprehensive job, but that having done a more comprehensive job, they have come out with an interesting conclusion about the way the world works.

PROFESSOR STANLEY BLACK: I appreciated Herring and Marston's verbal acknowledgment of my Princeton paper in which there were two-country markets, with interest rates variable in both countries and spot and forward rates. Having done this kind of work in the past, I am in a good position to comment on what they have done, which, it seems to me, is quite similar to my previous work.

I observe, along with Dr. Hodjera, that the Herring and Marston paper seems not to mention the level of the spot exchange rate. This leaves one wondering. Does the model imply a pegged exchange-rate system? The German central bank's holdings of bonds are supposed to be exogenous in the model. This seems to imply that any changes in reserve flows are going to have an immediate effect on bank reserves in Germany; in other words, the German central bank does not sterilize reserve flows. However, it would appear to me that a better way to deal with this matter is to build the spot market into the model more directly. That way, both reserve flow developments and the possibility of flexible rates can be handled.

Also, if the model included the spot exchange markets and examined changes in spot exchange rates a little more closely, one could pose questions about what effects policy changes will have on the current-account balance over time, which, presumably, will depend on the exchange-rate level. Certainly, the policy changes Herring and Marston talk about will tend to have effects on spot and forward exchange rates, and that should have some effect on trade balances over time.

186

PROFESSOR HERRING: In reply to Professor Stanley Black's comments: we could add flexible exchange rates to the model. But we have not been able to figure out a neat, clean way of doing it. We currently believe it would considerably complicate an already complicated model. We wanted to deal with arbitrage in this model. Perhaps we can deal with flexible exchange rates and central bank sterilization policy at another time.

Professor Black rightly points out that we have assumed that there is no central bank sterilization of reserve flows, but in a different paper—not concerned with arbitrage—we have dealt with what happens when there is partial or full sterilization by central banks. It is an interesting question, but, again, it is one which I think should be separated from the particular problem of arbitrage.

And finally, on the question of nontraded assets, several papers have dealt with what happens when there are nontraded assets in a model. We have done some work on what we consider a more general model which allows for a range of substitutability among different assets. When limited substitutability is allowed— say, between a German asset and a dollar security—the same results occur as in the case of a nontraded asset. Simply, the limited substitutability allows for more of a range and a more general result than the nontraded asset model.

PROFESSOR DUFEY: I have a specific question for Professor Herring. When you explained the example in your model, did I understand correctly that you implicitly assumed constant expectations about the change between the dollar and the mark exchange rate?

PROFESSOR HERRING: Yes.

PROFESSOR DUFEY: If one does not make that assumption—the assumption would not hold in the real world—would he be able, with your model, to pick up in empirical work the impact of an initial interest-rate change in the United States and the impact of an investor's expectations about changes in the mark-U.S. dollar exchange rate? On one hand, we have an interest-rate change, and the other case is a change in expectations about the mark-dollar exchange rate.

PROFESSOR HERRING: I am very reluctant to call the work at the end of the paper empirical work at all. It was merely an illustration of an assumption which we made that the arbitrage did not appear to be perfect through time. We have, in no sense, tested the model in any way. If you can tell me the way in which the expectations will change, we can produce a result from the model. But we have not thought in any great detail about separating empirically these two factors— impact of an initial interest-rate change in the United States and the impact of investors' expectations about the future dollar-mark exchange rate.

The Oil Funds Investment Problem

DR. WILLETT: A number of times I have gotten the impression from the many casual discussions I have heard about the oil money that there is quite a significant difference as to whether the oil-exporting countries' funds go into the Eurodollar market—this is usually associated with comments about recycling—or into the New York market—which is usually associated with comments about the funds being swallowed up. We have given a lot of thought at Treasury about this and have generally come to the conclusion that if the Eurodollar market and the New York market are as highly integrated as they would appear to be from all the evidence which we have examined, it basically should not make much difference which market the funds go into. I would like to throw this matter generally to the members of the panel and the audience. Does anyone feel there are factors which do make a difference as to whether the oil funds go into the New York market or the Eurodollar market?

Using a portfolio allocation model like Logue, Salant, and Sweeney have used, one would get the implication that, in the absence of changes in interest rates, an efficient portfolio would tend to be allocated roughly in proportion to the size of the financial market. In terms of liquid assets, the New York market represents the largest proportion of the world's financial markets and in the absence of interest-rate changes, one would expect a large proportion of the oil funds to end up ultimately in U.S. financial markets. Even if all the funds went into the Eurodollar market initially, they would be recycled out, and a large share—in this kind of scenario—would be recycled into the New York market. So, the manner in which funds were initially distributed would affect the movement of funds to the ultimate equilibrium, but the ultimate equilibrium would not be affected by the initial distribution.

A second question is—taking this efficient market model—how much of a change in interest rates would it take to make quite substantial alterations in the proportions in which funds are allocated among the various market alternatives?

DR. SWEENEY: Dr. Willett speaks of the New York market as though it is a well-defined, unitary entity. One might want to distinguish, in posing this question, between banks in New York, which are often the same institutions as the banks in the Eurocurrency markets, and U.S. Treasury bills. And there are the additional impacts of these funds flows, not only on interest rates on dollar-denominated assets, but on exchange rates, on bank capital adequacy, et cetera.

DR. WILLETT: The main question on which I wished to focus, however, is how would the ultimate distribution of the oil funds occur and what would that distribution be? Perhaps we could hold our distinctions to New York banks, U.S. Treasury bills, and the Eurodollar market.

DR. MAYER: In one sense, these funds cannot go into the United States because they are already there. They are already there right now in the form of Treasury bill holdings and bank deposit holdings of private nonbanks, commercial banks, and central banks. So, European money goes into the United States. There has merely been a shift of ownership of foreign assets held in the United States. The movement doesn't add at all to the money supply of the United States. But if the funds go somewhere else and increase the monetary base of the country involved, then there is a lot of difference.

PROFESSOR SWOBODA: I'm wondering if we aren't just chasing a red herring with this matter. What people are worried about with regard to the oil money and the recycling and so on is not the question of where does it go first and will it get distributed by perfect markets, as things usually do, and so forth. What they are really worried about is a change of major proportion in financial flows, together with the problems generated in particular sectors of the world economy: the fact that some countries' balance-of-payments problems are much more severe than others, that some countries are being put in severe financial and real strain in the face of such massive inflows and in a generally uncertain world, that banks may collapse here and there, that some banks—namely large banks—may pick up a much larger amount of the funds and let some of the smaller banks be squeezed out of business, and so forth. If there were plenty of time for adjustment, there would be no problem. The problem is really one of being short of time—of being faced with massive flows of funds, massive relative to the amount of time we have to respond to developments.

PROFESSOR KENEN: I agree in very large measure with Professor Swoboda, but let me go a step further and rephrase the question this way. Whether the oil money goes to the Euromoney market or goes to the U.S. money market—let's think of those two possibilities—is there any substantial difference in the probability of Italy getting some of it? My answer is "no." In terms of the efficiency of recycling—defined in terms of financing the deficit countries—there is very little difference, in my mind, between the oil funds going into the Euromarkets or the U.S. money market. Quite clearly, if it goes into the capital markets—in the sense that it goes long term into U.S. equities and corporate securities and so forth—it will go into the United States where these markets are large.

The chain of substitution by which funds move between the longer-term capital and the money markets is quite imperfect. No matter what one says about efficient markets and so forth, what and where the primary disturbance is does have some effect upon the final configuration of rates. Clearly, if the funds seek long-term outlets, not as much of them are going to seep back into the short-term markets—however those short-term markets are defined—and therefore not as much of them may be available for the financing of deficits. But my primary answer is that it does not make a lot of difference for solving the immediate financing problem, and the confusion between the U.S. market and the Euromarket—the distinction between those two—obscures the real distinction, which is whether it stays short term or whether it goes long term.

PROFESSOR NIEHANS: Just one brief remark. If this money moves through commercial channels, it seems to me the prototype of this question will be operation twist—between bills only or long-term or short-term or what not. The literature can be examined. But the nature of the problem very much depends on what exact assets are specified and what the degree of substitution is among them.

And if the money does not move through commercial channels, then it is a matter of international assistance. Operation twist does not apply. This analogy doesn't tell us very much. This is what came out in the Italian case.

PART
THREE

THE EUROCURRENCY MARKET, EXCHANGE-RATE SYSTEMS, AND NATIONAL FINANCIAL POLICIES

Thomas D. Willett

1. Introduction

Two major changes in the international economy in recent years have been the rapid increase in international capital mobility, facilitated in no small measure by the development of the Eurodollar market, and the switch from adjustably pegged to flexible exchange rates. Standard theorems in international economics indicate that both the degree of capital mobility and the exchange-rate system may have important effects on the efficacy of national monetary and fiscal policies.

The first section of this paper addresses the question of whether these changes are likely to have a significant impact on the way in which monetary and fiscal policies should be conducted. After reviewing the standard theorems, questions are posed concerning the empirical strength of various considerations and the possible extent to which a broader range of considerations may temper the conclusions of the standard analysis. For instance, an increase in capital mobility generally increases the strength of fiscal policy [1] under fixed rates while reducing it under flexible rates. A change from fixed to flexible rates will increase the strength of fiscal policy if capital mobility is fairly low, but will decrease it if capital mobility is high. Under current circumstances, is the switch from fixed to floating rates likely to increase or decrease the strength of U.S. fiscal policy or, perhaps, leave it roughly unchanged? Are these changes likely to increase or decrease the magnitude and frequency of disturbances which confront economic policy makers? And to what extent may the answers to these questions vary from country to country?

For many countries it has been argued that prior to floating rates, capital mobility had already increased to the point that there was little scope for

I would like to thank Ryan Amacher, Ralph Burgess, Vicki Farrell, Henry Goldstein, Gottfried Haberler, Jay Levin, Dennis Logue, John Makin, Richard Sweeney, and Edward Tower for helpful comments on portions of the included material and Ira Kaylin and Ron Meek for providing research assistance. Sole responsibility for the contents of the paper rests with the author. Official views of the U.S. Department of the Treasury are not necessarily implied.

[1] Throughout this paper fiscal policy is defined as an autonomous change in government expenditures or taxation with the money supply held constant. Monetary policy is defined as an autonomous change in the money supply. For a review of the standard results using alternative definitions, see John Helliwell, "Monetary and Fiscal Policies for an Open Economy," *Oxford Economic Papers*, March 1969.

autonomous monetary policy. On the other hand, at least until recently, the use of closed economy assumptions for the United States in the formulation of monetary and fiscal policy has not been far wrong. Further, in this same vein, questions may be raised about the extent to which there actually has been a substantial increase in international capital mobility as opposed to the international movement of capital.[2] Has capital mobility now increased to the point that this may have been a dangerous assumption on which to base U.S. financial policies under fixed rates? Even for smaller countries, had capital mobility really increased to the point that there was little scope for independence of monetary policy under fixed rates? And how substantially is this changed under floating rates? Should capital controls be used to reduce capital mobility under fixed rates? And do floating rates provide a more effective method of gaining greater monetary autonomy? Furthermore, how are these conclusions changed by considering not only the strength of monetary and fiscal policy but also the speed and variability of the effects of financial policy changes, criteria which are perhaps as, or even more, important? To the policy maker these questions may be compressed to what changes should be made in the conduct of monetary and fiscal policy in response to the changes in the operation of the international economic system, and what changes, if any, should be made to the international economic system.

Consideration of this last question must depend not only upon effects on policy leverages but also on the disturbances generated under alternative exchange-rate systems.[3] The second section focuses upon the effects which higher capital mobility has had on the disturbances facing national stabilization policy in an open economy and the implications of this analysis for the desirability of alternative exchange-rate systems. One of the key issues here is the effects of fixed versus floating exchange rates on the transmission of economic disturbances from one country to another. A critical analysis is presented of the recent argument by Modigliani and Askari that capital mobility has increased to the point where the traditional belief in greater transmission under fixed exchange rates must be reversed.

This section also considers the theorem that under flexible exchange rates the pursuit of tight money in one country will generate expansionary pressures abroad, as contrasted with the deflationary pressures which would be transmitted under fixed rates. If this scenario is applicable to current circumstances, then it

---

[2] See, for instance, Thomas D. Willett, Samuel I. Katz, and William H. Branson, "Exchange-Rate Systems, Interest Rates and Capital Flows," *Essays in International Finance*, no. 86 (June 1971); also see William H. Branson's commentary on this paper, pp. 254-257, below.

[3] Of course, the full question of the relative desirability of fixed versus floating rates embraces an even broader range of considerations. For recent discussions of the full range of issues involved, see Edward Tower and Thomas D. Willett, "The Theory of Optimum Currency Areas," *Princeton Studies in International Finance* (forthcoming); and Richard J. Sweeney and Thomas D. Willett, "The International Transmission of Inflation: A Survey of Mechanisms and Issues," prepared for the Conference on Bank Credit, Money and Inflation in Open Economies, Leuven, Belgium, 12-13 September 1974.

194

would have profound implications for the international coordination of macro-economic policies. For instance, one reads of considerable concern on the part of many European officials that U.S. policy makers may overdo the fight against domestic inflation and plunge both the United States and the rest of the world economy into serious recession. According to the standard analysis, however, under floating rates tight money in the United States would generate expansionary pressures abroad. If correct, this would suggest that European fears were generated by a failure to recognize one of the major implications of the change in exchange-rate systems.

While the titles of this session and of the conference focus on the Eurocurrency market, there will be little explicit discussion of the Eurocurrency markets throughout the first sections of this paper. However, the development of the Eurocurrency market has been an important factor in two recent events—namely, the increase in international capital mobility, and through this development, the switch from fixed to floating exchange rates. For analytic purposes, the development of the Eurocurrency market is treated as a general increase in interest-sensitive capital mobility. The development of the Euromarket has been a major factor in facilitating the increasing degree of international capital mobility and financial integration. Thus, while framed in more general terms, these sections are directly focused on major questions for macroeconomic policy posed by the rapid development of the Eurocurrency markets. The final section of the paper considers various effects on national financial policies which the development of the Eurocurrency markets may have over and above their general contribution to the increased international mobility of capital.

The key questions here are to what extent has the unregulated expansion of private and official liquidity, due to the operation of the Eurocurrency markets, undermined financial stability, as opposed to merely substituting for other forms of liquidity creation.

The major purpose of the paper is to provide some points of focus for the panel discussion. While in some cases I have indicated tentative judgments concerning some of the questions raised, the major objectives are to pose questions for the panelists and provide some background against which these questions may be addressed. For the most part, the presentation of background discussion is restricted to theoretical questions. References are given to a number of papers which report empirical results relevant to the question at hand. No systematic survey of empirical results is attempted, however.

2. The Effects of Capital Mobility on Monetary and Fiscal Policy under Fixed and Floating Exchange Rates

In recent years we have seen both a tremendous increase in international capital mobility and a switch from fixed to flexible exchange rates. Standard analysis suggests that under fixed exchange rates an increase in interest-sensitive capital mobility will decrease the efficacy of discretionary monetary policy while increasing the efficacy of fiscal policy. This can be explained quite intuitively along the lines developed by Marcus Fleming and Robert A. Mundell.[4] Under fixed rates an increase in capital mobility makes it more difficult for the monetary authorities to influence domestic interest rates. In other words, because of the offsetting effects of international capital flows, a greater change in domestic high-power money would be required to induce a given short-term change in interest rates. In the extreme case of infinite capital mobility, a change in domestic high-powered money would change neither the interest rate nor the domestic money supply, its only lasting effect being upon the level of international reserves.

For fiscal policy the leverage is increased because international capital mobility will dampen the interest-rate changes which would be brought about by government fiscal imbalances, thus reducing the extent to which the net effects of government surpluses or deficits on aggregate demand will be reduced by offsetting changes in private consumption and investment spending, which is crowded out or stimulated by the change in fiscal policy.

In other words, in the absence of sterilization policies, high capital mobility will "manufacture" monetary expansions to accompany budget deficits, thus converting a discretionary fiscal expansion into an expansionary monetary policy as well.[5] On the other hand, in the face of infinite capital mobility, a move to floating exchange rates will completely undermine the effectiveness of fiscal policy. Under any conditions of capital mobility, a move to floating rates will enhance the strength of monetary policy, while a switch to floating rates may either increase or decrease the effectiveness of fiscal policy.

Where capital flows are interest-sensitive, the necessary and sufficient condition for the strength of fiscal policy to be enhanced by a move to floating rates is that the capital inflow induced by the interest-rate increase accompanying the expansion of expenditures be less than the induced deterioration of the current account. Where income mobility of capital is present, the condition is that the sum of interest- and income-sensitive funds attracted be less than the current-account reduction. In most formal treatments, capital inflows are taken to be a positive function of increases in domestic income. However, due to the increase in investable funds associated with the increase in income, it is possible that the net

---

[4] J. Marcus Fleming, "Domestic Financial Policies under Fixed and Floating Exchange Rates," *IMF Staff Papers*, vol. 9 (1962), pp. 369-380; Robert A. Mundell, "Flexible Exchange Rates and Employment Policy," *Canadian Journal of Economics and Political Science*, vol. 27 (1961), pp. 509-517. For surveys of the current state of the literature and references to the major contributions, see Robert W. Bagley, Appendix A, in Richard Caves and Grant L. Reuber, *Capital Transfers and Economic Policy: Canada, 1951-1962* (Cambridge, Mass.: Harvard University Press, 1971), pp. 361-396; and Helliwell, "Monetary and Fiscal Policies for an Open Economy."

[5] For analysis of the effects of sterilization policies on the leverages of monetary and fiscal policy, see Bagley, Appendix A, in *Capital Transfers*.

income effect on capital flows could be of opposite sign. This is a topic on which much useful work could be done. Regardless of the degree of capital mobility, a move to floating rates will increase the comparative strength of monetary policy relative to fiscal policy. Under fixed rates an increase in capital mobility will always increase the strength of fiscal policy and reduce the strength of monetary policy, while under floating rates just the reverse will occur.

These qualitative conclusions are generally accepted within the profession. To advise policy makers usefully, however, we need to be able to indicate, at least roughly, the magnitude of differences in policy effects which the increase in capital mobility and the change in exchange-rate systems are likely to have. This task is made more difficult both by the general problem of a shortage of widely agreed upon estimates of many of the key parameters in the standard models, and by the fact that our current system is not one of freely floating rates, but rather the absence of official parities with continued substantial government intervention in many foreign exchange markets. A further crucial question concerns the behavior of speculators. As has been emphasized in recent literature, where private speculation is strongly stabilizing, floating rates may generate little change in policy leverages as compared with fixed rates.[6] On the other hand, destabilizing speculation can further increase the difference in policy leverages generated by a switch from fixed to floating rates.

There are two major mechanisms by which floating rates can increase the effectiveness of monetary policy. One is by allowing domestic interest rates to differ from the international interest-rate structure. The second is via the influence of capital flows on the exchange rate and hence on aggregate demand via the Keynesian trade-balance multiplier. A domestic monetary expansion, for instance, may lead to a capital outflow, depreciating the exchange rate and creating a trade surplus. In this way, even if the domestic interest rates are closely tied to international rates and cannot be influenced by the domestic authorities, monetary policy can influence aggregate demand.

Even under conditions of perfect capital mobility, exchange-rate flexibility may allow greater independence of domestic interest rates. There are two ways in which this can occur. The first applies to conditions of perfect covered arbitrage only. Unless exchange-rate expectations are held with certainty, then maintenance of interest parity conditions for covered arbitrage is quite consistent with the possibility of sizeable uncovered interest-rate differentials. If a move from fixed to floating rates is associated with a general increase in uncertainty

---

[6] See, for instance, Richard Caves, "Widening the Band for Permissible Exchange Rate Fluctuations: Discussion," *The International Adjustment Mechanism* (Federal Reserve Bank of Boston, 1969), pp. 135-140; Bagley, Appendix A, in *Capital Transfers;* Victor Argy and Michael G. Porter, "The Forward Exchange Market and the Effects of Domestic and External Disturbances under Alternative Exchange Rate Systems," *IMF Staff Papers*, vol. 19 (1972), pp. 503-533. As Argy and Porter note, this point is made in Fleming's classic paper, "Domestic Financial Policies under Fixed and Floating Exchange Rates," pp. 369-380, but has not been incorporated in most discussions of the subject.

concerning future exchange rates, then the elasticity of supply of uncovered arbitrage (spot speculation) funds would decline, allowing greater autonomy for monetary authorities in influencing domestic interest rates. The same forces reducing the elasticity of uncovered spot funds would also reduce the elasticity of supply of forward speculative funds. Where the supply of speculative funds to the forward market is quite inelastic, only a small movement of covered arbitrage funds would be necessary to move the forward rate sufficiently to close the covered differential generated by a change in one country's interest rates. Thus a highly elastic supply of covered arbitrage funds is not inconsistent with a considerable degree of domestic interest-rate autonomy if the supply of speculative funds is not also highly elastic.[7]

Of course, a priori it is difficult to predict how strong an effect of this type would be generated by a move from fixed to floating rates. With strongly held expectations under floating rates, there might be little difference at all. Indeed, in considering the change from an adjustable peg to a floating rate, one might even expect to find higher uncovered capital mobility under a float. In fact, work by Richard Caves and Grant Reuber suggests that this may well have been the case for Canada.[8]

Under the conditions of the recent generalized float, however, it appears that the effect of floating rates in dampening the uncovered interest-rate sensitivity of capital flows has been quite significant. Contrary to the emphasis placed by many analysts on interest-rate changes in explaining movements in spot exchange rates under the current float, our investigations have failed to find a significant, systematic influence of interest-rate changes on spot exchange rates (see Annex A). This would suggest that large net capital flows have not systematically accompanied interest-rate changes under the current float, and hence that the major contribution of floating rates so far to the strength of monetary policy has been through allowing greater scope for interest-rate changes. (As will be discussed in Section 3, the greatest contribution of floating rates to improving the workings of monetary policy may have come from the reduction in disturbances brought about by the elimination of attempts to maintain adjustable parities.)

Where the elasticity of speculative funds is high under floating rates, their effect on the strength of monetary policy will depend upon whether speculative exchange-rate expectations are elastic, inelastic, or neutral with respect to a change in exchange rates. Until recently, formal models had dealt only with the case of neutral expectations. Robert Bagley, as well as Victor Argy and Michael Porter, have shown rigorously, however, that inelastic expectations reduce the quantitative degree of difference between the leverages of monetary and fiscal policy under

---

[7] For further discussion and graphical illustration of this point, see Thomas D. Willett, "The Eurodollar Market, Speculation, and Forward Exchange: A Comment," *Journal of Money, Credit and Banking*, vol. 4 (August 1972), pp. 636-642.

[8] Caves and Reuber, *Capital Transfers.*

fixed and floating exchange rates, while elastic expectations increase these differences.[9] Completely inelastic expectations imply the exchange rate is expected to return to its former value, while elastic expectations refer to expectations that the rate will continue to move in the same direction. Neutral expectations refer to expectations that after the change the exchange rate will remain at its new level. Where expectations are inelastic, as appears likely to be the more general case, increases in the elasticity of supply of speculative funds will reduce the degree of additional leverage given to monetary policy by a move from fixed to floating exchange rates.

Even in the face of perfect capital mobility, completely inelastic expectations, and a perfectly elastic supply of speculative funds, monetary policy may gain some potency under floating rates. However, inelastic exchange-rate expectations in the face of an interest-rate increase would make economic sense only if interpreted as meaning that a permanent impact on the exchange rate is not anticipated, so that the exchange rate will at some point in the future return to its initial value. For instance, speculators might feel that an interest-rate change inspired by cyclical circumstances might have no effect on the long-run equilibrium exchange rate. It would not seem likely to make sense, however, to systematically expect changes to have no short-term impact on the exchange rate in the face of a high elasticity of uncovered arbitrage funds. Under such circumstances, a tightening of monetary policy would cause an initial appreciation of the exchange rate and would allow domestic interest rates to remain above international levels until the exchange rate had fallen back over time to its long-run expected value. The combination of the short-term appreciation of the exchange rate and its expected return to its initial value generates expectations of a gradual decline of the spot rate back to its initial value. In a world of perfect uncovered capital mobility, the equilibrium condition would be for domestic interest rates to exceed foreign rates by the expected amount of depreciation of the exchange rate. Thus exchange-rate expectations would determine the domestic term structure of interest rates and would allow monetary policy changes to have a short-term influence on interest rates.

Where the instrument of monetary policy is exchange-market intervention to generate the initial appreciation of the exchange rate, authorities are faced with a trade-off between the amount of interest-rate changes which can be generated and the length of time that the interest-rate differential can be maintained. For instance, securing an appreciation of the spot rate by 2 percent rather than 1 percent would maintain a 2 percent interest-rate differential on one-year maturities for one year or a 1 percent differential for two years. In either case the differential would be maintained by a steady rate of depreciation of the exchange rate back to its previous value.[10]

---

[9] Bagley, Appendix A, in *Capital Transfers,* and Argy and Porter, "The Forward Exchange Market."

[10] See, for instance, Ronald I. McKinnon, "Monetary Theory and Controlled Flexibility in the Foreign Exchanges," *Essays in International Finance,* no. 84 (April 1971).

Where the authorities do not directly manipulate the exchange rate, it becomes difficult to anticipate how great a degree of increased autonomy for interest rates can be secured under floating rates with strongly held speculative expectations. This would depend crucially upon the time horizon and term structure of expectations of speculators, about which we have little systematic knowledge at present.[11] Presumably in the case in question, "perfect" speculation would be based on estimates of the time period at which the "temporary" monetary change would be reversed. In practice it might prove that in such a world of extremely high elasticities of speculative and uncovered arbitrage funds, monetary authorities could not hope to gain much systematic control over domestic interest rates by directly or indirectly operating on exchange-rate expectations.

This discussion has by no means been exhaustive. But it should be sufficient to illustrate how important the strength and behavior of private speculation can be to the comparative effectiveness of monetary policy under fixed and floating exchange rates. In addressing this question, we must seek to judge the empirical behavior not only of interest-sensitive capital flows but also speculative reactions. Indeed, for many countries, it may be more the unpredictability than the changes in leverage of monetary policies which is the more important concomitant of higher capital mobility. This is due, not so much to higher and more variable interest sensitivity of international capital flows, as it is to the magnitude of such flows, which have risen sharply due to the increased volatility of speculative expectations about exchange rates.

Conceptually, this increase in speculative capital mobility has two components. One is implied by speculative responses to interest-rate or monetary policy changes. These are likely to be quite variable in strength and at various times may either offset or strengthen the effects of interest-sensitive capital flows. The second is an increase in the shocks or disturbances to which the domestic economic system is subjected. On both scores speculative capital flows under adjustably pegged exchange rates are likely to make domestic stabilization policy more difficult. Under such circumstances, the benefits to domestic stabilization from moving to a floating rate may not be so much the accompanying reduction in interest sensitivity of capital flows but rather the reduction in disturbances and in the variability of capital flows in response to domestic interest-rate changes.

This is quite important, because in judging the effectiveness of financial policy, greater certainty as to effects is probably much more important than average strength. Indeed, in the absence of the management costs attached to using policy

---

[11] For an innovative study in this area, see Michael G. Porter, "A Theoretical and Empirical Framework for Analyzing the Term Structure of Exchange Rate Expectations," *IMF Staff Papers*, November 1971, pp. 613-645. Discussions by participants in the foreign exchange market at the most recent meeting of the Bürgenstock group suggested that during the current float extremely short time horizons have domesticated speculative activity. This time horizon of speculators has many important implications for the behavior of floating rate systems which have not yet been systematically dealt with in the literature.

instruments, it is only the degree of certainty of effects, not strength, which would be important. One would just apply greater dosage to weaker instruments. In the absence of perfect certainty, both as to the effects of policy instruments and the future states of the economy, the speed with which policy instruments affect the economy may also be of considerable importance.[12]

It is sometimes argued that floating rates not only increase the strength of domestic macroeconomic policies, but also the speed with which they operate.[13] This argument may be overstated, however. It is true that under floating rates the exchange market will clear virtually instantaneously. It does not necessarily follow from this, however, that policy variables which influence the exchange rate will have their major effects on the domestic economy with equal speed. In the scenario under consideration, aggregate demand is influenced through changes in the current account, and the speeds of adjustment here may well be as long as or longer than those we find for the response to monetary and fiscal policies in a relatively closed economy such as that of the United States. Indeed, with low short-run trade elasticities, the initial effects via the current account could even be perverse. This is probably not the case for the major industrial countries, however, for as Henry Goldstein has recently argued, even if actual trade flows are initially perverse, flows of new orders will not be.[14]

I would suspect that floating rates may make a greater contribution to reducing the uncertainty of monetary policy effects than in increasing the speed with which these effects are felt. This is clearly a question, however, which requires a good deal more work, both to compare speeds of adjustment and to study the impact of exchange-rate systems on the behavior of speculative response to changes in financial policy. Both of these questions may be less important, however, than the effects of alternative exchange-rate systems in generating and mitigating disturbances.

What tentative judgments may we make at this point concerning the effectiveness of monetary and fiscal policy under fixed and flexible exchange rates? Based on the evidence discussed in Annex B, it appears that despite the substantial increase in capital movements in recent years, most major industrial countries have still not reached the point where a switch from fixed to floating exchange rates

---

[12] For recent discussions of the effects of lags and uncertainty on the optimal use of stabilization policies, see Arthur M. Okun, "Fiscal-Monetary Activism: Some Analytical Issues," *Brookings Papers on Economic Activity*, no. 1 (1972), pp. 123-172; and Stanley Fisher and Phillip J. Cooper, "Stabilization Policy and Lags," *Journal of Political Economy*, vol. 81 (July-August 1973), pp. 847-876.

[13] See, for instance, Egon Sohmen, *Flexible Exchange Rates* (Chicago: University of Chicago Press, 1969).

[14] Henry N. Goldstein, "Monetary Policy under Fixed and Floating Exchange Rates: Some Lessons from Recent Experience in the Leading Industrial Countries," *National Westminster Bank Quarterly Review*, November 1974, pp. 15-27; see also, however, Richard N. Cooper, "Currency Devaluation in Developing Countries," *Essays in International Finance*, no. 86 (June 1971).

will clearly cause a reduction in the absolute degree of effectiveness of fiscal policy. For the United States it appears unlikely that the flexibility of exchange rates will have a major quantitative impact on the value of fiscal multipliers.

With respect to monetary policy, there is considerable controversy over the extent to which monetary policy was independent under fixed rates. There have been two principal approaches to testing for the degree of monetary autonomy in an open economy. One is to estimate "offset coefficients" indicating the degree to which creation of high-powered money spills out of the economy. The second approach looks at the extent to which international reserve flows have influenced domestic money supplies. Unfortunately, as has been recently noted by Michele Fratianni, these two approaches, using the same data, are likely to suggest the opposite conclusions.[15] For instance, findings that the German money supply is little affected by changes in the proportions of the foreign and domestic components of the monetary bases could be viewed as showing either a high degree of offsets to domestic monetary changes due to high international capital mobility [16] or the considerable scope available for sterilizing capital inflows.[17] There is also the possibility of there being considerable scope for independent monetary policy under fixed exchange rates in periods of fairly stable monetary conditions, but much less scope when faced with large disturbances under less stable conditions. For instance, in his examination of the relationships between reserve changes and money-supply growth rates, Henry Goldstein found that there was little systematic relationship on a quarterly basis for the major industrial countries over the period 1959 through 1971 (see Table 1).[18] However, over the period 1972–73, Goldstein argues that the massive payments imbalances and reserve accumulations of the major industrial countries (other than the United States) were a major cause of the speedup in monetary growth rates in all major countries during that period. Goldstein notes that with the exception of Canada, the speedup in monetary growth in his group of industrial countries was associated with a substantial increase in reserve inflows. Even in this later period, however, it is not clear how dominant a role international developments played in domestic monetary expansion.

---

[15] Michele Fratianni, "Domestic Bank Credit, Money and the Open Economy," presented at the Conference on Bank Credit, Money and Inflation in Open Economies, Leuven, Belgium, 12-13 September 1974.

[16] See, for instance, Pentti J. K. Kouri and Michael G. Porter, "International Capital Flows and Portfolio Equilibrium," *Journal of Political Economy*, vol. 82 (May-June 1974). For recent reviews of some of the literature on offset coefficients and the degree of monetary independence under fixed rates, see Niels Thygesen, "Monetary Policy, Capital Flows and Internal Stability: Some Experiences from Large Industrial Countries," *Swedish Journal of Economics*, vol. 75 (March 1973), pp. 83-99, and the contribution to this conference by Logue, Salant and Sweeney.

[17] Manfred J. M. Neumann, "A Theoretical and Empirical Analysis of the German Money Supply Process, 1958-1972" (draft dated May 1974); Goldstein, "Monetary Policy under Fixed and Floating Exchange Rates."

[18] Goldstein, "Monetary Policy under Fixed and Floating Exchange Rates."

Table 1

CORRELATION BETWEEN QUARTERLY CHANGES IN EXTERNAL
RESERVES AND QUARTERLY CHANGES IN MONEY SUPPLY FOR
SIX DIFFERENT COUNTRIES (VALUE OF R^2 FOR FOUR
ALTERNATIVE EQUATION FORMS), 1959–71

Equation Form	Belgium	Nether-lands	Germany	France	Italy	Japan
(1) $\Delta M_t = a + b \, \Delta M_t$	.02	.13* (n)	.02	.00 (n)	.05	.11*
(2) $\Delta M_t = a + b \Delta R_{t-1}$	.00	.05	.01 (n)	.04	.00	.09*
(3) $\Delta \log M_t = a + b \Delta \log R_t$	.03	.08* (n)	.02	.00 (n)	.12	.02
(4) $\Delta \log \Delta M_t = a + b \Delta \log R_{t-1}$	.01	.01	.02 (n)	.04	.02 (n)	.01

(n) denotes a negative value of b.
* denotes an F statistic significant at the .05 level.
Source: Goldstein, "Monetary Policy under Fixed and Floating Exchange Rates."

A brief rundown of individual country experiences gives some flavor of the difficulty in accepting the view that countries have been severely constrained by international considerations in pursuing different rates of monetary expansion. Goldstein's tables indicate that for Belgium from 1967–68 to 1969–70, the two-year average reserve change improved by over $800 million, from −$163 million to +$660 million, but money supply growth remained unchanged. The inflow grew to slightly over $1 billion in 1971–72, and the monetary growth rate doubled from 5.3 percent to 10.9 percent.

Canada's monetary growth rate fell from 12.9 percent in 1966–68 to 3.5 percent in 1968–70, despite an increase in reserve inflows from $342 million to $1.6 billion. Then the rate of reserve inflow declined somewhat in 1971–72 to $1.37 billion, but the monetary expansion shot up to 23.2 percent.

France also does not fit the strong monetarist pattern well. Its international position strengthened from a $2.5 billion reserve loss in 1967–68 to a $759 million gain in 1969–70, but its rate of monetary expansion fell from 5.6 percent to 3.1 percent. France's accumulation of $5 billion in 1971–72 was, however, associated with a substantial acceleration in monetary growth to 12.5 percent.

Italy displayed an acceleration of monetary expansion from 1966–68 through 1970–72, but without huge changes in reserve flows. Reserve accumulations dropped from $429 million in 1967–68 to $11 million in 1969–70 without reducing monetary expansion. Nor did the more rapid rate of reserve accumulation in 1971–72 ($727 million) lead to an increase in the rate at which monetary expansion was accelerating. The rate of monetary expansion did increase, but by less than two percentage points, from 18.8 to 20.4, compared with the increase from 13.0 to 18.8 in the preceding biennium.

Neither does Japanese experience fit a strong monetarist model very well. Japan's rate of acceleration of monetary expansion was only slightly more rapid in 1970–72 than in 1968–70 (from 14.0 percent to 18.4 percent between 1966–68 and 1968–70, and from 18.4 percent to 23.7 percent, 5.3 percentage points, between 1968–70 and 1970–72), despite the growth of reserve accumulations during the biennium from $1.9 billion to $13.5 billion, as compared with a growth of only $0.9 billion to $1.9 billion in the preceding biennium.

The United Kingdom's rate of monetary expansion slowed between 1966–68 and 1968–70 despite the improvement in its international position from a reserve loss of $677 million to a gain of $405 million. Accumulations of $2.8 billion in the period 1970–72 were associated with a tripling of the rate of monetary expansion, however.

Germany, the Netherlands, and Switzerland all did display behavior consistent with the strong monetarist model. In each of the three biennia, they experienced increases both in the rate of domestic monetary expansion and in the rate of reserve accumulation.

As is indicated in Table 2, for the group as a whole, there is a negative correlation between the amount of reserve accumulation over the 1970–72 period and either the rate of monetary expansion or the absolute increase in the rate of monetary expansion. At this point we would seem to be left with considerable scope for disagreement as to the degree of monetary autonomy which existed in the last days of the fixed rate period.

Directions for useful further theoretical and empirical work on the efficacy of monetary and fiscal policy in open economies include better treatment of stock-flow relationships for capital flows and the timing of effects, dropping of small country assumptions, a consideration of credit as well as direct monetary effects along the lines of Karl Brunner and Allan Meltzer and their students, more systematic treatment of the broad range of effects which changes in aggregate demand may have on international capital, and incorporation of the effects of exchange-rate changes on incentives for portfolio rebalancing (which would act to complement the effects of inelastic speculative expectations).[19]

---

[19] For major efforts to date on the investigation of these questions under large country assumptions, see Robert A. Mundell, "A Reply: Capital Mobility and Size," *Canadian Journal of Economics and Political Science*, vol. 30 (1964), pp. 429-430, and Murray C. Kemp, "Monetary and Fiscal Policy under Alternative Assumptions about Capital Mobility," *Economic Record*, vol. 42 (1966), pp. 598-605. For recent contributions on credit and monetary effects, see Karl Brunner, "The Money Supply Process in Open Economies with Interdependent Security Markets: The Case of Imperfect Substitutability," presented at the Conference on Bank Credit, Money and Inflation in Open Economies, Leuven, Belgium, 12-13 September 1974, and Fratianni, "Domestic Bank Credit"; on rebalancing effects, see Dennis E. Logue and Thomas D. Willett, "The Effects of Exchange Rate Adjustment on International Investment," *The Effects of Exchange Rate Adjustments* (Washington, D.C.: U.S. Government Printing Office, 1976).

Table 2

RESERVE ACCUMULATION AND MONETARY EXPANSION

	(1) Changes in International Reserves, 1971–72		(2) Rate of Monetary Expansion, 1970–72		(3) Absolute Increase in Rate of Monetary Expansion from 1968–70 to 1970–72	
	Millions of dollars	Country rank	Percent increase	Country rank	Percent increase	Country rank
Belgium	+1,023	8	10.9	9	5.6	9
Canada	+1,371	7	23.2	2	10.3	1
France	+5,055	3	12.5	8	6.9	8
Germany	+10,175	2	13.1	7	7.6	6
Italy	+727	9	20.4	3	7.4	7
Japan	+13,525	1	23.7	1	9.7	2
Netherlands	+1,551	6	17.2	4	9.5	3
Switzerland	+2,356	5	15.9	5	7.5	5
United Kingdom	+2,820	4	14.6	6	8.8	4

Note: *Spearman's coefficient of rank correlation*   *Coefficient needed for 5% significance level*

Between (1) and (2)	−.150	.683
Between (1) and (3)	−.058	.683

Source: Goldstein, "Monetary Policy under Fixed and Floating Exchange Rates."

3. The Generation and Transmission of Disturbances and the Relative Desirability of Alternative Exchange-Rate Systems

There is considerable theoretical controversy concerning how increases in capital mobility affect the case for genuinely fixed versus floating exchange rates.[20] It seems to be fairly clear, however, that the increases in capital mobility brought about by the growth of multinational corporations and the Eurocurrency markets, et cetera, have considerably increased the case for floating exchange rates as compared with adjustable or crawling pegs.

Unless one believes that floating exchange rates are quite unstable due to instability in speculative expectations and/or the demand and supply of internationally mobile funds, conventional analysis suggests that floating exchange rates will dampen the international transmission of disturbances. Given the huge magnitude of payments imbalances which developed in the last days of the adjustable peg system, this would seem to be a powerful argument in favor of exchange-rate flexibility. Advocates of fixed rates or crawling pegs, however, have stressed the potential advantages of short-run fixity of exchange rates in spreading out disturbances over the international economy.

In large part this difference in point of view comes from emphasis on two alternative mechanisms by which disturbances are transmitted internationally. The first view stresses the monetary effects of capital flows and overall payments imbalances, while the second view emphasizes the Keynesian transmission mechanism of trade and current-account imbalances.[21] Ronald McKinnon has been one of the strongest advocates of the latter point of view, stressing the stabilizing effects of constrained exchange rates in the short run while granting the need for exchange-rate flexibility over the longer term.[22]

In a recent paper, Franco Modigliani and Hossein Askari reach this same outcome, but by a quite different route.[23] Modigliani and Askari adopt the alternative criterion of minimizing the extent to which disturbances are transmitted

---

[20] See Tower and Willett, "The Theory of Optimum Currency Areas."

[21] For a detailed discussion of the various mechanisms of international transmission, see Sweeney and Willett, "The International Transmission of Inflation."

[22] An argument sometimes made for the adjustable peg system is that it combines the advantages of exchange-rate stability in the short run with exchange-rate flexibility in the long run. However, to obtain this long-run flexibility required a discrete adjustment in some short-run periods. Thus, long-run flexibility was obtained in a technically inefficient manner as judged by most relevant criteria. The use of sliding parities would appear to be a much more satisfactory method of obtaining the objective of combining the major characteristics of a substantial degree of exchange-rate stability in the short run with flexibility in the long run.

[23] Franco Modigliani and Hossein Askari, "The International Transfer of Capital and the Propagation of Domestic Disturbances under Alternative Payments Systems," *Banca Nazionale del Lavoro Quarterly Review*, no. 107 (December 1973), pp. 295-310.

from one country to another.[24] Generally, this criterion has been used to argue for short-term flexibility rather than fixity of exchange rates. Modigliani and Askari, however, present an interesting argument that the propagation of disturbances will be greater under flexible than under fixed exchange rates.

Modigliani and Askari's reversal of the standard analysis rests upon two key ingredients. The first is high capital mobility. Consider the case of a shift in domestic investment. Under fixed rates, the trade balance will move in the direction opposite to that of the investment shift, tending to cushion the impact of the initial disturbance on GNP—for example, an investment boom would be dampened by a trade deficit—but the capital account is likely to move in the same direction.[25] Traditional analysis has tended to focus only upon the trade-account effects. As Gottfried Haberler and the present author argued several years ago, it is essential that capital-account effects also be taken into consideration. Our analysis was aimed against drawing too sharp a distinction between the stabilizing trade-balance effects of fixed versus flexible exchange rates. In the absence of capital flows, movements of the exchange rate would maintain trade balance and thus eliminate the automatic stabilizing impact of trade imbalances induced by domestic disturbances.[26] With capital mobility, however, incentives for opposing capital flows would normally be generated such that even with a freely floating exchange rate the trade balance would be likely to fluctuate in the direction desired on stabilization grounds. Thus we argued that the existence of capital mobility has reduced the difference between fixed and floating rates on this score.

Modigliani and Askari go further and consider the case of extremely high capital mobility, such that the initial changes in capital flows induced by a domestic disturbance exceed the size of change in the trade balance. Thus, in the case of a fall in domestic investment, the originating country's balance of payments would deteriorate under fixed rates and its currency would depreciate under floating rates. In this case, the country would secure a greater improvement in its trade balance under a floating rate than under a fixed rate. Under these circumstances, the international sector would provide a more potent automatic

---

[24] Another aspect of Modigliani and Askari's paper which will not be discussed in detail here is that countries will have a greater incentive to follow mutually beneficial macroeconomic policies under constrained exchange rates than under floating rates. This argument is not entirely convincing because it rests in part upon the assumption that countries under fixed rates must gear their macroeconomic policies toward external balance even in the short run.

[25] Negative income mobility of capital enhances the Modigliani-Askari result of a positive relationship between changes in exogenous expenditure and the exchange rate. In the case of a fall in investment, the attendant fall in income leads to a net capital inflow along with lower interest rates. Finally, a negative income mobility of capital enhances the comparative advantage of monetary over fiscal policy in obtaining external balance under fixed exchange rates. (For full results, see Table 1 in John H. Makin, "The Assignment Problem with Income Mobility of Capital and Limited Exchange Rate Flexibility," mimeo., University of Wisconsin—Milwaukee (March 1973), which considers systematically the impact upon the assignment problem of income mobility of capital under fixed and limited flexibility of exchange rates.)

[26] There would, of course, still exist other mechanisms by which disturbances would be transmitted internationally; for example, the Laursen-Metzler effect.

stabilizer under flexible than under fixed rates, and likewise the international propagation of disturbance would be greater under flexible rates.[27]

The condition for capital mobility to be high enough for fluctuations in the *IS* curve to be transmitted to a greater extent under flexible rates than under fixed rates is the same as for a switch from fixed to floating exchanges to decrease the strength of fiscal policy—that is, that the capital flows generated by a change in aggregate demand exceed the demand-induced change in the current account. The available evidence suggests that despite the increase in capital mobility over the postwar period, the sensitivity of international capital flows to changes in income and interest rates is still not clearly and generally above this critical value. Furthermore, in many countries we do not find a consistent tendency for the state of the domestic cycle to be systematically related to the overall state of the balance of payments under fixed rates. Thus, while it appears likely that fixed rates still give greater Keynesian transmission on average, this may vary from country to country and episode to episode.

Secondly, Modigliani and Askari focus on the Keynesian transmission mechanism of changes in the current account. Perhaps more important, however, for the international transmission of disturbances is the liquidity or monetary transmission mechanism caused by payments imbalances under constrained exchange-rate systems. Even if capital mobility were sufficiently high for Keynesian transmission to be less under fixed rates, the greater transmission of disturbances through overall payments imbalances would dominate the net outcome.

Thus, Modigliani and Askari's unambiguous conclusion—that with high capital mobility floating rates will be a stronger transmission mechanism—holds only if the effects via the Keynesian mechanism are greater than those via the

---

[27] As John Makin has emphasized to me in private correspondence, this discussion of the roles of monetary and fiscal policy under fixed and flexible exchange rates is drawn from a Keynesian fixed price *IS-LM* type framework.

That prices can make a difference is readily seen from a consideration of how they would affect the discussion of the Modigliani-Askari argument. There, under extremely high (interest) mobility of capital, a fall in investment (or government) expenditure would lead to exchange-rate depreciation as lower interest rates produced capital outflows which would dominate, in their negative impact upon the balance of payments, the positive impact of lower incomes on imports. The depreciation of the exchange rate that would occur under flexible exchange rates would result in a switching of expenditure *onto* domestic capacity, and would thereby serve as an automatic stabilizer to offset the initial fall in investment or government expenditure. With an effective reduction in aggregate demand and downwardly rigid prices, this result may follow smoothly enough while ignoring prices. If the events are reversed, with upwardly flexible prices, it could be incorrect to argue that a rise in investment leads to appreciation because of a high level of capital mobility that dominates the impact of income on the current account. In such a case it could occur that a rise in investment would lead to appreciation, even if income effects in the current account dominated the interest-rate effect on the capital account. Higher prices attendant upon increased aggregate demand create an excess demand for money which *ceteris paribus* raises the excess supply of bonds and goods, both of which, when sold abroad, will help the balance of payments. In short, when prices are considered, the Modigliani-Askari argument may not require a high interest mobility of capital. For further discussion of the price effects, see Sweeney and Willett, "The International Transmission of Inflation."

monetary mechanism. Their failure to focus on the effects of transmission through the monetary mechanism may have stemmed from their assumption that countries gear their macroeconomic policies toward external balance.[28] In the extreme, such macroeconomic behavior would neutralize the monetary transmission mechanism under fixed as well as floating rates (except for short-run timing questions which are not addressed by Modigliani and Askari). Thus under their assumptions the Keynesian transmission mechanism would clearly dominate the monetary mechanism.

However, the reasonableness of this assumption may be questioned. One of the traditional functions of international reserves is to finance temporary or cyclical imbalances under fixed rates. External balance is a long-run rather than a short-run requirement under fixed rates.[29] It would seem that the more relevant comparison for considering international transmission mechanisms lies not in the absence of payments imbalance under both fixed and floating rates, as analyzed by Modigliani and Askari, but rather payments imbalances and reserve flows under fixed rates with exchange-rate changes under floating rates.[30]

Where capital mobility is relatively low, the adoption of sliding parities is not incompatible with independent national monetary policies. However, where capital mobility is high relative to the size of national money markets, this is no longer the case in the sense of the ability to effectively undertake short-term discretionary policy. Crawling pegs would still allow countries to pick independently their long-run average rates of monetary growth. But even if this objective were considered sufficient for macroeconomic policy, high capital mobility could still present severe problems for domestic stabilization policy, unless sliding parities maintained their credibility at all times. Otherwise, large speculative capital flows could undermine attempts to maintain steady rates of monetary growth.[31]

While this is clearly an empirical question, it seems quite probable to me that sliding parities, as compared with freely floating rates, might be able to generate still further stability under conditions in the international economy which were fairly stable to begin with, but that in a reasonably unsettled world economic environment, constrained exchange rates would further increase instability. In a world of considerable instability in underlying economic and monetary relation-

---

[28] In general it would make a considerable difference for the transmission mechanism whether such adjustment was always required by the deficient country or the country in which the disturbance originates. In the example in the Modigliani-Askari paper, these are the same country. Their analysis will generalize, however, only if it is the country of origin which must always adjust, a rule which would be most difficult to make operational.

[29] This is emphasized in Thomas D. Willett and Francesco Forte, "Interest Rate Policy and External Balance," *Quarterly Journal of Economics*, vol. 83 (May 1969), pp. 242-262.

[30] It should be emphasized that for the purposes of this discussion fixed rates may refer to slowly moving, narrow band crawling pegs as well as genuinely fixed rates.

[31] On the effects of sliding parities on national monetary independence, see Willett, Katz, and Branson, "Exchange Rate Systems, Interest Rates, and Capital Flows."

ships, the prospect of large speculative capital flows under systems of highly constrained exchange-rate flexibility could generate stabilization costs through the magnification of monetary disturbances which would outweigh the greater stabilization benefits that might be gained in terms of the Keynesian trade-balance transmission mechanism.

In the last several years, the size of potential capital movements has reached a point where attempts to maintain exchange rates differing from market judgments can lead to capital flows of a size which can swamp many domestic money markets. As Branson and I noted in our earlier study, this is the point at which the rationale for official recycling of speculative capital flows is undercut.[32] Thus, while it seems to be quite likely that, at least through the 1950s and first half of the 1960s, a system of crawling pegs would have provided greater international stability than the adjustable peg and perhaps also floating rates, this is no longer the case. Given high capital mobility and the considerable uncertainties which now face the international monetary system, the prospective cost of giving speculators (or prudent businessmen) a parity at which to shoot seems far greater than the prospective gains to be had by occasionally fighting market pressures to maintain an "optimum" rate.

Phrased alternatively, my argument has two steps. First, given the more rapid pace of international economic change in recent years, it is now more difficult, if not impossible, to design a system of sliding parities which will keep exchange rates close to equilibrium levels as judged by responsible market participants. This has been caused in major part by the acceleration of worldwide inflation. Higher average rates of inflation tend to be associated with greater differences in rates of inflation among countries from year to year. There is considerable difficulty in designing a smoothly functioning sliding parity mechanism even under fairly stable circumstances, and this difficulty is compounded greatly when the degree of underlying uncertainty or instability increases. Given the rate of change in underlying economic factors during the fifties and early sixties, I believe it would have been possible to design relatively slow-moving sliding parities which would have kept most exchange rates from "getting out of line." Today variability in inflation rates can cause large changes in equilibrium exchange rates within a relatively short period of time. This has, of course, been compounded by the uncertainties associated with the oil situation. These make decisions about desirable discretionary exchange-rate adjustments more difficult, as well as making virtually impossible a smoothly working system of automatic parity adjustments.

Second, the increase in capital mobility makes it much more important to keep exchange rates from getting out of line. Today the capital flows which can be engendered by an exchange rate which appears out of line with the market can swamp the domestic money markets of many countries. Operationally, it seems that in today's world of high capital mobility and great uncertainty we must

---

[32] Ibid.

view the arguments for sliding parities as arguments concerning intervention policies under managed floats.

Abstracting from effects on speculative capital flows, the question becomes how much transmission of disturbances is desirable from the standpoint of the overall operation of the international monetary system. There are some genuine advantages to allowing some transmission via reserve changes according to the logic of McKinnon, Laffer, and others that the law of large numbers will operate to increase proportional stability for the group as a whole when transmission is allowed.[33] On the other hand, unlimited allowance for the transmission of disturbances could give rise to a severe problem of "moral hazard." Incentives for responsible domestic policies might be reduced and systematic tendencies toward overabsorption might appear. Thus one must balance the effects of any exchange-rate and reserve-flow mechanism on the costs of disturbances against the total quantity of disturbances generated over time. Conceptually, this trade-off may be addressed in the context of what limits should be placed on official intervention policies under floating rates. In other words, how wide should be the reserve bands within which countries may operate primarily at their own discretion?

The type of exchange-rate systems in operation can influence not only the leverages of national monetary and fiscal policies and the degree of international transmission of disturbances but also appropriate arrangements for the international coordination of macroeconomic policies. Under fixed exchange rates, increasing capital mobility increases the need for macroeconomic coordination. In general, floating exchange rates reduce the need for coordination of national monetary and fiscal policies, although they do not eliminate all potential gains from coordination.

Under fixed rates tight money in one country will generate deflationary tendencies abroad, whereas under floating rates monetary policy impacts, according to standard analysis, are transmitted with opposite sign. This may occur through the operation of the Laursen-Metzler effect even under conditions of no capital flows and balanced trade. What had generally been considered a theoretical curiosity was elevated to the status of an important policy question by consideration of the rate of capital flows in generating trade imbalance.[34] Tighter money in one country will attract capital, bidding up its exchange rate and leading to a worsening of its trade balance. Conversely, the trade balance of its trading partners would improve, leading to an expansion of economic activity. This suggests potential benefits from using monetary policy under floating exchange rates when countries differ in the directions of their objectives for macroeconomic policy. On the other hand, fiscal policies continue to transmit their effects abroad in the same direction under floating rates. Thus, we might conclude that where countries agree on macroeconomic objectives, it would be most desirable to rely more strongly

---

[33] McKinnon, "Monetary Theory in Controlled Flexibility."

[34] See Anne O. Krueger, "The Impact of Alternative Government Policies under Varying Exchange Systems," *Quarterly Journal of Economics*, vol. 79 (May 1965), pp. 195-208.

upon fiscal policy changes while, when they disagree, it would be more desirable to use changes in monetary policy.

Increases in capital mobility increase the desirability of consultation and coordination of both monetary and fiscal policy under floating rates because the capital-flows and current-account imbalances which reduce the domestic effects of fiscal policy changes increase their effects on foreign economies. In the extreme of perfect capital mobility under floating rates, the effects of domestic fiscal policy changes in a small economy would be entirely on income abroad.

Two caveats to the standard analysis should be considered. The first is that despite the adverse impact caused abroad by domestic monetary expansion, it would not seem that such monetary expansion should be viewed as a "beggar-thy-neighbor" policy. I strongly agree with Marcus Fleming's recent argument that this term should be applied only to measures such as trade restrictions, which if generalized would harm all countries without bringing about any improvement in the macroeconomic state of the world economy as a whole.[35] Monetary expansion by one country under floating rates does not inhibit the ability of other countries to follow the same type of policy. In this case economic expansion of all countries can be achieved by monetary expansion, but this is not so in the case of trade restrictions. The basic point here would seem to be that, even under floating exchange rates, spillovers from one country's macroeconomic situation to another's are not entirely eliminated and hence there remains a useful role for international consultation under floating rates.

A second caveat is that it does not seem correct that under all circumstances the effects of monetary changes will be transmitted internationally with an opposite sign under floating rates. Consider the case of a tightening of monetary policy in Country A which reduces domestic demand directly by, say, $10 billion and attracts a $1 billion inflow of capital. Suppose that the country had an 0.4 marginal propensity to import. Then the initial impact would be to reduce imports by $4 billion. The $1 billion capital inflow means that, in equilibrium, the trade balance would have to turn negative by $1 billion, while at constant exchange rates imports would initially drop by $4 billion. Therefore an appreciation of the exchange rate sufficient to worsen the trade balance by $5 billion would be required. Suppose this required change were divided equally between exports and imports, with exports falling by $2.5 billion and imports increasing by $2.5 billion. Then, in the new equilibrium, imports would be lower by $1.5 billion even though the trade balance would have moved into deficit. For the foreign country, exports would have fallen by $1.5 billion even though its trade balance had improved due to an even greater drop in imports. Unless the trade-balance multiplier were 1.5 or greater, the deflationary impact effect of the fall in exports would exceed the expansionary influence of the expansion in the trade balance.

---

[35] Fleming, "Domestic Financial Policies under Fixed and Floating Exchange Rates."

On the assumption that the effects of exchange-rate changes are divided equally between exports and imports and that exchange-rate changes have no effects on capital flows, the conditions for monetary policy to change aggregate demand in the same direction in both countries under floating rates is

$k < \dfrac{/M/-/C/}{2}$ where k is the trade-balance multiplier, C is the quantity of

capital attracted by a given change in money policy, and M is the change in imports generated by the effects of the change in monetary policy on domestic income.[36] The higher are trade-balance multipliers and capital mobility and the lower are marginal propensities to import and the direct responsiveness of domestic income to changes in monetary policy, the less likely are the effects of monetary policy on aggregate demand to be in the same direction for both countries. It should also be noted that, while for changes in fiscal policy income-sensitive and interest-rate-sensitive capital flows reinforce each other, in the case of monetary policy changes they will move in opposite directions (assuming a negatively sloped IS curve). Thus where income-sensitive flows are present, the value of M would be lowered in the above equation. Still it would appear that the results of the standard analysis would generally hold, that monetary policy will affect aggregate demand in opposite directions at home and abroad under floating rates.

In addition to considering the effects of recent changes on the international coordination of macroeconomic policies, a final topic concerns the desirability of attempting to use fiscal and administrative measures directly to reduce the effective degree of capital mobility.[37]

My own view is that this would not seem likely to be a wise policy. Fiscal or administrative measures which bear low welfare costs are not likely to be very effective, and measures which stand a chance of being effective are likely to carry quite high welfare cost. Thus, I would argue that the response to high international capital mobility should be floating exchange rates, not controls. Of course, floating rates with high capital mobility may not give a nation as much macroeconomic autonomy as floating rates with low capital mobility. (In other words, the increased leverage which high capital mobility gives monetary policy under floating rates may not be valued as highly as the reduction in disturbances to domestic monetary conditions and reductions in the amount of the fluctuations of the exchange rate which might be brought about by lower capital mobility.) But I am doubtful that economic efficiency or welfare is likely to be raised by attempting to combine floating rates with controls so as to give maximum domestic financial autonomy.

---

[36] The use of a trade-balance multiplier is not fully legitimate from a theoretical standpoint but greatly simplifies the presentation of the basic idea.

[37] This has recently been suggested, for instance, by James Tobin, *The New Economics One Decade Older* (Princeton: Princeton University Press, 1974), pp. 84-92.

4. The Possible Inflationary Impact of Eurocurrency Growth

In the view of a number of writers, the Eurocurrency market has been a major contributor to the acceleration of worldwide inflation, not only by its effects on increased capital mobility, which has made it more difficult for individual countries to pursue tight money policies under fixed exchange rates, but also because of its direct effects in creating private and official international liquidity outside of the control of national or international authorities.

As is indicated in Table 3, taken from the 1974 International Monetary Fund *Annual Report,* the creation of international reserves through the Eurocurrency market has reached sizable proportions.[38] The agreement among the countries of the Group of Ten not to increase official placements in the Eurocurrency market reduced for a time the rate of reserve creation from this source. More recently, however, the large accumulation of reserves by countries not in the Group of Ten has restored the scope for sizable further increases in foreign-exchange reserves from this source. From January through June of 1974, international foreign-exchange reserves grew by $20 billion, from $117.9 billion to $137.9 billion. The U.S. official settlements deficit contributed only about $2.6 billion over this period. Thus, while direct statistics are not yet available, it would appear likely that there has been a substantial amount of international reserve creation through the Eurocurrency markets this year.

As a source of private liquidity, the Eurocurrency markets have grown to a sizable proportion of the industrial countries' combined money supplies. As is indicated in the tables in Annex C, by 1970 the Eurocurrency market had grown to more than 10 percent of the combined money supplies (*M*1) of ten major industrial countries.[39] By 1973 this proportion had risen above 15 percent. Of the quantitative importance of the Eurocurrency markets, there can be no question. There is a considerable divergence of opinion, however, concerning to what extent this unregulated expansion of credit has undermined national financial policies and generated more expansionary financial pressures than were anticipated by national authorities. Warren McClam has recently argued quite strongly that the credit expansion in the Eurocurrency market has primarily been a substitute for, rather than an addition to, other forms of credit expansion.[40]

---

[38] For a discussion of the mechanics of such reserve creation, see Helmut W. Mayer, "Some Theoretical Problems Relating to the Euro-Dollar Market," *Essays in International Finance,* no. 84 (April 1971), pp. 12-14.

[39] The United States, the United Kingdom, Germany, Japan, France, Canada, Italy, Belgium, the Netherlands, and Sweden. It should be noted, however, that a substantial overstatement of global liquidity would occur from adding these Eurocurrency figures to a total of national monetary aggregates on a one-for-one basis. See Richard J. Sweeney and Thomas D. Willett, "Eurodollars, Petrodollars, and World Liquidity and Inflation," paper presented at the Carnegie-Rochester Monetary Conference, 14-15 November 1975.

[40] Warren D. McClam, "Credit Substitution and the Eurocurrency Market," *Banca Nazionale del Lavoro Quarterly Review,* vol. 25, no. 103 (December 1972), pp. 323-363.

There are two major aspects to the substitution question. One is the ability of national authorities to offset the domestic effects of international lending and borrowing by their residents. This is the question of how much autonomy for domestic monetary policy can national authorities obtain, discussed in Section 2. The second is to what extent may national authorities be misled in their policy actions by lack of knowledge of the effects of growth in the Eurocurrency market. For instance, by concentrating on national monetary and credit aggregates, do policy makers miss some of the expansionary effects of Eurocurrency market growth, so that they are misled into following more expansionary domestic policies than if they had a full picture of total credit expansion? In other words, how does the existence of the Eurocurrency markets and international capital mobility influence the way in which domestic monetary aggregates should be measured and interpreted? In the case of $M1$ the question concerns primarily differences between total and domestically owned money stocks.[41] Consider, for instance, an example associated with the financing of the oil deficits. It is possible that the financing of such payments could tighten the domestic money market even if the Organization of Petroleum Exporting Countries (OPEC) recipients put the money right back into the banks on which payments were drawn. In this case there would be no change in the total money supply; but, if the banks were initially fully loaned up, they would have to reduce demand deposits held by domestic residents by the amount of the transfer. There would be no change in high-powered money or total money stock, but since foreign held balances would have increased, domestically held balances would have to decline. As the ability of foreign-held balances to generate activity in the home country is likely to be well below average, perhaps even zero, aggregate velocity would drop. The supply of domestic balances would have fallen relative to demand, and a tightening of the money stock would be required.

This is not likely to be a very empirically realistic example, as the bulk of oil placements outside of the Eurocurrency markets is likely to go into financial instruments other than bank deposits. But it does illustrate the possible difficulties of interpreting monetary statistics in an open economy. Where the increase in foreign-held balances results from the placement of such funds for investment purposes, these balances appear likely to lead to a drop in the aggregate velocity associated with the total money stock. On the other hand, in many instances foreign-owned balances may be used to support economic activity to as great an extent as the average of domestically owned balances. Until recently the quantitative importance of such considerations has probably been trivial for most countries. This may be changing rapidly, however.

The existence of international capital mobility is likely, in and of itself, to also influence velocity, at least as related to the narrower monetary aggregates.

---

[41] For discussion of the measurement of the domestic money stock for the United States, see Albert E. Burger and Anatol Balbach, "Measurement of the Domestic Money Stock," *Federal Reserve Bank of St. Louis Review*, vol. 54 (May 1972), pp. 10-23.

Table 3

SOURCES OF RESERVE CHANGE, 1964–73
(billions of SDRs)

Annual Changes in	1964	1965	1966	1967	1968	1969	1970	1971	1972	1973	Outstanding Totals at End of 1973
1. GOLD RESERVES											
Monetary gold	0.7	0.2	—	−1.6	−0.7	0.1	0.3	−0.1	0.2	—	
Gold transactions (acquisitions −) by IMF, BIS, and European Fund	−0.1	0.8	−0.9	0.2	0.1	0.1	−2.2	−1.0	−0.5	—	
Countries' gold reserves	0.6	1.0	−0.9	−1.4	−0.6	0.2	−2.0	−1.1	−0.3	—	35.8
2. SPECIAL DRAWING RIGHTS											
Allocation of SDRs	—	—	—	—	—	—	3.4	3.0	3.0	—	
IMF holdings of SDRs (increase −)	—	—	—	—	—	—	−0.3	−0.2	−0.1	0.1	
Countries' SDR holdings	—	—	—	—	—	—	3.1	2.8	2.8	0.1	8.8
3. RESERVE POSITIONS IN THE FUND											
Use of IMF credit	0.4	1.6	—	−0.5	1.2	0.3	−0.8	−1.9	−0.3	−0.1	
IMF gold transactions (inflow +) [a]	−0.1	−0.3	1.0	0.1	−0.4	—	1.6	0.4	0.1	—	
IMF transactions in SDRs (inflow +)	—	—	—	—	—	—	0.3	0.2	0.1	−0.1	
IMF surplus (increase −)	—	−0.1	−0.1	−0.1	−0.1	−0.1	−0.1	—	—	—	
Reserve positions in the Fund	0.2	1.2	1.0	−0.6	0.7	0.2	1.0	−1.3	—	−0.2	6.2
4. FOREIGN EXCHANGE HOLDINGS											
Official claims on United States [b]											
U.S. deficit on official settlements [c]	1.5	1.3	−0.2	3.4	−1.6	−2.7	10.7	30.5	10.2	4.9	
U.S. reserve assets (including foreign exchange) used in transactions with countries	−0.2	−1.2	−0.7	−0.1	0.9	1.3	−2.9	−3.0[d]	−0.2	−0.2	
Official claims on United States [b]	1.4	—	−1.0	3.3	−0.8	−1.5	7.8	27.4[d]	10.0	4.7[e]	55.4
Official sterling claims on United Kingdom	−0.1	−0.4	−0.1	−0.5[f]	−0.5	0.8	0.5	1.7	0.6	0.2	6.5
Official deutsche mark claims on Germany	0.1	—	0.1	—	0.1	0.1	0.8	−0.4[d]	0.1	−0.7	0.6
Official French franc claims on France	−0.1	—	0.1	—	0.1	−0.2[g]	0.2	0.2	0.3	0.2	1.3

Foreign exchange claims arising from swap credits and related assistance	0.4	− 0.3	0.7	0.9	1.2	− 0.1	− 2.2	− 0.7	—	0.5[h]	0.5[h]
Correction for effect of valuation changes on stock of reserves	—	—	—	− 0.8	—	− 0.1	—	− 4.4	—	− 8.6	—
Identified official holdings of Euro-dollars	—	− 0.1	0.5	0.2	1.6	1.0	5.6	1.1[d]	6.8	2.0[e]	17.8
Identified official holdings of other Euro-currencies									1.9	1.7	5.3
Residual sources of reserves[i]	− 0.4	0.2	− 0.2	− 1.0[f]	0.1	1.1[g]	1.8	4.7[d]	1.6	7.0[e]	14.9
Countries' holdings of foreign exchange	1.3	− 0.6	0.2	2.1	1.8	1.2	14.5	29.7	21.3	7.0	102.1
Total reserve change	2.2	1.7	0.2	0.1	2.0	1.6	16.6	30.0	23.8	6.9	152.8

[a] Variations in IMF gold investments and gold deposits are excluded because they do not give rise to net creditor positions in the Fund.

[b] Covers only claims of countries, including those denominated in the claimants' own currency.

[c] Unlike the other components of reserve growth, the deficit is already a flow concept and therefore is not expressed as a change from the previous year. The U.S. deficit is shown before allocations of SDR 0.9 billion in 1970 and SDR 0.7 billion in both 1971 and 1972.

[d] Excluding the estimated impact of the December realignment on the value of amounts outstanding at that time.

[e] Excluding the estimated impact of the February devaluation of the U.S. dollar on the amounts outstanding at that time.

[f] Excluding the estimated impact of the November devaluation of the pound sterling on the amounts outstanding at that time.

[g] Excluding the estimated impact of the August devaluation of the French franc on the amounts outstanding at that time.

[h] Comprises official claims on the European Monetary Cooperation Fund.

[i] Includes asymmetries arising from the fact that data on U.S. and U.K. currency liabilities are more comprehensive than data on official foreign-exchange holdings shown in *International Financial Statistics*.

Note: Adjusted reserves. See International Monetary Fund, *Annual Report*, 1974, footnote 1, Table 10.

Sources: *International Financial Statistics* and International Monetary Fund staff information and estimates.

Table 4
INCOME VELOCITY OF MONEY (GNP/*M*1)
FOR NINE COUNTRIES, 1948–73
(annual data)

Date	Belgium	Canada	France	Italy	Japan	Nether-lands	Sweden	United King-dom	United States
1/48	—	4.08	—	—	—	2.04	4.93	—	2.34
1/49	—	4.35	—	—	—	2.34	5.16	—	2.33
1/50	—	4.41	3.22	—	—	2.78	5.39	—	2.47
1/51	—	5.08	3.33	3.60	—	3.08	5.52	2.61	2.67
1/52	—	5.42	3.48	3.36	—	2.92	5.81	2.80	2.67
1/53	2.28	5.75	3.26	3.36	3.64	2.93	5.82	2.91	2.79
1/54	2.33	5.38	3.04	3.30	3.89	3.05	6.10	2.96	2.70
1/55	2.37	5.58	2.88	3.33	3.70	3.16	6.52	3.21	2.88
1/56	2.46	6.32	2.91	3.36	3.58	3.53	6.71	3.46	3.01
1/57	2.61	6.33	2.98	3.43	3.92	3.91	7.09	3.72	3.18
1/58	2.49	5.85	3.28	3.31	3.62	3.54	7.30	3.78	3.10
1/59	2.40	6.41	3.28	3.08	3.48	3.63	7.14	3.67	3.32
1/60	2.60	6.41	3.18	2.94	3.74	3.78	6.82	3.88	3.44
1/61	2.55	5.88	3.00	2.82	3.90	3.68	7.27	4.07	3.44
1/62	2.55	6.11	2.84	2.70	3.70	3.67	7.23	4.52	3.61
1/63	2.50	6.10	2.78	2.72	3.18	3.66	7.13	4.20	3.69
1/64	2.62	6.09	2.84	2.76	3.32	3.98	7.32	4.43	3.76
1/65	2.66	5.87	2.79	2.56	3.11	4.08	7.66	4.58	3.89
1/66	2.69	6.10	2.81	2.44	3.14	4.10	7.71	4.88	4.17
1/67	2.79	5.68	2.90	2.32	3.26	4.24	7.68	4.79	4.10
1/68	2.78	5.45	2.94	2.24	3.41	4.21	8.29	4.95	4.14
1/69	3.01	6.37	3.42	2.13	3.30	4.41	9.34	5.29	4.30
1/70	3.10	6.00	3.44	1.87	3.32	4.43	9.58	5.28	4.29
1/71	3.05	5.12	3.42	1.70	7.86	4.34	9.41	5.10	4.37
1/72	2.99	4.91	3.31	1.50	2.68	4.28	9.53	4.93	4.44
1/73	—	4.96	—	—	2.80	—	—	5.35	4.62

Note: Income velocities of money are represented here by the ratio of GNP to *M*1.
Source: All data, unless otherwise noted, is from *International Financial Statistics*.

Capital mobility may be viewed as increasing the ease with which funds may be borrowed. This in turn may be expected to reduce the demand for owned balances—in other words, to increase velocity. This effect should be related primarily to changed options for borrowing, and its strength need not be closely related to the rate of growth of the Eurocurrency markets.

Table 5

INCOME VELOCITIES OF MONEY PLUS QUASI-MONEY [GNP/$M1$ + QUASI-MONEY] FOR TEN COUNTRIES, 1948–73

(annual data)

Date	Belgium	Canada	France	Germany	Italy	Japan	Netherlands	Sweden	United Kingdom	United States
1/48	—	2.05	—	—	—	—	1.83	2.31	—	1.78
1/49	—	2.11	—	—	—	—	2.12	2.23	—	1.77
1/50	—	2.21	3.16	4.39	—	—	2.06	2.31	1.80	1.89
1/51	—	2.53	3.26	4.17	—	—	2.20	2.44	1.89	2.06
1/52	—	2.69	3.40	3.71	—	—	2.09	2.66	1.95	2.05
1/53	0.95	2.79	3.17	3.33	2.29	1.79	2.10	2.45	1.98	2.11
1/54	0.95	2.58	2.94	3.32	2.18	1.72	2.15	2.47	2.18	2.02
1/55	0.95	2.66	2.79	3.28	2.15	1.60	2.20	2.64	2.33	2.15
1/56	0.95	2.89	2.81	3.00	2.09	1.48	2.39	2.74	2.39	2.22
1/57	0.95	2.94	2.83	2.78	2.05	1.46	2.53	2.74	2.40	2.27
1/58	0.95	2.72	3.06	2.58	1.92	1.27	2.24	2.62	2.39	2.17
1/59	0.94	2.91	3.01	2.81	1.77	1.18	2.16	2.46	2.48	2.30
1/60	0.93	2.91	2.85	2.73	1.68	1.50	2.16	2.59	2.57	2.32
1/61	0.92	2.76	2.65	2.66	1.61	1.56	2.09	2.86	2.76	2.25
1/62	0.92	2.87	2.49	2.53	1.54	1.44	2.05	2.80	2.69	2.24
1/63	0.92	2.74	2.45	2.46	1.55	1.31	2.00	2.78	2.79	2.20
1/64	0.92	2.72	2.48	2.39	1.56	1.34	2.13	2.84	2.78	2.18
1/65	0.91	2.72	2.40	2.29	1.45	1.26	2.17	2.98	2.86	2.16
1/66	0.91	2.81	2.36	2.02	1.37	1.25	2.20	3.02	2.72	2.25
1/67	0.89	2.61	2.25	1.90	1.32	1.28	2.14	2.90	2.74	2.15
1/68	0.89	2.50	2.21	1.90	1.27	1.32	2.07	2.73	2.84	2.13
1/69	0.88	2.59	2.37	1.94	1.25	1.30	2.10	2.90	2.84	2.31
1/70	0.88	2.51	2.30	1.86	1.22	1.31	2.12	3.10	2.79	2.15
1/71	0.87	2.48	2.16	1.77	1.13	1.18	2.09	3.00	2.40	2.08
1/72	0.86	2.43	2.03	7.09	1.01	1.08	2.07	2.90	2.15	2.04
1/73	—	2.38	—	—	—	1.15	—	—	—	2.03

Note: Income velocities of money plus quasi-money are a country's GNP divided by that country's $M1$ plus its quasi-money.

Table 6
AGGREGATE INDICES OF VELOCITY (*M*1),[a] 1948–73
(annual data)

Date	World	United States	World less United States	World plus Eurodollars
1/48	—	2.34	—	—
1/49	—	2.33	—	—
1/50	—	2.47	—	—
1/51	—	2.67	—	—
1/52	—	2.67	—	—
1/53	3.07	2.79	3.70	—
1/54	3.00	2.70	3.63	—
1/55	3.15	2.88	3.70	—
1/56	3.29	3.01	3.84	—
1/57	3.47	3.18	4.03	—
1/58	3.42	3.10	4.04	—
1/59	3.55	3.32	3.95	—
1/60	3.67	3.44	4.07	—
1/61	3.66	3.44	4.01	—
1/62	3.76	3.61	3.97	—
1/63	3.73	3.69	3.78	—
1/64	3.82	3.76	3.89	3.71
1/65	3.85	3.89	3.81	3.72
1/66	4.02	4.17	3.86	3.86
1/67	3.94	4.10	3.76	3.76
1/68	3.97	4.14	3.79	3.74
1/69	4.15	4.30	3.99	3.76
1/70	4.09	4.29	3.90	3.64
1/71	3.96	4.37	3.63	3.59
1/72	3.70	4.44	3.18	3.23
1/73	—	4.62	—	—

Note: For discussion of the construction of the aggregate money supply series, see Annex C.

The appropriate response to these possible problems for monetary management would be, at least in part, to obtain better statistical measures of the growth of monetary aggregates and to obtain the desired degree of financial tightness by adjusting the rate of growth of domestic monetary expansion to compensate for growth in international components and changes in velocity induced by international developments.

We might expect that if capital mobility and credit expansion in the Euro-currency market have had a major impact in undermining domestic monetary

Table 7

AGGREGATE INDICES OF VELOCITY, MONEY ($M1$)
PLUS QUASI-MONEY, 1948–73
(annual data)

Date	World	United States	World less United States	World plus Eurodollars
1/48	—	1.78	—	—
1/49	—	1.77	—	—
1/50	—	1.89	—	—
1/51	—	2.06	—	—
1/52	—	2.05	—	—
1/53	2.22	2.11	2.45	—
1/54	2.14	2.02	2.36	—
1/55	2.24	2.15	2.39	—
1/56	2.31	2.22	2.45	—
1/57	2.32	2.27	2.40	—
1/58	2.22	2.17	2.30	—
1/59	2.26	2.30	2.21	—
1/60	2.32	2.32	2.32	—
1/61	2.26	2.35	2.27	—
1/62	2.23	2.24	2.21	—
1/63	2.16	2.20	2.11	—
1/64	2.15	2.18	2.12	2.12
1/65	2.10	2.16	2.04	2.06
1/66	2.13	2.25	2.00	2.08
1/67	2.02	2.15	1.89	1.97
1/68	1.99	2.13	1.84	1.93
1/69	2.07	2.31	1.85	1.97
1/70	1.99	2.15	1.84	1.87
1/71	1.87	2.08	1.72	1.77
1/72	1.71	2.04	1.43	1.61
1/73	—	2.03	—	—

policies through these mechanisms, then the income velocities of the national monetary aggregates should have risen. As is shown in Tables 4 through 7, this has not been the case. Of course, the anticipated increase in velocity is a *ceteris paribus* proposition, and we should attempt to control for the major factors which may have influenced velocity. (We have a project under way on this.) The absence of an observed increase in velocity does, however, cast doubt on the proposition that the expansion of the Eurocurrency markets has had a major impact on world economic activity over and above any influence which it may have had on the growth of national monetary aggregates and foreign-exchange reserves.

ANNEXES

A: The Effect of Interest-Rate Changes on Exchange Rates during the Current Float

Ira J. Kaylin, Charles Pigott, Richard J. Sweeney, and *Thomas D. Willett*

An initial change in the uncovered short-term interest differential between two countries will lead to induced changes in spot and forward exchange rates, to changes in the flow of short-term capital, and finally to changes in home and foreign country interest rates. A natural question to ask is, in which markets are the induced changes relatively large and in which markets are they relatively small? Equivalently we can ask, what is the final effect of a change in uncovered differentials upon the covered differential and how is this divided between changes in current and forward exchange rates and changes in interest rates?

Popular analysis suggests a *systematic* relationship between interest-rate changes and movements in the spot rate. For example, depreciation of a country's currency is often attributed to a fall in interest rates relative to others' rates. However, our investigation of the current float has yielded little evidence of such a relationship that is either strong or systematic.

Not only do interest-rate changes explain only a small portion of the variance of exchange rates, but many of the estimated coefficients are of the wrong sign. Since the purpose of the estimation was not to test the hypothesized sign of its coefficients, but rather to get a handle on the magnitude of the effects, these poor results suggest that the simple estimates of the impact of interest-rate changes on spot rates are biased downwards, requiring a fuller estimation system to eliminate simultaneous equation bias. But the estimation also casts doubt upon assertions that interest-rate changes have been a dominant determinant of exchange-rate behavior under the current float.

The plan of this Annex is as follows. Section 1 reports some results of our statistical studies regarding spot exchange rates and interest rates. Included in this discussion are some preliminary results on the relation between trade-weighted

This is an interim report on some aspects of OASIA Research's ongoing investigation of foreign exchange markets.

exchange rates and interest rates. Section 2 shows how these results are compatible with other currently available evidence on spot and forward exchange markets.

1. Empirical Relationship between Spot Exchange Rates and Interest Rates.

The analysis of the introduction is normally applied to interest differentials and exchange rates for a pair of countries. In view of the increased interest in composite measures of exchange rates, that is, in trade-weighted exchange rates, the relation between these and interest rates was also examined. This work should, however, be regarded as preliminary, and future research in this area is planned.

Dollar exchange rates and interest rates. To examine the relationship between interest-rate differentials and the behavior of spot exchange rates, the following regressions were run:

(a) the *percent change* in the spot rate as a function of (1) the change in the interest differential and (2) the change in the interest differential lagged one and two weeks;

(b) the *absolute* change in the spot rate as a function of (1) the change in the interest differential and (2) the change in the interest differential lagged one and two weeks; and

(c) the *level* of the spot rate as a function of (1) the interest differential and (2) the interest differential lagged one and two weeks.

The spot rates tested are those of the United Kingdom, Germany, Switzerland, and Canada, expressed as dollars per unit of foreign currency. The interest differentials were calculated by subtracting the relevant three-month interest rate of each of the above countries from the U.S. ninety-day Treasury bill yield.[1] The data are weekly from February 1973 through May 1974.

A priori reasoning suggests that a *ceteris paribus* increase in, for example, the difference between the U.S. and the German interest rate should cause a *decrease* in the number of U.S. dollars that can be purchased with one D-mark. Whether monetary control over the interest differential gives strong leverage over the spot exchange rate depends on the magnitude of the appreciation of the mark due to, say, a 100 basis point increase in the differential. All of the regressions suggest that an increase in the interest-rate differential has a very minor effect on the exchange rate. Of the fifty-two regressions reported in Table A-1, twenty-one coefficients were *negative* and thirty-one positive. The negative coefficients had

---

[1] The assets for the United States, the United Kingdom, and Canada are 90-day Treasury bills; for Germany the interbank loan rate was used, while for Switzerland the deposit rate was used.

t-statistics greater than 2.00 in five cases, and the positive coefficients had *t*-statistics over 2.00 in seven cases.[2] This is particularly interesting in that a negative sign would have been theoretically expected.

These estimated coefficients measure the response of the spot rate to a 100 basis point change in the interest-rate differential. Except where the equation used the percent change in the spot rate as the dependent variable, the estimated coefficient of the interest-rate differential was divided by the spot rate, in order to show the percentage change in the spot rate due to a 100 basis point increase in the differential. Such a relatively major increase in the differential is seen to have only a very minor impact on spot rates, and the sign of the estimated impact varies with the form of the equation used. For example, as Table A-2 shows, if the interest-rate differential between the United States and Germany increases by 100 basis points, the estimated impact on the exchange rate is a depreciation (as expected) of approximately 0.09 percent in three cases, but *appreciations* of 0.02 percent and 2.1 percent in the other two cases. Given the relatively poor $\bar{R}^2$ and *t* statistics found in Table A-1, it is difficult to establish a strong systematic relationship between spot exchange rates and interest-rate differentials from these results.

Because the Treasury bill market is rather special in some countries, in particular Canada, it is interesting to compare these results with others using different, and perhaps more comparable, assets. For this purpose, the simple correlation coefficient of weekly changes in spot rates and interest differentials was calculated using the three-month Eurodollar deposit rate for the United States, the Finance Company yield for Canada, the interbank rates for the United Kingdom and Germany, and the deposit rate for Switzerland.[3] In this case the differential was calculated as the foreign minus the U.S. yield. The computations were made for two periods, 8 December 1972 through 18 April 1975 and 1 June 1973 through 18 April 1975; the latter period was examined in order to exclude the often chaotic interval following the adoption of generalized floating at the beginning of 1973.

As the results in Table A-3 indicate, in none of the cases was the correlation of changes in interest differentials and exchange rates significant at the 5 percent level; indeed, for the United Kingdom the correlation was negative (the opposite of that suggested by the simple theory) as it was for Switzerland, and for Germany it was virtually zero. As can be seen from the table, the results are not substantially altered by excluding the first five months of 1973.

---

[2] Notice that most of the significant coefficients occur for the regressions using levels of exchange and interest rates; thus the estimated standard errors are likely to be biased down since the Durbin-Watson figure indicates substantial serial correlation in the disturbances.

[3] These assets are used to calculate interest differentials by the Board of Governors of the Federal Reserve System for its H.13 series, "Selected Interest and Exchange Rates. . . ." Notice that although the assets used for Switzerland and Germany are the same as before, the interest differentials are altered, due to the change in U.S. assets used.

Table A-1

REGRESSION RESULTS

Country	Lag	(1) Interest Differential	(2) Constant	(3) Coefficient of (1)	(4) t of Constan
		Part A: The percent change of the spot rate as a function (			
Switzerland	—	US-SWDR	.0010	.0001	.8742
Germany	—	US-GIBLR	.001	−.0008	.9173
Canada	—	US-CTB	−6.3759E-05	.001 [a]	−.4547
United Kingdom	—	US-UKTB	−.02167	−.02075	−1.1074
		Part B: The change in the spot rate as a function (			
Switzerland	—	US-SWDR	.0335	.0048	.8696
Germany	—	US-GIBLR	.0413	−.0281	.8849
Canada	—	US-CTB	−.0065	.1000 [a]	−.4583
United Kingdom	—	US-UKTB	−.06973	.13100	−.6995
		Part C: The spot rate as a function of the interest differenti			
Switzerland	—	US-SWDR	32.057	−2.045E-08	143.67
Germany	—	US-GIBLR	37.402	−.32565	40.597
Canada	—	US-CTB	100.114	4.722E-07	11173.9
United Kingdom	—	US-UKTB	.0411	5.77310E-11	167.38
		Part D: Change in spot rate lagged one and two weeks as			
Switzerland	−1	US-SWDR	.03331	−.07625	.85697
	−2	US-SWDR	.03571	.01259	.89198
Germany	−1	US-GIBLR	.08653	−.00843	.76673
	−2	US-GIBLR	.04160	.01571	.85766
Canada	−1	US-CTB	−.0016	.0031	−.41058
	−2	US-CTB	.00006	.00017	−.40112
United Kingdom	−1	US-UKTB	−.07269	.04581	−.69959
	−2	US-UKTB	−.08331	−.11468	−.81992
		Part E: The spot rate lagged one and two weeks as			
Switzerland	−1	US-SWDR	32.106	−2.976E-08	144.6
	−2	US-SWDR	32.1489	−3.7938E-08	144.75
Germany	−1	US-GIBLR	37.3428	−.35171	41.0836
	−2	US-GIBLR	37.4352	−.34623	40.6123
Canada	−1	US-CTB	100.094	4.7599E-07	1183.42
	−2	US-CTB	100.0809	4.7855E-07	1175.7272
United Kingdom	−1	US-UKTB	.0041	5.805E-11	164.51
	−2	US-UKTB	.00411	5.7828E-11	40.597

[a] Significant at the 5 percent level.

(5) t of (1)	(6) Standard Error of Constant	(7) Standard Error of Coefficient of (1)	(8) R^2	(9) Adjusted R^2	(10) D.W.	(11) Standard Error of Estimate
ne change in the interest-rate differential						
.0629	.001	.0001	.0001	−.0199	1.9756	.0082
−.4558	.0011	.0018	.0053	−.0202	2.0522	.0072
2.33	.001	.004	.0986	.0806	2.0061	.001
−.57466	.01957	.03612	.00656	−.01331	1.99994	.13923
ne change in the interest-rate differential						
.0694	.0386	.0698	.0001	−.2199	1.9808	.2781
−3.772	.0466	.0744	.0036	−.0219	2.0525	.2985
2.3301	.0141	.0429	.0979	.0799	2.0065	.1065
.70783	.09967	.18508	.00992	.00988	1.78065	.71205
−.06541	.223	3.27E-07	.0008	−.01915	.19316	1.6244
−2.053	.9213	.1586	.095	.0727	.265	2.445
3.95	.08528	1.195-07	.2308	.21607	.43911	.62086
1.6777	.00002	3.44E-11	.05135	.03311	.1579	.00018
unction of the interest-rate differential						
−1.09409	—	—	.02385	.00393	2.0999	.27757
.17693	—	—	.00065	.02017	1.99461	.28309
−.11168	—	—	.00033	.02598	2.01857	.30131
.20623	—	—	.00115	−.02585	2.00926	.30203
.6809	—	—	.00919	−.01063	2.2657	.00106
.36724	—	—	.00274	−.01761	2.19885	.00108
.24052	—	—	.0012	−.01960	1.73094	.72941
−.61199	—	—	.00759	−.01267	1.78261	.71998
unction of the interest-rate differential						
−.09657	—	—	.00018	−.01942	.20224	1.60055
−.1292	—	—	.00031	−.01969	.17789	1.58605
−2.26565	—	—	.11631	.09365	.35469	2.37478
−2.2203	—	—	.11483	.09154	.39871	2.35245
4.05289	—	—	.24361	.23878	.46182	.60992
4.08576	—	—	.25030	.23531	.47494	.60816
1.67427	—	—	.0521	.03351	.14613	.00018
−2.0531	—	—	.0953	.07272	.26558	2.445

227

Table A-2
COMPARISON OF COEFFICIENTS

Item	United States	Switzer-land	t	Germany	t	Canada	t	United Kingdom	t
Part A: Percent response of the spot rate to a 1 percent change in the interest-rate differential									
Percent change in spot rate	—	+.01	.0629	−.08	−4.558	+.1	2.33	−2.0	−.57466
Absolute change in spot rate	—	.02	.0694	−.08	−3.772	.09	2.33	.05	.7078
Spot rate	—	a	−.065	−.09	−2.053	a	3.95	a	1.677
Absolute change in spot rate, lagged	—	.2	b	.02	—	.03	—	.02	—
Spot rate, lagged	—	a	—	2.1	—	a	—	a	—
Part B: Percent response of effective exchange rate to a 1 percent change in the interest-rate differential									
Effective exchange rate	−2.2	—	−5.399	1.44	3.279	.40	1.692	2.14	−9.874
Absolute change in effective exchange rate	.58	—	1.039	.52	1.73	1.31	4.01	−.38	−2.748
Effective exchange rate, lagged	−4.0119	—	b	2.4	—	.37	—	−2.5	—

+ appreciation.
− depreciation.
a Less than .001 percent.
b Program did not compute t statistic for sum of lag coefficients.

Table A-3

CORRELATION COEFFICIENTS OF WEEKLY CHANGES IN
INTEREST DIFFERENTIALS AND EXCHANGE RATES

	8 Dec. 1972– 18 Apr. 1975	1 June 1973– 18 Apr. 1975
Canada	0.13	0.17
Germany	0.03	0.04
United Kingdom	− 0.13	− 0.17
Switzerland	− 0.17	0.07

Effective exchange rates and interest rates.[4] In order to measure the relationship between a country's overall exchange-rate position, as represented by the effective exchange rate and its own interest rate, a series of regressions were run:

(a) the effective exchange as a function of (1) the interest rate and (2) the interest rate lagged one or two periods; and

(b) the change of the effective exchange rate as a function of the change in interest rates.

Canada, Germany, the United Kingdom and the United States were examined monthly from December 1973 to September 1974. Except for the United States, which was measured against the Group of Ten, each effective exchange rate was calculated vis-à-vis the Organization for Economic Cooperation and Development (OECD). Table A-4 lists the results.

The coefficient of the interest rate measures the response of the effective exchange rate to a 100-basis-point increase in the interest rate. Since the effective exchange rate is already expressed as a percent deviation from a base year value of 100, the coefficient can be interpreted as the percent response. When regressing the effective exchange rate of each currency on its respective interest rate, we find the coefficient significant in three of the four cases, but in two of the significant cases the signs were wrong. In response to a 100-basis-point increase in the interest rate, Germany shows a 1.4 percent appreciation, the United Kingdom a 2.14 percent depreciation and the United States a 2.2 percent depreciation of its currency. Canada showed a 0.4 percent appreciation but this was statistically insignificant. A negative coefficient could reflect the monetary authority's attempt to bolster a sagging exchange rate by raising interest rates (or raising rates to curb domestic inflation to accomplish the same goal). If, for instance, the pound remained weak, further attempts at exchange-rate strengthening would lead to further interest-rate increases, thus causing a significant negative relationship.

---

[4] The *effective exchange rate* refers to the trade-weighted rate for a given country; calculations of foreign interest-rate aggregates are planned in the future, from which appropriate differentials could be compared.

Table A-4

REGRESSION OF EFFECTIVE EXCHANGE RATE ON INTEREST RATE

Spot Rate of:	Constant	Coefficient of Interest	t of Constant	Standard Error of Constant	t of Interest	Standard Error of Interest	Adjusted R^2	D.W.	Standard Error of Estimate
Part A: Level of effective exchange rate on level of interest rate									
Canada	2.06432	0.396175	1.43441	1.43914	1.69255	0.234069	0.0316	0.2550	1.78295
Germany	-0.794730E-01	1.43714	-0.164292E-01	4.83732	3.27945	0.438227	0.3172	0.2983	4.81626
United Kingdom	5.47035	-2.13993	2.53645	2.15670	-9.87433	0.216710	0.8213	1.0411	2.11817
United States	-0.291742	-2.19743	-0.131827	2.21307	-5.39964	0.406959	0.4841	0.3843	3.39359
Part B: Change of level of exchange rate on change in interest rate									
Canada	-0.260321	1.31773	-0.999473	0.260457	4.01022	0.328593	0.4180	1.1235	1.06591
Germany	0.574465	0.517975	1.11532	0.515066	1.73424	0.298676	0.0873	1.8636	2.34691
United Kingdom	-0.434971	-0.381650	-0.855020	0.508726	-2.74859	0.320765	0.2379	2.6805	2.26873
United States	-0.518813	0.580326	-1.84308	0.281492	1.03967	0.558182	0.0027	1.5163	1.53636
Part C: Level of effective exchange rate on level of interest rate with one period lag									
Canada	3.15714	0.226692	2.65049	1.19115	1.11788	0.202787	0.0117	0.2316	1.84948
Germany	2.22973	1.27127	0.753553	2.95903	4.67017	0.272211	0.4977	0.4488	4.13070
United Kingdom	-1.53607	-1.49551	-0.892101	1.72186	-8.40874	0.177851	0.7635	1.5578	2.41091
United States	-1.60809	-2.03820	-0.911996	1.76327	-6.09741	0.334273	0.5467	0.6362	3.18126
Part D: Level of effective exchange rate on level of interest rate with two period lag									
Canada	3.69216	0.140341	3.51991	1.04394	0.744337	0.188545	-0.0217	0.2364	1.88051
Germany	4.01015	1.14589	1.84001	2.17942	5.62159	0.203835	0.5930	0.6858	3.71819
United Kingdom	-7.02926	-1.00547	-4.49478	1.56357	-5.87756	0.171069	0.6150	1.0375	3.10901
United States	-2.39594	-1.97371	-1.66993	1.43476	-7.02745	0.280058	0.6173	0.4961	2.92308

With traditionally strong currencies this would be less likely to occur, and indeed Germany and Canada showed a positive relationship.

When a change in the level of the effective exchange rate was run as a function of a change in the interest rate, the coefficient of Germany, the United Kingdom, and the United States all decreased to less than 0.6 percent with the German and U.S. results becoming insignificant. Only the Canadian result improved. In this case Canada had a significant coefficient of 1.3 percent.

Running the regression with lags of one and two months did not substantially alter the previously obtained results.

2. Relationship with Results Obtained by Other Researchers.

The results presented above suggest that changes in uncovered interest-rate differentials have little, if any, effect upon the spot rate of foreign exchange. This result might be expected if, for example, expectations as to the appropriate spot rate are very inelastic and strongly held, and the supply of speculative funds is very large at this rate, while expectations of the appropriate future rates are weakly held and the supply of speculative funds in the forward market is relatively small. A quick review of some of the currently available evidence on these matters is also suggestive (although not conclusive).

Indeed, it is interesting to note that some other attempts to estimate directly the relation between changes in the uncovered interest differential and the spot rate have yielded similarly inconclusive results. For example, Paul Wonnacott compared month-to-month changes in the uncovered differential between Canada and the United States with month-to-month changes in the spot rate for the period of October 1950 to December 1958 and found that the two were positively correlated for only fifty-eight of the ninety-six periods examined.[5] Similar, but more extensive comparisons were made by Oscar Morgenstern for the prewar (World War I) and intrawar (1925–31) periods for six pairs of countries with similarly inconclusive results.[6]

If spot exchange rates are largely unaffected by changes in the uncovered differential, adjustments are confined to forward or money markets. Some recent studies of the Canadian-American forward exchange market for the floating rate period of the 1950s indicate that the covered differential does not change much in response to changes in uncovered interest differentials. In particular, separate single equation studies by Stoll, by Kesselman, and by Tower and Pedersson indicate that the forward premium adjusts by about 80 to 100 percent of the

---

[5] Paul Wonnacott, *The Canadian Dollar, 1948-1958* (Toronto: University of Toronto Press, 1961), pp. 180-183. The result is consistent, at the 5 percent level, with the hypothesis that interest-rate and exchange-rate changes are independently distributed.

[6] Oscar Morgenstern, *International Financial Transactions and Business Cycles* (Princeton: Princeton University Press, 1959). Generally the prewar period shows the predicted relation while the intrawar period does not. The results quoted here are reported in Wonnacott, *The Canadian Dollar*, pp. 180-183.

change in the uncovered differential.[7] The studies of Stoll and Kesselman are typical: each estimated a relation of the form,

$$Ft = a1Se + a2F^*t, \tag{1}$$

where Ft is the current forward rate, Se is the spot rate expected at the time of maturity of the forward contract, and F^*t is the parity forward rate (that rate which makes the covered differential equal to zero). The expected future spot rate is estimated as a function of current and past actual spot rates.[8] Changes in Se and F^*t imply respectively shifts in the speculative supply schedule of forward exchange and in the arbitrage demand schedule for forward cover. Hence a large estimated value for $a2$ relative to $a1$ implies that changes in the parity forward rate, that is, shifts in the arbitrage schedule, dominate shifts in the speculative supply schedule in determining forward rates. When changes in expected spot rates are not extremely large relative to changes in the parity rate, the actual forward rate will move in line with changes in the parity rate; the results of the studies noted indicate in fact that $a2$ is rather close to, and often insignificantly different from, unity.[9]

Putting these two tentative pieces of evidence together, one is tempted to conclude that the principal impact of a change in the uncovered interest differential will be in the forward market. However, it is possible that induced capital flows will partially reverse the initial change in interest rates. A comprehensive evaluation of the different effects caused by a change in uncovered differentials should be made within the context of a simultaneous equation model that, at the least, includes separate relations determining forward and spot exchange rates and the uncovered interest differential. A comprehensive study of a similar nature for the Canadian floating rate period was done by Caves and Reuber, and it is interesting to examine the effects implied by their results.[10] They estimated relations of the form:

$$St = a1STK + e1E1, \tag{2a}$$
$$STK = b1DS + b2CFC + b3St + e2E2, \tag{2b}$$
$$DS = c1CFC + e3E3, \tag{2c}$$
$$CFC = d1DS + e4E4, \tag{2d}$$

---

[7] Hans Stoll, "An Empirical Study of the Foreign Exchange Market under Fixed and Flexible Exchange Rate Systems," *Canadian Journal of Economics*, vol. 1 (February 1968), pp. 55-78; Jonathan Kesselman, "The Role of Speculation in Forward-Rate Determination: The Canadian Flexible Dollar, 1953-1960," *Canadian Journal of Economics*, vol. 4 (August 1971), pp. 279-298; G. Pedersson and E. Tower, "On the Long and Short Run Relationship between the Forward Rate and Interest Parity," presented at the meetings of the Canadian Economics Association, Quebec, June 1976.

[8] Kesselman also attempts to parameterize expectations by "real world" variables such as levels of exports and imports.

[9] These studies take the spot rate as exogenous, which will lead to inconsistent parameter estimates if the forward rate itself influences the spot rate, for example, by affecting capital flows.

[10] Richard E. Caves and Grant L. Reuber, *Capital Transfers and Economic Policy: Canada, 1951-1962* (Cambridge, Mass.: Harvard University Press, 1971).

where *DS* is the uncovered interest differential in favor of Canada (in percent), *CFC* is the differential between spot and forward prices of Canadian dollars expressed as a percentage of the former, *St* is the spot rate, *STK* is short-term capital flows into Canada, and *Ei* is a vector of predetermined variables assumed to be unchanged in the following conceptual experiment.

To compute the effect of an initial change in the uncovered differential in Canada's favor, imagine that preferences for Canadian versus American securities change so that the schedule (2c) is shifted up by a factor *B*:

$$DS = c1CFC + e3E3 + B. \tag{2c$'$}$$

Substituting for *STK* in relation (2a) and solving for *DS* and *CFC* in terms of *B*, *E2*, and *E3*, we obtain the following expression for $d(St)/d(B)$:

$$d(St) = [a1/(1-a1b3)][b1d(DS)/dB+b2d(CFC)/dB]d(B), \tag{3a}$$
$$d(DS)/d(B) = 1/(1-c1d1); d(CFC)/d(B) = d1/(1-c1d1). \tag{3b}$$

Typical values found by Caves-Reuber for the parameters are: [11]

$$a1 = .000034; b1 = 683.1; b2 = -292.0; b3 = 35.57$$
$$c1 = .4785; d1 = 1.271. \tag{4}$$

These values imply that $d(St) = 0.027d(B)$, that is, that a rise of 1 percent (100 basis points) in the uncovered differential in favor of Canada led to an appreciation of the Canadian dollar of 2.7 cents, quite a large effect compared to Section 1's general results. These results, which tend to support the conclusion that Section 1's estimates were biased downward through neglecting the simultaneous equation problem, need to be taken with a grain of salt in view of some of the other implications of these estimates. For example, since the response of the uncovered differential to a change in the cost of forward cover (*c1*) is substantially smaller than the response of the latter to the former (*d1*), it also follows from these estimates that an initial rise in the uncovered yield in favor of Canada leads eventually to a *decline* in the covered differential; short-term capital still flows into Canada since the coefficient of *STK* on *DS* is substantially larger in absolute value than its coefficient on *CFC*.

However, the anomaly is eliminated by substituting for (2c) the relation (2″):

$$DS = C1\, STK + e3E3. \tag{2$''$}$$

Taking Caves's estimate for *c1*, -0.000226, which is not significantly different from zero at a 5 percent confidence level, the estimate of $d(RS)/d(B)$ is now approximately 0.09 cents.[12]

---

[11] See Caves-Reuber equations 2.11 and 3.27 through 3.29; the latter three were estimated by two-stage least squares.

[12] Results for other versions of the above relations were quite similar. The standard error of the estimate of $d(St)/d(B)$ involved the covariances of the parameters of relations 2, which are not known. However, *a1*, *c1*, and *d1* were not significant at the 5 percent level. Other,

Note that consideration of this rather self-contained model offers a possible reconciliation of the poor statistical relationships reported in Section 1 with the popular use of interest-rate changes to explain spot rate movements. The experiment just reported required an initial parametric shift in a schedule. It may be that for shifts in one schedule there is a stable, significant, and powerful relationship between changes in the differential and the spot rate, while for other schedule shifts there is also a good relationship but with the opposite sign. If our sample period then includes a random mixture of such shifts, it is to be expected that the statistical results would be poor. Popular analysis, then, may concentrate on the episodes where the shifts give the expected relationship, using other factors to explain different episodes.

B: Capital Mobility and the Efficacy of Fiscal Policy under Alternative Exchange-Rate Systems

Victoria S. Farrell

There are several means of determining whether or not a move from fixed to floating exchange rates tends to increase the efficacy of fiscal policy and also to decrease transmission of disturbances in the domestic *IS* curve to the rest of the world economy. The simplest kind of evidence is the historical experience of countries under fixed rate regimes. Disturbances in domestic output may be correlated with disturbances in the excess supply of foreign exchange; a positive correlation suggests that boom periods would be associated with an appreciation of the domestic currency, and a negative correlation suggests that boom periods would be associated with currency depreciation. The simplest kind of evidence, however, may be the most complicated to interpret. Historical data most probably contain instances of shocks to domestic *LM* curves as well as instances of shocks to *IS* curves.

Another test which abstracts from monetary disturbances is to simulate the effects of an increase in autonomous expenditures on income and interest-rate variables using domestic economy models, and then to introduce these results into balance-of-payments models to determine whether or not current-account deteriora-

---

generally lower, estimates of $a1$ are presented elsewhere in Caves. This would tend to change the estimate or $d(RS)/d(B)$ slightly.

It should also be noted that the magnitude of $d(RS)/d(B)$ is largely determined by the coefficient $a1$. The estimates generated here serve as approximate upper and lower bounds on $d(RS)/d(B)$ obtained from using alternative parameter estimates presented by Caves-Reuber, since calculations using alternative parameter estimates presented by them do not significantly alter these estimates.

234

tion is offset by a net surplus to the capital account. A few preliminary tests of this nature based on the DRI and Wharton models are discussed below for the United States. Measuring impacts on short-term rates alone, the DRI model suggests an improvement on capital account on the order of $1 billion greater than that suggested by the Wharton model. A greater difference, however, arises among the balance-of-payments models. For example, a Miller-Whitman formulation indicates a capital-account surplus within the period of a year on the order of $4 billion greater than that indicated by a Branson formulation.[1]

A superior test is simulation of a domestic economy model linked with a foreign sector that has been estimated during a floating rate period. Richard Caves and Grant Reuber have reported such an experiment for Canada. It suggests that capital mobility tends to reduce the effectiveness of fiscal policy in the short run but actually improves it over performance under a fixed rate in the long run.[2]

Edward Tower and Mark Courtney have examined annual data for fourteen developed countries during the period 1956 through 1970 to determine the effects of a move from fixed to flexible rates on the stability of economic activity.[3] They have expanded upon a model by Jerome Stein, who argued that fluctuations in output and fluctuations in the excess supply of foreign exchange under fixed rates should be positively correlated to foster stability in a less than full-employment economy.[4] Tower's and Courtney's model compares the variance of output under fixed rates to what the variance of output would have been during the same period if rates had been floating. They postulate that the deviation of output under flexible rates is identical to the deviation under fixed rates plus the change in output arising from a change in the balance-of-payments position. Unfortunately, their multiplier formulation assumes that the imposition of floating rates has no impact on a country's exports.

Tower and Courtney report the correlation between unanticipated excess supply of foreign exchange and unintended GNP under fixed rates for all fourteen countries, where unanticipated values are defined as deviations from trend. The correlation is unambiguously positive for four countries including the United States and Germany, and it is unambiguously negative for six countries including Italy and Japan.

---

[1] Norman C. Miller and Marina v. N. Whitman, "A Mean-Variance Analysis of United States Long-Term Portfolio Foreign Investments," *Quarterly Journal of Economics*, vol. 34 (May 1970), pp. 175-196; William H. Branson, *Financial Capital Flows in the U.S. Balance of Payments* (Amsterdam: North-Holland Publishing Company, 1968).

[2] Richard E. Caves and Grant L. Reuber, "International Capital Markets and Canadian Economic Policy under Flexible and Fixed Exchange Rates: 1951-1970," *Canadian-United States Financial Relationships* (Federal Reserve Bank of Boston, September 1971).

[3] Edward Tower and Mark M. Courtney, "Exchange Rate Flexibility and Macro-Economic Stability," *Review of Economics and Statistics*, vol. 56 (May 1974), pp. 215-224.

[4] Jerome L. Stein and Edward Tower, "Short-Run Stability of the Foreign Exchange Market," *Review of Economics and Statistics*, vol. 49 (May 1967), pp. 173-185.

Superficially, the simple correlation results suggest that a move to flexible rates would tend to increase internal stability, to decrease the efficacy of fiscal policy, and to transmit domestic disturbances to the rest of the world economy for countries such as the United States. However, deviations from trend in the data examined by Tower and Courtney may be the result of disturbances to domestic *LM* curves as well as to *IS* curves. Two countries, Belgium and Ireland, exhibit unambiguously positive correlations between unintended output and unanticipated excess supply of foreign exchange attributable to payments on goods and services alone; for Belgium, the overall correlation is unambiguously positive, but for Ireland it is unambiguously negative. In the case of Ireland, one might suspect that monetary policy was deliberately expansionary in a somewhat irregular pattern, creating substantial short-term capital outflows from time to time.

Five countries with unambiguously negative overall correlations exhibit unambiguously negative correlations on current account alone. This may be evidence that capital flows for these countries were not particularly interest sensitive. However, it may also be evidence of episodic monetary expansion. Countries exhibiting positive overall correlations may have been pursuing contractionary counter-cyclical monetary policies which can affect interest rates and output with substantially different time lags. In other words, the data may exhibit instances of improper assignment of government policies to internal and external balance goals.

One means of roughly gauging the effect of a move from fixed to floating rates on domestic stability versus stability of the rest of the world's economy for the United States is to measure the impact of a change in autonomous expenditures on GNP and interest rates, using domestic economy models, and then to measure the impact of changes in GNP and interest rates on private current and capital accounts, using balance-of-payments models under the assumption that foreign prices and interest rates are constant.

Simulation of the DRI model (Control 9/23) from the third quarter of 1974 to the second quarter of 1975, assuming a sustained $10 billion increase in federal purchases at an annual rate, changes the ninety-day Treasury bill rate by an average of 54 basis points over the four quarters, with most of the impact occurring in the first quarter; the average rate changes from 7.39 to 7.93—an increase of 7.3 percent. GNP increases by $16.2 billion over the four quarters from $1,469.3 to $1,485.5 billion, an increase of 1.1 percent, again with most of the impact occurring in the first quarter.

Simulation of the Wharton model as reported by Richard Herring and Richard Marston for the period from the first quarter of 1965 to the fourth quarter of 1969 suggests that a sustained $10 billion increase in current-dollar defense expenditures leads to an approximate increase in U.S. short-term interest rates of two basis points in the first year, rising to six basis points in the fifth year, a substantially different result from that given by the DRI model; the Treasury bill rate would rise from 7.39 to only 7.41 in this case in the year commencing with the third quarter of 1974, an increase of only 0.3 percent.[5]

The Branson model exhibits an interest-rate multiplier for net short-term capital inflows of 1.527, where capital flows are expressed in billions and the Treasury bill rate in percent per annum.[6] Net inflow in response to a change in the short-term interest rate takes place over six months. Private long-term portfolio liabilities to foreigners decrease by 0.015 for each billion dollar increase in GNP sustained over three quarters; long-term portfolio claims on foreigners decrease by 0.006 for each billion dollar increase in GNP lagged two quarters, and long-term banking claims on foreigners decrease by 0.046 for each billion dollar increase in GNP sustained over seven quarters.

Table B-1 lists approximate changes on current and capital account for the four quarters simulated by the DRI model, assuming various marginal propensities to import out of GNP in nominal terms. Table B-2 is similar to Table B-1 except that the response of the Treasury bill rate to increased government expenditure is taken from the Wharton model. Tables B-3 and B-4 are similar to Tables B-1 and B-2, respectively, except that it is assumed that long-term rates rise to the full extent that the short-term rate does; this assumption is perhaps strained but gives an upper bound to the surplus on capital account. Branson estimates that private long-term portfolio liabilities to foreigners increase by 0.693 for each percentage point rise in the long-term rate sustained over the past two quarters, and that long-term portfolio claims on foreigners decrease by 0.315 for each percentage point rise in the long-term rate in the current quarter.[7]

The interest sensitivity of long-term portfolio claims on foreigners, according to Miller and Whitman, is quite similar over the span of a year.[8] A one percentage point rise in the long rate reduces claims by $1.094 billion in the first quarter and by $0.021 billion in each succeeding quarter. They estimate that a

[5] Richard J. Herring and Richard C. Marston, *Monetary Interdependence Among Industrial Countries: A Study of Interest Rate Linkages*, research performed under contract to OASIA, U.S. Department of the Treasury, June 1974.

[6] Branson, *Financial Capital Flows in the U.S. Balance of Payments.*

[7] The U.S. long-term rate does not explicitly enter into formulations appearing in later capital flow equations for the United States by Branson and Hill. Consequently short-term coefficients reflect movements in long-term rates. William H. Branson and Raymond D. Hill, Jr., in "Capital Movements among Major OECD Countries: Some Preliminary Results," *Journal of Finance*, vol. 26 (May 1971), report an interest-rate multiplier for net U.S. capital flows excluding direct investment of 3.406, and in *Capital Movements in the OECD Area* (Paris: Organization for Economic Cooperation and Development, 1971), they report a multiplier of 2.169, both of which are significantly higher than the earlier Branson results. The former indicates an increase in capital-account surplus of $1.84 billion using the DRI model interest-rate response and an increase of $0.07 billion using the Wharton model response. The latter indicates an increase of $1.17 billion using the DRI model response and an increase of $0.04 billion using the Wharton model response.

Again, the Wharton model response indicates depreciation of the dollar; the DRI model response indicates appreciation of the dollar at low marginal propensities to import and depreciation of the dollar at high marginal propensities.

[8] Miller and Whitman, "A Mean-Variance Analysis."

Table B-1

CHANGE IN CURRENT- AND CAPITAL-ACCOUNT SURPLUSES USING RESPONSE OF TREASURY BILL RATE INDICATED BY THE DRI MODEL, III 74–II 75

Marginal Propensity to Import	Change in Current-Account Surplus	Change in Capital-Account Surplus	Change in Balance of Payments Surplus
.050	− .81	+ .96	+ .15
.075	− 1.22	+ .96	− .26
.100	− 1.62	+ .96	− .66
.125	− 2.02	+ .96	− 1.07
.150	− 2.43	+ .96	− 1.47

Table B-2

CHANGE IN CURRENT- AND CAPITAL-ACCOUNT SURPLUSES USING RESPONSE OF TREASURY BILL RATE INDICATED BY THE WHARTON MODEL, III 74–II 75

Marginal Propensity to Import	Change in Current-Account Surplus	Change in Capital-Account Surplus	Change in Balance of Payments Surplus
.050	− .81	+ .16	− .65
.075	− 1.22	+ .16	− 1.05
.100	− 1.62	+ .16	− 1.46
.125	− 2.02	+ .16	− 1.86
.150	− 2.43	+ .16	− 2.27

Table B-3

CHANGE IN CURRENT- AND CAPITAL-ACCOUNT SURPLUSES USING RESPONSE OF INTEREST RATES INDICATED BY THE DRI MODEL, III 74–II 75

Marginal Propensity to Import	Change in Current-Account Surplus	Change in Capital-Account Surplus	Change in Balance of Payments Surplus
.050	− .81	+ 2.39	+ 1.58
.075	− 1.22	+ 2.39	+ 1.17
.100	− 1.62	+ 2.39	+ .77
.125	− 2.02	+ 2.39	+ .36
.150	− 2.43	+ 2.39	− .04

Table B-4

CHANGE IN CURRENT- AND CAPITAL-ACCOUNT SURPLUSES
USING RESPONSE OF INTEREST RATES
INDICATED BY THE WHARTON MODEL, III 74–II 75

Marginal Propensity to Import	Change in Current-Account Surplus	Change in Capital-Account Surplus	Change in Balance of Payments Surplus
.050	− .81	+ .22	− .59
.075	− 1.22	+ .22	− 1.00
.100	− 1.62	+ .22	− 1.40
.125	− 2.02	+ .22	− 1.81
.150	− 2.43	+ .22	− 2.21

Table B-5

CHANGE IN CURRENT- AND CAPITAL-ACCOUNT SURPLUSES USING
RESPONSE OF INTEREST RATES INDICATED BY THE DRI MODEL
AND THE MILLER-WHITMAN RESULTS, III 74-II 75

Marginal Propensity to Import	Change in Current-Account Surplus	Change in Capital-Account Surplus	Change in Balance of Payments Surplus
.050	− .81	+ 6.33	+ 5.52
.075	− 1.22	+ 6.33	+ 5.11
.100	− 1.62	+ 6.33	+ 4.71
.125	− 2.02	+ 6.33	+ 4.30
.150	− 2.43	+ 6.33	+ 3.90

Table B-6

CHANGE IN CURRENT- AND CAPITAL-ACCOUNT SURPLUSES USING
RESPONSE OF INTEREST RATES INDICATED BY THE WHARTON
MODEL AND THE MILLER-WHITMAN RESULTS, III 74-II 75

Marginal Propensity to Import	Change in Current-Account Surplus	Change in Capital-Account Surplus	Change in Balance of Payments Surplus
.050	− .81	+ 4.21	+ 3.40
.075	− 1.22	+ 4.21	+ 3.00
.100	− 1.62	+ 4.21	+ 2.59
.125	− 2.02	+ 4.21	+ 2.19
.150	− 2.43	+ 4.21	+ 1.78

one billion dollar increase in U.S. income lowers long-term portfolio claims on foreigners by $1.011 billion in the first quarter and raises it by $0.004 billion in each succeeding quarter, a substantially larger response than that estimated by Branson. Tables B-5 and B-6 are similar to Tables B-3 and B-4, respectively, except that the Miller and Whitman results are substituted for Branson's with respect to long-term portfolio claims on foreigners.

Clearly, the evidence is mixed; according to the Miller and Whitman formulation, a shock to the domestic *IS* curve can generate appreciation of the dollar in the short or medium run. The Branson model indicates depreciation of the dollar if the relationship between autonomous expenditure and the short-term rate is best described by the Wharton model; the DRI model relationship can generate appreciation of the dollar in the medium run if long-term rates are sufficiently responsive to short-term rates.

Sung Y. Kwack and George Schink report simulations of a quarterly model of the U.S. balance of payments.[9] This model is far more disaggregated and more completely specified than is the Branson model, because it accounts for both direct investment flows and investment income in the current account. In this model, increases in GNP tend to unambiguously lower capital-account surpluses. The simulations of interest are those relating to Model A which treats foreign interest rates as exogenous, the relevant case when considering a switch to floating exchange rates.

With the Kwack and Schink model, a simulated 2.5 percent rise in U.S. income variables in billions of dollars at annual rates raises the current-account deficit by $0.933 billion and the capital-account deficit by $0.328 billion in Model A, and a simulated percentage point rise in the Treasury bill rate raises the current-account deficit by $0.460 billion and lowers the capital-account deficit by $2.461 billion. Table B-7 lists approximate current-account and capital-account changes for the four quarters corresponding to the DRI simulation and also for the Treasury bill rate change indicated by the Wharton model.

Herring and Marston report a significantly higher response of capital flows to the U.S. interest rate.[10] A sustained percentage point increase in the U.S. rate, foreign rates held exogenously, leads to a total net capital inflow of $4.85 billion in the first year. Table B-8 is similar to Table B-7, except that the Herring and Marston results with respect to the interest sensitivity of the capital account are substituted for those of Kwack and Schink.

Here again ambiguity arises as a consequence of the difference between the domestic economy model responses of the Treasury bill rate to a positive shock in the *IS* curve. Clearly, further research is indicated to determine the impact of

[9] Sung Y. Kwack and George R. Schink, *A Disaggregated Quarterly Model of U.S. Trade and Capital Flows: Simulations and Tests of Policy Effectiveness.* Prepared for the Brookings Conference on Econometric Model Building and Development, February 1972.

[10] Herring and Marston, *Monetary Interdependence among Industrial Countries.*

Table B-7

CHANGE IN BALANCE-OF-PAYMENTS SURPLUS USING
KWACK AND SCHINK PARAMETERS, III 74–II 75

Change in Treasury Bill Rate		Response to GNP Change		Response to Interest Change		Change in Balance of Payments Surplus
		Change in current-account surplus	Change in capital-account surplus	Change in current-account surplus	Change in capital-account surplus	
DRI	.54	−.41	−.14	−.25	+1.33	+.53
WHARTON	.02	−.41	−.14	−.01	+.05	−.51

Table B-8

CHANGE IN BALANCE-OF-PAYMENTS SURPLUS USING HERRING AND
MARSTON INTEREST SENSITIVITY OF CAPITAL ACCOUNT, III 74–II 75

Change in Treasury Bill Rate		Response to GNP Change		Response to Interest Change		Change in Balance of Payments Surplus
		Change in current-account surplus	Change in capital-account surplus	Change in current-account surplus	Change in capital-account surplus	
DRI	.54	−.41	−.14	−.25	+2.62	+1.82
WHARTON	.02	−.41	−.14	−.01	+.10	−.46

floating exchange rates on the efficacy of fiscal policy and on the extent to which domestic disturbances are transmitted abroad.

Canadian experience, as modeled by Caves and Reuber for the floating-rate period from 1951 to 1962, suggests that capital mobility does not nullify fiscal policy although it does reduce its effectiveness.[11] Caves and Reuber simulated an increase in government expenditure of $100 million assuming all other exogenous policy instruments unchanged. Without foreign capital flows, Canadian GNP rises by $110 million in the first quarter and by $202 million after six quarters have elapsed. With foreign capital flows, GNP rises by only $77 million in the first quarter, but after six quarters, it rises by $173 million. Capital flows have their greatest retarding effect in the first half year, but this effect subsequently tapers off. Similar simulations under the assumption of fixed exchange rates indicate that, after a year has elapsed, the effectiveness of fiscal policy is actually greater under flexible rates than under fixed. Capital mobility tended to stabilize short-run swings in the exchange rate for Canada.

---

[11] Caves and Reuber, *International Capital Markets and Canadian Economic Policy.*

The standard model indicates that a positive shock to the domestic *IS* curve will be fully transmitted abroad if an excess supply of foreign exchange resulting from capital inflows outweighs excess demand for foreign exchange resulting from deterioration of the current account. With high capital mobility, the domestic currency may continue to appreciate until interest rates are restored to their initial levels at the initial equilibrium level of income. An autonomous rise in government expenditure does increase the equilibrium level of income for Canada, however, suggesting that capital mobility does not create any substantial or continued appreciation of the domestic currency. If capital flows follow a one shot stock shift pattern in response to changing interest-rate differentials, even a high degree of interest sensitivity need not cause prolonged currency appreciation.

C: World Money Supply Statistics

Ronald Meek

Notes. These notes apply to the tables that follow.

(1) The world money supply aggregate ($M1$) consists of the total of the year-end money supply levels ($M1$) of ten industrial nations, converted to dollars at exchange rates prevailing at the end of each calendar year. The ten nations include the United States, the United Kingdom, Germany, Japan, France, Canada, Italy, Belgium, the Netherlands, and Sweden.

(2) The money supply aggregate labeled M^* consists of the sum of the series called "money" and "quasi money" in the IMF's *International Financial Statistics*. National currencies are converted to dollars in the manner described above.

(3) The levels of the Eurocurrency market come from the *40th Annual Report* (1970, p. 158) and the *44th Annual Report* (1974, p. 175) of the Bank for International Settlements, Basle, Switzerland. As is noted in footnote 39 on page 214, the true degree of global liquidity is substantially overstated by adding these figures for the Eurocurrency market to the total of national monetary aggregates on a one-for-one basis.

(4) The aggregate income velocity figures are the ratio of the sum total of GNP (in U.S. dollars) for ten industrial countries to the aggregate money supply levels described above.

M^* is a broadly defined monetary aggregate, consisting of the sum of the "money" and "quasi money" series of the IMF's *International Financial Statistics*. M^* is generally equivalent to $M2$, although for some countries it is closer to $M3$. The following defines "quasi money" for ten industrial countries:

242

Belgium	time and foreign currency deposits
Canada	time and foreign currency deposits
France	time deposits
Germany	time deposits
Italy	savings deposits
Japan	time deposits

Table C-1
AGGREGATE INDICES OF MONEY SUPPLY (*M*1), 1948–73

Date	World[a]	Eurodollars[b]	World plus Eurodollars[c]	Percent Eurodollars[d]
1/48	—	—	—	—
1/49	—	—	—	—
1/50	—	—	—	—
1/51	—	—	—	—
1/52	—	—	—	—
1/53	189.04	—	—	—
1/54	197.70	—	—	—
1/55	205.32	—	—	—
1/56	211.02	—	—	—
1/57	210.32	—	—	—
1/58	218.47	—	—	—
1/59	227.43	—	—	—
1/60	234.77	—	—	—
1/61	250.49	—	—	—
1/62	268.90	—	—	—
1/63	285.35	—	—	—
1/64	303.65	9.00	312.65	2.88
1/65	326.31	11.50	337.81	3.40
1/66	341.44	14.50	355.94	4.07
1/67	368.42	17.50	385.92	4.53
1/68	400.62	25.00	425.62	5.87
1/69	420.19	44.00	464.19	9.48
1/70	464.61	57.00	521.61	10.93
1/71	548.12	71.00	619.12	11.47
1/72	632.10	92.00	724.10	12.71
1/73	717.99	144.00	861.99	16.71

[a] Level of world money supply (*M*1) in U.S. dollars.
[b] Size of Eurodollar market, in U.S. dollars.
[c] World money supply (*M*1) + Eurodollar market.
[d] Eurodollar market as a percent of world money supply (*M*1) + Eurodollar market.

Netherlands	time, savings, and foreign currency deposits
Sweden	time deposits
United Kingdom	time deposits in banks and discount houses, plus overseas sector sterling deposits with banking sector
United States	time deposits

Table C-2
AGGREGATE INDICES OF MONEY SUPPLY, 1948–73
(money plus quasi-money)

Date	World[a]	Eurodollars[b]	World plus Eurodollars[c]	Percent Eurodollars[d]
1/48	—	—	—	—
1/49	—	—	—	—
1/50	—	—	—	—
1/51	—	—	—	—
1/52	—	—	—	—
1/53	260.93	—	—	—
1/54	277.07	—	—	—
1/55	289.04	—	—	—
1/56	300.95	—	—	—
1/57	314.00	—	—	—
1/58	336.87	—	—	—
1/59	356.86	—	—	—
1/60	372.15	—	—	—
1/61	406.08	—	—	—
1/62	445.47	—	—	—
1/63	492.96	—	—	—
1/64	538.31	9.00	547.81	1.64
1/65	597.67	11.50	609.17	1.89
1/66	644.41	14.50	658.91	2.20
1/67	718.37	17.50	735.87	2.38
1/68	800.02	25.00	825.82	3.03
1/69	842.95	44.00	886.95	4.96
1/70	957.20	57.00	1,014.20	5.62
1/71	1,156.77	71.00	1,227.77	5.78
1/72	1,362.95	92.00	1,454.95	6.32
1/73	1,630.14	144.00	1,774.14	8.12

[a] Level of world money supply (M2), in U.S. dollars.
[b] Size of Eurodollar market, in U.S. dollars.
[c] World money supply (M2) + Eurodollar market.
[d] Eurodollar market as a percent of world money supply (M2) plus Eurodollar market.

Table C-3

ANNUAL SERIES OF MONEY SUPPLY (M1) AND QUASI-MONEY, 1948–73

(in billions of national currency)

Date	United States		United Kingdom		Japan		Germany		Canada	
	M1	QM	M1	QM	M1	QM	M1	QM	M1	QM
1/48	110.30	34.60	—	—	—	—	11.80	—	3.80	3.75
1/49	109.90	34.90	—	—	—	—	14.20	—	3.86	4.09
1/50	115.30	35.00	—	—	—	—	16.80	—	4.19	4.18
1/51	122.80	36.60	5.65	2.56	—	—	19.10	8.10	4.26	4.30
1/52	129.20	39.50	5.67	2.72	—	—	21.10	11.70	4.54	4.60
1/53	130.80	42.30	5.85	2.90	1,937.00	2,015.00	23.20	16.50	4.49	4.76
1/54	134.90	45.60	6.07	3.03	2,013.00	2,543.00	26.40	21.00	4.82	5.22
1/55	138.00	47.00	6.01	2.82	2,331.00	3,064.00	29.10	25.30	5.11	5.63
1/56	139.40	49.20	6.04	2.93	2,714.00	3,837.00	30.80	29.80	5.07	6.01
1/57	138.70	55.20	5.94	3.32	2,824.00	4,767.00	35.10	37.00	5.29	6.11
1/58	144.30	62.20	6.09	3.49	3,185.00	5,870.00	39.70	43.70	5.95	6.84
1/59	145.60	64.90	6.59	3.54	3,711.00	7,236.00	44.40	52.60	5.75	6.90
1/60	146.60	70.50	6.62	3.74	4,146.00	6,178.00	47.40	60.40	5.98	7.22
1/61	151.40	79.80	6.76	3.94	4,909.00	7,365.00	54.40	67.30	6.74	7.62
1/62	155.20	94.90	6.39	4.08	5,725.00	8,968.00	58.00	77.30	7.03	7.93
1/63	160.20	108.50	7.32	4.08	7,703.00	10,965.00	62.20	89.40	7.54	9.24
1/64	168.00	121.90	7.55	4.46	8,704.00	12,818.00	67.70	103.10	8.25	10.26
1/65	176.10	141.40	7.84	5.08	10,287.00	15,107.00	72.50	120.40	9.43	10.94
1/66	180.00	153.30	7.84	5.55	11,716.00	17,806.00	74.20	140.30	10.13	11.87
1/67	193.50	175.90	8.44	6.39	13,369.00	20,729.00	81.60	163.80	11.70	13.71
1/68	208.90	196.80	8.70	7.12	15,155.00	23,999.00	88.40	196.20	13.32	15.66
1/69	216.30	186.60	8.81	7.58	18,282.00	28,117.00	93.70	223.80	12.53	18.29
1/70	227.80	226.00	9.63	8.31	21,358.00	32,877.00	102.70	250.30	14.27	19.81
1/71	241.80	266.70	11.10	9.21	27,692.00	39,705.00	115.80	291.00	18.23	19.48
1/72	260.40	306.40	12.65	13.32	34,526.00	49,514.00	131.90	337.40	21.05	21.53
1/73	279.10	356.20	13.30	19.82	40,311.00	57,877.00	132.90	390.00	23.95	27.60

Table C-3 *(continued)*

Date	Sweden M1	Sweden QM	Belgium M1	Belgium QM	Netherlands M1	Netherlands QM	Italy M1	Italy QM	France M1	France QM
1/48	5.21	5.92	150.10	—	7.39	0.84	1,989.00	—	21.71	0.20
1/49	5.22	6.87	155.90	—	7.29	0.78	2,298.00	—	27.12	0.38
1/50	5.55	7.39	156.10	14.60	6.81	2.38	2,568.00	—	31.29	0.60
1/51	6.63	8.39	168.70	16.50	7.04	2.82	2,983.00	—	36.95	0.80
1/52	6.94	8.21	174.60	20.20	7.76	3.12	3,452.00	—	41.88	0.99
1/53	7.11	9.75	180.40	22.00	8.27	3.27	3,817.00	1,779.00	46.58	1.36
1/54	7.23	10.61	183.70	23.20	8.86	3.72	4,134.00	2,119.00	52.98	1.67
1/55	7.26	10.68	192.60	25.80	9.59	4.16	4,519.00	2,495.00	59.69	2.00
1/56	7.67	11.12	198.20	25.50	9.23	4.39	4,883.00	2,974.00	65.85	2.32
1/57	7.82	12.44	198.00	26.50	9.05	4.94	5,132.00	3,457.00	71.37	3.98
1/58	7.98	14.27	209.50	30.00	10.14	5.91	5,712.00	4,148.00	74.58	5.38
1/59	8.69	16.52	216.30	35.90	10.59	7.20	6,529.00	4,844.00	83.11	7.55
1/60	9.91	16.24	220.40	42.00	11.30	8.49	7,421.00	5,545.00	94.87	10.94
1/61	10.72	16.54	237.40	51.60	12.18	9.25	8,611.00	6,500.00	109.60	14.44
1/62	11.72	18.50	254.50	55.90	13.09	10.37	10,129.00	7,631.00	129.50	17.69
1/63	12.83	20.11	278.90	64.10	14.29	11.87	11,507.00	8,657.00	148.29	19.59
1/64	13.91	21.95	297.40	70.20	15.44	13.49	12,374.00	9,533.00	160.57	23.76
1/65	14.61	22.28	318.60	81.80	17.00	14.57	14,406.00	11,016.00	175.66	28.78
1/66	15.84	24.53	339.70	94.70	18.16	15.71	16,322.00	12,750.00	189.28	36.77
1/67	17.14	28.20	350.50	116.20	19.29	18.92	18,890.00	14,346.00	198.32	57.30
1/68	16.92	34.48	376.60	134.50	21.48	22.27	21,124.00	16,084.00	214.16	71.07
1/69	16.28	36.20	386.30	164.00	23.21	25.47	24,472.00	17,189.00	211.80	93.66
1/70	17.76	37.14	418.50	176.90	25.95	28.38	31,185.00	16,673.00	235.33	116.71
1/71	19.40	41.40	645.00	208.40	29.85	32.17	37,099.00	18,701.00	263.19	153.03
1/72	20.86	47.61	530.30	251.80	35.11	36.10	46,006.00	22,102.00	302.52	191.30
1/73	22.99	55.92	573.70	310.30	35.05	47.40	54,067.00	27,142.00	332.21	235.61

Table C-4

PERCENTAGE CHANGES IN WORLD MONEY SUPPLY AGGREGATES (*M*1)

Date	World[a]	United States[b]	World less United States[c]	World plus Euro-dollars[d]	Euro-dollars[e]
1/48	—	—	—	—	—
1/49	—	−0.36	—	—	—
1/50	—	4.91	—	—	—
1/51	—	6.50	—	—	—
1/52	—	5.21	—	—	—
1/53	—	1.24	—	—	—
1/54	4.58	3.13	7.83	—	—
1/55	3.86	2.30	7.21	—	—
1/56	2.77	1.01	6.38	—	—
1/57	−0.33	−0.50	−0.00	—	—
1/58	3.87	4.04	3.56	—	—
1/59	4.10	0.90	10.33	—	—
1/60	3.23	0.69	7.76	—	—
1/61	6.70	3.27	12.38	—	—
1/62	5.35	2.51	9.70	—	—
1/63	8.13	3.22	15.14	—	—
1/64	6.41	4.87	8.39	—	—
1/65	7.46	4.82	10.73	8.05	27.78
1/66	4.64	2.21	7.48	5.37	26.09
1/67	7.90	7.50	8.35	8.42	20.69
1/68	8.74	7.96	9.60	10.29	42.86
1/69	4.88	3.54	6.35	9.06	76.00
1/70	10.57	5.32	16.15	12.37	29.55
1/71	17.97	6.15	29.35	18.69	24.56
1/72	15.32	7.69	21.34	16.96	29.58
1/73	13.59	7.18	18.08	19.04	56.52

[a] Percentage change in world money supply (*M*1).

[b] Percentage change in U.S. money supply (*M*1).

[c] Percentage change in world money supply less U.S.

[d] Percentage change in world money supply plus Eurodollar market.

[e] Percentage change in Eurodollar market.

Table C-5
PERCENTAGE CHANGES IN WORLD MONEY SUPPLY AGGREGATES (M2)

Date	World[a]	United States[b]	World less United States[c]	World plus Eurodollars[d]
1/48	—	—	—	—
1/49	—	−0.07	—	—
1/50	—	3.80	—	—
1/51	—	6.05	—	—
1/52	—	5.83	—	—
1/53	—	2.61	—	—
1/54	9.26	4.27	9.96	—
1/55	6.24	2.49	7.73	—
1/56	6.96	1.95	7.99	—
1/57	8.51	2.81	6.90	—
1/58	9.85	6.50	8.55	—
1/59	9.71	1.94	12.27	—
1/60	6.77	3.14	5.94	—
1/61	12.91	6.49	12.79	—
1/62	13.97	8.17	11.72	—
1/63	14.64	7.44	14.79	—
1/64	11.44	7.89	10.99	—
1/65	13.69	9.52	12.56	14.02
1/66	10.16	4.98	11.04	10.59
1/67	13.02	10.83	12.17	13.25
1/68	12.78	9.83	13.23	13.75
1/69	5.87	−0.69	11.37	8.71
1/70	16.40	12.63	14.40	17.26
1/71	25.44	12.05	28.78	25.38
1/72	20.50	11.47	22.81	21.15
1/73	22.54	12.09	24.96	25.15

[a] Percentage change in world money supply (M2).

[b] Percentage change in U.S. money supply (M2).

[c] Percentage change in world money supply (M2) less U.S.

[d] Percentage change in world money supply (M2) plus Eurodollars.

COMMENTARIES

Richard N. Cooper

Dr. Willett's paper is so rich in ideas and so broad in its coverage that it leaves a wide range of choice for comment. Yet it barely touches the topic of this session, and that gives me a further choice between commenting on the paper or on the topic of the session. I will do a bit of both.

One of the difficulties of monetary economics, and especially of international monetary economics, is that we are often more interested in the path we traverse than in the final resting point. Yet virtually all of our analytical tools are concerned with equilibrium points. Because of this difficulty, discussions of monetary economics often involve talking past each other rather than to one another, since one participant is addressing equilibrium while another is addressing the transitional dynamics.

I agree very much with the remark that Professor Swoboda made yesterday—that in the present situation, in which we have to make large and sudden payments for oil to the OPEC countries that will in turn flow back into financial markets, the more interesting immediate question is not whether the Eurocurrency market and the U.S. money market are ultimately unified through arbitrage, but whether either part of the market can absorb the great pressures created by such a massive shift in payments. If they cannot, the question of ultimate market unity becomes otiose. This kind of consideration applies more generally to our subject: the path by which we travel has a great bearing on where we end up and on our choice of policy instruments to influence the outcome.

I applaud Dr. Willett for the strong emphasis he gives to the influence of alternative monetary regimes on the pattern and magnitude of disturbances to the economic system, and for his relative downplaying of the question of effectiveness of given instruments of policy. I believe that the conditions governing whether monetary policy or fiscal policy is more effective under fixed or flexible exchange-rate regimes are much less interesting than the influence of those regimes both on the magnitude of disturbances and on the size of the structural coefficients that are often erroneously assumed to be unchanged in comparisons between regimes.

Indeed, if policy instruments were costless to use and were quick in their effects, we should not be concerned with the effectiveness of the instruments, since

249

they could be made as effective as we like by pushing them sufficiently hard. In fact, of course, policy instruments are not costless to use and are not often quick in their effects—a point that does not usually get incorporated into theoretical models—and therefore the more we can reduce the load that we put on them (that is, the disturbances to the system) the better.

To the extent that disturbances are monetary in origin—that is, a change in the money supply or switches in public preferences between money and goods or between money and securities—and to the extent that the public holds only domestic money, a system of freely floating exchange rates will tend to insulate the rest of the world from disturbances arising in the originating country. To the extent that the disturbances are nonmonetary in origin, however—that is, a change in supply of goods and services or a switch in public preferences between securities and goods—the insulation afforded by flexible exchange rates is both less complete and more complex in character. Under conditions of poor harvest in a major exporting country, for example, where foreign demand for the product is inelastic, a system of floating rates will lead to appreciation of the currency of the originating country and will therefore aggravate the disturbance in the rest of the world (for example, the rise in food prices), while mitigating it in the originating country. The same effect would result if the "shortage" arose from bond-financed government procurement of the crop in question.

In the case of a switch in public preference between bonds and goods, we need to compare the relative importance of the marginal propensity to import with the marginal propensity to purchase or sell foreign securities. When linkages between economies are high, it is unlikely that holdings of foreign securities will not be affected by changes in public behavior. Thus the net effect of such switches on the exchange rate will depend on two marginal propensities rather than one, and without quantification it is difficult to say whether a system of flexible rates will reduce or increase the transmission of disturbances of that type.

Thus flexible exchange rates tend to bottle up monetary disturbances in the country of origin, but the effect on real disturbances is more complicated. But do we always want to bottle up disturbances, if we can? Willett introduces the useful analogy to insurance. If disturbances throughout the world arise from unavoidable causes, perhaps we do not want to bottle them up; world welfare may be increased if they are widely dispersed. This is even more likely to be true when we allow for the fact that disturbances are occurring in many places at the same time, and some of them are likely to offset others in their effects, so that the total level of disturbance to the world economy is reduced if transmission is high among its various parts.

On the other hand, wide dispersal of disturbances reduces the incentive of governments to avoid creating disturbances, since their economies bear only part of the costs. Thus, as with any form of risk spreading, there is a problem of moral hazard. The existence of insurance may influence adversely the behavior of the insured. Thus to the extent that disturbances are unavoidable, we may want to spread them widely; to the extent that they arise from policy actions, we may want to bottle them up so as to encourage stabilizing behavior. One of the sources of dispute within the profession concerns the principal source of disturbances to the economy. To the extent that one believes, with many monetarists, that the major source of disturbances is inappropriate monetary policy, then a regime of flexible exchange rates represents a natural proposal, and it is undoubtedly no accident that monetarists also tend to espouse freely floating rates (but not all advocates of floating rates are monetarists).

I would suggest that one of the consequences of flexible exchange rates is to reduce international capital mobility, by which I mean the sensitivity of international capital movements both to uncovered interest-rate differentials and to differential movements in income. My comparison is with an adjustable peg (Bretton Woods) regime with credible parities. This conjecture follows from portfolio theory with aversion to risk, since a flexible rate system increases the short-run risk of holding assets denominated in foreign currencies, unless there are diversification reasons for holding foreign assets, either to reduce total variance of the portfolio or to cover risk in other transactions, such as future import payments.

If this view is correct, it means that focusing on a dividing line between upward and downward pressure on an exchange rate in response to various disturbances or policy actions under alternative exchange-rate regimes misses a central point, which is the change in behavioral parameters in response to alteration of the regime. It cannot be assumed that with a change in regime other features of the macroeconomy (as modeled) will remain unchanged.

I would like to make two more observations on Willett's paper before turning to some remarks on the Eurocurrency market. First, Willett neglected to deal with the possible impact on spending of the changing value of real balances under a flexible exchange-rate regime. If we have a moderately integrated world in which an important component of consumption in country A is goods from country B, monetary expansion in B, which leads to an incipient outflow of capital and a depreciation of its currency, will cheapen B's goods in A (assuming the exchange rate drops faster than B's domestic prices rise) and will therefore raise the real value of cash balances in A, thus encouraging additional spending there. To the extent that this effect is quantitatively important—an object of controversy ever since Gottfried Haberler identified a similar effect with respect to interest-rate movements thirty-five years ago in his *Prosperity and Depression*—it will qualify the suggestion made above that flexible exchange rates will insulate foreign economies from monetary disturbances in any one economy. Openness per se will result in the transmission of disturbances, and flexible rates will reduce that transmission only to the extent that they reduce openness.

Second, I take issue with Willett's observation that a regime of flexible rates will not differ much from a regime of fixed rates if private speculators in the former behave much like central banks in the latter, with the suggestion that they might well be expected to do so. There is one important reason why private speculators may not be expected to behave like central banks in today's world and why, therefore, a system of gliding parities or a managed float may be superior to a system of freely floating exchange rates.

The wage level in the modern economy is indeterminant because in the final analysis the monetary authorities must—for political reasons—provide a money supply adequate to ratify any given level of money wages, no matter how it was reached, in order to avoid excessive unemployment. One possible influence on money wages is the exchange rate, especially in an open economy, operating through its influence on the cost of living. In many countries the linkage between the cost of living and money wages is both direct and quick—partly through formal indexation of money wages, partly through strong conventions of wage bargaining.

Under these circumstances, a drop in the exchange rate large enough to make a noticeable impression on the cost of living, whatever the source of the change in exchange rate, will automatically become self-justifying because it gets reflected in a higher level of money wages. This is a feature of modern economies that speculators take as given, part of the economic environment, and their behavior is influenced accordingly. In contrast, it is presumably one of the objectives of the monetary authorities to limit the rise in money wages so as to avoid inflation. The central bank therefore has an incentive to engage in foreign-exchange transactions with this objective in mind, whereas private speculators have no such incentive. On the contrary, they expect that when a currency depreciates beyond a certain degree there will be an induced rise in wages. Under these circumstances, runs on a currency may be quite rational for private speculators, whereas a central bank will rightly be desirous of stopping the run. This is an example, incidentally, of how the adjustment path to a real disturbance may influence the final equilibrium—in this case, the equilibrium value of the exchange rate.

Let me turn now to the Eurocurrency market, first to raise a conceptual issue and then to discuss the performance of the Eurocurrency market in the face of large flows of petrodollars.

Part of the difficulty in assessing the impact of the Eurocurrency market on monetary policy and on aggregate demand is that we do not yet have a good theory concerning the role of money holdings in influencing aggregate demand. It is not known, for example, when an American firm holds balances in the Eurocurrency market, whether that does or does not satisfy some putative demand for money balances. Moreover, many nonresidents of the United States hold dollar balances abroad. Does that relate to aggregate demand in the United States, or in the home country? From many points of view, Eurocurrency holdings are just like the kinds of domestic assets included in the M_2 definition of the money supply, which is not limited to means of payment. In practice, foreign-held balances in the United States are counted in the U.S. money supply. Is this appropriate? If so, why not also American-owned dollar balances abroad, or even foreign-owned dollar balances abroad?

To pose these questions is simply to suggest that there is no clear conceptual framework for the microeconomics of money and hence for dealing with the relationship between changes in money holdings and the demand for goods and services. Until there is a better theory, there is bound to be a lot of floundering with respect to the influence of the Eurocurrency market on world aggregate demand. Indeed, perhaps such a degree of world economic integration has been reached that it is necessary to think in terms of a world money supply and a world demand for goods and services. But because of the partially insulating effects of flexible exchange rates, it seems premature to abandon the approach based on national economies. Some combination is needed.

Finally, let me turn to the question raised yesterday whether it really makes a difference to the final outcome where petrodollars are placed, in the Eurocurrency market or in the U.S. money market. General approval seemed to be given to the view that it does not make a difference, since the markets are fully unified through arbitrage. I would like to dissent from that view. I emphasize the current situation, not the situation that obtained, say, two years ago. At the present time financial markets, especially in Europe, are very jittery. This is because of a variety of reasons: the circumstances under which flexible rates came into being, the large increase in oil prices, and the substantial but still uncertain impact that it will have on national economies, the failure of a number of banks, the precipitous drop in equity values, and so on. For all these reasons, risk premia on various types of assets are very different from what they were a few years ago. There is a strong inclination of many investors to move into assets that they regard as absolutely safe, and the spreads between rates on Treasury bills and certificates of deposit (CDs) of the largest banks, on the one hand, and rates on other short-term assets have increased substantially. Default risks that were once considered negligible have now become significant. Aversion to the risk of bankruptcy is high. Arbitrage patterns of a few years ago no longer prevail.

As a result of a marked increase in perceived risk, there has been a shift in portfolio preferences, and under these circumstances it does make a difference to the pattern of spending where the OPEC money goes. The unity of markets has been broken. Purchases of U.S. Treasury bills or Chase Manhattan CDs will not result in the same pattern of spending as deposits in medium-sized non-American banks in the Eurocurrency market, for instance, because the customers of the latter banks do not have access to Chase, and at the borrowing rates they would have to pay if the funds go to the United States, many of them will withdraw from the market.

After a period of several years, things may settle down to where they would have been otherwise, regardless of where the funds were first placed, if present institutions survive the transition. But I return to my initial observation that the path can influence the outcome. Default risk is much higher now than it was a few years ago; bank failures alter the parameters under which the financial markets operate. Thus where the funds flow in the first instance, in a period of major strain, may have a strong influence not only on spending during the transition period but even in the longer run, by influencing which institutions will survive.

William H. Branson

The Willett paper is largely about the choice of exchange-rate systems and the effectiveness of different economic policy instruments. I will go through some of the points that Willett has made and try to add some information about empirical magnitudes in some of the areas.

First, I would like to question the assumption—which is implicit throughout Willett's paper—that capital mobility increased during the 1960s and up to the present time. It seems to me the capital movements which we have seen since the beginning of 1970 are not inconsistent with the magnitude of interest-sensitivity parameters which have been typically estimated from the data for the 1960s. Let me give an illustration to pin down what I mean.

A typical interest-sensitivity parameter estimated from data for the 1960s would indicate that a one percentage point change in the U.S. Treasury bill rate would lead to an inflow of about $3 billion in the U.S. capital account, with all of the other adjustments being made in other interest rates. This number is taken from a study which Raymond Hill and I did for the OECD in 1971.[1] But it is, roughly speaking, a typical empirical result.

Now that figure can be translated into the effect from expected changes in exchange rates on capital movements. Suppose a person expects that an exchange rate is going to change by 10 percent within the next six months, and he holds that expectation with 50 percent probability. The expected return on that exchange-rate change, if he can speculate, is at an annual rate of roughly 10 percent.

If that number—ten percentage points—is multiplied by the previous elasticity estimate that a one percentage point change in the U.S. Treasury bill rate generates a $3 billion capital inflow into the United States, the result is a $30 billion capital inflow, just using simple linear extrapolation. This sort of result is not inconsistent with what we have been seeing.

The point that tends to get missed in discussion about increasing capital mobility is the very point that led Fritz Machlup to title the conference that he held

---

[1] William H. Branson and Raymond D. Hill, *Capital Movements in the OECD Area* (Paris: Organization for Economic Cooperation and Development, 1971).

on capital movements in 1970 the way he did; it was a conference about mobility and movement of capital.[2] The point is that increased capital movements may occur either because capital flows are becoming more sensitive to given investment incentives or because investment incentives themselves have increased. My point here is that the investment incentives have been more important in the period since 1970 than in the earlier period, and, in fact, if typical parameters from the earlier period are applied to more recent investment incentives, orders of magnitude for capital flows will result that are roughly consistent with the movements actually observed.

Therefore, one cannot accept the size of recent capital flows as evidence of increased mobility of capital. It does not follow. Thus, in studying Willett's paper, the situation can be simplified somewhat because he has two dimensions to the story—one is increased mobility of capital and one is movement from fixed to flexible exchange rates. It seems to me we should concentrate on the movement from fixed to flexible exchange rates in our discussion.

The question of the effect of the movement from fixed to flexible rates on policy effectiveness, then, boils down to how mobile is capital. (And here I disagree with Professor Cooper to some extent. It seems to me that if we are going to use terms such as "relatively high mobility" of capital, it would be nice to define the terms more precisely.) Willett makes the point—which I think is correct—that moving from fixed to flexible rates in general improves the effectiveness of monetary policy. However, the effect of the change from fixed to flexible rates on the effectiveness of fiscal policy basically depends on the sensitivity of capital movements to interest rates relative to the sensitivity of the current account to income. If there is also some income sensitivity of capital movements, that must be added into the calculation.

Essentially, if capital movements are sufficiently insensitive to interest rates so that an expansionary fiscal policy causes a deficit in the overall balance of payments, then going from a fixed to a flexible rate system increases the power of fiscal policy as Willett has defined it; that is, more exchange-rate flexibility increases the multiplier effect of fiscal policy on GNP. This is basically because the devaluation which follows the incipient deficit will add a trade kick to the fiscal policy kick.

If an increase in government spending were to generate a balance-of-payments surplus through the capital-account effects, a move to flexible rates would reduce the unit impact of fiscal policy on GNP. So the question of whether or not the move from the old (more-or-less) fixed rate system to the new (more-or-less) flexible rate system made fiscal policy more or less effective can be boiled down to what one believes about an expansionary fiscal policy—whether it would cause a balance-of-payments surplus or deficit. If one believes it would generate a balance-of-payments deficit, then one believes that going from fixed rates to flexible

---

[2] Fritz Machlup, Walter S. Salant, and Lorie Tarshis, eds., *International Mobility and Movement of Capital* (New York: Columbia University Press, 1972).

rates *improves* the effectiveness of fiscal policy. Willett's Annex B generally suggests that this is the case—that capital mobility is sufficiently small so that going from fixed to flexible rates improves the effectiveness of fiscal policy. There are a few other bits of evidence that could be added to that annex. I did some calculations using the capital account estimates in the OECD study to which I just referred, and Kwack's current account estimates in the Brookings model and his obtained results are consistent with the low capital mobility case for the United States.

John Helliwell presented a paper reporting simulations combining the MIT-Penn-SSRC (MPS) model for the United States and the RDX2 model for Canada at a conference in Williamstown, Massachusetts, last spring.[3] In his summation he obtained a borderline result. His fiscal policy simulations for Canada showed no effect on the balance of payments of Canada. It seems to me that might be an extreme case because one generally thinks of Canada as a pretty open economy.

To summarize the results, my view is (1) that there is no particular evidence of increasing mobility of capital and (2) that capital is sufficiently immobile that, based on the old parameters estimated for the system of relatively pegged rates, moving from fixed to flexible rates would increase the effectiveness of fiscal policy. If Cooper is right—that making the change in regimes makes capital even less sensitive to interest rates—then my conclusion is reinforced by his considerations.

The second major point in the Willett work which I want to discuss is the question of the desirability of the transmission of economic disturbances. Most of the literature assumes that transmission is a bad thing—that countries which make economic policy mistakes ought to pay for them, and that if there is an excessively expansionary or contractionary policy in one country, it should not be allowed to spread to others. Usually the literature implies that it would be bad to let these effects spread to others. The implication of this is that it would be good to load all the effect on the originating country—which is to say, "they ought to pay for their mistakes." That was the presumption in the Modigliani and Askari paper to which Willett referred.[4] I believe this view of things assumes that all mistakes are avoidable, that they should not have been made in the first place, and that, therefore, they should be paid for.

However, it seems to me that if one faces the fact that many mistakes are not avoidable—that they were not made on purpose—then there is an insurance argument for the transmission of the effects of mistakes. Given that mistakes are going to be distributed randomly, it might be good for everyone to carry his proportionate load of each mistake on the usual insurance principles.

[3] John F. Helliwell, "Trade, Capital Flows, and Migration as Channels for International Transmission of Stabilization Policies," in A. Ando, R. Herring, R. Marston, eds., *International Aspects of Stabilization Policies* (Federal Reserve Bank of Boston, 1975).

[4] Franco Modigliani and H. Askari, "The International Transfer of Capital and the Propagation of Domestic Disturbances under Alternative Payments Systems," *Banca Nazionale del Lavoro Quarterly Review*, December 1973.

Willett and Cooper raised the argument about moral hazard, namely, that if the transmission is maximized and what each country pays for its mistakes is minimized, then the incentive to conduct good policy is reduced. That is certainly an argument which one has to take into consideration, and it is an argument which Professor Modigliani explicitly made in his paper with Askari.

In response to this objection about sharing the cost of mistakes on the insurance principle, I think there are two counters. One is that I really do not see policy makers making bad policy on purpose. But further, the insurance system we are talking about is coinsurance. In general, the effects of the policy mistake will make their appearance first in the country which made the mistake. And it will only subsequently spread. So, in general, the country which makes the mistake will pay something for it. We are not talking about a policy of lifting the whole load from them, but only spreading it somewhat. Thus the usual arguments supportive of the coinsurance principle would hold here.

The third point I want to make is a minor one which appeared in Willett's discussion. It concerns the question of whether or not a crawling peg makes sense in the current situation.

It ought to be almost obvious that a crawling peg makes sense in a situation in which there is relatively slow movement of the underlying economic structure of the world. In that situation the crawling peg can track the movement of the exchange rate, so that big jumps in the exchange rate are not necessary in order to restore equilibrium. On the other hand, if there are sudden significant changes in the economic structure underlying the exchange-rate system, then a crawling peg is not going to be able to handle the situation any better than a fixed peg. The exchange-rate system is going to break, and the rate is going to have to jump.

Thus it seems to me that anyone proposing a crawling peg system has to include the footnote or the reservation that from time to time—if the economic structure undergoes a big shift—the exchange-rate system may have to float for awhile until an equilibrium is reestablished, at which point the peg can start crawling again. If we are in a world which experiences sudden jumps in the economic structure, there is no point in supporting a gradually crawling peg with no provision for occasional floats.

Gottfried Haberler

I should like to comment on two problems which were raised in the Willett paper. The first deals with the theory that fiscal and monetary theory have different effects under a regime of fixed exchange rates than they have under a regime of flexible exchange rates. This theory reminds me of the related theory that under fixed exchange rates, it is possible to operate on the balance of payments and internal equilibrium simultaneously by changing the mix of monetary and fiscal policy. In other words, dilemma situations such as a weak balance of payments associated with a recession can be handled—without changing the exchange rate—by a tight money policy associated with an easy fiscal policy, for example, a tax cut. (Another gimmick that has been proposed is "operation twist"—twisting short-term and long-term interest rates to encourage short-term capital inflows without discouraging long-term domestic investment. This operation was tried out—unsuccessfully—in the United States in the 1960s.)

What is wrong with this theory is, I believe, that it forgets the monetary implications of an easy fiscal policy. Fiscal policy, a budget surplus or deficit, operates largely through the monetary mechanism. For example, if a government deficit is not financed in an inflationary way, it loses its stimulating effect. Hence the differential impact of monetary and fiscal policy—on which the criticized theory depends—is largely illusory. Let me remind you that this has prompted Harry Johnson, a prominent practitioner of the theory in question, to give it up. In the introduction to his volume, *Further Essays in Monetary Economics* (Harvard University Press, Cambridge, Massachusetts, 1973, p. 12) he referred to Robert Mundell's analysis of the effects of capital mobility on economic policy problems by assuming that international capital flows could be sensitive to movements of national income as well as to interest-rate differentials, and said: "I now think that the game of extending Keynesian international policy models by introducing further differentiation of the variables is both far too easy for the mathematically competent theorist and not very illuminating for the policy-maker."

My second comment concerns the Eurodollar market. How inflationary is it? Does it hamper anti-inflationary policies in the United States? I believe that the inflationary effects of the Eurodollar market have been greatly exaggerated, except in one particular respect: it can be said that the Eurodollar market has made it a little more difficult for the United States under certain circumstances to pursue an anti-inflation policy. Under a regime of fixed exchanges and free convertibility, the fight against inflation may be hampered by capital exports. Capital export controls have been used to close or narrow that leak. The Eurodollar market undercuts the capital export controls and thus makes it harder to maintain an overvalued currency that would have counteracted inflation by allowing a country to keep imports at a higher level and exports at a lower level than would be possible otherwise. However, for the United States this inflationary effect of the Eurodollar market would be negligible. For other countries the situation may be different.

There is an analogous situation in the commodity markets. Just as the uncontrolled Eurodollar market undercuts capital controls, commodity trade undercuts domestic price controls. Since export and import prices are usually uncontrolled, international trade provides an escape from price controls of rapidly growing magnitude.

Paul Wonnacott

I want to raise a question regarding the puzzling history of the last several years. I confess that I do not have an explanation for it, but I would like to throw the problem out for discussion and suggest a couple of lines along which an explanation might be sought.

The problem essentially is this. In the last few years, we have observed a significant movement toward greater flexibility of exchange rates. Obviously we do not have anything like the textbook case of freely floating exchange rates, but we certainly have a much higher degree of flexibility than we had in the past. According to accepted theory, greater exchange-rate flexibility should have led to greater policy independence. Yet, if you look at the policies of the OECD countries, you will find that they have been strikingly similar—although not identical, of course. (Germany made a movement to tighter monetary and fiscal policies significantly ahead of other countries.) There certainly has not been an identity of policies, but the record of the last several years has been one of strikingly similar policies and strikingly similar economic behavior by historical standards.

The question is: why has this been the case? It is obviously an important question. When countries have similar policies, the magnitude of their cyclical swings tends to increase. And the similarity of policy began before the oil problem was dumped on us. With every country responding to the oil crisis, the possibilities of an exaggerated cycle are increased.

There are a couple of possible explanations. I do not want to suggest that either of these is necessarily correct. But they are perhaps lines of argument that are worth thinking about.

One is that there are ties among national policies quite separate from, and in addition to, the ties which we normally think about. That is, there are ties which are not the result of changes in exports, imports, capital flows, or reserves. Maybe in a world of rapidly improving communications, national governments tend to look at things similarly at any particular time and, therefore, tend to behave similarly. I do not know how much weight to put on this possible explanation, but it seems to me we should try to broaden our horizons in dealing with the contacts among national economic policies and go beyond the variables which appear in the theoretical models.

The second possible explanation for similar policies goes back to changes in reserves, but puts the stress somewhat differently from the way it is put in the standard explanation. In the standard explanation, one argues that with fixed exchange rates countries tend to move in the same general direction for the following reason: if country A has expansive monetary and/or fiscal policies, it will tend to lose reserves. Country B will, therefore, tend to gain reserves. Then,

259

country B will follow the expansive policies of country A. Thus, A and B will tend to move together.

But there is another way of looking at a fixed exchange-rate regime. Generally if one country is gaining reserves, another country is losing reserves. Therefore, with fixed exchange rates, when one country is under pressure—because of its reserve position—to tighten up in policy, another country will be in a position where it simultaneously feels able to relax policy somewhat. This suggests that there may be a diffusion of behavior under fixed exchange rates which tends to be left out of the standard theoretical discussion.

I offer these two possible explanations for the policy similarities we have observed among the major industrial countries during the past few years as something that might be thought about, without making any attempt to evaluate them.

The second point on which I would like to comment is the debate between Professors Cooper and Kenen. Perhaps they are both right, if the proper distinction is made. One should distinguish between the Eurodollar-New York interest-rate differential, on the one hand, and the risk premium, on the other. Looking back over recent history, as I read it, the interest differential has not changed greatly. The really big change, rather, has been in risk premia, *everywhere*—in the Eurodollar market, in the New York market, in the German market, and so on—as a result of the general shaky state of confidence.

David I. Fand

My comments consider whether international reserves are adequate for the needs of the world economy. The acceleration of world inflation following the large increase in foreign reserves since 1970 would suggest that reserve expansion should be halted or slowed in order to stop spiraling world inflation. Yet, there is considerable concern about a potential reserve shortage and the unleashing of deflationary forces.

In assessing the adequacy of global reserves, we must factor in other changes that can affect the demand for international reserves, their potential supply, and their distribution among countries. The realignment of parities, the move to floating exchange rates, the rise in the market price of gold, the quadrupling of oil prices, and the massive deficits of the oil-importing countries are among the recent developments which need to be considered in evaluating the inflationary potential of the rapid growth in world reserves.

The question to be considered is whether world reserves are likely to accommodate or generate deflationary or inflationary tendencies. One view compares actual reserve holdings with the quantity that might be judged appropriate—using the procedures followed in setting up the SDRs—and suggests that the stock of reserves may be deficient and potentially deflationary. A second view evaluates reserve adequacy in terms of countries' use of exchange adjustments, exchange controls, demand management policies, and international borrowing. The pattern for 1973–75 is somewhat mixed, but the redistribution of reserves from the oil-importing to the exporting countries is seen as a factor that may cause some reserve stringency, at least for particular countries. A third view, which emphasizes the monetary aspects, associates the sharp 1968–73 growth in external reserves with the 1971–73 acceleration in world monetary growth and the 1974–75 jump in world inflation. It argues that the rapid buildup in aggregate liquidity must be stopped and reversed if we are to curb world inflation.

I shall assess the influence of several recent changes on the demand and supply of international reserves. These include (1) the impact of floating rates on the demand for international reserves, (2) the rise in the market price of gold and the supply of reserves, (3) the recycling of the oil surpluses and the distribution of reserves, (4) other factors which may affect world liquidity, and (5) recent developments in world reserves, world money, and world inflation. My conclusions summarizing the net effect of these influences are presented in the last section.

Floating Rates and the Demand for International Reserves. Consider the effect of moving to a floating exchange-rate regime on the demand for reserves. Central banks held approximately $226 billion of reserves at the end of 1974. The question is whether the March 1973 move to floating rates has converted some part of these external reserves into excess reserves. Greater flexibility in adjusting exchange rates should reduce the extent to which countries need or use international reserves to defend exchange parities. But if the monetary authorities are under less compulsion to maintain and defend existing exchange rates, some portion of the $226 billion, held as world reserves at the end of 1974, may be redundant and potentially inflationary.[1]

Redundant reserves can fuel inflationary impulses if the monetary authorities are committed to defend a set of exchange rates. But the move to floating rates should enable the authorities to regain control over their domestic monetary policies by breaking the link between the balance of payments and money growth. In the long run, floating rates should result in better money stock control in the world economy and, hopefully, less world inflation.[2]

---

[1] The transition to floating rates may lift world prices until the redundant reserves are eliminated. And while such transitional increases in the price level may continue for some time, they do not constitute permanent changes in the inflation rate.

[2] Some analysts argue that the move to floating rates has weakened monetary discipline and resulted in higher monetary growth rates. They point to Great Britain where the money stock has been growing very rapidly and the inflation rate now exceeds 20 percent. The argument is that with floating rates a deficit country may feel less constrained to curtail monetary growth and may choose instead to let its exchange rate depreciate. But it is not clear whether loss of reserves in a fixed rate system would have served as a more effective deterrent on the monetary authorities.

Some of the exchange-rate actions taken in 1973 lend some support to the view that reserve supply was growing relative to demand. Several countries imposed restrictions on exports; some removed restrictions on imports; and some curbed capital inflows and liberalized outflows—actions consistent with the hypothesis that reserves were growing relative to demand. This feeling of reserve adequacy may have changed at the end of 1973.

The national authorities may not yet have made a final determination as to what part of their international reserves are to be treated as excess reserves. The central banks are still learning how to operate in this relatively new system of floating rates, and their current demand for reserves may therefore exceed what they will ultimately regard as an appropriate level for a flexible exchange-rate regime. And some central banks may have additional motives for holding foreign reserves—either because they want to intervene in the currency markets or because larger reserves enable them to get large loans to finance their oil deficits on better terms, to name but two.

Our experience with floating rates is still too limited to assess their impact on the official demand for reserves and the extent to which some of the central bank holdings may be redundant. And the many disturbances in the world economy since March 1973 further complicate the analyses of official reserve holdings. The move to floating rates should have two kinds of effects. The short-run effect is to reduce the demand for reserves relative to supply and to generate excess reserves which may, *ceteris paribus*, contribute to more world inflation. But floating rates also break the automatic link between the balance of payments, the monetary base, and the domestic money supply, and therefore enable the national authorities to exercise much greater control over the domestic money stock. In the long run, a floating rate regime is consistent with greater control of the monetary bases and world money and therefore with less world inflation. It remains to be seen how the transitional and permanent effects of floating rates on the demand for official reserves, world money, and world inflation will work themselves out.[3]

Gold and World Reserves. The very sharp rise in gold prices from $35 in 1967 to $186 in 1974, and especially in the past four years, can substantially raise the stock of world reserves. At the end of 1974 central bank gold holdings, valued in dollars, were approximately $43.7 billion—assuming the official price of approximately $42 per ounce. At the current market price of $165 an ounce, these central bank gold holdings are worth approximately $170 billion. The sharp rise in the market price of gold relative to the official price in recent years opens up the potential of a $120 billion increase—over 50 percent—in world reserves.

---

[3] The analysis in this section permits the rationalization of the emergence of two opposing views on the relation between floating rates and inflation. The *transition* to floating rates may have reduced the demand for international reserves and could have been a contributing factor to the emergence of double-digit inflation, as claimed by its critics. At the same time, floating rates may still help us achieve less world inflation in the long run, as claimed by its defenders.

Although this increase has not yet occurred, gold valued at the market price is now being used as collateral for loans, and some countries, for example, France, have revalued their gold holdings at the market price.

The gap between the current market price of central bank gold stocks and the official price can therefore result in an increase of over 50 percent in world reserves and world liquidity. Such an increase in official reserves could generate, or accommodate, an increase in world inflation in the next five to ten years. Gold therefore has a very substantial potential for fueling further world inflation unless we develop a coordinated policy to deal with it.

The United States has sought to reduce and eventually eliminate gold's monetary role on the grounds that such a central role for gold was incompatible with a stable monetary system. There is at present broad agreement that the monetary role of gold should be reduced. The June 1975 communiqué of the IMF Interim Committee indicates the current status of the negotiations to enhance the role of the SDR as the central asset in the international monetary system and to reduce the role of gold. The principal remaining issues relate to the transitional arrangements and whether the IMF should be allowed to acquire gold from members.

The Financing of Oil Deficits and the Recycling of OPEC Surpluses. The financing of the oil deficits and the recycling of the oil surpluses can affect the stock of reserves and its distribution among countries. Recent estimates indicate that OPEC earned about $135 billion in 1974 and spent about $65 billion and that oil-importing countries had a current-account deficit of about $65 billion to finance. The 1974 deficit with OPEC was financed in large measure through short-term bank lending. Commercial banks in the United States, following the removal of the U.S. capital controls in January 1974, increased their claims on foreigners by $15 billion; and Eurocurrency loans totaled about $28 billion in 1974. But new international lending from the United States and Euromarkets has slowed in 1975. The slowdown in bank lending is the result of an increase in longer term financing through bond issues, increased direct lending from OPEC, and a decline in the OPEC surplus.

Effective intermediation by the Eurocurrency banks and the commercial banking system has enabled credit-worthy oil-importing countries to finance their 1974 deficits without undue difficulties. But—and this is a point which Professor Cooper stressed in his commentary—the international commercial banking system cannot be counted on to continue to increase its international intermediary role at its 1974 pace. The huge payments imbalance between the oil exporters and oil importers cannot be financed primarily through private short-term loans, and we may need to develop policies to hold down the buildup of OPEC assets, which have been estimated initially at almost one trillion dollars within ten years. More recent studies suggest that OPEC financial accumulations will not reach the large sums predicted last year.

263

The manner in which the oil deficits are financed may change the stock of global reserves. If the oil-importing countries use their foreign exchange to finance their deficits, there will be a redistribution of reserves from the oil importers to the oil exporters. But this transfer need not necessarily change the total stock of reserves, if the exporters choose to hold their reserves in the same places that the oil-importing countries hold them. The transfer would reduce the collective reserves of the oil importers by an amount equal to the surplus of the oil exporters, but it would leave the world total unchanged. And if the oil exporters are willing to lend their surpluses directly to importing countries, the financing of the oil deficits will not even lead to a reduction in the reserve holdings of the oil-importing countries.

But there are other cases in which the recycling of the oil surpluses will affect the stock of world reserves. World reserves will increase in the case where the oil importers transfer the foreign exchange that they hold in the *issuing* country, and the oil exporters place these funds in the *offshore* markets. And world reserves will decline if the oil importers transfer reserves previously held in *offshore* markets, and the oil exporters place these funds in the *issuing* country.

The very large 1974 increase of $43 billion in world reserves—$39 billion in the foreign-exchange component alone—does suggest a shift from the *issuing* country to the *offshore* market. The oil importers may have borrowed additional reserves, even though they suffered no reduction in their collective reserves. Uncertainty with regard to securing financing for their deficits, coupled with the need to hold reserves as a security for borrowing, account for the 1974 increase in the demand for reserves.[4]

We should note, however, that while the investment policies of the countries gaining and losing reserves may affect the stock of international reserves, the world impact can be lessened to the extent that capital is mobile. For example, a decision by the oil exporters to deposit additional reserves in the United States rather than in the offshore market would tend to reduce reserves. But if the oil importers can borrow in the United States, they can rebuild their reserve holdings. On the other hand, if U.S. policy seeks to sterilize such capital inflows, the oil importers may have difficulty restoring their liquidity.

The oil importers' demands for reserves are likely to rise, and their reserve holdings may, as in 1974, also grow with their deficits. The oil developments,

---

[4] Let me also comment on the question which was discussed earlier in the conference on whether it makes a difference if the oil funds initially go to country A or country B. Professor Cooper considered this question in terms of "does it make a difference in the kind of things which will happen in the real sector." I would like to consider this question in terms of "does it make a difference in terms of what is going to be happening to world liquidity and world money?" I think it does. But we cannot assess the different effects if money flows to country A or country B without indicating where the money is coming from. The question as posed cannot be answered. What needs to be asked is "how will world reserves be affected if we start here and end up there." In other words, we must consider whether the original funds were kept in the country of issue or in offshore markets relative to where the oil exporters are going to place them.

therefore, may bring about an increase in world reserves while simultaneously increasing reserve stringency, if the oil importers seek more reserves to offset their increasing indebtedness. An increased demand for reserves by the oil importers is one factor which tends to offset the growth in the global stock of reserves.

Other Influences on World Liquidity. One of the arguments used to suggest that there is a possible shortage in world liquidity is that the growth of international reserves has not kept pace with the growth of foreign trade imports. Now this is very similar to the argument that a monetary policy which causes money to grow at a lesser rate than money GNP is not inflationary. But everyone agrees today that U.S. monetary growth in 1972 was excessive, even though money growth was below the growth in nominal GNP. Yet using this kind of test, one would find that the 1972 GNP growth in the United States exceeded monetary growth and therefore conclude that monetary policy was not excessive. I do not think this kind of comparison can serve as an appropriate indicator of global liquidity. Furthermore, if floating rates do indeed reduce the demand for official reserves, the prefloating relationships imbedded in the data used in these tests would certainly tend to overestimate the demand for reserves.

Another question which we must consider is how to treat the private holdings of international liquid assets. These private holdings are fairly substantial, approximately 50 percent of central bank holdings, and can be substituted for official holdings to finance a payments deficit. But there are a number of different factors at work here. The demand for private international liquid assets that are used as a vehicle for transactions purposes may rise if central banks are no longer underwriting potential exchange-rate losses. On the other hand, the demand for private liquidity may decline under floating rates to the extent that it was held primarily in order to speculate against parities. I do not know how these things net out, but private holdings are substantial and have to be considered in any evaluation of whether world reserves are adequate or deficient.

Recent Changes in Reserves. In a recent paper entitled "Worldwide Inflation: A Monetarist View," Professor David Meiselman found that very high monetary growth rates in the major industrial countries in the 1970s followed large increases in their foreign reserves.[5] Waiving the question of cause or effect, there does appear to be a strong association. Total reserves increased very rapidly from 1968 on and accelerated sharply in 1971. Total reserves, and especially foreign-exchange holdings, grew rapidly, along with the dramatic increase in U.S. liabilities to foreigners and the rapid growth of Eurodollar holdings.

Monetary growth rates at the end of the 1968–73 period averaged somewhere between 10 and 20 percent, often closer to 20 percent, whereas at the beginning

[5] See *The Phenomenon of Worldwide Inflation*, eds. David I. Meiselman and Arthur B. Laffer (Washington, D. C.: American Enterprise Institute, 1975), pp. 69-112.

of the period the rates were closer to 10 percent. This rapid explosion in world money came at a time when the annual increase in international reserves averaged close to $35 billion a year, starting with a total stock of about $75 billion in 1968. The central banks of the major countries abandoned fixed exchange rates in early 1973, and the move to floating rates was followed by a deceleration in monetary growth rates. The linkage between excess foreign-exchange reserves, monetary growth, aggregate demand policies, and worldwide inflation is certainly controversial. But inflation rates have been ranging from 7 percent to 16 percent in the industrial countries even before the oil price impact was felt. And while granting that inflation may have many causes, this 1974–75 jump in world inflation to double-digit levels appears to reflect the very same process which produced the 1971–73 acceleration in world money and the explosion in world reserves starting in 1970. I would like to quote the Bank for International Settlements (BIS), which cannot be accused of having a monetarist bias. It describes the 1971–74 period as follows: "One of the limitations on the monetary restraint in recent years has been the huge volume of external flows of funds largely associated with exchange rate uncertainties. . . . The strength of monetary expansion by early 1973 was based largely on cumulative foreign exchange inflows showing up in the banking system's net acquisitions of foreign assets." [6]

The BIS view is that the buildup of foreign-exchange holdings led to rapid world monetary growth and a speedup of world inflation. From this point of view, the stock of global reserves has certainly been adequate in recent years. There are, however, two provisos to consider for the future. First, the real value of global reserves has been declining, both because of the depreciation of the reserve currencies and of inflation. Secondly, the oil price developments may have further increased the demand for reserves relative to the supply.

Several developments in 1974 may be symptomatic of less reserve redundancy and of greater stringency. But there is no evidence, as yet, of inappropriate deflationary policies being dictated by a stringency of reserves. Indeed, several countries have used their reserves on a large scale to prevent the depreciation of their currencies. Import restrictions do not appear to have spread to countries that are not suffering from non-oil balance-of-payments deficits.

The distribution of reserves has worsened in recent years because of the oil developments, and some observers think that the demand for reserves is currently rising. But a sense of world stringency may not develop if the private intermediaries and the official agencies facilitate the recycling of the surpluses and continue to supply some of this demand. Further, if the effective liquidity of official gold holdings is increased, this may generate a dramatic increase in reserves.

Summary. World liquidity has been subject to opposing forces. The move to floating rates and the gold price developments tend to increase supply relative to

---

[6] Bank for International Settlements, *Forty-fourth Annual Report* (Basle: BIS, June 1974), p. 24.

demand and may operate in the direction of generating excessive reserves. On the other hand, the oil price developments tend to increase the demand relative to the supply. Now, if these two forces have just about offset each other in the past year, we may be fortunate. But there is no inherent reason why the oil impact—increasing the demand for global liquidity—should just offset the other factors which tend to increase the supply of reserves. Accordingly, there may be a potential inflationary force here which needs to be monitored.[7]

If the oil developments should dominate and the world turns out to be short of international liquidity, it is necessary to be alert to recognize any restrictive economic policies which will emerge. But it is equally important to be alert to monitor and detect evidences of excessive liquidity.

---

[7] For further elaboration, see David I. Fand, "World Reserves and World Inflation," *Banca Nazionale del Lavoro Quarterly Review*, December 1975, pp. 347-370.

DISCUSSION

International Capital Mobility and Exchange-Rate Systems

DR. WILLETT: Let me respond to a few points brought up in the discussion of my paper. First, the matter of international capital mobility, since this is—following along in the tradition of the literature—somewhat ambiguous in the paper. Within the context of the types of questions dealt with in this session, of primary interest is the extent to which capital will be attracted by a change in uncovered national interest rates. That is, how much interest-rate independence is there on the basis of uncovered interest differentials? (This is the reason, I believe, why the Logue, Salant, and Sweeney paper looks at the uncovered interest-rate differentials.) For some of the questions we are addressing, the income mobility of capital—in other words, the income sensitivity of capital—also becomes relevant. If one examines the effects of expansionary fiscal policy on international capital flows, one needs to look both at the interest-rate effect and the income effect in these capital flows.

The income effect on capital flows is an area in which we need to do considerably more work because we really do not know what the sign should be. This is a point which Paul Wonnacott made very nicely at a conference several years ago. In our models, we have generally assumed that an increase in national income attracts capital. But if an increase in income is taken as a proxy for an increase in portfolio size or in the volume of investable funds, the opposite conclusion may fall out of the analysis. And if one focuses on the direct investment account, the cyclical relationship between, say, direct investment and domestic economic activity will depend very much on whether the direct investment substitutes for or complements domestic production. During a domestic boom, for example, one would expect some increase in direct investment abroad to the extent there is an increased need for raw materials from abroad. Direct investment abroad will complement the domestic boom in this case.

The two standard definitions of capital mobility, though, will refer either to the uncovered arbitrage schedule or the covered arbitrage schedule. Following on Professor Cooper's point, I would expect, by and large, a move from adjustable pegs to floating exchange rates to increase the elasticity of the covered arbitrage schedule and to decrease the elasticity of the uncovered arbitrage schedule or the

269

spot speculation schedule. The presumption for an increase in the elasticity of the covered arbitrage schedule is based on the conclusions that for covered arbitrage there would be no change in exchange risk in a move from pegged to floating exchange rates and that since exchange-rate flexibility is a partial substitute for controls, there would be a decrease in the probability of exchange controls.

On the other hand, there could be a perfectly infinitely elastic covered arbitrage schedule and almost no international interest-rate interdependence. Suppose, for example, that there is a highly inelastic speculative expectations schedule in terms of the forward market and the willingness to move uncovered funds in the spot market—called spot speculating. In this case, a domestic interest-rate increase will show up almost entirely as a shift in the forward exchange rate. Very little capital will move. The forward exchange rate will move, and there will still be a good deal of interest-rate independence.

I certainly agree with Professor Branson that we must be very careful not to misinterpret increases in the volume of the international movement of funds as necessarily representing increases in the mobility of funds. I believe there is a great deal of evidence that capital mobility is higher today than it was in the late forties or early fifties. There are fewer exchange controls, and there has certainly been a broadening of investment horizons. But the extent to which capital mobility is higher today than it was three or four years ago is very much an open question.

PROFESSOR NIEHANS: Perhaps I can simplify a bit the points Professors Branson and Cooper made about capital mobility. I think that one of the main effects on capital flows of the transition to flexible exchange rates is to make expected future exchange-rate changes one of the very normal factors influencing capital flows. Under the pegged exchange-rate system, expected future exchange-rate changes were an extraordinary factor influencing capital flows. But now they are a normal feature of everyday life.

This means that by changing the current exchange rate—making it low enough—any amount of capital inflow desired may always be produced, whatever the interest rate may be, and by making the exchange rate high enough, any amount of outflow may always be produced, whatever the interest rate may be. For example, Germany today has a strong mark and a very strong capital outflow which, on the basis of interest-rate differentials, does not appear justified.

Connected with this is a basic change in behavior which I believe to be quite important—that is, that the reactions of trade flows (commodity flows) to exchange-rate changes may be even slower today with floating rates than they were under a pegged exchange-rate system. These reactions may, in the long run, still be fairly high, but they are probably lower with respect to current changes in the exchange rate than before because under a floating or flexible rate system,

270

exchange-rate changes may be considered just temporary and of no lasting importance, whereas under a pegged system, changes were considered more permanent. This means that the greater effectiveness of monetary policy on domestic stabilization—which is expected under flexible rates—may not materialize because changes in interest rates and exchange rates will not affect current trade flows except after a very long time. The whole effect of monetary policy will be taken up through capital flows: capital outflows, which it would be hoped would come from interest-rate changes, will be neutralized by capital inflows which are generated through exchange-rate changes. So, not only are there no changes in net capital flows, but there are no changes in commodity flows, and monetary policy does not gain in effectiveness compared with a pegged exchange-rate system.

DR. WILLETT: I am very sympathetic to Professor Niehans's comments about the reactions of trade flows to exchange-rate changes under a floating system, certainly in the matter of investment decisions and production planning and so forth. But there is a possible countereffect which might speed up trade flow responses to floating rates. Under floating rates, a change in the rate may in part be viewed as sort of a temporary excise tax. Clearly, there will be less response to exchange-rate changes under a floating system—where they may be viewed as temporary in the case of basic production runs and investment planning. On the other hand, with regard to current inventory—depending on how it is handled—there may be a quicker response to a temporary exchange-rate change than there would be in the case of a more permanent change in the rate. That may be muted to the extent that there are strong customer relations and trading patterns reflecting the extent to which high priority is put on keeping stable trade flows to regular customers.

PROFESSOR STANLEY BLACK: It would appear to me there is a difference of opinion between Professor Cooper and Dr. Willett about the elasticity of arbitrage flows. This is a matter which is very important to the efficiency of the flexible exchange-rate system. One of the things which can increase the efficiency of a flexible rate system is high elasticity of interest arbitrage flows. So if, as Professor Cooper thinks, the arbitrage schedule becomes less elastic as a result of a shift from pegged to flexible rates, that is bad. On the other hand, if the arbitrage schedule becomes more elastic, as Dr. Willett seems to think—at least for covered arbitrage—that is good for the system. Which is correct appears to me to be an empirical question to some extent.

DR. WILLETT: I do not think there is really any disagreement between Professor Cooper and myself. Whether one thinks of high capital mobility as good or bad really depends on one's objectives. At times international economists have

271

demonstrated a type of schizophrenia. We like to talk about well-functioning exchange-rate systems, by which we mean systems that generate very stable exchange rates and give greater monetary independence, but it is very difficult for both characteristics to be realized at the same time. The more stable the rates tend to be—in terms of stabilizing speculation—the lower is the degree of monetary independence, and the more monetary independence there is, the more likely are fluctuations in the exchange rate. This is one of the basic welfare trade-offs which we face.

PROFESSOR FISCHER BLACK: I am utterly confused by this discussion of capital mobility. Let me make just two points. First, both Willett and Cooper said they would define capital mobility—in one sense at least—as the responsiveness of capital movements to uncovered interest-rate differentials. I have trouble making any sense of that definition. Presumably, the idea is that a person who owns an asset which is earning a low interest rate in one country will switch his asset to another country in which he is able to earn a higher rate of return. However, he would certainly take into account factors other than the interest-rate differential. He would take into account any possible changes in exchange rates, controls, taxes, expropriation of assets, and so on. In talking about capital mobility, I would think one would have to include all of these factors when examining the possibilities for capital flows to occur.

Secondly, another thing that has been omitted from the discussion to this point is the matter of offsetting transactions, those on the other side of the balance sheet from the capital movements. This is particularly important in a floating rate regime where there are no gold or reserve flows. In a floating rate system, presumably capital flows are offset by trade flows. So when one hypothesizes that higher interest rates in one country will induce investors to move capital into that country—that is, acquire that country's securities—one needs to specify, in return for what. In a floating rate system presumably that can only be in return for exports of goods and services.

DR. WILLETT: Professor Black is certainly correct in asserting that we should be concerned with all the factors—possible controls, tax laws, and so forth—if we want to explain the *entire* volume of a capital movement. But one may want to analyze capital flows with respect to only one variable or a particular set of variables. If one is concerned with changing tax laws, one would want to look at tax law sensitivity of capital flows. In the sense in which it is used here, though, the main variable with which to be concerned is changing monetary policy. For the kinds of decisions with which we are concerned here, it is necessary to know how much a change in monetary policy will change capital flows.

Clearly, what the net capital-flow effect will be depends in part on the impact the interest-rate changes have on speculative expectations. That is one of the things

I stress in my paper—that these speculative expectations will not always be consistent over time. For instance, speculators could interpret an interest-rate increase as a sign that the government intends to defend the existing exchange rate, and it might have a very stabilizing effect on expectations. On the other hand, there have been historical episodes in which an interest-rate change—particularly when it was done on an unusual day, as it was once done in the United Kingdom—was taken as a sign that things were even worse than people had thought, and it shifted speculative expectations in the opposite direction.

With regard to what will offset the capital flows in the balance of payments—particularly under floating rates—one of the points I tried to make in the paper in several places is that very frequently, in the short run what may be offsetting this is not trade flows but capital flows going in the opposite direction which result from exchange-rate expectations.

PROFESSOR BRANSON: I hate to leave confusion about the interest elasticity of capital flows. Perhaps my remarks could help a little bit.

We have had some mention of the elasticity approach and the absorption approach for analyzing trade flows. The elasticity approach focuses on the price elasticity of imports and exports. In contrast, the absorption approach would say, let's look at the other side of the balance sheet—let's look at domestic excess demand in the market. And then there is the synthesis where one looks at both sides. We all would agree that the price elasticity of exports and imports is not *pure* price elasticity but a rather complicated animal reflecting many things.

In our discussion today, we have been using much the same approach to the analysis of capital flows. Some have looked at capital flows, estimating what purports to be the interest elasticity. Others have looked at the other side of the balance sheet, the exports and imports, and claimed that these must accommodate capital flows. Of course, again, a synthesis approach must be used and it should be recognized that both sides at the same time, capital flows and commodity flows, have to be in balance and that there has to be some mechanism to bring them into balance.

PROFESSOR NUSSBAUMER: We have been discussing differences between fixed and flexible exchange-rate systems, practically always making one assumption: that there is a high mobility of capital. But is that assumption justified in light of all that is known about financial markets today and recent market developments? For instance, we have referred in these discussions to government intervention in financial markets, and we know that whenever such occurs it generates splits in the markets. And we have referred to the fact that interest differentials do not offset differences in risk. There obviously is not sufficient mobility of capital, otherwise these circumstances would not persist. There have been remarks in this discussion about the difference between resident and nonresident holding of assets and about the problem of the oil funds—conditions and developments which attest to the immobility of capital.

Now, whenever there is limited mobility of capital, of course, there is an increased demand for reserves. And what impact does an increased demand for reserves have on inflation? It will bring down inflation rates.

The agreement of European central banks not to engage in borrowing and lending in the Eurodollar market is just an attempt to limit the mobility of capital, at least at the central bank level, and thereby limit the potential size of the Eurocurrency credit multiplier. Actually, are we not well on the way to limiting increasingly the mobility of capital for all sorts of reasons and with all sorts of instruments, which individually may not be spectacular but when taken all together may be very important?

The State of Eurocurrency Markets in 1974

PROFESSOR LEVIN: This morning there has been some mention of the oil money problem currently facing us, as it relates to capital mobility and the relationship between financial markets. I wonder, does it really make a difference whether the Arab oil money goes first to the U.S. market or to the Eurodollar market?

On the face of it, it would appear to me that when the funds are deposited in the Eurodollar market, the liquidity is created in the Eurodollar market without affecting the money supply or liquidity in the U.S. market. True, international liquidity is affected, and thereby other sectors of the economy are affected. In this sense, I agree with Professor Cooper when he says that it does make a difference whether the funds go initially into the Eurodollar market or the U.S. market.

On the other hand, suppose there is an equilibrium amount of Eurodollar deposits associated with the given interest differential between the Eurodollar interest rate and the U.S. interest rate and with given risk coefficients for the U.S. and the Eurodollar markets. Then an increased supply of funds—oil funds, for example—to the Eurodollar market will depress the Eurodollar rate relative to the U.S. interest rate and encourage a flow of funds from Eurodollars to the U.S. market. So, in this sense, the total volume of Eurodollar funds is not affected by whether the Arab oil funds are initially deposited as Eurodollars, and I agree with Professor Kenen that where the funds go initially has no effect on the liquidity in other sectors.

My point is that the matter would appear to come down to an empirical question: what happens if all the Arab oil money flows initially to the Eurodollar market rather than to the U.S. market? Are parameters such as the interest differential and the risk coefficients between the Eurodollar and U.S. markets affected, thus changing the size of the Eurodollar market or not? I would like to hear Professor Cooper comment on this.

PROFESSOR COOPER: The only thing I would add is the conjecture that the parameters have been affected. I thought I made clear that I was talking about the Eurodollar market today and not the Eurodollar market two years ago. One of the consequences of a series of developments—including high and differential rates of inflation from country to country, associated foreign-exchange-rate changes, the increase in oil prices, and now a number of bank failures—is to give financial markets in general a degree of the jitters which they have not had for forty years. And that higher degree of jitters has affected the arbitrage schedule between the New York market and the Eurocurrency market.

Paul Wonnacott mentioned that he had looked at some data which indicated that the interest differential between the Eurodollar and U.S. markets, while it was higher in the first half of 1974 than it was during 1973, was not higher than it was, say, two years ago. I would question, however, the source of the data recorded in the newspaper, because my impression is that the Eurocurrency market has now become a two or even a three-tiered market with very substantial risk premia associated with different participants in the market. And that being so, the unity of the market—as connected up by a set of stable arbitrage schedules— has broken down or is in the process of breaking down. This means more fragmentation in the market, and, in these circumstances, how the money goes out depends in part—to a greater extent than used to be the case—on how it comes in. Further, I would agree with Professor Fand's explanation of that: how the money goes out also depends on where it originally came from. It may be necessary to trace it back to the source.

One other point I would make—and this applies more to the U.S. market than to the Eurocurrency market, although since we are comparing the two, it is relevant. We have had so far this year—but this may be changing right now—a considerable degree of credit rationing by American banks. Whenever such a condition exists, those borrowers who are on the priority list of customers of the banks are the preferred customers by assumption. Funds coming into a certain group of banks then go to the preferred customers of those banks rather than to the preferred customers of a different set of banks. Thus, in a period of credit rationing, there is fragmentation in the model of perfect markets which we use and which is frequently a reasonable approximation to the real world. It is necessary to be aware of such developments and their impact on the assumptions.

Putting the matter a little more formally, the model of perfect markets usually makes a lot of background assumptions about the structure of relationships—one of which is that default risk remains unchanged. Normally, economists do not think about default risk, in fact. But default risk has recently increased considerably as perceived by market participants. There has occurred a change in a parameter which analysts normally take as constant and which they, therefore, neglect entirely.

PROFESSOR LOGUE: About the distribution of the OPEC funds among the world's financial markets, my studies drew me very rapidly to the conclusion that the distribution of the funds would roughly correspond to the relative sizes of the markets. Some rough calculations suggest that perhaps 75 percent of the total OPEC current-account surplus will be placed in either the Eurodollar or the New York markets. The question then becomes, how will this 75 percent be distributed among those two markets.

It seems to me that irrespective of where the funds are initially placed— whether they go into the Eurodollar market or the U.S. market first—they will be distributed eventually in relation to the relative sizes of these two markets. If they are put into Eurodollars and there is not a queue of borrowers standing outside the London banks, there would just be an increase in the deposits of the London banks with banks in the United States. Some rough calculations suggest that the size of the flow from the Eurodollar market to the U.S. market that is needed to maintain the rough relative sizes of these two markets would not have to be any larger than the amount of funds transferred during 1969 and 1970 between Eurobanks and U.S. banks—usually via U.S. bank overseas branches operating in the Eurodollar market. So, I do not see any real problem with this giant flow of funds even if it is distributed by its initial depositors in a pattern which, in ultimate terms, is unbalanced. The markets have the capacity to redistribute the funds to reflect real requirements.

As for the bank failures and the jitters in the markets about which Professor Cooper spoke, I am not overly concerned. Anyone who is familiar with these failures—such as Franklin National and Herrstatt—knows they were the result of incredibly poor management, and it was appropriate that they failed. I am personally not sure that bank failures are something to be more concerned with than failures of industrial firms of equivalent size.

DR. HEWSON: I would like to put a question to Professor Cooper. I agree with him that the recent jitters in world financial markets have changed the basic parameters of the markets. But have they changed the relative position of New York vis-à-vis London? True, they have changed the relative position of large commercial banks vis-à-vis smaller commercial banks or some other types of institutions. But we should take into account the multinational characteristics of the banks in London and New York. Do the jitters really change the relative position of London branches of the Bank of America to their head office? And do they really change the position of some New York branches of some of the banks in London? My answer would tend to be No.

PROFESSOR COOPER: I do not know whether all the developments which I have subsumed under the term "jitters" have changed the relationship between the Bank of America, London, and the Bank of America, New York or San Francisco.

What I am suggesting though is that that is only part of the picture. In former times the Bank of America, London, on receiving funds would quickly distribute them to the interbank market in London. But that market is not functioning now the way it functioned, say, two years ago. (The change in its functioning is a quantitative question, but then there is the question of how far you go quantitatively before you call it a qualitative change.) The London branch is more likely now to send the funds to its head office than it is to put them into the interbank market in London.

And to the extent that credit rationing is occurring in the United States, it is more likely that the funds will be lent to domestic customers here in the United States rather than to borrowers in, say, the Kingdom of Denmark. It seems to me that this type of thing is the real change which has occurred. The impact can be traced through the world system, and if you abstract from all other factors, U.S. imports of Danish goods may go up because of the impact such changes have had on financial flows. In the meantime, Denmark may have to impose import controls before that happens because it cannot borrow the funds.

So, the matter gets back to the point I made earlier—the point that we are interested primarily in the path of developments. I think the path has been changed. And as long as there are lags in the system and the system is as jittery as it now is, we have to worry about a breakdown in the system, I believe.

PROFESSOR ALLEN: In support of what Professor Cooper is saying, I believe that the interest-rate differential now existing between the Eurocurrency market and the New York market is an indication of a risk premium which did not exist earlier. The U.S. capital controls were terminated in January 1974. Prior to that time, the differential by which Eurodollar rates exceeded U.S. rates was taken to be partly due to the fact that the markets were divided by the capital controls. When the controls were removed, the Eurodollar and U.S. interest rates went almost completely together. But starting in June 1974, they separated again. This was just about the time of the Herrstatt failure and the growth of a lot of nervousness in the Eurocurrency market.

The growing differential of Eurodollar rates above U.S. rates is attributed by many bankers to several developments. It may be an indication of worry that the British will impose some kind of capital controls which would interefere with the use of dollar funds deposited in London. It may also reflect a worry on the part of the market that perhaps the Federal Reserve Board would be more supportive of New York banks than it would be of the U.S. subsidiaries in London. That is, there is a lender of last resort in New York but not a clearly defined one in London.

DR. KLOPSTOCK: There are a number of unanswered questions about the Eurocurrency market on which we should focus in a discussion like this. The market has expanded at a tremendous rate during the last three years, at a much faster rate than it did during the regime of fixed rates. Why? We have had—with floating exchange rates—a tremendous increase in the risk associated with the placement of funds in the market. And yet, in spite of this greater risk—which at one time I thought would be an impediment to the growth and expansion of the market—the market has expanded at a fantastic rate. Why?

I also wonder about the effect of the creation of credit and deposits in the market on capital movements and on interest rates. And in what respect do interest rates serve as a limiting factor to the expansion of credit and deposits in the market?

Questions have been raised about capital mobility and the Euromarket which still need to be answered. It has been well demonstrated that capital mobility—as a result of the emergence of the Euromarket—has continuously increased. Look at what happened in 1974—fantastic amounts of money have moved through the market from country to country this year! Tens of billions of dollars have moved in a very short period of time—through both developed and less developed countries—under the specter of floating rates. Why?

With regard to the current state of the market, the multitiered market is not one or two tiers, and not even one of three tiers. It is one of at least seven tiers. We are seeing tremendous changes, perhaps not in the size of the market, but in the distribution of funds within the market and in distribution between institutions. And there is a tremendous distinction between placing funds in the Euromarket or in the U.S. money market. The Euromarket is a pass-through market. The Euromarket distributes funds immediately or simultaneously; there is simultaneous action between receiving funds and lending them in the Euromarket. All of these factors and developments need to be given closer analytical attention.

DR. SAVONA: Dr. Willett and perhaps others have brought up the matter of credit substitution in the Eurocurrency market. So often the credit substitution notion is used to play down the inflationary impact of the Eurocurrency system or the idea that it makes a net contribution to credit expansion. I believe that the use of the credit substitution notion in either of these two ways is wrong. If there is credit substitution occurring in the Eurocurrency system, it finds its source in the credit multiplication which occurs in the system, just as domestic credit is the result of credit multiplication in a domestic credit system.

The problem is that if European countries, for example, want to curb domestic credit availability, they have a hard time of it because of the credit substitution from the Eurocurrency market. This is the inflationary aspect of the market. Take the case of Germany. In order to curb domestic credit availability it has had to resort to administrative tools, which moreover are very unsettling on the markets. Germany has resorted to the *bardepôt* system and many other instruments. Italy, too, has resorted to a lot of administrative tools to keep funds from moving out of the country into the international financial markets.

Finally, it should be noted that an exchange of official reserves among central banks is not neutral in terms of the impact on either interest rates or on the level of liquidity, because there is the possibility that the central bank making the transfer will use deposits in the Eurodollar market—thus switching an amount of liquidity from London to New York. Total official reserves will remain unchanged. But the volume of international liquidity, broadly defined, is changed. This is why I, together with Professor Fratianni, have proposed the concept of what we are calling an international monetary-base market into which all the international high-powered liquidity is grouped. This concept of international high-powered liquidity is also consistent with the Bank of Italy's call for the official planning of the use of international liquidity to enhance the proper—in terms of policy objectives—control of the international money stock.

PART
FOUR

SOME EUROCURRENCY PROBLEMS: CREDIT EXPANSION, THE REGULATORY FRAMEWORK, LIQUIDITY, AND PETRODOLLARS

Carl H. Stem

Eurocurrency banking—also called external currency or foreign currency banking—has been around now for a little more than fifteen years. From a meager $500 million or so in 1959,[1] total outstanding Eurocurrency deposit liabilities of eight reporting European countries had grown to an estimated $185 billion by the end of March 1975—and to approximately $220 billion if the Eurocurrency centers outside Europe, such as the Bahamas and Singapore, are included. The Eurodollar component, although it has grown more slowly since 1969 than the nondollar Eurocurrency component, is estimated worldwide at about $170 billion at the end of March 1975.[2] As recently as December 1967, it was estimated at approximately $22 billion.

Eurocurrency banking has grown particularly rapidly since the beginning of 1969, with the rate of growth accelerating during 1972, 1973, and early 1974. The amount of Eurocurrency deposits outstanding worldwide increased by approximately $25 billion during 1972 and by an estimated $50 billion during 1973. During the first half of 1974, worldwide Eurocurrency volume grew at an estimated annual rate of slightly more than $50 billion. However, heightened uncertainties in Eurocurrency markets in the summer of 1974—generated by some widely publicized bank failures and tightening credit conditions—led to a slight contraction of Eurocurrency volume in the third quarter of that year and reduced the gain in Eurocurrency volume for 1974 as a whole to approximately $35 billion.[3] Very

---

I wish to acknowledge a personal indebtedness to many academic and former government colleagues for stimulating thoughts on some of the topics discussed in this paper. In particular, I want to thank Mr. Robert H. Enslow, former director of the Office of Foreign Direct Investments (OFDI), U.S. Department of Commerce, Mr. C. Dirck Keyser, former director of the Research and Policy Division, OFDI, Dr. Richard Erb, former assistant director of the Council on International Economic Policy, and Dr. Rodney Mills, Division of International Finance, Board of Governors of the Federal Reserve System.

[1] *The Economist*, 11 July 1959, pp. 109-110.

[2] Bank for International Settlements, *Forty-Fifth Annual Report* (Basle: BIS, June 1975), pp. 129-130. The eight reporting European countries are Belgium, France, Germany, Italy, the Netherlands, Sweden, Switzerland and the United Kingdom.

[3] It is generally conceded that the contraction in Eurocurrency volume during the second half of 1974 was the result of retrenchment in interbank positions. See Morgan Guaranty Trust Company of New York, *World Financial Markets*, 15 April 1975, p. 6.

preliminary data indicate a reviving of Eurocurrency growth during the first half of 1975 with a rate of expansion only slightly less than that of the first half of 1974.[4]

A buildup of numerous developments during 1973 and 1974—at the same time that Eurocurrency volume appeared to be increasing its rate of growth—focused renewed attention on the workings of the Eurocurrency system and intensified concern about the impact of Eurocurrency banking. The following summarizes the developments of major concern to international bankers and national regulatory and monetary authorities.

(1) The very rapid growth of the volume of Eurocurrency credit at a time of accelerating worldwide inflationary pressures and anti-inflationary monetary policy in much of the industrialized world has raised anew the question of the nature of Eurocurrency expansion and its inflationary implications and revived interest in the possible control of Eurocurrency expansion.

(2) The termination of U.S. capital controls, the growing internationalization of U.S. corporate borrowing, and the expansion of foreign banking in the United States has raised concern about the competitiveness of U.S.-based institutions, given the U.S. regulatory environment to which they are subject.

(3) The rapidly growing volume of Eurocurrency loans extended to borrowers in the developing countries and the considerable lengthening of the average maturity of Euroloans—particularly up to mid-1974—has raised questions about the liquidity and viability of the Eurocurrency system especially during a period of worldwide credit stringency and heightened financial market uncertainty.[5]

(4) The failure of several small banks in the United Kingdom, Germany, and Austria because of bad management, overexpansion, or foreign-exchange losses in 1974 has raised the fear that a liquidity problem in the Eurocurrency system might lead to a domino-type collapse of the world banking system à la 1931.

(5) The sharp increase in the price of oil from the major oil-exporting nations, with the attendant transfer of wealth from the oil importers to the oil exporters, has posed the problems of financing the necessary payments flows and investing the proceeds and has raised the questions of the extent to which the Eurocurrency market might serve these financial needs and of the nature of the impact of these developments on Eurocurrency banking.

This paper focuses on some of the issues raised by these developments and attempts to analyze the relevant factors with a view to determining possible

---

[4] Ibid.

[5] Until the heightened uncertainties which developed in international financial markets about mid-1974, it was quite common for Euroloans to have final maturities of 10 years. However, by August 1974 it was very difficult to syndicate a loan with a final maturity greater than seven to eight years.

scenarios of future developments. First, an in-depth analysis of Eurocurrency expansion is undertaken with a view to determining the possible effectiveness of various instruments which, it has been suggested, might be implemented to control Eurocurrency expansion. (The presumption underlying the concern about Eurocurrency expansion is that this expansion, like domestic credit expansion, is inflationary.) Second, the impact of the U.S. regulatory framework on the relative competitiveness of U.S.-based banks vis-à-vis foreign banks is examined. This matter follows quite closely on the first question since the conclusions drawn from the study of possible control of Eurocurrency expansion are that the best way to "control" Eurocurrency expansion is to recapture deposit-loan business from the external banking function for the domestic currency banking functions of the world by enhancing the competitiveness of domestic currency banking institutions vis-à-vis Eurobanks. Third, the Eurocurrency system's liquidity problem and the prospects for a "lender (or lenders) of last resort" are discussed. Finally, the problems and prospects associated with the possible role of the Eurocurrency system in petrodollar recycling are very briefly explored primarily to set the stage for the discussion to follow.

Controlling Eurocurrency Expansion

Time and again during the global expansion of Eurocurrency banking, concern has been expressed that this expansion has been "uncontrolled" and "unregulated." A variety of developments and circumstances have prompted the call for control and regulation of Eurocurrency markets.

Circumstances Generating Calls for Control of Eurocurrency Activity. Prior to 1966 there was general concern among international monetary authorities and analysts that Eurocurrency expansion was occurring outside the oversight of a central bank or group of central banks. Not only did the depositing and lending activity of Eurobanks take place without the supervisory surveillance of an individual central bank or group of cooperating central banks, but many observers thought that the credit mass being generated by Eurocurrency lending activity was not tethered directly to a finite monetary base as is the case with domestic credit expansion.

In 1969 relatively tight credit conditions and very high interest rates in the United States attracted a massive volume of financial flows—mostly through the Eurodollar market—out of foreign currency investments into U.S. dollar-denominated assets, drawing significant amounts of official reserves from numerous countries. At about this time, calls for controls on Eurocurrency expansion became more specific. In 1969 the U.S. Federal Reserve Board, through its monetary policy and by maintaining Regulation Q ceilings on interest rates offered to depositors by U.S. banks, caused the competition of U.S. banks for funds among dollar depositors—which normally is confined to domestic U.S. markets—to spill over into the nonregulated Eurodollar market. Competitive bidding in the Eurodollar market—where there were no deposit rate ceilings—drove Eurodollar deposit rates to unprecedented levels and significantly above comparable deposit rates in the United States. This made dollar investments even more attractive than they would have been in the absence of the Eurodollar market.

Also, since there was no reserve requirement on the liabilities of U.S. bank home offices to their foreign branches, there was a relative cost advantage associated with the absence of the reserve requirement for U.S. banks to borrow in the Eurodollar market rather than in domestic U.S. funds markets.[6]

This state of affairs—particularly the severe drain imposed by these flows of funds to the United States on foreign central bank reserves—prompted a call that U.S. authorities reduce the incentive for U.S. banks to borrow in the Eurodollar market. The Federal Reserve then placed marginal reserve requirements on U.S. banks' liabilities to foreign branches effective in September 1969, in a move to make Eurodollar funds prohibitively expensive for U.S. banks. In 1970 the Federal Reserve removed Regulation Q ceilings on large-denomination time deposits at U.S. banks, effectively eliminating the incentive for U.S. banks to move their competition for funds to the unregulated Eurodollar market during periods of monetary stringency and elevated interest rates in the United States.

During the 1970 to 1973 period of foreign-exchange-market turmoil and uncertainty about currency parities, speculation on possible parity changes generated massive flows of funds through foreign exchange markets, a large part of which—it was believed by many observers—was deposited in or borrowed from the Eurocurrency system. These massive flows of speculative funds were disruptive to foreign exchange and money markets, and they interfered with the normal business of financing and clearing international payments. Again, a call arose to control the Eurocurrency system and to reduce the destabilizing speculative flows of funds which were emanating from Eurocurrency activity.[7]

In the spring of 1971, the Group of Ten central banks jointly agreed not to place additional funds into the Eurodollar market. Some of these banks even

---

[6] A rather complete empirical analysis of this state of affairs and the ensuing flows of funds is found in Richard C. Marston, *American Monetary Policy and the Structure of the Eurodollar Market,* Princeton Studies in International Finance, No. 34 (Princeton: Princeton University Press, 1974).

[7] An excellent review of foreign-exchange-market and Eurocurrency market developments during the 1970-73 period of exchange-market turmoil may be found in the *Forty-First, Forty-Second,* and *Forty-Third Annual Reports* of the Bank for International Settlements (BIS), Basle, Switzerland, in the appropriate chapters on foreign exchange and the Eurocurrency market. The data collected and analyzed by the BIS have led it to minimize the disruptive importance of Eurocurrency activity on foreign exchange markets during this period. However, at the time of the exchange-market "crises," there was considerable opinion that the liquidity furnished by the Eurocurrency system was making matters worse than they would have been in the absence of the Eurocurrency system.

withdrew funds from the Eurocurrency markets.[8] But the major control-type actions against short-term capital flows were taken on an individual country basis: countries subject to speculative inflows of funds undertook defensive measures to restrain residents from borrowing abroad and repatriating funds from abroad and to restrain nonresidents from the inward movement of funds. Countries subject to speculative outflows of funds undertook measures to moderate or restrain the outward movement of funds.

From time to time there have been calls for control of Eurocurrency banking on grounds that the growth of Eurocurrency credit (deposit liquidity) is inflationary. Concern about the possible inflationary impact of Eurocurrency expansion heightened particularly in 1973 and 1974 as the pace of inflation quickened generally throughout the industrial world. In late August 1974, West German Chancellor Schmidt called for control of the rapidly burgeoning Eurocurrency market, indicating that it could soon surpass in outstanding volume the gross national product of Germany.[9] Indicating that "Eurocurrencies can expand by the process of money creation, even without infusions from oil nations or payments deficits," the *Wall Street Journal* called in August 1974 for an international review of Eurocurrency expansion and an examination of the possibility of imposing reserve requirements and perhaps other regulations which apply to loans and deposits denominated in domestic currencies. It concluded: "Yet ultimately a dollar created in Zurich bids for the same world supply of goods as a dollar created in New York, and somewhere sooner or later must have the same inflationary effect.[10]

The development of the tightly integrated, worldwide Eurocurrency marketplace may have increased to some degree the sensitivity of liquid and intermediate-term funds to interest-rate differentials. The highly organized Eurocurrency marketplace makes it mechanically easier for investors to shift funds in response to interest-rate changes and/or speculative situations, and the information system associated with the market probably makes investors more sensitive—in that it makes them more aware—to changes in interest rates and speculative conditions than they would be in the absence of the Eurocurrency system.

However, even in the absence of the Eurocurrency system, international short-term capital flows would develop to take advantage of interest-rate differentials among nations or among regions of the world and/or speculative conditions in foreign exchange and/or financial markets. Funds would move directly from one national (domestic currency) banking system to another without the intermediation of the Eurocurrency system if it did not exist. Thus the existence of the Eurocurrency system is an institutional factor which probably means that the

---

[8] Bank for International Settlements, *Forty-Second Annual Report* (Basle: BIS, June 1972), p. 149.

[9] *New York Times,* 22 August 1974, p. 47.

[10] "Controlling Eurocurrencies," *Wall Street Journal,* 30 August 1974, p. 4.

short-term capital flows which do develop for any given interest differential or speculative condition may be somewhat greater than they would be in its absence. How much greater—significantly greater, insignificantly greater—it is impossible to know.

In addition to this increased mechanical efficiency which the Eurocurrency system contributes to international short-term capital flows, the credit volume which it makes available—a volume that would not be available in its absence—no doubt supplies liquidity which, for any given interest-rate differential and/or speculative condition, results in larger international capital flows than would be the case in the absence of Eurocurrency banking.

However, destabilizing speculative short-term capital flows—motivated by speculative conditions in foreign exchange markets—may be little problem today with the exchange rates of the major economic and financial powers in a generally floating situation. What speculation on possible exchange-rate changes that does occur may be largely reflected in the exchange rates themselves, depending on the extent to which the relevant central bank wants to distribute the exchange-market pressure between its exchange rate and its reserve holdings. The same state of affairs also generally applies to short-term capital flows generated by interest rate differentials. The affected country may let the capital flows be reflected in its exchange rate or be reflected in its international reserves or a combination of both, or it may use control techniques to moderate the capital flows themselves.

Controlling International Short-Term Capital Flows. In controlling international short-term capital flows, the initiation or action point continues to remain entirely at the national level—as was the case during the periods of tumultuous short-term capital flows prior to the general floating of exchange rates in March 1973. National controls take as their points of impact:

(1) resident banks which, by changing their net foreign currency positions, may effect inflows and outflows of funds from a country;

(2) nonbank residents—corporations, businesses and individuals—which may invest and borrow abroad or repatriate funds and pay off loans abroad; and

(3) foreign residents—banks, corporations, businesses and individuals—which may invest in, lend to, borrow from, and repay loans from the target country.

National authorities have developed a variety of techniques to implement control of short-term capital flows which may occur through these three channels.

National monetary or regulatory authorities may restrict the extent to which *resident banks* may convert foreign currency assets into domestic currency or vice versa by placing limits on the banks' net foreign currency positions. Italian authorities have successfully applied such techniques in the past, and the Bank of

England perennially limits the net foreign currency position of British banks. Under a regime of floating rates, however, a national banking system as a whole cannot gain any additional domestic currency liquidity by selling foreign currency assets (or reduce domestic currency liquidity by purchasing foreign currency assets) if its central bank maintains a complete noninterventionary foreign-exchange-market policy. Only if the domestic banking system as a whole sells its foreign currency assets to its central bank, does it realize any additional domestic currency liquidity. With the central bank out of the exchange market, bank selling of foreign currency assets merely drives the exchange rate down, other things equal.[11]

Various techniques may be used to discourage *residents* of a country from placing funds abroad or borrowing funds from abroad when the moderation of such flows of funds is judged in the best interests of a country's domestic stabilization and/or balance-of-payments policy. To discourage residents from borrowing abroad, German authorities have instituted at times a *bardepôt*.[12] In Great Britain, where a rather sophisticated exchange control system has continued in effect since World War II, residents have been limited at times to foreign borrowings with a maturity of five years or longer to discourage borrowing abroad. Exchange control measures may be instituted by national authorities to prohibit residents from placing funds abroad. The United States for example, instituted a direct controls program which limited the extent to which U.S. corporations could keep liquid balances outside the United States. The program remained in effect in various forms from 1965 until January 1974.

A variety of measures have been used in the past by national authorities to discourage *foreign residents* from borrowing funds from or placing funds in a country when the flow of funds would have an adverse impact on national financial markets and/or a country's balance of payments. In countries with established exchange controls, nonresident borrowing and placing of funds may be fairly easily regulated. Other techniques include prohibition of nonresident purchase of domestic financial assets—implemented at times by Germany—and the institution of service charges or taxes on foreign-owned domestic depository assets—utilized by various European countries at various times.

The existence of short-term capital flows which may be considered destabilizing or disruptive and the problem of their effective control at the national level is not unique to the existence of Eurocurrency banking. As mentioned above, the Eurocurrency system may have aggravated the problem by causing, in at least two ways, short-term capital flows to be larger than would be the case in its

---

[11] Detailed discussion of the various short-term capital control techniques used in recent years by the major European countries may be found in the appropriate chapters of Donald R. Hodgman, *National Monetary Policies and International Monetary Cooperation* (Boston: Little, Brown and Company, 1974).

[12] A *bardepôt* requires the resident borrowing unit to place on non-interest-bearing deposit with the stipulated government agency—usually the treasury or central bank of a country—a certain percent of the amount borrowed from abroad. It has the effect of raising the effective interest rate the borrower must pay on the funds available for his use.

absence: (1) by providing a better mechanism and information system for international short-term capital flows than would otherwise exist and (2) by providing—through credit expansion—liquidity for movement among countries which would not have been available in the system's absence.

The control problem in the forefront of discussions today (1974/1975), however, is concerned with the general expansiveness of Eurocurrency liquidity and credit—because of its perceived inflationary implications—and the possibility of its cooperative international control on a global basis. The concern is not so much with destabilizing or disruptive—to foreign-exchange and financial markets—short-term capital flows.

Controlling Eurocurrency Expansion on a Global Basis. It is to the problem of global control of Eurocurrency expansion that the rest of this section of the paper is devoted.

The nature of Eurocurrency expansion. The following analysis of the possibilities for control of Eurocurrency expansion on a global basis is conducted in terms of Eurodollar banking because of the need to focus on external currency financial intermediation in a single currency in our work. However, the analysis developed in terms of Eurodollars is generally applicable to nondollar Eurocurrency financial intermediation, also. The exception is the special way in which U.S. resident banks have used the Eurodollar market as a source of funds for the internal liquidity management of head offices in the United States. Other Eurocurrency markets have not come to be used by the commercial banks of the home countries of the currencies involved as sources of funds for the internal liquidity management of the home offices in the same way U.S. banks have used the Eurodollar market.[13]

Analysis of the possible inflationary implications of global Eurodollar expansion requires distinguishing clearly between three types of financial phenomena which occur simultaneously in the Eurodollar system and which are reflected in the net liabilities and assets data for the Eurodollar system:

(1) U.S. bank borrowing in the Eurodollar market. As mentioned above, during 1966 and again in 1969, U.S. resident banks turned to the Eurodollar market to bid for time deposits for which they were precluded from bidding in U.S. domestic financial markets because of the Regulation Q interest-rate ceilings in the United States. As Eurodollar rates rose to unprecedented heights, investors—U.S. residents, as well as nonresidents—shifted funds from dollar deposits held in banks in the United States and from other financial assets in the United States into the Eurodollar market. In addition, investors shifted funds from nondollar currency investments into Eurodollars by buying U.S. dollars in their respective foreign

---

[13] See the article by Fred Klopstock, *Monthly Review*, Federal Reserve Bank of New York, July 1968, pp. 130-138, for a discussion of the ways in which U.S. resident banks have used Eurodollar-source funds in their internal liquidity management.

exchange markets. Operating as the world was at that time on a par value exchange-rate system, the massive purchases of U.S. dollars to invest in high-yielding Eurodollar deposits shifted official dollar reserves into the hands of private investors who in turn shifted them into Eurodollar deposits.

The Bank for International Settlements (BIS) estimates that during 1969 the net volume of Eurodollar deposits outstanding increased about $13 billion.[14] However, this increase in Eurodollar volume did not reflect the intermediation by the Eurodollar system of credit—which some analysts would consider inflationary—available to support net additional transactions in goods and services. U.S. resident banks' liabilities to foreign branches in the Eurodollar market rose about $13 billion during 1969. But these Eurodollar funds taken up by U.S. resident banks were not available to Eurobanks for loans to credit end-users. These funds, newly attracted to the Eurodollar market, were not used to extend credit to credit end-users; they were allowed to build up in intrabank accounts between U.S. resident banks and their branches outside the United States.

What we would call "Eurodollar banking" in a limited sense, at least—accepting dollar deposits and making loans to credit end-users—ceased to expand during 1969 and may have even contracted though the recorded volume of net Eurodollar deposits rose sharply during this period. The expansion of Eurodollar volume in 1969 merely reflected the function of the Eurodollar market as an external and unregulated market in interbank funds for U.S. resident banks. The overall balance sheet of the Eurodollar system expanded, but that part of the Eurodollar system which intermediates credit from savers to nonbank credit end-users ceased to expand and may have even decreased.

To the extent that Eurodollar funds are "pulled into U.S. resident banks" as liabilities to foreign branches (or to foreign Eurobanks), they are not available to be used for loan extensions to credit end-users, and hence they may not increase inflationary pressures directly.

(2) Interbank chaining of deposits. A second financial phenomenon reflected in the Eurodollar data is the interbank chaining of deposits. Through the process of interbank redepositing, funds are shifted within the Eurodollar system from Eurobanks which have funds in excess of final loan demand to Eurobanks which have inadequate funds to meet their loan demand. Although the interbank deposit markets—and the buildup of interbank deposits—is a vital part of the Eurodollar financial intermediary process, the interbank deposits built up in this process do not directly, in and of themselves, increase the volume of credit available to support worldwide aggregate demand since they do not reflect loans to credit end-users. Obviously, to the extent they reflect interbank redepositing which supports Eurobank lending to credit end-users, they indirectly contribute to

---

[14] Bank for International Settlements, *Fortieth Annual Report* (Basle: BIS, June 1970), pp. 145-146.

an additional volume of credit to support aggregate demand which might not otherwise be available.

The BIS data for the eight reporting European countries net out interbank balances among banks in the eight countries. However, they do not net out interbank balances between banks within the eight-country reporting area and the rest of the world. Thus, the BIS worldwide estimates of Eurodollar size will include some unknown volume of interbank deposits.

(3) Bank loans to credit end-users. The third financial phenomenon reflected in the Eurodollar data collected by the BIS is the credit intermediation performed by Eurobanks in the process of accepting deposits from investors and making loans to credit end-users. When this credit is used to support transactions in goods and services which add to worldwide aggregate demand, it may be considered inflationary; that is, it tends to support a larger aggregate demand than could exist in the absence of the credit.

Two points need to be kept in mind at this stage of our analysis, however. First, credit extended by Eurobanks to so-called credit end-users may be used in such a way that it does not add to the aggregate demand for goods and services. The best example of this is the loans made by Eurobanks to currency speculators during the periods of massive speculation on possible currency par value changes during the early 1970s. The proceeds of the loans were used by the borrowers to purchase foreign exchange—generally provided under the par value exchange-rate regime in existence at that time by the respective central banks involved. Such loans supported currency speculation and provided fodder for the massive flows of short-term capital which disrupted foreign exchange and money markets. But they did not add to demand pressures for goods and services anywhere in the world.

The second point is that credit extended by Eurobanks to credit end-users to finance purchases of goods and services may not add to inflationary aggregate demand pressures per se if the Eurodollar credit is a substitute for credit which would have been made available to the borrower in the absence of Eurodollar banking, either by banks in the United States in dollars or by banks in nondollar currencies. It is not possible to measure, not even possible to guesstimate, the extent to which Eurodollar—or Eurocurrency credit in general—substitutes for credit that would otherwise have been provided by national banking and credit markets in the absence of Eurodollar banking.

It would appear safe to say though that some part of the Eurodollar credit volume outstanding at any point in time adds to the net volume of financing available on a worldwide basis merely because the greater competition among lending institutions inherent in the presence of Eurodollar banking probably means that some borrowers are able to get loans who would not be able to do so in the absence of the Eurodollar system. To the extent this net addition to credit availability provided by Eurodollar banking is used to finance purchases of goods and services, it supports a larger volume of aggregate demand than would exist if

Table 1

SUMMARY

THE IMPACT OF EURODOLLAR INTERMEDIATION ON CREDIT AVAILABILITY TO SUPPORT AGGREGATE DEMAND DEPENDS ON THE DISPOSITION OF EUROLOANS

I. *Funds from the Eurodollar Market Used by U.S. Resident Bank Home Offices:* Funds lent through foreign branches and/or correspondents to banks in the United States do not add to net credit availability to support aggregate demand.

II. *Funds from the Eurodollar Market Used by Non-U.S. Banks:* Dollar funds converted on a net basis by a national banking system into domestic currency increase the domestic currency reserve base of the banking system to the extent the respective central bank intervenes in its exchange market, thus increasing its credit expansion potential. Under a floating exchange-rate system, foreign currency conversion into domestic currency by a national banking system does not affect the country's monetary base.

III. *Euroloans Made to U.S. Residents:* This credit will add to general credit availability to the extent it does *not* substitute for credit which would have been furnished in the absence of the Euroloans by banks in the United States.

IV. *Euroloans Made to Other Borrowers Than U.S. Residents:* (a) Loans, the proceeds of which are converted into domestic currency by the borrowers, may largely reflect credit that would not have been available from the domestic banking system; hence these may largely add to net credit availability.

(b) Loans, the proceeds of which are used as dollars to finance international trade and other transactions, again may add to net credit availability if they are a net addition to the volume of credit which would be available in the absence of Eurodollar lending.

Eurodollar credit were not available. (A summary of the impact of Eurodollar credit intermediation on credit availability and an analysis of its inflationary potential is given in Table 1.)

Bernstein has questioned "whether the Eurodollar market is a banking system in the same sense that the banks of the United States or other countries constitute a system. This seems to me the heart of the problem . . ." he says.[15] He points out that the holding of deposits in commercial banks in the various Federal Reserve districts of the United States is closely related to production, consumption, and investment in these regions individually. He further observes that a bank credit system traditionally supports a relatively self-contained economic system, seeming to imply that since the Eurodollar system does not support economic activity in a self-contained "national" system, it perhaps has no net effect on credit availability and aggregate demand.

---

[15] E. M. Bernstein in Fritz Machlup, Armin Gutowski, and Friedrich Lutz, *International Monetary Problems* (Washington: American Enterprise Institute, 1972), p. 37.

293

However, Bernstein may have focused in his analysis too strongly on the depositor/asset side of Eurodollar intermediation and not enough on the bank loan side. He points out that "the geographic distribution of Eurodollar deposits does not conform to the relative importance of countries in international trade and investment, nor to their relative output, nor to their domestic money supply. Of the $31 billion of Eurodollar deposits in London at the end of 1970, Switzerland held 22.2 percent, Canada 9.5 percent, the United States 9.3 percent, Italy 8.4 percent, France 5.0 percent, Germany 2.5 percent, and Japan 1.2 percent." [16]

There is the problem though—if one focuses attention on the money supply or the supply of near-monies of individual national economic systems—of how to parcel Eurodollar deposits among the various nations of the world. Should they be allocated on the basis of the country of ownership of the deposits, or the country in whose banks they are deposited, or the country in which the credit extended was used to generate demand for goods and services? There may be times at which each approach is appropriate to the problem at hand.

With respect to the problem of the inflationary pressures generated by Euro-currency expansion, it would appear that it is the geographical region or country in which the credit extended is used to generate demand for goods and services that is important. When the Eurodollar system makes credit available that would not have otherwise been available to finance transactions in goods and services, it supports greater aggregate demand on a worldwide basis than could be supported in its absence. But unless a geographical breakdown of the loan portfolio of the Eurodollar system were to be available—indicating the residency of the borrower and hence the likely location of the expenditures financed by the Eurodollar credit—it is not possible to know the nation in which aggregate demand is affected by Eurodollar expansion.

There is less question within a national economic context of the incidence of the credit extension which is counterpart to the money and near-monies generated by the expansion of domestic financial intermediaries. By far, the largest share of the credit generated by domestic intermediary institutions supports increased aggregate demand for domestically produced goods and services. Some part of any given credit increase will impact on import demand, of course, the proportion depending on the economy's propensity to import. Although the financing of a country's imports may be shared by domestic and foreign credit institutions, in general it is probably correct to conclude—in the absence of empirical evidence— that for most countries the major burden for financing imports is borne by domestic financial institutions.[17] Likewise, a given national economy will be stimulated by

---

[16] Ibid.

[17] The balance-of-payments problems generated for many countries by the sharp rise in the price of oil from the OPEC countries may well have increased since 1973 the percent of imports financed from external financing sources for many of the substantial importers of oil. Some of the major oil-importing countries have borrowed substantially from abroad to finance their higher priced oil imports.

export demand, some part of which is supported by credit supplied by domestic credit institutions.

Some national financial intermediaries have historically assumed international roles and engaged in extending credit to support economic transactions among third countries. Such was the case with the British banking system, particularly prior to the world wars. But even in the British case, sterling continued to fill a reduced role in third country financing until 1957 when, for balance-of-payments reasons, United Kingdom authorities were forced to restrict this function of sterling.

Banks in the United States have also engaged in considerable international credit extension to support transactions among third countries although this role of U.S. resident banks was severely limited during the 1963–74 period by the U.S. capital controls implemented to shore up the U.S. international payments position. Since the termination of the U.S. capital controls in January 1974, U.S. resident banks have expanded considerably their lending to support trade among third countries.

In fact, one of the main forces behind the development of Eurocurrency banking has been the existence of regulatory factors and agreements among bankers governing their practices which limit the competitiveness of domestic banks relative to their foreign counterparts. For example, when the British authorities forbade British banks in 1957 from financing in sterling trade among third countries, banks in the United Kingdom turned to using dollars for this part of their business instead of sterling.[18] And all the U.S. capital controls—the voluntary Foreign Credit Restraint Program and the Foreign Direct Investment Program— had the effect of pushing bank loan business which would have otherwise been done by banks in the United States to offshore banks—banks in the Eurocurrency system.

An appropriate model of Eurodollar expansion. There is considerable ambiguity in the concept "Eurodollar credit expansion," ambiguity which has contributed to significant confusion about the nature of Eurodollar growth and the prospects for its control. The literature is replete with different models and analogies explaining the nature of Eurodollar credit multiplication. The nature of the Eurodollar (or Eurocurrency) expansionary process is important to the problem of its control, for it is difficult to institute effective control over Eurodollar expansion if it is not known how the expansionary process of intermediation works.

A prime concern all analysts have about the Eurodollar expansion mechanism is the nature of the factors internal to the mechanism which limit or harness its expansion. Is there any harness on its growth? If so, how does it work and how

---

[18] See Milton Gilbert, "The Eurocurrency Market," a speech presented at the Conference on the Future of the European Capital Market sponsored by the Federal Trust for Education and Research, London, 23-24 November 1966, p. 6.

might it be manipulated by monetary authorities to regulate Eurodollar expansion congruent with the demand management requirements of the world economy?

Perhaps the most common model of financial intermediation currently is that of bank credit expansion within a domestic context, expansion on the basis of a required reserve base held with a nation's central bank, the Federal Reserve in the case of the United States. The simple textbook explanation of the commercial bank multiplier usually assumes that the depository assets, created as banks make loans on the basis of an increased amount of reserves at the Federal Reserve (or a reduction in required reserves), are *demand deposits* ("money") and, for simplicity's sake, that there is little or no currency and coin leakage from the banking system.[19] The proceeds of all loans made are always redeposited in the banking system; in fact, they are never withdrawn from the system except for the public's marginal demand for coin and currency. Payments merely cause a shifting of deposits—and their related reserve balances at the Federal Reserve— from one commercial bank to another.

The simple textbook bank multiplier gives the *maximum potential amount of credit* (or deposit) *expansion* which can occur for a given increase in bank reserves held at the Federal Reserve. (The value of the multiplier is the inverse of the reserve requirement.) *This expansionary process is a mechanical process.* If sufficient loan demand is present, the actual amount of credit expansion which occurs will equal the maximum potential credit expansion which can be supported by the increase in the banking system's reserve base. But the *actual* amount of multiplication which occurs during a specific time period on the basis of a given increase in bank reserves is a function of economic conditions (including stabilization policy conditions), more specifically, loan demand. The monetary base may be increased by the Federal Reserve through open market operations, but if loan demand is not there, bank credit and the money supply will not grow as anticipated. It is like "pushing on a string" as Chairman William McChesney Martin of the Board of Governors of the Federal Reserve System used to say.[20]

The Federal Reserve has considerable grip, though, on the U.S. financial system when it wishes to pull on the string at a time that the financial system is fully expanded on its available reserve base. Then, contracting the monetary base or increasing reserve requirements reduces the maximum potential amount of credit which the banking system can provide and forces it to contract the actual volume of outstanding credit to the maximum potential level.

---

[19] For a typical textbook explanation of the commercial bank multiplier see George G. Kaufman, *Money, the Financial System, and the Economy* (Chicago: Rand McNally and Company, 1973), chapter 7.

[20] The money supply may also grow—when free reserves are available—even in the absence of growth in the banking system's loan portfolio if the system as a whole increases its holdings of other financial assets, such as U.S. Treasury bills, notes and bonds, by net purchases either from the nonbank private sector of the economy or from new supplies being issued by the federal government to finance its budget deficit.

There is considerable interest among Eurodollar analysts in identifying a reserve base for the Eurodollar system. This interest probably reflects the universal familiarity with the domestic commercial bank multiplication model and the importance of the idea which springs from this model—*that if some clearly defined base can be identified to which Eurodollar expansion can be linked, then the manipulation of this base would restrain Eurodollar credit expansion when restraint is desired and would allow Eurodollar credit expansion when a stepped-up rate of growth in credit availability is desired.* The analogy with the commercial bank multiplication process also would appear to imply that roughly the same process of internal generation of deposits applies in the Eurodollar system as applies in a commercial banking system. It was this implication of the commercial bank analogy which was at the heart of the Friedman-Klopstock controversy several years ago about the nature of Eurodollar expansion.[21]

We shall propose below that the commercial bank multiplication model is not the most useful model for analysis of the Eurodollar system. It would appear that the Eurodollar system is more analogous to a system of nonbank financial intermediaries. There is no reserve base for the Eurodollar system comparable to the reserves of commercial banks at the central bank. Thus it is unlikely that successful control of Eurodollar credit volume may be realized through manipulation of a reserve base in the same way as is done in a commercial banking system. But, first, let us look at some of the definitions and concepts of a Eurodollar base which analysts have proposed.

(1) First National City Bank (FNCB). Analysts at FNCB have published an analysis of Eurodollar multiplication in which Eurodollar expansion is linked to growth in the U.S. monetary base—the reserves of member banks at the Federal Reserve and the coin and currency held by the U.S. public.[22] Their correlation analysis of actual changes in the U.S. monetary base with actual changes in total Eurodollar deposits during the period 1957 to 1973 showed a fairly stable association between the two variables.

Using the domestic bank multiplication model, they define a "Eurodollar multiplier" as the volume of Eurodollar deposits created per dollar of change (increase) in the U.S. monetary base. They show that this multiplier, so defined, has changed from zero in 1957 to slightly more than one in 1974.[23] Growth in Eurodollar volume since 1957 is then explained in terms of the increase in the

---

[21] Milton Friedman, "The Eurodollar Market: Some First Principles," *Morgan Guaranty Survey,* October 1969, pp. 4-14; and Fred Klopstock, "Money Creation in the Eurodollar Market: A Note on Professor Friedman's Views," *Monthly Review,* Federal Reserve Bank of New York, January 1970, pp. 12-15.

[22] First National City Bank, *Monthly Economic Letter,* July 1974, pp. 9-15.

[23] It is important to note that the historical change in this ex post Eurodollar multiplier did not derive from a change in the required reserves for any bank, either in the United States or in the Eurodollar system, as is the case with the ex ante textbook commercial bank multiplier.

U.S. monetary base together with the increase in the Eurodollar multiplier which has occurred during this period.

The FNCB Eurodollar multiplier is vastly different from the simple commercial bank multiplier model, however. First, in actuality there is no direct link between Eurobanks—the institutions engaged in the credit multiplication—and the U.S. monetary base. Eurobanks do not hold reserves directly at the Federal Reserve. Thus, there is no internal mechanical process *directly* linking a change in the U.S. monetary base with the Eurodollar loan process. In the domestic commercial bank model, there is first an increase in the monetary base and then an associated expansion of bank credit (given that the necessary loan demand exists). But in the Eurodollar case, there is first an increase in the U.S. monetary base, then a multiplication of U.S. resident banks' deposit liabilities (given that the necessary loan demand exists), and then a shift of these deposits to the Eurodollar system before Eurodollar credit expansion can occur (given that the necessary Euroloan demand exists).

Secondly, unlike the simple commercial bank multiplier—which is a "theoretical optimal or maximum multiplier," an ex ante type multiplier—the FNCB Eurodollar multiplier is an ex post or historical multiplier reflecting, as the writers partially recognize, all the many factors which have caused depositors since the late 1950s to shift funds from various other financial assets into Eurodollars. These factors are: (a) the investing public's growing awareness of the Eurodollar investment opportunity, (b) the technological advances in communications and transportation which have enabled the worldwide Eurodollar marketplace to develop, (c) the U.S. regulations which forced U.S. resident bank bidding for funds into the unregulated Eurodollar market in 1966 and again in 1969, (d) the vast volume of funds being paid to the oil-exporting countries after the 1974 price increase and their preference for Eurodollar deposits, and (e) all the other institutional and regulatory factors which have affected the shift of funds into and out of Eurodollars.

For the FNCB Eurodollar multiplier to be useful in a policy way, one would have to be convinced that historical, regulatory, and institutional developments would occur in the future to keep investors shifting deposits into Eurodollars at roughly the same rate of increase per dollar increase in the U.S. monetary base as has occurred since the late 1950s. It may well happen that during the next twenty years such developments will come to pass and that the FNCB Eurodollar multiplier will grow at roughly the same rate as it has grown during the past seventeen years. On the other hand, the developments may not occur. The tenuous nature of this multiplier concept would appear to limit substantially its usefulness in policy making.

The FNCB analysts present a possible explanation for the mechanism which they feel may link an increase in the U.S. monetary base with an expansion of Eurodollar credit. They focus on factors which possibly affect the expansion of

U.S. resident banks' activity in the Eurodollar market. "It could be that U.S. banks try to spread their risks and earnings in some balanced way between their domestic and foreign operations. Thus, as the U.S. base expanded and their domestic activity increased, they would invest more capital abroad, raising their ceilings on foreign borrowing and lending," the FNCB suggests.[24]

This explanation, however, depends entirely on U.S. resident banks performing the role of "developers" of Eurodollar banking; it does not explain the growth of Eurodollar banking on the part of banks based outside the United States. True, U.S. resident banks—through their foreign branches and consortium banks—are the most important bank group in the Eurodollar system. At the end of April 1975, foreign branches of U.S. resident banks had approximately $110 billion of Eurodollar deposit liabilities—about 65 percent—out of an estimated total net Eurodollar deposit liabilities for all banks worldwide of $170 billion.[25] Approximately $60 billion of Eurodollar business had developed up to that date with Eurobanks which are unrelated to banks based in the United States. This business is not explained by the FNCB hypothesis.

The actual mechanism by which Eurodollar growth occurs, however, is more of a problem for the FNCB thesis that Eurodollar expansion is linked to the growth of the U.S. monetary base. Eurodollar growth is started when U.S. residents and foreign residents (banks and nonbanks) shift U.S. dollar deposits from institutions—and nondepository type assets—in the United States to banks outside the United States. The resources of foreign branches of U.S. resident banks and of nonbranches—banks unaffiliated with U.S.-based banks—are derived from deposits being shifted by investors to them from banks in the United States.

Thus it would appear that the FNCB thesis for a possible link between Eurodollar growth and growth of the U.S. monetary base needs to explain how changes in the U.S. monetary base *cause* or *influence* investors to shift dollar deposits from institutions in the United States to Eurobanks. The most important motivations behind such shifts are (a) investor preference for Eurodollar deposits over deposits in the United States (there are many factors affecting preference) and (b) the higher interest rates paid on Eurodollar deposits than on deposits in the United States.[26] The FNCB thesis needs to link causally the existence of these factors or

---

[24] First National City Bank, *Monthly Economic Letter*, p. 12. International bankers with whom I have talked recently pointed out that although the growth of U.S.-based bank activity outside the United States may reflect banks' efforts to spread their risks and earnings in some balanced way between domestic and foreign operations, it equally reflects the relative attractiveness of profit opportunities in foreign markets over those within the United States.

[25] Board of Governors of the Federal Reserve System, *Federal Reserve Bulletin,* August 1975, p. A71.

[26] The vast majority of international bankers and Eurocurrency analysts that I have interviewed seem to think that the dominant factor attracting funds into Eurodollar deposits is the higher interest rate paid in the Euromarket. The sovereign risk factor, it is thought, is the major factor discouraging the holding of dollar deposit assets outside the United States.

changes in these factors to changes in the U.S. monetary base to establish its credibility.

There is a connection between the high-powered U.S. monetary base and the maximum volume of U.S. dollar-denominated liquid assets which can be extended on any given volume of monetary base. The liquid asset multiplier—an extension of the simple demand deposit multiplier—relates the maximum potential expansion of total depository claims to changes in the reserves of commercial banks at the central bank, *given the proportions in which the public holds cash and various depository claims and the reserve ratios behind these depository claims.*[27] (The reserves of the nonbank financial intermediaries are the deposits they hold with commercial banks of the system.) Eurodollar deposits could be incorporated into the liquid asset multiplier, assuming (a) a fairly stable proportion of Eurodollar deposits to the total volume of U.S. dollar deposits of all kinds and (b) a given reserve ratio for the Eurobanks (ratio of Eurobank reserve dollar deposits with banks in the United States to total deposit liabilities of Eurobanks).

An increase in the high-powered reserve base (reserves of U.S. member banks at the Federal Reserve) of the U.S. dollar depository system increases the potential for U.S. dollar credit expansion. But the actual amount of expansion which occurs for a given reserve increase depends on the strength of loan demand at each of the depository institutions composing the system. On the other hand, if the credit system is fully expanded and all the reserve and liquid asset ratios remain unchanged, a reduction in the high-powered U.S. monetary base would cause a contraction in the total amount of U.S. dollar credit actually extended by the system—including Eurodollar credit.

If, however, as the U.S. dollar monetary base is contracted by the Federal Reserve, dollar depositors shift more and more deposits into the Eurodollar system (that is, increase the proportion of Eurodollar deposits to total U.S. dollar deposits), the total volume of U.S. dollar credit available to the world economy can continue to expand even though the U.S. monetary base is declining (or growing at a slower rate). This is because Eurodollar deposits do not require direct backing with high-powered reserves, reserves at the Federal Reserve. The Federal Reserve's influence over the maximum potential volume of U.S. dollar credit—including Eurodollar credit—which can be extended is heavily dependent on the dollar-holding public's choice of type of dollar deposits.

(2) The Lee Base. Boyden E. Lee has suggested "that net Eurodollar deposits are related to a Eurodollar base in the same way that the domestic money supply is related to a domestic monetary base." [28] His model assumes (a) that the demand deposit liabilities of New York banks to foreign banks are the actual

---

[27] For a discussion of the liquid asset multiplier and claims shift multipliers, see Warren L. Smith, "Financial Intermediaries and Monetary Controls," *Quarterly Journal of Economics,* vol. 73, no. 4 (November 1959), pp. 533-553.

[28] Boyden E. Lee, "The Eurodollar Multiplier," *Journal of Finance,* vol. 28, no. 4 (September 1973), pp. 867-874.

"cash" reserves maintained by Eurobanks against net Eurodollar deposit liabilities and (b) that U.S. short-term liquid liabilities to U.S. nonresidents perform the same function in the Eurodollar system as cash—reserves at the Federal Reserve—does in domestic money models. He defines the Eurodollar base as the "sum of all short-term U.S. liabilities to nonresidents."

Lee computes—on a quarterly basis from 1963 through 1969—a value for his Eurodollar "multiplier," defined as the ratio of net Eurodollar deposit liabilities to the total volume of U.S. short-term liabilities to foreigners. The value of the Lee multiplier grew fairly continuously from 1.27 in March 1963 to 1.92 in December 1969.

The Lee multiplier, like the FNCB multiplier, is an ex post, historical multiplier. It is conceptually different from the liquid asset multiplier and would be useful as an analytical or policy tool only if (a) we could feel confident that the historical relationship it captures in the past between net Eurodollar deposit volume and U.S. short-term liabilities to foreigners will hold for the future and (b) that the U.S. short-term liabilities to foreigners could be manipulated by monetary authorities in a way similar to the manner in which the domestic monetary base can be manipulated. Its major fault, however, is that it apparently assumes that Eurodollars are generated only by U.S. nonresident shifts of funds to Eurobanks. It appears to disregard the possibility that U.S. residents may shift funds to Eurobanks and thus set in motion Eurodollar expansion.

(3) The Makin Base. Professor John H. Makin has suggested analysis of the Eurodollar system by making an analogy in certain respects to the multiple deposit expansion process in a closed economy.[29] He hypothesizes that the demand deposit claims of Eurobanks on U.S. resident banks, exclusive of U.S. foreign branch loans to U.S. home offices, are essentially the cash or base money of the Eurodollar system. He develops a model of Eurobank behavior which he uses to calculate the demand of Eurobanks for precautionary reserves between 1964 and 1970. The level of precautionary reserve holdings of Eurobanks is a decision of bank management since there are no legal reserve requirements for Eurobanks.

Makin's investigation found a drop—from 14 percent in 1964 to about 5 percent in 1970—in the ratio of Eurobanks' demand deposit claims on banks in the United States to the net volume of Eurodollars. He finds this consistent with the effective economies of scale which may be realized in the management of precautionary balances as the volume of receipts and disbursements of a financial intermediary rises over time. This falling reserve ratio implies an increase in the "multiplier"—defined as the increase in Eurodollar deposits associated with a one dollar increase in the demand deposit claims of Eurobanks on banks in the

---

[29] John H. Makin, "Identifying a Reserve Base for the Eurodollar System," *Journal of Finance*, vol. 28, no. 3 (June 1973), pp. 609-617. Makin identifies three factors which explicitly determine the optimal size of bank precautionary balances: the cost of running out of precautionary balances, the opportunity cost of holding precautionary balances, and the probability that net disbursements will exceed precautionary balances.

United States—unless one assumes increasing leakages from the system, which he says may have been the case until 1969. Makin suggests that since 1969 the size of Eurodollar leakages may have been substantially reduced and that if the level of leakages merely stabilizes, his study shows that the Eurodollar credit multiplier—on the base of Eurobanks' precautionary balances with banks in the United States—will increase.

Although it is an ex post multiplier—reflecting behavioral characteristics of Eurobanks during the 1964–70 period—the Makin multiplier is substantially different in concept from the FNCB and Lee multipliers. Unlike those multipliers, Makin's is developed from a model which incorporates profit-maximizing banks engaged in the efficient management of liquid dollar reserves. It is also conceptually different from the simple textbook definition of commercial bank multipliers which defines the "base" as commercial bank reserve holdings at the central bank. Makin's "base" is the demand deposit claims of Eurobanks on banks in the United States.

The Makin analysis is compatible with the liquid asset multiplier approach to the analysis of Eurodollar expansion in which the Eurodollar system is incorporated as one of several nonbank dollar-deposit generating financial intermediaries (savings and loan associations and mutual savings banks would be others) which hold their precautionary reserve balances as demand deposits with U.S. commercial banks, which in turn hold their reserves at the Federal Reserve. In fact, the reserve ratio Makin calculates for the Eurodollar system is a necessary ingredient for the computation of a value for the worldwide U.S. dollar liquid asset multiplier. This reserve ratio is the link between the volume of demand deposits in banks in the United States and the volume of the Eurodollar portion of the total U.S. dollar depository assets which can be supported on a given U.S. monetary base (that is, reserves of U.S. commercial banks at the Federal Reserve plus the coin and currency held by the public). The stability of the Makin reserve ratio is important to the stability of the worldwide liquid asset multiplier for U.S. dollars.

(4) The Fratianni and Savona International Monetary Base. Professor Michele Fratianni and Dr. Paolo Savona have hypothesized a special relationship between a financial aggregate which they call the "international monetary base" (IMB) and the expansion of Eurodollar credit. The IMB—a wide-ranging group of financial assets—is defined, under a par value international monetary arrangement, to include:

> the gold stock net of private uses and gold deposits at the IMF, SDR's, the IMF Reserve position plus credits granted by the IMF, unused credit lines at the Federal Reserve Bank of New York, all dollars and convertible currencies held by nonresidents (i.e., held by people for whom the currencies are not part of their country's monetary base) and in principle any financial asset which can be transformed into vehicle currency (ies) at sight and without capital loss, provided such a trans-

formation represents an addition to the existing stock of international monetary base.[30]

Their Eurodollar credit multiplier—which measures the relationship between a dollar change in the IMB and the change in the volume of Eurocredit—is estimated very roughly to range between 1.87 and 5.27, depending on the conditions obtaining.

Many of the same problems exist for Fratianni's and Savona's Eurodollar base and multiplier concepts as for those mentioned previously. The base is ill-defined, is difficult to conceptualize, and would be very difficult to manipulate by a monetary authority. The multiplier really captures historical, institutional, and policy developments. It is not a factor indicating the theoretical optimal volume of credit expansion which can develop for any given change in the base. It is compatible with neither the simple textbook definition of the commercial bank multiplier nor the liquid asset multiplier.

Perhaps the best model for analyzing Eurodollar expansion with a view to its possible control is that of the liquid asset multiplier, mentioned earlier. The base in this case is well defined; it is the reserve balances held by U.S. member banks at the Federal Reserve plus coin and currency held by the public. But more importantly, this model of expansion focuses our attention on the variables most instrumental in Eurodollar expansion—(a) the coefficient depicting the public's preference for Eurodollar deposits as a proportion of the public's total holdings of U.S. dollar deposits and (b) the ratio of Eurobank precautionary balances—held in banks in the United States—to total Eurobank deposit liabilities (the Makin reserve ratio). If these proportions were to be constant, then—given adequate loan demand—we could predict the maximum Eurodollar expansion which could occur for any given increase in the U.S. monetary base and, likewise, the amount of contraction in Eurodollar credit which would occur when the U.S. monetary base decreased.

If, however, the public's preference for Eurodollar deposits increases as the U.S. monetary base expands, the potential for Eurodollar expansion—as well as the total expansive potential for the worldwide dollar liquid asset multiplier— grows faster than the rate of increase in the monetary base. Given adequate loan demand, the actual amount of credit expansion—both Eurodollar and total dollar— will grow at an increasing rate. If the public's preference for Eurodollar deposits increases as the U.S. monetary base decreases, the potential for Eurodollar expansion—as well as the total expansive potential for the worldwide dollar liquid asset multiplier—will increase even though the monetary base is declining.

The opposite results would obtain under similarly hypothesized conditions if the public's preference for Eurodollar deposits were to decrease as a proportion of total dollar deposits.

[30] Michele Fratianni and Paolo Savona, "International Liquidity: An Analytical and Empirical Reinterpretation," *A Debate on the Eurodollar Market* (Rome: Ente per gli Studi Monetari, Bancari e Finanziari, 1972), pp. 37-121.

Likewise, the maximum potential for Eurodollar expansion also depends on the ratio of precautionary reserve balances which Eurobanks hold with banks in the United States to their Eurodollar deposit liabilities, the Makin-type ratio. If this ratio increases as the U.S. monetary base expands—with the public's preference for Eurodollar deposits unchanged—the expansive potential of the worldwide dollar liquid asset multiplier will not expand in proportion to the expansion of the U.S. monetary base. It will expand more slowly. If the Eurobank reserve ratio decreases—with the public's preference for Eurodollar deposits unchanged—as the U.S. monetary base expands, the expansive potential of the worldwide dollar liquid asset multiplier will expand more rapidly than the monetary base.

Eurodollar expansion can be affected by introducing factors which change the public's propensity to hold Eurodollar deposits—either reduce or increase the public's holdings of Eurodollar deposits as a proportion of total dollar deposits—and/or which change the Eurobank's reserve ratios. Hence, concern for reducing or increasing the expansive potential of Eurodollar banking would cause one to look for policy measures which would affect the public's propensity to hold Eurodollar deposits and/or the reserve ratios of Eurobanks.

The potential effectiveness of legal reserve requirements and open market operations in the global control of Eurocurrency expansion. Two techniques of monetary control which have been mentioned more frequently than others as having potential applicability in the regulation of Eurodollar credit expansion are (1) legal reserve requirements for Eurobanks and (2) open-market operations. Let us now examine these possibilities.

(1) Legal Reserve Requirements. Eurobanks could be required by their respective regulatory authorities to maintain U.S. dollar reserves against their U.S. dollar deposit liabilities either with (a) the U.S. Federal Reserve or (b) their respective central banks. Requiring Eurobanks to maintain dollar reserves with the Federal Reserve would put them under direct control of the Federal Reserve just like banks in the United States and would incorporate Eurobank reserve holdings into the U.S. monetary base. The Eurodollar system then would be subject to the same contractive and expansive influences emanating from changes in the U.S. monetary base—caused by U.S. open-market operations, for example— as are banks in the United States. Eurobanks could use the Federal Reserve payments mechanism, supplementing it with clearing house transfers. This would reduce to some extent the correspondent balances which Eurobanks would need to hold with U.S. commercial banks.

With Eurobanks holding reserves at the Federal Reserve, a shift of funds by depositors from U.S. resident banks to Eurobanks would drain resources from banks in the United States—reduce their reserves and ability to make loans—to the same extent resources were made available to the Eurobanks receiving the funds. The global U.S. dollar credit system would operate on a more uniform basis— without regard to national borders—than it does today. Today, a shift of funds from a U.S. resident bank to Eurobanks reduces only marginally, and by less than the amount of the funds shifted, the ability of the U.S. resident bank to make loans. This occurs as the proportion of demand deposits—requiring higher reserves—at U.S. resident banks rises, reflecting the increased transactions use by Eurobanks of balances held with U.S. resident banks. The familiar pyramiding of Eurobank reserve deposits at U.S. resident banks—on top of the "high-powered" reserves of U.S. resident banks at the Federal Reserve—enables Eurobanks to expand credit without an equal reduction in the credit which U.S. resident banks can extend.

It is highly unlikely though that monetary authorities worldwide could be enticed to require their Eurobanks to hold reserves at the Federal Reserve. There would probably be great reluctance to give the Federal Reserve any greater domination of world monetary and credit conditions than it already exercises. Possibly in the future when (or if) the world has moved to the centralization of world money management, some kind of cooperative arrangement requiring centralized reserve holdings for all commercial banks may be established.[31]

In addition, most countries in which the major volume of Eurodollar banking is conducted would more than likely be reluctant to take away from their banks the cost advantage they derive from having no reserve requirements on their foreign currency deposit liabilities. This cost advantage gives their banks a competitive advantage vis-à-vis banks in the United States—in the case of U.S. dollar business—which is vital to their existence. The Bank of England, for example, has encouraged the development of London as a Eurodollar center by minimizing the regulatory factors applicable to the external currency business of British banks. It would appear unlikely that British authorities would undertake restrictive measures on Eurocurrency business which would have a contradictory effect on its development.

Even if the major industrial countries where most of the external currency banking business is currently located were to agree cooperatively to impose legal reserve requirements on Eurobanks, the business could be moved to any number of other localities in the world from Monaco to the New Hebrides. It would be highly unlikely that all nations and governmental entities throughout the world would agree to impose uniform legal reserve requirements in such a way as not to cause foreign currency business to move to the most advantageous locations.

Requiring Eurobanks to maintain U.S. dollar reserves against their U.S. dollar liabilities at their respective central banks has much reduced implications for controlling Eurodollar expansiveness compared with requiring Eurobanks to maintain reserves at the Federal Reserve. Requiring reserves at the Federal Reserve would change the Eurobanks' relationship to the high-powered U.S. monetary base: it would "plug them directly into" the U.S. monetary base. Requiring

---

[31] Presumably this would entail the establishment of a world central bank with adequate authority and sovereignty.

reserves at their respective central banks would not change the Eurobanks' arms-length or indirect relationship to the U.S. monetary base.

The ultimate impact on Eurodollar expansiveness of a requirement for Euro-banks to maintain U.S. dollar reserves with their respective national central banks depends on the foreign central banks' disposition of the U.S. dollars they receive as Eurobank reserves. If these dollars are merely kept on deposit with banks in the United States or invested in money market securities in the United States, a shift of deposits to Eurodollars does not reduce the U.S. banking system's ability to lend at the same time that the lending ability of the Eurodollar system is expanded by the shifting of funds to it. The main impact of this type of reserve require-ment—in addition to increasing the cost of funds to Eurobanks—would be to skim off a small percentage of any given shift of funds to Eurodollar deposits and to prevent them from being used by Eurobanks to make loans to credit end-users. Such a requirement would in effect slightly increase the leakage of funds from the Eurodollar system for any given volume of inflow.

However, a 10 percent reserve requirement on Eurodollar deposits, with the reserves held at respective central banks, would *not* have nearly the contractive potential on the Eurodollar system as would a 10 percent reserve requirement, with the reserves held directly at the Federal Reserve. A reserve requirement for Eurobanks with the reserves held at foreign central banks is functionally different from a reserve requirement with the reserves held at the Federal Reserve.

If foreign central banks were to keep the Eurobank reserve balances placed with them at the Federal Reserve, the contractive impact of the reserve requirement would be increased from the case in which foreign central banks kept none of these balances at the Federal Reserve. But the contractive impact would be only a fraction of that which would occur if Eurobank reserves were kept by Eurobanks directly with the Federal Reserve. This can be seen by comparing the impact of a $100 shift of deposits from U.S. resident banks to Eurobanks. If Eurobanks were to keep reserves directly at the Federal Reserve, a $100 shift to Eurodollars would shift $100 of reserves away from U.S. resident banks to Eurobanks. Credit would have to decrease in the United States by some multiple of the $100 shift and would be able to expand by a multiple of $100 in the Eurodollar system. However, if Eurobanks were to keep reserves with their respective central banks—which in turn kept the dollars on deposit at the Federal Reserve—a $100 shift of funds to Eurodollars would reduce the reserves of U.S. resident banks by only some fraction of the shift, say, 10 percent, whereas the Eurobank would have close to 90 percent of the shifted funds to use in extending credit.

Perhaps the most important and effective impact of a Eurodollar reserve requirement would be to increase the cost of funds for Eurobanks and hence, other things equal, to reduce their profit margins, thus reducing their competitive advantage vis-à-vis banks in the United States. This feature of the reserve require-

306

ment will be discussed in the next major section of the paper which deals with the matter of competitiveness between U.S. resident banks and Eurobanks.

(2) Open-Market Operations. On several occasions in the past, national monetary authorities have undertaken actions both to infuse funds into the Eurodollar market and to withdraw funds from the market to reduce the availability of credit therein—types of open-market operations, one could say. Prior to December 1968, the Federal Reserve made small amounts of funds available from time to time to the BIS through its swap arrangements with that institution for placement in the Eurodollar market when the Federal Reserve wished to exert downward pressure on rising Eurodollar rates. These funds were withdrawn from the market when the rise in deposit rates moderated.[32]

During 1971, foreign branches of U.S. resident banks were sold short-term Export-Import Bank paper and U.S. Treasury notes by U.S. authorities at favorable rates in an effort to absorb liquidity from the Eurodollar market. Had the U.S. foreign branches not purchased these securities, the funds with which they were purchased would have been available to support Euroloans. In June 1971 the central banks of the Group of Ten countries indicated they would gradually withdraw the funds they then had on deposit in Eurocurrency markets. This move had the once-and-for-all impact of reducing the availability of funds in the Eurodollar and other Eurocurrency markets.[33]

However, open-market operations in the Eurodollar (or Eurocurrency) system functionally would be entirely different from central bank open-market operations within a domestic context. In contrast to such Eurodollar "open-market operations" as cited in the two previous paragraphs, Federal Reserve open-market operations directly affect a finite financial aggregate, the reserves of U.S. commercial banks held at the Federal Reserve. Public shifts of deposits from high-reserve demand deposits to low-reserve time deposits or vice versa change the aggregate required reserves of the U.S. banking system and may work to offset Federal Reserve open-market operations—which affect the actual volume of bank reserves available. But there is no doubt about the Federal Reserve's ability significantly to affect the available volume of bank reserves.

In the case of the Eurodollar system, the financial aggregate which an individual monetary authority or group of monetary authorities can affect through open-market operations is much more amorphous than the monetary base of a national banking system. Assume, for example, that a group of central banks offers to sell some sort of special security to Eurobanks and that circumstances are such that Eurobanks are inclined to purchase the security instead of making loans with their available funds. This operation would tend to drive the Eurodollar

---

[32] For discussions of Federal Reserve operations in the Eurocurrency markets, see the quarterly reports by Charles A. Coombs, "Treasury-Federal Reserve Foreign Exchange Operations," *Federal Reserve Bulletin,* March, June, September, and December issues of respective years.
[33] Bank for International Settlements, *Forty-Second Annual Report,* p. 149.

rate up relative to interest rates in the United States and other national money centers, and this would tend to attract more funds into Eurodollars. The operation might not be too dissimilar to bailing out a boat with a hole in its bottom. Funds would tend to flow into the Eurodollar pool as fast as open-market operations would bail them out.

Because the shifting of funds into Eurodollars from deposits in banks in the United States does not significantly reduce U.S. resident banks' ability to make loans, the shifting of funds into Eurodollars expands the U.S. dollar liquid asset multiplier—for a given U.S. monetary base. The point is that, although Eurodollar open-market operations will reduce Eurodollar credit availability from what it would be in the absence of the open-market operations, a more effective technique for reducing general U.S. dollar credit availability would be to undertake policies which would cause interest rates in the United States to rise relative to Eurodollar interest rates. Thus, funds would shift back to U.S. resident banks—relatively—reducing the U.S. dollar liquid asset multiplier at the same time the Federal Reserve was reducing the U.S. monetary base.

Reducing, through open-market operations, the flow of funds into the Eurodollar system which are available for lending to credit end-users would not have the multiple contractive impact as does the reduction of the monetary base of a national banking system. This is because there is no Eurodollar base exactly analogous—particularly in respect to its relationship to the multiplication process—to the commercial bank reserve base.

There are several other problems with conducting open-market operations in the Eurodollar system which would require some institutional innovations. Some are of a mechanical nature: what instruments would be used to take up and release funds, for example? There is nothing comparable to the well-developed government securities market in the United States, which is at the heart of Federal Reserve open-market operations.[34] The matter of who would undertake the operations and how they would be coordinated among the various central banks—monetary policy coordination—would have to be worked out. But if open-market operations were a practical antedote to the regulation of Eurodollar credit expansion—which I doubt—the mechanical features of the operations no doubt could be worked out.

Reducing the expansiveness of Eurodollar (and external currency) banking. So far in our analysis, we have approached the problem of controlling Eurodollar credit expansion with a view to *extending to the Eurodollar system some of the monetary control techniques commonly used in domestic banking systems: reserve requirements and open-market operations.* Because the Eurodollar system is in effect a nonbank financial intermediation system—standing in the same relation

---

[34] The interbank Eurodollar market—centered in London—is highly developed, perhaps as much so as the U.S. government securities market. Perhaps the open-market instrument that could be used by the authorities would be to take out loans from Eurobanks through the interbank market.

to the U.S. banking system and the U.S. monetary base as nonbank financial intermediaries in the United States (savings and loan associations, for example) these central bank monetary policy instruments will not function in the same way when applied to the Eurodollar system as they function for monetary control in the United States.[35]

I would propose that the best way of moderating Eurodollar expansiveness and hence reducing the Eurodollar system's inflationary implications, if they exist, would be to reduce the factors tending to cause the system to grow rather than to attempt to extend to it monetary control measures employed in domestic banking systems. For example, instead of attempting to extend reserve requirements over the Eurocurrency system—an attempt which probably would be futile—perhaps U.S. authorities should examine ways of making a U.S.-located bank more competitive in international deposit and loan markets. The cost of holding reserves, which is currently borne by the banking system itself in the United States, could be shifted to society as a whole by paying interest to banks for reserves they hold at the Federal Reserve. An important competitive advantage Eurobanks have over banks in the United States is the ability to pay interest on deposits with less than thirty-day maturity. U.S. resident banks could be given authority to pay interest on such accounts. Other domestic currency banking systems—the British, the Swiss, et cetera—should also work to enhance their competitiveness in international markets.

The proposal, then, is to attempt to recapture deposit-loan business from the external currency banking function for the domestic currency banking functions of the world by enhancing the competitiveness of the domestic currency banking institutions vis-à-vis Eurobanks. The recovery of Eurocurrency business to domestic institutions will bring credit expansion back to institutions which are directly linked to the monetary bases of their banking systems and hence are directly under the influence of central bank monetary policy.

The matter of the competitiveness of U.S. banks in international markets is discussed in the next section.

Relative Competitiveness between Internal and External Currency Banking

Eurodollar, or external currency, banking developed to a large extent because of opportunities outside the United States which did not exist for banks located in the United States. Freedom from regulations applicable to banks in the United States have given Eurobanks a competitive edge in several respects over banks in the United States.

---

[35] Open-market operations in the United States will have an impact on credit expansion in the Eurodollar system. But open-market operations in the Eurodollar system—although reducing credit availability—*ceteris paribus*—will not have an impact comparable to open-market operations in the United States because they do not affect "high-powered" bank reserves, as do open-market operations in the United States.

The U.S. balance-of-payments controls played an important role in creating demand for the services of Eurobanks. The Interest Equalization Tax (IET), which effectively closed U.S. capital markets to foreigners, was primarily responsible for the development of the Eurobond market, but it may well have created some demand for loans from Eurobanks which would not have existed in the absence of the IET. The Federal Reserve's Voluntary Foreign Credit Restraint Program (VFCR), imposed in 1965, restricted U.S.-located banks in their loan extensions to nonresidents of the United States, causing loan demand—which in the absence of the VFCR would have been met by U.S. institutions—to shift to Eurobanks. The Commerce Department's Foreign Direct Investment Program (FDIP), instituted on a voluntary basis in 1965 and made mandatory in 1968, restricted U.S. corporations from taking internally generated or borrowed funds out of the United States, above a certain limit, thus forcing them to finance external capital needs through the external dollar markets, including the Eurodollar market.[36]

The U.S. capital controls were terminated in January 1974, thus opening up new scope for arbitrage between the U.S. and Eurodollar deposit and loan markets by depositors and borrowers. This means new scope for lending outside the United States for banks located in the United States.

In several important respects though, the U.S. banking system is not competitive with the Eurodollar system in business involving both U.S. residents and nonresidents of the United States. Eurobanks offer several services and advantages which U.S. resident banks do not or cannot offer because of regulatory restrictions. The competitive edge of the Eurodollar system has become particularly important now that the U.S. capital controls have been terminated, enabling U.S.-located institutions to compete in foreign markets and U.S. depositors to shift funds between U.S. and foreign markets in response to interest rate differentials and to the relative convenience of the financial instruments offered.

U.S. Limitations on Paying Interest on Less-than-30-Day Deposits. An important advantage of the Eurodollar system is the ability to offer interest-bearing time deposits of less than thirty-day maturities, unavailable in the United States because of Regulation Q restrictions on U.S. resident banks. It is difficult to measure precisely the volume of such funds on deposit in the Eurodollar system because of the inadequacy of the data. However, at the end of August 1973, the volume of overnight and call deposits and deposits maturing within thirty days in foreign branches of U.S. banks totaled $19 billion, compared with a total net Eurodollar deposit volume of $100 billion.[37] Including such deposits with other Eurobanks—

---

[36] The U.S. capital controls interfered in other ways with the arbitrage between internal and external dollar credit markets. The VFCR kept U.S. nonbank financial institutions from moving funds into the Eurodollar market, and the FDIP restricted U.S. corporations from moving funds into the Eurodollar deposit market.

[37] This figure includes deposits with an original maturity of more than thirty days which have remaining maturity at the time of the report of thirty days or less. Board of Governors of the Federal Reserve System, *Federal Reserve Bulletin,* December 1973, p. A88.

other than foreign branches of U.S. resident banks—would enlarge the total even more.

The availability of this investment opportunity in the Eurodollar system and the lack of it in the U.S. banking system attracts funds to support Eurodollar expansion which would otherwise have been left with the U.S. banking system. Thus, allowing U.S. banks to be competitive with Eurobanks by offering interest-bearing less-than-thirty-day deposits would reduce the expansiveness of the Eurodollar system on a once-and-for-all basis.

The Problem of U.S. Reserve Requirements. Another important respect in which U.S. regulations reduce the attractiveness of domestic banking business relative to Eurobanking is in the matter of reserve requirements. Eurobanks are in a position—should market conditions require it—to offer slightly higher interest rates on deposits or to offer loans at lower rates on competitive business than U.S.-located banks, which may have to work on a narrower profit margin because of Regulation D and Regulation M reserve requirements.[38] In addition to its regular reserve requirements on demand and time deposits, effective in September 1969, the Federal Reserve established a reserve requirement on U.S. banks' borrowings from the Eurodollar market—under Regulation M, a reserve requirement on borrowings from overseas branches (liabilities to foreign branches) and under Regulation D, a reserve requirement on borrowings directly from banks outside the United States—and set it at 10 percent. At the same time, under Regulation M, it established a 10 percent reserve requirement for a U.S. bank on the loans which its overseas branches make to residents of the United States.

Briefly, the Regulation D and Regulation M reserve requirements have the effect of increasing—from what they would be in the absence of the regulations—(1) the cost of funds which U.S.-based banks use in all loan markets and (2) the cost of funds which U.S. foreign branches use to make loans in the United States. Eurobanks operating in the Eurodollar system are not subject to reserve requirements (although they do keep necessary working and reserve dollar balances with commercial banks in the United States). Thus, if deposit rates happened to be equal in the Eurodollar and U.S. markets, Eurobanks would have a cost-of-funds advantage over U.S.-based banks in all loan markets.

In the U.S. loan market foreign-based banks have a permanent cost-of-funds advantage over U.S. foreign branches since both U.S. foreign branches and other Eurobanks are faced with the same deposit rates for funds in the Eurodollar

---

[38] Actual rates paid depositors and charged borrowers in both markets—U.S. and Eurodollar markets—will be determined by relevant supply and demand conditions in each market. The actual profit margin realized by a bank on each loan made will be determined by the deposit rate paid and the loan charge made. For example, Eurobanks may have to pay a higher deposit rate than U.S. resident banks to attract funds because of risk factors. But they may do so and still experience the same profit margin as banks in the United States—assuming loan rates are the same in each market—because U.S. banks must keep reserves against their deposits.

market. As long as foreign-based banks did not actively compete for business in the domestic U.S. loan market, the advantage of foreign-based banks over U.S. resident banks and their foreign branches in the U.S. market emanating from Regulations D and M was not of great importance.[39] However, foreign banks have shown increasing interest in competing in the U.S. loan market in the last two years. First, the number of foreign bank branches and subsidiaries in the United States has grown rapidly. Secondly, and more important to the Regulation M problem, foreign-based banks have—during the past two years or so—shown increasing interest in booking loans for U.S. residents at their overseas locations, hence avoiding the impact of Regulations D and M.[40]

The existence of U.S. dollar banking outside the United States and the easy access of U.S. depositors and borrowers to the Eurodollar system create a dilemma for U.S. monetary authorities. If the integrity of the reserve requirements of Regulations D and M are maintained for U.S. resident banks—these regulations are instruments of Federal Reserve monetary control—U.S. resident banks and their foreign branches are put at a disadvantage relative to foreign-based banks both in the domestic U.S. loan business and in foreign markets. On the other hand, the maintenance of the cost-increasing reserve requirements for U.S. resident banks may be a factor causing the shift of U.S. dollar banking—which would have otherwise been done by institutions in the United States—to Eurobanks. The shift of U.S. dollar banking from the United States to institutions abroad has increased the potential expansiveness—and no doubt the actual availability of dollar credit—and complicated the ability of monetary authorities to exercise control over worldwide credit expansion, as discussed in the previous section of this paper.

Existing U.S. regulations and reserve requirements result in adverse effects on U.S.-based banks and their overseas branches. These effects are discussed in greater detail below.

The impact of Regulation D and Regulation M on the competitive position of banks in the United States. The impact of Regulation D reserve requirements on a U.S. resident bank is illustrated in Figure 1 under assumptions of (1) equality of real loan rates in the U.S. and Eurodollar loan markets and (2) equality of deposit rates in the two markets. These assumptions obviously are based on the further assumption of perfect arbitrage between the appropriate markets of the two banking systems.

The impact of Regulation D reserve requirements is to produce a wider gross margin on U.S. dollar loan business in the Eurodollar system than in the United States. Unless U.S. resident banks can more than offset the cost disadvantage attributable to the reserve requirement with greater operating efficiency

---

[39] Until 29 January 1974, when they were terminated, U.S. capital controls may have contributed to keeping Eurodollar rates above equivalent domestic rates, thus putting Eurobanks at a cost-of-funds disadvantage relative to banks in the United States.

[40] The lending banks and the borrowers also avoid the hassle over compensating balances by booking loans out of their overseas locations.

Figure 1

IMPACT OF *REGULATION D* ON A BANK IN THE UNITED STATES [a]

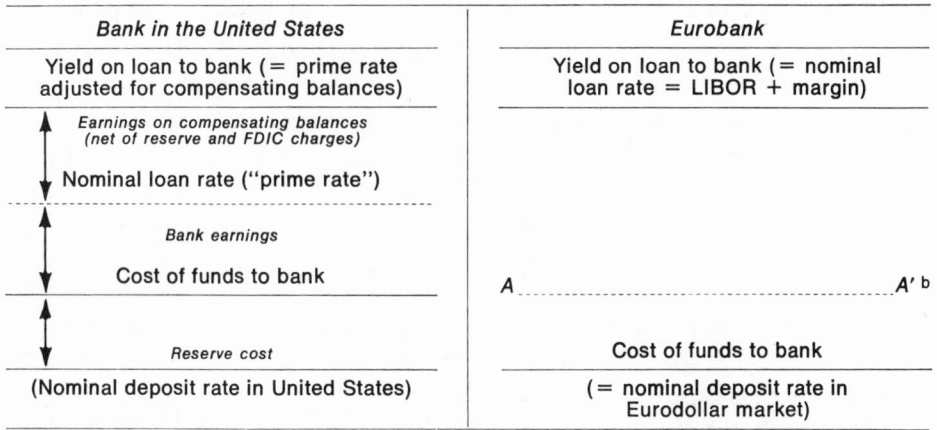

Bank in the United States	Eurobank
Yield on loan to bank (= prime rate adjusted for compensating balances)	Yield on loan to bank (= nominal loan rate = LIBOR + margin)
▲ *Earnings on compensating balances (net of reserve and FDIC charges)* ▼ Nominal loan rate ("prime rate")	
▲ *Bank earnings* ▼ Cost of funds to bank	A..A′ [b]
▲ ▼ *Reserve cost*	Cost of funds to bank
(Nominal deposit rate in United States)	(= nominal deposit rate in Eurodollar market)

[a] This diagram assumes that unimpeded flows of funds between the U.S. and Eurodollar loan markets equalize real loan rates and that flows of funds between the U.S. and Eurodollar deposit markets equalize deposit rates.

[b] Explained in fourth paragraph on page 314.

or lower overhead costs than their Eurobank competitors, U.S. dollar loan business in the Eurodollar market will tend to grow to the detriment of U.S. dollar loan business in the United States. U.S. banks will foster as much of their loan growth in their overseas branches as possible (with the exception of loans to U.S. residents, to be discussed later) to the detriment of loan growth in the United States. Foreign-based banks would outcompete banks in the United States for this loan business.[41]

On the deposit side, Eurobanks, in competition with U.S. resident banks, would tend to bid deposit rates above those in the United States as their need for funds continued to grow. On the loan side, Eurobanks would tend to undercut their U.S. resident competitors by offering lower loan rates to attract the profitable business. Loan rates for loans equally available in both systems would fall, and deposit rates would rise in both systems under the pressure of competition, causing the shift of loan business to the Eurodollar system until the profit margin on loan business in the United States is eliminated. In the extreme, U.S. resident institutions would go out of the loan business for which Eurobanks could compete with them.[42]

---

[41] A factor which may work to offset the cost disadvantage inherent in the reserve requirement for U.S. resident banks is the increased risk depositors may—and likely do—associate with U.S. dollar deposits with institutions outside the United States. Eurobanks may need to offer a higher deposit rate than U.S. resident banks in order to attract funds. This risk factor would work to moderate the growth of Eurodollar banking.

[42] In actuality matters are not as clean-cut as they appear in this theoretical analysis. The loan market is not completely homogeneous, as the analysis assumes. In fact, the deposit market—which undoubtedly is more homogeneous than the loan market—is probably characterized by a large degree of nonhomogeneity.

Eurobanks—in the extreme case—would put U.S. banks out of business. Obviously this will not occur because much of the U.S. resident bank business is domestic—not internationally competitive—and hence not subject to inroads from Eurobanks. But for that part of the bank business (both deposits and loans) for which U.S. resident banks and Eurobanks are equally competitive, the Eurobank has an advantage—beyond that which would otherwise be the case—over the U.S. resident bank emanating from the absence of reserve requirements.

The apparent attraction to foreign business of U.S. resident banks would tend to support the foregoing analysis, although actual conditions in the world today do not embrace all the assumptions made in this analysis. Under actual conditions, the relative competitiveness of U.S. resident banks and Eurobanks depends heavily on the relationship between deposit rates in the United States and the Eurodollar deposit rate structure. The deposit markets in the United States and the Eurodollar system are separate and the ideal state of perfect arbitrage between these markets does not exist.

Historically the Eurodollar deposit rate has been higher than the comparable U.S. deposit rate. During the latter half of 1972 and again during the latter half of 1973, when the difference between deposit rates in the United States and in the Eurodollar market appeared "normal" (by historic standards), the ninety-day Eurodollar deposit rate averaged between 50 to 75 basis points *above* the CD rate in the United States *adjusted* for Regulation D reserve requirements.

At times when the Eurodollar deposit rate is *above* the U.S. deposit rate by a margin equal to the impact of the Regulation D reserve requirement on the cost of funds for a U.S. resident bank, the cost disadvantage of the U.S. resident bank relative to the Eurobank—associated with the Regulation D reserve requirement— disappears. Historically, U.S. resident banks have seldom experienced a cost-of-funds disadvantage relative to their Eurodollar competitors even after taking the Regulation D reserve requirements into account.

From February through June of 1974, however, U.S. and Eurodollar deposit rates were very close. And recent developments affecting the historical structure of flows between the U.S. and Eurodollar banking systems raise the possibility of a much narrower spread between U.S. and Eurodollar deposit rates in the future than has existed in the past.

If new conditions result in less difference between U.S. and Eurodollar deposit rates in the future than historically, the anticompetitive impact on U.S. resident banks of Regulation D reserve requirements will be more serious than it has been in the past.

The impact that *Regulation M* reserve requirements have on the net balances of U.S. banks due to their foreign branches is illustrated in Figure 2 under the assumption of equality of real loan rates in the U.S. and Eurodollar loan markets. The Regulation M reserve requirement on net balances due foreign branches is functionally an extension of the general Regulation D reserve requirement. It has

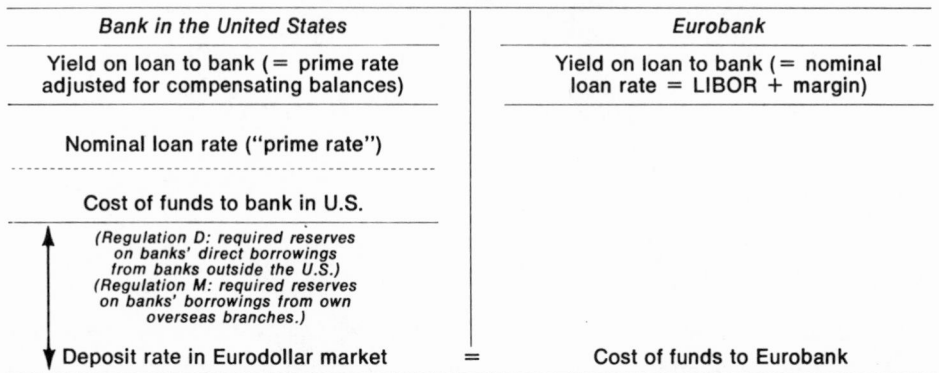

Figure 2

IMPACT OF *REGULATIONS D* and *M* ON A BANK
IN THE UNITED STATES [a]

Bank in the United States	Eurobank
Yield on loan to bank (= prime rate adjusted for compensating balances)	Yield on loan to bank (= nominal loan rate = LIBOR + margin)
Nominal loan rate ("prime rate")	
Cost of funds to bank in U.S.	
(Regulation D: required reserves on banks' direct borrowings from banks outside the U.S.) *(Regulation M: required reserves on banks' borrowings from own overseas branches.)*	
Deposit rate in Eurodollar market =	Cost of funds to Eurobank

[a] This diagram assumes unimpeded flows of funds between the U.S. and Eurodollar loan markets equalize real loan rates.

the same cost-increasing impact on U.S. bank funds sourced from the Eurodollar market as Regulation D has on U.S. resident bank funds sourced from domestic U.S. money markets. Hence, the U.S. resident bank's gross margin on loans sourced from the Eurodollar market is narrower than the gross margin of a Eurobank, which is not subject to Regulation M reserve requirements.[43]

By varying Regulation M reserve requirements relative to Regulation D reserve requirements on time deposits, the Federal Reserve has a mechanism for influencing U.S. resident banks' selection of sources of funds if the Federal Reserve ever wishes to exert such influence. For example, if deposit rates in the Eurodollar market are below comparable market rates in the United States— the call and/or overnight Eurodollar deposit rate at times in the past has been lower than the federal funds rate in the United States—the Federal Reserve could neutralize the relative attractiveness to U.S. banks of Eurodollar-source funds by raising the Regulation M reserve requirement relative to the Regulation D reserve requirement. On the other hand, the Federal Reserve could make Eurodollar-source funds relatively more attractive to U.S. resident banks than domestic-source funds, if there were ever a reason to do so, by lowering the Regulation M reserve requirement relative to the Regulation D requirement.

The impact of Regulation M on the competitive position of U.S. foreign branches. The impact of *Regulation M* reserve requirements on loans made by

---

[43] Some analysts point out that Regulation M also has an equity function. Small U.S. banks without overseas branches do not have easy access to the Eurodollar market and hence could not very well avail themselves of nonreservable Eurodollar funds in the absence of Regulation M. Regulation M puts large and small U.S. banks on the same cost-of-funds footing in this regard.

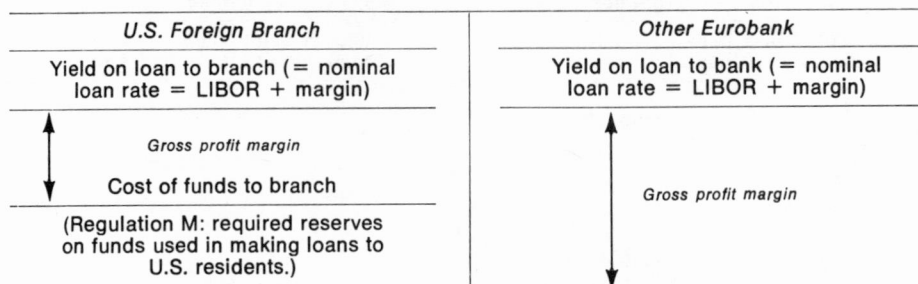

Figure 3

IMPACT OF *REGULATION M* ON A FOREIGN BRANCH
OF A U.S. BANK
LOAN TO RESIDENT OF THE UNITED STATES [a]

U.S. Foreign Branch	Other Eurobank
Yield on loan to branch (= nominal loan rate = LIBOR + margin)	Yield on loan to bank (= nominal loan rate = LIBOR + margin)
↕ *Gross profit margin*	↑
Cost of funds to branch	*Gross profit margin*
(Regulation M: required reserves on funds used in making loans to U.S. residents.)	
Deposit rate in Eurodollar market =	↓ Cost of funds to "other Eurobank"

[a] This diagram assumes that competition between U.S. foreign branches and other Euro-banks equalizes real rates on loans offered by the branches and other Eurobanks.

U.S. foreign branches to U.S. residents is illustrated in Figure 3 under the assumption of equality of rates on loans offered by U.S. foreign branches and other Eurobanks. This is a fairly realistic assumption since competition for loan business between these two groups of Eurobanks would probably keep their loan rates to customers of equal credit worthiness from differing significantly.

Through their foreign branches, U.S. resident banks can escape the cost-increasing impact of Regulation D reserve requirements on funds used to extend loans to nonresidents of the United States and thus gain a cost-of-funds parity with Eurobanks (assuming equal rates in the U.S. and Eurodollar deposit markets.) *However, the Regulation M reserve requirement precludes U.S. banks from gaining—through their foreign branches—a cost-of-funds parity with Eurobanks in the matter of loans made to residents of the United States.*

There are two general conditions under which the cost-increasing impact of Regulation M reserve requirements on funds of U.S. foreign branches used to extend loans to U.S. residents is of no practical import:

(1) Segmentation of the U.S. dollar bank loan markets. If U.S. borrowers are not aware of the lower-cost loans available from Eurobanks or for institutional or other reasons are not inclined to take up lines of credit from Eurobanks and/or if Eurobanks do not advertise and solicit the loan business of U.S. residents, U.S. resident banks may lose little or no U.S. resident loan business to foreign-based banks even though U.S. banks extend loans at higher interest rates than Eurobanks because of the cost-increasing impact of Regulation D reserve requirements.

(2) Eurodollar deposit rates are equal to or greater than U.S. deposit rates adjusted for reserve requirements. As long as Eurodollar deposit rates are

above comparable deposit rates in the United States by a margin equal to or greater than the cost disadvantage accruing to U.S. resident banks from the Regulation D reserve requirements, the cost of funds to the U.S. resident bank is equal to or less than the cost of funds for the Eurobank.

However, the general trend toward greater internationalization of banking and business and the expansion of instant communications systems tying investors, borrowers, and financial intermediaries more closely together, regardless of physical location, all tend to erode the segmentation which exists in the U.S. dollar bank loan markets. Likewise, these factors will tend to eliminate differences in loan rates and deposit rates between U.S. markets and markets external to the United States. There is increased likelihood that the anticompetitive impact of Regulation D and Regulation M reserve requirements will be a greater problem in the future than it has been historically.

Possible solutions to the dilemma. The shifting of dollar loan business—for both U.S. resident and U.S. nonresident borrowers—from U.S. resident banks to banks outside the United States brings up two main issues: (1) the problem of central bank control over Eurodollar credit expansiveness (as the Eurodollar system makes credit available both to U.S. residents and to U.S. nonresidents) and (2) the problem of the competitiveness of U.S. resident banks versus Eurobanks. U.S. resident banks may extend their operations outside the United States by various vehicles—foreign branches, ownership of foreign banks, and participation in consortium banks—to gain the advantages which Eurobanks have with regard to business with U.S. nonresidents. However, the Regulation M reserve requirement forecloses their being able to gain competitive equality with Eurobanks in the matter of domestic U.S. loan business.

To take action to make U.S. resident banks more competitive with Eurobanks would also tend to moderate the expansive potential of Eurodollar banking by recapturing for U.S. institutions—which fall directly under the policy influence of the Federal Reserve—business which would otherwise go to Eurobanks which are not *directly* influenced by Federal Reserve monetary policy actions. The subproblem of Eurobanks' comparative advantage over U.S. banks in the U.S. domestic loan market—emanating from the Regulation M reserve requirement—would also be remedied.

Solutions to these problems obviously involve either extending to banks outside the United States the same regulatory structure—reserve requirements, et cetera—which applies internally or neutralizing the noncompetitive impact of the U.S. requirements. U.S. authorities could attempt to use moral suasion on foreign authorities to gain their support in extending U.S. regulatory requirements abroad. The success of this, I would suggest, is highly unlikely though. Let us look, therefore, at possible internal changes in the United States.

(1) Eliminate Reserve Requirements. The elimination of required reserves for banks located in the United States would have implications for the Federal

317

Reserve's exercise of monetary policy. To the extent that the nonrequired reserves which banks would hold at the Federal Reserve would be smaller than required reserves, the commercial bank multiplier would be higher.

In the past, however, the Federal Reserve has not changed the level of reserve requirements too frequently, apparently relying more on open-market operations than reserve requirement changes to effectuate monetary policy. Thus, a loss of the reserve requirement monetary policy tool may not be too significant a loss for the Federal Reserve. A higher multiplier would mean that it would not have to work as hard at its open-market operations to change the maximum expansive potential of the U.S. banking system as it does with a lower multiplier.[44] However, monetary management is considerably complex, and the impact of the elimination of required reserves on the exercise of monetary policy would have to be seriously examined from all angles.

(2) Federal Reserve Pay Interest on Required Reserves. A technique for neutralizing the anticompetitive impact of required reserves would be for the Federal Reserve to pay U.S. banks interest on their required reserves. The market CD rate could be used as the rate to be paid. Perhaps rather than payment on the full amount of reserve holdings, payment could be made only on some portion under the assumption that non-interest-earning transactions balances would have to be maintained at the Federal Reserve even in the absence of required reserves.[45]

This option in effect transfers the cost of maintaining reserves from the banking system to the Federal Reserve and hence to American society as a whole. The funds which the Federal Reserve would use to pay interest to U.S. banks under this option currently are turned over to the U.S. Treasury to support federal government spending. The costs of this option would need to be evaluated against the cost of the negative consequences of Eurodollar credit growth for the American economy and society. The latter would be very difficult to evaluate, but some idea of its value would be needed to compare against the loss of revenue to the U.S. Treasury.

(3) Regulation M Impact on U.S. Foreign Branches. There are several additional possible solutions to the subproblem of the foreign bank advantage over the U.S. foreign branch in the domestic U.S. loan market. (Regulation M requires reserves against U.S. foreign branches' loans to U.S. residents.) (a) U.S. authorities could attempt to use moral suasion to convince foreign authorities that they should bring pressure on their banks not to lend in the U.S. market. (b) U.S. residents are currently allowed to deduct from taxable income interest paid on outstanding borrowings. By varying the amount of deduction allowed on interest paid to foreigners, the cost of borrowing from abroad could be raised to the point

---

[44] That is, a given change in the reserve base will—everything else being equal—produce a larger expansion or contraction in the maximum expansive potential of the U.S. dollar depository credit system than would be the case with a smaller multiplier.

[45] Or a lower rate of interest could be paid on the entire amount of reserve holdings.

that it would become cheaper for the U.S. resident to borrow domestically. (c) Finally, U.S. resident borrowers could be required to put up reserves on loans from banks and branches outside the United States—a *bardepôt*—which has the effect of increasing the cost of foreign-source funds for the U.S. resident borrower.

All these techniques involve trying to isolate the U.S. borrower from the outside world, a task that runs against the integrative currents which have developed in the past decade, that would be costly, and that probably could not be accomplished short of an extensive network of controls—which would, in turn, have significant costs and disadvantages.

Eurocurrency Liquidity and A Lender of Last Resort

Several factors have generated increased concern about the stability and liquidity of the Eurocurrency system. The very rapid rate of growth of total deposits, particularly during the past three to four years, and the enormous size of the system—absolutely and relative to major national banking systems—have raised apprehension about the stability of the system. The extension of loans at longer and longer term and to what some observers feel are higher and higher credit risks has raised the level of concern about liquidity. The cycles of historically high interest rates and reduced availability of credit which have been experienced in most major industrial countries since 1969—with the attendant demise of several banks for various reasons—have raised anew the question of the toughness of the fabric of Eurocurrency liquidity. Finally there has always been the nagging question: what national or international authority will come to the rescue of the system if it gets into "trouble"?

"Liquidity" is a multifaceted characteristic of a financial system. It obviously is a function of the maturity structure of assets, particularly loans—in a consolidated balance sheet of a financial system—relative to the maturity structure of deposits. At the same time, it depends on the prospect for the repayment of loans as they have been scheduled, that is, the credit worthiness of the borrowers. The public's confidence in a system is extremely important to liquidity: will the failure or "trouble" of several banks trip off a general and massive withdrawal of funds or is the fabric of confidence strong enough to withstand that? Is there a lender of last resort generally pledged to support the system if adverse circumstances were to arise? The mere existence of a proclaimed lender of last resort will contribute to confidence and reduce the prospect of it ever having to function. All these factors interrelate to determine what may be called the "state of liquidity" of any financial system at a point in time.

We have precious little information about each of these factors relative to the liquidity of the Eurocurrency system. Perhaps this absence of fact and knowledge is what most disturbs observers about Eurocurrency liquidity. There is no consolidated balance sheet for the system giving maturity structures for assets and liabilities. Tradition holds that most Eurocurrency loans are matched against deposits of the same maturity, hence there is little liquidity risk in the balance sheet of an individual bank or the system as a whole. But indications have been made to me in interviews with Eurobankers during the past two or three years that there has been considerable movement away from loans matched by deposits, particularly during periods of heightened competition for loan business such as 1972 and early 1973. Also, there is the risk that a non-U.S. Eurobank may not be able to find U.S. dollar resources at some loan's future rollover date or may be forced to pay exorbitant rates for funds to meet its rollover obligations.[46]

Likewise, little is known about the prospect for repayment of Euroloans as scheduled, even by national regulatory authorities. No single examinations authority has an overview of the loan repayment situation in the Eurocurrency system as, for example, U.S. bank examiners should have for the U.S. banking system. How many Euroloans would currently be classified, if a classification system were in use? Concern with credit worthiness apparently began to increase among bankers, regulatory authorities, and observers about 1972 coincident with the growing volume of Euroloans to borrowers among the developing countries, which have special problems in servicing external debt. The International Bank for Reconstruction and Development (IBRD) compiles data on Euroloans to developing countries which may be useful—in the absence of anything else—in analyzing this particular exposure of the Eurocurrency system.

Another element of concern with regard to credit worthiness involves the manner in which Euroloan syndication occurs. For several years the syndication approach to making Euroloans has been very popular. In most cases, I understand, the evaluation of borrower credit worthiness is left entirely to the bank serving as the syndicate leader. This approach could result—some Eurobankers have indicated to me it has resulted—in inadequate independent evaluation of major loan extensions. However, most serious banks review and validate the research and credit analysis of the syndicate leader.

Confidence in the system and the availability of a lender of last resort are closely linked. It would appear there is considerable confidence in the system today in spite of the talk of a liquidity squeeze, the development of several bank failures, the concern about credit worthiness and the lack of an official lender of last resort. There is no indication of any significant movement of funds out of Eurocurrencies at this time. Perhaps this is a case of the proof of the pudding being in the eating.

The Liquidity Problem of An Individual Bank. An individual Eurobank may find itself with a liquidity problem if (1) it has excessive loan losses, or (2) it has

---

[46] Some analysts have mentioned to me that the application of the portfolio theoretic approach would suggest that the matters mentioned in this paragraph may not be such a bad problem.

excessive loans on which repayment has been deferred beyond original maturity, or (3) it has a massive unexpected withdrawal of deposits, either by other banks or by nonbank depositors. Since Eurobanks hold little if any reserves against foreign currency liabilities in the form of marketable securities, an unexpected cash drain on a Eurobank must be met—at least theoretically—in one of the following ways or a combination of all:

(1) utilizing foreign currency deposits held with other Eurobanks,

(2) utilizing funds held with banks in the home country of the currency involved,

(3) drawing on established lines of credit with other Eurobanks,

(4) drawing on established lines of credit with banks in the home country of the currency involved,

(5) aggressive bidding for funds in the interbank Eurocurrency market,

(6) converting, in the exchange market, domestic currency funds into foreign currencies to meet the foreign currency drain. (The Eurobank may draw on its own domestic currency liquidity, borrow domestic currency from local banks or borrow from its central bank; however, the conversion of domestic currency funds into foreign currencies to meet a foreign currency drain may be subject to exchange controls or other regulatory provisions of its central bank.)

Although all the above possibilities are at least theoretically available to the Eurobank in a liquidity squeeze, it would be unlikely that a Eurobank with liquidity problems—primarily in terms of U.S. dollars, let us say—could depend on drawing on lines of credit with U.S. resident banks or Eurobanks, successfully bidding for U.S. dollar funds in the interbank Eurodollar market, or converting significant amounts of domestic currency funds into dollars. Once word spread that a particular Eurobank was in "trouble," I would doubt that a U.S. correspondent would want to lend it funds.[47] Depositors, including interbank depositors, would probably avoid it like the plague. Just as the federal funds market has suddenly become "unavailable" to U.S. resident banks which have found themselves in trouble, so would the interbank Eurodollar market become unavailable to a Eurobank in trouble.

Traditionally interbank markets for funds—the federal funds market in the United States or the interbank Eurodollar market—have been held up as sources of liquidity for banks, substituting to some extent for asset liquidity. This may be true for the bank which occasionally dips into these markets. But for the bank in dire need of liquidity—such as Franklin National Bank in the United States—

---

[47] In the case of a consortium Eurobank in which a U.S. resident bank has an interest, the U.S. shareholding bank may be inclined to make a temporary loan to the Eurobank up to some limit merely to attempt to protect its investment.

the well suddenly becomes dry when the thirst is greatest. In cases of dire need, liability liquidity cannot substitute for asset liquidity.

The lines of credit which major Eurobanks have with correspondent banks in the United States—and banks in other countries in the case of other currencies—have frequently been cited as the second line of reserves for Eurobanks, their first line of reserves being the funds on deposit with banks in the United States and banks in other countries in the case of other currencies. The pertinent question is, to what degree will the U.S. correspondent (or other correspondents in the case of other currencies) feel committed to honor a loan arrangement with a Eurobank which is caught in a liquidity squeeze? It could be that these lines of credit are a second line of reserves only in theory.[48]

Most Eurobanks operate in countries with various degrees of exchange controls.[49] The conversion of any sizable amount of domestic currency funds into U.S. dollars (or any other foreign currency) to meet a liquidity squeeze could more than likely require approval of the Eurobank's domestic monetary authorities. Furthermore, under the floating exchange-rate regime, a bank may have problems making the needed conversions without moving the exchange rate adversely against itself. Obviously, the extent to which this would be a problem would depend on the foreign currency involved and the size of the conversions attempted.

It would appear most likely that once its own resources are used up in a liquidity squeeze, an ailing Eurobank would have little alternative but to call on its own central bank or regulatory authorities for assistance. The national authorities would have the final responsibility in determining the merits of the case—that is, should it prop the ailing bank up by making U.S. dollars or other foreign currencies available to it. Is the bank's existence important to the public's confidence in the system? Or is the bank unimportant to the confidence factor and there exist no extenuating circumstances which merit saving it?

In a world in which such life-or-death decisions for an ailing Eurobank are made by individual national regulatory authorities, it would be expected that the criteria involved in such judgments would vary from country to country. There would also be the possibility that a national authority could misjudge the importance of a particular Eurobank's troubles to the public's confidence in the system. For such reasons—to develop less disparate criteria for the life-or-death decision and to reduce the possibility of a misjudgment—it might be well for national regulatory authorities to develop a formal coordinating mechanism for such

---

[48] Some Eurobankers have suggested that I not be so pessimistic about the usefulness of lines of credit with correspondent banks in a liquidity crisis. Obviously, the usefulness of such lines depends on how bad the problem is, which is my point. The worse the problem, the less likely the availability of funds under such lines.

[49] See Bank for International Settlements, Monetary and Economics Department, *Regulations and Policies Relating to Eurocurrency Markets* (Basle: BIS, 7 April 1967 and later editions) for a detailed description of the regulations applicable to Eurobanks in the countries in which they are located.

problems, particularly for times when there is heightened liquidity stress in both national and international financial systems.

Because of its special relationship to its parent U.S. bank, a U.S. foreign branch—a special type of Eurobank—has an alternative during a liquidity crisis not available to the nonbranch Eurobank. It may look to its U.S. parent for U.S. dollar liquidity. Although the Federal Reserve has ruled that payment of a deposit at a foreign branch may not be guaranteed by the U.S. resident parent as if it were a deposit at the U.S. home office itself, it would appear unlikely that U.S. authorities would allow a foreign branch of a U.S. bank to fail without the home office being able to come to its assistance. It could be that some local or national regulations might interfere with the U.S. parent's assistance to a foreign branch, but again it would be unlikely that national authorities ultimately would not allow the U.S. head office to rescue a foreign branch. In fact, the reverse is the likely case, foreign authorities probably look to U.S. parent banks to come to the assistance of their foreign branches when they are in trouble. British authorities have recently called on U.S. banks with interests in banks in the United Kingdom, particularly in the consortium banks in the United Kingdom, to give assurances they will assume responsibility for their share of U.K. banking operations in case of a liquidity squeeze on these institutions.

The Liquidity Problem of the Eurocurrency System. The Eurocurrency system would suffer from a liquidity crisis if there were to be a general and massive withdrawal of funds from the system as a whole. What kind of developments could trip off a massive withdrawal of funds? Presumably such a withdrawal could result from failures of major Eurobanks with substantial depositor losses and growing belief that more major Eurobank failures were likely. The impact of general withdrawals would spread quickly through the system via the network of interbank deposits. No single Eurobank would be immune from the pressures of such a general liquidity squeeze on the whole system.

The scenario of subsequent developments, once a complete loss of confidence in the system began to generate a massive shift of funds from the Euro-currency system, could take various forms. A lender or group of lenders of last resort could come into play to shore up the failing banks. However, before we consider the alternatives for lenders of last resort, let us discuss the possible role of U.S. foreign branches and their U.S. resident parent banks in such a crisis.

Where would the funds go that were being withdrawn en masse from the Eurodollar system, for example? For those depositors who would want to maintain balances in U.S. dollars, there would be only one alternative—to shift their deposits to banks in the United States. Those depositors desiring to move their Eurodollar funds into deposits in other currencies would have to go through the respective foreign-exchange-markets to acquire such deposits. Massive flows from Eurodollar deposits into nondollar national financial markets would cause a sharp appreciation in the exchange rates for the foreign currencies involved, which would tend to moderate the extent of the deposit shifts into nondollar financial assets. Therefore we might not be too much in error to conclude that massive withdrawals from Eurodollars would be shifted primarily into banks in the United States in the case of a complete loss of confidence in the Eurodollar system.

Foreign branches of U.S. banks hold roughly 65 percent of the total U.S. dollar deposit liabilities of Eurobanks to nonbanks. In a general withdrawal of Eurodollar funds, a little less than three dollars in four would be withdrawn from a U.S. foreign branch. Assuming the U.S. parents come to the rescue of their Eurodollar branches, about 65 percent of the total rescue effort would be taken care of automatically in this manner. (Even in the case of a massive withdrawal of Eurodollar funds, it would appear unlikely that 100 percent of Eurodollar funds would be shifted out of the market.)

What would be the mechanics of an infusion of funds from U.S. home offices to foreign branches? As the branch would lose deposits, it would draw down its balances at its home office. The home office could replenish these balances by writing up its "due from branch" accounts or actually acquiring the loans on its branch's books and incorporating them into the home office accounts. Either approach would expand the consolidated U.S. banking system—as it in fact absorbs the part of the Eurodollar system being shifted to it—and would require extra reserves (or lower reserve requirements) unless the U.S. banking system had ample excess reserves. The Federal Reserve would have to be sensitive to this impact and to the need for extra reserves by U.S. banks under such circumstances.

The Lenders of Last Resort. Much has been written about the multinational character of Eurodollar banking precluding it from having a lender of last resort, with the additional contribution to confidence which such a lender would give the system. Some European officials have even called for the Federal Reserve to assume, and presumably to announce publicly, such a role.

One would wonder why, for Eurobanks located in countries with an ample share of the U.S. dollar overhang, the Federal Reserve should serve as lender of last resort in a general crisis situation. The central banks of these countries could well afford—that is they have the necessary U.S. dollar resources available—to provide their banks with the U.S. dollars necessary to shore them up in case of a general withdrawal of funds from the system. They could assume the U.S. dollar loans of their banks in exchange for the dollars, if they so desired, in effect exchanging one kind of U.S. dollar asset for another.

For those countries which have an inadequate supply of U.S. dollars to shore up the general withdrawal of dollars from their banks, the Federal Reserve or the International Monetary Fund could provide the necessary dollars for shoring up the banks. It would be difficult for the Federal Reserve to serve directly as the lender of last resort for these Eurobanks since the banks do not have direct

324

access to the Federal Reserve nor does the Federal Reserve have the necessary surveillance over the banks to give it the kind of information it would need to fill the direct lending role. (U.S. law would probably prevent it from functioning in this direct way.) The Federal Reserve could make funds available, perhaps under some kind of swap arrangement, to those foreign central banks in need of dollar resources.

However, there might be merit in internationalizing such a rescue attempt and having those central banks needing U.S. dollars borrow them through the International Monetary Fund.

No matter what kind of lender of last resort arrangements are produced, the authorities will be faced with walking the very narrow path between bailing out bad management and maintaining confidence in the system. Which way they lean in the exercise of their lender of last resort function depends on their judgment of how fragile the system is at any moment in time. Monitoring the degree of fragility is where collaboration would be desirable among national monetary authorities.

The Eurocurrency System and Petrodollars

An Overview of the Problem. The scope and complexity of the petrodollar problem extends far beyond the current involvement of the Eurocurrency system. The problem, which stems from the steep and rather abrupt increase in the price of oil during 1972–74 by the Organization of Petroleum Exporting Countries (OPEC), has several facets.

First, there is the matter of the size of the collective current-account surplus of OPEC members vis-à-vis the oil importing countries. How large will this surplus be? Current estimates indicate that it will be in the range of $50 to $65 billion in 1974.[50] The surpluses in future years will depend on (1) the strength of non-OPEC demand for OPEC oil, (2) the future price of OPEC oil, which will depend on the supply-demand relationships and the viability of the OPEC cartel, and (3) the volume of OPEC expenditures on goods and services from abroad.

Many different scenarios have been developed for the OPEC current-account surplus during the next ten to fifteen years, each based on assumptions and analysis with high degrees of uncertainty. Developments which cannot be determined today—either in their occurrence or the magnitude of their impact—will determine the size of future OPEC current-account surpluses: the extent to which non-OPEC sources of energy will be developed, the politics of the OPEC cartel, and the development and success of OPEC spending plans, for example.[51]

---

[50] The OPEC current-account surplus for 1974 turned out to be $66 billion. See First National City Bank, *Monthly Economic Letter*, June 1975, p. 12.

[51] By summer 1975 most analysts had revised downward their estimates of OPEC current-account surpluses through 1985. See, for example, First National City Bank, "Why OPEC's Rocket Will Lose Its Thrust," *Monthly Economic Letter*, June 1975, pp. 11-15.

Second, there is the matter of how the non-OPEC countries will handle their side of the OPEC current-account surplus—their deficit. How will the OPEC deficit be distributed among the oil-importing countries? This depends on the policies adopted by the importing countries. There are three ways the oil consumers may respond to the higher oil prices: They may attempt through various policies to reduce non-oil imports and increase exports to pay for the higher priced oil. They may continue existing trade and exchange rate policies and attempt to borrow the funds needed to pay for the higher priced oil. (Their economies would hence gradually adjust to the higher priced oil with a concomitant impact on exports and imports.) Or they may attempt to reduce oil imports from OPEC by developing additional internal supplies of energy. (This alternative is not one which can be utilized in the short run because of the time needed to explore and bring on stream new sources of energy.)

The magnitude of the problem facing the oil-importing countries in future years obviously depends not only on the action they take and the policies they adopt, but also on what happens with OPEC imports and on the investment policies implemented by OPEC members for the investable surpluses with which they find themselves. But, whatever the size of their deficit, the importing countries will have the policy options mentioned above.

The United States is in a somewhat unique position in that its currency is being used as the main means of payment in the transactions between oil-exporting and oil-importing countries.[52] As long as the exporting countries hold their receipts—or the major share of them—in U.S. dollars, there is no overall balance-of-payments problem for the United States. The U.S. balance-of-trade deficit reflects the increased payments of U.S. residents to the OPEC members, and the official reserves transactions balance will reflect any transfer of privately held foreign dollar balances—together with U.S. resident transfers—to the governmental agencies and central banks or monetary boards of the exporting nations. To the extent the exporting nations sell their dollar proceeds for other currencies, either to pay for imports from these countries or to make direct investments, there is a depressing impact on the exchange rate for the dollar under the current floating exchange-rate arrangements.

In the very short run it is most likely—as in fact we have seen already—that the oil-importing countries will attempt to minimize the potentially disruptive impact of the higher oil prices on their trade flows and their domestic economies by borrowing to meet their higher oil import bills. Theoretically, at least, those oil importers needing to borrow would acquire the surplus funds of the OPEC members. This is what is called recycling. The nature of the recycling vehicle to be used—that is, private financial markets and intermediaries or official international

---

[52] It is commonly accepted knowledge that as of mid-1974 the oil payments are being made to the OPEC countries about 75 percent in dollars and 25 percent in sterling.

agencies or government bodies—is still open to question.[53] By borrowing to meet their oil payments deficits, the importing countries are able to buy time to allow the necessary internal adjustments to their economies and lifestyles to be made.

This brings us to a third aspect of the problem created by the OPEC price increases—what may be called the financial, or financial markets, aspect. Here we are concerned with the implications for financial markets, in particular the Eurocurrency markets, of the OPEC investment of its accumulating payments surpluses and of the recycling—or financing of oil imports—required by the oil-importing nations.

The first two problem areas mentioned above—the size of future OPEC surpluses and the policy alternatives available to the importing nations for dividing their collective deficit among themselves—have been treated in some of the other papers of this conference and by several of the discussants and fall outside the scope of our focus. Briefly let us summarize some of the Eurocurrency market aspects of the oil problem, primarily with a view to setting the stage for further discussion of the problem rather than to being definitive.

Eurocurrency Markets and Petrodollars: Deposit Distribution and Recycling. The Eurocurrency system is involved in the current oil payments situation because Eurocurrency deposits—primarily Eurodollar deposits—have served as a substantial investment vehicle to date for the oil exporters. In addition, a substantial amount of financing for oil payments has been undertaken through the Euro-currency markets.[54]

On the investment side, the disposition by the OPEC members of the massive volume of investable funds with which they have suddenly found themselves has accentuated strains and problems already extant in major financial markets, and particularly in the Eurocurrency markets, although the period of peak pressures would appear to have already passed. Early in 1974 alarmists cautioned—and still do to some extent—that the Eurocurrency markets might be on the verge of "chaos" or "total breakdown," whatever that might mean. Before the oil funds began to be shifted into the Euromarkets, strains had begun to develop there under the pressure of growing credit stringency emanating from general anti-inflationary monetary policy in the major industrial countries. There was growing concern among observers and officials that some less well-situated Eurobanks would

---

[53] By summer 1975, with sharply downward revised estimates of the OPEC surpluses fairly prevalent, there was much less focus on recycling by international agencies or government bodies.

[54] The BIS estimates that in 1974 alone about $24 billion of new Eurocurrency deposits were placed in the Eurocurrency markets by the oil-exporting countries. During the first half of 1974, new long- and medium-term credit lines obtained in the Euromarkets by governments and public sector institutions approximated $16.5 billion, with the United Kingdom, France and Italy doing most of the borrowing. In addition, some governments encouraged banks and other enterprises to draw on foreign credit sources during the year. See Bank for International Settlements, *Forty-Fifth Annual Report* (Basle: 9 June 1975), pp. 130-132.

not be able to acquire funds to meet withdrawals or to meet roll-over obligations under stringent credit conditions. There was concern that a few bank failures might snowball into a general withdrawal of funds from the Eurocurrency markets, which would test the viability of the entire system.

Into this kind of environment came the OPEC investors with their massive deposits, generally reacting as any prudent investor would. By spring and summer 1974 there had been several widely publicized bank failures in several countries—including Germany and the United Kingdom—and U.K. authorities had had to initiate rescue operations for numerous smaller Eurobanks operating in London. OPEC investors showed a decided preference for depositing funds only with the bluest-chip Eurobanks—thus minimizing their risk. This preference left the recipient Eurobanks with a larger volume of funds than they could profitably employ in making loans to nonbanks.

Normally funds are redistributed through the Eurocurrency system—from banks with excess funds to banks with a need for funds to meet loan demand—through the interbank redepositing process. However, given the heightened concerns about the viability of many Eurobanks during this period of liquidity tightness, the recipient blue chip Eurobanks were reluctant to serve as risk takers between the export-nation depositors and the low-tiered Eurobanks which needed the funds to meet loan demand.[55] The immediate impact—as was to be expected—was lower deposit rates at the prime banks, those receiving the oil country deposits, and higher deposit rates at the lower-tiered Eurobanks. There were even reports from the market that certain banks were "refusing" to take deposits from potential oil-exporting depositors.

There was also a preference among the oil-exporting depositors, along with most other depositors in the highly uncertain markets, for very short-term deposits—overnight and call deposits. The recipient Eurobanks were reluctant to take the risk involved in converting these very liquid deposits—given the massive volumes involved—into longer-term loans, particularly for some of the potential borrowers who needed longer-term credits. Again, market forces came into play and interest rates on the popular shorter-term deposits fell very sharply relative to those on longer-term deposits. In other words, the preferences of the depositors shifted the yield curve sharply downward on the short end.

The indigestion created in the Eurocurrency markets by the depositor preferences and market segmentation mentioned above would appear to have already passed its peak. These markets are highly efficient and have displayed an ability to serve well the financial needs of a world subject to abrupt developments, such as the rapid sharp increase in the price of OPEC oil. In fact, the sharp changes

---

[55] Tiering—or the grouping of Eurobanks by their credit worthiness as perceived by other banks—developed on a large-scale basis in the interbank market during 1973-74 and interfered considerably with the efficient transfer of funds through the Eurocurrency system.

in the level and the direction of movement of yields—which was experienced in the Euromarkets during 1973–74—are quite consistent with efficient financial markets where rates adjust very rapidly to new information. We would not expect gradual and prolonged interest rate or yield changes in an efficient market. Such would indicate imperfection in the markets.[56]

To the extent the OPEC members have an increasing volume of funds to invest and prefer the Eurodollar market, for example, to the placement of funds with U.S. resident banks, there should be a general lowering of Eurodollar rates relative to U.S. deposit rates, *ceteris paribus*.[57] Historically, Eurodollar deposit rates have been marginally higher than U.S. deposit rates, a factor generally attributed to the risk associated with having dollar deposits with institutions outside the home country of the dollar. The OPEC preference for Eurodollar deposits—if it persists—will work in the opposite direction. This development, to the extent it significantly lowers Eurodollar rates, would favorably reduce the cost of funds for Eurobanks and further enhance their competitive position vis-à-vis resident banks for loan business both in the United States and abroad.

On the other hand, foreign central banks may need to draw down foreign currency holdings to meet their countries' higher oil bills. To the extent these holdings are withdrawn from the Eurocurrency markets, there would be upward pressure on Eurocurrency rates relative to domestic currency deposit rates. Thus, it is impossible to assess quantitatively the net impact of the oil funds development on the margin by which Eurodollar rates are normally above domestic U.S. deposit rates.

There has also been some concern expressed about the ability of the Eurocurrency markets to absorb over the long term the volume of investable funds which the OPEC members will acquire. Eurobanks will need large infusions of additional capital to take on the volume of new funds expected. Will this be forthcoming in a capital short world at rates the Eurobanks will be willing to pay? Obviously, the severity of the capital adequacy problem will depend on the magnitude of the OPEC current-account surpluses in the future—something we can only hypothesize about today. I would suspect, though, that if the additional business is profitable enough, additional long-term capital—both equity and borrowed capital—will be forthcoming.

---

[56] Following a statement in September 1974 by the Group of Ten central bank governors confirming their responsibility for the Eurocurrency markets and their willingness and ability to help in the case of need, sentiment in the Eurocurrency markets began to improve. The BIS reports that interbank business began to pick up in the final quarter of 1974 and that "in the first quarter of 1975 the recovery of confidence made further progress. The premium of Eurorates over U.S. rates contracted, the multi-tier interest rate structure became much narrower, and both nonbank and interbank assets and liabilities appear to have recorded substantial increases." (Bank for International Settlements, *Forty-fifth Annual Report*, p. 134.)

[57] As mentioned in footnote 51, by mid-1975 most estimates of the buildup of OPEC investable funds were sharply lower than they had been earlier.

With regard to recycling, what can be the role of the Eurocurrency markets? Again, the need for recycling will depend on the size of the collective OPEC current-account surpluses in future years and the geographical distribution of the OPEC investments. In the matter of marketable financial investments, the OPEC members do not have a great many alternatives. They must stick with those countries which have well-developed financial markets, mainly the major industrialized countries. Direct investment opportunities are available with wider geographical scope. Many complex factors, which we will not discuss here, will determine the pattern of the payments flows to the oil-consuming nations emanating from OPEC direct investments. These flows will, of course, reduce recycling needs.

The financing approach to the importers' problem of oil payments is fraught with potentially severe difficulties—the main one being that the continual borrowing, if it persists, by the importing nations to pay for a consumable import produces the specter of a rapidly pyramiding debt. This generates an equally rapidly growing requirement for debt servicing in addition to the borrowing which must be continually undertaken to keep the currently needed volume of oil imports flowing. The volumes of financing, interest, and payments flows which will be involved boggle the mind if current price and payments estimates hold.[58]

There are some problem areas developing out of the Eurocurrency system's participation in petrodollar recycling. Unless Eurobanks change their traditional approach of largely matching loans against deposits of the same maturity—I understand they have changed in recent years to some extent—they would appear to be in a position to provide only minimal medium-term financing for the oil importers. There have been suggestions that by denominating deposits in some new unit of account, which would protect the depositor against inflation, Eurobanks may provide an attractive asset which would give some stability to the system.[59] Although the deposit might contain some inflation protection for the depositor, nothing in the unit-of-account approach alters the risk the Eurobank would be taking in transforming short-term deposits into long-term loans, particularly in the massive volumes which it is currently foreseen will be needed.

The Eurocurrency system has made a signal contribution to world stability in the role it has played during the initial financial adjustments called for by the oil payments problem. I would foresee it continuing as a major vehicle for the investment of OPEC funds and for the recycling of petrodollars among the major industrial countries. However, the extent of its recycling role will depend on how large a volume of recycling is needed and how the risk involved evolves through time. Its role in recycling to the less developed countries will probably be a considerably limited one, given the acute problems of these countries and the unusual nature of the risk involved.

---

[58] As mentioned previously, by mid-1975 these estimates had been sharply reduced by most analysts.

[59] See the editorial, "The IMF, the Euromarket or Both," *Euromoney*, February 1974, p. 3.

Summary

This paper reviews four current problem areas of the Eurocurrency system: (1) the nature of credit expansion in the system and proposals for its control, (2) the bank regulatory framework in the United States and its impact on the competitiveness of U.S. resident banks with Eurobanks, (3) the problem of Eurocurrency liquidity and a lender of last resort for the system, and (4) the impact of petrodollars on the Eurocurrency system and its possible role in recycling the oil funds.

The various conditions which have generated calls for control of Eurocurrency banking are reviewed. The nature of Eurocredit expansion is analyzed with particular attention to the attempts by various analysts to define a "base" for the Eurocurrency system. It is suggested that there is no "base" in the Eurocurrency system comparable to the monetary base—primarily the reserves of commercial banks with their central bank—in a domestic fractional reserve banking system and that the nonbank financial intermediary credit expansion model is appropriate for analysis of the Eurocurrency system. Possible control instruments—required reserves and open-market operations—are analyzed within the context of the nonbank intermediary model. It is concluded that the best way to control Eurocurrency expansion—if that is desired—is to enable banks in the home countries of the currencies involved, the United States, for example, to "compete away" the deposit and loan business from Eurobanks.

In the second section of the paper, regulations which limit the competitiveness of U.S. resident banks vis-à-vis Eurobanks—in particular Federal Reserve Regulations D, M, and Q—are analyzed. Their impact on the profit margins of U.S. resident banks relative to Eurobanks is shown, and possible options for neutralizing this impact are examined. It is concluded that the most likely way of establishing competitive conditions for U.S. resident banks roughly equal to those of Eurobanks would be to reduce or eliminate the U.S. regulations which put U.S. resident banks at a disadvantage.

Thirdly, the nature of liquidity for an individual Eurobank and for the Eurocurrency system as a whole is examined. The special role that U.S. head offices—and indirectly the Federal Reserve—would play with regard to U.S. foreign branches in the Eurocurrency markets in case of a liquidity squeeze is analyzed. Various possibilities for lenders of last resort in the Eurocurrency system are discussed.

Finally, the nature and scope of the problem generated by the sharp increase in the price of oil from the OPEC countries during the 1972–74 period is reviewed. The involvement of the Eurocurrency system in this matter has occurred because Eurocurrency deposits have served as a substantial investment vehicle for the oil exporters and because a substantial amount of financing for oil payments has been undertaken through the Eurocurrency markets. The impact of the OPEC

331

funds on the Eurocurrency markets is discussed. The special problems of the Euromarkets accentuated during 1974 by the OPEC funds—depositor preferences and market segmentation—appeared to have passed their peak by late September 1974. It is concluded that the Euromarkets have been very efficient and have displayed an ability to serve well the financial needs of a world subject to abrupt developments.

The petrodollar recycling role of the Eurocurrency markets is briefly reviewed. The extent of the need for recycling depends on the OPEC current-account surpluses in future years. The Eurocurrency system has made a signal contribution to world stability, it is concluded, during the initial financial adjustments called for by the oil payments problem. However, the extent of its recycling role in the future will depend on how large a volume of recycling is needed and how the attendant risk evolves through time. The system's role in recycling to the less developed countries will probably be a considerably limited one.

COMMENTARIES

Hamish McRae

Let me start by thanking Professor Stem and by saying how impressed I am by the breadth and depth of his paper. Just to have gotten the whole subject into one paper was a very considerable achievement, and I think we should all be most grateful to Professor Stem for having done it.

What I am going to talk about will be the back part of the paper, sections three and four. I shall suggest four areas where there could be further comment. My main reason for so doing is the crucial role of the Euromarket in recycling oil dollars.

It has been an amusing transformation: three or four years ago the market was regarded as a scar on the face of the world money scene, something that central bankers did not like to think about too much because it was awkward, unplanned, and had suddenly grown up without their playing any part in its growth. Now for us in Britain, we simply thank God that the market exists, for it has saved our bacon in the last couple of years. In Britain there is very much less talk about control of the market, because you cannot very well talk about controlling a market when you have to go cap in hand to it frequently for a loan.

In this comment I intend to talk, first, about the degree of maturity transformation that takes place in the market, second, about the experience we had in London last year of a run on the sterling money market, third, about the relationship between central banks in the Euromarket, and fourth, about the recycling of oil funds. On the first, I thought it might help if I explained two quite separate stages, or types, of maturity transformation.

There is, to begin with, a range of maturities from one week—the preferred Arab oil funds maturity—to six months. This range exists within the money markets, and in practice within the money market divisions of the commercial banks. Professor Stem mentioned that the old idea was that banks would match their money market deposits on a maturity basis but that there is evidence that Eurobanks had not done so quite as much in the last couple of years. I think he is absolutely right about this, but that is only the first stage of maturity transformation.

333

The second stage, or type of maturity transformation—quite separate—is between six months and seven years and takes place through the medium-term loan market. The rate on the medium-term loan is set at a certain margin over the interbank deposit rate. So, a lending bank goes back to the deposit market every six months, borrows its chunk of the funds behind the loan, charges its three-quarters percent or 1 percent margin and then passes the loan on to the client. The borrower thinks he has a loan for seven years, and the bank says, Well, we are merely making a loan for six months. This is a marvelous conjuring trick, providing the bank can go back to the deposit market every six months for the funds. Medium-term Eurocurrency loans, which many countries have used to finance oil purchases are, in fact, merely a series of six-month loans.

The dangers of the first stage of maturity transformation are obvious. The dangers of the second stage become obvious when you consider the growth of the medium-term loan market during the last three years.

The second point I want to make is about the run on the money markets which can occur and which, indeed, did occur late last year. A secondary bank in London, London and County Securities, had to be rescued. We then found a wave of panic sweeping through the markets. This sterling market is identical to the Euromarket in its organization and, although substantially smaller than the London Eurodollar market, it is still sizable.

Because of the failure of that one bank, every small bank in London, though perhaps perfectly sound, quite suddenly found it could not go back to the money market to roll over its loans. The good suffered with the bad. Banks had to be rescued, and then the banks which had rescued them had to be rescued. Finally, some of the ones that had already been rescued once had to be rescued again. It was only by the Bank of England's rallying of the clearing banks to the rescue of these fringe banks that the London sterling market was saved from disaster. I mention this to demonstrate that a run on these banks can happen. And the particular point I want to stress is that such a panic is completely irrational. Perfectly sound banks suffer with unsound ones. All that is needed is a rumor.

The next matter I want to explore is central bank support for banks in the Euromarket. You may recall there was a central bankers' meeting in Basle in July 1974, the regular monthly meeting at the Bank for International Settlements. At this meeting, the question of support for banks in the Euromarket was discussed and a rather woolly agreement came out at the end of it. My understanding of what transpired is that both the German and American authorities showed severe resistance to such support, which was why no firm communique could be issued. There then followed the Herstatt mess, the ramifications of which only gradually became clear during the months of July and August 1974. Later at the September 1974 meeting of the central banks, there apparently was a substantial change of view in favor of support for commercial banks in the Euromarket. I understand there were five parts to this agreement:

(1) Banks that get into liquidity difficulties within national boundaries will automatically be supported by their respective central banks.

(2) Banks that get into difficulties through fraud will not necessarily be bailed out by their respective central banks, but all depositors will be protected, large and small.

(3) Where the difficulty is at a foreign branch of a bank, the parent bank will be bullied by its central bank into making good any losses, and it will, if necessary, be supported by the central bank of the parent bank.

(4) Where the loss is sustained by an overseas subsidiary, the parent bank will again be responsible and supported by the parent's central bank if necessary.

(5) The consortium banks will be supported on a pro-rata basis by their parents (that is, pro rata their shareholdings), again with central bank support if necessary.

Now, this agreement never appeared in print. It could not be published in this form because of domestic considerations within the United States and within Germany.

The final area I want to talk about concerns the oil billions. The U.S. Treasury figures are well known: $10 billion to $13 billion out of $25 billion to $28 billion to, I think, mid-September of this year (1974) were placed through the Euromarkets. This squares with U.K. estimates of the amount that has gone through the Euromarkets.

There are a number of reasons why it is impossible for the Euromarket to continue to recycle this volume of funds. First, there is the liquidity preference of the Arabs: a vast proportion of these $13 billion are in deposits with maturities of less than one week.

Second, there is the obvious credit risk. There is an important distinction between lending to a country—recycling oil funds—and lending to a company. If you lend to a company, you are usually doing so on the basis of some project which is going to repay the loan; if you lend to a country, there is no such project. You merely make a political judgment about the country. Clearly a country which has to borrow on the Euromarkets to finance its oil deficit will be the country least able to repay the loan. To illustrate this, a word about the British position: I think the market view would be that it is now impossible for Britain to go back to the Euromarkets to raise $2.5 billion as it did in the early part of this year. If it could do so, it certainly would not be able to get the same rates.

The third reason why the Euromarkets cannot handle the oil funds involves the balance sheet considerations of commercial banks. Every Euromarket loan has to be carried on the balance sheet of a commercial bank. If I recall correctly, the OECD reckons the oil money will cumulate $350 billion by 1980, and the World Bank estimates $650 billion. If you look at the total capital and reserves and the expected growth in the capital and reserves of the world's top fifty banks during this period, you can see the mathematical impossibility of their inter-mediating this volume of funds.

So, what will happen? I have two suggestions to make. I think there is a statistical inevitability that there will be a major default on a loan in the Euromarket in the reasonably near future. I am not predicting this. I am merely saying that it is like the chance of a hurricane in the West Indies. It *must* happen sooner or later, but we do not know when. I think we have to face the fact that when this occurs, it will create severe difficulties for major commercial banks, difficulties on a scale not seen before.

Finally, I want to echo Professor Stem's view that the Euromarket is quite incapable of continuing to carry out the recycling task in the volume currently envisaged. I suggest it will instead return to its original job of providing funds for economic development—both in developing countries and in the developed coun-tries around the world. The Euromarket will come through a full circle, for this is where it began.

Fischer Black

I generally agree with the conclusions Professor Stem has reached. He claims that regulation of banks in the United States and in other countries is a major reason for the growth of the Eurocurrency market. It follows then that if we want to control its growth, the best thing to do is to reduce or eliminate the controls on domestic banks, such as reserve requirements and interest-rate ceilings.

Professor Stem talks about Eurocurrency markets as credit markets rather than as money markets. There is little reason to think of Eurocurrency deposits as money. If Eurocurrency deposits are money, then by symmetry, Eurocurrency loans must be negative money. If the banks have some capital, so that their loans exceed their deposits, the net amount of money represented in the Eurocurrency markets is negative. In other words, it is appropriate to think of the Eurocurrency markets as credit markets. Thus, I prefer to view the issue as one of "Eurocredit."

Stem's discussion of the effects of the growth of Eurocredit assumes that growth in Eurocredit tends to cause an increase in aggregate demand or an increase in inflationary pressure. This view is very common. Many writers feel that uncon-trolled growth of domestic credit leads to an increase in domestic income and that uncontrolled growth of international credit leads to an increase in international income. With full employment, an increase in income means an increase in the price level.

I want to quarrel with the notion that a credit expansion leads to an increase in aggregate demand or an increase in inflationary pressure. The arguments that credit expansion has these effects are partial equilibrium arguments. They look only at one side of the coin. They consider the effects of new credit on the borrower but not on the lender.

Let us assume, as is customary, that intermediaries have no assets other than loans and no liabilities other than deposits. We will assume the type of intermediary that exists in the Eurocredit market. That means that there are no restrictions on the maturities and interest rates of deposits and no reserve requirements. At most, there is a requirement that there be approximate balance between the currencies or maturities of the assets and liabilities. This means that aggregate borrowing through these intermediaries equals aggregate lending. The net amount of credit supplied by such intermediaries is zero. This is true whether we count interbank credit or not. Even for nonbanks, the amount they borrow in total equals the amount they lend in total. Any increase in credit increases the amount of borrowing and the amount of lending equally.

The usual argument is that an increase in available credit will increase aggregate demand because the borrower will use the money to buy more goods and services than he bought before. But this ignores the lender. The new lender must buy fewer goods and services than he bought before. Together, the borrower and the lender may have either more or less total demand than they had before. But we cannot tell which way it will go. An increase in credit may cause an increase in aggregate demand, no change in aggregate demand, or a decrease in aggregate demand.

It is hard to test theories in this area because there is so much reverse causation. An increase in income or wealth will tend to cause an increase in the demand for credit. An individual who is borrowing against future income will want to borrow more when his expected income goes up, and the individual who is lending will have more to lend. An individual who is borrowing to invest in risky assets will want to borrow more when the value of his risky assets goes up, and the individual who is combining holdings of risky assets with lending will generally want to lend more.

It is the same with inflation. An increase in the price level will lead to a corresponding increase in the demand for nominal borrowing and lending, assuming that other factors remain the same. So we cannot tell empirically whether the inflation caused the expansion of credit or the expansion of credit caused the inflation.

Since there is no reason to believe that control of credit means control of aggregate demand or inflationary pressure, it is not obvious why we would want to control the Eurocredit market at all. Indeed, it would be better to concentrate our efforts on decontrolling the domestic banking system. If we had a domestic equivalent of the Eurocredit market, both borrowers and lenders would be better off—especially lenders.

Helmut W. Mayer

The emphasis in Professor Stem's excellent paper is on credit creation and multiplier effects in the Eurocurrency system and on the possibility of controlling the market's potential inflationary impact by keeping down its growth. I must admit I find his argument very lucid, and I agree with him on many points, although as can only be expected when dealing with such a complex and controversial subject, there are also some points of disagreement. However, rather than dwelling on these points and getting into some analytically complicated, technical details, I probably can make a more positive contribution to this session by trying to say a few words about the present state of the Eurocurrency markets and about their prospects and likely future problems.

To start, let me point out that as a result of the oil price situation and the greater flexibility of exchange rates, a rather remarkable metamorphosis seems to have occurred in official concern about the market. With one or two possible exceptions, there is to my knowledge hardly any government that is greatly concerned at present about the potential inflationary impact of the Eurocurrency markets on its country; instead it is generally feared that the official sector or the private residents of certain countries may not be able to borrow enough funds in these markets to cover their oil-induced deficits. If there is still a lot of talk about control of the markets, "control" now means something different. Its primary aim would no longer be to keep the growth of the markets and their alleged inflationary impact in check, but to safeguard the markets' health and stability, since difficulties in either of these areas would undoubtedly aggravate the problem of financing the oil deficits. Similarly there does not seem to be much concern right now about a shift of business away from U.S.-based banks to banks in the Eurocurrency markets. On the contrary, most of the big U.S. banks themselves would probably be quite happy if some of the oil funds offered to them in the United States were offered abroad instead and preferably not to their own foreign branches.

Let me add two remarks in this context. One is that the statistics collected by the Bank for International Settlements (BIS) indicate that, after a rapid expansion in the first four months of 1974, the growth of the Eurobanks' balance sheet slowed during May and June and recorded an absolute contraction during July and August. This occurred despite large flows of new oil funds into the markets. Although the figures are still very incomplete and details are not yet available, I would expect that the contraction affected mainly the non-U.S.-owned Eurobanks and that, coming in the aftermath of the Herstatt failure, it occurred mainly in the interbank sector of the market. Nevertheless, on the basis of the BIS estimate of $155 billion for the end of 1973, I would be inclined to place the so-called net size of the markets (including the Caribbean area, Singapore, et cetera) in the neighborhood of $175 billion at the end of August. This means that there has been, on balance, hardly any growth of the markets since the end of March 1974.

Let me also add that, with market confidence improving right now and with the premium Eurobanks have to pay for funds becoming smaller, I do not think that the contraction of the markets will continue for very long. On the other hand, for reasons I will mention shortly, I do not feel that the markets will come anywhere near achieving the high growth rates experienced during 1973 and early 1974.

The second remark I want to add is that on taking a close look at individual countries, there is—contrary to what many economists like Professor Friedman, Professor Machlup and, although to a much more limited extent, perhaps also Professor Stem would lead one to expect—little evidence that the Eurocurrency markets have been a major causal factor in the sharp aggravation of the problem of inflation with which the world economy has been plagued in recent years. This is particularly true of countries such as the United States, Japan, Italy, the United Kingdom and France, where inflation must be blamed on other influences. The only major country where, to my knowledge, the credit injections from the Euromarket made a major contribution to domestic inflationary problems some time ago—that is, before the recourse to floating—is Germany. But this is also the country that has often been blamed, though in my view unjustifiably so, for putting the international monetary system under strain by not inflating enough. I might also add that it is quite out of the question that the intermediation by the Euromarkets of part of the oil funds is inflationary; all that it will do is offset to a partial extent the deflationary impact of the oil-induced balance-of-payments deficits. In fact, it is quite likely that there will not be enough funds available in the market to protect all the oil-importing countries from reserve losses.

However, let me return to the topic of this session, namely, current problems and prospects. I take it that one of the reasons why Professor Stem has hardly touched upon the question of the future development of the market is that the world has become largely unpredictable. As a result of what has happened in the field of oil prices and inflation, the past is no longer a very useful guide to the future. Extrapolation of the recent progress of inflation seems to lead to the conclusion that monetary chaos is imminent and, similarly, it is hard to see how without additional official financing schemes, the oil-price induced external payments disequilibria can be managed.

Since we have to assume that we will continue to have a viable economic system, the conclusion must be that there will take place some quite dramatic changes in trends and policies. But what these changes will be is hard to predict. For example, will we be able to return to the relatively low and stable rates of inflation of the fifties and sixties without a pronounced depression, or will it take a major economic shake-out to produce the necessary moderation and downward revision of expectations? Or has the social fabric degenerated too much for a return to the old system, with bureaucratic and centralized control of wages, prices, and interest rates being the only means to achieve an acceptable degree of price stability? Similarly, how will the oil price situation be managed? Will it be possible after all to reach agreement on a reduction of oil prices; and if not, what form will the necessary international cooperation and the new institutional arrangements take? Will they bypass the Eurocurrency markets or will they take advantage of the existing mechanisms of the markets for the intermediation of the oil funds? Last but not least, will the necessary changes come about as a result of foresight and reason or will it take a further acceleration of inflation and a further degeneration of the international monetary system to produce the necessary responses?

To a large extent, the answer to these questions is, of course, also the answer to the question about the future development of the Eurocurrency markets. With some exaggeration, it might even be contended that whereas in the relatively stable economic environment of some years ago the growth and health of the markets depended mainly on microeconomic considerations, that is, on the internal dynamics of the markets and the soundness of the business conducted in them, their development in the near future will be largely influenced by macroeconomic factors outside their control. This, however, does not acquit the Eurobankers of any responsibility for the health of the markets. On the contrary, since rough times may be ahead, it will be as important as ever that the markets start out from a position of strength. In fact, Eurobankers seem to be highly aware of the potential dangers inherent in the present general economic situation and, despite the challenge of the oil funds, they are likely to put safety before growth.

One thing that seems to be quite certain is that in real terms the supply of *non*-oil funds to the markets will slow down. There are three main reasons for this. First, the oil price increase has reduced the oil-importing countries' real income. Second, non-Group of Ten countries' placements of their reserve accruals in the Eurocurrency markets have in the past been one of the main factors behind the markets' growth. As a result of the oil price situation, the growth of these countries' reserves will undoubtedly slow down, and some countries may actually have to draw down their reserves. To the extent that such drawings are financed out of reserves held in the Euromarkets, there may even be negative multiplier effects, that is, a multiple contraction of official non-oil funds deposited in the Eurocurrency markets. Third, the precarious balance-of-payments positions and rapidly increasing foreign indebtedness of the oil-importing countries will tend to induce them to tighten up their measures against capital outflows, which would, of course, also affect supplies to the Eurocurrency markets.

On the other hand, a major role in the intermediation of oil funds could give a strong fillip to the growth of the markets. However, there are a number of important factors, some of which are mentioned in Professor Stem's paper, that will probably limit the participation by the market in this kind of business.

First, the challenge of oil funds comes at a time when, after a period of extremely rapid growth in a climate of inflation, exchange-rate speculation, fierce interbank competition, and very generous maturity transformation, the markets could do with a pause for consolidation. Inflation has undermined the capital base of many of the Eurobanks' corporate customers and has thus reduced the Euro-banks' enthusiasm for increasing their claims on these borrowers. Massive foreign exchange losses by some banks, though not related to Eurocurrency business, have weakened public confidence in the health of the markets and particularly in that of the smaller Eurobanks. The resultant sharp rise in the interest rates these smaller banks have had to pay for foreign funds has subjected them to a severe profit squeeze, the memory of which will undoubtedly influence their attitudes toward new business in the future. Moreover, the rapid growth of their balance sheets, together with very narrow profit margins, has led to a more general deterioration in the relationship between the Eurobanks' risk capital and their loans. Particu-larly in view of the depressed state of the equity markets, these stretched loan-to-capital ratios will tend to act as a brake on the further growth of the market.

Second, the oil price situation itself has undermined the international financial strength and, viewed from the standpoint of the Eurobanks, the credit rating of many of the oil-importing countries. The Eurobanks already seem to be quite reluctant to lend to a number of countries, and the impending rapid decline in the ratio between the oil-importing countries' official reserves and their foreign indebtedness will aggravate this situation.

Third, from a microeconomic point of view, the financing of the oil deficits does not seem to be in line with traditional banking standards. It does not itself generate a future flow of foreign exchange for the borrowing countries which will permit the servicing and ultimate repayment of these loans. On the contrary, since the oil-importing countries will have to go on increasing their foreign indebt-edness, they will only be able to service and repay the loans out of the proceeds of ever larger borrowings. Moreover, the countries which need to borrow most, that is, the large deficit countries, will be, according to banking standards, the least credit worthy ones.

Fourth, on the liabilities side, the growth of the Eurobanks' balance sheets would be concentrated on a small number of large depositors, namely, the govern-ments of the oil-exporting countries. The banks could therefore no longer depend on the law of large numbers. Sudden massive withdrawals or shifts of these funds might not only render illiquid individual or whole groups of Eurobanks but would pose a very serious threat to international monetary stability in general.

Fifth, the oil-exporting countries have shown a strong preference for liquidity, whereas the oil-importing countries' borrowing requirements are of an extremely long-term nature. Consequently, large participation in the intermediation of the oil funds might threaten to involve the Eurobanks in an excessive amount of maturity transformation, which could turn out to be a very serious problem when the oil-exporting countries start to move this money around.

The conclusion to be drawn from all this, and here I think I am fully in agreement with Professor Stem, is that in the future the role played by the Euro-banks in the intermediation of oil funds will be much more modest than it was in the first nine months of this year—*unless* there are some joint international guarantees protecting the banks against the consequences of payments difficulties on the part of the borrowing countries and against sudden shifts of funds by the oil-exporting countries. Without such guarantees, the practical consequence of the various considerations I have just enumerated will be that the Eurobanks will reduce the interest yields they are willing to offer on deposits, particularly on short-term deposits from the oil-exporting countries and will raise the interest on their loans to the large deficit countries. The increase in margins charged by the Eurobanks, together with outright refusals to accept on deposit additional funds from the oil producers, will tend to divert the flow of oil funds to other channels. The transactions still handled by the market will be the cream of the crop, will involve less maturity transformation, and will be carried out with margins that permit the buildup of adequate reserves against risk.

This, of course, leaves open the problem of recycling the oil surpluses, which, however, is a macro- and not a microeconomic problem. Whether the intermediation of the oil funds is effected with or without large-scale participation of the Euromarkets, in the interest of the preservation of a viable international economic system, there will be a need for dramatic official efforts and international cooperation in the field of credit assistance, joint official guarantees, and credit facilities.

Polly Reynolds Allen

My comments will be quite brief, partly because, being the last discussant, some of the things I had planned to say have been nicely taken care of by Helmut Mayer. He has described what I, too, believe are some of the limitations on the growth of the Eurocurrency markets in the coming period of oil funds recycling. I also generally agree with Professor Black's comments on the nature of the Eurodollar market as a credit market, rather than a money market. This leads me to what may be appropriate concluding comments for the session—a few suggestions of where we need to go in terms of further research on the Eurocurrency markets.

Although this conference has ostensibly been on the Eurocurrency markets, that subject has not been discussed very much here. Professor Cooper was probably correct when he suggested that one reason for this may be that we do not have a good theory of the use of money. We also do not have a good theory of where the Eurocurrency markets fit into the national money and credit markets. As a result, economists, who do not like to talk in generalities, may perhaps feel that they do not have much to say about the Eurocurrency markets.

There is, I think, a real need for further work in developing general equilibrium kinds of models to deal with the Eurocurrency markets. The multiplier models that have been used have serious difficulties, partly because they are partial equilibrium models. In addition, I have doubts as to the appropriateness of the underlying assumptions in many of these multiplier models about the demand and supply functions for Eurocurrency deposits and loans. It is inappropriate to treat the Eurocurrency markets as if they were a closed banking system, in which banks are not allowed to pay interest on demand deposits and thus have perfectly elastic supply functions for loans—at whatever interest rate they can get—up to the maximum allowed by reserve requirements.

Professor Stem, in his proposal for a model with a liquid asset multiplier, seems to be suggesting that we should incorporate the Eurocurrency model into an overall model of the U.S. financial markets. I think that is going in the right direction, but not far enough. We need to develop models that include, minimally, the money and financial markets of the United States, the Eurocurrency markets, and one other country—as the rest of the world—and to examine the interrelationships among these markets. There is a high degree of substitutability, most certainly between dollar-denominated assets in the United States and in the Eurodollar market. There is also substitutability of some unknown degree between assets in the Eurodollar market and in the national money and credit markets of other countries. Some promising work in this direction has been done by Hewson and Sakakibara at the International Monetary Fund.

The other area in which I would suggest we need more work is the development of models that are not based on assumptions of perfectly competitive financial markets. Probably one of the reasons that we have not talked more about the Eurocurrency markets is that our models do not incorporate many of the constraints that are currently appearing in these markets. There is the important problem with the oil funds, mentioned by Dr. Mayer, that there are only a small number of depositors for such a large volume of funds. Financial intermediation between the short maturities of deposits and the long maturities of assets is usually based on the assumption that there is a fairly stable deposit base, resulting from a large number of depositors. Such an assumption is inappropriate for the oil funds. For individual institutions this makes a real difference in their risk, and it makes a difference in how these markets behave.

Another recent development in the Eurocurrency markets is the consideration of what bankers are calling sovereign risk, which is the risk of loaning to a particular country. This applies not only to loans to the governments of countries that have been borrowing heavily to finance oil deficits, but it is also being applied to the banks and the firms in these countries, which individually may have sound projects and good prospects. The balance-of-payments outlook for the country as a whole and the ability of the country to generate the necessary foreign exchange to pay back its loans in the future define sovereign risk. If a country has been borrowing too heavily, perhaps for consumption of oil rather than for investment, then loans to anyone in that country are being lumped together as risky assets.

So we have here another kind of market imperfection that involves the problem of small numbers. Because such borrowing is by a relatively small number of countries, risk cannot be reduced simply by charging a higher rate of interest and expecting that a few will fail, but the rest will come through.

The problem of small numbers, both of depositors and of risky borrowers, suggests the need to develop theoretical models of international capital flows that include some monopoly elements and that give greater attention to the role of risk.

Finally, I would like to make a comment regarding oil financing which is not really a Eurocurrency consideration. While it is reasonable to assume that the oil-producing countries will invest their current-account surpluses somewhere in the oil-consuming world, in all probability the oil funds will not be distributed in the same manner as the oil deficits. This certainly presents problems for the oil-deficit countries, those countries whose current-account deficits exceed their net capital inflows. And it also presents potential problems for oil surplus countries, of which the United States may be a major one.

If the United States finds itself fighting inflation as its major domestic economic problem, which may or may not be the case, then it may face a classical dilemma problem. With a net capital inflow exceeding our current-account deficit, external balance would call for an expansionary monetary policy; but this would be out of line with our domestic goals. The alternatives would be (1) to allow the surplus to continue, which would reduce world liquidity, be contractionary, and perhaps highly disruptive to the world economy; (2) to let the dollar appreciate which, although quite appropriate over some longer period, could present serious adjustment problems in the short run; or (3) to initiate some kind of government intervention to move these funds out of the United States and to the oil-deficit countries. I think this is a problem that has not been given adequate attention and needs to be considered further.

An exchange-rate change, sufficient for the United States to generate a current-account deficit that would offset its net capital inflow might be impractical in the short run. The limitations of short-run exchange-rate adjustment are greater than in the past because of the magnitudes of the immediate surpluses of the oil-producing countries—currently estimated at something like $60 to $70 billion a year.

About six months ago, one heard expressions of concern to the effect that the oil-producing nations were a kind of black hole which would suck up the oil funds and into which these funds would disappear. That, of course, will not happen: the oil-producing countries will have to invest the funds somewhere. But, in a sense, if the United States would not allow an appreciation of the dollar relative to oil-deficit countries, but would run a substantial balance-of-payments surplus, the dollar's position as a reserve currency could permit the United States to become a kind of black hole. Dollars could continue to flow into the United States and yet have no effect on the U.S. money supply. I have suggested the need to consider measures that would prevent such a situation. However, the need to develop some kind of financing beyond what the market may do, as an alternative to depending wholly on exchange-rate adjustment, is basically a short-run rather than a long-run problem.

Finally, the fact deserves mention that to force the oil-deficit countries to cut back consumption in the short run and bring their balance of payments into equilibrium through current-account adjustments presents two kinds of problems. There is, first, a moral problem for some of the developing countries, whose difficulties involve questions literally of survival. For other countries, whose problems are less disastrous, the issue revolves more around the externalities that may be generated by serious economic disruptions to certain economies. Even if we felt inclined to say, "That is their problem," there will be sizable external effects from such disruptions because of the enormous degree of interaction among world economies. Oil imports are not a consumption good that can easily be cut back; oil is an intermediate good for much of the production of an industrialized nation. There are also potential political repercussions from severe economic disturbances, the impact of which may be of concern to many other countries. There is no reason, of course, to think that these countries should be financed indefinitely, but in the short run there are externalities that need to be considered.

DISCUSSION

Multiplier Aspects of Eurocurrencies

PROFESSOR SWOBODA: Professor Allen has told us that we do not have an adequate theory of the Eurodollar market. I agree. But neither do we have an adequate theory of any particular economic phenomenon that is a general theory. That is, we have particular theories when we try to explain particular phenomena and we have general theories when we try to explain general phenomena. We have quite a few general theories about international monetary economics, capital movements, et cetera into which we can—within the framework of those theories— put the Eurodollar market or some of its salient features. But then we need to turn to the principles of industrial organization for valuable analysis when trying to explain some of the more particular things about Eurodollars.

Professor Allen and others have commented that multiplier models are inadequate in Eurocurrency analysis. We all agree, but these—like other simple models—are a little bit the poetry of science. They try to catch some phenomena but not everything. We do have, if you are willing to play around with multipliers, adequate multiplier theories applicable to Eurodollars and Eurocurrencies. And there is even a general equilibrium one of which I am the producer. This brings me to my last comment, which concerns the inflationary impact of the Eurodollar market.

In my particular version, the Eurodollar multiplier is just part of the more general multiplier, which I call the world money-supply multiplier under fixed exchange rates. In this model it is necessary to decide what is exogenous and what is endogenous. One of the problems with Eurodollar multipliers to date is that the base has been treated as exogenous. It is not very helpful to say that if we could only control the base, then we could control Eurodollar expansion, because we do not have any idea how to control the base.

In my simple model—and it is inadequate for any practical policy purposes— four things are exogenous: (1) domestic credit creation in the United States, (2) domestic credit creation in Europe, (3) the supply of gold or other outside assets in the world, and (4) particular currency preferences of the public—or in various countries, preferences between holding national currency deposits, foreign currency deposits, et cetera—and some reserve preference ratios for central banks.

Given these four elements, everything else in the system becomes endogenous, and what one finds is that an increase in the world money stock can be due to a number of causes. It can be due to an increase in the supply of any of three of the exogenous variables in the system—that is, an increase in U.S. domestic credit availability, an increase in European domestic credit availability, or an increase in the quantity of outside assets. The basic source of inflation in such a model of money, including Eurodollars, is domestic credit creation or outside assets.

The relevant question is, Will changes in the exogenous variables have a stronger or weaker impact on the world money supply in the presence of the Eurodollar system or in its absence? Obviously, the impact is going to be more with a Eurodollar market than without because some of what is high-powered money in the Eurodollar system—claims on commercial banks in the United States—is low-powered money somewhere else. You get multiplier effects that turn out to be rather minor compared with the increase in the world money supply generated either by the neutralizing of reserve flows by the United States—when it is in a balance-of-payments deficit situation—or the holding by central banks of reserves in U.S. Treasury bills or in deposits with the U.S. commercial banking system, which has about the same effect as neutralization of a balance-of-payments deficit on the money supply of the United States.

Let me conclude by mentioning yet another source of increase in the world money supply and inflation: a shift in currency preferences. If the public starts to change its asset preferences, there may be an inflationary impact. If the public decides to shift deposits toward the Eurodollar market from national money markets, for example, there will tend to be some inflationary repercussions.

But barring that, the basic conclusion is that what is inflationary at the origin is really domestic credit creation, which will then—with the existence of the Eurodollar market—tend to spread more rapidly into the rest of the world.

DR. JOHN HEWSON: Let me raise a point about multipliers which I feel has been neglected in the literature, a point which Professor Niehans raised a couple of years ago. This concerns the essential nature of the banking process implicit in the simple multiplier model. In general, domestic commercial banks, as envisaged by the model, borrow essentially demand deposits, while on the asset side, they lend at longer term in the form of commercial loans, mortgages, et cetera. As a system, the essence of the process is liquidity creation in terms of maturity transformation.

On the liability side, banks borrow demand deposits. In other words, the depositors still maintain their right to purchasing power. But on the asset side, banks lend longer term. They are taking, in a sense, an illiquid position and thereby enhancing the liquidity position of the nonbank sector.

If this model is applied to the Eurocurrency system, we find a banking system, it is true, that may be a fractional reserve banking system. But its assets and its liabilities can be divided into clearly delineated maturity classes. And as far as I can determine, checking accounts or demand deposits are a very small—if not a zero—part of Eurocurrency liabilities.

The Eurocurrency market is a time deposit market. Eurobanks borrow time funds and lend time funds. The implication of this is that when we use the domestic multiplier model, we concentrate on the gross deposit figure—which gives us a good idea of the extent of the liquidity transformation in the case of a domestic banking system with demand deposits. But in the Eurocurrency market, the gross deposit figure is really irrelevant because what we should be taking into consideration is a net position; we should be comparing the liquidity of assets to the liquidity of liabilities. As Professor Black said, on one side we have positive money and on the other we have negative money. For every deposit there is a claim of much the same maturity.

The point I want to make is that Eurobanks tend to balance their maturity structures, that is the maturities of their liabilities and claims. Unfortunately the evidence is not as good as we would like it to be. But if you take Bank of England data on the maturity structure of assets and liabilities for London-based Eurobanks and compare it with that for domestic banking systems, one receives the fairly clear impression that maturity transformation is a much smaller factor in the Eurocurrency system.

We should, however, make a distinction in this matter of maturity transformation between "normal times" and "crisis times." In normal times, I believe it is correct to say, Eurobanks maintain fairly close maturity balance in their assets and liabilities. Mr. McRae referred, on the other hand, to the present crisis situation in Eurocurrency markets exemplified by the preference of Arab depositors for very short-term deposits, generally with maturities of less than thirty days. Eurobanks are lending these funds medium-term, out to eight or ten years. What can we infer from this situation?

First, we really do not know what percentage of the Arab funds are actually taking the form of deposits of one month or less. Secondly, there is a feature of Eurocurrency lending called "rollover loans," a technique whereby Eurobanks minimize their liquidity risk—in a sense—by adjusting periodically the interest rate on their loans to reflect the cost of funds, that is, the current deposit rate. A rollover loan may be viewed in some respects as a series of three-month loans up to the commitment period, say ten years.

Finally, let me mention briefly a point raised in Professor Stem's paper about U.S. commercial bank borrowing from the Eurocurrency market. He mentioned the special security issues which the Federal Reserve System offered foreign branches of U.S. commercial banks in 1970, with the intention of discouraging the re-flow of funds from the U.S. banking system to the Eurocurrency markets. The work done on estimating equations for U.S. commercial bank borrowing from their foreign branches suggests that since the U.S. banks were allowed to include these security holdings as part of their reserve-free base, the same re-flow of funds to the Eurocurrency market occurred as would have occurred in the absence of the special security issues.

PROFESSOR NIEHANS: Perhaps I could generalize a little more on Dr. Hewson's remarks. In discussing the Eurodollar market, a misleading paradigm is used—a paradigm which used to be quite helpful in analyzing domestic money creation but which does not happen to be very helpful in discussing the Eurodollar market. People have tried for about six years to capture the essence of the Eurodollar market in terms of the domestic money creation paradigm and have, I believe, had very serious troubles with it.

One of the problems is the following: if one goes back in banking literature about 100 years, or maybe 90 years, one will find that banking was discussed generally in terms of the distribution of credit—like the distribution of cigarettes or some other good. Then people such as Irving Fisher and others came along and discovered there is something called credit "creation" in the business, which they suggested is based on the credit transformation which occurs in an individual bank. People believed it. Economists believed it. Bankers never did, but economists came to believe in credit creation based on credit transformation. And for professional economists, the attention to credit creation completely overshadowed the earlier concern with the distribution of credit.

Now, turning to the Eurocurrency markets: until several years ago, this' system tended to be generally a pure case of a distribution system in which funds came in through deposits and were lent out again—generally with the same maturity as the deposits—with very little credit transformation or credit creation involved. This can be shown statistically. (Of course, there is the loan rollover practice and all that it involves.) What this means is that we do not have an adequate theory for this type of banking system today because we have forgotten about the distributive banking function during the last quarter century or so.

If one looks at the Eurocurrency statistics, one can dream up some more or less plausible monetary base and put down a number. One can find some reasonably plausible figure for the total volume of deposits or credit in the system. Thus, one can divide the latter by the former and get a figure for a multiplier, but this multiplier, in a credit distribution network, does not mean a thing. The monetary base does not mean a thing. These are meaningless numbers.

There is some credit transformation in the Eurocurrency system today—we have heard of some rather critical cases—so I do not want to go all the other way and leave out credit creation entirely. But the problem is that we have not yet developed adequate concepts. Our current banking concepts are in terms of banks which have two classes of assets and liabilities, one class which is perfect money—complete money—and another class which is non-money. We relate the perfect money to the non-money and get a multiplier.

350

But there is part of the banking system which has no complete money. This part barely has any reserves. It has no checking accounts. Its deposit liabilities are entirely time deposits. What you have are different shades of maturities and liquidity. One does not know what to relate to what. The multiplier concept cannot be employed fruitfully. Instead there are very complex relationships with many dimensions, relationships with which we have not yet learned to work. We had better try to figure out the basic theory.

PROFESSOR STEM: I am sympathetic with Professor Niehans's comment to the effect that we need to work diligently to develop the theory necessary for Euro-currency analysis. Perhaps I should explain that my attempt to analyze the possi-bility of controls on Eurocurrency banking within the context of the traditional liquid asset multiplier model was an attempt to meet the enemy on its own ground, so to speak—that is, to employ a model which is clearly recognizable and widely understood and used. It is within the context of the multiplier model that sug-gestions have been made in the press and literature for applying reserve require-ments or using open-market operations in the Eurocurrency system to limit expansion. Implicit in these suggestions is the assumption that such policies would have the same impact on credit expansion—whatever credit expansion might mean and whatever impact its control might have on aggregate demand—as would occur within a domestic context.

Of course, my reasons for using this model grow out of the extant state of affairs discussed by Professor Niehans. Most of us cut our teeth on this model, and it is very difficult for us to get away from it.

My point, though, is that when one examines—within the context of a multiplier model—the types of operations traditionally implemented domestically in an attempt to constrain credit expansion, one must conclude that such opera-tions will produce little control of Eurocurrency credit expansion if that be the goal. Professor Black has questioned whether control of credit expansion should even be a goal. But if it is your goal, you will not get within the Eurocurrency system the kind of impact from the traditional operations which is gotten within a domestic financial system where there is a finite monetary base over which the central bank has some kind of control.

PROFESSOR MAKIN: Just one last comment on the multiplier matter. Given the way Professor Niehans derives his multiplier, it is meaningless. If one identifies an arbitrary base and divides it into the total stock of either liabilities or assets in the system, the resultant multiplier is meaningless. That is a nonsensical type of multiplier, from which I want to distinguish myself sharply.

Finally, there is a distinction between the question of liquidity creation and the question of identifying a stable part of the total portfolio of a financial inter-mediary which has a stable relationship, not a stable multiplier, with the total portfolio itself. This stable relationship is relevant when there is a desire to control the total quantity of credit outstanding. The distinction between these two questions should be kept clearly in mind.

Petrodollar Recycling

PROFESSOR GUNTER DUFEY: In discussion about the ability of private capital markets—particularly the Eurodollar market plus national credit markets in different countries—to handle the so-called recycling problem adequately, there always appears to be an implicit assumption that this adequacy should be judged in terms of whether the additional funds—that is, those funds not transferred through exports to the oil-producing nations—get distributed among the oil-importing countries according to the distribution of oil imports. I wonder whether there is any reason—if I may put it provocatively—why these funds should not go to a few deserving countries, like Switzerland, Germany, and the United States, and whether there is any economic law which might prevent that or which would tell us whether, if such were to occur, we would get into problems that would severely shake the world financial system.

PROFESSOR ALLEN: I think the underlying assumption behind this kind of statement—to the effect that oil funds should be recycled in a pattern roughly similar to that of the oil imports—is that to ask the oil-importing countries to cut back consumption and adjust their current accounts sufficiently to give themselves balance in their international accounts presents problems in the short run. There is, perhaps, a kind of moral problem for some of the developing countries. For some of these countries it is literally a matter of survival. For countries not in quite such dire circumstances, I think the question boils down to one of very serious economic disruptions. And for those who might say, Well, that is their problem, I must reply by pointing out the large external effects which might develop from any one country's problem because of the enormous degree of interaction among the world's national economies.

If, for example, Italy were forced to bring its current account into line within the next year, the Italian economy most likely would be put in very serious disarray. Oil imports are not a consumption good a country can easily cut back. Oil is an intermediate good which is used in production of other goods.

There are also political externalities to be considered; there are political implications in forcing such short-run adjustment on these economies. There is no reason to think these countries should be financed indefinitely, but I think there are many considerations which support financing in the short run.

Furthermore, there are the practical problems of the economic disruptions which those "few" who might receive the bulk of the oil funds might experience. Remember, we are talking about a surplus currently estimated at $50 to $60 billion this year. Would it be in the interest of, say, Germany, with an already large current-account surplus, to receive any significant amount of this massive OPEC surplus? Think of the effect on Germany's domestic credit situation, on its own inflation problem. Or, if the German surplus were reflected in a rapidly rising D-mark, it would cause enormous disruptions, not only in the deficit countries but also in the surplus country.

PROFESSOR WILLIAM FELLNER: Generally speaking, this kind of model—one in which the oil funds are concentrated in a few countries—of course assumes that the current-account deficits for the oil-importing countries would come out quite differently than is now expected. If all these funds go into two or three countries, this would reshuffle the current-account deficits of the oil importers completely. So, it is not so much an absurdity, I think, as a matter of the amount of time required to adjust.

PROFESSOR ALLEN: Well, it would be an absurdity if the D-mark were to increase in value by the amount required to produce the needed German current-account deficit. The normal exchange-rate effects take two years to materialize. Furthermore, we have seen in Europe in the past two or three years that those currencies which have appreciated have seen a widening of current-account surpluses and those which have depreciated have seen a widening of current-account deficits. Just take the United Kingdom and Italy, and Germany, on the other side. They tried to help their international payments positions by changing their exchange rates, but it has not worked.

PROFESSOR FELLNER: On this point one has to be very careful to distinguish between a revaluation of a currency and an appreciation (or depreciation) of a currency operating on the basis of flexible exchange rates.

PROFESSOR ALIBER: It seems we should be careful of becoming too deserving. Taking the United States along with the Swiss and the Germans, I find it incredible to think of what a $50 billion trade deficit for these three countries together amounts to in terms of its domestic employment effect. If, on a flow basis, the OPEC countries are going to have a $50 billion trade surplus and it has to find its reflection someplace else in the world—and it finds its reflection in only three countries—then it seems to me the sectoral employment implications for those three countries are such that their governments are going to be impelled to react.

PROFESSOR BRANSON: Let me make a few remarks without the overtones of deserving and nondeserving countries. It appears to me, in talking about the oil problem, that everyone takes the distribution of payments deficits as given. And then we discuss how to move the money around. Now, if money is tending to flow—just to stay close to home—into the United States disproportionally, why does not the United States allow the dollar to appreciate and develop a larger current-account deficit? This would ease the current-account deficit problem of countries like Italy, which would then have less need to borrow funds.

The upvaluation of the dollar would tend to be—I hesitate to say, deflationary. It would tend to reduce the price in the United States—the rate of the increase in the price level from the cost side. And the increase in imports would be deflationary on the demand side. If the deflationary impact were deemed to be a little too much, policies which would have an expansionary impact on aggregate demand could be instituted to take care of that problem and even further increase the U.S. deficit, which would improve the situation of other oil-importing countries.

The same kind of proposition could be applied to Germany and a few other countries. One could, instead of merely talking about redistributing funds—given the distribution of current-account deficits—do a little bit about the current-account deficits in order to ease the problem of redistributing the funds.

PROFESSOR LOGUE: I would like to follow up on Professor Branson's point and take this discussion to what I see could be the next stage. Let us suppose that the United States takes the major role—that it might have to—and proceeded to run a $25 or $30 billion trade deficit in 1975 or 1976. This would have the dislocations and employment impacts already mentioned. The United States will run this deficit because, presumably, it is being favored by capital flows from the oil exporters. But capital flows are, in turn, a function of expectations and psychological elements.

What would happen to these expectations and psychological elements if the United States were to start to run a $25 or $30 billion trade deficit? What would happen if the psychological factors were to turn such as to discourage capital flows to the United States? The United States would be left with little capital inflow, perhaps with capital outflows, as in the early seventies, and a $25 or $30 billion trade deficit.

Obviously the United States could not have such a large trade deficit without capital inflows. The balance of payments, after all, is an accounting identity. What I am saying is that there would be severe economic dislocations for the United States if there were to be a change in psychology affecting capital inflows after the United States had started to run any major current-account deficit which was deliberately induced because it was the recipient of massive OPEC funds.

I think the other countries will try to push their current-account deficits to the United States. It is a question of how much deficit the United States is going to accept, and I have my doubts that it will be much because of the domestic considerations.

PROFESSOR STEM: Perhaps we should keep in mind the mutual interdependence involved in this state of affairs. An exchange rate involves two countries. Any given level of an exchange rate can exist for a substantial length of time only with the mutual consent of both countries involved. If the "other" oil importers are going to push their trade deficits off on the United States, letting the value of their currencies drop against the dollar, the United States must consent, either actively or passively, to the appreciation of the dollar. Of course, the high degree of interdependence also makes for possible economic conflict among the oil-importing countries. These countries must be cautious so that severely damaging economic conflict does not break out.

On the other hand, there is some limit to which Italy, for example, can afford to let its currency depreciate to push its trade deficit off on the United States. A depreciating currency has implications for domestic employment, inflation, et cetera, and is particularly important to the cost of necessary imports such as oil. Perhaps we should focus a bit on the depreciation limits allowable in the "other" countries—as well as on what the United States would do—to get a better fix on the overall parameters of this problem.

PROFESSOR ALLEN: Since I started some of this discussion, perhaps I should clarify my position. My original comments were based on the assumption that it would not be possible, in the short run, for the United States to realize sufficient exchange-rate changes to generate a current-account deficit which would match the OPEC funds inflow. The reason is that we are talking to the tune of about $50 to $60 billion a year, which would create problems of extreme magnitudes if short-run adjustment were to be forced.

There was, maybe six months ago—perhaps not so much now—talk about the black hole into which the OPEC countries sucked up funds, and the funds disappeared. Of course, that is not going to happen; the OPEC countries have to invest the funds somewhere.

But if the U.S. were not to allow exchange-rate changes and it were to run a balance-of-payments surplus—with its position as a reserve currency—it would in a sense be a kind of black hole. The OPEC dollars would come to the United States. They would not increase the U.S. money supply. Our task then is to develop some kind of financing arrangements to supplement the recycling the markets might be able to do, instead of allowing exchange-rate changes to generate the necessary balancing payments flows. Sharp exchange-rate changes in the short run would generate severe economic dislocations both for the United States and the other oil-importing nations.

SPECIAL NOTES

The "Multiplier" Versus the "New-View" Analysis of Eurocurrencies

John H. Makin

Characterizing the Two Views. As might be expected, a lively dispute has developed over attempts to model the Eurocurrency system, a dispute which parallels a broad dispute among monetary theorists over how monetary policy works in general. In view of the preponderance of heat over light that has come out of much of the past discussion in this area, it seems worthwhile to suggest that the disputants make an effort to spare themselves, as well as the profession and those who hope to learn something from the profession, the tedious and sterile ordeal of the continued expounding of notions that the "other" view is naive or misguided or that only one way exists to understand the Eurocurrency system.

Admittedly, this will not be easy. There are basic differences in the approaches to Eurocurrency analysis, but perhaps the best way to begin to improve communication is to present—hopefully in a reasonably unbiased manner—the stereotypical view of each side and then to try to point out ways in which the stereotypes are wrong. We frequently assume that the "others" are homogeneous and therefore particularly easy to disagree with. If nothing else, my own prejudices may prove revealing.

Perhaps most unfortunate for the stereotypical reinforcement which it provides is the tendency to assume an institutional nominal association for members of each of the two groups. "Multiplier" proponents are taken to be Chicago-Friedman types, while "new view" proponents are taken to be Yale-Tobin types. If there is any doubt about the potential for disagreement among these groups, one need only look at the acidity of the interchanges between their nominal heads to be reassured of the "fundamental" differences that exist.

On more important, substantive matters, the stereotypes are perhaps more revealing. Multiplier types are "naive" because they attempt to apply a model which is in all the textbooks. Leaving aside the implications of this view for the integrity of a profession which fills its textbooks with models which "everyone" knows are wrong, the basic quarrel is with the implicit or explicit exogeniety of the

357

monetary or credit base. More specifically, it is argued that one cannot simply calculate a ratio of total deposits to some measure of reserves and deduce an ex post multiplier.[1]

Characterizing the "new view," one finds an application of the Markowitz portfolio theory to the behavior of economic units, including financial intermediaries. A major implication of the approach is the necessity "to regard the structure of interest rates, asset yields and credit availabilities rather than the quantity of money as the linkage between monetary and financial institutions, on the one hand, and the real economy on the other." [2] The negative aspects of this characterization, as reported by Harry Johnson, are as follows: "the 'new view' is long on elegant analysis of theoretical possibilities, but remarkably short on testable or tested theoretical propositions about the way the economy works and specifically how it responds to monetary impulses when the interaction of the monetary and real sectors is taken into account." [3]

I shall try to defuse the stereotypical view of multiplier analysis with references to my own work on the Eurodollar system. First, let me say that the bulk of that work is not directly concerned with identifying "a" multiplier since such a notion is naive indeed, implying as it does stable feedbacks of funds to the Eurodollar system, which my empirical evidence suggests do not exist. My 1972 article attempts first to identify stable stock demand and supply functions for Eurodollars.[4] A stable stock demand function for *holdings* of Eurodollars is, after all, a necessary but not a sufficient condition for reflows of deposits to the Eurodollar system from Eurodollar loan proceeds and therefore is a necessary condition for the operation of *some* multiplier process.

The stock model of the Eurodollar market which I employ specifically states that Eurobank reserve stocks are endogenous variables whose equilibrium values are determined simultaneously along with the interest on Eurodollars and total Eurodollar deposits supplied. Critics of the multiplier approach appear to assume that a multiplier can exist only in a regulated system of financial intermediaries where some part of reserves is required and therefore is exogenous. This is simply not so if by a "multiplier" one means a stable relationship—based on some predictable reflow to intermediaries of loaned funds—between an identifiable asset

---

[1] This approach is, indeed, appropriately viewed as naive and could be dismissed as a straw man were it not for the existence of a patently absurd article which follows exactly such an approach. (See Boyden E. Lee, "The Eurodollar Multiplier," *Journal of Finance,* September 1973, pp. 867-874.) Inference from this piece only illustrates the danger of assuming the "other side" holds homogeneous views.

[2] J. Tobin, "Commercial Banks as Creators of 'Money'," Cowles Foundation Monograph 21 (New York: John Wiley and Sons, 1967), p. 3. This characterization is drawn from Harry Johnson's discussion of the " 'New View' of Monetary Theory and Policy" in *Money in Britain* eds. D. R. Croome and H. G. Johnson (Oxford, 1970), pp. 101-105.

[3] Johnson, " 'New View' of Monetary Theory," p. 105.

[4] J. H. Makin, "Demand and Supply Functions for Stocks of Euro-dollar Deposits: An Empirical Study," *The Review of Economics and Statistics,* November 1972, pp. 381-393.

of a system of financial intermediaries and the total assets or liabilities of that system.

The reason to identify such a stable relationship would be to provide a basis for prediction of growth of total Eurodollar deposits, based on an increase in Eurobank reserves and from that to infer a possible impact on levels of economic activity in general. Prediction is important and necessary since, among other things, my empirical results suggest that only about one-fourth of the adjustment of Eurodollar deposits supplied, given changes in Eurobank reserves, is completed in one quarter, with a mean lag for total adjustment of about two-and-a-half quarters. It is precisely because equilibrium Eurobank reserves are endogenous that a predictable change in total Eurodollars may be said to arise from a disequilibrium introduced by a change in such reserves. At the same time, the share of reserves in total assets is not stable, but it is a stable function of an identifiable set of variables, as is explicitly stated in my 1972 and 1973 papers.[5]

The existence of a reserve base for Eurodollars, based on a theory developed by Whalen, cannot be rejected on the basis of a hypothesis that such a magnitude composes precautionary reserves for a group of unregulated financial intermediaries.[6] The base is composed of demand deposits of private foreign banks at U.S. commercial banks, exclusive of claims on home offices of branch banks.[7] When these deposits change—leaving aside the significance of the reason for the change, which will be taken up below—there follows, with some lag as already indicated, a predictable response of total Eurodollar deposits.[8]

Alternatively, if all markets adjust instantaneously, any change in portfolio holdings—say in the form of a change in reserves—represents a movement to a new equilibrium position. Therefore no subsequent change will occur. There would be no increase in loans and no reflow of funds to the system of intermediaries from loan proceeds. The new view appears not to go quite so far as to suggest such a prompt move to equilibrium but rather argues that the results of, say, an open-market operation, arise from the depression of interest rates required to induce the commercial bank to exchange securities for cash. The reduction in interest rates then stimulates economic activity as banks lend their new reserves on easier terms. This description suggests the basis for the new view that interest rates, and not the quantity of money, serve as the linkage between the financial and the real sectors of the economy.

---

[5] For the 1972 paper, see footnote 4. For the 1973 paper, see J. H. Makin, "Identifying a Reserve Base for the Euro-dollar System," *The Journal of Finance*, June 1973, pp. 609-617.

[6] E. L. Whalen, "A Rationalization of the Precautionary Demand for Cash," *Quarterly Journal of Economics*, May 1966, pp. 314-324.

[7] Claims on home offices of branch banks are really loans to the parent bank, not readily available for use as working balances. The hypothesis that these claims serve as precautionary reserves is not supported by the data, as reported in my 1973 *Journal of Finance* paper.

[8] One could say deposits or loans if the balance sheet identity is borne in mind. This assumption may not be strictly correct for single Eurobanks since they may not balance dollar loans with dollar deposits.

Operational Significance of the Different Approaches. Probably the greatest difficulty arises in distinguishing the difference in the operational significance of the new view and the old (multiplier) view. In both cases a shock to reserves is seen to lead to new loans. The multiplier view emphasizes the effects of changes in the quantity of money implicit in such a response, while the new view emphasizes the effects of changes in the price of bonds (the interest rate). Both results suggest an expansion of economic activity in response to an expansionary open-market operation. It is further argued by the new view that the extension of more loans will lower earnable interest rates and thereby "diminish" the incentives for banks to keep fully loaned up or to borrow reserves and will make banks content to hold, on the average, higher excess reserves.[9] This last result, which appears to assume a static demand for loans, suggests that the "full" multiplier effect of an open-market operation may not materialize.

An Attempted Reconciliation: Dynamics. Some reconciliation of the two views may be sought by considering disequilibrium dynamics. Suppose an expansionary open-market operation increases banks' liquidity, while simultaneously lowering the return on short-term financial instruments. If capital markets across real and financial sectors were perfect, all rates of return on financial and real assets would instantaneously be adjusted to the same equilibrium levels by virtue of all portfolio managers and investors adjusting the prices of their assets. Complete, instantaneous, and uniformly correct adjustment of asset prices would eliminate any quantity response to the monetary shock borne of different expected responses to asset prices. In fact if, given a doubling of the monetary base, all money prices were doubled instantaneously, the result suggested by the classical dichotomy would be preserved.

But such perfect markets do not exist. A change in commercial bank reserves affects short-term interest rates and, subsequently, the quantity of loans (demand deposits) and money outstanding. If the change in the quantity of money is effected by expansionary loan activities of the banks before all prices have readjusted to equilibrium levels, there exists an excess supply of money which further excites purchases of financial and real assets and commodities. Indeed, these results may affect the demand for loans, which the new view holds constant while arguing that increased lending activity by banks will depress interest rates. In short, changes in both asset prices (interest rates) and the quantity of money accompany an open-market operation and the latter, as well as the former, in the absence of perfect capital markets, excite subsequent changes in spending and are therefore *both* connected with the real sector. Such a situation does not preclude the possibility of a stable relationship between changes in some subset of assets, called reserves, and total liabilities or assets of financial intermediaries which may, in addition, as the new view suggests, depend on rates of return. Such a relationship

---

[9] Tobin, "Commercial Banks as Creators of 'Money'," p. 10.

may in fact be shown empirically to exist. In addition, a systematic relationship may be shown to exist directly between changes in the quantity of money and economic variables such as incomes, prices, and interest rates.

Let us return now to the reserve base for Eurobanks, taken to be their demand deposits at U.S. commercial banks. Exogenous forces, such as an increased rate of U.S. monetary expansion which leads to increased inflows of funds to Eurobanks, will lead to, among other things, an increase in such reserves. The subsequent response of Eurobanks can be described in the same way as the response of banks to open-market operations described above. In both cases, liquidity is enhanced by increased holdings of liquid assets, induced by a sale of some earnings asset, which could indeed be a U.S. Treasury bill for a Eurobank. For example, large open-market purchases of Treasury bills by the Federal Reserve could drive down returns on such assets to a level that Eurobanks subsequently sell their holdings for cash to some party other than the Federal Reserve. The cash may then be reinvested in Eurodollar loans, leading to a subsequent increase in total deposits whose total size is governed by the level of reflows to the Eurodollar system from those loans. Not all Eurodollar expansion, however, need be at the expense of U.S. liquidity, since the Treasury bills need not be sold to U.S. institutions. Indeed, sales for dollar proceeds may take the form of sales of nondollar assets which may have appreciated to an attractive level in terms of dollars. Such nondollar assets may be sold and converted into dollars to make Eurodollar loans. The dollar price of nondollars may be high due to expected further depreciation of the dollar which the bank—selling nondollar assets—views as unrealistic. Here again it is important to realize that existence of truly perfect capital markets would preclude such an operation since all expectations would instantly be correctly reflected in asset prices.

This admittedly simplified discussion of the impact of reserve changes identifies considerable common ground for the multiplier and new view approaches to analysis of the impact of monetary disturbances on the real sector of the economy, while at the same time suggesting the different emphasis of each approach. Both views see a change in reserves of a financial intermediary disturbing equilibrium in the financial sector. As we have seen, the multiplier approach emphasizes the impact on the real sector of changes in the quantity of money while the new view emphasizes the impact on the real sector of changes in the price of bonds. The multiplier approach must, and often fails to, contend with the fact that a shock to reserve holdings must be accompanied by a change in rates of return since such holdings are part of the portfolio of financial intermediaries. Where equilibrium portfolio shares are determined by rates of return, and by their variances and covariances, some price adjustment—in the form generally of a change in rates of return—must accompany portfolio reallocation toward the holding of more reserves.

On the other hand, the new view often fails to contend with the empirical fact that, conditional upon portfolio rates of return, there exists a stable relationship between identifiable reserves and total liabilities of financial intermediaries. The level of these liabilities may in turn be shown to be systematically related to economic activity. It does, then, seem useful to attempt to investigate the predictability of total credit expansion based upon the behavior of some subset intermediary reserves.

Final Remarks. In sum, risking some fairly broad generalizations, changes in both asset prices and total deposit liabilities must accompany shocks to the reserves of financial intermediaries in the absence of perfect capital markets—which would accommodate all shocks with instantaneous price adjustments—and imply, in turn, an effective dichotomy between financial and real sectors of the economy. Since perfect capital markets do not exist, effects of shocks to the financial sector are transmitted to the real sector both by price and quantity changes. To consider both the multiplier and new view approaches seems to be as soundly based as the notion that shocks to market equilibrium are accommodated by simultaneous adjustments of prices and quantities. In view of this, it would be of considerable interest to have some empirical information on the time paths of price and quantity adjustments to such shocks. Until the simultaneity of the results implied in each of the approaches is recognized, we shall probably go on hearing from different parties that the multiplier approach is "naive" or a "black box" while the new view is "empirically empty."

Flexible Exchange Rates and the Recycling of Petrodollars

Gottfried Haberler

In the discussion several speakers expressed doubts about whether a country which is confronted with a sudden deterioration of its balance of payments—due, for example, to a crop failure or an abrupt rise in oil prices—can rely on flexible exchange rates to restore equilibrium. This view seems to be based on the assumption that according to standard theory—which allegedly concentrates on the current balance and neglects capital flows—under flexible rates, the current balance is continuously kept in equilibrium; this, it is said, may not always be possible and is at any rate not desirable.

But this is not how floating works nor what standard theory says about how it works.[1] It is like arguing that a free market for wheat cannot work because it

---

[1] The charge that standard theory overemphasizes the current or trade balance and neglects induced capital flows has been recently made by M. Modigliani and H. Askari in their paper "The International Transfer of Capital and the Propagation of Domestic Disturbances Under Alternative Payments Systems," *Banca Nazionale del Lavoro Quarterly Review,* no. 107, (December 1973), pp. 295-310. However, the point has been made before, for example, in

would continuously equate consumption and production, thus exposing a country to the danger of extreme hardship or even famine and leading to excessive seasonal and erratic price fluctuations. Actually, in a free market stocks are being held by private traders. These stocks are continuously adjusted to changing circumstances and this tends to moderate price fluctuations. It is possible to argue that the market sometimes makes mistakes and that therefore the government should stockpile to guard against emergencies and promote greater stability. (Whether the government does a better job than the market is very doubtful but need not be discussed here.) Similarly under flexible exchange rates, private business will hold stocks of foreign monies and maintain credit lines, but it can be argued that even under floating, the monetary authorities should keep an ample international reserve in order not only to smooth out day-to-day fluctuations but also to moderate, although not suppress, medium-term movements. (However, I shall not discuss here the problem of managed *versus* free or clean *versus* dirty floating. I have expressed my views on this problem elsewhere.) [2]

Take the case of Italy, which is often mentioned in this connection. Floating has not prevented Italy from borrowing large sums, over $10 billion, in the Eurodollar market and elsewhere to finance a large trade deficit, thus cushioning and spreading out the impact of the sudden rise in oil prices on the standard of living. In addition, Italy has applied a stiff dose of direct controls to imports in violation of the International Monetary Fund, General Agreement on Tariffs and Trade, and European Economic Community regulations.[3] These restrictions could have been avoided by letting the lira float down in exchange markets. While running a trade deficit financed by borrowing can be defended on the grounds that it helps temporarily to keep down inflation and keep up the standard of living, import restrictions do neither; they are a messy kind of disguised depreciation. The reason for using controls was probably the wish to protect certain branches of industry and agriculture from foreign competition. Protectionist measures can

---

Robert Triffin's paper "National Central Banking and the International Economy," *International Monetary Policies*, Postwar Economic Studies No. 7, September 1947, Board of Governors of the Federal Reserve System, Washington, D. C., pp. 46-81. In my comments on Triffin's paper (in the same volume, pp. 82-100) I show, quoting J. S. Mill, R. G. Hawtrey and J. Viner, that the influence of changes in exchange rates and monetary policy on capital flows has often been taken into consideration in the literature. It has been recognized by the writers mentioned and many others that induced capital flows may change the sequence of events with respect to price movements, et cetera, that one would expect if there were no induced capital flows. In my book, *Prosperity and Depression*, 4th ed. (Cambridge, Mass.: Harvard University Press, 1958), chapter 12, "Foreign Aspects of the Business Cycle," I tried to analyze the adjustment mechanism under flexible exchange rates with and without capital mobility. Egon Sohmen in his monograph *Flexible Exchange Rates*, rev. ed. (Chicago: University of Chicago, 1969), chapter 5, section 2, presents a general equilibrium model in which capital movements are treated as an endogenous variable.

[2] See my "The Case against Capital Controls for Balance of Payments Reasons," *Geneva Conference on Capital Movements and Their Control*, forthcoming.

[3] These restrictions were later removed (under prodding of EEC, GATT, and IMF) when the balance of payments improved because the Banca d'Italia applied the monetary brakes.

conceivably be justified on terms-of-trade grounds or grounds of unemployment or external economies, but they cannot be justified on balance-of-trade grounds.[4]

There are, of course, limits to the amount that any country can borrow from abroad through the market. That is why there is so much demand for official lending—called "recycling"—through special oil facilities provided by the IMF, IBRD, BIS, et cetera, or by special swaps between central banks. Floating, it is said, can make no contribution to the settlement of oil deficits; non-oil deficits often necessitate depreciation or floating, but oil deficits call for recycling.

This argument is vitiated by the failure to make a vital distinction. Are oil-exporting and importing countries each taken as a unit or is the differential impact of the oil price rise on different oil-importing countries considered?

When treating oil exporters and importers as units, it makes indeed little or no sense to propose that the transfer problems should be solved by depreciating the currencies of the oil importers collectively vis-à-vis the currencies of the oil exporters. In that respect the popular analogy with the case of the German reparations in the 1920s obscures the problem. For unlike the recipients of the German reparations, the oil-exporting countries, especially the Arab ones, are highly specialized, wide open economies. The governments receive the oil income and must decide how much of it they want to use for additional imports; as for the rest they have no choice but to invest in one form or another in the oil-importing countries. Under these circumstances, the transfer problem, as distinguished from the problem of raising the money in local currency, would be easy—much easier than it was in the German case—and it would not make much sense to appreciate the Saudi riyal or the Kuwaiti dinar vis-à-vis the dollar.[5]

The situation is, however, quite different when we consider the differential impact of the oil price rise on different importing countries. Some are hit much harder than others in three different respects: first, the burden of having to pay more for imported oil, second, the opportunity to pay for part of the higher oil bill by exporting more to the oil countries, and third, the chance of receiving investment funds ("petrodollars") from the oil countries.

The basic burden of having to reduce other expenditures in order to pay more for imported oil is, of course, very different for different countries. For the

---

[4] The relative merits of import restrictions and exchange-rate changes has become a hot issue in Great Britain. Import restrictions, in preference to devaluation or floating are being strongly urged by labor unions, the left wing of the labor party and advocates of comprehensive planning. See for example *Economic Policy Review*, no. 1, February 1975 (University of Cambridge, Department of Applied Economics), and the devastating criticism that this plea for restrictions has received in W. M. Corden, M. M. D. Little and M. F. G. Scott, *Import Controls versus Devaluation and Britain's Economic Prospects* (London: Trade Policy Research Center, 1975).

[5] It could be argued, however, that appreciating the riyal would be one way to let the Saudi population share in the windfall by making imports cheaper. For oil countries with a more diversified economy and larger populations such as Iran or Venezuela, an appreciation makes more sense. But both countries seem to *prefer inflation to appreciation* as a solution to their surplus problem.

United States it is, though not negligible, surely not a heavy burden—about 1.5 percent of GNP. For other industrial countries the burden is heavier but not crushing. For some less developed countries it may be really crushing. However, I confine my discussion to the problems of the industrial countries.

If the oil price does not come down, some belt tightening is unavoidable. But for no industrial country is the burden so high that it cannot be taken care of by one or two years' normal annual growth of GNP. For the United States it is perhaps one-half of a normal annual increase in GNP. In other words, in a short period of time, GNP and the standard of living could be back where they were before the oil price was raised and growth could be resumed, provided the adjustment to the new situation—including the transfer—can be made smoothly.[6] To the extent that the oil countries use their new incomes not to import more but to invest abroad, the basic burden on the oil-importing countries is postponed and spread out.[7]

Everybody knows that the oil-importing countries collectively have to accept a deficit in their current balance to match the surplus of the oil-exporting countries. But the petrodollars will not be distributed among the importing countries in proportion to their oil created balance-of-payments gap (additional cost of oil imports minus additional exports to the oil countries), let alone in proportion to the basic burden (additional cost of oil imports in percent of GNP). Suppose that all petrodollars go to one country. Then in the absence of recycling, this country would enjoy a temporary reduction of the basic burden. Theoretically the burden could initially even become negative, more petrodollar investments being attracted than the additional cost of oil imports. This fortunate country would have to accept a current-account deficit equal to the current surplus of the oil countries, and the other oil-importing countries would have to develop an export surplus vis-à-vis the sole recipient of the petrodollars, equal to their oil deficit, matching the corresponding surplus of the oil countries.

It stands to reason that in the process of allocating the collective current-account deficit among the oil-importing countries, unlike the case where the importers are treated as a unit, exchange-rate changes and floating cannot be excluded. In fact, in our hypothetical example, an appreciation or upward float of the currency of the sole recipient of the petrodollars might be the easiest method of adjustment.

---

[6] These guesses have been confirmed by Hollis B. Chenery's analysis "Restructuring the World Economy," *Foreign Affairs*, vol. 53, no. 2 (January 1975), pp. 242-263.

[7] It is conceivable that the burden be permanently reduced (not only spread out). This could be the case if the petrodollars are productively invested and become a *net* addition to the annual investment stream which would, of course, require that the consumers of the oil-importing countries (including the government) cut down their consumption rather than their savings to pay their increased oil bill. Whether and to what extent this will actually happen depends, as Thomas Willett has pointed out, on the domestic policies in the oil-importing countries. It does not require that petrodollars be invested in equities.

It is widely assumed that the United States will receive the lion's share of the petrodollars, and it is concluded that it should share its riches with other countries through official recycling. Nobody can know beforehand, however, how large the lion's share will be, and even ex post it may be difficult to ascertain its magnitude. Oil related deficits and non-oil deficits are not easily separable. Floating surely should not be ruled out as a mechanism of adjustment. But as already mentioned, floating does not exclude that a country may borrow abroad to stretch out the burden of adjusting to the high price of oil. Some countries, especially Great Britain and Italy, have made extensive if not profligate use of this opportunity.[8] True, the possibility to borrow abroad is not unlimited, but the barrier to further borrowing is not rigid but elastic, depending largely on the policies pursued by the country in question. With prudent internal policies, many countries should be able to attract a good share of petrodollars either directly from the oil countries or in some roundabout way. Great Britain, if it could manage its inflation, would be in an especially favorable position in that respect, owing to the efficient financial machinery of the City of London and the historical ties with the principal oil producers.

The question whether recycling of petrodollars should be done mainly through the market or through official channels raises many difficult questions, some of which go beyond technical economics. Only a few will be briefly discussed here. There is the political question as to whether the large recipients of petrodollars have some sort of obligation to share them with less fortunate countries. It is difficult to see why oil should be treated differently from other commodities. But even if the question is answered in the affirmative, as many people would find reasonable, it does not necessarily follow that the redistribution—recycling—should be done mainly through official lending. It could be argued that, given the complexity and uncertainties of the situation, the market will do a better job of the recycling that may be needed or desirable than national or international official agencies.

Among the questions involved here is the capacity, or readiness, of the Euro-banks and U.S. banks to handle such a large job of intermediation. As indicated above, this will to a large extent depend on how the countries concerned manage their internal economic problems. Countries that manage well without much inflation would attract petrodollars directly or through the intermediation of Euro-banks and U.S. banks. Domestic policies, in turn, may be influenced by the method used for recycling. Easy availability of official financing may well foster laxity of national stabilization policies. On the other hand, it can be argued that international financing through the IMF can effectively be used to induce the borrowing countries to put their financial house in order. If the Eurodollar market

---

[8] The British policy could be characterized as "dirty fixing" rather than "dirty floating" of the exchange rate.

becomes saturated with petrodollars, interest rates will decline and the petrodollars will be diverted into other assets. This process has already started.

Whatever the final solution of the recycling problem, floating of some currencies as a method of balance-of-payments adjustment surely cannot be excluded. Even if the flow of petrodollars is fully and equitably redistributed through the market or official recycling and assuming that there are no non-oil deficits to adjust, floating of some currencies is almost certain to be required to effect the transfer of that part of the additional oil bill which is settled by the larger imports of the oil countries. The reason is that the increased exports to the oil countries, in general, will necessitate some reshuffling of trade among the oil-importing countries, because we would not want a bilateral settlement. That is to say, it would be inefficient if each oil-importing country tried to reach a bilateral equilibrium with the oil-exporting countries in the sense that for each oil-importing country the additional oil bill would equal its own additional exports to the oil countries plus its share of the pool of petrodollars. A multilateral settlement implies that some oil-importing countries will export more to the oil countries, and others will export less than their share of the total additional exports to the oil countries. In other words, some oil importers will run a deficit, others a surplus with the oil countries— these surpluses and deficits being matched by corresponding balances among the oil-*importing* countries. Nobody can tell beforehand what the equilibrium pattern of trade surpluses and deficits will be. But if each country keeps its own overall balance in equilibrium, the general equilibrium will be established by the market. This will surely require that some currencies be allowed to float, especially if we keep in mind that oil and non-oil deficits coexist and are difficult to disentangle ex post and practically impossible to separate ex ante. Fortunately there is no real need to separate them, for there is no economic justification for treating oil and non-oil deficits differently.

Does It Make a Difference Whether Petrodollars Are Channeled to the Eurodollar Market or to U.S. Financial Markets?

Dennis E. Logue

The large payments that the OPEC countries have begun to receive for their oil exports raise the issue of where the OPEC investors will likely invest their continuing surpluses. The collective current-account surpluses of the OPEC investors fell within the range of $50 to $65 billion during 1974. In view of such magnitudes, the choice of investment haven(s) may have a significant impact on monetary conditions, employment, and income in the receiving countries and in countries whose import bills have soared but which do not receive investment oil funds. While a broad spectrum of issues may be raised in any general examination of OPEC investment strategies, this paper addresses only one: What difference does it make whether OPEC countries invest in the Eurodollar market or directly in U.S. financial markets? It treats as a subsidiary issue the effect of Federal Reserve policy on recycling.

Most analyses of possible OPEC investment strategies have stressed that a huge portion, perhaps up to 85 percent, of the OPEC current-account surplus will ultimately be invested in dollar-denominated assets.[1] Principally, this is because of the size, liquidity, and depth of the U.S. and Eurodollar markets. Moreover, because of its relative size, the U.S. market was presumed to receive a significantly larger proportion of OPEC's investable funds than the Eurodollar market. U.S. financial markets are roughly fifteen times the size of the Eurodollar market (roughly $3 trillion versus $200 billion), and hence the U.S. would ultimately receive perhaps fifteen times more funds than the Eurodollar market.

However, the analysis supporting the foregoing assumed that economic investment behavior would not be constrained by political considerations. This may, in fact, not be the case. Accordingly, a far greater than proportional amount may initially be placed in the Euromarkets, for these funds could be less easily blocked or confiscated by an irate U.S. government. Further, the more equally are funds placed in various national capital markets, the less hold do any of the host governments have through confiscation threats. A central question is whether the initial placement of these funds in, say, the Eurodollar market rather than in U.S. markets will have any persistent effects on differentials in interest rates and credit availability in the two markets.

The U.S. financial market and the Eurodollar market should be perfectly integrated. There are currently no controls preventing the free flow of capital between the two markets, so the interest rate and credit availability effect of a large withdrawal or deposit in one market should be immediately dispersed through both markets. Accordingly, even though the Eurodollar market is much smaller than the U.S. market, the impact of a large transaction there should be immediately dispersed among U.S. money and capital markets as well as the Euromarkets. There should be no segmentation among the markets.

If institutional differences are ignored, pursuit of this line of reasoning would ultimately lead one to expect that interest rates in the two markets should be identical. Experience, however, reveals that they are not. Several quite practical reasons explain this phenomenon. Note, though, that perfect integration of the markets does not require equal rates in the presence of institutional differences. It really means that the rates vary together in a relatively predictable way.[2]

---

[1] See, for example, "Petrodollars and U.S. Financial Markets," U.S. Department of the Treasury, Office of the Assistant Secretary for International Affairs, Special Report, July 1974.

[2] See D. E. Logue, M. A. Salant, and R. J. Sweeney, "International Integration of Financial Markets: Survey, Synthesis and Results," this volume.

The Difference between Eurodollar and U.S. Interest Rates. The rates paid depositors by Eurobanks tend to be higher than those paid depositors (large certificate of deposit holders) at U.S. commercial banks. This is a result of several factors. First, there are no reserve requirements on Eurodollar deposits, whereas U.S. commercial banks must hold a certain percentage of each deposit as a reserve against withdrawal of that or other deposits. To the extent that the desired level of reserves—presumably the level actually held by Eurobanks—is less than that which must be held by domestic commercial banks, they are able to afford higher deposit rates. Bear in mind, however, that the riskiness of a bank generally tends to be inversely related to its level of reserves, so Eurobanks are likely to be riskier in addition to paying higher rates. Also, there is in general no formal lender of last resort for Eurobanks. This contrasts with the domestic situation where commercial banks can always look to the Federal Reserve System to mitigate temporary liquidity crises. Further, there exists no equivalent for Eurobanks of the U.S. Federal Deposit Insurance Corporation, which guarantees that deposits in member banks will ultimately be honored. All in all, the higher yield on Eurobank deposits may be justified by the greater risk and need not be an indication of even partial segmentation between the two markets.

On the lending side, Eurobanks tend to charge higher rates than U.S. commercial banks, but this difference does not necessarily mean that the rates are different after adjusting for risk and different methods of bank operation.

The maturity structure of Eurobank loans tends to be longer than the maturity structure of U.S. commercial bank loans. For example, Eurobanks have not in the past been especially reluctant to offer loans with maturities of ten years, whereas U.S. commercial banks virtually never go beyond five. Similarly, while U.S. commercial banks normally require pledges of assets and often impose operational restrictions (for example dividend payment restrictions), Eurobanks very rarely do.

In addition to the differential riskiness of loans, U.S. commercial banks tend normally to require borrowers to maintain compensating balances (which increase the effective cost of the loan), whereas Eurobanks generally do not require them.

On balance, after adjusting the differential in lending rates for risk and bank requirements, this differential will tend to equal zero.

The Effect of Federal Reserve Policy on Interest Rate Levels. The degree to which the average differential in rates can be altered through Federal Reserve behavior depends largely on the effect of changing bank *regulations* or *selective* measures of control. For example, if reserve requirements are altered, there would be a change in the relative riskiness of deposits in U.S. and Eurodollar banks. Similarly, if the Federal Reserve prohibits compensating balance requirements, this would tend to result in a higher average level of interest rates in the United States relative to the Eurodollar market. But such changes would essentially cause once-and-for-all types of shifts in relative interest rates and not reduce the covariability of rates in the two markets.

Broad-based monetary policy—in particular, open-market operations—should have no effect on interest-rate differentials since increases or decreases in domestic liquidity should be immediately transmitted to both markets.

The Arbitrage Schedule. To say that the Eurodollar market and U.S. financial markets are highly integrated is equivalent to saying that the elasticity of the arbitrage schedule between the two markets is very high. As a deposit is made in the Eurodollar market, which depresses interest rates there and thus narrows the differential between Eurodollar rates and rates prevailing in the United States, funds would immediately flow out of the Eurodollar market and into the U.S. market to restore the former equilibrium differential. Although the shift in wealth to oil producers, who have preferences for short-term financial assets, may lower the relative level of short-term interest rates, this is a separate question.

What the scant existing empirical evidence—for the most part casual and impressionistic—suggests is that the elasticity of the arbitrage schedule between the two markets is quite high and that disturbances in one market tend to be reflected immediately in the other. However, the size of the disturbance (deposit or withdrawal) has tended to be small relative to the size of the markets. Accordingly, not much arbitrage (or speculative) money had to move to bring the markets back into line. Some fears have, however, been expressed that the potential magnitude of OPEC investment funds—$50 to $65 billion in 1974 alone— and the potential disruption they may cause may prove to be too large to be arbitraged fully and immediately if largely desposited in the Eurodollar market.

Of great relevance is the fact that these funds will not all come into the market at one time but rather will be distributed over the entire year as oil payments are made. Assuming OPEC invests its funds on, say, a quarterly basis, each quarter the Eurodollar market could potentially receive $12.5 to $16.25 billion. Compared to the approximately $200 billion size of the Eurodollar market in April 1974, the possible investment flows represent roughly 6.25 to 8.125 percent of the market. This is not an incredibly large percentage, although it is substantial.

Let us assume that the ultimate distribution of these funds will be according to the relative size of markets and, for the worst possible case, that the only two markets which will receive these funds are the U.S. and Eurodollar markets.[3] Accordingly, given the relative sizes of the two markets—$3 trillion versus $200

---

[3] Two measures of relative size are possible: the first is the absolute size of each market; the second is the growth in the size of each market or size of the new issue market. Since the Eurodollar market is growing substantially faster than the U.S. market, if growth determined allocation, less funds would have to be arbitraged, that is, transmitted to the U.S. Accordingly, the worst case, that is, the greatest amount of arbitrage, would occur if fund allocation were based on absolute size of the relevant markets. This is the one chosen here.

billion, the United States should ultimately receive approximately 94 percent of the invested funds, or between $11.75 and $15.775 billion per quarter. In fact, if the markets were perfectly integrated, the United States would either receive these funds immediately or U.S. firms which were planning to borrow domestically would immediately shift their borrowing plans, or foreign branches of U.S. banks would remit balances to their home operations for lending.

In general, the arbitrage can take place in several ways, all of which have been alluded to above. To see this, suppose OPEC deposits a disproportionate share of its funds in Eurodollars. First, the recipients of the funds (Eurobanks) could transfer the funds back to the United States. As they receive funds, the deposit rates Eurobanks offer would decline. At some point it will be possible to relend the funds in the United States at advantage. U.S. rates would thus decline. The relending in the United States would continue until the structure of rates in the two markets reflected risk differences, et cetera. The decline in the general level of short-term interest rates would reflect the presumably greater OPEC preference for short-term assets—relative to the preference of those who are less wealthy and are reducing their relative holdings of the world's assets due to the oil price rise.

A second arbitrage channel is that firms just about to borrow in the U.S. markets would switch their borrowing plans, borrowing instead in the Eurodollar market where rates would have declined—reflecting a decline in the rate which banks are paying on deposits. This arbitrage would tend to eliminate systematic differences in rates not attributable to risk or bank characteristics. However, this possibility is likely to be much slower to take hold than the former arbitrage, since borrowing arrangements normally tend to take a good deal more time to negotiate.

Third, non-OPEC Eurodollar holders would tend to switch to dollar deposits in the United States if the Eurodollar deposit rate is depressed by OPEC deposits relative to the dollar deposit rate in the United States. And, fourth, OPEC depositors should feel some of the same influence, though they might resist moving funds to the United States for nonfinancial reasons.

In practice, the arbitrage mechanism between U.S. and Eurodollar markets is potentially much smoother than outlined above. The principal reason for this is that a large portion of the major Eurodollar banks are subsidiaries of U.S. commercial banks. Accordingly, if a U.S. subsidiary receives a large deposit, it can either lend it abroad or redeposit it in a matter of hours at its U.S. headquarters. In addition, non-U.S. subsidiary Eurodollar banks have close working relationships with U.S. commercial banks as well, and funds can be transferred among them virtually immediately. Moreover, these funds can either be transferred by an interbank demand or time deposit or via the Federal Funds market.

Returning to the empirical evidence (scanty as it may be): in the past, liabilities of U.S. banks to foreign branches changed by as much as $5 billion in a quarter. For example, at the end of December 1970, these liabilities stood at \$7.7 billion, but by the end of March 1971, they were down to \$2.8 billion. At the time, the size of the Eurodollar market was roughly \$100 billion, so an amount representing 5 percent of the market had been arbitraged. There are several other instances as well where relatively large amounts were arbitraged without distorting the relationship between domestic and Eurodollar rates. To the extent that these relative magnitudes do not differ by large amounts from those relative magnitudes possible under the worst case outlined above, this evidence suggests no persistent problems are likely to arise as a result of OPEC investment policy.

Some insight also may be gained by examining quarterly data to see if there is a relationship between flows into and out of Eurobanks and interest-rate differentials between comparable U.S. domestic and Eurodollar instruments. Figure 1 depicts this relationship and essentially shows no correlation.

In the figure, the quarterly change in U.S. banks' liabilities to foreign branches is used as a surrogate for U.S.-originated inflows and outflows from the Eurodollar market. The interest differential is taken as the difference between the Eurodollar deposit rate and the rate on short-term U.S. finance company paper privately placed. The reason for this pairing is that both represent liabilities of financial intermediaries which are not members of the Federal Reserve System. Moreover, both Eurodollar deposit rates and private placement rates are privately negotiated. Hence this pair of interest rates probably represents at least as good a pair as would be possible to develop from publicly available sources.

Both sets of data are plotted during the period from the first quarter of 1969 through the second quarter of 1974. If there is a strong relationship between flows and differentials, the two series should move in opposite directions. But this is not the case. Indeed, the two time series appear to be independent. (The choice of quarterly data reflects only a graphical convenience. Monthly data show virtually the same type of relationship.)

From this admittedly sketchy evidence, the inference can be drawn that factors aside from bank-type arbitrage account for differentials in interest rates between the U.S. and Eurodollar markets. Stretching this evidence a little suggests that bank flows between the two markets do not appear to have much effect on differentials. And the chief implication of this finding is that it matters little whether the OPEC investors deposit in the U.S. or in the Eurodollar market, for the funds will ultimately be allocated between the two markets efficiently by the relevant banks with minimal interest-rate distortions.

Temporary Distortions. So far, the analysis has focused on persistent distortions, but the conclusions reached are likely to apply to transient phenomena as well. Given no hindrances to capital flows between the U.S. and Eurodollar markets, and given that the major Eurodollar banks are either subsidiaries of or have close working relationships with U.S. banks—thereby being able to transfer funds elec-

Figure 1

RELATIONSHIP BETWEEN CHANGES IN LIABILITIES OF U.S. BANKS
TO FOREIGN BRANCHES AND INTEREST RATE DIFFERENTIALS.

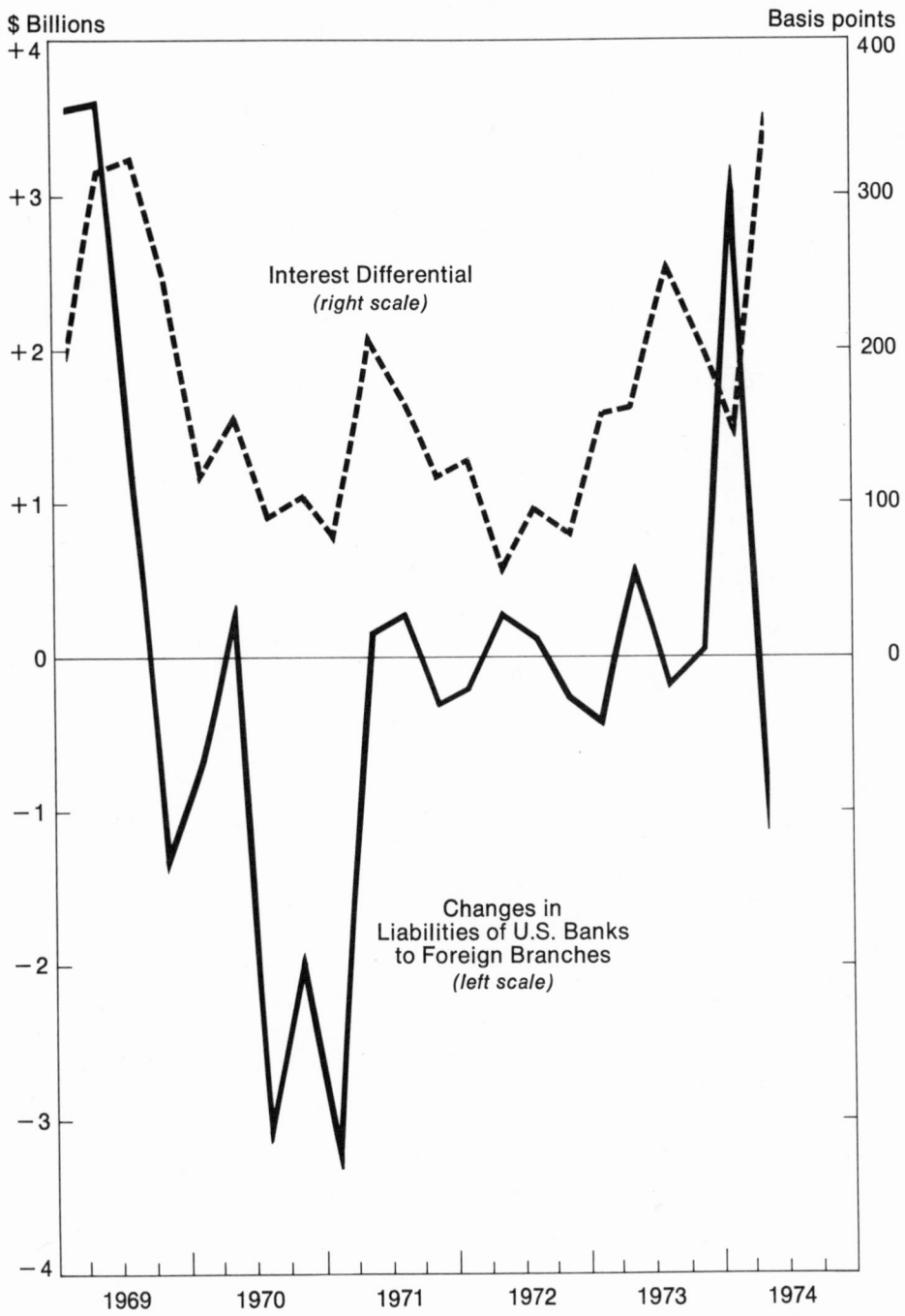

tronically and virtually instantly—there does not seem to be any reason to expect distortions in interest-rate differentials to be other than very fleeting. That is, there does not seem to be any practicable limit—aside from the absolute availability of funds—to the amount that can be transferred among dollar banking centers.

The Effect of Federal Reserve Policy on Recycling. As noted previously, specific types of Federal Reserve policy can have an effect on the level of U.S. interest rates relative to Eurodollar rates. Hence, given investors' risk and return preferences, Federal Reserve policy can have an effect on where investors will initially place their funds. Furthermore, Federal Reserve policy can have an effect on the total availability of funds for recycling (that is, the volume of funds reallocatable from the wealthy countries to those needing the funds to meet oil import needs). For example, if the Federal Reserve engages in open-market operations which increase the liquidity of the banking system, more funds will be available for recycling, or lending to foreign countries. Similarly, if reserve requirements are changed domestically or with respect to domestic banks' liabilities to foreign branches, there will be an aggregate effect on the availability of funds. In addition, specific policies can alter the availability of funds.

However, aside from the distributional effects of relative interest-rate levels, there are unlikely to be additional distributional effects of Federal Reserve policy, provided capital controls or other policies designed to segment world financial markets are not introduced. Because of the current ease with which domestic banks can transfer funds into and out of the Eurodollar market, anti-recycling types of policies imposed only in the United States should not hinder international recycling. Analogously, pro-recycling policies are unlikely to have much additional effect because banks will attempt to circumvent these policies by using their Eurodollar market affiliates to channel funds to their highest valued uses.

To the extent that funds will be "recycled" to the neediest nations on the basis of market interest rates and the countries' ability to repay, recycling poses no problem and will be accomplished virtually automatically. However, to the extent that a government wants to undercut market allocation and recycle on a political or equity basis, then either new controls on Eurobanks or an incredible array of controls to segment the domestic from the Eurodollar market will have to be imposed. It simply does not seem possible, given the existing array of measures available to the Federal Reserve and other government agencies, to accomplish a nonmarket allocation of funds to any large degree.

It should be pointed out that commercial banks themselves may find it desirable to allocate on other than a market basis. For example, a major bank with substantial investments in a given country may decide to attempt to protect and preserve the value of those investments by lending the relevant government a substantial amount of funds to meet its oil-related balance-of-payments deficit at an interest rate the government can afford rather than of a market-determined rate. Although such activity may be occurring, it is difficult to identify the extent to which it will occur and even more difficult to expect any substantial magnitude of funds (in the aggregate sense) to be recycled on this basis.

Conclusion. Concern has been generated by the possibility that, for a number of reasons, OPEC countries will invest a disproportionate share of their current-account surpluses in the Eurodollar market rather than in U.S. financial markets and that this may result in divergences in interest rates between the two markets. Evidence was provided to show that the relative magnitudes of the maximum amount of funds (the worst case) that must be transferred to keep the two markets in rough balance does not differ substantially from the relative size of transfers which have taken place in the past. Evidence also was presented suggesting that interest-rate differentials and the magnitude of funds transfers from one market to the other are independent. Similarly, it was argued that because of the relationship between Eurobanks and U.S. commercial banks, funds transfers (arbitrage) could occur almost instantaneously. Disturbances to the Eurodollar market should be diffused over both that market and the U.S. market quite rapidly, resulting perhaps in rather small net disturbances to the U.S. dollar-denominated assets market in general.

BIBLIOGRAPHY

Compiled by
Ragnhild Mowill, John H. Makin, and Carl H. Stem

I. Annotated Citations.[1]

Altman, Oscar L. "Foreign Markets for Dollars, Sterling, and Other Currencies." International Monetary Fund, *Staff Papers,* vol. 8, no. 3 (December 1961), pp. 313–352.

This is a fairly comprehensive article—one of the first major articles written—covering Eurodollar developments through March 1961. It defines Eurodollars and discusses such topics as types of transactions, advantages to lenders and borrowers, interest-rate differentials, structure of interest rates, size of the market, and positions of individual countries in the market. Also, it discusses the foreign deposit market for other convertible currencies.

————. "Canadian Markets for U.S. Dollars." International Monetary Fund, *Staff Papers,* vol. 9, no. 3 (November 1962), pp. 297–316.

This article explains in detail the business conducted by Canadian chartered banks in U.S. dollar-denominated deposits and loans. Although some students of Eurodollars would exclude the Canadian banks because of their special relationship to the U.S. money market, any comprehensive view of the overseas U.S. dollar deposit and loan business would have to include them as an important factor.

————. "Recent Developments in Foreign Markets for Dollars and Other Currencies." International Monetary Fund, *Staff Papers,* vol. 10, no. 1 (March 1963), pp. 48–96.

This paper, which for the most part is based on discussions with officials in central and commercial banks, discusses the developments in the foreign markets for dollars, sterling, and other currencies from the spring of 1961 through the summer of 1962. It emphasizes the effects of operations in foreign currencies, largely U.S. dollars, on interest rates and short-term capital markets in Europe and elsewhere, the significance of these operations for monetary policy, and the limitations on the use of Eurodollars.

————. "Eurodollars: Some Further Comments." International Monetary Fund, *Staff Papers,* vol. 12, no. 1 (March 1965), pp. 1–16.

A speech delivered at the Conference on International Financing. It discusses the major uses for Eurodollars and their role as a money market instrument, and talks about the tendency to borrow short and lend long. Interest-rate determination in the Eurodollar market is explained.

Bank of England. "U.K. Banks' External Liabilities and Claims in Foreign Currencies." *Quarterly Bulletin,* June 1964, pp. 100–108.

This article introduces the Bank of England statistical series on the external liabilities

---

[1] A very small selected group of articles dealing specifically with Eurocurrency topics has been briefly annotated for the reader's convenience. The citations included in this annotated section have also been included in the appropriate part of Section II of this bibliography. All articles listed are in English unless otherwise noted.

and claims of financial institutions in the United Kingdom—mainly accepting houses, overseas banks and branches of foreign banks doing business in London. The data—given quarterly, going back to December 1962—are broken down by country for U.S. dollars and by area for all currencies.

Bank for International Settlements. "The Eurocurrency Market." *Thirty-fourth Annual Report,* June 8, 1964, pp. 127–141.

This is the first of the BIS annual articles on Eurocurrencies. Its main contribution is the data it presents on the size of the market. Liabilities and assets in U.S. dollars, Swiss francs, sterling, DM and Dutch guilders are given for financial institutions in the nine countries which make up the largest share of activity as of the end of September 1963. Also, there is an excellent discussion of definitional problems, sources and uses of funds, and of interest-rate developments.

Bell, Goeffrey L. "Credit Creation Through Eurodollars?" *The Banker,* vol. 114 (August 1964), pp. 494–502.

This is a good discussion of a very widely misunderstood aspect of the Eurodollar system, that is, whether Eurodollar transactions actually result in the multiple "creation" of credit or whether they merely result in the "passing on" of credit in the financial intermediation sense.

Black, Stanley W. "An Econometric Study of Eurodollar Borrowing by New York Banks and the Rate of Interest on Eurodollars." *Journal of Finance,* vol. 26, no. 1 (March 1971), pp. 83–88.

This paper attempts to quantify supply and demand functions for the Eurodollar funds borrowed by New York banks from their foreign branches. Reduced form equations are estimated from weekly data covering the period 1966–68 and are tested by predicting the first seven months of 1969.

Carli, Guido. "Il mercato dell'eurodollaro e il suo controllo" ["The Eurodollar Market and its Control," with English summary.] *Bancaria,* vol. 28, no. 1 (January 1972), pp. 7–12.

Carli claims that care must be taken to keep the Eurodollar market from continuing to have the possibility of upsetting the equilibrium of the international monetary system and from hindering a European monetary union. He suggests that steps should be taken to try to control the rate of growth of Eurodeposits.

Clendenning, E. Wayne. "Eurodollars and Credit Creation." *International Currency Review,* vol. 3 (March/April 1971), pp. 12–19.

The purpose of this article is to examine the credit-creating possibilities of the Euro-dollar market, to point out the areas of conflict and uncertainty about credit creation, and to present a possible method of reconciling the opposing views which have perpetuated these uncertainties. The conclusion drawn is that the Eurodollar market has had a significant expansion impact on the world credit base through its ability to attract both new deposits and a substantial, but delayed, deposit reflow of Euro-dollar loan proceeds.

Cohen, Benjamin J. "Eurodollar, the Common Market, and Currency Unification." *Journal of Finance,* vol. 28, no. 4 (December 1963), pp. 605–621.

This article originally formed part of a doctoral dissertation written at Columbia University in 1961–62. It argues that the lag in the formal monetary unification in

378

the growing European Economic Community is partly due to the coincidental emergence of the Eurodollar market and to the Eurodollar having some of the benefits of a de facto common currency.

Cooper, Richard N. "Eurodollars, Reserve Dollars, and Asymmetries in the International Monetary System." *Journal of International Economics,* vol. 2, no. 4 (September 1972), pp. 325–344.

Attention is drawn to the fundamental asymmetries in the world financial system which are generating a growing demand in the European press and public discussions for putting on Britain and the United States the same financial burdens and responsibilities that fall on other countries with respect to their foreign payments. The reasons for these asymmetries are given, and their implications for official monetary arrangements are discussed. The radical changes needed to achieve symmetry are sketched, and attention is drawn to some of the difficulties created for reserve consolidation by the existing asymmetries. Some possible resolutions to these difficulties are offered.

Einzig, Paul. "Dollar Deposits in London." *The Banker,* vol. 110 (January 1960), pp. 23–27.

This is the first widely published article on Eurodollars. It is a short piece which deals with some of the more important factors behind the development of Eurodollars, such as the ban imposed by U.K. authorities in September 1957 on credits to finance trade between foreign countries and on "refinance" credits. Also, it discusses the impact of Eurodollar business on London as an international financial center and the possibilities the market provides for adding liquidity to the U.K. commercial banking system.

————. "Statics and Dynamics of the Eurodollar Market." *Economic Journal,* vol. 71, no. 3 (September 1961), pp. 592–595.

Einzig contends that the Eurodollar system goes a long way towards creating a truly international money market in conformity with the static assumption of a basic trend toward the elimination of discrepancies between interest rates in different countries. However, a close examination of its dynamic aspects leads to some highly perturbing conclusions. The amounts held are particularly loose and liquid and are being used for speculative and arbitrage transactions, Einzig claims.

————. "Some Recent Changes in the Eurodollar System." *Journal of Finance,* vol. 19, no. 3 (September 1964), pp. 443–449.

Einzig claims that Eurodollars have come to stay, and that there is a need for close study of the organization of the market. The development of this new, important credit and financing system—described in the article—has not yet found its definite form, Einzig believes, and should be followed with close attention.

Fellner, William. "The Dollar's Place in the International System: Suggested Criteria for the Appraisal of Emerging Views." *Journal of Economic Literature,* vol. 10, no. 3 (September 1972), pp. 735–756.

Fellner suggests that the emerging views on the international role of the dollar in the post-1971 period differ from each other with respect to favored links of exchange-rate policy as well as with respect to the question of the convertibility of foreign official dollar holdings. He claims that the various criteria suggested for appraisal of the role of the U.S. dollar will have to take these differing views into consideration.

Formuzis, Peter A. "The Demand for Eurodollars and the Optimum Stock of Bank Liabilities." *Journal of Money, Credit, and Banking,* vol. 5, no. 3 (August 1973), pp. 806–818.

This paper attempts to extend in a simple but precise fashion the microeconomic theory of banking to the use of Eurodollar funds by U.S. resident banks under the assumption that a bank has control over the size of its total liabilities—which are assumed to be composed of exogenously given deposits and the endogenously controlled Eurodollar borrowings which U.S. banks purchase in the market.

Fratianni, Michele and Savona, Paolo. "Una struttura formale per l'analisi della capacita moltiplicativa del mercato dell' eurodollaro," ["A Formal Analysis of the Multiplicative Potential Within the Eurodollar Market," with English summary]. *L'Industria,* vol. 3, no. 3 (July–September 1970), pp. 345–356.

The concept of "international liquidity" is abandoned by the authors and replaced with one which has properties similar—they claim—to a country's monetary base. A formulation of Eurocredit and Eurodeposit multipliers is developed within the context of their new international monetary base framework of analysis.

Friedman, Milton. "The Eurodollar Market: Some First Principles." *Federal Reserve Bank of St. Louis Review,* vol. 53, no. 7 (July 1971), pp. 16–24.

This article attempts to present the general reader with a basic understanding of the Eurodollar market. The author makes a distinction between Eurodollar creation and the Eurodollar multiplier within the context of analogy with a domestic commercial banking system. This article was originally published in Morgan Guaranty Trust, *Survey,* October 1969, and was the subject of a reply by Fred Klopstock of the Federal Reserve Bank of New York, cited below.

Friedrich, Klaus. "The Eurodollar System and International Liquidity." *Journal of Money, Credit, and Banking,* vol. 2, no. 3 (August 1970), pp. 337–347.

The author feels that since one of the most widely noted functions of the Eurodollar system is the financing of international transactions, the system must therefore have important implications for international liquidity. Definitional and conceptual aspects of the links between the Eurodollar system and international liquidity are discussed, and a model which elaborates on the details of these links is developed.

Gibson, William E. "Eurodollars and U.S. Monetary Policy." *Journal of Money, Credit, and Banking,* vol. 3, no. 3 (August 1971), pp. 649–665.

This paper investigates the relationship between the Eurodollar market and money and credit markets in the United States and tries to answer the question whether Eurodollars have had deleterious consequences for monetary control in the United States.

————. "The Eurodollar Market and the Foreign Demand for Liquid Dollar Assets: Comment." *Journal of Money, Credit, and Banking,* vol. 4, no. 3 (August 1972), pp. 684–687.

This is a critique of the Mikesell and Rich articles, cited below. A factor not clearly stated by Mikesell is that U.S. short-term liabilities to foreigners rise when Eurodollar volume increases, contributing to the U.S. balance-of-payments deficit. Rich does not take into account in his analysis that the U.S. balance of payments and the volume of Eurodollars are simultaneously determined along with the forward foreign exchange discount or premium on the dollar. In the Eurodollar market, the United

States supplies reserves to intermediaries, a function something like a central bank, but without the controls normally associated with it, Gibson suggests.

Havrilesky, Thomas and Clark, P. "Eurodollar Borrowings and the Effectiveness of Monetary Policy." *Mississippi Valley Journal of Business and Economics,* vol. 7, no. 1 (Fall 1971), pp. 74–81.

The purpose of this note is to develop, within a simple, deterministic, Keynesian model of the money sector, an analysis of the effect that an increase in U.S. bank borrowing of Eurodollars has on the effectiveness of monetary policy in the United States—effectiveness being measured by the impact on the interest rate or the equilibrium stock of demand deposits of a change in the monetary base.

Hendershott, Patric H. "The Structure of International Interest Rates: The U.S. Treasury Bill Rate and the Eurodollar Deposit Rate." *Journal of Finance,* vol. 22, no. 3 (September 1967), pp. 455–465.

Earlier investigations into the estimated sensitivity of short-term international capital movements to international interest-rate differentials are extended into the closely related area of the impact of changes in the U.S. Treasury bill rate on the Eurodollar deposit rate. Stock-flow considerations suggest that the Eurodollar deposit rate adjusts gradually to changes in the U.S. bill rate.

Hinshaw, Randall. "The Eurodollar Market and the Foreign Demand for Liquid Dollar Assets: Comment." *Journal of Money, Credit, and Banking,* vol. 4, no. 3 (August 1972), pp. 688–690.

Hinshaw's comment tries to place the statistical conclusions of Professors Rich and Mikesell in a broader perspective, emphasizing the impressive size of the market and the strong impact of changes in Eurodollar deposit rates on foreign currency conversions.

Hodjera, Zoran. "International Short-Term Capital Movements: A Survey of Theory and Empirical Analysis." International Monetary Fund, *Staff Papers,* vol. 20, no. 3 (November 1973), pp. 683–740.

The writer contends that a comparable and fairly rigorous statistical inquiry and quantitative projection, as given to the trade balance on an individual country level and on a general equilibrium multicountry basis, is not yet possible for the capital account, in general, but progress has been made regarding short-term capital movements. This study is limited to short-term capital movements between industrial countries since these play an important role in the domestic and international adjustment process of these countries.

Holmes, Allen R. and Klopstock, Fred H. "The Market for Dollar Deposits in Europe." *Federal Reserve Bank of New York, Monthly Review,* November 1960, pp. 197–202.

This is one of the earliest articles on Eurodollars. It is based on observations during a tour of major European financial centers made by the authors in June 1960. Basically a descriptive article, it discusses very briefly such topics as the history and mechanics of the market, the supply and demand for funds in the market, and the banks' functions as financial intermediaries.

Ingram, James C. "The Dollar and the International Monetary System: A Retrospective View." *Southern Economic Journal,* vol. 40, no. 4 (April 1974), pp. 531–543.

This is the presidential address delivered by the author at the 43rd Annual Meeting

381

of the Southern Economic Association in November 1973, which includes comments on some aspects of the postwar (World War II) international monetary experience—particularly the role of the dollar—and some tentative comments about the future. New institutions and practices in world money and capital markets—like the Eurodollar, Eurocurrency markets, et cetera—may progressively curtail national monetary autonomy and thus produce, de facto, a kind of informal policy coordination among nations.

Kindleberger, Charles P. "The Eurodollar and the Internationalization of United States' Monetary Policy." *Banca Nazionale del Lavoro Quarterly Review,* vol. 22, no. 88 (March 1969), pp. 3–15.

Kindleberger contends the fixed exchange-rate system requires harmonized policies with respect to domestic price levels and target figures for balance of payments. Ultimately, crisis liquidity should be provided by an international central bank, but meanwhile the Eurodollar market and the Basle swap arrangements are rudimentary substitutes. The joining of international money markets calls for internationalization of monetary policy, he says. Comments are furnished on flexible exchange rates and changing the price of gold.

Klopstock, Fred H. "The International Money Market: Structure, Scope and Instruments." *Journal of Finance,* vol. 20, no. 2 (May 1965), pp. 182–208.

This is a very comprehensive review of international money markets with particular attention to their scope and supply and demand structures. It discusses the different behavioral characteristics of potential suppliers of funds, and the scattered material available on the geographical origins of funds invested in money market instruments. It gives profiles of three major internationally oriented money markets, two of the traditional type—New York and London—and the Eurocurrency market. Perhaps the most valuable part of the article is the detailed account of the ways in which the existence of Eurocurrency markets increases the interlinkage of national money markets.

————. "Impact of Euromarkets on the United States' Balance of Payments." *Law and Contemporary Problems,* vol. 34, no. 1 (Winter 1969), pp. 157–171.

This article describes the Eurodollar, the Eurocurrency and the Eurobond markets, which provide good examples of institutional arrangements that emerge in response to legal barriers which impede the free flow of international capital across national borders. Little did those who designed these legal roadblocks perceive the dynamic market processes that would evolve as a result. Special attention is given to the capital movements through the Eurodollar and the Eurobond market.

————. "Money Creation in the Eurodollar Market—A Note on Professor Friedman's Views." *Federal Reserve Bank of New York, Monthly Review,* vol. 52, no. 1 (January 1970), pp. 12–15.

Klopstock contends that the absence of basic data on the Eurodollar market has given rise to many misunderstandings about its workings. The forces behind monetary expansion in the United States and in the Eurodollar system differ in many important respects, a fact disregarded by Professor Friedman.

Kwack, Sung Y. "The Structure of International Interest Rates: An Extension of Hendershott's Tests." *Journal of Finance,* vol. 26, no. 4 (September 1971), pp. 897–900.

The empirical results of this study consolidate Hendershott's conclusion that the

Eurodollar rate adjusts to changes in the U.S. interest rate. Whether this adjustment is complete or partial depends on whether the U.S. bill rate represents the corresponding foreign rates.

Levin, Jay H. "The Marginal Cost of International Short-Term Capital Movements." *International Economic Review,* vol. 12, no. 3 (June 1971), pp. 227–238.

This paper demonstrates that knowledge of the actual amount of capital flow and subsequent changes in interest payments are insufficient for an adequate determination of the marginal cost of short-term capital movements. It is also shown that increased responsiveness of the actual capital flow to changes in interest rates does not necessarily lower the marginal cost. The marginal cost of higher interest rates is compared with that of forward intervention undertaken for the same purpose, and the two are proven to be identical.

————. "A Financial Sector Analysis of the Eurodollar Market." *Journal of Finance,* vol. 29, no. 1 (March 1974), pp. 103–115.

In an attempt to clarify the functioning of the Eurodollar market, this paper presents two models in which Eurobanks are viewed as a special type of intermediary in the financial sector of the United States. These models are used to determine how the behavior of transactors in the Eurodollar market affects the impact on U.S. rates of monetary disturbances in the United States, how the size of the market is affected by these disturbances, whether switches into Eurodollar deposits by the public are likely to lead to an induced expansion of the market, whether raising Regulation Q ceilings is expansionary or contractionary, and the importance of these ceilings to the size of the market.

————. "The Eurodollar Market and the International Transmission of Interest Rates." *Canadian Journal of Economics,* vol. 7, no. 2 (May 1974), pp. 205–223.

In the context of a two-country financial sector model of the United States, the rest of the world, and a Eurodollar market, this paper investigates the link between U.S. and foreign interest rates in a system of pegged exchange rates. The model is also used to examine the argument that the Eurodollar market tends to narrow international interest-rate differentials and to explore the effect of official open-market operations in this market.

Machlup, Fritz. "Eurodollar Creation: A Mystery Story." *Banca Nazionale del Lavoro Quarterly Review,* vol. 23, no. 94 (September 1970), pp. 219–260.

The difficulty in judging the different explanations of the fast growth of the volume of Eurodollars and other controversies regarding Eurodollars is due to a lack of conceptual clarity and a lack of statistical information. The author formulates several propositions which contradict the views of other analysts, and he invites criticism.

————. "Eurodollars, Once Again." *Banca Nazionale del Lavoro Quarterly Review,* vol. 25, no. 101 (June 1972), pp. 119–137.

The author gives five different results, and many more shown to be possible, depending on alternative methods of measuring "deposit creation" through Eurobanks, with or without redepositing by recipients of funds derived from loans. Analysts of effects of Eurodollar banking on the balance of payments confuse "transactions mechanics," giving rise to entries in foreign accounts, with "market processes," attributable to particular reactions of transactors.

Makin, John H. "Demand and Supply Functions for Stocks of Eurodollar Deposits: An Empirical Study." *Review of Economics and Statistics,* vol. 54, no. 4 (November 1972), pp. 381–391.

This study considers the market for Eurodollar deposits as a structural system with determinate demand and supply relations. The article makes a distinction between the stock demand for Eurodollar deposits and the flow demand for Eurodollar credit, concentrating on the former. The empirical results suggest that there exists a stable stock-demand function and a stable stock-supply function for Eurodollar deposits. The evidence does not permit rejection of the hypothesis that Eurodollar deposits serve as an international medium of exchange substitute and as an international store of value. The multiple deposit expansion process is also discussed.

————. "Identifying a Reserve Base for the Eurodollar System." *Journal of Finance,* vol. 28, no. 3 (June 1973), pp. 609–617.

This paper presents evidence that the reserve ratio in the Eurodollar system is low and falling and is determined by bank behavior which is consistent with the hypothesis that Eurobank dollar deposits in U.S. commercial banks are held as precautionary reserves. Evidence suggests that the behavior of liabilities to foreign branches of U.S. resident banks is not consistent with the profit maximization principle.

Mayer, Helmut W. "Multiplier Effects and Credit Creation in the Eurodollar Market." *Banca Nazionale del Lavoro Quarterly Review,* vol. 24, no. 98 (September 1971), pp. 233–262.

This paper attempts to show that the analogy of endogenous credit creation in a largely self-contained commercial banking system cannot be applied to credit creation in the Eurodollar market. Three major reasons why the self-contained commercial banking model cannot be applied to Eurodollars are suggested.

McClam, Warren D. "Credit Substitution and the Eurocurrency Market." *Banca Nazionale del Lavoro Quarterly Review,* vol. 25, no. 103 (December 1972), pp. 323–363.

McClam suggests that Eurocurrency credits serve partly as a true substitute for other forms of credit in the strict sense that, in the absence of Eurocurrency credits, national authorities would have had to expand domestic credit more in order to achieve their domestic objectives. He argues that the net growth of the Eurocurrency market is a misleading indicator of the market's influence on "world" credit expansion and international inflation.

Meltzer, Allan H. "The Dollar as an International Money." *Banca Nazionale del Lavoro Quarterly Review,* vol. 26, no. 104 (March 1973), pp. 21–28.

This paper restates some recent developments in monetary theory and draws conclusions for the international monetary system. Problems of seigniorage and management of the system are discussed briefly.

Mikesell, Raymond F. "The Eurodollar Market and the Foreign Demand for Liquid Dollar Assets." *Journal of Money, Credit, and Banking,* vol. 4, no. 3 (August 1972), pp. 643–683.

The foreign demand for liquid dollar assets and the substitutability among American dollars, Eurodollars, and nondollar liquid assets are discussed. The impact of the Eurodollar market on the U.S. balance of payments is the concern of the latter part of the article.

Rich, George. "A Theoretical and Empirical Analysis of the Eurodollar Market." *Journal of Money, Credit, and Banking,* vol. 4, no. 3 (August 1972), pp. 616–635.

A theoretical model of the Eurodollar market is developed which is consistent with the available empirical evidence but there is no discussion of the implications of Eurodollar transactions for the balance of payments and monetary policy. Some reasons behind the emergence of the Eurodollar market are also given.

Schaffner, P. P. "Eurobank Credit Expansion." *Euromoney,* July 1970, pp. 61–63.

An explanation is given of why there is very little data available relating to the credit expansion capacity of the Eurodollar system. The process which occurs following receipt by a Eurobank of additional liquid dollar assets in connection with a so-called "primary" deposit is summarized.

Schloss, B. H. "The Eurobond Market and the United States' Balance of Payments." *Economia Internazionale,* vol. 25, no. 1 (February 1972), pp. 115–119.

This paper gives an analytical description of the Eurobond market and evaluates the impact of this market on the U.S. balance of payments. Conceptual problems arise since—as in all financial markets—there exist no clear boundaries between short-term and long-term markets, and because of the more troublesome issue relating to the question of what constitutes a Eurobond issue as distinguished from what in Europe is now called a "classical" international issue.

Stem, Carl H. "The Eurodollar Market and the Foreign Demand for Liquid Dollar Assets: Comment." *Journal of Money, Credit, and Banking,* vol. 4, no. 3 (August 1972), pp. 691–703.

Mikesell's analytical model and the general problem of analyzing the impact of the Eurodollar market on several components of the U.S. balance of payments are discussed. Stem cautions about the conclusions drawn from the many regressions run by Mikesell.

Thygesen, M. "Monetary Policy, Capital Flows, and Internal Stability: Some Experiences from Large Industrial Countries." *Swedish Journal of Economics,* vol. 75, no. 1 (March 1973), pp. 83–99.

This note reviews the experiences of Germany, Italy, and Japan in the conduct of monetary policy in an open economy. The starting point is the monetary theory of balance of payments as formulated by Mundell, Swoboda, and others. Extensions are made incorporating some important aspects of the transmission mechanism by which changes in monetary instruments are reflected via domestic financial markets in the capital account and in private expenditures. Some comparisons between Eurodollar and domestic interest rates are made.

Valentini, John J. and Hunt, Lacy H. "Eurodollar Borrowing by New York Banks and the Rate of Interest on Eurodollars: Comment." *Journal of Finance,* vol. 27, no. 1 (March 1972), pp. 130–133.

Two important qualifications about Stanley Black's article are mentioned: (1) two of the equations describe an overidentified structural model, and (2) there are problems with the market equality assumption necessary in the solution of Black's structural model. Unless the total market is described and estimated, no legitimate rate or supply equation can be found, the writers suggest.

Willett, Thomas D. "A Theoretical and Empirical Analysis of the Eurodollar Market: Comment." *Journal of Money, Credit, and Banking,* vol. 4, no. 3 (August 1972), pp. 636–642.

This comment is directed primarily to some issues raised in Rich's theoretical and empirical analysis of the Eurodollar market, displaying optimism about the fact that some general agreement over the rough magnitudes of a number of major parameters will emerge as the number of empirical studies increases. Relating to Mikesell's article, Willett feels that given the international position of the dollar, it makes very little difference what the effects of the Eurodollar market are on the U.S. balance of payments.

II. Selected Citations

Books and Booklets

Aliber, Robert Z. *The Management of the Dollar in International Finance.* Princeton Studies in International Finance, no. 13. Princeton: Princeton University Press, 1964.

———. ed. *The International Market for Foreign Exchange.* New York: Praeger Publishers, 1969.

———. *The International Money Game.* New York: Basic Books, 1973.

Anderson, Clay J. *Defending the Dollar.* Philadelphia: Federal Reserve Bank of Philadelphia, 1962.

Aschinger, Franz E. *Zurich as a Center of Finance.* Zurich: Neue Zürcher Zeitung, 1959.

Aubrey, Henry G. *The Dollar in World Affairs: An Essay in International Financial Policy.* New York: Harper and Row, 1964.

———. *Behind the Veil of International Money.* Essays in International Finance, no. 71. Princeton: Princeton University Press, 1969.

Backman, Jules and Bloch, Ernest, eds. *Multinational Corporations, Trade and the Dollar.* New York: New York University Press, 1974.

Bank for International Settlements, Monetary and Economics Department. *Regulations and Policies Relating to Eurocurrency Markets.* Basle: Bank for International Settlements, April 7, 1967.

———. *Some Questions Relating to the Structure of Interest Rates.* Basle: Bank for International Settlements, July 1968.

Bell, Geoffrey. *The Eurodollar Market and the International Financial System.* London: Macmillan & Co., Ltd., 1973.

Bergsten, C. F.; Cairncross, Sir A.; Casanova, J. C.; Colonna di Paliano, D. G.; Cooper, R. N.; Fried, E. R.; Kaji, M.; Kioten, N.; Machlup, F.; Matthews, R.; Okita, S. and Saeki, K. *Tripartite Report on Reshaping the International Economic Order.* Washington, D. C.: Brookings Institution, 1971.

Bergsten, C. Fred. *Reforming the Dollar: An International Monetary Policy for the United States.* Council Papers on International Affairs. New York: Council on Foreign Relations, 1972.

Bergsten, C. Fred and Tyler, William G., eds. *Leading Issues in International Economic Policy: Essays in Honor of George N. Halm.* Lexington: D. C. Heath, 1973.

Black, Stanley W. *An Econometric Study of Eurodollar Borrowing by New York Banks and the Rate of Interest on Eurodollars.* Reprints in International Finance, no. 17. Princeton: Princeton University Press, 1971. (Reprinted from *The Journal of Finance,* vol. 26, March 1971.)

Blancpain, J. P. *Die Eurogeldmarkte an einem Wendepunkt.* Zurich: Buch Verlag Neue Zürcher Zeitung, 1966.

Bloch, Ernest. *Eurodollars: An Emerging International Money Market.* New York: New York University Graduate School of Business Administration, C. J. Devine Institute of Finance, 1966.

Brandes, Henning. *Der Eurodollarmarkt: eine Analyse seiner Entstehungsgrunde, seiner Struktur, seiner Marktelemente und seiner einzelwirtschaftlichen und währungspolitischen Bedeutung.* Wiesbaden: Betriebwirtschaftlicher Verlag Th. Gabler, 1968.

Branson, William H. *Financial Capital Flows in the U.S. Balance of Payments.* Amsterdam: North-Holland Publishing Co., 1968.

Brown, Weir M. *The External Liquidity of an Advanced Country.* Princeton Studies in International Finance, no. 14. Princeton: Princeton University Press, 1964.

Bryant, Ralph C. and Hendershott, Patric H. *Financial Capital Flows in the Balance of Payments of the United States: An Exploratory Empirical Study.* Princeton Studies in International Finance, no. 25. Princeton: Princeton University Press, 1970.

Cairncross, Sir Alec. *Control of Long-Term International Capital Movements.* Washington, D. C.: Brookings Institution, 1973.

Canterbury, E. Ray. *Foreign Exchange, Capital Flows, and Monetary Policy.* Princeton Studies in International Finance, no. 15. Princeton: Princeton University Press, 1965.

Carli, Guido; Fratianni, Michele; Masera, Francesco; Masera, Rainer S., and Savona, Paolo. *A Debate on the Eurodollar Market.* Quaderni di Ricerche no. 11. Rome: Ente per Gli Studi Monetari, Bancari e Finanziari-Luigi Einaudi, December 1972.

Carnemark, Curt. *Eurodollar Market.* Uppsala, Sweden: Institute of Business Studies, University of Uppsala, November 1962.

Chalmers, Eric B., ed. *Readings in the Eurodollar.* London: W. P. Griffith & Sons, Ltd., 1969.

————. *International Interest Rate War.* London: Macmillan & Co., Ltd., 1972.

Chase Manhattan Bank, N.A. *Eurodollar Financing.* New York, 1968.

Chown, John F. and Valentine, Robert. *The International Bond Market in the 1960's: Its development and operation.* New York and London: Praeger Publishers, 1968.

Clarke, William M. and Pulay, George. *The World's Money: How It Works.* New York: Praeger Publishers, Inc., 1971. (Ch. 20: "How the Eurodollar Market Works.")

Clendenning, E. Wayne. *The Eurodollar Market*. Oxford: Clarendon Press, 1970.

Committee for Economic Development. *The International Position of the Dollar*. New York, 1961.

Cooper, R. N., ed. *International Finance: Selected Readings*. Baltimore, Md. and Harmondsworth, Middlesex: Penguin, 1969.

Diebold, William. *The United States and the Industrial World: American Foreign Economic Policy in the 1970's*. London and New York: Praeger Publishers for the Council on Foreign Relations, 1972.

Dufey, Gunter. *The Eurobond Market: Function and Future*. International Business Series, no. 7, Studies in Finance. Seattle, Wash.: Graduate School of Business Administration, University of Washington, 1969.

Dunn, Robert M., Jr. *Canada's Experience with Fixed and Flexible Exchange Rates in a North American Capital Market*. Canadian-American Committee of the National Planning Association and the Private Planning Association of Canada. Washington, D. C. and Montreal, 1971.

Einzig, Paul. *Foreign Dollar Loans in Europe*. New York: St. Martin's Press, 1965.

———. *A Dynamic Theory of Forward Exchange*. 2nd ed. London: Macmillan & Co., Ltd., 1967.

———. *The Eurobond Market*. 2nd ed. London: Macmillan & Co., 1969.

———. *A Textbook on Foreign Exchange*. 2nd ed. New York: St. Martin's Press, 1969. (Ch. 14, "The Eurodollar Market.")

———. *The Case Against Floating Exchanges*. London: Macmillan & Co., Ltd., 1970.

———. *Foreign Exchange Crises: An Essay in Economic Pathology*. 2nd ed. London: Macmillan & Co., Ltd., 1970.

———. *The Destiny of the Dollar*. New York: St. Martin's Press, 1972.

———. *Roll-Over Credits*. London: Macmillan & Co., Ltd., 1973.

———. *The Eurodollar System: Practice and Theory of International Interest Rates*. 5th ed. London: Macmillan & Co., Ltd., 1973.

Fatemi, Nasrollah S.; Saint Phalle, Thibaut de; Keeffe, Grace M. *The Dollar Crisis: The United States' Balance of Payments and Dollar Stability*. Rutherford, N. J.: Fairleigh Dickinson University Press, 1963.

Federal Reserve Bank of Boston. *The International Adjustment Mechanism*. Boston: 1970.

Friedrich, Klaus. *The Eurodollar System*. Ithaca, N. Y.: Cornell University Press, 1968.

———. *A Quantitative Framework for the Eurodollar System*. Princeton Studies in International Finance, no. 26. Princeton: Princeton University Press, 1970.

German Council of Economic Experts. *Toward a New Basis for International Monetary Policy*. Princeton Studies in International Finance, no. 31. Princeton: Princeton University Press, 1972.

Gilbert, Milton. *Problems of the International Monetary System.* Essays in International Finance, no. 53. Princeton: Princeton University Press, 1966.

―――. *The Gold-Dollar System: Conditions of Equilibrium and the Price of Gold.* Essays in International Finance, no. 70. Princeton: Princeton University Press, 1968.

Haberler, Gottfried, and Willett, Thomas D. *U.S. Balance-of-Payments Policies and International Monetary Reform: A Critical Analysis.* Washington, D. C.: American Enterprise Institute for Public Policy Research, 1968.

―――. *A Strategy for U.S. Balance of Payments Policy.* Washington, D. C.: American Enterprise Institute for Public Policy Research, February 1971.

Halm, George N., ed. *Approaches to Greater Flexibility of Exchange Rates.* Proceedings of the Conference on Exchange Rates at Burgenstock, Switzerland. Princeton: Princeton University Press, 1970.

Haubold, Dietmar. *Direct Investments and the Balance of Payments: Effects of U.S. Investments in Europe on the American Balance of Payments.* Hamburg: Verlag Weltarchiv, 1972.

Hayek, Friedrich A. *Monetary Nationalism and International Stability.* (Reprinted.) Clifton, N. J.: Augustus M. Kelley, 1971 (1937).

Hinshaw, Randall, ed. *Inflation as a Global Problem.* Baltimore, Md.: The Johns Hopkins University Press, 1972.

Hirsch, Fred. *An SDR Standard: Impetus, Elements, and Impediments.* Essays in International Finance, no. 99. Princeton: Princeton University Press, 1973.

Hodgman, Donald R. *Eurodollars and National Monetary Policies.* An Irving Economic Study. New York: Irving Trust Company, 1970.

―――. *National Monetary Policies and International Monetary Cooperation.* Boston: Little, Brown & Company, 1974.

Holbik, Karel, ed. *Monetary Policy in Twelve Industrial Countries.* Boston: Federal Reserve Bank of Boston, 1973.

Holmes, Alan R. and Schott, Francis H. *The New York Foreign Exchange Market.* New York: Federal Reserve Bank of New York, 1965.

International Economic Policy Association. *The United States' Balance of Payments: From Crisis to Controversy.* New York: Walker and Company, 1972.

International Monetary Fund, Committee on Reform of the International Monetary System and Related Issues [Committee of Twenty]. *International Monetary Reform: Documents of the Committee of Twenty.* Washington, D. C.: International Monetary Fund, 1974.

Johnson, Harry and Swoboda, Alexander K. *The Economics of Common Currencies.* Proceedings of the Madrid Conference on Optimum Currency Areas. Cambridge: Harvard University Press, 1973.

Johnson, Norris O. *Eurodollars in the New International Money Market.* New York: First National City Bank, 1964.

389

Kafka, Alexandre. *The IMF: The Second Coming?* Essays in International Finance, no. 94. Princeton: Princeton University Press, 1972.

Katz, Samuel I. *External Surpluses, Capital Flows, and Credit Policy in the European Economic Community.* Princeton Studies in International Finance, no. 22. Princeton: Princeton University Press, 1969.

Kindleberger, Charles P. *Europe and the Dollar.* Cambridge: M.I.T. Press, 1966.

Klopstock, Fred H. *The International Status of the Dollar.* Essays in International Finance, no. 28. Princeton: Princeton University Press, 1957.

———. *The Eurodollar Market: Some Unresolved Issues.* Essays in International Finance, no. 65. Princeton: Princeton University Press, 1968.

Krause, Lawrence B. *Sequel to Bretton Woods: A Proposal to Reform the World Monetary System.* A Staff Paper. Washington, D. C.: Brookings Institution, 1971.

Krause, Lawrence B. and Salant, Walter S., eds. *European Monetary Unification and its Meaning for the United States.* Washington, D. C.: Brookings Institution, 1973.

Lees, Francis A. *International Banking and Finance.* New York: John Wiley & Sons, 1974.

Lipfert, Helmut. *Internationales Devisen- und Geldhandel.* Frankfurt: F. Knapp Verlag, 1969.

Little, Jane Sneddon. *Eurodollars: The Money Market Gypsies.* New York: Harper & Row, 1975.

MacDougall, Sir Donald. *The Dollar Problem: A Reappraisal.* Essays in International Finance, no. 35. Princeton: Princeton University Press, 1960.

Machlup, Fritz. *Plans for Reform of the International Monetary System.* Special Papers in International Economics, no. 3. Princeton: Princeton University Press, 1964.

———. *Remaking the International Monetary System: The Rio Agreement and Beyond.* Baltimore, Md.: The Johns Hopkins Press with the Committee for Economic Development, 1968.

———. *Eurodollar Creation: A Mystery Story.* Reprints in International Finance, no. 16. Reprinted from *Banca Nazionale del Lavoro Quarterly Review,* no. 94, 1970. Princeton: Princeton University Press, 1970.

Machlup, Fritz; Gutowski, Armin; and Lutz, Friedrich A. *International Monetary Problems.* A conference sponsored by the American Enterprise Institute for Public Policy Research. Washington, D. C.: American Enterprise Institute for Public Policy Research, 1972.

Machlup, Fritz; Salant, Walter S.; and Tarshis, Lorie, eds. *International Mobility and Movement of Capital.* NBER-Universities National Bureau Conference Series, no. 24. New York and London: Columbia University Press for National Bureau of Economic Research, Inc., 1972.

Marston, Richard C. *American Monetary Policy and the Structure of the Eurodollar Market.* Princeton Studies in International Finance, no. 34. Princeton: Princeton University Press, 1974.

Martenson, G. Carroll. *The Eurodollar Market*. Boston: Bankers Publishing Co., 1964.

Mayer, Helmut W. *Some Theoretical Problems Relating to the Eurodollar Markets*. Essays in International Finance, no. 79. Princeton: Princeton University Press, 1970.

McKinnon, Ronald I. *Private and Official International Money: The Case for the Dollar*. Essays in International Finance, no. 74. Princeton: Princeton University Press, 1969.

van Meerhaeghe, M. A. G. *International Economics*. New York: Crane, Russak, 1972.

Meier, Gerald M., ed. *International Economic Reform. Collected Papers of Emile Despres*. New York, London, and Toronto: Oxford University Press, 1973.

Michael, Walther P. *Measuring International Capital Movements*. NBER Occasional Paper No. 114. New York and London: Columbia University Press for the National Bureau of Economic Research, 1971. (One third of the book contains statistical information.)

Mikesell, Raymond F. *The Emerging Pattern of International Payments*. Essays in International Finance, no. 18. Princeton: Princeton University Press, 1954.

———. *The U.S. Balance of Payments and the International Role of the Dollar*. Washington, D. C.: American Enterprise Institute for Public Policy Research, 1970.

Mikesell, Raymond F. and Furth, J. Herbert. *Foreign Dollar Balances and the International Role of the Dollar*. New York: Columbia University Press for the National Bureau of Economic Research, 1974.

Mills, Rodney H., Jr. *Explaining Changes in Eurodollar Positions: A Study of Banks in Four European Countries*. Staff Economic Studies, no. 71. Washington, D. C.: Board of Governors of the Federal Reserve System, August 1971.

Modigliani, Franco and Askari, Hossein. *The Reform of the International Payments System*. Essays in International Finance, no. 89. Princeton: Princeton University Press, 1971.

Morgan Guaranty Trust Company. *The Financing of Business with Eurodollars*. New York, 1967.

Naley-Cohen, Stephen and Marten, Jenny, eds. *The Hambro Euromoney Directory 1974*. 3rd ed. London: Euromoney Publications, 1974.

Officer, Lawrence H. and Willett, Thomas D., eds. *The International Monetary System: Problems and Proposals*. Englewood Cliffs, N. J.: Prentice-Hall, 1969.

Ossola, Rinaldo. *Towards New Monetary Relationships*. Essays in International Finance, no. 87. Princeton: Princeton University Press, 1971.

Parker, Hans J. *The Eurodollar Market*. Detroit: City National Bank of Detroit, 1964.

Posner, Michael V. *The World Monetary System: A Minimal Reform Program*. Essays in International Finance, no. 96. Princeton: Princeton University Press, 1972.

Prochnow, Herbert V., ed. *The Eurodollar*. Chicago: Rand McNally & Co., 1970.

Reierson, Roy L. *The Eurodollar Market*. New York: Bankers Trust Company, 1964.

Robbins, Sidney M. and Stobaugh, Robert B. *Money in the Multinational Enterprise: A Study of Financial Policy*. New York: Basic Books, 1973.

Robinson, Stuart W., Jr. *Multinational Banking.* Leiden: A. W. Sijthoff, 1972.

Roosa, Robert V. *Monetary Reform for the World Economy.* New York: Harper & Row, 1965.

Schafer, Wolf. *Der Eurodollarmarkt.* Tubingen: Mohr, 1971.

Schmitz, Wolfgang, ed. *Convertibility, Multilateralism, and Freedom.* New York: Springer-Verlag, 1972.

Simha, S. L. N. *International Monetary Reform: An Introduction.* Madras, India: Vora & Co. for the Institute for Financial Management and Research, 1973.

Sohmen, Egon. *International Monetary Problems and the Foreign Exchanges.* Special Papers in International Economics, no. 4. Princeton: Princeton University Press, 1963.

Stevens, Robert Warren A. *A Primer on the Dollar in the World Economy: United States Balance of Payments and International Monetary Reform.* New York: Random House, 1972.

Strange, Susan. *Sterling and British Policy.* London: Oxford University Press, 1971.

Swoboda, Alexander. *The Eurodollar Market: An Interpretation.* Essays in International Finance, no. 64. Princeton: Princeton University Press, 1968.

Tobin, James. *National Economic Policy.* New Haven: Yale University Press, 1966.

Triffin, Robert. *The Evolution of the International Monetary System: Historical Reappraisal and Future Perspectives.* Princeton Studies in International Finance, no. 12. Princeton: Princeton University Press, 1964.

Triffin, R. *Our International Monetary System Yesterday, Today, and Tomorrow.* New York: Random House, 1968.

Willett, Thomas D.; Katz, Samuel I. and Branson, William H. *Exchange-Rate Systems, Interest Rates, and Capital Flows.* Essays in International Finance, no. 78. Princeton: Princeton University Press, 1970.

Yeager, Leland. *International Monetary Relations: Theory, History and Policy.* New York: Harper & Row, 1966.

Articles

Abboud, Robert A. "Significance of Eurodollars in Today's World Markets." *Bankers Monthly,* vol. 81, no. 2 (February 1964), pp. 28–40.

———. "Eurodollars and the Payments Deficit." *Bankers Monthly,* vol. 82, no. 11 (November 1965), pp. 28–30 ff.

van den Adel, M. "The Eurco-Jury Still Out." *Euromoney,* April 1974, pp. 39–43.

Aliber, Robert Z. "The Costs and Benefits of the U.S. Role as a Reserve Currency Country." *Quarterly Journal of Economics,* vol. 78, no. 3 (August 1964), pp. 442–456.

"All About Eurodollars." *The Economist,* vol. 207 (May 25, 1963), p. 790 ff.

Altman, Oscar L. "Foreign Markets for Dollars, Sterling and Other Currencies." International Monetary Fund, *Staff Papers*, vol. 8, no. 3 (December 1961), pp. 313–352.

————. "Canadian Markets for U.S. Dollars." International Monetary Fund, *Staff Papers*, vol. 9, no. 3 (November 1962), pp. 297–316.

————. "Recent Developments in Foreign Markets for Dollars and Other Currencies." International Monetary Fund, *Staff Papers*, vol. 10, no. 1 (March 1963), pp. 48–96.

————. "Eurodollars Knit Together Many National Markets." *Journal of Commerce*, December 14, 1964, p. 22 ff.

————. "Eurodollars: Some Further Comments." International Monetary Fund, *Staff Papers*, vol. 12 (March 1965), pp. 1–16.

————. "What Does It Really Mean?—Eurodollars." *Finance and Development: The Fund and Bank Review*, vol. 4 (March 1967), pp. 9–16.

————. "New Peripatetic on Eurodollars." *Weekly Bond Buyer*, vol. 168 (April 3, 1967), pp. 6–7 ff.

Andersen, Leonall C. and Burger, Albert E. "Asset Management and Commercial Bank Portfolio Behavior: Theory and Practice." *Journal of Finance*, vol. 24, no. 2 (May 1969), pp. 207–222.

"Another Term for Your Glossary, Eurodollar," *Banking*, vol. 60, no. 11 (May 1968), p. 57 ff.

Argy, Victor and Hodjera, Zoran. "Financial Integration and Interest Rate Linkages in Industrial Countries, 1958–71." International Monetary Fund, *Staff Papers*, vol. 20, no. 1 (March 1973), pp. 1–77.

Ashby, David. "The $300 Billion Super-Dollar Market." *The Banker*, vol. 124, no. 5 (May 1974), pp. 449–454.

"Australia Hopeful on Financing." *American Banker*, vol. 132, no. 44 (March 6, 1967), p. 3 ff.

Bach, C. L. "Foreign Exchange and U.S. Balance of Payments Developments in 1972 and Early 1973." *Federal Reserve Bank of St. Louis Review*, vol. 55, no. 4 (April 1973), pp. 14–20.

Bade, Robert. "Optimal Growth and Foreign Borrowing with Restricted Mobility of Foreign Capital." *International Economic Review*, vol. 13, no. 3 (October 1972), pp. 544–552.

Bame, Jack. "How Growing Use of Eurodollars Helps to Produce Greater International Liquidity." *The Magazine of Wall Street and Business Analysts*, vol. 118 (June 11, 1966), pp. 296–297.

Banks, F. E. "A Note on Income, Capital Mobility, and the Theory of Economic Policy." *Kyklos*, vol. 22, no. 4 (1969), pp. 767–773.

Bank of England. "U.K. Banks' External Liabilities and Claims in Foreign Currencies." *Quarterly Bulletin* (June 1964), pp. 100–108.

"Bank for International Settlements Report: More About Eurodollars." *The Economist* vol. 211 (June 13, 1964), pp. 1265–1266.

Barattieri, V. "Deficit USA, eurodollari e crisi del sistema." (U.S. Deficit, Eurodollars and Crisis of the System, with English summary.) *Bancaria,* vol. 27, no. 11 (November 1971), pp. 1387–1395.

———. "The Oil Exporters and the Euromarkets." *Euromoney,* May 1974, pp. 27–28.

Bareau, Paul. "The Eurocurrency Market." *Finance,* June 19, 1964.

———. "Foreign Currency Deposits in London." *Finance,* June 26, 1964.

Barrand, Harry P. "Getting Funds Via Commercial Banking." *Finance,* May 1968, pp. 28–29.

Baumol, William J. "The Transactions Demand for Cash: An Inventory Theoretic Approach." *Quarterly Journal of Economics,* vol. 66, no. 4 (November 1952), pp. 545–556.

Bell, Geoffrey L. "The Eurodollar Market." *Federal Reserve Bank of St. Louis Review,* vol. 45, no. 12 (December 1963), pp. 5–8.

———. "Credit Creation Through Eurodollars?" *The Banker,* vol. 114, no. 8 August 1964), pp. 494–502.

———. "The Eurodollar Market and the United States." *Business Scope,* vol. 8, no. 12 (August 22, 1964).

———. "The Eurodollar Market and the United States." *Business Scope,* vol. 8, no. 13 (September 5, 1964).

———. "The Forgotten Issues—Dollars and Gold." *The Times* (London), October 29, 1969, p. 10.

———. "Eurodollars." *The Times* (London), December 19, 1969, p. 11.

———. "The Eurocurrency Markets in 1974." *Euromoney,* February 1974, pp. 4–7.

Bennett, Alfred R. "Federal Funds and Eurodollars." *Euromoney,* vol. 1, no. 8 (January 1970), pp. 22–31.

Bennett, Robert A. "U.S. Banks Find Eurodollars in the Bahamas." *American Banker,* April 18, 1968.

Bernstein, Edward M. "The Eurodollar Market and National Credit Policy." Model, Roland and Co., Inc., *Quarterly Review and Investment Survey,* Second Quarter, 1969, pp. 1–5.

———. "Convertibility and the International Role of the Dollar." Model, Roland and Co., Inc. *Quarterly Review and Investment Survey,* First Quarter, 1972, p. 1 ff.

Bhagwati, Jagdish N. "The International Monetary System: Issues in the Symposium." *Journal of International Economics,* vol. 2, no. 4 (September 1972), pp. 315–323.

Black, Stanley W. "An Econometric Study of Eurodollar Borrowing by New York Banks and the Rate of Interest on Eurodollars." *Journal of Finance,* vol. 26, no. 1 (March 1971), pp. 83–88.

———. "Eurodollar Borrowing by New York Banks and the Rate of Interest on Eurodollars: Reply." *Journal of Finance,* vol. 27, no. 1 (March 1972), pp. 134–135.

————. "An Econometric Study of Eurodollar Borrowing by New York Banks and the Rate of Interest on Eurodollars: Reply." *Journal of Finance,* vol. 27, no. 4 (September 1972), pp. 931–932.

Bloomfield, Arthur I. "Official Intervention in the Forward Exchange Market: Some Recent Experiences." *Banca Nazionale del Lavoro Quarterly Review,* vol. 17, no. 86 (March 1964), pp. 3–42.

Bolton, Sir G. "The International Money Markets." Bank of London and South America, *Quarterly Review,* March 1963.

————. "The International Money Market." *The European Capital Market.* Federal Trust Report, Special Series, No. 2. London: Federal Trust for Education and Research, 1967, pp. 1–10.

Borcich, J. "Capital Flows, Devaluation, and the Balance of Payments." *Canadian Journal of Economics,* vol. 5, no. 2 (May 1972), pp. 227–236.

Branson, William H. "Monetary Policy and the New View of International Capital Movements." *Brookings Papers on Economic Activity* (2) (1970), pp. 235–270.

Branson, William H. and Hill, Robert D. "Capital Movements among Major OECD Countries: Some Preliminary Results." *Journal of Finance,* vol. 26, no. 2 (May 1971), pp. 269–286.

Brimmer, Andrew F. "International Capital Markets and the Financing of Economic Development." *Revue de la Banque* (Brussels), vol. 2 (1974), pp. 1–12.

————. "Multi-National Banks and the Management of Monetary Policy in the United States." *Journal of Finance,* vol. 28, no. 2 (May 1973), pp. 439–454.

"Brokers Discover Eurodollars." *The Economist,* vol. 212 (September 19, 1964), p. 1155.

Bross, S. R., Jr. "The United States Borrower in the Eurobond Market—A Lawyer's Point of View." *Law and Contemporary Problems,* vol. 34, no. 1 (Winter 1969), pp. 172–202.

Buonomio, M. "Problemi Europei: Sui rapporti economici fra l'Europa e gli Stati Uniti (Con particolare riferimento all'attivita bancaria)." [On Economic Relationships between Europe and the USA (with particular reference to banking), with English summary.] *Bancaria,* vol. 28, no. 7 (July 1972), pp. 910–923.

Butler, William F. and Deaver, J. V. "Gold and the Dollar." *Foreign Affairs,* vol. 46, no. 1 (October 1967), pp. 181–192.

Cameron, Juan. "Roosa Asks Action on Interest to Counteract Eurodollar Mart." *American Banker,* vol. 127, no. 132 (July 11, 1962), p. 1 ff.

Canterbery, E. Ray. "Exchange Rates, Capital Flows, and Monetary Policy." *American Economic Review,* vol. 59, no. 3 (June 1969), pp. 426–435.

"The Capacity of the Euromarket." *Euromoney,* June 1974, p. 3 ff.

Carli, Guido. "Mobilita Internazionale dei Capitali e Stabilita Monetaria Interna." [International Mobility of Capital and Internal Monetary Stability.] *Bancaria Rassegna,* vol. 25, no. 10 (October 1969), pp. 1216–1220.

———. "Eurodollars: A Paper Pyramid." *Banca Nazionale del Lavoro Quarterly Review,* vol. 24, no. 97 (June 1971), pp. 95–109.

———. "Il mercato dell'eurodollaro e il suo controllo." [The Eurodollar Market and its Control, with English summary.] *Bancaria,* vol. 28, no. 1 (January 1972), pp. 7–12.

———. "Riflession sulle recenti vicende monetarie." [Some reflections on recent monetary events, with English summary.] *Bancaria,* vol. 28, no. 9 (September 1972), pp. 1099–1112.

Carvallo, R. "Les contraintes de l'environment exterieur: le mecanisme de l'eurodollar." (With English summary.) *Revue Economique,* vol. 22, no. 4 (July 1971), pp. 613–656.

"CD's, Eurodollars, and Monetary Policy." *Morgan Guaranty Survey,* February 1969, pp. 4–9.

"Central Bank Swaps—A Bulwark of International Monetary Cooperation." *Federal Reserve Bank of Atlanta Monthly Review,* vol. 52, no. 12 (December 1967).

Chen, C. "Diversified Currency Holdings and Flexible Exchanges." *Quarterly Journal of Economics,* vol. 87, no. 1 (February 1973), pp. 96–111.

Christie, Herbert. "Eurodollars and the Balance of Payments." *The Banker,* vol. 117, no. 1 (January 1967), pp. 34–45.

Clark, Peter B. "The Effects of International Monetary Developments on Capital Movements." *Law and Contemporary Problems,* vol. 34, no. 1 (Winter 1969), pp. 18–32.

Clark, J. B. "Eurobonds: The Changing Face of the Market." *Euromoney,* April 1974, pp. 25–29.

Clendenning, E. Wayne. "Eurodollars: The Problem of Control." *The Banker,* vol. 118, no. 4 (April 1968), pp. 321–329.

———. "Eurodollars and Credit Creation." *International Currency Review,* vol. 3, no. 1 (March/April 1971), pp. 12–19.

Cohen, Benjamin J. "The Eurodollar, the Common Market, and Currency Unification." *Journal of Finance,* vol. 18, no. 4 (December 1963), pp. 605–621.

Cohen, Jerome B. "Restructuring the International Monetary System." *The Bankers Magazine,* vol. 157, no. 1 (Winter 1974), pp. 15–17.

Colombo, E. "America's Economic Measures and Their Effects on the Italian Economy." *Review of the Economic Conditions in Italy,* vol. 22, no. 2 (March 1968), pp. 79–97.

"Commercial Banking Trends in Western Europe." Chase Manhattan Bank, *Report on Western Europe,* vol. 34 (February–March 1965).

"Concern about Eurodollar Borrowing—Heavy Industrial Obligations." *Financial Times* (London), November 13, 1963, p. 17.

Cooper, John. "How Foreign Exchange Operations Can Go Wrong." *Euromoney,* May 1974, pp. 4–7.

Cooper, Richard N. "Eurodollars, Reserve Dollars, and Asymmetrics in the International Monetary System." *Journal of International Economics,* vol. 2, no. 4 (September 1972), pp. 325–344.

Cox, Albert H., Jr., and Leach, Ralph F. "Defensive Open Market Operations." *Journal of Finance,* vol. 19, no. 1 (March 1964), pp. 76–93.

Dach, Joseph. "Legal Nature of the Eurodollar." *American Journal of Comparative Law,* vol. 13, no. 1 (Winter 1964), pp. 30–43.

Davis, S. I. "A Buyer's Market in Eurodollars." *Harvard Business Review,* vol. 51, no. 3 (May–June 1973), pp. 119–130.

"Decade of the Eurodollar." *The Economist,* vol. 224 (July 8, 1967), pp. 126–127.

De Gunzburg, Dimitri. "Eurodollar Market Role Is Diversifying." *Journal of Commerce,* March 20, 1967, p. 2A ff.

"Demand for Eurodollars." *The Economist,* vol. 197 (October 1, 1960), p. 78.

Deweirdt, E. "Le marche des euro-obligations." [The Eurobond market, with English summary.] *Rivista Internazionale di Scienze Economiche e Commerciali,* vol. 16, no. 11 (November 1969), pp. 1033–1052.

Divoy, I. "les mesures americaines en matiere d'exportation de capitaux prives." [The U.S. measures affecting private capital exports.] *Revue d'Economie Politique,* vol. 79, no. 1 (January/February 1969), pp. 27–65.

"Dollar Defense Aims at Killing Eurodollars." *Journal of Commerce,* July 17, 1962.

"A Double Threat to the Eurodollar." *Financial Times* (London), March 5, 1963, p. 19.

Doucet, Jean. "The Growth and Challenge of Carribean Off-Shore Banking." *The Banker,* vol. 121, no. 5 (May 1971), pp. 507–515.

Dreyer, H. Peter. "Eurodollar." *European Community,* vol. 120 (February 1969), pp. 3–5.

Duell, Dennis C. and Pfannestiel, Maurice. "U.S. Short-Term Capital Movements: A Distributed Lag Approach." *Quarterly Review of Economics and Business,* vol. 12, no. 1, pp. 77–85.

Einzig, Paul. "Dollar Deposits in London." *The Banker,* vol. 110, no. 1 (January 1960), pp. 23–27.

———. "Statics and Dynamics of the Eurodollar Market." *Economic Journal,* vol. 71, no. 3 (September 1961), pp. 592–595.

———. "Towards an International Money Market." *Statist,* vol. 174 (November 17, 1961), pp. 925–926.

———. "Some Recent Developments in Official Forward Exchange Operations." *Economic Journal,* vol. 73, no. 2 (June 1963), pp. 241–253.

———. "Has the Eurodollar a Future?" *Statist,* vol. 182, (October 11, 1963), pp. 121–122.

———. "Some Recent Changes in the Eurodollar System." *Journal of Finance,* vol. 19, no. 3 (September 1964), pp. 443–449.

————. "London Dollar Certificates of Deposit." *Banca Nazionale del Lavoro Quarterly Review*, vol. 19, no. 79 (December 1966), pp. 328–345.

————. "The Declining Use of Sterling as a Trading Currency." *Westminster Bank Review*, May 1968, pp. 2–10.

————. "Correspondence." *Economic Journal*, March 1969, pp. 140–141.

————. "Extensive Market in Foreign Currency Deposits." *Commercial and Financial Chronicle*, vol. 193 (April 20, 1961), p. 1751.

————. "Dangerous Possibilities of the Eurodollar System." *Commercial and Financial Chronicle*, vol. 195 (January 25, 1962), p. 11.

————. "Eurodollar Market Has Achieved Permanency." *Commercial and Financial Chronicle*, vol. 197 (March 14, 1963), p. 1083.

————. "Communist Borrowing in the Eurodollar Market." *Commercial and Financial Chronicle*, vol. 197 (April 18, 1963), p. 1595.

————. "Euroexchange Sought by Firms in the U.S." *Commercial and Financial Chronicle*, vol. 198 (August 15, 1963), p. 633.

————. "Muddle and Misunderstanding about Eurodollars." *Commercial and Financial Chronicle*, vol. 198 (September 19, 1963), p. 1104.

————. "Why Eurodollars Are Returning to Normal." *Commercial and Financial Chronicle*, vol. 199 (January 23, 1964), p. 282.

————. "Bank for International Settlements Hopes Eurodollar Market is Here to Stay." *Commercial and Financial Chronicle*, vol. 199 (February 13, 1964), p. 637.

————. "Eurodollars Receive Official Blessing Abroad." *Commercial and Financial Chronicle*, vol. 199 (June 18, 1964), p. 2445.

————. "Character and Significance of the Eurodollar Market." *Commercial and Financial Chronicle*, vol. 200 (September 24, 1964).

————. "Eurodollar System Is Making Further Progress." *Commercial and Financial Chronicle*, vol. 206 (July 6, 1967), p. 61.

————. "A Eurodollar Market Dominated by Americans." *Commercial and Financial Chronicle*, vol. 208 (October 31, 1968), p. 1728.

Emminger, O. H. "Short-term Capital Flows: A Threat to International Equilibrium." *Euromoney*, May 1971, pp. 6–8.

"Eurocurrencies: Broking Club Rules." *The Economist*, vol. 211 (November 12, 1966), p. 718.

"The Eurocurrency and Eurobond Markets." Bank for International Settlements, Thirty-fourth and successive *Annual Reports*. Basle: Bank for International Settlements.

"Eurodollar Deposits an Active Market—Changes in Monetary Policy." *Financial Times* (London), February 5, 1962, p. 20.

"Eurodollar Float." Chemical Bank, *U.S. Banking Developments*, August 11, 1969.

"Eurodollar and International Capital Markets Today." First National City Bank, *Monthly Economic Letter,* August 1967, pp. 89–92.

"Eurodollar Loss Slowed in Japan." *New York Times,* March 9, 1964, p. 45.

"The Eurodollar Market." *Federal Reserve Bank of Richmond Monthly Review,* April 1967, pp. 8–10.

"The Eurodollar Market." Svenska Handelsbanken, *Index,* vol. 7 (1969).

"The Eurodollar Market." Chase Manhattan Bank, *World Business,* October 1969, pp. 9–11.

"The Eurodollar Market—I: Anatomy of a Deposit and Loan Market." *Federal Reserve Bank of Cleveland Economic Review,* March 1970.

"The Eurodollar Market—II." *Federal Reserve Bank of Cleveland Economic Review,* April 1970, pp. 3–18.

"The Eurodollar Market—III." *Federal Reserve Bank of Cleveland Economic Review,* May 1970, pp. 3–14.

"The Eurodollar Market's Big Test." First National City Bank, *Monthly Economic Letter,* July 1974, pp. 9–15.

"Eurodollar Mart Seen as Threat to Stability." *American Banker,* March 20, 1967, p. 3.

"Eurodollar Operations." The First National Bank of Chicago. *International Economic Review,* September/October, 1962, p. 24.

"Eurodollar Traffic—Have Margins Been Cut Too Fine?" *Financial Times* (London), May 30, 1963, p. 25.

"Eurodollar Works for Both Sides." *Business Week,* July 28, 1962, pp. 108–110.

"Eurodollar's Future." *The Economist,* vol. 203 (May 26, 1962), p. 821.

"Eurodollars—Here to Stay? New Kind of International Currency." *The Economist,* vol. 203 (June 2, 1962), pp. 908–910.

"Eurodollars: Counsel for the Defense." *The Economist,* vol. 204 (August 4, 1962), p. 466.

"Eurodollars for Belgium." *The Economist,* vol. 209 (December 14, 1963), p. 1200.

"Eurodollars in London." *The Economist,* vol. 211 (June 20, 1964), p. 1434.

"Eurodollars: Canadian Switch-back." *The Economist,* vol. 219 (April 9, 1966), p. 174.

"Eurodollars Go Home." *The Economist,* vol. 232 (August 30, 1969), pp. 40–41.

"Eurodollars: Full Exposure." *The Economist,* vol. 235 (June 22, 1974), p. 68.

"Eurodollars: A Changing Market." *Federal Reserve Bulletin,* vol. 55, no. 10 (October 1969), pp. 765–784.

"Euromarkets: Arabs Pressing for New Debt Instruments." *International Currency Review,* vol. 6, no. 1 (January–February 1974), pp. 19–21.

"Euromarkets: Some Implications of Arab Financial Power." *International Currency Review,* vol. 6, no. 2 (March–April 1974), pp. 26–28.

"Euromarkets: Talking Points at the FT Conference." *The Banker,* vol. 124, no. 4 (April 1974), pp. 315–317.

"Euromoney Market Tight Again." Frankfurter Bank, *Monthly Economic Letter,* December 1969.

Faith, Nicholas. "The Eurobond Market Becomes Respectable at Last." *Euromoney,* May 1974, pp. 56–57.

Farnsworth, Clyde H. "National City to Bid for Dollars in London with its Certificates." *New York Times,* May 24, 1966, pp. 65, 72.

Fellner, William. "The Dollar's Place in the International System: Suggested Criteria for the Appraisal of Emerging Views." *Journal of Economic Literature,* vol. 10, no. 3 (September 1972), pp. 735–756.

"Fight to Preserve Pound Seen Won; '66 Eurodollar Crisis Move Revealed." *American Banker,* March 9, 1967, p. 1 ff.

Fink, W. H. "The International Transfer of Capital." *Revista Internazionale di Scienze Economiche e Commerciali,* vol. 18, no. 5 (May 1971), pp. 472–486.

———. "Dollar Surplus and Devaluation." *Revista Internazionale di Scienze Economiche e Commerciali,* vol. 20, no. 7 (July 1973), pp. 625–639.

Fleming, J. Marcus. "Towards a New Regime for International Payments." *Journal of International Economics,* vol. 2, no. 4 (September 1972), pp. 345–374.

Floyd, J. E. "International Capital Movements and Monetary Equilibrium." *American Economic Review,* vol. 59, no. 4 (September 1969), pp. 472–492.

———. "International Capital Movements and Monetary Equilibrium: Reply." *American Economic Review,* vol. 60, no. 5 (December 1970), pp. 2–18.

"Foreign Banks in London—A Survey." *The Banker,* vol. 117, no. 11 (November 1967), pp. 1321–1365.

Formuzis, Peter K. "The Demand for Eurodollars and the Optimum Stock of Bank Liabilities." *Journal of Money, Credit, and Banking,* vol. 5, no. 3 (August 1973), pp. 806–818.

Forte, Francesco, and Scott, Ira O., Jr. "The Use of Selective Taxes as a Means of Achieving Balance of Payments Equilibrium." *National Banking Review,* vol. 3, no. 4 (June 1966), pp. 439–447.

Fowler, Henry H. "Intervento." (International Capital Movements—Past, Present, Future: Discussion.) *Bancaria,* vol. 28, no. 3 (March 1972), pp. 315–320.

Fratianni, Michele and Savona, Paolo. "Uno struttura formale per l'analisi della capacita moltiplicativa del mercato dell'eurodollaro." [A Formal Analysis of the Multiplicative Potential Within the Eurodollar Market, with English summary.] *L'Industria,* July–September 1970, pp. 345–356.

———. "Eurodollar Creation: Comments on Professor Machlup's Proposition and Developments." *Banca Nazionale del Lavoro Quarterly Review,* vol. 24, no. 97 (June 1971), pp. 110–128.

Friedman, Milton. "The Eurodollar Market: Some First Principles." *Morgan Guaranty Survey,* October 1969, pp. 4–14.

Friedrich, Klaus. "The Eurodollar System and International Liquidity." *Journal of Money, Credit, and Banking,* vol. 2 (August 1970), pp. 337–347.

Fujita, M. "International Money and Gold Market." (In Japanese.) *Kokumin-Keizai Zasshi,* vol. 121, no. 5 (May 1970), pp. 93–107.

Furth, J. Herbert. "International Dollar Liquidity and the Eurodollar Market." *De Economist,* vol. 121, no. 4 (July–August 1973), pp. 347–361.

"The Future of the Dollar." C. J. Divine Institute of Finance, New York University, *The Bulletin,* no. 21 (September 1962).

Gaines, Tilford C. "Eurodollar Developments in Fresh Perspective." *Bankers Monthly Magazine,* vol. 86, no. 7 (July 15, 1969), pp. 12–16.

Ganoe, Charles S. "The Eurodollar Market: A New Source of Financing." *Journal of Commercial Bank Lending,* vol. 50 (July 1968), pp. 11–20.

"Germany Warned on Money Inflow." *New York Times,* February 7, 1964, p. 41.

Ghosh, U. N. "The Dollar Politics." *Economic Affairs,* vol. 17, nos. 1–2 (January–February 1972), pp. 92–100.

Gibson, William E. "Eurodollars and U.S. Monetary Policy." *Journal of Money, Credit, and Banking,* vol. 3, no. 3 (August 1971), pp. 649–665.

———. "The Eurodollar Market and the Foreign Demand for Liquid Dollar Assets: Comment." *Journal of Money, Credit, and Banking,* vol. 4, no. 3 (August 1972), pp. 684–687.

Gilbert, Milton. "The Eurocurrency Market." *The European Capital Market,* Federal Trust Report, Special Series, No. 2. (London: Federal Trust for Education and Research, 1967), pp. 11–23.

———. "Control of the Euromarket," *Euromoney,* October 1973, pp. 58–62.

Gobbato, O. "Relazioni tra euroemissioni e Mercato dell'eurodollar." *Rassegna Economica,* vol. 32, no. 1 (January–February 1968), pp. 29–68.

Guth, W. "Intervento." [International Capital Movements—Past, Present, Future: Discussion, with English summary.] *Bancaria,* vol. 28, no. 3 (March 1972), pp. 310–314.

———. "Betrachtungen zur Aussenwirtschaftspolitik: II." [Current Issues of International Monetary Policy.] *Aussen-wirtschaft,* vol. 29, no. 4 (Dectmber 1972), pp. 366–369.

Gynt, F. E. "Problem of Extracting Clearing House Monkey Wrench from the Foreign Exchange and Eurodollar Markets." *Weekly Bond Buyer,* September 11, 1967.

Haberler, Gottfried. "Prospects for the Dollar Standard." *Lloyds Bank Review,* no. 105 (July 1972), pp. 1–17.

Hacker, George L. "Some Glaring Abuses in the Use of Eurodollars Arouse Bankers." *New York Herald Tribune,* January 26, 1964.

Hagemann, Harold A. "Reserve Policies of Central Banks and Their Implications for U.S. Balance of Payments Policy." *American Economic Review,* vol. 59, no. 1 (March 1969), pp. 62–77.

———. "N. Y. Bankers Eye Eurodollar Use." *American Banker,* April 1, 1963, pp. 1–2.

Hambleton, James R. "The Eurodollar and Wall Street." *American Banker,* December 2, 1963, pp. 1–2.

———. "Fed Moves to Draw Dollars Back from Germany, Lift U.S. Reserves." *American Banker,* March 9, 1964, pp. 1–2.

———. "Gold Rush Financing Debt—and Dangerous." *American Banker,* March 22, 1968.

Havrilesky, Thomas and Clark, Peter. "Eurodollar Borrowings and the Effectiveness of Monetary Policy." *Mississippi Valley Journal of Business and Economics,* vol. 7, no. 1 (Fall 1971), pp. 74–81.

Hayes, Alfred. "The Dollar: National and International Bulwark." *Federal Reserve Bank of New York, Monthly Review,* vol. 45, no. 5 (May 1963), pp. 70–74.

Heckerman, D. G. " 'Inefficient' European Capital Markets as an Explanation of International Capital Movements: Comment." *Journal of Money, Credit, and Banking,* vol. 1, no. 1 (February 1969), pp. 121–123.

Heineman, H. Erich. "Loan Rates Fall for Eurodollars." *New York Times,* January 17, 1967, p. 57 ff.

———. "Eurodollar Loophole." *New York Times,* July 16, 1968, p. 30.

Heller, H. Robert. "Foreign Bond Issues in Europe." *Lloyd's Bank Review,* no. 91 (October 1967), pp. 49–62.

———. "International Capital Movements and Monetary Equilibrium: Comment." *American Economic Review,* vol. 60, no. 5 (December 1970), p. 984.

———. "The Costs and Benefits of the Dollar as a Reserve Currency: Discussion." *American Economic Review,* vol. 63, no. 2 (May 1973), pp. 212–214.

Helliwell, John F. "Dollars as Reserve Assets: What Next? *American Economic Review,* vol. 63, no. 2 (May 1973), pp. 206–211.

Helliwell, John and Maxwell, Tom. "Short-Term Capital Flows and the Foreign Exchange Market." *Canadian Journal of Economics,* vol. 5, no. 2 (May 1972), pp. 199–214.

Hendershott, Patric H. "The Structure of International Interest Rates: The U.S. Treasury Bill Rate and the Eurodollar Deposit Rate." *Journal of Finance,* vol. 22, no. 3 (September 1967), pp. 455–465.

Hill, Samuel & Co. "Foreign Exchange: Dollar Boom Gets Underway." *Euromoney,* February 1974, pp. 76–77.

Hinshaw, Randell. "The Eurodollar Market and the Foreign Demand for Liquid Dollar Assets: Comment." *Journal of Money, Credit, and Banking,* vol. 4, no. 3 (August 1972), pp. 688–690.

Hodjera, Zoran. "Basic Balances, Short-Term Capital Flows, and International Reserves of Industrial Countries." International Monetary Fund, *Staff Papers,* vol. 16, no. 3 (November 1969), pp. 582–611.

————. "International Short-Term Capital Movements: A Survey of Theory and Empirical Analysis." International Monetary Fund, *Staff Papers,* vol. 20, no. 3 (November 1973), pp. 683–740.

Hoffmeyer, Erik. "The Eurocurrency Market and Monetary Control." *Euromoney,* June 1973, p. 15 ff.

Holmes, Alan R. and Klopstock, Fred H. "The Market for Dollar Deposits in Europe." *Federal Reserve Bank of New York, Monthly Review,* vol. 42, no. 11 (November 1960), pp. 197–202.

Holtrop, Marius W. "Central Banking and Economic Integration." Per Jacobson Foundation Lecture, Stockholm, May 16, 1968. International Monetary Fund, *Supplement to International Financial News Survey,* vol. 20, no. 19 (May 17, 1968).

Hoott, Pieter C. "North Sea Oil and the Euromarkets." *Euromoney,* April 1974, pp. 51–53.

Horsfall, Turner J. "New Trends in Eurodollar Loan Agreements." *Euromoney,* March 1974, pp. 28–31.

"How Serious Is the Danger of a Eurodollar Explosion?" *Financial Times* (London), November 18, 1963, p. 31.

Ingram, James C. "The Dollar and the International Monetary System: A Retrospective View." *Southern Economic Journal,* vol. 40, no. 4 (April 1974), pp. 531–543.

"International Gold and Dollar Flows." *Federal Reserve Bulletin,* vol. 44 (March 1958), pp. 241–247.

"The IMF, the Euromarket or Both." *Euromoney,* February 1974, p. 3.

"International Money: Eurodollars Are Our Dollars." *The Economist,* vol. 206 (March 2, 1963), p. 828.

"Interest Rate Developments since Sterling Devaluation." Morgan Guaranty Trust Company, *World Financial Markets,* January 18, 1968.

"The International Relationship of Interest Rates." Model, Roland and Company. *Quarterly Review and Investment Survey,* Fourth Quarter, 1968.

Johnson, Harry G. "Current Issues in Monetary Policy." *Bankers' Magazine,* vol. 151, no. 4 (Autumn 1968) pp. 251–257.

————. "The International Monetary Crisis of 1971." *Journal of Business,* vol. 46, no. 1 (January 1973), pp. 11–23.

Kahn, R. "The International Monetary System." *American Economic Review,* vol. 63, no. 2 (May 1973), pp. 181–188.

Kaufman, Henry. "Interest Rates and the Defense of the Dollar." *University of Washington Business Review,* vol. 27, no. 1 (Autumn 1967, suppl.), pp. 13–22.

Kazmi, A. A. "Special Drawing Rights and International Liquidity." *Punjab University Economist,* vol. 8, no. 2 (December 1970), pp. 153–160.

Keran, Michael W. "An Appropriate International Currency—Gold, Dollars, or SDRs?" *Federal Reserve Bank of St. Louis Review,* vol. 54, no. 8 (August 1972), pp. 8–19.

Kern, D. "International Finance and the Eurodollar Market," *National Westminster Bank Quarterly Review,* November 1971, pp. 6–21.

Kindleberger, Charles P. "The Eurodollar and the Internationalization of United States' Monetary Policy." *Banca Nazionale del Lavoro Quarterly Review,* vol. 22, no. 88 (March 1969), pp. 3–15.

————. "The Dollar System." Federal Reserve Bank of Boston, *New England Economic Review,* September–October 1970, pp. 3–9.

————. "The Benefits of International Money." *Journal of International Economics,* vol. 2, no. 4 (September 1972), pp. 425–442.

————. "A New Look at Foreign and International Banking in the United States." In *Private Financial Institutions,* edited by Bernard Fox. Englewood Cliffs, N.J.: Prentice-Hall, 1963, pp. 338-382.

Klopstock, Fred H. "The International Money Market: Structure, Scope, and Instruments." *Journal of Finance,* vol. 20, no. 2 (May 1965), pp. 182–208.

————. "Eurodollars in the Liquidity and Reserve Management of United States Banks." *Federal Reserve Bank of New York, Monthly Review,* vol. 50, no. 7 (July 1968), pp. 130–138. [Reprinted in *American Banker,* vol. 133, no. 146 (July 31, 1968), p. 84 ff.]

————. "Impact of Euromarkets on the United States' Balance of Payments." *Law and Contemporary Problems,* vol. 34, no. 1 (Winter 1969), pp. 157–171.

————. "Money Creation in the Eurodollar Market—A Note on Professor Friedman's Views." *Federal Reserve Bank of New York, Monthly Review,* vol. 52, no. 1 (January 1970), pp. 12–15.

————. "The Wiring of the Eurodollar Market." *Euromoney,* August 1970, pp. 16–20.

————. "Outlook for the Euromarket: 1." *International Monetary Review,* vol. 5 (March–April 1973), pp. 7–11.

Kohn, Donald L. "Capital Flows in a Foreign Exchange Crisis." *Federal Reserve Bank of Kansas City, Monthly Review,* February 1973, pp. 14–23.

Koszul, Julien. "La tendance sur la marche de l'Eurodollar." Extrait de la *Review de la Societé d'Etudes et d'Expansion,* no. 217 (September–October 1965), pp. 611–617.

Kraus, Albert. "Eurodollars in Demand." *New York Times,* July 15, 1962, Sec. 3, pp. 1, 5.

Kreinin, Mordechai E. and Gilbert, Roy F. "The Demand for Foreign Currency Holdings by European Banks." *Southern Economic Journal,* vol. 38, no. 1 (July 1971), pp. 101–104.

Kriz, Miroslov A. "Gold, the Dollar, and 'Paper Gold'." *University of Washington Business Review*, vol. 20, no. 2 (Winter 1970), pp. 5–12.

Kurihara, K. K. "The Gold-Dollar Problem and World Monetary Reform." *Journal of Economic Issues*, vol. 1, no. 4 (December 1967), pp. 269–279.

Kvasnicka, Joseph G. "Banking Goes International." Federal Reserve Bank of Chicago, *Business Conditions*, April 1967, pp. 7–16.

————. "Eurodollars: An Important Source of Funds for American Banks." Federal Reserve Bank of Chicago, *Business Conditions*, June 1969, pp. 9–20.

Kwack, Sung Y. "The Structure of International Interest Rates: An Extension of Hendershott's Tests." *Journal of Finance*, vol. 26, no. 4 (September 1971), pp. 897–900.

Laffargue, J. "Une explication economique des flux d'investissements directs entre pays hautement industrialises." *Revue Economique*, vol. 22, no. 3 (May 1971), pp. 476–518.

Lalwani, K. C. "International Monetary System: Present Position and Future Outlook." *Economic Affairs*, vol. 18, nos. 1–2, pp. 29–38.

Lee, Boyden E. "The Eurodollar Market Revisited." *The Bankers' Magazine*, vol. 156, no. 4 (Autumn 1973).

————. "The Eurodollar Multiplier." *Journal of Finance*, vol. 28, no. 4 (September 1973), pp. 867–874.

Lee, C. H. "The Balance of Trade, Interest Rates, and Capital Movements." *Kyklos*, vol. 23, no. 1 (1970), pp. 65–74.

Leimone, John E. "The Eurodollar Market: An Element in Monetary Policy." *Federal Reserve Bank of Atlanta, Monthly Review*, vol. 53, no. 8 (August 1968), pp. 102–107. [Also in *Weekly Bond Buyer*, vol. 173, no. 3934 (September 3, 1968), p. 12 ff.]

Levin, Jay H. "The Marginal Cost of International Short-Term Capital Movements." *International Economic Review*, vol. 12, no. 2 (June 1971), pp. 227–238.

————. "A Financial Sector Analysis of the Eurodollar Market." *Journal of Finance*, vol. 29, no. 1 (March 1974), pp. 103–115.

————. "The Eurodollar Market and the International Transmission of Interest Rates." *The Canadian Journal of Economics*, vol. 7, no. 2 (May 1974), pp. 205–223.

Little, Jane Sneddon. "The Eurodollar Market: Its Nature and Impact." Federal Reserve Bank of Boston, *New England Economic Review*, May/June 1969.

"Local Finance—A New Choice," *The Economist*, vol. 204 (August 18, 1962), pp. 631–633.

Lombard (pseud). "How Serious Is the Danger of a 'Eurodollar Explosion'?" *Financial Times* (London), November 19, 1963, p. 37.

"London Bank Arranges $15 Million Norway Power Loan in U.S. Dollars." *Wall Street Journal*, January 24, 1967, p. 23.

Lutz, Alfred. "Eurobonds: Self-Regulation the Key to Survival." *Euromoney*, April 1974, pp. 30–32.

Lutz, R. H. "Le banche e i mercati monetari e finanziari internazionali." [Banks on the international money and capital markets, with English summary.] *Bancaria*, vol. 27, no. 9 (September 1971), pp. 1104–1112.

Machlup, Fritz. "Eurodollar Creation: A Mystery Story." *Banca Nazionale del Lavoro Quarterly Review*, vol. 23, no. 94 (September 1970), pp. 219–260.

———. "The Magicians and Their Rabbits." *Morgan Guaranty Survey*, May 1971, pp. 3–13.

———. "Il dollaro convertible . . . in che cosa?" [Dollar convertible . . . into what? with English summary.] *Bancaria*, vol. 28, no. 1 (January 1972), pp. 13–15.

———. "Eurodollars, Once Again." *Banca Nazionale del Lavoro Quarterly Review*, vol. 25, no. 101 (June 1972), pp. 119–137.

———. "Eurodollars, Once Again: A Correction." *Banca Nazionale del Lavoro Quarterly Review*, vol. 25, no. 103 (December 1972), pp. 4–40.

Magnani, L. "Considerazioni sui flussi e sulle disponibilita." [Money flows and asset formation, with English summary.] *Bancaria Rassegna*, vol. 25, no. 2 (February 1969), pp. 206–226.

———. "Considerazioni sui flussi e sulle disponibilita." [Money flows and asset formation, with English summary.] *Bancaria Rassegna*, vol. 25, no. 3 (March 1969), pp. 227–243.

Main, Jeremy. "The First Real International Bankers." *Fortune*, vol. 76, no. 7 (December 1967), p. 143.

Makin, John H. "The Composition of International Reserve Holdings: A Problem of Choice Involving Risk." *American Economic Review*, vol. 61, no. 5 (December 1971), pp. 818–832.

———. "The Problem of Coexistence of SDRs and a Reserve Currency." *Journal of Money, Credit, and Banking*, vol. 4, no. 3 (August 1972), pp. 509–528.

———. "Demand and Supply Functions for Stocks of Eurodollar Deposits: An Empirical Study." *Review of Economics and Statistics*, vol. 54, no. 4 (November 1972), pp. 381–391.

———. "Identifying a Reserve Base for the Eurodollar System." *Journal of Finance*, vol. 28, no. 3 (June 1973), pp. 609–617.

Makkonen, V. "Eurodollarit kansainvalisilla rahamarkkinoilla." [Eurodollars in the international money market, with English summary.] *Kansantaloudellinen Aikakauskirja*, vol. 64, no. 2 (1968), pp. 95–104.

Makowski, Werner M. M. "The Eurodollar Market: Methods and Prospects." In *The Challenge of International Finance*, edited by Guenter Reiman and Edwin F. Wigglesworth. New York: McGraw-Hill Company, 1966.

Manson, P. A. "Eurodollars." *Scottish Bankers Magazine*, vol. 54, no. 213 (May 1962), pp. 16–20.

Marcus, Edward, and Marcus, Mildred R. "New Directions: The International Monetary Scene Since March 1968." *Journal of Economic Issues,* vol. 5, no. 2 (June 1971), pp. 31–40.

"Market in Eurodollars." *The Economist,* vol. 195 (April 9, 1960), p. 190.

Masera, Francesco. "International Movements of Bank Funds and Monetary Policy in Italy." *Banca Nazionale del Lavoro Quarterly Review,* vol. 19, no. 79 (December 1966), pp. 311–327.

Massaro, Vincent G. "Eurodollars and U.S. Banks." *The Conference Board Record,* vol. 7, no. 10 (October 1970), pp. 15–22.

———. "An Econometric Study of Eurodollar Borrowing by New York Banks and the Rate of Interest on Eurodollars: Comment." *Journal of Finance,* vol. 27, no. 4 (September 1972), pp. 927–930.

Mayer, Helmut W. "Multiplier Effects and Credit Creation in the Eurodollar Market." *Banca Nazionale del Lavoro Quarterly Review,* vol. 24, no. 98 (September 1971), pp. 233–262.

Mayer, Lawrence A. "The World's Freest Money Market: Eurodollars and Eurobonds Are Being Chased Hard by U.S. Business." *Fortune,* vol. 77, no. 4 (April 1968), p. 113 ff.

McClam, Warren D. "Credit Substitution and the Eurocurrency Market." *Banca Nazionale del Lavoro Quarterly Review,* vol. 25, no. 103 (December 1972), pp. 323–363.

Meade, James E. "The International Monetary Mechanism." *The Three Banks Review,* September 1964, pp. 3–25.

Meltzer, Allan H. "The Dollar as an International Money." *Banca Nazionale del Lavoro Quarterly Review,* vol. 26, no. 104 (March 1973), pp. 21–28.

Mendenhall, W. Kenneth. "Eurodollars—Are Controls Needed?" An address before the European Atlantic Group, London, June 30, 1971.

Mendershausen, Horst. "Transfers of United States Dollars between Foreign Regions." *Weltwirtshaftliches Archiv,* vol. 71 (Heft 1, 1957), pp. 84–101.

Mendelsohn, M. S. "London's Many Money Markets." *The Banker,* vol. 117, no. 5 (May 1967), pp. 411–417.

Mendelson, Morris. "Some Tax Considerations in American Eurobond Flotations." *National Tax Journal,* vol. 22, no. 2 (June 1969), pp. 303–310.

———. "The Eurobond and Capital Market Integration." *Journal of Finance,* vol. 27, no. 1 (March 1972), pp. 110–126.

Mikesell, Raymond F. "Sterling Devaluation and the Dollar." *Oregon Business Review,* March 1968, pp. 1–4.

———. "The Eurodollar Market and the Foreign Demand for Liquid Dollar Assets." *Journal of Money, Credit, and Banking,* vol. 4, no. 3 (August 1972), pp. 643–683.

Miller, N. C. "A General Equilibrium Theory of International Capital Flows." *Economic Journal,* vol. 78, no. 2 (June 1968), pp. 312–320.

Mohammed, Azizali F. and Saccomanni, Fabrizio. "Short-term Banking and Euro-currency Credits to Developing Countries." International Monetary Fund, *Staff Papers*, vol. 20, no. 3 (November 1973), pp. 612–638.

Montanaro, E. "Le Banche cantonali nel quadro del sistema bancario svizzero e il mercato dell'eurodollaro (1968–1970)—I." [Cantonal banks in the Swiss banking system and the Eurodollar market (1968–1970)—I, with English summary.] *Bancaria*, vol. 28, no. 3 (March 1972), pp. 321–328.

―――. "Le Banche cantonali nel quadro del sistema bancario svizzero e il mercato dell'eurodollaro (1968–1970)—II." [Cantonal banks in the Swiss banking system and the Eurodollar market (1968–1970)—II, with English summary.] *Bancaria*, vol. 28, no. 4 (April 1972), pp. 447–456.

Morgan Guaranty Trust Company. "Dollars That Go Abroad—But Not Really." *Morgan Guaranty Survey*, December 1961, pp. 4–6.

Morris, Frank E., and Little, Jane S. "The Role of the Eurodollar." In *The Changing World of Banking*, edited by Herbert V. Prochnow and Herbert V. Prochnow, Jr. New York: Harper & Row, 1974, pp. 98–125.

Mosse, R. "Storia del dollaro." (History of the dollar, with English summary.) *Bancaria Rassegna*, vol. 26, no. 5 (May 1970), pp. 556–561.

Mundell, Robert A. "The Appropriate Use of Monetary and Fiscal Policy for Internal and External Stability." International Monetary Fund, *Staff Papers*, vol. 9, no. 1 (March 1962), pp. 70–76.

―――. "The Future of Gold: Real Gold, Dollars and Paper Gold." *American Economic Review*, vol. 59, no. 2 (May 1969), pp. 324–331.

Nars, K. "Valutakrisen i perspektiv och 1970—talets valutasystem." [The monetary crisis in perspective and the currency system in the 1970s, with English summary.] *Ekonomiska Samfundets Tidsskrift*, vol. 25, no. 3 (January 1972), pp. 85–96.

Neme, C. "Les euro-marches." [With English summary.] *Rivista Internazionale di Scienze Economiche e Commerciali*, December 1967, pp. 1177–1193.

"New Eurodollars?" *The Economist*, vol. 207 (June 29, 1963), p. 1409.

"A New Seasonal." Salomon Brothers and Hutzler, *Comments on Credit*, November 14, 1969.

"The New Settlement Arrangements for Member Banks." *Morgan Guaranty Survey*, May 1968.

"No Raid on Eurodollars." *The Economist*, vol. 205 (December 29, 1962), p. 1296.

Nysten, J. "Katsaus eurodollarmarkkinoihin." [Review of the Eurodollar market, with English summary.] *Kansantaloudellinen Aikakauskirja*, vol. 66, no. 2 (1970), pp. 137–143.

"Oil and Money: Your Questions Answered." *The Banker*, vol. 124, no. 3 (March 1974), pp. 257–261.

Olson, Ernest. "Devaluation of the Dollar." *Federal Reserve Bank of San Francisco Review*, vol. 58, no. 11 (November 1972), pp. 955–956.

Oppenheimer, Peter M. "Short-term Capital Flows." *The Banker,* vol. 117, no. 8 (August 1967), p. 670 ff.

Organization for Economic Cooperation and Development. "The International Transmission of Inflation." OECD *Economic Outlook,* July 1973, pp. 81–96.

Orosa, Ramon S. "Manila: A New Asia-Dollar Dealing Centre." *Euromoney,* February 1974, pp. 71–73.

Ossola, Rinaldo. "Central Bank Interventions and Eurocurrency Markets." *Banca Nazionale del Lavoro Quarterly Review,* vol. 26, no. 104 (March 1973), pp. 29–45.

O'Toole, Edward T. "Experts to Meet Over Eurodollars." *New York Times,* October 5, 1962, p. 47 ff.

Pandit, S. A. "The Asian Dollar and Free Gold Markets in Singapore," *Finance and Development,* vol. 8, no. 2 (June 1971), pp. 32–36.

Park, Yoon S. "Background Briefing: Structure and Function of the Eurocredit Market." *Euromoney,* April 1974, pp. 73–81.

"Philadelphia Bankers Are International Bankers." *Federal Reserve Bank of Philadelphia Business Review,* May 1968, p. 43.

Pippenger, John E. "Reparation Payments and International Capital Flows." *Australian Economic Papers,* vol. 10, no. 17 (December 1971), pp. 142–152.

"Playing for Big Chips in Eurodollars." *Business Week,* December 10, 1966, pp. 61–64.

Porter, Michael G. "Capital Flows as an Offset to Monetary Policy: The German Experience." International Monetary Fund, *Staff Papers,* vol. 19, no. 2 (July 1972), pp. 395–424.

Potter, David R. W. "The London Dollar CD—Liquid Tool for International Cash Management." *Columbia Journal of Business,* vol. 8, no. 2 (Summer 1973), pp. 5–10.

Quinn, G. "The Eurodollar Market." *Irish Banking Review,* March 1970, pp. 10–15.

Reading, Brian. "Eurodollars—Tonic or Toxic?" *Bankers Magazine* (London), vol. 204, no. 1484 (November 1967), pp. 233–237.

Readman, Peter; Hoare, Michael; Poole, David; and Davies, Jonathan. "Banking Developments in the EEC." *Euromoney,* November 1971, pp. 21–26.

"Recent Developments in the U.S. Balance of Payments: Capital Flows." *Federal Reserve Bulletin,* vol. 60, no. 4 (April 1974), pp. 243–244.

Regier, Donald W. "Dollar's Changing Role and International Trade." *Agricultural Finance Review,* vol. 33 (July 1972), pp. 27–31.

Rettaroli, R. "Il mercato delle euro-emissioni e i sistemi di compensazione internazionale tipo CEDEL." [The Eurodollar market and the international clearing systems of the CEDEL type, with English summary.] *Bancaria,* vol. 27, no. 5 (May 1971), pp. 616–630.

de Ribet, C. "Place financière multicephale et monnaie europèenne de l'euro-dévise à l'unité de compte." [Pluricentered Financial Market and European Money: From the

Eurocurrency to the Unit of Account.] *Economie Appliquée,* vol. 23, nos. 2–3 (1970), pp. 385–416.

Rich, Georg. "A Theoretical and Empirical Analysis of the Eurodollar Market." *Journal of Money, Credit, and Banking,* vol. 4, no. 3 (August 1972), pp. 616–635.

Roeber, Joe. "The New British Lion of World Banking." *Finance,* vol. 89, no. 6 (June 1971), pp. 6–15.

Rogers, Augustus J., III. "The Eurodollar Market." Michigan State University, *Business Topics,* vol. 15, no. 1 (Winter 1967), pp. 30–34.

Rogers, Forrest L. "Canadian Banks Overseas." *The Banker,* vol. 121, no. 10 (October 1971), pp. 1216–1221.

Roll, Eric. "Movimenti internazionali di capital: passato, presente, futuro." [International capital movements: past, present, future, with English summary.] *Bancaria,* vol. 28, no. 3 (March 1972), pp. 293–309.

Roosa, Robert V. "Capital Movements and Balance-of-Payments Adjustment." *Federal Reserve Bank of Philadelphia Business Review,* September 1970, pp. 21–38.

Ross, Stanley D. L. "Future of the Eurobond Market." *International Currency Review,* vol. 6, no. 1 (January–February 1974), pp. 7–11.

Rudloff, M. "Un nouveau soutien du dollar-standard: le marche des euro-dollars." *Revue Economique de Madagascar,* vol. 3–4 (1968–1969), pp. 249–263.

Saini, K. G. "The Case for the International Dollar Standard." *Economia Internazionale,* vol. 24, nos. 3–4 (August–November 1971), pp. 560–591.

Saunders, Philip. "American Banks in London's Eurodollar Market." *National Banking Review,* vol. 4, no. 1 (September 1966), pp. 21–28.

Schaffner, Philip P. "Eurobank Credit Expansion." *Euromoney,* July 1970, pp. 61–63.

Schloss, B. H. "The Eurobond Market and the United States' Balance of Payments." *Economia Internazionale,* vol. 25, no. 1 (February 1972), pp. 115–119.

Schreiber, Hans Joachim. "Der Begehrte Donnerstag-Dollar." *Zeitschrift fur das Gesamte Kreditwesen,* July 1, 1967, pp. 606–608.

Scott, Ira O., Jr. "That Controversial Eurodollar Market." *National Westminster Bank Quarterly Review,* August 1969, pp. 2–22.

"Secret Report on Eurodollar Market Finds its Virtues Outweigh its Vices." *Business Week,* February 22, 1964, p. 58 ff.

Sergeant, Patrick. "Will Cairo Become the Financial Centre of the Arab World?" *Euromoney,* June 1974, pp. 79–80.

"Shake Up in Eurodollars." *The Economist,* vol. 215 (June 19, 1965), pp. xiii–xiv.

Shannon, I. "The Challenge of the International Monetary System." *Zeitschrift fur die Gesamte Staatswissenschaft,* vol. 123, no. 4 (October 1967).

"Sharp Rise in Overseas Deposits of New York Banks." *The Times* (London), January 18, 1961, p. 46.

"Shift in Eurodollar Loans." *American Banker,* vol. 132, no. 51 (March 15, 1967), p. 3.

"Sizing Up The Euromarket." *The Banker,* vol. 116, no. 12 (December 1966), p. 834.

Stem, Carl H. "The Eurodollar Market and the Foreign Demand for Liquid Dollar Assets: Comment." *Journal of Money, Credit, and Banking,* vol. 4, no. 3 (August 1972), pp. 691–703.

Stevenson, R. B. "The Eurocurrency Market." *Journal of the Institute of Bankers,* vol. 85, part 4 (August 1964), pp. 299–303.

"Sustained Expansion in Eurodollar Banking." First National City Bank, *Monthly Economic Letter,* October 1968, pp. 116–119.

"Swiss Eurodollar Control." *American Banker,* March 13, 1967, p. 3.

Swoboda, Alexander K. "Multinational Banking, the Eurodollar Market and Economic Policy." *Journal of World Trade Law,* vol. 5, no. 2 (March–April 1971), pp. 121–130.

————. "Monetary Policy under Fixed Exchange Rates: Effectiveness, the Speed of Adjustment and Proper Use." *Economica,* vol. 40, no. 158 (May 1973), pp. 136–154.

Tether, C. Gordon. "Dollars—Hard, Soft and Euro." *The Banker,* vol. 111, no. 6 (June 1961), pp. 395–404.

Thomas, Luke E. "London's Capital Come-back." *Banking,* vol. 56, no. 9 (March 1964), pp. 60–61, 107.

Thygesen, N. "Monetary Policy, Capital Flows, and Internal Stability: Some Experiences from Large Industrial Countries." *Swedish Journal of Economics,* vol. 75, no. 1 (March 1973), pp. 83–99.

"Tougher Going on Eurodollars?" *The Economist,* vol. 217 (October 30, 1965), pp. 539–540.

"Trends in the Eurodollar Market." First National City Bank, *Monthly Economic Letter,* July 1966, pp. 81–83.

"Trends in the Eurodollar Market." Continental Illinois National Bank and Trust Company, *Continental Comment,* November 7, 1969.

Trestrail, Richard W. "The Eurodollar Obsoletes the Definition of Money." *Financial Analysts Journal,* vol. 28, no. 3 (May–June 1972), pp. 55–63.

Triffin, Robert. "Toward a Viable International Monetary System." *New York Times,* January 23, 1973, p. 48.

————. "The Collapse of the International Monetary System: Structural Causes and Remedies." *De Economist,* vol. 121, no. 4 (1973), pp. 362–374.

Turot, Paul. "Le Marche des capitaux a court terme en Europe et l'Eurodollar." *Banque* (Paris), April 1961.

Underwood, Trevor. "International Money—How the Talks on Reform Stand Now." *The Banker,* vol. 124, no. 576 (February 1974), pp. 95–98.

"U.S. Banks' Eurodollar Redepositing." Morgan Guaranty Trust Company, *World Financial Markets,* April 30, 1968.

"U.S. Pessimism over Eurodollar Market." *Financial Times* (London), December 19, 1962, p. 50.

Valentini, John J., and Hunt, Lacy H. "Eurodollar Borrowing by New York Banks and the Rate of Interest on Eurodollars: Comment." *Journal of Finance,* vol. 27, no. 1 (March 1972), pp. 130–133.

Vernucci, Alfredo. "The Impact of the U.S.A. Federal Funds' Market on the International Exchange Market." *Banca Nazionale del Lavoro Quarterly Review,* vol. 19, no. 79 (December 1966), pp. 346–361.

————. "La Lira a termine e il mercato delle eurolire." (The Forward Lira and the Eurolira Market, with English summary.) *Bancaria,* vol. 27, no. 8 (August 1971), pp. 1000–1004.

Vicker, Ray. "Dealings in 'Eurodollars' Spurt in Wake of U.S. Curb on Outlays Abroad." *Wall Street Journal,* January 15, 1968, p. 1 ff.

Vinney, L. C. "Credit Creation in the Eurodollar Market: An Unresolved Issue." *Rivista Internazionale di Scienze Economiche e Commerciali,* vol. 20, no. 12 (January 1973), pp. 33–47.

Von Clemm, Michael. "The Rise of Consortium Banking." *Harvard Business Review,* vol. 49, no. 3 (May–June 1971), pp. 125–142.

Walters, A. A. "Floating Rates, World Liquidity and Inflation." *Euromoney,* July 1973, pp. 9–15.

Weberman, Ben. "Banks Using Brokers to Get Eurodollars." *American Banker,* May 2, 1968.

"Where Eurodollars Are Held." *The Economist,* vol. 204 (September 15, 1962), p. 1042.

"Who Lends in London." *The Economist,* vol. 210 (January 18, 1964), p. 235.

Willes, Mark H. "Balance of Payments—In Deficit or Surplus." *Federal Reserve Bank of Philadelphia, Business Review,* November 1969, pp. 26–31.

Willett, Thomas D. "A Theoretical and Empirical Analysis of the Eurodollar Market: Comments." *Journal of Money, Credit, and Banking,* vol. 4, no. 3 (August 1972), pp. 636–642.

Williams, Harold R. "Exchange Rate Systems, the Marginal Efficiency of Investment, and Foreign Direct Capital Movements." *Kyklos,* vol. 26, no. 1 (1973), pp. 58–74.

Wilson, John D. "Latest Development In U.S. Bank Loan Pricing." *Euromoney,* May 1974, pp. 62–64.

Wilson, Stanley. "Despite Forebodings, Eurodollar Fortified for Market Ravages." *Journal of Commerce,* January 10, 1964.

Other Sources

Brimmer, Andrew F. "Eurodollar Flows and the Efficiency of U.S. Monetary Policy." A paper presented to a Conference on Wall Street and the Economy 1969 at the New School for Social Research, New York, March 8, 1969.

―――. "The Eurodollar Market and the United States Balance of Payments." A paper presented at the London School of Economics, University of London, November 17, 1969.

―――. "Monetary Policy and Bank Credit Flows in 1970." Remarks before a Bankers' Lunch sponsored by The Detroit Branch of the Federal Reserve Bank of Chicago, Detroit, December 30, 1970.

―――. "Commercial Bank Lending and Monetary Management." Remarks to the 57th Annual Fall Conference of the Robert Morris Associates, Los Angeles, California, October 25, 1971.

―――. "Commercial Bank Lending Abroad and the U.S. Balance of Payments." Remarks before a Symposium on the International Monetary System in Transition sponsored by the Federal Reserve Bank of Chicago, Chicago, March 16, 1972.

―――. "American International Banking: Trends and Prospects." A paper presented to the 51st Annual Meeting of the Bankers' Association for Foreign Trade, Boca Raton, Florida, April 2, 1973.

―――. "Prospects for Commercial Banks in International Money and Capital Markets: An American Perspective." A paper presented at the Conference on World Banking organized by *The Financial Times* with *The Banker, American Bankers Magazine, The Investors Chronicle* and British Airways, London, England, January 1974.

Fieleke, Norman S. "The Performance of the Foreign Exchange Market in Five European Countries: Interviews with Private Foreign Exchange Traders and with Central Bankers." Federal Reserve Bank of Boston, 1973 (xeroxed).

Gemmill, Robert F. "Liabilities to Foreign Branches as a Means of Adjusting Reserve Positions." A paper presented to a meeting of the Federal Reserve System Committee on Banking and Credit Policy, February 17, 1969 (mimeographed).

Hamburger, Michael J. "The Demand for Money in an Open Economy: Germany and the United Kingdom." A paper presented to the Federal Reserve System Committee on International Research and Analysis, Chicago, December 4, 1973.

Klopstock, Fred H., Manager, International Research Department, Federal Reserve Bank of New York. Statement before the Subcommittee on International Exchange and Payments of the Joint Economic Committee, Washington, D. C., June 22, 1971.

Kouri, Pentii J. K., and Porter, Michael G. "International Capital Flows and Portfolio Equilibrium." International Monetary Fund, May 23, 1973 (mimeographed).

Scott, Ira O., Jr. *The Eurodollar Market and Its Public Policy Implications.* Economic Policies and Practices, paper no. 12, U.S. Congress, Joint Economic Committee, 91st Cong., 2nd sess., February 25, 1970.

Stem, Carl H. "The Eurodollar System: An Analysis of Its Credit Function and Impact on the International Financial Position of the United States." Ph.D. dissertation, Harvard University, 1968.

―――. "The Eurodollar System: Some Credit Aspects." An unpublished paper, February 1970.

U.S. Congress, House, Committee on Banking and Currency. *Higher Interest Rates on Time Deposits of Foreign Currencies.* Hearings. 87th Cong., 2nd sess., 1962.